REAL ESTATE PRINCIPLES AND PRACTICES

JAMES E. LARSEN
Wright State University

www.wiley.com/college/larsen

Acquisitions Editor *Leslie Kraham*
Marketing Manager *Charity Robey*
Production Manager *Lari Bishop*
Designer *Shoshanna Turek*
Illustration Editor *Benjamin Reece*
Copy Editor *Martha Collins*
Cover Design *Kris Pauls*
Cover Images *Copyright © Corbis Digital Stock*

This book was set in Minion and printed and bound by R.R.Donnelley & Sons Company. The cover was printed by Phoenix Color Corp.

This book is printed on acid free paper.∞

ISBN 0471-22379-4

Printed in the United States of America

10 9 8 7 6 5 4 3 2 1

This book is dedicated to my former, current, and future real estate students.

Brief Contents

Contents

Part II

Real Estate Ownership and the Law   37

Chapter 7

■ INCOME TAXES   96

Part III

Real Estate Transactions   135

Chapter 9

■ Real Estate Agency And Brokerage   136

Chapter 11

REAL ESTATE CONTRACTS   178

Chapter 14

■ CLOSING THE REAL ESTATE TRANSACTION   230

Part IV

REAL ESTATE FINANCING 247

Chapter 15

■ MORTGAGES AND DEEDS OF TRUST 248

Chapter 17

MORTGAGE CALCULATIONS   294

Preface

Virtually all students enrolled in introductory real estate courses find the subject matter interesting. Perhaps this is because they have an inherent understanding of the economic importance of real estate, and also because they plan to actually use the information. Some students take this course in preparation for a real estate career, while many hope to use the information in making housing, investment, or other real estate related decisions. *Real Estate Principles and Practices* was written for both of these groups, as well as anyone interested in learning more about real estate.

Real Estate Principles and Practices was developed explicitly for a first undergraduate course in real estate. A primary objective in writing this text was to provide clarity and understanding of the theories and practices used in real estate to students who have no previous experience in this field of study. Our vision for this introduction to real estate was a book that is relevant and comprehensive, and that balances practical information with academic rigor.

PEDAGOGY

Each chapter begins with a list of learning objectives for the material to come. A summary at the end of the chapter emphasizes coverage of these objectives. Following the summary, the key terms, which have been in **boldface** throughout the chapter, are listed for review. End-of-chapter questions and problems provide students with the opportunity to test their comprehension of the material. Web assignments encourage students to be familiar with real estate related Web sites, and selected readings are provided for additional study.

As concepts are discussed, they are illustrated extensively with examples. This constant application of concepts helps solidify the student's grasp of the material. In addition to these standard pedagogical features, *Real Estate Principles and Practices* contains numerous special features that distinguish it from its competitors.

SPECIAL FEATURES

From the Wire—most chapters begin with an actual real estate issue or newsworthy item. These high-interest features keep the chapter topics tied to current events of importance in the world of real estate. For instance, one chapter opens with a discussion of the "home buyer bill of rights" proposed by President Bush (Chapter 14).

Decision Points—Each chapter requires students to exercise their own judgment while using the information just covered. For example, after a discussion of forms of ownership, a Decision Point in Chapter 4 begins: "Your Uncle Jake has a fee simple absolute interest in a gold mine. He has decided to sell to your cousin . . ." In the situation that follows, students are asked to use their knowledge of types of ownership to increase their chances of owning the gold mine.

Practitioner Profiles—Profiles of individuals who have made their names in real estate provide a high-interest start to some chapters. Chapter 2 begins with the story of a student running a large real estate company's Web site from his dorm room, while a later chapter profiles the current president of the Counselors of Real Estate.

Doing Business sidebars—These sidebars offer an inside look at the practice of real estate. Each Doing Business sidebar presents an application of the real estate concepts being discussed. Some vignettes present new technology, like how AVM systems are used to speed the work of appraisers, while another may inform the reader about the "junk fees" included in some settlement statements.

Ethical Issues—This is the first real estate text to explicitly incorporate ethics. Ethics have an important place today in the education of real estate professionals, as anyone who has dealt with the accrediting bodies of business schools knows. Responsive to this and to the recent high profile of ethical problems in the business world, most chapters in this text pose ethical questions for the reader to consider. In one of these, students are challenged to decide whether to disclose property defects to a purchaser (Chapter 3). The Ethical Issues feature can provoke lively class discussions.

Consumer Checklists—These highly useful checklists provide items to investigate before entering into transactions. Students will appreciate a tool like the list of potential problems in older houses presented in Chapter 2.

State-by-State Tables—Tables throughout the text show side-by-side comparisons of states' treatment of real estate issues. Chapter 4 compares the time required to gain title through adverse possession, and Chapter 9 shows the number of real estate licensees in each state.

Internet Exercises—Each Practitioner Profile, From the Wire, and Doing Business sidebar has an Internet assignment that directs the students to a particular web site to perform an activity. For example, on a visit to the Web site of the Department of Housing and Urban Development, students research down payment assistance programs (Chapter 15).

Real Estate on the Web—These end-of-chapter exercises prompt students to explore the Web and familiarize themselves with leading real estate sites. In these activities, students will compare the types of mortgage loans available locally and discover whether there is a real estate investor's club in their area.

ORGANIZATION AND COVERAGE

Real Estate Principles and Practices uses a **steps-in-the-process approach.** Part I, "An Introduction to Real Estate," acquaints the student with the basics of real estate. An understanding of real estate markets and the service providers working within these markets is a necessary prerequisite for anyone contemplating the sale, purchase, or leasing of real property. Chapter 3, "Home Ownership," covers an area that stimulates the interest of students, many of whom have the goal of eventual home ownership. Part II, "Real Estate Ownership and the Law," provides information that all should be aware of before entering into a real estate transaction. Armed with the information in Parts I and II, the student is ready for Part III, "Real Estate Transactions," in which the details of a real estate purchase/sale are described. Since most people cannot pay cash in real estate acquisitions, securing financing can be an important part of the transaction process. However, since borrowing money is not necessarily an essential step in a purchase, we examine mortgage lending separately in

Part IV, "Real Estate Financing." Finally, several topics of interest to those who own real estate are presented in Part V, "Real Estate Development and Investment."

PART I: AN INTRODUCTION TO REAL ESTATE

The three chapters of Part I present basic information about real estate that is of value whether you plan a career in the field or just want to make better decisions concerning real estate for your personal use. Chapter 1, "An Introduction to Real Estate," discusses the variety and significant economic importance of real estate markets. Basic terms and ideas, like the difference between real property and personal property, and important determinants of real property value, are also explained in Chapter 1. In any market involving valuable assets, there is usually a demand for specialists to assist market participants, and this is the case in real estate markets. The student is introduced to a variety of specialists who operate in the real estate markets in Chapter 2, "Real Estate Services." Because home ownership is a goal of many people, the information provided in Chapter 3 should be of interest. In Chapter 3, "Home Ownership," we explain how the government promotes home ownership and we examine the advantages and disadvantages of ownership. In addition, we look at methods purchasers can use to estimate how much they can afford to pay for a home and to formulate an informed purchase offer.

PART II: REAL ESTATE OWNERSHIP AND THE LAW

Part II contains five chapters that cover the important topic of real property rights. Of the many valuable lessons in this Part, paramount is that the most important thing gained when one acquires an interest in real property is the set of property rights associated with the interest. Without these rights, which are presented in Chapter 4, "Interests in Real Estate," there would be little incentive to own real property. However, real property rights are not unlimited. Chapter 4 outlines the ways property rights are affected by the estate (ownership interest) one possesses. In addition, the form of ownership employed may affect the owner's real property rights. Therefore, the various forms of real property ownership are presented in Chapter 5, "Forms of Ownership." In Chapter 6, "Limitations on Ownership," we show that property rights may also be limited either by the government or by private parties. Along with rights comes responsibilities, and while most people in the United States are legally obligated to least file an income tax return, real estate ownership affects the amount of tax owed. Therefore, Chapter 7, "Income Taxes," explores this effect of real estate ownership on income tax. All of this presumes that we have some way to distinguish one owner's property from that of another. Fortunately, we do, and Chapter 8, "Legal Descriptions," presents various methods that may be used to provide a legal real property description.

PART III: REAL ESTATE TRANSACTIONS

Part III contains six chapters that describe the details involved in a real estate purchase/sale. Most people buy or sell real estate infrequently and are unfamiliar with the details needed to complete a transaction. Therefore, they can benefit from the services provided by real estate specialists. In Chapter 9, "Real Estate Agency and Brokerage," the role played by brokers is explained, and the contracts between brokers and customers are described. An independently determined estimate of the value of real property is a frequent concern. Therefore, this topic is examined in Chapter 10, "Property Appraisal." Because of the high value of real estate, it is important that transactions involving the transfer of ownership satisfy all legal requirements. Hence, a basic understanding of the material presented in Chapter 11, "Contracts," is essential. Chapter 12, "Deeds," examines the transfer of real property ownership by deed (or according to the provisions of a will). You will note that the promises made by the seller depend on the type of deed used. But, because we are unsure whether sellers will be able to honor their promises, most people will take additional steps to ensure the quality of the title being acquired. Methods by which this can be accomplished are reviewed in Chapter 13, "Preparation for the Real Estate Closing." Finally, the actual transfer of property ownership may take place with or without a meeting of the seller and buyer, as described in Chapter 14, "Closing the Real Estate Transaction."

PART IV: REAL ESTATE FINANCING

Part IV contains three chapters that present information about several elements of financing real estate transactions. Lenders require borrowers to sign a number of documents, including a promissory note and either a mortgage or a deed of trust. These documents are described in Chapter 15, "Mortgages and Deeds of Trust." Also included in Chapter 15 is a description of the various types of mortgage contracts, and, in case things go badly, an explanation of the mortgage foreclosure process. You will see that borrowers are faced with a variety of mortgage loan products and lending institutions. Basic information about many of these lenders and products is presented in Chapter 16, "Financing Real Estate Transactions." Chapter 17, "Mortgage Calculations," covers the math skills required to calculate solutions to a variety of mortgage-related problems.

PART V: REAL ESTATE DEVELOPMENT AND INVESTMENT

Part V of this text contains four chapters that should be of interest both to those who own real estate and those who want to create improvements or invest in real estate. Chapter 18, "Property Management and Leasing," provides a description of the responsibilities of real property managers. Leasing is an integral part of the property manager's job; information concerning lease transactions and the landlord-tenant relationship is also presented. Real property ownership entails the risk that fire or some other catastrophe may damage the property, or that someone may be injured while on the property. In order to manage these risks, real property owners can enter various types of contracts, which are covered in Chapter 19, "Property Insurance." In Chapter 20, "Property Development and Market Analysis," important regulations and issues faced by real estate developers are described, and an explanation of the steps in the development process is provided. Finally, in Chapter 21, "Investment Analysis," we describe the advantages, disadvantages, and risk factors associated with direct investments in real estate, and demonstrate how to determine whether such an investment makes good financial sense. A number of indirect real estate investment possibilities are also presented.

SUPPLEMENTAL MATERIAL

Web site materials for the Instructor can be found at http://www.wiley.com/college/larsen and include:

- **Instructor's manual**—Teaching supplements are available chapter-by-chapter on the instructors' web site as Adobe Acrobat files. They can be viewed online or downloaded and printed. Each chapter of the manual includes definitions of key terms, answers to end-of-chapter questions and problems, suggested class discussion topics, and comments on Decision Points and Ethical Issues.

- **Test bank**—This bank of more than 1,000 multiple-choice questions, 200 true/false questions, and 100 open-ended questions is available in Microsoft Word format for download or viewing and printing.

The Students' Companion Web site (also found at http://www.wiley.com/college/larsen) provides a range of review materials, exercises, and additional resources. We have tried to make the Web site a learning tool and resource that provides both content that is integrated with the textbook and additional current topics that students will find useful and interesting. For instance, at the top level of the site, the student will find real estate career information, including Pre-licensing and Continuing Education Requirements for real estate licensees. The Web site is then organized by chapter. Each chapter has a review of key topics and a series of features. These can be relevant articles and questions to answer about them, Internet research activities and other exercises, extensions of textbook exercises, and links to useful real estate sites. The Web site reinforces key concepts of the book, provides further opportunities to connect these concepts to real world applications, and provides additional resources and information that students will find personally and professionally useful.

ACKNOWLEDGMENTS

I am indebted to many people whose efforts helped bring about the publication of this text. Numerous people at Leyh Publishing were instrumental in this effort. In particular, I extend my gratitude to Rick Leyh, Lari Bishop, Kris Pauls, and Camille McMorrow for their editorial and project management services. In addition, I would like to acknowledge Susan Elbe, Leslie Kraham, and Charity Robey at John Wiley & Sons, Inc. for their support of this project. Finally, thanks are due to my colleagues, listed below, who reviewed various drafts of the manuscript and offered helpful comments.

Maryanne Cunningham, University of Rhode Island

Thomas Springer, Florida Atlantic University

C. Griffin, Metropolitan State College of Denver

Jon Crunkleton, Old Dominion University

Jay Butler, Arizona State University

James Short, San Diego State University

Sidney Rosenberg, University of North Florida

David Downs, University of Georgia

Jay Butler, Arizona State University

Edward Lawrence, University of Missouri, St. Louis

I hope you enjoy the text, and I encourage anyone with suggestions that would improve the material to contact me at james.larsen@wright.edu.

- J.E.L.

About the Author

James E. Larsen, Professor of Finance in the Raj Soin College of Business at Wright State University in Dayton, Ohio, received his Ph.D. from the University of Nebraska-Lincoln. He was previously on the faculty at Marquette University, Creighton University, and the University of Nebraska-Lincoln. Professor Larsen has written dozens of papers published in a variety of real estate journals. His research focuses on real estate brokerage and appraisal. He currently serves on the editorial board of several academic journals and is on the Board of Directors of the Academy of Financial Services. He is also an Associate Member of the Dayton Area Board of REALTORS® and a member of the Ohio Real Estate Commission's Research and Education Advisory Committee. When not attending to his academic duties, Professor Larsen enjoys conducting "field research" on golf courses across the country and hiking with his dog, Algebra. He is the proud father of Erin, Kristin, and Douglas, and lucky to be the husband of Christine.

An Introduction to Real Estate

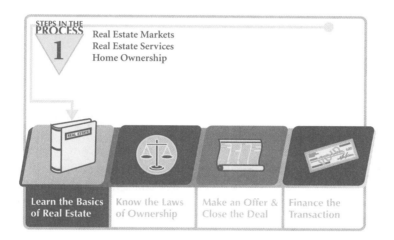

Part I of this text contains three chapters that present basic information about real estate that should be of value whether you plan a career in the field or just want to make better decisions concerning real estate for your personal use. As shown in Chapter 1, "An Introduction to Real Estate," there are many real estate markets. These markets can be defined either by property usage or location. Whether viewed separately or together, these markets are of significant economic importance. The difference between real property and personal property, and important determinants of real property value, are also explained in Chapter 1.

Within any market involving valuable assets, there is usually a demand for specialists to help market participants acquire, manage, and sell those assets. This is certainly the case with real estate. Therefore, in Chapter 2, "Real Estate Services," we introduce you to a variety of specialists that operate in the real estate markets. Some of you may end up working in one of these occupations, and most of you will eventually use the services provided by these individuals. Several of these service providers are usually employed to facilitate a home sale/purchase. Because home ownership is a goal of many people, the information provided in Chapter 3 should be of interest. In Chapter 3, "Home Ownership," we explain how the government promotes home ownership, as well as examining the advantages and disadvantages of ownership. In addition, we explain how purchasers can estimate how much they can afford to pay for a home, and describe how they can formulate an informed purchase offer.

CHAPTER 1

Real Estate Markets

Learning Objectives

After studying this chapter, you should be able to:

- Recognize the economic importance of the real estate industry.
- Distinguish real property from personal property.
- Explain how personal property may become real property, and vice versa.
- Understand the tests used to determine if an item is a fixture.
- Describe the various value-influencing characteristics of real property.
- Explain how geographic location and property use result in real property submarkets.

FROM THE WIRE

The year 2001 was a tough one for the extremely rich. The number of billionaires worldwide dropped from 538 in 2000 to a mere 497 in 2001. However, the number of billionaires whose wealth was attributed primarily to real estate increased from thirty-two in 2000 to thirty-three in 2001. Fifteen of the thirty-three were citizens of the United States. Another six called Hong Kong home; four were from Japan; three from Germany; two each from the United Kingdom and Singapore; and one from Australia.

Some of the people on the real estate billionaires' list have achieved a degree of celebrity, including Donald Trump ($1.8 billion) and Leona Helmsley ($1.9 billion). Most, however, are unknown to the general public. The Kwok brothers (Walter,

Thomas, and Raymond) from Hong Kong have the largest fortune, estimated at $9.2 billion (down from $11.5 billion in 2000). And while 2001 saw most of the billionaires' fortunes drop or remain unchanged, there were notable exceptions. Singapore's Kwek Leng Beng's wealth increased from $1.6 to $2 billion, and the United Kingdom's Gerald Cavendish Grosvenor's wealth increased from $6.5 to $6.7 billion (second place on the real estate billionaires' list).

Go to www.forbes.com to view the complete list of billionaires.

INTRODUCTION

Real estate ownership is a source of great pride for many; a source of great disappointment for a few; and a seemingly impossible dream for others. And consider this, no single class of assets is more valuable than real estate. It is estimated that real estate accounts for approximately 45 percent of total wealth in the United States, and about 54 percent worldwide.

An informed consumer or competent businessperson should have a basic understanding of the real estate market prior to entering any transaction, and the odds are that the real estate billionaires mentioned in the chapter opener, "From the Wire," have such an understanding. The wealth accumulated by these people is impressive but, as demonstrated in the following sections, they own only a small fraction of all real estate.

In this chapter, we provide you with some evidence of the economic importance of real estate. In addition, we explain the difference between real property and personal property (and how one may become the other) as well as important characteristics of real estate that influence its value.

THE ECONOMIC IMPORTANCE OF REAL ESTATE

The federal government identifies "real estate" as one sector of our economy in compiling gross domestic product (GDP) and other economic data. GDP is the value of all goods and services produced within a country during the year, expressed in current prices. The value of services provided by real estate brokers, managers, lessors, operators, subdividers, and developers, is included in the real estate sector figures shown in Exhibit 1.1. In 2000, the $1,116.3 billion of output by the real estate sector represented 11.3 percent of GDP. The performance of the industry in 2000 is typical of its contribution to GDP each year. The importance of real estate to our economy is even greater than these numbers indicate, however, because there are extensive links between the real estate sector and other sectors, including: construction, banking, insurance, and the manufacture of durable goods such as furniture and home appliances.

To illustrate the importance of these links consider the value of total new construction shown in Exhibit 1.2 by property type for selected years. The construction and building supplies trade is also affected as owners of improved real property protect their investment by making expenditures to maintain and repair their properties. In 2000, for example, owners of residential property alone spent more than $100 billion for repairs, maintenance and making alterations and additions to structures.

| EXHIBIT | 1.1 | **2000 GROSS DOMESTIC PRODUCT AND RECEIPTS FOR SELECTED INDUSTRIES (IN BILLIONS OF DOLLARS)** |

Sector	Dollar Output	Percentage of GDP
Gross Domestic Product	$9,872.9	100.0
Real Estate	1,116.3	11.3
Finance and Insurance	819.9	8.3
Manufacturing: Durable Goods	901.7	9.1

Source: Survey of Current Business. December, 2001. Bureau of Economic Analysis of the U. S. Department of Commerce.

| EXHIBIT | 1.2 | **NEW CONSTRUCTION ACTIVITY (IN BILLIONS OF DOLLARS)** |

	2000	1995	1990	1985
Total new construction	$825.0	$555.6	$476.8	$403.4
Total private construction	639.2	425.7	369.3	325.6
Residential	252.5	171.4	132.1	115.9
Commercial	136.9	75.4	85.8	88.1
Industrial	44.6	34.0	33.6	24.1
Other	97.1	68.9	58.8	52.9
Total public construction	185.8	129.9	107.5	77.8
Federal	15.4	15.8	12.1	12.0
State and local	170.4	114.2	95.4	65.8

Source: (various issues) Economic Report of the President, U. S. Government Printing Office.

Employment figures, compiled by the United States Department of Labor, also attest to the importance of the real estate sector. In the year 2000, more than 1.8 million people were employed in the real estate sector, 754,810 in brokerage and management, 576,090 as operators or lessors, and 123,390 as subdividers and developers. In addition, there were 6.7 million employed in construction, 83,970 employed in the title insurance industry, and 348,590 mortgage bankers. The people employed in the real estate and real-estate-related sectors represented approximately 6 percent of total employment. Jobs in other sectors of the economy are affected by activity in the real estate sector. For example, because real estate is relatively expensive, buyers use at least some borrowed funds in most acquisitions.

In the United States, at the beginning of 2000, there were $6.5 trillion in outstanding mortgage loans. In any year, real estate loans account for a significant share of our total private (nongovernment) borrowing. In 1999, for example, total net borrowing by the private nonfinancial sector increased by $1,191.6 billion. Approximately 51 percent of this increase was due to a $607.8 million increase in real estate mortgages. In comparison, all state and local governments increased their net borrowing by only $52.3 billion during 1999. Obviously, the livelihood of many people working in the private finance sector depends on originating real estate loans. Decisions made by governments and private parties concerning a resource of this magnitude have a major impact on both the public and private sectors of our economy.

REAL PROPERTY CLASSIFICATION AND SUBMARKETS

Examination of Exhibit 1.2 reveals that the real estate "market" is stratified; it actually consists of many markets. One way to classify real estate is according to whether it has been improved. Unimproved land, sometimes called raw land, is real property in its unused natural state. Improved land is land whose value has been increased by the addition of improvements such as grading, sewers, utilities, roads, and buildings.

Another way to classify real estate markets is by the use to which the property is or will be put. Based on this criterion, a number of markets can be identified, including residential, hotel/motel, commercial, industrial, recreational, institutional, and agricultural (Chapter 20). Because properties within a particular classification are not necessarily good substitutes, submarkets within each classification also exist. For example, within the residential market, starter homes constitute a different market than executive homes. Likewise, townhouses may be considered a submarket separate from single-family detached housing. Real estate submarkets may also be identified geographically. The markets for residential properties and small commercial properties tend to be local. A house in Los Angeles may not be considered a good substitute for a house in San Francisco, and a parking lot in Atlanta would do commuters in Boston little good. Therefore, these properties are said to be located in different submarkets. Geographic submarkets for other property classifications may be local, regional, national, or even international. A large corporation, for example, may consider buying (or leasing) office space in New York, Chicago, Tokyo, or London.

The presence of submarkets complicates the task of making an informed decision. Participants face a market with stratified demand; the value of property in each submarket may be affected by demand factors different from those in other submarkets. For example, knowing the demand factors for housing is of little value if the object is to develop a hotel because the pertinent demand factors in these markets differ significantly. In addition, in most cases, good decision-making requires market participants to consider not only general economic conditions, but also local competitive factors.

REAL PROPERTY VS. PERSONAL PROPERTY

As the above information indicates, real property is an important part of our economy. So what exactly constitutes real property? Let's start with the basics. **Property** is anything that is, or can be, owned or possessed. All property may be classified into one of two categories: real and personal. The ability to distinguish real property from personal property is important for a number of reasons. Both the contract law that applies to a particular transaction and the documentation needed for a valid transfer of ownership are governed by the specific type of property involved. Personal property contracts are governed by the Uniform Commercial Code while real property contracts are subject to the Statute of Frauds. Therefore, contracts involving the sale of personal property may be either written or oral, and when written, ordinarily need not be recorded in the public records. Contracts involving real property, however, must be in writing, and should be recorded (Chapter 11). When a document is used to transfer ownership of personal property, it is called a **bill of sale,** whereas the document used to convey ownership of real property is a **deed** (Chapter 12). In addition, our income tax law makes important distinctions between personal and real property (Chapter 7).

REAL PROPERTY

Real property includes both land and anything permanently attached to the land, such as a house, barn, or tree. Permanent attachments to land, intended to enhance the value of the land, are referred to as **improvements.** Improvements may be grouped into two categories: improvements in common, and improvements to land. As the name implies, an **improvement in common** is an improvement that benefits more than a single parcel of real property. Highways, utility lines, and sewers are all examples of improvements in common. An improvement that benefits a particular parcel is referred to as an **improvement to land.** Examples of improvements to land include such things as buildings, fences, driveways, and landscaping.

"Real estate" and "realty" are two terms commonly used as synonyms for the term "real property." In certain contexts, however, a particular term may be employed more frequently. For example, people who assist others in the sale of real property in exchange for a fee are usually referred to as real estate brokers, not real property brokers (Chapter 9).

PERSONAL PROPERTY

Personal property is all property that is not real property. Examples of personal property include: jewelry, calculators, and textbooks. A characteristic of most personal property is that it is movable. A notable exception to this generalization is an emblement, which is a growing crop, produced annually, such as corn or wheat. Because the crop is growing it is obviously attached to the land, but the legal doctrine of emblements treats the crop as personal property; the person who plants and cultivates a crop has the right to harvest it. For example, a tenant farmer would have the right to harvest his crop.

Personal property can be either tangible or intangible. **Intangible property** is property that has no material being, or no intrinsic value. Examples of intangible assets include: a copyright, a common stock, a patent, and a promissory note. **Tangible property** includes items of material substance. Examples of tangible property include: clothing, automobiles, and furniture. As we explain in the next sections, tangible personal property can be attached to real property in such a manner that legally it becomes real property, and real property can be converted into personal property by severing it from the real property.

CONVERTING PERSONAL PROPERTY TO REAL PROPERTY

Before being assembled into a building, or other improvement; all of the components used in the construction of an improvement (bricks, nails, lumber, etc.) are personal property. When an item of personal property is so affixed to real property that it is deemed a part of the real property, it is known as a **fixture.**

In most cases, there is no question that the attachment of an item of personal property, such as lumber, electrical wiring, and roofing material, effectively converts the item to real property status. It is not uncommon, however, for disputes to arise between real property buyers and sellers (and between tenants and landlords, Chapter 18) concerning whether a particular item is real property (and included in the transaction) or personal property. For example, disagreements may occur over such items as: track lighting, carpeting, draperies, and appliances. Sometimes, a real property seller will attempt to replace an item with a similar (perhaps cheaper) item after accepting an offer, but before delivering title to the buyer. This practice can upset the purchaser and result in a costly lawsuit. To help avoid such problems, the seller should specify in the sales contract which, if any, items the seller intends to remove. Likewise, a buyer can help avoid problems by inserting a clause in the purchase offer that states that "the buyer is to receive all appliances and fixtures as currently installed and used on the premises."

TESTS OF A FIXTURE

For such a clause in a purchase offer to be effective, one must be able to determine whether an item is personal property or a fixture. When disputes result in legal actions, courts use several tests for this purpose. As previously suggested, one test of a fixture is the intention of the parties. Under this test, one must determine what the parties intended: did they intend for the item to be considered a part of the real property. To illustrate, a homeowner had bookshelves custom-made so that they fit perfectly against a wall. The shelves looked built-in, but were actually not attached to the wall. The home-owner had the shelves constructed in such a manner because he intended to take them with him when he moved. If the seller does not make this intention clear to prospective purchasers, courts today are likely to decide that the bookshelves are a fixture. Again, the best way to establish intent is for the parties to agree in writing as to which items are a part of the transaction.

Another test to determine whether property is a fixture is based on the manner of attachment. Under this test, if the item can be removed from the real property without causing material damage, it is personal property, if not, it is a fixture. In applying this test, it is important to remember, however, that the test really depends on the firmness of the item's installation rather than the size of the hole that may be caused by its removal. Plumbing, for example, would qualify as a fixture under this test because its removal would, in all likelihood, cause material structural damage to floors, ceilings, and walls. For discussion purposes, consider the removal of a ceiling fan. Properly done, the removal of the fan would result in little or no structural damage, but the buyer would be financially damaged if a cheaper fan was used as a replacement, or if no replacement was made. The permanence of the ceiling fan's attachment suggests it is a fixture. For other items, such as custom-made draperies and refrigerators, the manner of attachment test is usually inadequate and other tests must be applied.

One such test is the adaptation of the item to the real property. Under this test, courts usually deem custom-made draperies and custom-built cabinets to be fixtures because they were specifically designed for, and adapted to, a specific building. Even if a seller could remove such items without materially damaging the building they would be less useful elsewhere because they are not readily adaptable to other structures. Local custom frequently dictates whether home appliances are considered personal property or fixtures. In some areas, for example, refrigerators are routinely considered fixtures, while stoves are considered personal property. In other areas, the reverse is true. In most areas, all appliances in rental properties are considered a part of the real property.

Under another test, fixtures may be identified according to the effect of removal of the item on the usefulness of the property to the next occupant. If, for example, the removal of wall-to-wall carpeting reveals an attractive hardwood floor, the carpet may be classified as personal property. If however, removal of the carpeting reveals a cement slab or unattractive flooring material, the carpet will be classified as a fixture.

Finally, some items that are not attached in any way to the real property are considered fixtures under the constructive annexation test because they are so closely associated with a structure. House keys and remote garage door openers are examples.

FIXTURES IN RENTAL PROPERTY

Unless otherwise agreed, a tenant must leave fixtures in the leased premises at the termination of the lease. This includes any fixtures the tenant adds during the lease period; ownership of such fixtures reverts to the landlord at the termination of the lease. This rule also applies regardless of who installed the fixtures, or whether the fixtures were additions to the property or replacements. If, for example, a tenant installs a new counter to replace an old counter in a drug store leased by the tenant; the tenant cannot remove the new counter from the property at the expiration of the lease.

A **trade fixture** is an item of personal property affixed to leased premises by a tenant as a necessary part of the tenant's business. Examples of trade fixtures include ovens and walk-in refrigerators used in restaurants, and floor-mounted shelving, tables, and seating used in commercial buildings. Trade fixtures are an exception to the general rule regarding fixtures described in the preceding paragraph in that the tenant may usually remove them. The tenant is, however, responsible for any damage resulting from the removal of trade fixtures. Trade fixtures not removed by the tenant within a reasonable time after the lease expires are considered abandoned and ownership reverts to the landlord.

Decision Point

Assume that you, as a tenant, are about to enter into a business lease that is silent with regard to the removal of trade fixtures. What steps would you take before signing the lease? Would your answer be different if you were the landlord? Why?

CONVERTING REAL PROPERTY TO PERSONAL PROPERTY

As the preceding sections suggest, nothing is so permanently attached to real property that it is impossible for it to be removed. Virtually all real property can be converted to personal property by severing it from the real property. When you cut down a tree for firewood, you convert real property into personal property. Likewise, if you dig up and pot trees, shrubs, or other landscaping, you convert it from real to personal property. However, only the owner of the real property has the legal right to make such a conversion.

DETERMINANTS OF REAL PROPERTY VALUE

Many things influence the value of real property, including the use to which the property is put, the ownership form employed, and claims that other parties may have on the property. These factors, and others, are examined throughout the text. In the following sections, we briefly explain several factors that influence the value of real property.

SCARCITY

Scarcity describes the situation in which a commodity or service is in limited supply. Scarcity frequently means that, because demand exceeds supply, individuals cannot own or control as much of a particular item as they would like. This results in competition for ownership that, in turn, makes scarce items more valuable as competitors bid up prices. Conversely, low prices are associated with goods and services in abundant supply.

Scarcity in real estate markets is important for two reasons. First, as previously explained, real property values may increase because of competition. Second, scarcity may affect the manner in which real property is used. To justify the higher cost of real property that results from scarcity, owners have an incentive to operate the property in the manner that will generate the most income. In many cases, this is accomplished by using real property more intensively. Farmers, for example, may irrigate formerly unirrigated land or employ more modern technology (including chemical fertilizers and pesticides) in an attempt to generate more profit. Similarly, the skylines of modern cities are the result of real property owners using their land more intensively; replacing single-story office buildings with high-rise office buildings.

MODIFICATION

An important characteristic of real property is the fact that it is subject to modification. Examples of modifications that can be made to real property include changing the contour of the land, and constructing, altering, or removing structures or other improvements. Modifications are usually made to enhance the value of the owner's real property, but they may also influence the value of other parcels. The value of nearby parcels may either increase or decrease depending upon their proximity to the modified property and the nature of the modification.

   Many modifications have a positive impact on nearby parcels. For example, extending utilities and roads into a new housing subdivision may reduce the development costs associated with the surrounding land; thereby, increasing the value of the surrounding property. In this case, the extent of the increase in value is certainly a function of the proximity of the surrounding land to the new development. While development costs may be reduced dramatically for property adjacent to the new development, the impact on development costs of property located a mile away is likely to be minimal.

   If the modifications made to a property are not compatible with the use to which surrounding land is put, the value of the surrounding property may be negatively affected. Many people, for example, react with outrage at the notion of locating a land fill even remotely close to their home because they fear the impact it will have on the value of their property (especially those located down wind from the proposed land fill). Because modifications to one property can adversely affect the value of others, owners may not be completely free to make modifications. Restrictions may be placed on their ability to do so either by the party from whom they receive ownership or by government regulation (Chapter 6).

   Certain modifications may affect one type of property positively and other types negatively. A street widening to accommodate more traffic, for example, may be welcome by owners of business property, but disdained by homeowners on the street.

IMMOBILITY

As suggested earlier, a characteristic that distinguishes real from personal property is the immobility of real property. It is possible for owners of most personal property to increase selling price by transporting the property to an area where greater relative scarcity for the item exists. For example, a car owner may discover that used car prices are relatively low in the area, but learn that used cars are commanding higher prices in another location. If the price difference exceeds the transportation costs, the car owner may increase the net sales price by transporting and selling the vehicle in the higher-price market.

It is difficult, or impossible, however, to physically move real property. Although some structures can be moved, it is not usually cost-effective to do so. In addition, some items such as natural gas, minerals, timber, and soil can be removed from land. It is not possible, however, to alter the value of a particular parcel of real property by moving it, since the location of the land is fixed. If people wish to own and use real property they must go to it, it cannot be delivered to them.

Closely related to the physical characteristic of immobility of real property is the economic concept of situs, which refers to the preference by people for a certain location. A number of factors may affect one's preference for one real property location over another. In selecting a home site, for example, people may consider a number of factors, including: the proximity of the property to highways, public transportation, employment, schools, churches, police and fire protection, and shopping opportunities. A desire for open space and privacy may also be important in selecting a home site and partially explains the population migration from city centers to suburban areas that has occurred in recent decades. The planned use to which a property is to be put may also affect the particular parcel one decides to purchase. A remotely located mountaintop may be an excellent site for an astronomical observatory, but a site along a heavily traveled street will likely be preferred if the intended use is a fast-food restaurant. The implication of physical immobility and situs for real property values is captured in a well-known adage: "The three most important determinants of real property value are location, location, and location."

HETEROGENEITY

Heterogeneity refers to the fact that no two parcels of real property are identical. The size, shape, and topography of any parcel may vary from others, making it more, or less, desirable for a particular use. In addition, as suggested in the preceding section, the location of every parcel is unique, and this may also affect value. To illustrate the implications of heterogeneity, consider two parcels of undeveloped land located on opposite sides of town; each has the same size, shape, and topography. The announcement of plans to construct a shopping mall next to one of the tracts is likely to increase its value, but not the value of the other.

DURABILITY

Another important characteristic of real property is its durability. Most real property improvements are long-lived. Improvements do, however, wear out with time, become functionally obsolete, or may be destroyed by a natural calamity. Even after improvements have lost their economic usefulness, however, the land will remain; it is virtually indestructible. Institutional recognition of this fact is provided by accountants who, in the course of their duties, periodically depreciate (or write off) the cost of improvements, but do not depreciate the land.

The physical durability of real property has important economic consequences. Some investors will pay a premium for real property compared to other less durable investments (Chapter 21). Similarly, many lenders, in assessing loan collateral value, view the durable nature of real estate favorably. The continued physical existence of land, however, does not guarantee that the land will retain its value. The value of real estate, like any other asset, can go down as well as up. The long-term nature of real property means that people may have to live with good, and bad, land use choices for a long time.

Decision Point

Assume that the economy is healthy and growing. Rank the real property characteristics described above in order of their potential influence on real property value. How, if at all, would your ranking change if the economy were in a recession?

Which, if any, of these characteristics do you think may influence property value in one direction: up or down?

SUMMARY

A first step toward learning about real estate is the ability to distinguish real property from personal property. Real property includes land and all things permanently attached to the land; all other property is personal property. It is, however, possible for personal property to become real property and vice versa. As a result, disputes sometimes arise between parties to a transaction regarding whether a particular item is personal property or a fixture (real property). One may employ several tests to make such a determination. These tests include: local custom, the intention of the parties, whether the removal of the article would damage the structure or cause the real property to be less useful to the next occupant, and whether the article is uniquely adapted to the property.

Real-estate-related businesses account for an important share of our total economic activity. To be successful in most real-estate-related pursuits, a person must have specialized knowledge. Acquisition of such knowledge requires an ongoing effort because the real estate market is dynamic; the value of real estate is subject to constant change. Several determinants of real property value were explained in this chapter including scarcity, immobility, durability, heterogeneity, and modification. Acquisition of the knowledge necessary for sound decision-making may be complicated by the fact that the real estate market actually consists of several submarkets, each of which may be subject to unique supply and demand factors.

KEY TERMS

bill of sale	improvement in common	property
deed	improvement to land	real property
fixture	intangible property	tangible property
improvements	personal property	trade fixture

REVIEW QUESTIONS

1. What is real property?
2. How does real property differ from personal property?
3. What is a fixture?
4. What tests are used to determine whether an item is personal property or a fixture?
5. Classify the following items as real or personal property:

   a. automobile;
   b. classroom desk;
   c. dishwasher;
   d. swing set; and
   e. tree.
   f. What assumption did you make in classifying these items? Under what assumptions could the items you classified as real property be considered personal property, and vice versa?

6. Describe the characteristics of real property and comment on how each might influence the value of real property.

7. If a developer announced plans to build a regional shopping mall on the vacant land next to your home, what do you think would happen to the value of your property as a home site? What do you think would happen to the value of your property as a commercial site? What characteristics of real property help explain the change in value of your property?

8. List several examples that demonstrate the economic importance of real estate.

9. How are real property submarkets defined? Give at least three examples of real property submarkets.

10. What are your answers to the questions in the two "Decision Point" sections in this chapter?

REAL ESTATE ON THE WEB

Use your favorite search engine to:

1. Determine the land area (e.g., square miles, acres) of your city, county, and state.

2. Determine the proportion of land in each of the jurisdictions in Web assignment 1 that is devoted to various property uses (e.g., residential, commercial, industrial, etc.).

3. Locate an example in which one (or more) of the real property characteristics described in the chapter affected the value of a particular property.

4. Find an example in which rehabilitation of a real property probably changed the property's submarket classification (e.g., a school converted to an apartment building).

5. Find out more about one (or more) of the 33 billionaires referred to in the "From the Newswire" material at the beginning of the chapter.

Refer to the companion Web site at www.wiley.com/college/larsen for a variety of online activities including additional chapter content, review materials, assignments, and related links.

ADDITIONAL READINGS

Anonymous. "The Impact of the September 11th Tragedy." *Real Estate Issues* (Fall 2001): 1–4.

Cymrot, A. "Our Current Economy: What's the Real Story?" *Real Estate Review* (Spring 2000): 15–19.

Fulman, R. "Sponsors Plan to Reduce Real Estate, Value Stocks." *Pensions & Investments* (July 10, 2000): 2, 56.

Rikon, M. "The Law of Trade Fixtures." *Real Estate Law Journal* (Fall 1997): 161–171.

Ziobroski, A. J. "Real Estate Holdings of United States Senators." *The Appraisal Journal* (January 2002): 76–85.

CHAPTER

2

Real Estate Services

Learning Objectives

After studying this chapter, you should be able to:

- Identify three groups of consumers who use real estate services.
- List the real estate service providers who usually have direct contact with a home seller and buyer and explain the service each provides.
- List the real estate service providers who work behind the scenes to facilitate a real estate transaction and explain the service each provides.
- Describe the roles of other real estate service providers.

PRACTITIONER PROFILE

The Prudential Arizona Relocation Center Internet site serves as a hub for about 120 community-based Web sites that provide information about properties listed for sale throughout the state. The popular Web site is run by Keegan Miller, a University of Arizona freshman, who developed and sold commercial Web sites while still in high school and is majoring in computer science. He spends about twelve hours a week on the project, doing most of the programming from his dormitory room using a laptop computer supplied by Prudential. He plans to telecommute and continue to program the site during his sophomore year while he attends Hunter College in New York City, then return to the University of Arizona to finish his degree requirements.

Keegan began playing around with computers at age eight and four years later set up his first Web page. Technically, Keegan is not in the real estate business, nor does he plan to

14

enter it. After graduation, he wants to start his own company and be a Web-site consultant. But the service he provides enables Prudential to offer a service that benefits home sellers and buyers.

Go to www.arizonawebpage.com to check out Keegan's work. While there, find a modestly priced house and an expensive house that are currently available for purchase.

INTRODUCTION

In the previous chapter, you learned about the economic importance of real estate and the characteristics that affect its value. When dealing with an asset of such importance, most parties employ specialists to assist them. In this chapter, we first briefly describe the parties who utilize the services of real estate specialists. Then, we describe a variety of service providers.

Many of these specialists, like Keegan Miller, described in the chapter opener "Practitioner Profile," provide services that most home sellers and buyers utilize. Miller, like some other specialists, provides a valuable service even though he is unlikely to have direct contact with buyers and sellers. Examples of other indirect service providers include appraisers, title abstractors, and title insurance companies.

Most sellers and buyers will have direct dealings with a number of specialists including a real estate broker, and perhaps a home inspector, and an attorney. Buyers are also likely to have direct dealings with a mortgage lender, and those purchasing a new home are likely to have direct dealings with a contractor/builder, and perhaps an architect.

WHO EMPLOYS REAL ESTATE SERVICE PROVIDERS?

The short answer to this question is—just about everyone. Government, businesses, organizations, and individuals may all choose to employ specialists to assist them in purchasing, leasing, selling, improving, managing, and investing in real estate.

A number of government agencies and departments require the knowledge these service providers possess. Many of these specialists are employed in-house. For example, at the federal level, the General Services Administration and the Bureau of Land Management need real property managers because they are responsible for managing federally owned land (about one-third of our nation's land—mostly located in western states). The Federal Deposit Insurance Corporation, and the Department of Housing and Urban Development also need people to manage real properties they acquire due to the failures of financial institutions and individual mortgage defaults. State and local governments also require people well trained in real estate to serve as members of planning commissions, building commissions, zoning boards, and in property tax departments. In addition, some larger cities have real estate management offices. For example, such an office in New York City manages the more than 33,000 parcels of real estate owned by the city.

Business executives have long realized the importance of real estate in many corporate decisions and, historically, they have hired outside real estate consultants on a periodic basis to assist them in the decision-making process. More recently, large corporations are hiring individuals skilled in real estate to work in-house. They need these people not only at the time of property acquisition and disposition, but also to evaluate and manage the company's real property on an ongoing basis. Organizations such as J.C. Penney, Jiffy Lube, KinderCare, Exxon, and McDonald's have active real estate departments. In addition, many large businesses hire relocation companies to assist employees transferred from one location to another. The main function of most relocation companies is real estate brokerage (described later). The relocation company provides all the services of a brokerage firm (including trying to find a buyer, and helping the transferee find a home in the new location). In the case of an employee relocation, however, the relocation company will also maintain and clean the house before it is shown to prospects. And, depending on the contract between the relocation company and the business, the relocation company will agree to purchase the house at a fixed price if they are unable to sell it.

Individual consumers of real estate services include those making investment and housing decisions. The most expensive purchase most individuals will make during their lifetime is their home, but because this is not an everyday event the average person may be unfamiliar with the way that the real estate market works. For this reason, most people employ specialists to assist them in their real estate transactions. To facilitate our presentation of real estate service providers, we have classified them into three categories: direct contact service providers, those with whom home sellers and buyers are likely to have direct dealings; indirect service providers, those working behind the scenes to facilitate the transaction; and other service providers.

DIRECT CONTACT SERVICE PROVIDERS

When purchasing or selling a home, you are likely to have direct contact with several providers of specialized real estate services. Most sellers and buyers will have direct dealings with a real estate broker, and perhaps a home inspector and an attorney. Buyers of new or existing homes are also likely to have direct dealings with a mortgage lender, and those purchasing a new home are likely to have direct dealings with a contractor/builder, and perhaps an architect.

BROKER

One of the most visible occupations in the real estate industry is brokerage. In fact, when most people hear that somebody "works in real estate," they assume that the person works in real estate brokerage. But, brokerage is just one of numerous specializations within the real estate industry. Because brokers provide such an important service, and because some people reading this text may be contemplating a career in this field, we provide more details about real estate brokerage in Chapter 9. But for now, here is some basic information.

Real estate brokers assist others in the selling, leasing, or acquisition of real property. In a typical home sale, brokers actually provide a bundle of services. These services include assisting the home owner in establishing a price at which the property will be listed, marketing the property (e.g., newspaper ads, open houses), locating other service providers (e.g., lender, attorney), serving as a conduit in negotiations between the buyer and seller, and, in general, coordinating the transaction. Historically, brokers have been employed to represent the seller in a real estate transaction, and they usually are compensated for their services by a commission paid by the seller. In 2002, the average real estate commission nationwide equaled 5.4 percent of selling price. A relatively recent development is "buyers' brokers" who, instead of following the traditional role, contract with home purchasers to represent them in the transaction. Real estate brokers recognize the complexities resulting from market stratification, as described in Chapter 1. While many brokers deal in all property classes, most specialize in a particular class such as residential or commercial real estate. In addition, because real property value is largely a function of local economic,

DOING BUSINESS

TECHNOLOGY

The Internet has changed the way many people approach home buying and selling. According to a survey conducted in 2001 by the National Association of REALTORS (NAR), 67 percent of buyers plan to use the Internet as a source of information in their home search. Many Web sites allow buyers to discover details about available properties such as the list price, commute times, shopping opportunities, school district, and other demographic and property information. With increasing frequency it is also possible to take a virtual tour of the house. The increased exposure afforded by the Internet makes it a marketing tool that is becoming valued by sellers. This development motivated NAR to introduce a new designation for some of their members, e-PRO agents, which is awarded by NAR to an agent it has certified as an Internet expert.

Go to www.realtor.org, click on e-Pro Internet Professionalism Certification, and then click on FAQs to learn more about e-Pro certification.

political, and social conditions, brokers usually limit their activities to a relatively small geographic area.

To help ensure that people in the brokerage industry are qualified, every state requires that individuals be licensed in order to provide brokerage services for compensation. And states also protect licensees from non-licensed competition. You could use the information in this text to assist someone in a real estate transaction, as long as you do so for free! But, in general, only licensed individuals can be paid for their service (exceptions may include attorneys, and someone acting as the administrator of an estate). Licensing requirements vary by state, but in general they specify two classes of licensees: brokers and sales associates **(agents)**. Brokers employ agents to act in their behalf, but the broker is ultimately responsible for the actions of his or her agents. To be licensed, both classes must meet specified prerequisites: a certain amount of pre-testing education and successful completion of a written examination. An experience requirement (e.g., two years of successful work as an agent) is also customary before one can sit for the broker's exam. Finally, to keep the broker's and agent's skills sharp, most states require that they attend a certain number of continuing education classes following licensure.

MORTGAGE LENDER

Mortgage lenders serve an extremely important function; they provide (at least some of) the money individuals and businesses need for the acquisition, or improvement of, real property. You could obtain the funds you need to purchase a house from a relative, friend, or neighbor and, in that case, technically, that individual would be a mortgage lender. But most mortgage money is provided by institutional mortgage lenders. These lending institutions include commercial banks, savings and loan associations, mutual savings banks, life insurance companies, mortgage bankers, credit unions, and finance companies.

There are three primary functions involved in the loan application process. Ignoring the possibility that you may locate and deal with a lender via the Internet, which is becoming more common, the individual with whom you will have face-to-face contact is the person who takes your application—the loan originator. It is the loan originator who puts your application and supporting documentation together in a "loan package." A loan processor assists the originator in putting the package together. The loan package is then submitted to the person who makes the final decision regarding the loan—the loan underwriter. You may never actually see the underwriter or processor, but the success of your application depends just as much on their efforts as those of the originator.

There are no special educational requirements for these service providers, although it is becoming more common for originators and underwriters to hold college degrees. The financial institutions for which these people work provide them with the needed training. Loan processors usually work on salary. Compensation for underwriters and originators may be in the form of salary and/or commission. Borrowers effectively pay these service providers by fees charged in association with the loan.

The mortgage lending business is in a continual state of evolution, so lenders must keep current. They must be familiar with an array of lending regulations and loan products (e.g., fixed-rate loans, adjustable-rate loans, etc.) The material in Chapters 15, 16, and 17 provides you with more details on mortgage loan documents, the mortgage business, and mortgage calculations.

HOME INSPECTOR (AND HOME WARRANTIES)

Historically, the principle of caveat emptor (let the buyer beware) applied to home sales. In essence, a buyer who purchased a home with some defect(s) was stuck with it. In recent years, however, buyers have shown less reluctance to pursue legal action against a seller who sold them a lemon. But lawsuits can be expensive and time consuming. The relatively recent development of the home inspection industry enables all parties to reduce the likelihood of such problems by having a qualified **home inspector** examine the property and prepare a report that details its condition prior to title transfer. Initially, home inspections were commissioned as buyers requested inspections to avoid potential problems. Today, other interested parties employ home inspectors. Some lenders now require home inspections as a prerequisite to loan approval. Agents and sellers are also ordering home inspections. They benefit by identifying and addressing potential problems to ensure that the home is ready to market.

Many agents use a good inspection as a marketing tool, advertising the home as "pre-inspected." Inspection of a used home will frequently locate several major defects, but discovery of these defects prior to marketing the property allows the seller to be proactive rather than reactive. No seller or agent likes to be in the position of reacting to a negative report obtained by a potential buyer. A disadvantage of home inspections for the seller who is unwilling to correct defects (and his agent) is that most states now require both agents and sellers to disclose any known defects to potential buyers.

A good inspection report does not guarantee that the buyer will not have problems with their purchase. Therefore, some sellers obtain a home warranty policy for buyers to reduce their fears concerning breakdowns of appliances and major systems (although buyers can purchase a policy for themselves). A **home warranty policy** is an insurance policy that will pay to repair or replace most appliances and major systems if they become inoperative due to normal wear and tear during the term of coverage. Typically, items covered include plumbing, heating and air conditioning systems, electrical system, hot water heater, garbage disposal, dishwasher, and oven/range. Other items may be offered as an option. Most policies are for a term of one year, and annual premiums usually range from $300 to $500. Some sellers include a one-year home warranty policy as a part of the purchase price. This may enable them to sell their home faster or for a better price because the policy provides the buyer with some peace of mind. Such policies can be invaluable. In one case, the text author purchased a very nice home where the seller provided a home warranty policy. Within one year, the garbage disposal stopped working, the self-cleaning unit in the oven shorted out, the heat pump failed (twice), and the water heater quit heating. Fortunately all of these problems were repaired or replaced at little cost to the new owner.

REAL ESTATE ATTORNEY

Real estate transactions are fairly complex and usually involve large amounts of money. Some attorneys, therefore, specialize in the practice of real estate law. When you think of an attorney, you probably think "lawsuit." And when one party fails to honor a contract, an attorney may be needed. But representing individuals involved in a legal action is just one service attorneys provide. Other services they offer may help avoid a lawsuit. Prudent people have a competent attorney review contracts, deeds, leases, and other real estate documents before signing the documents. In some cases, buyers will hire an attorney to help ensure that the seller is able to deliver a marketable title (one that is reasonably free of problems). The attorney reviews the documentation put together by an abstractor (described later) and provides the client with a letter, called an "opinion of title." In the letter, the attorney provides his or her opinion regarding the marketability of the seller's title and lists any claims on the property that others appear to have.

The service provided by an attorney requires a high degree of skill. To help ensure that they do have these skills, each state requires that (after graduating from law school) attorneys pass a state bar examination before they begin practicing law. The fees charged by an attorney may be on an hourly basis or may be a flat fee. Many of the common legal rules that affect real estate and real estate transactions are described throughout the remainder of the text. When dealing with real estate, you do not need a law degree, but all individual sellers, buyers, and investors, as well as real estate professionals should have a basic understanding of real estate law, even if just in order to ask attorneys relevant questions.

CONTRACTOR/BUILDER

A **contractor** contracts with another to supply labor and materials for the construction or rehabilitation of improvements on a property. Such contracts are frequently the result of a

CONSUMER CHECKLIST
HOME INSPECTIONS

When shopping for a home, first-time homebuyers frequently face disadvantages compared to experienced homebuyers. To compensate for a shortage of money first-timers often select older homes at bargain prices. Lack of experience in home ownership means they often do not recognize signs of serious defects and they often are not cognizant of the cost to repair defects. Many home inspection companies conduct surveys that indicate the prevalence of serious defects in older homes. Some of the more common defects found in homes at least thirty years old are shown in tabular form below, along with the percentage of homes in which the problem appears and the estimated cost to repair each problem.

One precaution recommended for older-home shoppers is to insist on a professional home inspection. Many prospective purchasers make a purchase contingent on a satisfactory inspection report. Inspectors are not infallible, however, and they sometimes overlook or misjudge problems. An inspection can, however, greatly reduce a buyer's chances of purchasing a home that needs expensive repairs. In most locations home inspectors are listed in the yellow pages under "Building Inspection Service."

Problem	Percentage of Older Homes with Problem	Estimated Cost to Repair Problem
Basement water	32	$600–$5,000
Defective plumbing	44	$3,000–$4,000
Inadequate roof insulation	34	$800–$1,100
Faulty heating system	31	$1,500–$2,500
Roofing defects	27	$1,500–$4,000
Plumbing, other than pipes	25	$350–$1,600
Electrical problems	19	$250–$1,200
Faulty cooling system	11	$800–$2,000
Foundation problems	8	$3,000–$10,000

process whereby the party who desires the construction solicits bids from several contractors. Contractors may be classified according to the role they play in a particular project. The term prime contractor describes one who contracts the complete job. However, a prime contractor may or may not actually perform all of the work. When the prime contractor hires others to perform certain tasks, the prime contractor may assume the role of general contractor, a contractor who uses or supervises the work of two or more unrelated building trades (e.g., plumbers, masons, carpenters).

Subcontractors are the contractors hired by a prime contractor. The roles of general contractor and subcontractors may also be created if a job is originally bid by task rather than as a complete job. Like brokers, many contractors specialize in a particular type of property (e.g., industrial, commercial, apartments, single-family homes). No matter what property type is involved, in order to ensure the attractiveness of their product, contractors/builders must be aware of innovations in building materials and features that consumers demand.

ARCHITECT

For those who plan to have their home (or other structure) built to their specifications, contact with an architect is a good idea. With the expertise architects possess, they may be able to provide some valuable guidance. For example, an architect could determine whether something is feasible, or will be very expensive to accomplish. In such cases, they are likely to be able to suggest a better option.

Architects, who provide designs for individual buildings or more complex projects, also play an important role in shaping the character of an area. In designing a structure, architects must balance function with aesthetic appeal. In many cases, the final results of their work are breathtaking. Consider the work of architects who designed the Sears Tower in Chicago, the Saint Louis Arch, the Empire State Building, or the Sydney Opera House in Australia.

INDIRECT CONTACT SERVICE PROVIDERS

While the services provided by the specialists described so far are important, there are also a number of people working behind the scenes to facilitate each transaction. Most (if not all) transactions could not be consummated without the effort of these professionals, including appraisers, title abstractors, and title insurance companies.

DOING BUSINESS
THE FUTURE

According to a survey of their membership, the International Furnishings and Design Association predicts that, in order to meet the needs of our aging population, houses of the future will be smaller, attached or clustered together, and more multifunctional. In addition, respondents to the survey offered the following predictions about homes of the future:

40 percent see movable walls replacing permanent interior walls.

51 percent predict eat-in kitchens will replace dining rooms.

71 percent believe great rooms will eclipse living rooms.

72 percent predict larger kitchens.

73 percent see a move toward more open-plan home designs.

87 percent believe that homes will include a separate media room.

Go to www.hud.gov, click on Search/Index and use the keywords "housing trends" to learn more about recent developments and anticipated changes in the housing market.

APPRAISER

A real estate **appraiser** is a person who gives a professional opinion of the value of a particular parcel of real property. A number of groups use the services of appraisers, including real property owners, investors, mortgage lenders, insurance companies, and the government. For example, sellers or buyers may be interested in the appraised value as some assurance that they are not selling or buying the property for too little or too much. Mortgage lenders routinely employ in-house or independent appraisers to help ensure that the real property has sufficient value to serve as collateral for a loan. Insurance companies need an independent estimate of value to write policies and to settle damage claims. And when the government forces a private property owner to sell their land to the government for a public purpose (e.g., highway system) it needs an estimate of value to determine the compensation owed to the private property owner.

Like brokers, appraisers frequently specialize in a particular type of property, and limit the geographic scope of their activities. Another similarity to brokers is that appraisers must be licensed by the state in which they conduct their business. Prerequisites to obtaining a license vary by state. But, in general, to be able to appraise any type of property a candidate must complete a certain amount of pre-testing education, successfully complete a written examination, and satisfy an experience requirement. Appraisers usually work for a predetermined fee. In the case of a home sale, the fee is paid from funds collected from the buyer at the closing. Recently, there has been a high demand for competent real estate appraisers. Low mortgage interest rates in 2001 spurred homeowners to refinance existing mortgages and first-time buyers to enter the housing market. More details about appraisers and how they provide their service is presented in Chapter 10.

TITLE ABSTRACTOR

Anytime ownership of real property is conveyed from one party to another, or when real property is to be used as collateral for a loan, a title abstractor's services are needed. An **abstractor** searches through the public records for all documents that have been filed involving the property in question. This requires visits to the County Tax Assessor's Office, the County Recorder's Office, and the County Court House. Upon completion of the title search, the abstractor prepares a document, the abstract of title, that summarizes the results of the search. The abstractor's work allows knowledgeable parties, such as an attorney or a title insurance company, to make a judgment regarding the quality and extent of the title held by the current property owner. There are no special educational requirements for title abstractors. As we show in the next chapter, you can search the same

DOING BUSINESS

TRADE ASSOCIATIONS

Members of almost all of the service providers discussed in this chapter can be affiliated with a number of professional associations. Generally, these associations were formed to foster professionalism within the industry. To realize this goal, many associations offer educational programs to their members, and award designations to members who demonstrate expertise. Many organizations, as well as some real estate trade associations, sponsor and/or publish research designed to benefit real estate practitioners and the public.

Go to www.wiley.com/college/larsen to find out what designations the various professional associations offer and to learn about periodicals that specialize in real estate issues.

offices that the abstractor searches before you make an offer on a property. This should enable you to make an informed offer, and perhaps avoid some unwanted surprises.

TITLE INSURER

As we will see in Chapter 12, sellers make certain promises about the quality of the title that they are conveying to the buyer. But few buyers rely on these promises (mainly because their mortgage lender will not let them). Therefore, buyers usually take additional steps to assure the quality of the title they receive. In a few areas of the country, the attorney's letter of opinion (described previously) is used. But, the most widely used method of assuring title quality is with title insurance.

In most cases, a **title insurance** company will issue a policy that provides financial protection to mortgage lenders and/or real property buyers who may subsequently suffer a loss due to title defects (i.e., if someone shows up later with a better claim to the property). In some cases, however, the company may decline to offer a policy if the title search suggests that the risk of a loss is too high. The one-time premium for a title insurance policy is usually paid by the buyer at the closing. Title insurance and other forms of title assurance are explained in Chapter 13.

SETTLEMENT/ESCROW AGENT

As previously mentioned, title is conveyed at the "closing" or "settlement." In many areas, it is common practice for the company providing the title insurance for the transaction to act as the **settlement agent.** Prior to the closing, it is the settlement agent's job to ensure that all parties accomplish whatever they need to do to finalize the transaction. At the closing, the interested parties (seller, buyer, their attorneys, brokers, and lender) meet, and the settlement agent passes documents to them for their signatures. After the closing, the settlement agent makes sure that any documents that need to be entered into the public record are recorded. There are no special educational requirements for settlement agents, and they are usually paid a fee at the closing.

In some areas of the country, a physical meeting of the parties is not required. Instead, an independent third party, known as an **escrow agent,** or escrow company, is responsible for ensuring that all parties perform in accordance with the contract, and for processing the paperwork associated with the transaction. In this type of closing, none of the parties must devote time to a meeting. They simply mail required documents to the escrow agent, who in turn forwards them to the appropriate party. More information about the closing process is provided in Chapter 14.

Decision Point

If the only career opportunities available to you were in real estate, which do you think you would enjoy pursuing? Why?

OTHER REAL ESTATE SERVICES

There are a number of other service providers in the real estate industry. These include surveyors, subdividers and developers, property managers, counselors, researchers and educators, as well as those who provide syndication and real estate securities services.

SURVEYOR

Surveyors also play a comparatively small, but important, part in the real estate industry. Surveyors locate real property boundaries called for in deeds and other legal documents that affect the ownership of real property. Lenders often require an accurate survey before they will lend money to finance the acquisition or construction of property. Surveyors also provide the information needed to develop legal descriptions for real property (Chapter 8).

SUBDIVIDER AND PROPERTY DEVELOPER

A subdivider buys a large tract of land, divides it into smaller parcels (usually for the purpose of home sites), installs streets and utilities within the subdivision, and then sells the lots to individuals, builders, or developers. Subdividers and developers play an important role in shaping the character of an area because they determine factors such as: lot sizes and shapes, the retention (or creation) of green-space, and the location of roads within the subdivision. Of course, if they are to be successful, the subdivision plan they submit to the local building inspector's office must conform to local ordinances, and appeal to potential purchasers.

The role some developers play in developing an area may be even greater than the role of a subdivider. A **developer** attempts to put land to its most profitable use by acquiring the land, supervising construction, and selling the developed property. In some cases, developers even provide maintenance for the project after the sale. The complex nature of real estate development often requires developers to work with finance and construction experts.

PROPERTY MANAGER

Many owners of income-producing real property (e.g., apartment buildings, shopping centers, office buildings) do not have the time, desire, or expertise required to manage their real property investments successfully. Instead, they hire a firm, or individual, to manage their property. Real property management companies provide a number of services. They advertise for and screen prospective tenants, collect rents, recommend needed improvements, and oversee building repairs and more comprehensive building rehabilitations. Property management companies have become increasingly important in recent years. Many lenders become unwilling property owners when they foreclose on a loan, and they rely on the expertise of professional property management firms. Many government agencies and private corporations also employ property managers on a full-time basis.

REAL ESTATE ADVISOR/COUNSELOR

Real estate advisors/counselors evaluate, and provide advice on, a variety of real estate problems including development, redevelopment, and other real estate investment opportunities. To be effective, they must have extensive knowledge of all phases of real estate, finance, tax law, and other aspects of investment. Such knowledge usually only comes with decades of experience. When providing advice, real estate advisors must also consider the personal circumstances and investment objectives of the client. Real estate counseling is a relatively recent specialty, and only about 1,100 individuals worldwide have earned the Counselor of Real Estate (CRE) designation conferred by the American Society of Real Estate Counselors (www.cre.org).

RESEARCHER AND EDUCATOR

One factor that distinguishes a job from a profession is the level of education required. High educational requirements are prerequisites for admission into most professions (e.g., medicine, accountancy, and teaching). Historically, educational requirements for entry into most real estate fields have been minimal, and many people have viewed real estate occupations as jobs rather than professions. Recently, educational standards have been increased for many real estate specializations in an attempt to increase professionalism within the industry. As a result, there is a need for people knowledgeable in the various specializations to train others. In addition, there is a need for people to teach courses such as this one as well as advanced real estate classes. Universities, junior colleges, and proprietary schools employ people who are knowledgeable in real estate for this purpose. Many university professors, and researchers employed by businesses, also conduct theoretical and empirical research that benefits the real estate industry.

SYNDICATION AND REAL ESTATE SECURITIES

Real estate can be an excellent investment, but the financial requirements of most large real estate projects prevent most individuals from investing in such projects directly. As a result, a variety of investment vehicles have been developed which pool the funds of various individuals in order to make such investments. The real estate investment trust, REIT (Chapter 21) is a popular indirect investment vehicle. REITs need people with a variety of skills. Such enterprises are routinely involved in property acquisition and disposition, and property management. In addition, these organizations need people to sell ownership interests in the organization, and to handle investor relations. The development of the secondary mortgage market (Chapter 16) provides another indirect investment opportunity for those interested in participating in the mortgage loan market. A number of mortgage-related securities are described in Chapter 21.

SUMMARY

Knowledge of the market is important in making good decisions about the acquisition, use, and sale of real estate. But most of us cannot find the time to acquire this knowledge because we are too busy with other things. The same problem confronts those thinking of making an investment in income-producing real estate or real-estate-related securities. If you fit into the "too busy" category, it is suggested that before making any decision concerning real estate you surround yourself with a team of qualified real estate service providers. Selling your home? Getting a good real estate broker, an attorney, and perhaps a home inspector would be helpful. Buying an existing home? Perhaps you should employ a buyer's broker, and line up a mortgage lender to prequalify you for a loan before you start shopping. A home inspector would be a good idea also. When buying a new home, you might want to add a contractor and an architect to your team. There are a number of additional service providers that may be helpful in other real estate endeavors.

KEY TERMS

abstractor	contractor	mortgage lender
agent (real estate)	developer	settlement agent
appraiser	escrow agent	title insurer
architect	home inspector	
broker (real estate)	home warranty policy	

REVIEW QUESTIONS

1. Which real estate service providers usually work directly with real estate sellers and buyers?
2. Describe the services provided by a real estate broker.
3. Describe the service provided by a mortgage lender.
4. Describe the service provided by home inspectors
5. Which real estate service providers usually work behind the scenes to facilitate a transaction?
6. Describe the service provided by a real estate appraiser.
7. Describe the service provided by a real estate attorney.
8. What is the difference between a contractor and a developer?
9. Describe the service provided by a real property management company.
10. Do you intend to pursue a career in real estate? Why?
11. What is your answer to the two questions in the "Decision Point" section of the chapter?

REAL ESTATE ON THE WEB

Use your favorite search engine to:
1. Identify the residential and commercial real estate brokerage firms in your area.
2. Identify and describe local mortgage lenders.
3. Identify and describe local home inspection companies.
4. Identify and describe real estate appraisal firms in your area.
5. Identify and describe local real property management companies.
6. Identify and describe local real estate counselors.
7. Identify and describe a local real estate investors' association.
8. Determine which of the real estate service providers described in this chapter must be licensed to operate in your state.

Refer to the companion Web site at www.wiley.com/college/larsen for a variety of online activities including additional chapter content, review materials, assignments, and related links.

ADDITIONAL READINGS

Barasch, C. S. "Real Estate Mortgage Brokerage: Legal Relationships Between Broker and Borrower." *Real Estate Finance Journal* (Winter 2000): 42–45.

Benjamin, J. D., G. D. Jud, K. A. Roth and D. T. Winkler. "Technology and Realtor® Income." *Journal of Real Estate Finance and Economics* (2002): 51–65.

Downs, A. "Some Principles of Real Estate Counseling." *Real Estate Issues* (Fall 2000): 56–59.

Hill, K. "Forward-Thinking Daniel Jones Meets Industry Challenges Head On." *Canadian Appraiser* (2001): 16–18.

Pomerleano, M. "Back to the Basics: Critical Financial Sector Professions Required in the Aftermath of an Asset Bubble." *Appraisal Journal* (2002): 173–181.

Wyatt, P. "An Investigation of the Nature of the Valuation Service Offered to Business Occupiers." *Journal of Property Investment and Finance* (2001): 100–126.

CHAPTER

3

Home Ownership

Learning Objectives

After studying this chapter you should be able to:

- Explain the ways our government supports home ownership.
- List the advantages and disadvantages of home ownership.
- Estimate how much a prospective purchaser can afford to pay for a home.
- Formulate an informed purchase offer.

FROM THE WIRE

To take a step up the corporate ladder, Larry and Jean Gutman moved from San Diego to St. Louis. Eight years later, another step up required them to move back to San Diego. As they were house hunting in San Diego, they were surprised to find their old house back on the market. Perhaps they should not have sold it. The house that they had sold for $60,000 was now listed at $600,000! Such a dramatic increase may not be typical, but the National Association of REALTORS® recent survey on the wealth effects of home ownership provides some interesting data. In 2001, as people watched the value of their stock portfolios drop, the median price for an existing home increased by 5.5 percent. A record 5.3 million existing homes sold in 2001. It is important to remember that the value of an individual house can go up or down (just like the price of an individual security), but the national median home price has risen every year since record keeping began in 1968.

Go to www.REALTOR.org /realtormag, and search "price trends" to discover what has happened and what is expected to happen to housing prices.

INTRODUCTION

After being introduced to the broad aspects of real estate markets and services, a more personal question may be on your mind—whether (or when) to purchase a residence? To properly answer this question, you should have a basic understanding of the language of real estate and real estate law, and know the steps involved in purchasing real estate. That is a lot of required information. Whether you are planning on buying or selling real estate personally or professionally, or both, the remaining chapters in this book will follow a logical progression of the process involved.

To start, in this chapter, we present some basic information that you should be aware of when considering home ownership. An integral part of the American dream is home ownership. First, we take a look at ways the government facilitates ownership. Then, we describe the advantages of home ownership. One obvious advantage, demonstrated in the chapter opener, "From the Wire," is the possibility that your home will increase in value. There are other advantages associated with home ownership, but there can be disadvantages as well and these are also described. In addition, we explain how you can estimate the maximum amount you are likely to be able to afford to spend on a home, and describe how you can take advantage of information in the public record to formulate a purchase offer.

GOVERNMENT SUPPORT OF HOME OWNERSHIP

Our federal government encourages home ownership and Congress has enacted numerous pieces of legislation to facilitate it. In fact, we have a national home ownership policy; the National Housing Act of 1949 established a national housing goal of a "decent home and a suitable living environment for every American." The theory underlying such legislation is that home ownership results in an improved citizenry because it vests owners with a greater stake in the country.

One way that Congress has encouraged home ownership is through favorable provisions in the federal income tax code. In Chapter 7, we present the details of the tax benefits afforded homeowners, such as the deductability of both mortgage interest and real property taxes in calculating one's federal income tax liability. Congress also periodically comes up with additional tax breaks to help make home ownership more attainable. For example, in 1997, they passed legislation that allows first-time home buyers to make a penalty-free withdrawal of up to $10,000 from an Individual Retirement Account for the down payment on a home (normally a 10 percent penalty applies for early withdrawals from an IRA).

There are several other tax-related ways in which home ownership is encouraged in the United States. In some countries, not including the United States, homeowners must pay taxes on the imputed rent for their home. **Imputed rent** is the rent that owners would have to pay to lease their homes if they did not own them. From a global perspective, the absence of imputed rents in our tax code is an advantage for American homeowners. Examples of imputed rents, or their equivalent, in the Code that have particular importance for students and their instructors include fellowships for graduate students, and tuition remission for family members of faculty attending graduate school. Each is considered taxable income. Because our tax code contains few such provisions for any type of asset ownership, the absence of imputed home rent provisions provides no relative advantage for the ownership of a home versus other goods. Homeowners do, however, receive some relative benefit from other forms of taxation. For example, real property, unlike many other goods, is usually not subject to federal or state excise taxes. An **excise tax** is a direct tax that is imposed on the manufacture, sale, or consumption of a commodity. Examples of excise taxes are: sales taxes, license fees, and the so-called "sin taxes." Sin taxes can add more than 20 percent to the cost of items such as gasoline, alcohol, and tobacco products. Since these items generally do not provide reasonable substitutes for a home, you may wonder how homeowners benefit from the imposition of sales and excise taxes on other goods. First, homes are relatively more affordable because neither the sales tax nor excise taxes generally apply to home purchases. There are exceptions, of course. New York, for example, charges a 1 percent sales tax on the sale of a residential property valued at more than $1,000,000. Second, to the extent that these taxes are used to fund local projects, the revenue generated by these taxes means that real property taxes can be set lower than they would be otherwise. Another way Congress encourages home ownership is through innovative mortgage loan products and programs. In Chapter 16, we will discuss available mortgage loan products, many of which were designed to make home ownership more affordable. The federal government has developed programs to assist households that tend to have difficulty obtaining home ownership. An example of such an effort is the "3-2 mortgage" program designed for first-time, low- and moderate-income buyers. Usually, for a conventional mortgage to qualify for secondary trading (Chapter 16) the minimum down payment is 5 percent. Mortgages written under the 3-2 mortgage program are eligible for secondary trading although the borrower needs only a 3-percent cash down payment. The other 2 percent may be borrowed at the same rate and term as the mortgage, or the borrower can apply money received as a gift. In many cases, the federal government coordinates its efforts with state housing authorities.

State Housing Finance Agencies (SHFA) have been created in almost every state. They address a broad spectrum of housing needs through financing the development and preservation of affordable rental and ownership housing for lower-income citizens. These agencies help fund low- and moderate-income rental housing units and provide low-interest-rate home mortgages. SHFAs operate a number of programs, the most important for potential homeowners being the Mortgage Revenue Bond program. Under this program, the agencies periodically issue tax-exempt bonds and use the funds to make mortgages at below market interest rates to lower-income, first-time buyers of modestly priced homes. The interest rate on such loans can be as much as 2.5 percentage points below conventional rates, which can result in monthly savings of up to $100 on a typical mortgage.

Home ownership has increased because of the programs mentioned above and also because of mortgage industry innovation and outreach to low-income borrowers. With the introduction of low-down-payment products, flexible underwriting standards, and improved risk-assessment tools (Chapters 15-17), more loans are being approved and the goal of home ownership attained by more households. In 2001, 68 percent of Americans owned their own homes, an all-time high. Powered by strong income and employment growth, all age groups, racial and ethnic groups, and geographic regions benefited as part of this trend. In fact, 40 percent of the net growth in home ownership in the final half of the 1990s was among minorities. Loans to low-income buyers in metropolitan areas increased by 55 percent between 1993 and 1998.

HOME OWNERSHIP IN THE UNITED STATES AND OTHER COUNTRIES

Housing is a bargain in the United States compared to many other countries. For example, mortgage payments for the typical American equal 30 percent of household income, while in Australia, mortgage payments amount to 44 percent of household income. Unlike the United States, most other countries do not allow tax deductions for mortgage interest. The Netherlands is one of the few other countries that share the view that the tax system should subsidize home ownership. In addition, the United States is one of the few countries in the world where a 30-year fixed-rate mortgage is available. Lenders in Canada, by contrast, match a five-year fixed-rate home loan with the current rate being offered by banks on deposits (similar to the renegotiable rate mortgage described in Chapter 16). As indicated in Exhibit 3.1, the 68 percent rate of home ownership in the United States compares favorably with home ownership rates in other countries (although we have a long way to go to match Mongolia). In many countries, private ownership of real property is not allowed, and in others it is prohibitively expensive.

ADVANTAGES OF HOME OWNERSHIP

Home ownership is an important part of the traditional American dream. Some value home ownership because a home fulfills a basic human need—the need for shelter. Although this need can also be met with rental property, ownership offers a number of financial and nonfinancial advantages over renting. Nonfinancial advantages include the owner's right to modify the property to suit personal tastes, increased privacy, and the pride of ownership.

The financial advantages of home ownership are numerous. One advantage pertains to owners who employ a fixed-interest-rate mortgage loan. By doing so they lock in the major component of their monthly housing costs. Financial planners and other experts have long suggested that home ownership is one of the best long-run inflation hedges available. An **inflation hedge** is any investment that preserves one's purchasing power by increasing in value by at least the same rate as general price levels. In fact, from 1980 to 2000, home prices, on average, did more than maintain purchasing power. Over this time period, consumer prices increased at an annual rate of 3.8 percent, while selling prices for new and existing homes increased at 4.9 percent and 4.1 percent, respectively. Exhibit 3.2

| EXHIBIT | 3.1 | **HOME OWNERSHIP RATES IN SELECTED COUNTRIES** |

Country	Percentage of Owner-Occupied Housing Stock	Country	Percentage of Owner-Occupied Housing Stock
Australia	61.6	Mexico	66.8
Canada	62.1	Mongolia	100.0
China	18.5	Nigeria	8.0
France	50.7	Norway	66.6
Israel	72.9	Switzerland	29.9
Japan	62.4	United Kingdom	51.1

Source: United Nation's Construction Statistics Yearbook
These figures are for 1988, the last time the United Nations conducted such a survey. At the time this text went to print, the U. N. was contemplating updating the survey.

compares the Consumer Price Index, and the median sale prices of new and existing one-family houses from 1980 to 2000.

While Exhibit 3.2 demonstrates a persistent upward trend in housing prices, it is important to note that, just like any other asset, home prices can decrease as well as increase during a particular holding period. Fortunately, for owners, housing prices have historically been less affected by recessions than many other assets. Even in economically troubled times, the demand for housing tends to remain at a significant level because people need a place to live. Pride of ownership and the tax advantages associated with ownership also motivate some to purchase homes even during periods when home values are decreasing. One of the financial advantages of home ownership is that owners may build equity in the property. **Equity buildup** can occur in one, or both, of two ways: by reducing the mortgage principal, or with increases in the value of the property. An owner's net worth increases as equity buildup occurs and a homeowner may use this to his or her advantage. Equity may be used to secure additional debt, or it may result in increased purchasing power when the property is sold. Finally, homeowners accrue several tax advantages (Chapter 8). For example, the federal government subsidizes homeowners by allowing them to deduct property tax payments and mortgage interest payments for federal income tax purposes (which effectively decreases the cost of housing for homeowners). And homeowners may avoid or postpone income taxes resulting from the sale of a home at a gain.

DISADVANTAGES OF HOME OWNERSHIP

There are disadvantages associated with home ownership that may offset some of the advantages. For example, because homes are a relatively illiquid asset (i.e., it is difficult to secure fair market value quickly), owners tend to be less mobile than renters. Home ownership requires one to be responsible. An owner is fully liable for things for which renters may be only partially responsible, such as: personal injuries suffered by others on the property, repairs, and maintenance. In addition, ownership carries the risk of loss. Judgments, liens, natural disasters, eminent domain condemnation, and many other hazards may threaten one's continued ownership. All of these limitations are described in later chapters.

For many people, financial constraints are another disadvantage of ownership. As demonstrated in Exhibit 3.3, the cost of homes today presents a formidable obstacle for many. Even those who can afford to purchase a home are likely to be able to afford fewer

EXHIBIT 3.2	HOME OWNERSHIP AS AN INFLATION HEDGE: 1980–2000		
Year	Consumer Price Index (% change from previous period)	Median Selling Price of New Single-Family Houses (% change from previous period)	Median Selling Price of Existing Single-Family Houses (% change from previous period)
1980	82.4 (n.a.)	$ 64,000 (n.a.)	$ 62,200 (n.a.)
1985	107.6 (30.6)	84,300 (31.7)	75,500 (21.4)
1990	130.7 (21.5)	122,900 (45.8)	92,000 (21.9)
1995	152.4 (16.6)	133,900 (9.0)	110,500 (20.1)
2000	172.2 (13.0)	169,000 (26.2)	139,000 (25.8)

Sources:

CPI: Monthly Labor Review and Handbook of Labor Statistics. Bureau of Labor Statistics.

New house prices: Current Construction Reports. Series C25 Characteristics of New Housing, and New Family Housing. U. S. Census Bureau & U. S. Department of Housing and Urban Development.

Existing house prices: Real Estate Outlook, Market Trends and Insights. National Association of REALTORS®

EXHIBIT	3.3	WHO CAN AFFORD A MODESTLY-PRICED HOME?

Percent Unable to Afford a Modestly-Priced Home	Group
42	All families
67	Unrelated individuals
87	Female heads of households with children
88	Renter (families)
88	Renter (unrelated individuals)
36	Current homeowners
30	Married couples with no children
30	Households whose members were 55 years of age or older
94	Families with income of $60,000 or more
9	Households whose members were younger than 25 years of age

Source: Savage and Howard. "Who can Afford to Buy a House," Series H121/97–1 (July 1997). Bureau of the Census, Current Housing Reports.

amenities (such as a swimming pool or tennis court) than they could obtain by renting. In financing the acquisition of a home, some people extend themselves to the point where they cannot afford to do much more than live in the home. Such owners are said to be **house poor.**

Unfortunately, for too many people in the United States, the advantages and disadvantages described earlier are not pertinent because a home purchase is beyond their means. The United States Bureau of the Census (the Census Bureau) released a report in 1997 that suggests that the purchase of a modestly-priced home (25 percent of all owner-occupied houses in the area are below this value and 75 percent are above), financed with a 5 percent down payment, 30-year fixed-rate conventional mortgage, is more difficult for some groups than others. For example, they found that renters and single people are less able to afford a home purchase compared to those who already own a home and married couples. Three obstacles to potential home ownership were identified: lack of cash or other financial assets for the down payment and closing costs, insufficient income to make the mortgage payments, and other debt payments that reduce the amount of income available for the mortgage payment. Exhibit 3.3 shows the percentages of various groups that could not afford to purchase a modestly priced home in the area in which they live.

HOW MUCH HOUSE CAN ONE AFFORD?

The maximum price one can afford to pay for a home depends on a number of factors: the extent to which the purchaser will use borrowed funds, the loan terms, the purchaser's income, wealth, and other obligations. A number of criteria have been developed regarding housing affordability. A traditional rule of thumb holds that if one is to avoid becoming house poor, the house price should not exceed 2.5 times annual gross household income. For example, this rule suggests that a family earning $50,000 annually should not purchase a home that costs more than $125,000. Recently, however, it appears that rule is being stretched to three times annual gross household income.

When one uses borrowed funds to finance a home purchase, lender-imposed restrictions are likely to determine the maximum affordable home price. Historically, there were considerable differences between lenders' requirements, but one result of the development of the secondary mortgage market is more uniform underwriting standards. Lenders who wish to sell their loans on the secondary market (which now includes most institutional mortgage originators) have formal income rules that they must use to qualify mortgage loan applicants. The specific income rules depend on the type of loan. For example, with a conventional fixed-rate mortgage, the monthly mortgage payment (including escrow deposits for property taxes and insurance premiums) can be no more than 28 percent of the borrower's monthly gross income. And the combination of the mortgage payment and other recurring obligations (e.g., payments for car loans, student loans, and alimony) can be no more than 36 percent of the borrower's gross monthly income. Similar requirements are applicable for FHA-insured (Federal Housing Authority) and VA-guaranteed (Veterans Administration) loans.

Decision Point

You are contemplating purchasing a home. What is a realistic upper price limit for you if your annual gross income is $36,000 and you want to avoid becoming house poor?

MAKING AN INFORMED PURCHASE OFFER

Traditionally, prospective buyers have begun their home search by scanning classified newspaper advertisements or calling a real estate agent. At some point, a property is identified and the would-be purchaser makes an offer of an amount less than the list price. If the offer is accepted, did the buyer get a good deal? Maybe, and maybe not. In this section, we present a strategy that may save buyers money and prevent unwanted surprises. Our legal system requires that all documentation concerning real property be filed at the County level. The strategy involves gathering information at various County offices that will enable prospective owners to make a more informed purchase offer than under the traditional scenario.

After identifying one or more potential properties, a good starting point for gathering useful information is the County Auditor's Office. (The exact title of this and other offices may vary with location. For example, in some areas this office is known as the County Tax

DOING BUSINESS
QUALIFYING A LOAN APPLICATION

Douglas Charles had some bad news for Fred and Barbara White, the very first mortgage loan applicants he dealt with in his new job as a loan officer with the First National Mortgage Corporation in Des Moines, Iowa. The White's had applied for a 30-year, conventional home loan and reported monthly gross income of $5,000. Douglas calculated that the monthly payment for the White's loan was just pennies under $1,400. This was good because, according to the income rule he had to use in qualifying applicants, the White's loan payment could amount to no more than 28 percent of their gross monthly income ($1,400 = $5,000 x .28). Unfortunately, the White's other recurring monthly obligations amounted to $800. If Douglas was going to write the loan, these obligations could amount to no more than $400 [($5,000 x .36) − $1,400].

The White's were disappointed, but there was no way they could increase their down payment or eliminate their other recurring obligations. However, using the Internet, with the words "mortgage lender" as a key-word search term, Fred discovered other lenders willing to write a loan using less stringent criteria.

Some lenders do write loans that do not conform to the guidelines Douglas had to follow (and these loans will not qualify for secondary trading). They are sometimes called nonconforming lenders. Douglas wished the Whites well and silently hoped they realized that the interest rate and points that nonconforming lenders charge can be quite high.

Go to www.clarkhoward.com, and search "subprime mortgage lending" to learn more about this topic.

Assessor's Office.) Identifying more than one acceptable property rather than "falling in love" with a single property may increase the purchaser's bargaining position and also enable the purchaser to sequence offers to maximize consumer surplus. **Consumer surplus** is the difference between what one must pay for a property and the amount at which they value the property. Armed with the street address, or in some cases a "key number" (which can be determined at the office), one can learn several potentially useful pieces of information, including: when the house was built; the current owner's name; the legal description of the property (Chapter 8); various property characteristics (e.g., lot size, number of rooms, etc.); and the property's assessed value.

Decision Point

You are considering a home purchase and have narrowed the possible candidates down to three. Given the following information, how would you sequence your offers to maximize consumer surplus?

House	List Price	Price You Will Offer	Your Estimate of House Value
One	$100,000	$95,000	$96,000
Two	$105,000	$95,000	$95,000
Three	$98,000	$96,000	$99,000

The first four pieces of information mentioned in the previous paragraph are usually found on the property-listing sheet, which is available from the listing agent. It is important, however, to compare the official information to the sales information; any differences may cause one to question the seller's veracity. For example, the listing sheet might claim that the property is thirty years old, but the official records indicate that it is fifty years old. Likewise, if a physical inspection of the property reveals two and one-half bathrooms, but the official records show only one and one-half, the buyer may wish to ensure that the additional bathroom was installed according to local building codes. This requires a stop at the Building Inspector's Office, which will be explained shortly. In many cases, the assessed value indicates a floor, or minimum, price that the seller might entertain. This depends on market conditions, however, and other information discovered through your research might suggest that the seller would accept a lower offer.

The purchaser must ask two important questions regarding the assessed value. First, does the assessed value represent the Assessor's estimate of fair market value (FMV)? And second, when was the assessment made? In many locations the assessed value represents only a fraction of what the Assessor thinks is FMV. For example, assume that the assessed

AN ETHICAL ISSUE
DISCLOSURE OF PROPERTY DEFECTS

"Buyer beware" is an appropriate motto for home purchases. Sellers are in a much better position to know about a property's defects because they have lived there. Some defects may be quite difficult to detect. Historically, most sellers have not made much effort to disclose defects to potential buyers. To provide buyers with better information, some states have adopted laws that require home sellers to disclose in writing any known defects to the buyer.

1. If you were selling your home and were required by law to disclose any defects would you disclose them all? Why? What kind of property defects would you not disclose?

2. If you were selling your home and were not required by law to disclose any defects would you disclose any of them? Why? What kind of property defects would you not disclose?

value of a property is $70,000, but that all property in the area is assessed at 75 percent of FMV: Therefore, in the Assessor's opinion, FMV equals $93,333 ($70,000 is 75 percent of $93,333). If the assessment was made recently this value could be used to formulate a purchase offer. An adjustment for inflation may be required, however, if some time has elapsed since the last assessment date.

Using the legal description of the property obtained at the Assessor's Office, you can obtain several additional pieces of information at the Office of the Registrar of Deeds (County Recorder), including: the ownership history of the property; the date the current owner acquired title; the type of deed held by the current owner; and the price the current owner paid. Although there may be other explanations, frequent ownership turnover could indicate a hidden problem with the property. The price the current owner paid for the property may be of particular importance in formulating a purchase offer, because research suggests that home owners with extended tenure in the property may be more willing to accept low offers.

To illustrate this point, consider the owners of two identical homes with FMV of $100,000 who have listed their property with a broker. Owner A purchased his property two years ago for $93,000. Owner B purchased his home fifteen years ago for $55,000. Each receives an offer of $96,000 for his property. Although both owners may be unhappy with what they consider a low offer, owner A is more likely to reject it because he can easily calculate that he will incur a loss after paying the brokerage commission. Owner B may rationalize acceptance of the offer by comparing it to his purchase price; he may ignore the fact that he may incur a loss in purchasing power.

Inquiry at other public offices will result in additional pieces of useful information. The exact amount of property taxes for the previous tax year, and any delinquent property taxes, can be found at the County Treasurer's Office. Again, a prospective purchaser can compare the tax bill to the information on the listing sheet; delinquent taxes are likely to indicate what people in the real estate industry refer to as a "motivated seller." Any paperwork on work performed on the property that involves local codes can be discovered at the Building Inspector's Office. In addition, it should be possible to determine the original cost to build the improvements to the property, which may be particularly useful if one is considering a new home. The Planning and Zoning Commission will provide information regarding any planned zoning, or other, changes (e.g., installation of sidewalks, sewer, or water-lines; and street-widening) that may negatively affect the value of the property or result in a special assessment being levied. Finally, examination of the judgment rolls and lis pendens file at the County Courthouse will reveal whether the seller has any existing or pending obligations which, again, may indicate a motivated seller.

DOING BUSINESS

TECHNOLOGY

In some cases, a physical visit to the public records offices mentioned above can be truncated because at least some of the information needed to pursue our purchase offer strategy can be obtained via a virtual trip. Many County Assessors and Treasurers offices in metropolitan areas make their information available on their web site. In less populace counties, a real trip is still required because the offices do not have a web site. Even in most metropolitan areas, while the County court, Building Inspector, and other offices mentioned above may have web sites containing useful information, almost none include the detailed information that you need to pursue our strategy.

Go to www.alta.org, click on search and enter "title search," to learn about automated title search processes.

SUMMARY

Most American households own their own home, which is a tribute to their industriousness. Some have achieved this goal with a bit of assistance from our government, which encourages home ownership and facilitates it principally through tax benefits and innovative mortgage loan products and programs. These efforts, and the effort of our citizenry, have resulted in a home ownership rate in the United States that compares favorably with other developed countries. In this chapter, we detailed the advantages and disadvantages of home ownership. Since nearly seven of ten households in the United States own their own homes, for them, the advantages of ownership apparently outweigh the disadvantages. However, despite the fact that there are federal and state programs designed to facilitate home ownership, it is beyond the reach of many Americans, so additional efforts need to be made.

There are a number of steps prospective homeowners can take to increase the possibility of owning a home. First, while improved savings habits would eventually make ownership more affordable for everyone, lower- and middle-income households may be able to purchase a home sooner by taking advantage of government loan programs. In addition, better home-shopping habits may increase ownership possibilities. Review of the public records can enable one to acquire property at a reduced cost, and/or avoid unwanted surprises. Another way to acquire one's dream home is to settle for a small home for a short period of time. One can build up equity in a smaller home, and eventually use it to acquire one's dream home.

KEY TERMS

consumer surplus

excise tax

equity build-up

house poor

imputed rent

inflation hedge

State Housing Finance
Agencies

REVIEW QUESTIONS

1. Do you own or rent your dwelling? Why?
2. How does our government support home ownership?
3. What are the advantages of home ownership?
4. What are the disadvantages of home ownership?
5. What do you consider to be the primary advantage and disadvantage of owning a home?
6. What factors affect the affordability of home ownership for a particular individual?
7. In what public office would you look if you wanted to know the assessed value of a property?
8. In what public office would you look if you wanted to see a copy of a property owner's deed?
9. In what public office would you look if you wanted to know the amount of the annual property taxes for a property?
10. In what public office would you look if you wanted to know whether there are any current or pending lawsuits against a property owner?
11. In what public office would you look if you wanted to know how a property is zoned?
12. In what public office would you look if you wanted to verify that an addition to a home was constructed in compliance with the building code?
13. What are your answers to the questions in the two "Decision Point" sections in this chapter?

PROBLEMS

1. Assume you have identified three properties that you are considering purchasing as your home. Properties A, B, and C are listed at $140,000, $145,000, and $150,000, respectively.

Also assume that you believe property A is worth $137,000, that property B is worth $142,000, and that property C is worth $141,000. If you were willing to offer as much as $137,000 for any of the houses:

    a. What is your consumer surplus for each house?

    b. If you want to maximize consumer surplus, how should you sequence your offers?

2. Using the 2.5 times earnings rule of thumb, what is the most you should pay for a home if:

    a. Your annual gross income is $45,000?

    b. Your monthly gross income is $8,000?

    c. Your weekly gross income is $1,500?

REAL ESTATE ON THE WEB

Use your favorite search engine to:

1. Determine the official title of the state housing finance agency in your state, and describe the programs they currently offer to assist home purchasers.

2. Determine what percentage of homes in your area and state are owner-occupied.

3. Find a house currently for sale in your area that you:

    a. Would like to own regardless of price.

    b. Could afford to purchase given the 2.5 times income rule of thumb mentioned in the chapter.

4. Determine which of your County Records' Offices have Web sites and discover what information is available on their sites.

Refer to the companion Web site at www.wiley.com/college/larsen for a variety of online activities including additional chapter content, review materials, assignments, and related links.

ADDITIONAL READINGS

Arimah, Ben C. "Housing-Sector Performance in a Global Perspective: A Cross-City Investigation." *Urban Studies* (December 2000): 2551–2579.

Fong, Eric and Kumiko Shibuya. "Suburbanization and Home Ownership: The Spatial Assimilation Process in U. S. Metropolitan Areas." *Sociological Perspectives* (Spring 2000): 137–157.

Francese, Peter. "The Coming Boom in Second-Home Ownership." *American Demographics* (October 2001): 26–27.

Lang, Susan S. "High Home Prices are the Result of Bigger Houses and More Amenities." *Human Ecology* (Summer 2000): 3.

Leon, Hortense. "High Hopes for Immigrant Homeownership." *Mortgage Banking* (October 1999): 24–31.

Sloan, Bill. "So You Want to Buy a Home." *USA Today,* vol. 130 no. 2680 (January 2002): 72–74.

Real Estate Ownership And the Law

P A R T

II

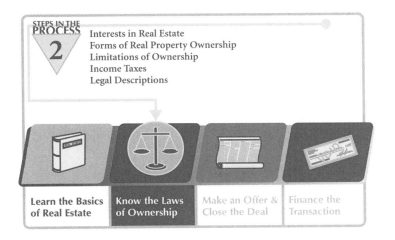

STEPS IN THE PROCESS

2

Interests in Real Estate
Forms of Real Property Ownership
Limitations of Ownership
Income Taxes
Legal Descriptions

Learn the Basics of Real Estate | **Know the Laws of Ownership** | Make an Offer & Close the Deal | Finance the Transaction

In Part II, several important topics regarding real property rights are presented. There are many valuable lessons to be learned in here. Paramount is that the most important asset gained when one acquires an interest in real property is the set of property rights associated with the interest. Without these rights, which are presented in Chapter 4, Interests In Real Estate, there would be little incentive to own real property. The material in Part II makes it clear, however, that real property rights are not unlimited. Chapter 4 outlines the ways property rights are affected by the estate or ownership interest one possesses. In addition, the form of ownership employed may affect the owner's real property rights. Therefore, the various forms of real property ownership are presented in Chapter 5, Forms of Ownership. In Chapter 6, Limitations on Ownership, we show that property rights may also be limited either by the government or by private parties. Most people in the United States are legally obligated to pay taxes, or at least file an income tax return, and real estate ownership affects the amount of tax owed. Therefore, Chapter 7, Income Taxes, presents information about income taxes. All of this presumes that we have some way to distinguish one owner's property from property owned by others. Fortunately, we do, and Chapter 8, Legal Descriptions, presents various methods that may be used to describe real property.

CHAPTER 4

Interests in Real Estate

Learning Objectives

After studying this chapter you should be able to:

- Describe the property rights associated with real property ownership.
- Identify the parties to a deed.
- Identify and describe the various estates in land.
- Describe the process of taking title by adverse possession.

FROM THE WIRE

The Kiesels purchased a riverfront property in Lee County, Florida, and built a home on it. Later, the county built a bridge that crossed the river at an angle. The bridge did not physically encroach upon the Kiesel's property, but it obstructed their view of the river. Therefore, the Kiesels initiated a lawsuit, alleging that the county had (effectively) taken their property without compensation. At trial, their expert witness testified that the placement of the bridge had reduced the value of the Kiesel's property by $300,000. The court agreed, and the decision was upheld upon appeal. The decision was based on the court's interpretation of Florida's riparian rights (discussed in this chapter under "water rights"). The court held that these rights constitute property, and that the county had intruded on this right of the Kiesel's property ownership.

Go to water.usgs.gov, click on "Local Websites & USGS Contacts in Your State," then click on your state on the map to learn about water resources and regulations in your state.

INTRODUCTION

When one obtains ownership of real property the most important thing acquired is not the physical property, but the property rights associated with the property. To illustrate this important point, assume that property rights do not exist, and that you purchased the nicest home in the neighborhood. There is a maxim in real estate that suggests one should never buy the best home in a neighborhood because every other property in the neighborhood will act as a negative externality on that home. An externality is an external factor that affects the value of the subject property. A negative externality depresses the value of the subject property, while a positive externality enhances the value of the subject property. But you ignored this advice, and hope to enjoy a relaxing evening when you hear a party being held by your neighbors around the pool in your backyard. They decided to have the party at your house because it is so much nicer than their own. Without property rights you are powerless to prevent such an occurrence and it is not likely that you would choose to own real property.

In this chapter, the property rights associated with real property ownership are described. An interest in real property is referred to as an **estate,** and the rights one is entitled to depend upon the type of estate held. All estates may be classified into one of two categories. One category is a **freehold estate,** and represents an ownership interest in real property. The other category is a **leasehold estate,** and entitles the holder to use the property for a period of time, but without ownership of the property. Those who rent real property have a leasehold estate (Chapter 18).

Freehold estates can be classified into the following categories: possessory interests, future interests, potential interests, and nonpossessory interests. This chapter focuses on possessory and future interests. A possessory interest entitles the owner to current possession of the property, while a future interest entitles the interest holder to possession of the property at some time in the future. Potential and nonpossessory interests, discussed further in Chapter 7, both act to restrict the rights of the possessory interest holder. The concept of title and the parties to a deed are introduced to facilitate the discussion of estates.

REAL PROPERTY RIGHTS

One usually acquires a number of rights with the acquisition of real property. These rights empower the owner to use (and/or dispose of) the property in any legal manner. They include the right of possession, the right of control, the right of quiet enjoyment, and the right of disposition.

The right of possession gives the owner the right to physically occupy the property and use it as desired, including the right to keep all others out. The right of possession is not unlimited, however, as a property cannot be used as a nuisance. A nuisance is a use that prevents others from enjoying their property.

The right of control gives the owner the right to physically alter the property as well as the right to control property use even if he or she chooses not to physically possess the property. For example, a property owner may choose to rent the property to others.

The right of quiet enjoyment protects the owner from interference by previous owners or others. The right of quiet enjoyment does not involve noise levels, which are controlled by local ordinances.

The right of disposition enables the owner to transfer his or her ownership in the real property, either during his or her lifetime or upon his or her death. The right of disposition includes the right to give the property away. In addition, the right of disposition enables the owner to transfer an interest of less than full ownership to another.

Real property ownership entitles the owner to property rights at three different physical levels: the property surface, the subsurface, and the supersurface or airspace. Exhibit 4.1 illustrates the three areas associated with a hypothetical property.

The **subsurface** area of a particular property is defined by imaginary straight lines that converge at the center of the planet from the property boundaries at the surface. The subsurface rights associated with real property ownership include the right to remove oil, coal, gravel, gas, sand, and minerals from the subsurface. The owner of a property may exercise this right or sell the right to another party without affecting the owner's surface or supersurface rights. However, as the following section, "DOING BUSINESS: Legal Issues," demonstrates, if an owner sells such rights, it would be wise to specify a method of removal that minimizes interference with the surface owner's activities.

The **supersurface** area of a particular property is defined by extending the imaginary lines that marked the subsurface area out into space. Supersurface rights include air rights, solar rights, and other rights to use the space above the surface of the land. These rights extend upward to include an area that can reasonably be expected to be used by the owner. Parties other than the property owner, aircraft for example, are entitled to use the space above the owner's point of reasonable use. Supersurface rights within the owner's reasonable point of use may be sold, leased, or have easements (Chapter 6) placed on them. In recent decades, buildings have been erected using unique combinations of surface, subsurface and supersurface rights. For example, buildings have been built in the airspace above highways and railroads in metropolitan areas where land is both expensive and scarce. The building housing the Chicago Stock Exchange, for example, is constructed above a highway.

WATER RIGHTS

The right to use water is frequently associated with real property ownership. Water rights vary, however, depending on specific state laws and the water source. Water

| EXHIBIT | 4.1 | **PHYSICAL LEVELS OF REAL PROPERTY RIGHTS** |

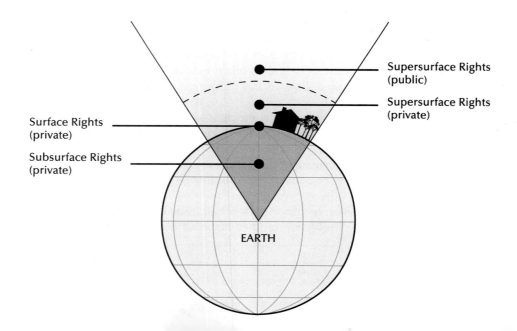

sources may be classified into one of three categories: riparian, surface, and percolating ground water.

Riparian water refers to water in a natural stream or lake. There are two basic systems that govern the use of riparian water. One system, sometimes called the riparian system, is used in many eastern states. Under the riparian system all landowners with property adjacent to the riparian water have the right to make a reasonable use of the riparian water source, subject only to the limitation that the owner may not interrupt or change the flow of the water, and may not contaminate it. And as the "From the Wire" chapter opener indicates "reasonable use," at least in some jurisdictions, includes an unobstructed view of the water.

The other system, sometimes referred to as prior appropriation, is used by many western states. Under the prior appropriation system, a permit, issued by the state, is required for the right to use riparian water, except for normal domestic use. This system is based on the prior appropriation doctrine, which means during water shortages the prior permit holders are given priority over those who began their use at a later time. A special set of water use rights, known as littoral rights, has been developed for those who own property next to very large, non-flowing bodies of water. Littoral rights entitle the owners of such land to use nonflowing bodies of water without restriction.

Surface water is water on the surface of the land but not yet a part of a riparian source. Most states allow property owners to use as much surface water as they can capture. On the other hand, one may not discharge surface water onto another's property in a manner that would cause damage to a neighboring property.

Water beneath the surface that is not in an underground stream or lake is known as percolating ground water. Most states allow real property owners to remove and use percolating ground water.

LIMITATIONS ON PROPERTY RIGHTS

The various possessory and future interests one can hold in real property provide the owner with a set of property rights. Some property interests have limited rights compared to others. All possible limitations are not discussed in this chapter. Additional limitations are detailed throughout the text. The limitations discussed in this chapter stem from a number of sources and may restrict an owner's right to: possession, control, quiet enjoyment, or disposition. In some cases, they may even affect the owner's continued ownership of the property.

TITLE TO REAL PROPERTY

In real estate, **title** is synonymous with ownership. In the United States, title to real property may be held either publicly (by a governmental body) or privately (by any entity other

DOING BUSINESS
LEGAL ISSUES

The fact that real property rights below the surface can be transferred separately from the surface rights can cause problems. To illustrate this, consider the dilemma faced by a real property developer in Texas. The developer was forced to abandon plans to build a shopping mall, after the land for the mall had been acquired and substantial costs incurred, upon learning that a previous landowner had sold the mineral rights to the property to a drilling company. The drilling company was unwilling to sell the valuable rights to the developer. The developer concluded that while drilling rigs in the parking lot, or in the mall, would provide a unique shopping experience, it was not compatible with the shopping atmosphere he wished to develop.

Go to www.caprep.com, and click on one of the headlines to learn more about mineral rights or other current environmental issues.

than the government). Private title can be held in severalty, by one owner, or concurrently, by two or more owners. A variety of organizational forms may hold title, including among others: corporations, partnerships, and trusts.

Titles may be divided into two broad categories: original, and derivative. Only nations can hold original title. Our focus is on derivative titles that are derived from original titles and are the only type of title an individual can hold. Original titles are important, however, because if a derivative title cannot be traced back to an original title, the owner's interest may be in jeopardy.

Derivative titles can be classified into two groups: title by descent, and title by purchase. Title by descent occurs when one obtains ownership from a relative who died intestate (without a valid will). Title by purchase includes titles acquired by all other methods except by descent. Titles acquired by will, gift, or outright purchases are titles by purchase.

HOW ORIGINAL TITLE IS ACQUIRED

Nations acquire original title to land in a number of ways. One way is by discovery. The first country to find and claim ownership to real property acquires original title by discovery. For example, the European nations acquired original title to much of the Western Hemisphere centuries ago. Few opportunities remain to acquire original title by discovery. Another way original title is acquired is by occupancy. When a nation's people actually live on the land they acquire original title by occupancy. One nation may claim original title by occupancy although another has previously claimed title by discovery. In this context, the word "original" is not synonymous with the words "initial" or "first." Original title refers to the title a particular nation claims.

Numerous wars have been fought to settle title disputes between nations, both claiming title either by discovery or occupancy. Another way original title may be acquired is by conquest. Nations have gone to war over disagreements other than real property title. A frequent outcome of these disputes is the transfer of ownership of the loser's land to the winner. Private titles are often unaffected in such cases. For example, the United States gained title to a substantial amount of land as a result of the Spanish-American War, yet private land grants that predated the war were honored by the American government.

Finally, original title may be acquired by cession. Original title by cession is acquired when one nation grants title to another nation. For example, the United States purchased, from Russia, the territory that is now the state of Alaska.

TRANSFERRING TITLE

When title to real property is conveyed from one party to another the transaction is referred to as a grant. A grant may be accomplished by a deed and by will (Chapter 12). A deed is the legal document used to grant, or convey, title to real property. In a deed, the grantor is the person transferring title, and the person receiving title is the grantee. When the individual who transfers title is deceased, the intention to transfer title to real property is made by devise—a will, or a clause in a will, conveying real property. In this case, a deed would be prepared by the executor of the deceased's estate.

PUBLIC GRANTS

Most of the land in the United States was originally titled to the federal government, which still holds title to approximately one-third of it. Transfer of title to private hands is accomplished through a public grant. The distinguishing feature of a public grant is that the grantor is a governmental body. The authority to grant title of public land to private parties is given either by Congress or a particular state legislature, and is accomplished in one of two ways—either a general or a special act.

A general act expresses the means by which a private party may acquire title to public land. For example, portions of Oklahoma were transferred to private ownership through a general act that specified that title would be given to those who were the first to mark and inhabit tracts of land (the Homestead Act, passed in 1862 to encourage settlement of the frontier, was repealed in 1976).

A special act expressly transfers certain land to certain parties. Parties acquiring land from the government receive a patent. A patent is the instrument by which a government grants land to private parties.

PRIVATE GRANTS

When the grantor is a private party the transfer is referred to as a private grant. Most transfers or grants of title to real property are between individuals. Therefore, most grants are private grants and both parties to the deed are private individuals. In some cases, a private party makes a grant to the public called a dedication. A dedication is a private grant because the grantor is a private party. For a dedication to be effective the wording of the deed must make the grantor's intention to surrender the property to the public clear, and the public must accept the grant. Acceptance of a dedication is particularly important considering recent problems involving the clean up of toxic waste. An unscrupulous party could dedicate polluted property in an effort to transfer future clean-up costs to the government.

FREEHOLD ESTATES

Estates that represent an ownership interest in real property are called freehold estates. There are several kinds of freehold estates: absolute fees, defeasible fees, and life estates. Each type of estate has a unique set of property rights.

FEE SIMPLE ABSOLUTE

A **fee simple absolute** (also known as fee simple, fee absolute, absolute fee, and fee) is the most desirable estate to hold because the owner usually has all of the property rights that attach to land. While possible limitations to such property rights are described in subsequent chapters, when one has an absolute fee no one can own or use the real property without the permission of the owner. The fee simple owner may use the real property or dispose of it in any legal manner, and the property rights held by a fee simple owner continue for an unlimited duration of time. The feature of unlimited duration distinguishes the fee simple absolute from other estates in real property. Fee simple is the most prevalent estate in real property. The fee simple is usually acquired in a residential real estate transaction, and ownership in fee simple is what most people perceive as "real property ownership."

The holder of a fee simple interest can transfer the interest to another party either by executing a deed, or by will. No specific language or wording is required to convey a fee simple interest, but it must be apparent from the language in the document that no conditions or limitations are placed on the ownership interest conveyed. A fee simple absolute may be transferred using words such as the following:

> "This tract of real estate is hereby transferred from Peggy and Eugene Shoemaker to Earl and Wanda Brown, their heirs and assigns."

DEFEASIBLE FEES

A **defeasible fee,** also known as a qualified fee, is a freehold estate because it is of indefinite duration, but it is less than a fee simple because the holder's right to use the property is restricted in some way. Such interests are called defeasible fees because they can be defeated or defeased in the future should a stated condition occur, or fail to occur. The condition that creates the qualified fee is imposed by the person creating the estate, and the condition may continue for a specified period of time or it may be permanent.

While defeasible fees are relatively rare, they merit study because, if the condition or conditions are not met, the holder of the defeasible fee may lose his or her interest in the property. A defeasible fee occurs when the property rights of an absolute fee are divided and spread among different parties. Two major types of defeasible fees are fee simple determinable, and fee simple subject to a condition subsequent.

Fee Simple Determinable

A **fee simple determinable** (also called: base fee, fee on limitation, or determinable fee) is an ownership interest that continues until the occurrence of some event. The event usually, but not always, involves the use to which the property can be put. Classic examples of the fee simple determinable involve transfer of title to a church, school, or governmental body. The named event creating the determinable fee must be a contingency and not a certainty, because one of the essential characteristics of the determinable fee is that it may last forever.

A fee simple determinable is created when the legal instrument transferring title contains words effective to create a fee simple and, in addition, a provision for automatic expiration of the estate upon the occurrence of a stated event. The common phrases used to create a fee simple determinable are, "so long as," "until," and "as long as." For example:

> This tract of real estate is hereby transferred from Fred Dean and Barbara
> Dean to the First Church so long as such tract is used as the site for a church
> and no longer.

The above language indicates that the First Church did not receive a fee simple absolute ownership because the Deans did not grant an ownership interest that was intended to last forever, although it may. The holder of a determinable fee has all the real property rights normally associated with fee simple absolute ownership, except the right to change the use.

A fee simple determinable, as illustrated in Exhibit 4.2, occurs as the result of a division of a fee simple absolute into two parts: the determinable fee, and the possibility of reverter that is retained by the grantor. Until the named event occurs, the possibility of reverter is a **future interest,** the holder of which has no current rights to the property.

Termination of Fee Simple Determinable

If the named event occurs, the determinable fee reverts to the owner of the possibility of reverter, and the estate from which both interests evolved is restored to the grantor or his or her heirs. The fee simple absolute from which the fee determinable evolved can be restored in two other ways: first, if either the determinable fee owner or the owner of the possibility of reverter transfers their interest to the other; or second, if both the determinable fee owner and the owner of the possibility of reverter transfer their respective interest to the same third party.

Technically, the determinable fee is terminated automatically upon the happening of the contingent event; no legal proceedings are required to accomplish the reversion of title.

EXHIBIT   4.2   **CREATION OF A FEE SIMPLE DETERMINABLE**

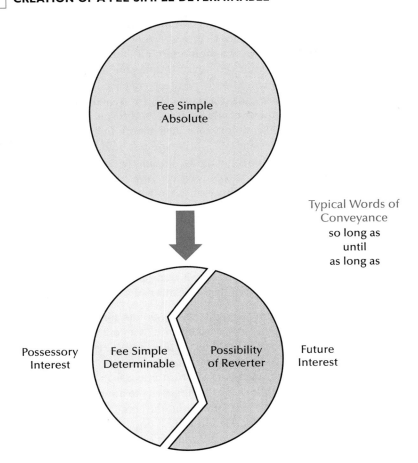

Recently, however, courts have been reluctant to enforce a fee simple determinable literally. The courts consider it harsh to automatically divest ownership from the violating owner without compensation for any improvements made, but it does occur. For example, several years ago a municipal government sought to maintain ownership of land that was deeded to it nearly a hundred years earlier. In that conveyance, the grantor specified that the municipality's ownership interest was to continue "so long as the land is used as a railroad station." Railroad service was discontinued to the community and the municipality wanted to sell the land that would then be put to another use. The court affirmed the grantor's heirs' claim that ownership of the land reverted to them.

It may also be possible to prevent automatic reversion of title in a fee simple determinable. In certain cases, including those that are factually similar to the situation described in the "Doing Business: Legal Issues" box, actions can be taken to prevent this occurrence.

Fee Simple Subject to a Condition Subsequent

A **fee simple subject to a condition subsequent** (also known as: fee simple conditional, fee on condition, or fee on condition subsequent) is similar to the fee simple determinable in several respects. As illustrated in Exhibit 4.3, the grant splits a fee simple absolute into two parts. In this case, however, the future interest retained by the grantor is known as a **right of entry for condition broken,** or more simply as a **right of entry.** A grantor may use this type of grant to exercise some control over the property. Under this grant, the grantee can exercise all the rights associated with a fee simple interest, except that which would violate the stated condition. The absolute fee from which the conditional fee evolved can be restored in ways similar to those previously discussed for a determinable fee.

There is, however, an important difference between a fee simple conditional and a fee simple determinable. For a fee simple conditional, the right of entry does not become active until the condition is violated, and even then only if the person with the right or his or her heirs takes positive action. This is done by suing the grantee and proving in court that the subsequent condition has been broken. However, the holder of the right of entry is under no obligation to take such action. In essence, given the occurrence of the stated condition, reversion to the future interest holder is not automatic.

One rarely finds the terms "fee simple determinable," or "fee simple subject to a condition subsequent," in a conveyance. Instead, grantors use certain language to imply one or the other. Common phrases used to create a fee simple subject to a condition subsequent include; "subject to the following," "but if," "subject to the condition(s) and restriction(s) that," "on the condition that," and "provided that." Compare these phrases to the language used to imply a fee simple determinable. An example of the language used to create a fee simple subject to a condition subsequent is as follows:

> "This tract of real estate is transferred from Kenneth Savage to my son, David Savage, provided that he is married before reaching the age of thirty."

This example highlights several points. First, note that in this case, it is the nonoccurrence of an event, not the occurrence of an event, which can terminate the grantee's interest. If David is not married by the time he reaches the age of thirty, he could lose his interest in the property. Second, note that the condition is not permanent. While David initially receives a defeasible fee, it will turn into a fee absolute upon his marriage. Last, note that the wording implies a fee simple subject to a subsequent condition, and, therefore, if David does not marry in the allotted time, the grantor must take action, exercise the right of entry, to reclaim his original interest. If he does not, David will retain the defeasible fee and in several states his interest will convert to an absolute fee with the passage of time.

Economic Consequences of Defeasible Fees

Determinable fees are freely transferable, but it is impossible for one to legally transfer a greater ownership interest than one's own interest in real property. Therefore, until the occurrence of the event, parties whose titles derive from a defeasible fee also hold a defeasible fee.

DOING BUSINESS
LEGAL ISSUES

Mr. Hardesty was a nature lover. He also owned a considerable amount of land. Upon his death, his will specified that ownership to some of his land be transferred to the city so long as the land be used only as a public park and that no structures be erected upon the land or else ownership of the land would revert to his estate. As a result, the city received a fee simple determinable. Two decades passed before the community decided to build a picnic shelter in the park. Fortunately, someone recalled the restriction on the property use and Mr. Hardesty's heirs were contacted. The heirs concluded that a picnic shelter would not violate the intention of Mr. Hardesty and signed a release so the structure could be built.

Go to www.lexis-nexis.com/universe, (using your university computer system), click on Legal Research, then click on Area of Law By Topic and enter the key words "fee simple determinable" (or whatever type of ownership interest that you wish to investigate) to learn about other court cases involving these concepts.

EXHIBIT 4.3 CREATION OF A FEE SIMPLE SUBJECT TO A CONDITION SUBSEQUENT

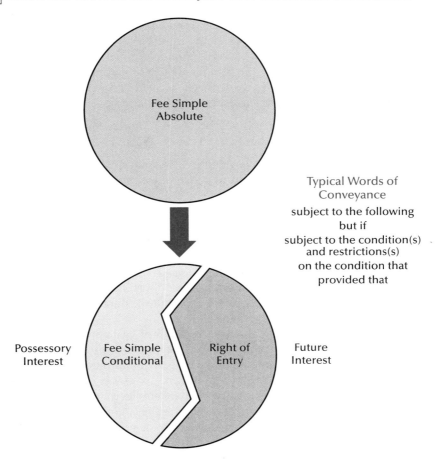

Real property purchasers and mortgage lenders prefer real estate to be owned in fee simple absolute rather than as a fee simple determinable or conditional. Why? Because it is possible for owners of defeasible fees to lose title, with no compensation for loss, because of the occurrence of a contingent event. Therefore, purchasers may offer less, and lenders may lend less for property owned under a defeasible fee.

LIFE ESTATE

A **life estate** is an ownership interest that is limited to the natural life of a person. This feature distinguishes most life estates from the estates described previously, all of which can be passed on by will or probate. A life estate is a freehold estate because it is of indeterminate length, but the owner of a life estate, the **life tenant,** can generally not transfer the interest by will because the estate ends with his or her life. An exception to termination of a life estate upon the life tenant's death is the life estate pour autre vie (which is explained later). As illustrated in Exhibit 4.4, for most life estates there are three parties with an interest in the property; the grantor (or his or her estate) retains a right of reversion, the grantee has the life estate, and a third party, the remainderman, has a future interest. Life estates may be classified into three categories: conventional, legal, and pour autre vie.

Conventional Life Estate

A conventional life estate, sometimes called an ordinary life estate, is created when a grantor uses the appropriate words of conveyance. To illustrate a life estate, assume that Richard Harrison has ownership in fee simple of a tract of land with a house. He wishes to ensure that his wife, Kay, has a place to live for the rest of her life, but would also like to ensure that his favorite nephew, William, gets the property after his wife dies. He can accomplish both objectives with language similar to the following:

> "This tract of real estate is transferred from Richard Harrison to Kay Harrison for life, and then to William Harrison."

In this example, the life tenant grantee, Kay, received an ordinary life estate because the life estate was created by a grantor exercising his right to dispose of the property. William has a remainder interest, and Richard (or his estate) retains a reversionary interest. The same conventional life estate could also be created after Richard's death with appropriate instructions specified in his will.

Rights and Duties of the Life Tenant With a few exceptions, the life tenant has full ownership rights for life. A life tenant has the right to use and control the property, mortgage it, rent it to others, or sell his or her interest. If a life estate is sold, the new grantee will hold a life estate pour autre vie, but the duration of the new life estate is still determined by the life of the original life tenant.

Life tenants also have a number of legal responsibilities. They have the duty to pay any property taxes, and to pay any interest on any mortgage on the property. In addition, and because their interest in the property is of limited duration, life tenants have the duty not to commit waste on the property. Waste is defined as any action that would unreasonably lower the value of the property. Examples of waste include: the removal of a structure, or the failure to maintain a structure in a usable condition for its intended purpose. The clear-cutting of timber, or the removal of sand, gravel or minerals from the property may also be waste. If such removal existed when the life estate was created, and the life tenant was not specifically prevented from such removal in the conveyance, such removal would not constitute waste. If, however, the removal is prohibited in the conveyance, or occurs from new mines or wells, the removal is waste. Either the party who has a reversionary interest or a vested remainderman may take legal action to stop waste from being committed on the property.

Remainderman One who has a remainder interest is called a **remainderman** (although the politically correct now refer to these individuals as remainderperson). A remainder is an example of a future interest in real property; the remainderman has no current right to possess or use the property. While the life tenant is alive the remainder interest is inactive, but upon the death of the life tenant the remainder interest automatically converts to the estate held by the grantor who created the life estate. This is one way the estate from which the life estate evolved (normally a fee simple absolute) will be restored. The original estate will also be restored if either the life tenant or the remainderman convey their interest to the other, or if both interests are transferred to the same third party.

Remaindermen can be classified into two categories: vested and contingent. If the remainderman can be determined at the time the life estate is created, then the remainderman is said to be a vested remainderman. In the previous example, William is a vested remainderman. A vested remainder interest is inheritable, so if the remainder dies before the life tenant, the interest of the life tenant is unaffected and the remainderman's heirs inherit the remainderman's interest.

EXHIBIT | **4.4** | **CREATION OF A CONVENTIONAL LIFE ESTATE**

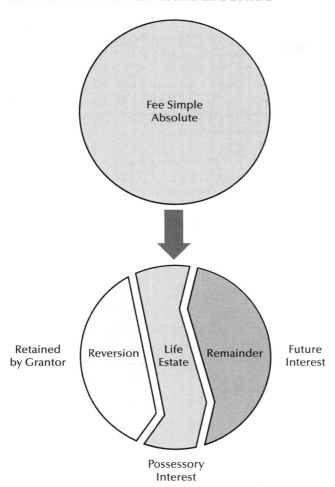

If the remainderman cannot be determined at the time the life estate is created, then the remainderman is said to be a contingent remainderman. Language in the following conveyance would result in a contingent remainderman, if at the time of the grant Mary does not have a daughter.

> "This tract of real estate is transferred from Dan Kaufman to Sally Kaufman for life, and a remainder to Sally's eldest daughter."

In this case, the remainder is contingent until Sally has a daughter. If Sally has a daughter, the remainder becomes vested. If Sally never has a daughter, at her death, the interest of the original grantor would revest in the grantor or his estate.

Another example of language that would result in a contingent remainderman is:

> "This tract of real estate is transferred from Ron Faul to Beverly Faul for life, and a remainder to Beverly's eldest living daughter at the time of Beverly's death."

In this case, the remainderman remains contingent until the life tenant's death, regardless of whether or not Beverly has a daughter at the time of the grant. Only upon Beverly's death can one determine who is the eldest living daughter.

Economic and Estate Tax Consequences of a Life Estate The creation of a life estate may significantly affect the short-term marketability of a property because purchasers may hesitate to bid much for an interest of uncertain duration. Lenders may also be reluctant to lend much to a party if a life estate is offered as the primary collateral because the duration of the estate is uncertain. As it is the interest in a property that is being mortgaged and not the property itself, the lender's lien expires automatically upon the expiration of the estate. Conventional life estates are usually created when the grantor's goal is to provide the life tenant with a place to live or financial security from the income generated by the real estate on which the life estate is placed, not for the purpose of enhancing the marketability of the property.

Life estates can be useful as a means to reduce estate taxes. If, for example, a life estate is created by will, and the property placed in trust for the remainderman, estate taxes on the property must be paid upon the grantor's death. Upon the life tenant's death, however, no additional tax is due because only a life estate is possessed. This may result in substantial tax savings particularly if the property increases in value significantly after the grantor's death. Occasionally, someone, while still living, will deed a property to another party and reserve to him or herself a life estate. In this manner the grantor can use the property during his or her life, can specify who takes title after his or her death, and saves on the expense of probating a will. In this case, the reversion and the life estate are held by the same party.

Decision Point

Your Uncle Jake has a fee simple absolute interest in a gold mine. He has decided to sell the property to your cousin, but in doing so plans to create either a fee simple determinable or an ordinary life estate. In either case, you are to be named the future interest holder. Which of the two estates do you recommend be established? Why?

Legal Life Estates

A legal life estate is a life estate created by operation of the law. Simply, legal life estates are property rights that automatically arise because someone was married to a real property owner at the time of the property owner's death. Traditionally, legal life estates evolved out of two concepts: dower and curtesy. These concepts were developed in England centuries ago under the common law. Common law comprises the body of principles and rules of action, relating to the government and security of property and persons, which derive their authority solely from custom, or from the judgments and decrees of courts recognizing, affirming, and enforcing such customs, as opposed to law that stems from the enactments of legislatures.

Dower refers to the right of a surviving wife to a life estate in the real property of her deceased husband. To prevent widows from becoming a financial burden on the community, common law provided the widow with an automatic life estate in one-third of all real property owned by her husband during the marriage, although some or all of the property had been disposed of prior to her husband's death, and regardless of whether or not an interest was conveyed to her, or anyone else, by will. The concept of dower has been abolished in most states. Exhibit 4.5 shows those states that still recognize dower. In those states that recognize dower, for a dower interest to exist there must be a valid marriage, and ownership of real property by the husband. Until the husband's death the dower interest is inactive, but the interest attaches with the marriage or as soon as property is acquired, and cannot be terminated without the consent of the wife. Therefore, in most states that still recognize dower, if the wife does not sign the deed conveying real property owned by the husband, the dower interest is not terminated. If a grantee does not secure the signature of the grantor's wife on a deed, he or she may be surprised to learn that at some time in the future ownership of the property is encumbered by the widow's life estate.

English common law also gave husbands a life estate in any real property owned as a fee estate by the wife during the marriage. This right, known as **curtesy,** has also been abolished in most states. Exhibit 4.5 indicates the states that still recognize curtesy rights. Curtesy rights provide widowers with substantially less protection than dower rights provide widows. The requirements for curtesy rights to apply include: a valid marriage and the birth of a child; sole ownership of the property by the wife at the time of her death; and her death. Unlike the husband, the wife may, during her life, convey any property she owns to others without her husband's permission, or signature on a deed, and such property is not subject to curtesy rights. In addition, the wife may defeat curtesy, by specifying disposition of the property in a will. An important reason for the abolition of dower and curtesy is that their operation can result in multiple chains of title that can complicate subsequent transfers of title. In states where dower and curtesy rights are used, the division of property in a divorce terminates the rights.

Some states have replaced the traditional concepts of dower and curtesy with probate homesteads. Under modern homestead laws, a homestead is the house and the adjoining land where the head of the family lives. Most states set a maximum limit on either the size or value of homesteads. A homestead right is an artificial estate in land that protects the owner's use of the property by exempting it from forced sale resulting from the claims of creditors, except mortgage and tax liens. In some states, homesteads are exempt from property taxes up to a certain assessed value. The homestead exemption is not the same as homestead rights.

To qualify for the homestead right, a homeowner must submit a written declaration of homestead and occupy the dwelling as the family home. Death of either spouse is not a prerequisite for the homestead right. Probate homesteads, however, come into existence only when a homeowner dies.

A probate homestead is a homestead set apart from the common property, or out of the real estate belonging to the deceased, by a court, for the use of a surviving spouse and the minor children. In essence, it provides a widow, or widower, with a home for life. The details vary from state to state, but generally the requirements for the creation of a probate homestead are that a written declaration of homestead be filed and that the dwelling be occupied as the family home. The state of Florida, for example, allows for probate homesteads. Under Florida law, a surviving spouse is entitled to a life estate in the couple's residence only, and only if the title was held by the deceased spouse at the time of death. This homestead right applies regardless of any other disposition of the property made by the deceased spouse in a will.

Other states have replaced dower and curtesy with an approach called statutory interest. Synonyms for statutory interest include statutory share and elective share. Under this approach, if the surviving spouse was either precluded from the deceased spouse's will entirely, or was given less than the elective share (established by statute) of the estate, both personal and real property, the surviving spouse may claim the allowed statutory share. For example, the statutory share may be one-third interest of all property owned by the deceased spouse at the time of his or her death.

Life Estate Pour Autre Vie

When the length of time that a life estate exists is dependent upon the life span of someone other than the current life tenant, the ownership interest is called a life estate pour autre vie. The French phrase, pour autre vie, roughly translates to "based on the life of another." Usually, a life estate pour autre vie comes into existence when the original life tenant from either a conventional or legal life estate conveys the estate to someone other than the

| EXHIBIT | 4.5 | **ACQUIRING AN INTEREST IN LAND** |

	Dower Rights	Courtesy Rights	Homestead Protection Limits	Years to Acquire Title by Adverse Possession	
				Without Color of Title	With Color of Title
Alabama	yes	no	$ 2,000	20	10
Alaska	no	no	27,000	10	7
Arizona	no	no	50,000	10a	3
Arkansas	yes	yes	1,250#@	15	7
California	no	no	55,000*	NA	5
Colorado	no	no	20,000	18	7
Connecticut	no	no	NA	15	15
Delaware	no	no	NA	20	20
Florida	no	no	@	NA	7
Georgia	yes	no	5,000	20	7
Hawaii	yes	yes	30,000#*@	20	20
Idaho	no	no	25,000#	5	5
Illinois	no	no	7,500	20	7
Indiana	no	no	7,500	NA	10
Iowa	no	no	500@	10	10
Kansas	yes	yes	@	15	15
Kentucky	no	no	50,000	15	7
Louisiana	no	no	15,000	30	10
Maine	no	no	7,500	20	20
Maryland	no	no	5,500	20	20
Massachusetts	yes	yes	50,000	20	20
Michigan	yes	no	10,000	15	5
Minnesota	no	no	@	15	15
Mississippi	no	no	30,000@	10	10
Missouri	no	no	8,000	10	10
Montana	yes	no	40,000@	NA	10
Nebraska	no	no	6,500@	10	10
New Hampshire	yes	yes	5,000	20	20
New Jersey	yes	yes	NA	60	30
New Mexico	no	no	20,000	10	10
New York	no	no	10,000	10	10
N. Carolina	yes	yes	7,500	20	7
N. Dakota	no	no	80,000	20	10
Ohio	yes	yes	5,000	21	21
Oklahoma	yes	no	5,000@	15	15c
Oregon	yes	yes	20,000@	10	10
Pennsylvania	yes	no	NA	21	21d
Rhode Island	yes	yes	NA	10	10
S. Carolina	yes	no	5,000	20	10
S. Dakota	no	no	yes	20	20
Tennessee	yes	yes	7,500#	20	7
Texas	no	no	@	25	5
Utah	no	no	8,000#	NA	7

EXHIBIT 4.5 **ACQUIRING AN INTEREST IN LAND (CONTINUED)**

	Dower Rights	Courtesy Rights	Homestead Protection Limits	Years to Acquire Title by Adverse Possession	
				Without Color of Title	With Color of Title
Vermont	yes	no	30,000	15	15
Virginia	yes	yes	5,000	10	10[e]
Washington	no	no	20,000	10	7
West Virginia	yes	yes	7,500	10	10
Wisconsin	yes	yes	25,000	20	10
Wyoming	no	no	10,000	10	10

NA title may not be acquired without color of title; homestead protection not available
[a] 5 years if adverse user pays property taxes, 15 years for unimproved land
[b] 2 years on mining claims
[c] 7 years for property outside the city limits
[d] 40 years for property in Philadelphia
[e] 15 years for property located east of the Allegheny Mountains
[#] amount varies according to marital status
[*] amount varies according to age and disability of property owner
[@] also a limit on the size of the property protected
Source: various state statutes

remainder. It is possible, however, that a life estate pour autre vie was acquired from another holder in pour autre vie or, rarely, the original grantor will create the estate in this manner.

The owner of a life estate pour autre vie is subject to the same duties as the owner of an ordinary life estate. The pour autre vie owner enjoys all the rights of an ordinary life estate owner, and may transfer the interest to another by will as long as the person on whose life the estate is based is alive. Termination of the life estate pour autre vie may be accomplished in any of the same ways that an ordinary life estate is terminated.

ADVERSE POSSESSION

The estates in land discussed thus far are commonly acquired by deed or by inheritance. In such cases, the public records will show a complete and perfect succession of deeds from the government down to the current owner of record. The party whose name appears in the public records as the owner of real property is said to hold paper title or record title to the land. True ownership of the land may, however, be vested in another party who holds possession of the land without any documentation to support his or her ownership claim. This occurs when the other party acquired ownership through adverse possession.

Adverse possession is the right of one who occupies land, without the permission of the record owner, to acquire title to the property. In the United States, title to any private property or government property used for a proprietary purpose may be acquired through adverse possession. Why? For two reasons: first, historically, land records were not always kept and ownership of real property often depended on transactions that occurred so long ago that witnesses who were familiar with the transaction had either forgotten the facts or were dead. Second, adverse possession furthers the public policy that land should be used rather than sit idle.

Before purchasing real property you should answer the following questions.

1. Is the estate to be acquired a fee simple absolute?
2. If a defeasible fee is to be acquired, will the condition that would end the interest allow you to use the property as you wish? What is the probability that the condition will occur?
3. Will all of the property rights, including subsurface and supersurface rights, come with the property or were they sold separately?
4. Does a physical inspection of the property indicate that anyone other than the record owner is claiming ownership of the property?

While ownership of an entire tract of land may be acquired by adverse possession, most recent cases of adverse possession involve boundary disputes and cases where building encroachments are discovered rather than entire tracts. Today, adverse possession is an unusual means to acquire title to an entire tract because of the lack of wide-open space property and the availability of land records.

Title by adverse possession may be acquired if the adverse user meets several tests of possession. Specifically, the possession must be: actual, continuous, visible, exclusive, and hostile for the required statutory time period.

Actual possession means that the adverse user must enter and make actual use of the land in a manner that is appropriate given the locality and nature of the land. For example, for farmland, the adverse user is required to farm the acres sought to be acquired; for residential property, the adverse user must reside in an appropriate structure on the property. In most states, courts decide what constitutes actual possession on a case-by-case basis. In some states, however, the type of possession required is specified by statute. Under California law, for example, possession occurs only if the property is protected by a substantial enclosure, or if it has been improved or cultivated.

Continuous possession refers to the requirement that an adverse user use the property continuously for the required statutory time period. As shown in Exhibit 4.5, the time requirement varies by state, and in many states depends on whether the adverse use is with color of title or without color of title. Color of title refers to a situation where the adverse user believes they have good title to the land, but because of some defect it is, in fact, invalid. For example, Mr. Pike takes title from Mrs. Paul, unaware that Mrs. Paul held title under a wild (forged) deed. In this case, Mr. Pike has color of title and although his title is not valid he may gain valid title; depending on the state in which the property is located, he may gain it more quickly than if he were without color of title.

Continuous possession does not mean that the adverse user can never leave the property; travel to perform normal activities will not prevent an adverse user from gaining title. However, the requirement does preclude a claim of ownership through adverse possession if the use was abandoned before the full statutory time requirement is met. For example, assume twenty-one years are required to acquire title through adverse possession. If an adverse user used the property for ten years, abandoned use for two years, and then used the property again for another eleven years; the continuous possession requirement has not been met even though the adverse user has used the property for twenty-one years.

The test of visible possession requires that the actual use of the property be visible enough that the owner, inspecting the property, would know that it was being claimed, and that the use is generally known by people living in the area. In an interesting case that relates to this point [Marenga Cave Co. v. Ross, 212 Ind. 624,10 N.E.2d 917 (1937)], a company used a cave that extended below an adjoining property for the time period required for adverse possession. The court denied the company's application for adverse possession on the grounds that the adverse use was not visible.

Exclusive possession means that the adverse user may not share possession of the land with the owner or with other parties. For example, a person could not claim adverse possession of a public park just because he visited the property on a regular basis for the statutory time period.

Decision Point

If you owned a valuable parcel of real property located in a distant state, what steps would you take to ensure that no one could gain title through adverse possession?

Different states apply the test of hostile possession in different ways. Some still apply the traditional test of hostility that has two parts: one, that the adverse user occupy the land without the permission of the owner; and two, that the adverse user do so with the intention of claiming ownership. In most states, however, the intent to claim ownership is no longer a requirement of hostile possession. To illustrate the difference between these requirements consider the following example. Sam and Ralph own adjoining properties. Sam erects a fence on what he thinks is the property boundary, but it is actually on Ralph 's property, twenty feet beyond the true boundary line. After the statutory period required for adverse possession has been met, Ralph realizes the fence is on his property and orders Sam to remove it. In most states, courts have decided that actual possession of the strip of land meets the requirement of hostility although the adverse user did not intend to take his neighbor's property, and Sam would take title to the twenty-foot strip of land. In those states that apply the traditional test, Sam would move the fence.

If all the requirements of adverse possession are met, the adverse user becomes the owner of the real estate although his interest is not written in a deed or recorded in the public record, and a purchaser from the record owner acquires no property rights. The adverse user turned owner can even become the record owner by proving in court that all the requirements were met.

SUMMARY

When one acquires real property, the most important part of the acquisition is the set of property rights associated with the property. Property rights enable the property owner to enjoy the benefits of real property ownership. The full set of property ownership rights

AN ETHICAL ISSUE
ADVERSE POSSESSION

Assume your neighbor plants a row of shrubs on his property five feet from your property line. You, and only you, use and maintain the property on your side of the shrubs for the time period required to perfect adverse possession.

1. Would you claim the strip of land?
2. What if circumstances gave you the opportunity to claim the most valuable parcel of real property in the entire town by adverse possession? Would you claim the property?
3. If you answered "yes" to either 1 or 2, how would you feel about the situation if you were the record owner of either property?
4. If your answer to 1 was different from your answer to 2, why?

includes: the right of possession, the right of control, the right of quiet enjoyment, and the right of disposition. Each of these rights applies to three different physical levels: the property surface, the subsurface, and the supersurface.

The estate, or interest one has in real property, affects the set of property rights. Freehold estates represent an ownership interest; the freehold estate that entitles the holder to the most complete set of property rights is the fee simple absolute. A limited set of property rights is associated with every other type of freehold estate.

The major distinction between a fee simple absolute estate and the other freehold estates is that the interest of the absolute fee is not split into two or more parts. For all other types of freehold estates, defeasible fees, and life estates, there is both a possessory interest and a future interest. If and when the future interest becomes active, the right of possession is transferred to another party. To preclude the possibility of transfer, the defeasible fee holder must often use the property in a certain manner not necessarily of his or her own choosing. Similarly, the use to which the life tenant in a life estate can put the property is restricted in that waste cannot be committed on the property. In addition, life estates cannot usually be transferred by will, and lenders are reluctant to use property held either in defeasible fee or life tenancy as collateral for mortgage loans.

Any freehold estate may be lost, involuntarily, through adverse possession. To successfully exercise adverse possession, the possession must be: actual, continuous, visible, exclusive, and hostile for a required statutory time period.

KEY TERMS

adverse possession	fee simple subject to a con-	possessory interest
curtesy	dition subsequent	remainderman
defeasible fee	freehold estate	right of entry for condition
dower	future interest	broken
estate	leasehold estate	subsurface
fee simple absolute	life estate	supersurface
fee simple determinable	life tenant	title

REVIEW QUESTIONS

1. What estate would exist if either a life estate or a life estate pour autre vie were transferred to the remainder?

2. Given the following language in a deed:

   "This tract of real estate is transferred from Won Park to Barbara Dean for life, and a remainder to her eldest living daughter at the time of Barbara's death."

   a. What is Barbara's interest?

   b. Is the remainder contingent or vested?

   c. Regarding the remainder, would it make a difference if the daughter were natural or adopted?

3. In states that recognize curtesy rights, what conditions would have to prevail for the widower to receive a life estate? Is it fair that these conditions are more stringent than those required for a widow?

4. Given the following language in a deed:

   "This tract of real estate is transferred from Joe Coleman to my daughter, Joy Coleman, provided that she is married before reaching the age of thirty."

   a. What type of estate does Joy hold?

   b. What happens if Joy is married and divorced before age thirty?

5. A popular comedian suggests that the Middle-Eastern countries do not own the oil beneath their land, they are just closer to it than we are. He suggests that the United States should ensure its oil supply by drilling a well and pumping it out from underneath them. Ignoring technical difficulties, would this be legal?

6. There are probably a thousand stars in the supersurface over your property. If you own the property in fee simple absolute, do you own the stars?

7. List three ways a determinable fee can be restored to a fee simple absolute.

8. List and describe the tests of possession used in adverse possession. What is the statutory time period for adverse possession in your state, with and without color of title?

9. How does the presence of a future interest affect the value of a possessory interest? Why?

10. What is the future interest associated with: a life estate, a fee simple determinable, and a fee simple subject to a condition subsequent? How do these future interests differ?

11. What are your answers to the questions in the two "Decision Point" sections in this chapter?

12. What are your answers to the questions in the "Ethical Issue" section in this chapter?

REAL ESTATE ON THE WEB

Use your favorite search engine to:

1. Find an example of disputed water rights.

2. Find an example of adverse possession.

3. Find an example of subsurface or supersurface (solar or air) rights being conveyed separate from the rest of a property.

4. Find an example of a private citizen giving (dedicating) real property to a governmental unit.

Refer to the companion Web site at www.wiley.com/college/larsen for a variety of online activities including additional chapter content, review materials, assignments, and related links.

ADDITIONAL READINGS

Andersen, R. W. "Present and Future Interests: A Graphic Explanation". 19 *Seattle University Law Review* 101 (Fall 1995).

Baker, M, T. Miceli, C. F. Sirmans and G. K Turnbull. "Property Rights by Squatting: Land Ownership Risk and Adverse Possession Statutes." *Land Economics* (August 2001): 360–370.

Hopperton, R. J. "Teaching Present and Future Interests: A Methodology for Students that Unifies Estates in Land Concepts, Structures, and Principles." 26 *University of Toledo Law Review* 621 (September 1995).

Porter, J. W. "Will Property Rights Legislation Endanger Smart Growth Efforts?" *Real Estate Law Journal* (Spring 2002): 275–302.

Reinstein, E. J. "Owning Outer Space." *Northwestern Journal of International Law & Business* (Fall 1999): 59–98.

Sprankling, J. G. "An Environmental Critique of Adverse Possession." 79 *Cornell Law Review* 816 (May 1994).

Sterk, S. E. "How Defeasible Fees Can Create Potential for Disputes." *New York Real Estate Law Reporter* (May 1999): 10+.

5

Forms of Real Property Ownership

FROM THE WIRE

On June 21, 2002, Full Spectrum Building and Development, an African-American real estate developer, held a groundbreaking ceremony for a $40-million condominium development at 1400 5th Street in New York City. The developers claim that the project will be the nation's largest affordable energy efficient ("green") condominium. Seventy percent of the building will be constructed from recycled or renewable resources, and reliance on geothermal energy for heating and air conditioning means it will use 35 percent less energy than is permitted by the New York State Energy Code. The 225,000-square-foot development, which will include 30,000 square feet of retail space, will be the first affordable urban mid-rise to qualify for the New York State Green Building Tax Credit. The tax credit for each homeowner is expected to amount to $24,000 over a five-year period. Eighty-five of the 128 residential units are reserved for middle-income (annual incomes between $53,000 and $103,000) families.

The condominium development will also be a "smart" building. Among a wide assortment of smart features, each home will have connectivity to broadband Internet access, as well as to the building's local area network (LAN). Washing machines on each floor will be connected to the LAN so owners can check on their availability from desktop computers. The project is scheduled to be complete by the summer of 2003. Does this sound like an attractive place to live? Apparently it did to lots of others. To make it fair for everyone, a lottery was held to determine who could buy the residential units.

Go to www.dec.state.ny.us/website/ppu/grnbldg/legis.html to learn more about the New York State Green Building tax credit.

INTRODUCTION

The benefits that owners derive from real property can be greatly influenced by the form of ownership they employ. Title to real estate can be held either individually or by groups. When title is held by one person, that person is said to have sole ownership, or **ownership in severalty** (i.e., one's ownership is severed from the ownership of others). Perhaps the primary advantage of ownership in severalty is that a sole owner does not have to be concerned with the rights of co-owners. In certain situations, however, it may be both appropriate and advantageous for two or more parties to become co-owners of real property. Title held by more than one party, is referred to as co-ownership, or **concurrent ownership.** This chapter focuses on concurrent ownership forms.

Several different forms of concurrent ownership are possible, including: joint tenancy, tenancy in common, tenancy by the entireties, tenancy in partnership, corporation, cooperative, trust, and condominium, the form being used for the project described in the chapter opener "From the Wire." It is important to understand the rights and responsibilities of co-owners under each concurrent ownership form because they may affect one's right to use, or convey a property.

JOINT TENANCY

Joint tenancy is a widely used form of concurrent ownership, especially for property held by married couples. Under joint tenancy two or more parties, the joint tenants, are considered to have a single estate in land, and each is considered to be the owner of the entire estate. (Note that in several forms of concurrent ownership, the owners are referred to as tenants. This should not be confused with the term tenant in the context of a leasehold). In general, for joint tenancy to exist, four criteria must be met. These criteria, sometimes called the four unities of joint tenancy, are: the unity of title, the unity of time, the unity of interest, and the unity of possession. Although in some states, under certain circumstances, ownership can be held in joint tenancy although all four of the unities are not met.

THE UNITIES OF JOINT TENANCY

The unity of title requires that all owners derive their title from the same grantor. For example, if Al conveys property to Bruce and Charles, they can be joint tenants. However, a joint tenancy is destroyed if a joint tenant transfers his or her interest to a third party. If, for example, Bruce later conveys his interest to Eric, Charles and Eric are not joint tenants because they acquired title from different grantors.

The unity of time requires that all joint tenants take title to the property at the same time. Assume, for example, that a grantor conveys title to a half interest in a property to Bob on August 1, and then conveys title to the other half to Carol on August 15. Bob and Carol are not joint tenants even though both received title from the same grantor because the unity of time was not met. When one person owns property in severalty before a marriage, the unity of time requirement may present problems. To illustrate, suppose Ted owns a home in severalty, and after his marriage to Alice he seeks to transfer title so that he and Alice are joint tenants. Som states have enacted laws that eliminate the unity of time requirement in such cases and a direct transfer to Alice would enable Ted and Alice to be joint tenants. In other states, a joint tenancy can only be achieved through a straw man transaction. A straw man is a third party who, for a fee, takes title temporarily and then reconveys the property to the designated parties.

The unity of interest requires that all joint tenants have an equal interest in the property. For example, with two owners, each must have a 50 percent interest, and with three owners, each must have a one-third interest for a joint tenancy to exist. Unequal interests preclude the possibility of a joint tenancy. Two owners with interests of 75 percent and 25 percent, respectively, cannot be joint tenants.

The unity of possession requires that each owner have one and the same undivided possession of the property. Recall that the unity of interest requires equal interests. Do not be tempted to visualize each tenant's interest by dividing the land into equal portions. "Undivided" right of possession means that each tenant has an equal right to every atom of the land. If ownership of the land is divided geographically, the unity of possession is violated and the parties are no longer co-owners. Instead, they are neighbors and owners in severalty of the individual parcels. Further, if the property is divided by time into present and future interests the unity of possession is not met and, again, the parties are not co-owners. For example, if a life estate (Chapter 4) is created, the present interest holder and the future interest holder are not joint tenants even though their interests were created at the same time and with the same instrument.

THE RIGHT OF SURVIVORSHIP

Sometimes joint tenancy is referred to as the "poor man's probate" because in most states upon the death of one of the joint tenants, the deceased's ownership share is not subject to probate. Instead, it automatically passes to the remaining joint tenant or tenants. For example, if there were five joint tenants, each with an undivided 20 percent interest, and one died, the deceased's interest would pass to the remaining joint tenants, each of whom would then have an undivided 25 percent interest.

The right of survivorship is sometimes referred to as the "grand incident" of joint tenancy because it enables the surviving joint tenant to avoid the hassle of probate court (at least for property owned as joint tenants). However, the right of survivorship no longer automatically applies to joint tenancy. Many states require that the deed expressly state that the property shall pass to the surviving grantees (Alabama, Arizona, Florida, Georgia, Kansas, Kentucky, Maine, North Carolina, Ohio, Oregon, Pennsylvania, South Carolina, Tennessee, Texas, Virginia, and West Virginia).

Therefore, it is generally a good idea and required in certain states that if joint tenancy with the right of survivorship is desired that it be explicitly stated in a deed. Some states have specific language requirements to create a valid joint tenancy. In general, words similar to the following create a joint tenancy with the right of survivorship:

> "to Paul Ollier and Mary Ann Ollier not as tenants in common and not as a community property estate, but as joint tenants with right of survivorship in the following described property."

TENANCY BY THE ENTIRETIES

For **tenancy by the entireties,** also known as tenancy by the entirety, to exist the four unities required for joint tenancy must be met and one more: the unity of person. Unity of person requires that the tenants be married. Therefore, only married couples can use this form of ownership. Tenancy by the entirety is similar to joint tenancy because the right of survivorship applies; upon the death of one spouse, the surviving spouse becomes the sole owner. Tenancy by the entireties is, however, different from joint tenancy because when property is owned in this form, neither party is individually able to mortgage or transfer his or her interest to another party. For property held in tenancy by the entireties, both spouses must sign the deed for the transfer to be valid. Further, unlike a joint tenancy, a tenancy by the entireties cannot be terminated by an action for partition. If the couple divorce, the tenancy by the entireties ends because the unity of person no longer exists. In some states, divorce results in a conversion of a tenancy by the entireties to a tenancy in common (described below), in others it results in a conversion to a joint tenancy.

Every state that recognizes tenancy by the entireties has language requirements for its creation, therefore, those who wish to establish this form of ownership should seek competent legal advice. Some states assume that a tenancy by the entireties is created when a married couple purchases real estate. To avoid subsequent questions regarding whether the parties intended to create such a tenancy, it is best to make their intent clear by using words similar to the following in the deed or other conveyance:

> "to Ronald Faul and Beverly Faul, husband and wife, as tenants by the entireties with the right of survivorship the following described property."

There are advantages and potential disadvantages associated with tenancy by the entireties. One advantage is that it usually features automatic survivorship, although some states may require the phrase "with the right of survivorship." Another advantage of tenancy by the entireties is that in many states, property held in this form is protected from claims advanced by the creditors of only one spouse. Assume, for example, that a husband has a judgment rendered against him in a matter in which the wife was completely uninvolved. If the couple owns real property in joint tenancy, upon the husband's death, title to the property passes to the wife, but the judgment creditor can still force the sale of the property to satisfy the judgment. If, instead, they hold the property as tenants by the entireties, upon the husband's death, title passes to the wife, and the judgment creditor cannot foreclose on the property. And, as mentioned above, an uninformed spouse is protected against the sale or mortgaging of the property. An example of a disadvantage is the situation in which a seller discovered that his ex-wife, rather than his current wife, was named on the deed to the property to be conveyed. To fix the problem, it cost him $10,000 plus legal fees. Whether this was a problem caused by the ownership form or a bad divorce attorney is debatable.

TENANCY IN COMMON

Tenancy in common is another form under which two or more parties may hold concurrent ownership in real property. This tenancy is the most common form of concurrent ownership; it is the relationship that is created unless the parties clearly specify their intent to create another form of ownership, and meet the requirements of the specified form. In the description of joint tenancy earlier, examples were presented to demonstrate circumstances that do not result in the creation of a joint tenancy. In each case, one of the unities required for joint tenancy was violated. Therefore, the parties may have intended to be joint tenants, but legally they will be considered tenants in common.

The primary distinction between tenancy in common and joint tenancy is that the only unity required for a tenancy in common is the unity of possession. That is, each tenant in common must have an undivided right to possess the property and each has the right to a share in any rents or profits derived from the property. Unlike joint tenants, tenants in common may acquire their interests from different grantors or from different conveyances, although tenants in common may, and frequently do, acquire title from the same conveyance. Tenants in common, unlike joint tenants, may hold unequal ownership interests. For example, if two people own a property as tenants in common, their ownership shares could be split 90/10, 75/25, or any other combination including 50/50. When the conveyance does not specify the extent of each owner's interest, there is a rebuttable presumption that the ownership shares are equal.

Another difference between joint tenancy and tenancy in common is that survivorship does not apply to tenancy in common. Each tenant in common can pass his or her interest on by will; each tenant's share does not automatically pass to the surviving tenants in common. To illustrate, assume that Doris, Beth, and Frank hold title as tenants in common. Beth dies leaving, by will, her interest to Gwen. Doris, Frank, and Gwen are then tenants in common. Compare this to the case where Doris, Beth, and Frank hold title as joint tenants. Upon Beth's death her interest passes to the remaining joint tenants who now each have a fifty percent interest.

In most states, the language used in a deed or other conveyance to create a tenancy in common, with each owner having an equal interest, is similar to the following:

> "to Jeri Parrott and Wanda Brown as tenants in common in the following described property."

To create unequal interests, the share of ownership must be specified. For example:

> "to Jeri Parrott, an undivided one-quarter interest and to Wanda Brown, an undivided three-quarters interest as tenants in common in the following described property. "

One may consider other features of tenancy in common advantageous or disadvantageous, depending on personal circumstances. If one of the owners no longer wants to be a tenant in common, several options are available. Under tenancy in common, any owner may convey his or her interest to others at any time without the permission of the other co-owners. No tenant in common, however, may transfer the entire property without the permission of the other owners. Alternatively, an owner could sell his or her interest to the other tenants in common. If they are unwilling or unable to purchase the interest, the owner can bring an action for **partition.** In such actions a court will decide whether to divide and sell part or all of the property. An action for partition can be lengthy and expensive, therefore, tenants may choose to conduct an auction after which each tenant in common receives his or her share of the proceeds.

For several reasons, tenancy in common is not generally recommended for business purposes. If one or more of the tenants in common fails to pay their share of taxes and assessments, the other tenants must make up the difference or risk losing the property to foreclosure. Conversely, if one of the tenants pays taxes or assessments above his or her own share, then that tenant generally has a lien on the interests of the other tenant or tenants. In addition, lenders generally do not consider a tenant in common's interest to be desireable security, because in the event of foreclosure, the lender has the additional expense of forcing a partition proceeding to recover on the security interest. Finally, the fact that the interest of a deceased tenant in common is subject to probate can create problems that could be avoided by holding title either in the form of a partnership or trust. For example, three people purchase a property as tenants in common intending to eventually sell the property to a developer. Just as the tenants in common are ready to sell, one of the tenants dies intestate. The deceased tenant had ten heirs. Shortly thereafter, one of the original ten heirs dies leaving eight heirs of his own. Before the property can be sold to the developer the signatures of all of these parties may have to be secured in order to release every possible interest.

Decision Point

You, a business acquaintance, and your spouse plan to invest in a tract of real property. Under which of the following ownership forms do you recommend title be acquired: joint tenancy, tenancy in common, or tenancy by the entireties? Why?

COMMUNITY PROPERTY

The types of concurrent ownership discussed above are rooted in English common law. Another type of concurrent ownership derived from Spanish and French law is known as **community property.** This form of ownership is similar to tenancy by the entireties in that both are designed to protect the interest of an uninformed spouse.

Under community property law, each spouse is presumed to have an equal interest in property acquired by either spouse during the marriage and each is equally responsible for any debts incurred during the marriage. Each spouse has an equal interest regardless of whether either was unemployed or employed during the marriage, and regardless of whether record title is held in only one spouse's name. States using community property law are referred to as community property states. There are only nine community property states: Arizona, California, Idaho, Louisiana, Nevada, New Mexico, Texas, Washington, and Wisconsin.

Even in community property states spouses may have **separate property** for which they hold complete title. Separate property includes any property that was acquired by either spouse before the marriage, as well as any gifts or inheritances received by either spouse during the marriage. A spouse may transfer separate property without the other spouse's signature on the deed. Lenders, title insurance companies, and other institutions do, however, prefer the signature of both spouses to eliminate subsequent questions about whether the property was community or separate property.

Community property laws affect every aspect of real property. Therefore, to be valid, the signature of both spouses is required for any transaction involving community property. This includes listing real property for sale, as well as leasing, mortgaging, improving, or selling real property. Real estate partnerships operating in community property states must secure a waiver from the spouse of each partner so that title to partnership property can be transferred without the risk that a spouse will later exercise his or her community property right. Real estate practitioners in community property states suggest that an unmarried grantor's marital status be described in conveyances to make it clear that community property it not involved. For example:

"The grantor, Donna Boyer, divorced, conveys to…, or

The grantor, Michael Muscato, bachelor, conveys to… .or

The grantor, Mary Brown, widow, conveys to…"

Neither curtesy, nor dower rights (Chapter 4) are recognized in community property states. When one spouse dies with a valid will, the surviving spouse retains his or her half share of the community property and the other half goes to the deceased's heirs as specified in the will. Under such circumstances the other half does not have to pass to the surviving spouse, although it may if so specified. In three community property states, Arizona,

Louisiana, and Texas, if a spouse dies intestate, the deceased's descendants are the primary recipients. In the other community property states, if a spouse dies intestate, the deceased's interest passes to the surviving spouse.

CONDOMINIUMS AND COOPERATIVES

The focus of the following section is on condominiums and cooperatives owned as residential real estate. These ownership forms can, however, be used for any kind of real property. Commercial applications of the condominium form are increasingly popular, especially for professional office space.

CONDOMINIUMS

A **condominium** is an estate in real property that consists of individual ownership of a residential or commercial unit and an undivided joint interest in the common areas in the condominium project, such as: the land, elevators, stairways, hallways, lobby, parking area, any recreational area, and structure exterior. A residential condominium can take many physical forms, including an apartment, a duplex, or a townhouse, but the physical form does not affect the owner's legal status or rights. With respect to his or her dwelling, the condominium owner has all the rights and duties associated with a fee simple interest. The interest can be mortgaged, leased, sold, or given away, and the interest is subject to foreclosure and homestead rights. Although the owner holds a fee simple interest, there may be restrictions on the use of the dwelling, which are imposed by deed, or by the homeowners' association.

A condominium development begins with the drafting and recording of a **master deed.** The master deed, sometimes called the declaration of condominium, or declaration of horizontal property regime and covenants, describes the real property involved and the number of units located therein. Individual deeds to every condominium unit owner refer to the master deed for a complete legal description of the unit owner's interest. Once the master deed is recorded, no variations in the uses of the structure of the property are permitted unless one follows the amendment procedures specified in the master deed.

Once the master deed is complete, the developer must adopt **condominium bylaws** for the unit owners. The bylaws provide rules and regulations for the unit owners and for the operation of the units. They also include rules for the governing body of the dwelling units: the homeowners' association. The homeowners' association, comprised of elected

CONSUMER CHECKLIST
ITEMS USUALLY CONTAINED IN A CONDOMINIUM MASTER DEED

1. A legal description of the property
2. A detailed description of the building or buildings of the complex
3. The monetary value of the buildings and each unit
4. A detailed description of the common areas
5. Any limitations on the use of the common areas
6. Any land use restrictions
7. The mailing address and a physical description of each unit
8. The name and address of the legal representative for the development
9. How votes are to be assigned, based on unit value or the number of units owned
10. Voting procedures
11. Procedures for amending the master deed

condominium unit owners, is responsible for issues such as: noise, property use, and maintenance of the common areas. For example, the association may set rules that regulate the times at which recreational facilities can be used, or the placement of "for sale" signs. Some may consider such restrictions a disadvantage of condominium ownership. Despite these limitations, the popularity of the condominium ownership form for residential property has increased among older and younger people. Some older people are attracted to the ownership form by the fact that most maintenance is performed by others, and many young people find condominiums an affordable alternative to the traditional detached, single-family home.

COOPERATIVES

A **cooperative** is a living arrangement in which the dwellers purchase ownership shares in a business organization (corporation, partnership, or trust) the principal asset of which is the building. Unlike a condominium, the individuals who inhabit a cooperative do not have fee simple ownership of any real property. Instead, ownership of the property is usually held by the (nonprofit) business organization, and share ownership in the organization entitles the holder to a proprietary lease on a dwelling unit.

A **proprietary lease** differs from an ordinary lease in two ways. First, no provision for rent is made in a proprietary lease. Instead of rent payments, the periodic payments made by the cooperative tenant to the corporation are called a maintenance fee. While this fee may be fixed for the term of the lease, it is common for the lease to provide for possible increases in the fee. This may be accomplished by basing the fee on a cost-of-living scale. The second way in which a proprietary lease differs from an ordinary lease involves the termination date of the lease. Many proprietary leases do not stipulate a specific termination date. The termination of the lease is usually tied to either the transfer of the tenant's interest, or the tenant's death. When a termination date is included in a proprietary lease, the date is usually in the distant future.

While either the condominium or cooperative form can be used for residential dwellings, there are important differences between the two. Condominium owners actually own their own units. They are, therefore, less restricted than cooperative shareholders in the use of their unit. In addition, the condominium owner is free to sell his interest to whomever he or she chooses. The cooperative shareholder may be able to freely sell his or her shares,

DOING BUSINESS

LEGAL ISSUES

Some states allow a form of ownership that combines features of the condominium and townhouse. A townhouse is a type of dwelling unit that usually has two stories, but sometimes has three. Usually, the unit is connected to a similar structure by a common wall. Each townhouse owner owns their own unit, the land under their unit, and an undivided joint interest in the common grounds, such as the surrounding land, clubhouse, and swimming pool. Ownership of the land under the townhouse distinguishes this type of multi-unit housing from the condominium where there is individual ownership of airspace only.

Various names have been given to this hybrid form of ownership, including garden homes, attached homes, landominiums, and patio homes. Under this form of ownership, each owner owns his or her dwelling, the land under the dwelling, and usually a very small frontyard and backyard. State laws vary on who owns the joint walls between properties. In some states this form of ownership is treated as a townhouse and a party wall agreement is employed. In other states the walls are treated as if the property were a condominium.

Go to www.lexis-nexis.com/universe (using your university computer system), and search "legal research" to learn the results of court cases involving any of the real property ownership forms discussed in this chapter.

but such transfers are usually restricted. The cooperative shareholder may be required to first offer the shares to the cooperative, or to obtain permission from the cooperative before he or she sells them. There may also be restrictions regarding disposition of the shares upon the death of the shareholder. All condominium owners obtain their own financing and are individually responsible for property taxes on their own units, therefore, they are not responsible for any other owner's default on their mortgage or property tax. If shareholders in a cooperative default on their share of the cooperative's mortgage or tax payments, the other shareholders must cure the default or risk losing the entire project through a tax sale or mortgage foreclosure. For these reasons, the cooperative is not as popular as the condominium, although it is used, primarily in large cities on the East Coast.

BUSINESS ENTITIES THAT CAN OWN REAL ESTATE

The focus to this point has been on forms of real estate ownership and most of the examples have emphasized the use of these forms by individuals. In the remainder of the chapter, our focus shifts to an examination of business entities that can own real property, including: general, limited, and limited liability partnerships, corporations, limited liability companies, and trusts. These entities are usually formed for business and/or investment purposes.

PARTNERSHIP

A **partnership** exists when two or more parties agree to combine their time, effort, money, and property for the purpose of operating a business. The agreement between the partners may be either written or oral, although a written **partnership agreement** that clearly delineates the duties and responsibilities of each partner is preferable.

There are both advantages and disadvantages associated with a partnership owning property. One advantage is that partnerships are relatively easy to form. Another is that a partnership is not subject to income taxes on any profits it generates. Instead, each partner is taxed on his or her share of the partnership's profits. This avoids the double taxation that occurs under the corporate form of organization. Another advantage is that by investing in a partnership many people can participate in investments they would otherwise be unable to, such as a shopping mall, or a large apartment complex. There are, however, factors that may offset these advantages. First, partners are generally taxed on their share of the partnership profits regardless of whether the profits are distributed to them or retained by the partnership. Second, for real estate partnerships in particular, the ability to use partnership losses to offset other taxable income is restricted (Chapter 7).

Several ownership forms are available for the real property owned by partners or a partnership. When the partners decide to hold the property in the partnership's name the ownership form is called a tenancy in partnership. If the tenancy in partnership is used, the name of the partnership, as well as the name of all partners, must be published in the public records of each county and state where the partnership owns property. In large partnerships, it is common to specify that a few of the partners have the authority to contract for the entire partnership. Otherwise, all partners would be required to sign every document.

A tenancy in partnership is similar to the tenancies described previously. Each partner has the right to possess and use the property for partnership purposes, and one partner cannot dispossess the partnership or other partners from the property without their permission. Tenancy in partnership is similar to joint tenancy in that if one partner dies, the remaining partners are entitled to the deceased partner's interest. While the heirs of the deceased partner have no right to the partnership property, they may be entitled to compensation for the deceased partner's interest in the partnership. Alternatively, the partners may choose to hold the property in their own names. In this case, either tenancy in common or joint tenancy may be used, assuming that the required unities are met.

There are three types of partnerships: general, limited, and limited liability. A **general partnership** is what most people consider a partnership. Perhaps the biggest disadvantage of a general partnership is that each partner has personal liability for the debts of the partnership. Personal liability means that general partners may be forced to use their personal assets to satisfy the debts of the partnership. In real estate partnerships, this personal liability is limited to the extent that the partnership uses non-recourse financing. Non-recourse financing occurs when a lender agrees to use real property as collateral for a loan, and further agrees that in the event of default on the loan the lender may only rely on the property to satisfy the debt without recourse to the borrower. Another potential disadvantage of a general partnership is the possibility that a partner will have to spend time managing the partnership. If a partner is otherwise employed, this may be a burden. Finally, ownership interests in partnerships tend to involve large amounts of money and to be illiquid. As explained later in this chapter, none of these problems exist under the corporate form of ownership. These disadvantages of a general partnership can be reduced or eliminated by employing a limited partnership.

A **limited partnership** is similar to a general partnership except that in the case of a limited partnership there are two classes of partners: limited partners and general partners. A limited partner does not have any management responsibilities, and is not subject to personal liability for partnership debts. The most a limited partner can lose is the amount he or she invested or promised to invest in the future. In these respects limited partners are similar to stockholders in a corporation. Every limited partnership must have at least one general partner who is subject to personal liability for the debts of the partnership. The general partner's risk exposure can be limited by having a corporation act as general partner, or using non-recourse debt to finance investments. In the early 1980s, the limited partnership was a very popular real estate investment vehicle. But changes to the income tax code in 1986 changed that dramatically. Today, there are very few real estate limited partnerships still in existence, and a major concern of many limited partners is how to get out of the partnership.

CORPORATION

A **corporation** is another organizational form that may hold property when two or more individuals agree to combine their efforts in a business venture (although single stockholder corporations are also allowed). It is a popular method of organization for real estate developers and brokerage firms; several large real estate corporations are traded on the New York Stock Exchange.

Forming a corporation may be more time consuming than forming a partnership. To achieve corporate status the corporation organizers must first draft and adopt **articles of incorporation** that specify the powers of the corporation. The organizers must then apply for a corporate charter, and the articles must be filed with the state or federal government chartering authority. A corporate charter is, effectively, a license to do business as a corporation. If the articles of incorporation conform to the chartering agency's requirements, a charter is granted. Once chartered, a corporation is considered a separate legal entity; the corporation has independent capacity to contract and hold title to real estate if entering contracts is within the powers granted by the articles of incorporation.

There are several advantages associated with doing business as a corporation. Large corporations have access to the capital markets making it possible to raise large sums of money. Perhaps the biggest advantage is that the owners of the corporation, the stockholders, have no personal liability for the debts of the corporation. The most each stockholder can lose is the amount he or she invests in the company. Some business novices are attracted by this feature and form a corporation. Lenders do, however, almost always require that the major stockholders of small corporations personally co-sign any debt obligation the corporation incurs, thus eliminating the shield from personal liability. Other advantages of the corporate form include: a good secondary market for shares of publicly traded corporations, making it possible to quickly convert one's ownership interest into cash, and low capital requirements to become a stockholder. One might have to invest several thousand dollars to become a partner in a partnership, whereas, the purchase of a single share provides an ownership interest in a corporation.

A disadvantage of the corporate form is the fact that the corporation must pay income taxes on any profits it generates. These payments occur before any distribution of dividends to the stockholders, who are again taxed on any dividends they receive. "Double taxation " is one of the reasons why most real estate investors avoid the corporate form of organization.

One should take certain precautionary measures when contracting with a corporation. When selling property to a corporation, you should verify that the organizers have filed the articles of incorporation and a corporate charter has been granted. Otherwise, the contract may be invalid for lack of a grantee. It is important to determine whether the person signing the contract on behalf of the corporation is authorized to sign, and also whether the corporation is authorized under its articles of incorporation to enter into the contract. You can verify these points by obtaining a copy of the certificate of resolution from the corporation's board of directors.

Sub-Chapter S Corporation

A sub-chapter S corporation, or more simply an S corporation, is a special type of corporation, so called because the rules that govern them are located in sub-chapter S of the Internal Revenue Service Code. The primary advantage of a sub-chapter S corporation is that it is taxed as if it were a partnership. Therefore, the stockholders are not personally liable for corporate debts and avoid double taxation of earnings. Sub-chapter S corporations are sometimes referred to as tax-option corporations because of these benefits.

With individual income tax rates currently lower than corporate income tax rates you may wonder why all corporations are not organized in this fashion. The answer is straightforward; this organizational form is not appropriate for all business ventures because of several requirements in the tax code. First, all stockholders must be individuals and residents of the United States (other corporations, partnerships, and non-U.S. residents cannot be stockholders). Second, these corporations must restrict their activities to domestic operations. Third, S corporations cannot own more than 80 percent of another corporation. Additionally, the maximum number of stockholders permitted in an S corporation is seventy-five, which is why they are sometimes referred to as a small business corporation. In recent years, many S corporations have converted to limited liability companies because these restrictions do not apply to that organizational form.

Limited Liability Company

A relatively new form of business organization that is gaining popularity with real estate investors is the **limited liability company** (LLC). The first state to enact legislation allowing this form of business organization was Texas, which did so largely in response to the liability that had been imposed on partners in partnerships sued by government agencies as a result of the massive savings and loan association failures of the 1980s. By 1999, forty-eight states had enacted legislation allowing this (or the LLP—limited liability partnership) organizational form. In general, an LLC (or LLP) is a hybrid between a corporation and a partnership in that it combines the income/loss pass through treatment of a partnership with the limited legal liability of a corporation. In other words, double taxation of income may be avoided, and the LLC is recognized as a separate legal entity from its members (owners).

Technically, an LLC may be organized as a sole proprietorship, a corporation, or a partnership. A limited liability partnership (LLP) is essentially a general partnership with one important difference. As its name implies, an LLP provides each partner protection against personal liability for certain partnership liabilities (e.g., claims due to the negligence, errors, omissions, or incompetence of a copartner, employee or other agent). But, this protection does not extend to cover a partner's own negligence or incompetence or to the partner's involvement in supervising wrongful conduct. It is also important to realize that, because of the limited liability feature of the organizational form, parties dealing with an LLC are likely to take actions that will reduce their own risk. If, for example, the LLC is relatively new and/or with no credit history, landlords about to lease space to it or creditors about to provide it with borrowed funds are likely to demand a personal guarantee from one (or more) of the members before entering into the transaction. To help reduce problems associated with limited liability, before granting permission to operate as an LLC, some states require proof that the organization has adequate assets or has obtained adequate liability insurance to satisfy potential claims.

There are other important features that are peculiar to LLCs. The federal tax code classifies any LLC with two or more members as a partnership unless the LLC elects to be taxed as a corporation (or was formed before 1997 and was taxed as a corporation). But, an LLC with one member is not treated as a separate entity for tax purposes (most states require that an LLC have at least two members although some allow a single member). A potential drawback of this organizational form is the possibility of a limited life. Although many states now allow an LLC to have a perpetual existence, traditionally LLCs were required to specify the date on which the LLC's existence would terminate. In most cases, an LLC is dissolved at the withdrawal, resignation, expulsion, bankruptcy, or death of a member.

Decision Point

Five of your classmates have decided to start a real estate brokerage. They have asked for your advice concerning the organizational form to employ. One person favors a general partnership, another favors a limited partnership, the third believes the corporate form should be used, the fourth wants to form an S corporation, and the fifth thinks a limited liability company is the way to go. Which organizational form do you recommend? Why?

TRUST

A **trust** is an arrangement whereby the owner of real and/or personal property transfers title to another party who manages the property for the benefit of a third party. The trustor is the party who contributes property to the trust. The trustee is the party responsible for administering the trust property or trust estate. The beneficiary is the party who benefits from the trust. The trustor may create a trust while living or upon his or her death. A trust that takes effect while the trustor is living is referred to as an inter vivos trust, a trust that takes effect after the trustor's death is referred to as a testamentary trust.

Trusts are popular because they provide the trustor with a way to provide for the well being of another party while having a number of estate planning and tax advantages. In administering the trust, the trustee must follow the instructions specified in the written trust agreement executed between the trustor and the trustee. These instructions can include such things as the designation of the beneficiaries, how the assets are to be managed, and how often and in what amount distributions are to be made to the beneficiaries. While virtually anyone may serve as a trustee, trustors commonly select the trust department of a commercial bank. A responsible party should serve as trustee because legal and equitable title to the trust property is in the trustee's name under a deed of trust.

A land trust is a specialized type of trust. Several features distinguish land trusts from intervivos and testamentary trusts. The only asset in a land trust is real property, and generally only living persons can create a land trust. The trustor is usually the beneficiary and has the right to the possession, income, and proceeds of the sale of the property in trust. In a land trust, the trustee cannot deal with the property without the beneficiary's written direction.

LAND TRUST

Land trusts are growing in popularity and there are several reasons they are used. In a land trust, one can transfer the beneficial interest by assignment instead of by deed and thereby avoid all the formal requirements associated with deeds. Also, if one uses a collateral assignment, the beneficiary can effectively use the property as collateral for a loan without a mortgage being placed on the record.

Sometimes, owners who wish to keep their ownership a secret use land trusts. For example, developers occasionally desire anonymity if they are trying to acquire a number of parcels for a single development. They are concerned that if the seller of a property knows their identity that the price of the land they need will skyrocket.

Another feature of the land trust is that the trust is not subject to attachment. So, if a judgement is rendered against the owner of property in a land trust, the property in the trust is not in jeopardy. A land trust is also a vehicle for multiple owners who seek protection from the effects of bankruptcy, divorce, or judgements against co-owners. A land trust may also simplify probate procedures for people who own land in one state but live in another.

REAL ESTATE INVESTMENT TRUSTS

A **Real Estate Investment Trust** (REIT), pronounced "reet," is an investment vehicle that enables investors with relatively limited means to pool their funds and invest in real estate projects that require substantial sums of money. A REIT is similar to a mutual fund in the securities markets except that instead of specializing in stocks and bonds, REITs specialize in real property investments. Some REITs specialize in physical real property investments. They are referred to as "equity REITs." Within this group, you can probably locate a REIT that specializes in any type of real property (e.g., office buildings, apartments, and retail shopping malls) or geographical area of the country that you are interested in. Other REITs specialize in mortgages and mortgage related securities investments. They are called "mortgage REITs." Still other REITs spread their investments between physical real property and mortgages. They are known as "hybrid REITs." Ownership in a REIT is acquired by purchasing the beneficial shares issued by the REIT. These beneficial shares usually sell for less than $100 each, and the shares of many REITs are traded on stock markets just like the common shares of a corporation.

REITs have been used as an investment vehicle for many years. In the mid-1800s, Massachusetts law did not permit corporations to hold real property for investment purposes. Massachusetts's lawyers invented the real estate trust for investors to pool their funds and gain such corporate advantages as enterprise continuity, limited shareholder

AN ETHICAL ISSUE
LAND TRUSTS

Obviously, land trusts are valuable for the people who establish them, but do you think it is ethical to hide assets in a land trust? If so, would your opinion change if you were just severely injured by an uninsured person whose only valuable asset is in a land trust?

liability, and free transferability of interests. However, it was not until 1960 that Congress made it clear that a REIT is not subject to income tax if it the follows the rules described in the following "DOING BUSINESS." If it qualifies, a REIT is treated similarly to a partnership for income tax purposes; it pays no income tax on the profit it generates and the shareholders are required to pay income tax on the distributions of REIT profits. However, unlike a partnership, REIT losses may not be passed on to the investors. Some investment counselors recommend REITs as appropriate ownership vehicles for individual retirement accounts and other small pension funds, but investment in REITs requires some degree of investment sophistication. Additional information about REITs is presented in Chapter 21.

REAL ESTATE SYNDICATES AND JOINT VENTURES

In real estate, the terms **syndicate** and **joint venture** are frequently used in a way that implies that they are ownership forms, but each merely describes the pooling of resources for investment purposes. A syndicate may be made up of from two to several hundred or more investors. Real estate owned by a syndicate can be held in a number of forms, including: joint tenancy, tenancy in common, or by a corporation or partnership.

A joint venture generally describes a business relationship between a real property operator or developer and a financial institution, although more than two parties may be involved. The parties to the joint venture are known as joint venturers. A joint venture is very similar to a partnership, and as such either an oral or written agreement is needed concerning how any profits or losses are to be shared among the joint venturers. Like the partners in a partnership, each joint venturer contributes money, property, or expertise to the venture. Another similarity is that for tax purposes a joint venture is treated as if it were a partnership. Examples of joint ventures in real estate include; the association of a contractor and lender to purchase land and construct buildings on it to sell to investors; and the purchase of raw land by two or more parties to be subdivided and sold as building lots.

DOING BUSINESS
REIT TAXES

In order to qualify for tax avoidance, REITs:

1. Must be unincorporated trusts
2. Must be managed by trustees
3. Must have at least 100 shareholders
4. May not have more than 50 percent of the ownership held by five or fewer shareholders

In addition, two tests of income must be met:

1. The 90 percent test: at least 90 percent of the REIT's gross income must be derived from investment sources including dividends, interest, rents from real property, gains from the sale of stock securities and real property, and abatements and refunds of taxes on real property.
2. The 75 percent test: at least 75 percent of the REIT's gross income must be derived from investment in real property, including rents from real property, interest on obligations secured by mortgages on real property, gains from the sale or other disposition of real property, and dividends or other distributions on, and gains from, the sale or other disposition of shares in other real estate trusts, and abatements and refunds of taxes on real property.

Finally, a REIT must annually distribute at least 90 percent of its taxable income to its shareholders. Go to www.nareit.com, to find out more about REITs in general and to link to specific REIT Web sites.

Co-ownership of property can complicate real estate transactions. Before entering into a contract to purchase, sell or finance real property one must answer the following questions.
If you are purchasing real property:

1. Is the property co-owned?

If so:

1. Who are the co-owners?
2. What type of ownership form is title held in and what interest does each co-owner have in the property?

Is one co-owner authorized to transfer complete title?

1. Can one co-owner transfer his or her interest without permission of the other co-owners?
2. Are all the required signatures on the listing agreement, purchase offer, sales contract, note payable, and mortgage? Failure to acquire all necessary signatures may result in a costly legal dispute.

If you are taking title as a co-owner:

1. Which form of co-ownership is available?
2. Which of the available forms of co-ownership is best for you?

A joint venture differs from a partnership in that a partnership describes a group pursuing ongoing investment opportunities while a joint venture is formed to invest in a single project such as a shopping center or a condominium project. Upon completion of the project the joint venture is dissolved. In effect, a joint venture is like a "one-shot partnership." Unlike a general partnership, however, where all of the partners can be bound by the contract of one of the general partners, a joint venturer cannot bind the other joint venturers.

SUMMARY

While title to real property can be held by an individual in severalty, frequently a number of parties wish to share ownership of the same piece of real estate. Concurrent ownership commonly occurs when a married couple purchases a home. However, any number of parties, having a variety of legal relationships with each other, can be co-owners of real property.

A variety of concurrent ownership forms are available. People frequently own real property in either joint tenancy, tenancy in common, tenancy by the entireties, or as community property. The latter two forms only apply to married couples. In addition, the condominium and cooperative are available as ownership forms. Both commercial and residential properties can be owned in either of these forms although they are most used for residential buildings.

Concurrent ownership of real property for business purposes can be accomplished using any of several legal entities: a corporation, general partnership, limited partnership, limited liability company, and various trusts. Each entity has different advantages and tax characteristics that are important in structuring the ideal vehicle to accomplish a particular investment objective. Perhaps the most important advantage of all of these entities is that they provide a means for the pooling of capital from a number of individuals. Another advantage is that, with the exception of the general partnership, they insulate investors from personal liability for any losses incurred by the organization. In addition, these ownership forms enable an inexperienced investor to benefit from the expertise of professional managers.

KEY TERMS

articles of incorporation
community property
concurrent ownership
condominium
condominium bylaws
cooperative
corporation
general partnership

joint tenancy
joint venture
limited liability company
limited partnership
master deed
ownership in severalty
partition
partnership

partnership agreement
proprietary lease
real estate investment trust
separate property
syndicate
tenancy by the entireties
tenancy in common
trust

REVIEW QUESTIONS

1. List and explain the four unities of joint tenancy. What is the extra unity required for a tenancy by the entireties?
2. Doris, Beth, and Frank are joint tenants. Assume that Beth sells her interest to Gwen. What is the relationship between Doris, Frank, and Gwen?
3. What is a condominium? How does it differ from a cooperative, and from sole ownership?
4. Explain all of the possible methods of acquiring separate property in a community property state.
5. X and Y are tenants in common. X dies leaving his widow, W, as his only heir. Who now holds title to the property? Would your answer be different if X and Y were joint tenants?
6. How is a limited partner different from a general partner?
7. How is a joint venture different from a partnership?
8. What are the requirements for forming a real estate syndicate? What is the maximum number of participants in a real estate syndicate?
9. How is a subchapter S corporation different from a regular corporation?
10. How is a limited liability company different from a corporation?
11. Who are the parties to a land trust? How does a land trust differ from a regular trust?
12. What are your answers to the questions in the two "Decision Point" sections in this chapter?
13. What are your answers to the questions in the "Ethical Issue" section in this chapter?

REAL ESTATE ON THE WEB

Use your favorite search engine to:
1. Locate residential condominiums in your area.
2. Discover investment experiences people have had with real estate limited partnerships.
3. Determine if there are any real estate cooperatives in your area.
4. Discover whether your state allows LLCs, or LLPs and the filing requirements to form them.
5. Find out more about land trusts.

Refer to the companion Web site at www.wiley.com/college/larsen for a variety of online activities including additional chapter content, review materials, assignments, and related links.

ADDITIONAL READINGS

Giniss, R. J., "Putting a Stop to 'Asset Protection' Trusts," 51 *Baylor Law Review* 987 (1999).
Orth, J. V., "Tenancy by the Entirety: The Strange Career of the Common Law Marital Estate." *Brigham Young University Law Review* 35 (1997).
Womack, L. and D. Timmons, "Homeowner Associations: Are They Private Governments?" *Real Estate Law Journal* (Spring 2001): 322337.

CHAPTER

6

Limitations on Ownership

Learning Objectives

After studying this chapter, you should be able to do the following:

- Describe the various nonpossessory and potential interests in real estate.
- Understand the difference between an appurtenant easement and an easement in gross.
- Describe how easements are created and terminated.
- Explain the reason for, and enforceability of, dead restrictions.
- Describe the various types of liens that may attach to real property.
- Describe the powers retained by the government that affect land use.

FROM THE WIRE

In February 2001, five contractors took legal action against the Walt Disney Company, alleging that the entertainment giant owed them $12.6 million for work done on the new California Adventure theme park. The contractors filed four mechanic's liens and one lawsuit for unpaid construction on Paradise Pier, a section of the $1.4 billion park and resort 30 miles south of Los Angeles. A Disney spokesman said such actions are common with large projects because of differences in billing and payment cycles. "We anticipate that everything will get paid and the liens will be released," the spokesman said. The largest lien seeks $10.6 million for Steiny and Company, an electrical firm. Owner, Susan Steiny, said her firm was obligated by contract to do extra work on charge orders without first settling on the cost. "That way they can renegotiate you down" after the work is done, she said. An Anaheim real estate lawyer, Michael Migan, said it is not uncommon for liens to be filed over construction projects and that typically the parties later compromise on the payment.

Go to www.lienlawonline.com, to examine an example of an Internet service designed to assist those who wish to file a mechanic's lien, and click on FAQ to evaluate the advantages and disadvantages of using such a service.

INTRODUCTION

Previously you learned that the property rights of the present interest holder in real property may be limited by the presence of future interests. In this chapter, additional limitations on the rights of the present interest owner are discussed. Nonpossessory interests, such as easements, and potential interests in real estate, such as mechanic's liens, may restrict either the use to which the property is put, or the transfer of ownership. The property rights of the present interest owner may also be limited by the government's exercise of eminent domain, escheat, police power, or taxation.

Nonpossessory interests and potential interests in real estate act as encumbrances on the present interest. An **encumbrance** is any interest in, or right to, real property held by anyone other than the present interest owner, which reduces the value of the title. In addition to nonpossessory and potential interests, encumbrances include encroachments, leases, and title defects (Chapter 13). A knowledge of encumbrances is important because they may limit the use to which the property can be put or hamper the title transfer. The more binding the restriction, the greater impact it has on the value of the owner's title. Some encumbrances may even result in a loss of title. For example, failure to pay a mechanic's lien can result in the forced sale of the property to satisfy the lien. So, if things work out really badly for Disney in the "From the Wire" chapter opener, maybe on your next visit to Disneyland all the park workers will be electricians.

NONPOSSESSORY LAND INTERESTS

The holder of a **nonpossessory land interest** has certain rights which allow limited use and enjoyment of the property, but the given rights fall short of possession of the land. Easements, profits, licenses, and deed restrictions are nonpossessory land interests.

EASEMENTS

An **easement** is a right to use another's property for a specific purpose. While the easement holder's right is nonpossessory, the right may be permanent. Easements may be classified in many ways. An easement may be classified as an appurtenant easement or an easement in gross. The major distinction between these two categories is whether the easement benefits another parcel of land, regardless of who owns the other parcel, or benefits a particular individual, regardless of whether adjacent property is owned by the holder of the easement.

Appurtenant Easement

An appurtenant easement benefits another parcel of land. The property on which the easement is placed is referred to as the **servient tenement** and its owner as the servient tenant. The property that benefits from the easement is called the **dominant tenement** and its owner the dominant tenant. If ownership of either tenement is transferred to another the easement remains because the benefit applies to the dominant tenement, not the individual who owned the dominant tenement at the time the easement was created. This is the case even if the deed used to transfer ownership of the dominant tenement does not mention the easement because the easement is an appurtenance of the dominant tenement. An **appurtenance** is something that is deemed incidental to the land when it is used with the land for its benefit, such as access to a roadway across another's property. Therefore, it makes sense that such an easement cannot be sold separately from the dominant tenement.

The dominant tenement usually adjoins the servient tenement, although, as Exhibit 6.1 illustrates, it need not. In Exhibit 6.1, both property X and property Y are landlocked and have an easement on property Z for access to the road. Note that X does not adjoin Z. In addition, X has an easement on Y for road access. In this case, X is a dominant tenement for both of the other properties, Z is a servient tenement for both the other properties, and Y is both a dominant and servient tenement.

Traditionally, the most important uses permitted by easements concern rights to flowing water and rights of way. Easements can, however, be acquired for other purposes such as VORTAC stations, from which radio signals are sent to track the position of overhead planes. For the stations to function properly no object within approximately a half-mile of the station may be higher than six feet. When a station is established, the government acquires an easement to assure the required open air space. Another example is a solar access easement, generally granted for the collection of solar energy for use in heating devices. Both of these examples are easements on the supersurface, not the surface, but these types of easements can severely restrict the potential development of the servient tenement because the easement could prevent the construction of buildings, fences, or even the planting of certain types of vegetation. If this is the case, you may question why one would grant such an easement. There is more than one answer to that question. In some

| EXHIBIT | 6.1 | APPURTENANT EASEMENT EXAMPLE |

cases, like the VORTAC system easements or where the government obtains scenic easements surrounding public recreation areas, the property owner has no choice. The government has the power to acquire the easement through an eminent domain proceeding that is discussed later in this chapter. In other cases, an easement may be granted voluntarily. In either case, the property owner receives some compensation for the easement. In addition, there are tax benefits associated with such easements. The servient tenant can deduct the reduction in property value from the tax basis of the property that may lower income tax at the time the property is sold. Also, if the easement is granted to a charitable organization, the servient tenant could claim the reduction in property value currently as a charitable contribution in the year the easement is created.

Easement in Gross

An easement in gross differs from an appurtenant easement in that only servient tenements are involved. Either a person or a commercial entity has the right to use, or dominate, the servient tenement. Commercial easements in gross are commonplace. Utility companies, for example, obtain an easement to run lines for improvements. This particular type of easement presents an interesting exception to the definition of an encumbrance. Technically, utility company easements are an encumbrance, but few would argue that access to power and water reduces the value of most properties. An example of a private easement in gross would be a grantor who transfers ownership of a tract of wooded land, but reserves the right to walk on the land. Private easements in gross usually cease with the death of the grantor.

Affirmative and Negative Easements

Easements can also be classified based on whether they are affirmative or negative easements. A negative easement is one in which the servient tenant is prevented from using the property in a particular way. A solar access easement is an example of such a negative easement. An affirmative easement is one in which the dominant tenant can use the servient tenement. The right to use a portion of another's property as access to a roadway is an example of an affirmative easement.

Methods of Creating Easements

Easements may also be classified according to the manner in which they come into existence. Easements may be created in one of a number of ways, including: by express grant, by necessity, by express reservation, by implied grant or implied reservation, and by prescriptive right.

Easement by Express Grant An easement by express grant is created by a written document; most easements are created in this way. The party granting the easement is called the grantor and the party that receives the easement, the grantee. Because an easement creates an interest in land, the document used to create an easement by express grant must comply with all the formal requirements of the state in which the property is located. No particular words are necessary to create an easement, but it is essential that the parties make clear their intent to create an easement. A well-written document should include: an accurate description of the location, width, and length of the easement; the intended use of the easement and any limits on the use of the easement; specification of any conditions that would terminate the easement; and a statement about who is responsible for maintaining the easement. In addition, the document should be signed by the grantor, sealed, witnessed, acknowledged and delivered to the grantee. The term "acknowledged" means that the document is witnessed, or notarized, by a notary public. To perfect the easement, the document should be recorded in accordance with the local rules governing deeds (Chapter 12). An express easement can be terminated by obtaining a written release from the owner of the dominant tenement, which should also be recorded.

Easement by Necessity   An easement by necessity is created when a parcel of land conveyed by a grantor has no direct access to or from any road. For example, Dr. Fall owns a property that adjoins a lake. The lake is completely surrounded by privately owned properties. Dr. Fall decides to subdivide the property into two parts, A and B, as shown in Exhibit 6.2. Dr. Fall enjoys being near the lake, but does not require lakefront property, so she retains parcel B and sells parcel A to Mr. Spring. Unless Mr. Spring is qualified as a pilot, examination of Exhibit 6.2 illustrates his dilemma; there is no access to parcel A. In this case, Mr. Spring would be entitled to an easement by necessity across parcel B. What if Dr. Fall decides to prevent access? In some states, condemnation procedures are available to help property owners who need access to their land.

Another example of an easement by necessity is when a farmer cultivates property with no road access and must cross the property of another to get in and out of a field. Easements by necessity last only as long as the necessity. In this example, if a road were constructed adjacent to the formerly landlocked acreage, the necessity no longer exists and the easement by necessity is terminated.

Easement by Reservation   An easement by reservation is created when a property owner, in selling part of his or her land, reserves in the deed an easement in favor of the land retained. In the example illustrated in Exhibit 6.2, Dr. Fall's access to the lake was cut off when parcel A was sold. Change the example slightly and assume that she wants to retain access to the lake. This can be done by inserting a clause in the deed to the effect that a portion of parcel A is reserved as a means of access to, and egress from, the lake. Consider another scenario, again referring to the example in Exhibit 6.2. If the grantor decides to sell parcel B and retain parcel A, access to parcel A could be ensured by including a clause in the deed that allows use of a portion of parcel B as a means of access.

Implied Easements   As the phrase suggests, an implied easement exists although there is no written mention of an easement in the document used to convey title. An implied easement is created when one part of a property is used by a property owner for the benefit of another part, and this use is such that if the parts were owned by different parties, an

| EXHIBIT | 6.2 | **EXAMPLE: EASEMENT BY RESERVATION AND EASEMENT BY NECESSITY** |

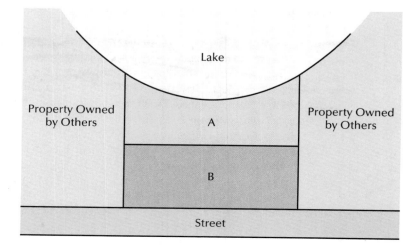

easement would be required in order for one of the owners to enjoy the beneficial use to which the property is put under sole ownership.

To create an implied easement four requirements must be met.

1. The prior use of one part of the land for the benefit of the other part must have been such that it would be disclosed by a reasonable inspection of the premises.
2. The prior use must have been continuous.
3. The easement must be necessary in that a substitute for the easement cannot be obtained without unreasonable trouble and expense.
4. The multiple parcels must have been owned by one party when the use began and ownership of the land separated after the use began, such that one party owns the burdened parcel and another owns the benefited parcel.

A common application of the implied easement is provided in the following example. A developer subdivides a property into building lots and contours the development so that all rain water in the development flows to a sewer drain located on a particular lot. The developer then sells the lots to other parties. All of the other lots in the development have an implied easement on the lot with the drain, and the owner of the lot with the drain cannot redirect the flow away from the drain.

In one case, a court determined that an implied easement existed based on the following circumstances. One party owned two lots and had a building erected on each. To save on construction expense, stairs for both two-story buildings were contained in only one of the buildings. The owner later sold the building with the stairs to another party, retaining ownership of the building with no direct access to the second floor. In this case, the court determined that an easement was created through implied reservation.

Easement by Prescription An easement by prescription is acquired by continuously using another's property for some purpose, without the owner's permission. Acquiring an easement by prescription is similar to acquiring title to property through adverse possession. But, remember that adverse possession results in a possessory interest, while an easement by prescription results in a nonpossessory interest. Several requirements, similar to those for taking title by adverse possession, must be met for an easement by prescription to be created.

- The use must continue for the required statutory (prescriptive) time period. In most states, the time required to establish an easement by prescription generally corresponds to the state's adverse possession period.
- The use of the easement must be visible. In most states, this means that the user must use the property in a way that the owner would, under normal circumstances, be aware of the use.
- The use must be adverse. In other words, without the permission of the owner.
- The use must be exclusive. The exclusivity requirement forces the user to consistently confine use to a particular area.
- The use must be continuous. A prescriptive claim can be based solely on the user's use and not on use by others. Tacking is an exception to this requirement that courts sometimes allow. The rule of tacking enables either those who inherit or purchase title to add, or tack on, their use to the use of the former prescriptive user under certain circumstances. An easement by prescription is terminated if the use is abandoned. In addition, the servient tenant could, for a price, secure a written release from the dominant tenant.

The following example points out other important aspects of easements by prescription. Mr. Jones uses a neighboring property, owned by Mrs. Brown, as a short-cut footpath from his property to the grocery store. Mr. Jones uses the footpath without the permission of Mrs. Brown and she would prefer that he not cut across her land. Until the prescriptive time requirement has been met, Mr. Jones is a trespasser and Mrs. Brown may take legal action to prevent the trespass. Courts in the majority of states would recognize most of the following: a written protest presented to Mr. Jones, putting up a fence, or Mrs. Brown could get a court order to prevent the trespass. However, if Mrs. Brown fails to prevent the unauthorized use before the prescriptive time requirement is met, Mr. Jones's unauthorized use ripens into a prescriptive easement. He is then able to continue the use of the footpath and Mrs. Brown has no legal power to stop him. For example, if she were to erect a fence after the prescriptive easement is obtained, Mr. Jones could force her to have it removed. The extent of an easement is determined by the type of use made during the prescriptive period. Mr. Jones's prescriptive use was as a footpath. After the easement is acquired he would not have the right to use the footpath for vehicular travel.

Perhaps the use of the footpath does not bother Mrs. Brown, but she is concerned that it may ripen into a prescriptive easement. To prevent this she could give Mr. Jones oral permission or a license for the use; such permission prevents the use from qualifying for prescription. To prevent an easement by prescription, the parties must mutually agree upon permission to use the property for a specific use. For example, if Mrs. Brown only posts a permission sign, Mr. Jones's prescriptive right would not be cutoff.

PROFITS

The holder of a **profit** has the right not only to access another's property, but also to remove something from the land, for example: water, oil, minerals, or some other element of the property. In essence, a profit is an easement with the right of removal. A profit is different from ownership of subsurface rights because ownership of subsurface rights is unlimited and exclusive. In contrast, more than one party may hold a profit in a particular property, and a profit can be restricted by the time allowed for removal, the type of item that may be removed, or the quantity that may be removed.

Similar to easements, profits can be classified as: in gross, or appurtenant. Examples of a profit in gross would be an oil company given the right to remove oil from a property, or the right to move cattle onto another's land for grazing purposes. An example of an appurtenant profit is the right to remove water for use on an adjoining property.

LICENSE

A **license** legalizes certain conduct on another's property. Examples of activities for which one receives a license are: fishing, hunting, attending a sporting or entertainment event, or just being on the land. The party giving the license is the licensor and the party receiving the license is the licensee.

There are important differences between a license and an easement. Easement rights are mandatory and relatively permanent in nature, while license rights are acquired only with the permission of the property owner and are generally temporary. In essence, the rights or privilege of the licensee may be revoked at any time by the licensor. In addition, while ownership of an easement changes with the ownership of the dominant tenement, a license is a purely personal right and cannot be sold. Finally, a license may be created by oral agreement. In fact, a license generally results if parties attempt to create an easement by oral agreement.

DEED RESTRICTIONS

Many restrictions on real property use are included in deeds executed by private landowners. In this way, a grantor can control some aspect of the land use by subsequent owners.

This is accomplished by placing a clause in a deed known as a **deed restriction.** Common examples of such restrictions include: limiting improvements to a particular type of structure; specification of some minimum square footage for the improvement; and restrictions on the maximum building height. Other examples of restrictions include, but are not limited to: the type of exterior construction material which may be used; whether or not garages may face the street; minimum amounts of landscaping for a property; and whether large pets, such as horses, may be kept on the premises. Such clauses create a nonpossessory interest in land in that the grantor has no right of possession.

The primary purpose of most deed restrictions that limit use is to protect property values. These restrictions help to assure, for example, that a home with a very low value is not constructed next to a very expensive one, thereby negatively affecting the value of the expensive home. Such restrictions are often imposed by developers, and well-considered deed restrictions often enhance the marketability of real property. These restrictions may apply to all subsequent owners of the property, or the deed might specify a time period after which they are no longer applicable.

POTENTIAL INTERESTS IN REAL PROPERTY

The holder of a **potential interest in real property** has a claim on property that may ripen into a present interest if certain conditions are not met by the property owner. Mortgages

AN ETHICAL ISSUE
DEED RESTRICTIONS CONTROLLING OWNERSHIP

In addition to restrictions concerning the use to which property can be put, some deeds contain clauses that place restrictions on the classes of people, based on race, creed, color, or country of national origin, to whom ownership of real property can be transferred. The following example demonstrates the lack of legitimacy of such restrictions.

The Congressional hearings held to evaluate Justice William Rehnquist's nomination for the position of Chief Justice of the United States Supreme Court were televised nationwide. Opponents of the nomination criticized Rehnquist for, among other things, his record on civil rights for minorities. His critics cited covenants in deeds to two properties as evidence of his insensitivity. One deed, for a property located in the southwestern part of the country, which the Justice no longer owned at the time of his confirmation hearings, had a covenant that prohibited transfer of the property to people of Hispanic origin. Another deed, for property located in the northeastern part of the country, prohibited transfer of the property to anyone of the Jewish faith. Justice Rehnquist had not placed either of these covenants in the deeds; he merely took title with the covenants already in the deeds.

Each time an opponent to the nomination raised this issue, a Rehnquist supporter quickly pointed out that the deed restrictions did not demonstrate insensitivity on the part of Rehnquist toward the civil rights of minorities. Instead, Rehnquist's supporters argued that such covenants are irrelevant because they are unenforceable, but they did not provide a case reference to support their assertion. Perhaps the legislators were all familiar with the unenforceability of the clauses, but the critics' persistence must have confused the general public. Such covenants were declared unenforceable by the 1947 United States Supreme Court decision of Shelly v. Kramer [334 U.S. 1 (1947)]. However, one could still question why someone with political ambitions did not have the offensive clauses removed with a correction deed (Chapter 12).

If you were to acquire title to property with a deed that includes such a covenant, would you file a correction deed to have the offensive covenant removed? A filing fee is required to record a correction deed. If you answered "yes" to the above question, how high would the filing cost have to be before your answer becomes "no"?

and security interests (Chapter 15) are potential interests in real property, as are liens. The most common types of liens are discussed in the following sections.

LIENS

A **lien** is a claim by one party on the property of another that serves as security for the repayment of a debt. Liens on real property can be classified as either general or specific. A general lien is a claim that applies to all real property owned by the debtor, whereas a specific lien applies only to a particular parcel. Common examples of general liens include: judgment liens, federal income tax liens, and federal estate tax liens. Examples of specific liens include: mechanic's liens, property tax liens, and vendor's liens. In many states, a specific lien is created when a mortgage is used to secure financing for real property.

There are two parties to a lien. The party who holds a claim on another's property is referred to as the lienor or lien creditor. The person on whose property the claim is placed is known as the lienee or lien debtor. It is important to note that the filing of a lien does not transfer title to the lienor. A lien is a financial security interest, not an ownership interest in the property. If a property on which a lien exists is sold, however, the lien creditor receives payment before any money passes to the seller.

Real property liens can be created either by contract or by operation of the law. A mortgage lien is an example of a lien created by contract. Liens created by operation of the law can be classified as statutory liens, common law liens, or equitable liens, depending upon whether the relation of the parties to the lien is governed by a statute, the rules of common law, or equity. Sometimes, liens created by operation of the law are called involuntary liens because, unlike a lien created by contract, the lien is created without the stipulation of the parties, in particular the lienee. The three most common types of liens created by operation of the law are mechanic's, judgment, and tax liens.

MECHANIC'S LIEN

A **mechanic's lien** is a claim placed on real property for the purpose of securing payment for materials and labor supplied for improvements to the real property such as new construction, additions, or repairs to existing improvements. The most widely used term for this type of lien is "mechanic's," but some states use other terminology, including: construction liens, laborer's lien, architect's lien, or materialman's lien. As these names imply, parties who may be entitled to file a mechanic's lien include: contractors, subcontractors, architects, engineers, laborers, and those who supply material for the job. Mechanic's liens are statutory liens because they are governed by state statutes. Further, they are specific liens; other real property owned by the lienee is not subject to the lien. For the property involved, however, they apply not only to the improvements, but also to the land.

In one case, a college professor was attracted by a contractor's low interest rate on new home loans. The professor bought one of the homes, and within a few months of moving in received notice of eleven different mechanic's liens on his property. The contractor was having cash flow problems, and he attempted to solve this problem in two ways—attracting sales with his low interest rates and not paying his subcontractors. In cases like this, it is possible that the owner will have to pay for the property twice. Whether double payment is required depends upon the lien system used in the state in which the property is located.

There are two basic lien systems: the New York system and the Pennsylvania system. Real property owners in states that follow the Pennsylvania system are subject to double jeopardy. Under this system, a subcontractor has the right to file a mechanic's lien even if the owner paid the full contract price to the contractor. Of course, the property owner can bring suit against the contractor in an attempt to recover the payment made. The New York system provides property owners with considerably more protection against unscrupulous

The following suggestions are for those who wish to reduce the possibility of acquiring mechanic's liens when they purchase real property. Some suggestions are more practical than others, some more effective than others and, of course, the author cannot guarantee that any provide absolute protection.

For New Construction

- If you can, build the improvements yourself.
- Deal only with reputable contractors.
- Sign a "no-lien contract" with the contractor. To be effective against subcontractors, the no-lien contract must be recorded.
- Insist that the contractor post a performance bond to ensure completion of the work at the agreed price.
- Secure lien waivers from the subcontractors.
- Have the lender distribute payments.

For Used Property

- Ask the seller if any improvements or repairs have been made and verify payment was made to the correct party.
- Do not hold the closing until the statutory period to file a lien has elapsed. Warning—contractors and subcontractors often save some work in order to prevent the statutory time clock from starting

In Either Case

- Obtain an affidavit from the seller that all contractors have been paid.
- Secure competent legal advice.

---

contractors. A subcontractor's recourse to the owner under this system depends on whether or not the subcontractor gave the owner notice of the amount that would be due to him under his contract with the contractor. If the subcontractor does not present the owner with notice of the amount that will be owed, the subcontractor is precluded from collecting the amount from the owner. However, if the subcontractor gives the owner notice of the amount that will be due to him from the contractor, the owner may withhold that amount from payments to the contractor until proof is provided that the subcontractor has been paid. In some states, the system followed depends on the type of property involved. In Ohio, for example, one- to four-unit residential dwellings are covered by the New York system while other properties are governed by the Pennsylvania system.

Mechanic's liens do not come into existence automatically upon the failure to receive payment; the claimant must take action. In order to file a lien, the claimant must show: that a contract for the work existed, that the work was done, and that payment was not received. Imagine what might happen if a contract were not required. Home repairmen might watch people leave their homes, do unwanted work on the unoccupied houses, and send bills which when unpaid would be used to file a mechanic's lien. The degree of contractual arrangement required to file a mechanic's lien varies significantly among states. Some states have "contract statutes" which require that the owner of the property sign a contract for the work or materials. Other states with "consent statutes" will allow a lien to be filed if there was an implied agreement. For example, the owner permitted work to continue after witnessing the work being initiated or continued.

In most states, the process requires that each claimant file an affidavit, or notice, of mechanic's lien with the county clerk in the county in which the property is located. Although requirements vary by state, the affidavit generally must include: the name of the lienor, the services or material provided and when it was delivered, a legal description of the property where the materials were used or services performed, the identity of the owner of the property, the name of the person with whom the lienor contracted, the contract price, any amount paid, and the amount still due. Anyone filing a mechanic's lien must do so within the statutory time period. This time period varies by state and is usually measured from the date of completion of the project. In addition, written notice of the filing usually must be given to the property owner and the contractor, if applicable, within a statutory time period. A valid lien against the property is created after all of the filing and notice requirements have been met.

The mere filing of the lien does not guarantee payment of the debt, but mechanic's liens provide substantial protection for those who provide material and labor. If the lienee does not pay on the lien, the lienor can normally force the sale of the property and collect the amount owed from the sale proceeds. However, in states that provide homestead exemptions, homesteads are protected from forced sale for satisfaction of a mechanic's lien. Similarly, in those states that still recognize dower and curtesy interests, a mechanic's lien may not attach to the interest, or cause the sale of the interest. But in cases where a lien can result in a forced sale, foreclosure proceedings could begin at once or at any time up to the maximum period allowed by law, which ranges from six months to three years. If legal action is not commenced within the statutory time period the lien expires and is worthless.

Sometimes, in order to collect some cash quickly, the lienor will sell the lien to another, who may then pursue the claim. In any case, the lienor initiates the foreclosure process by filing a lis pendens notice. The filing of this notice prevents the lien from lapsing although the claim has not been heard in court. It also gives potential purchasers, and other interested parties, constructive notice that a lawsuit is pending that may affect the title to the property. Constructive (or legal) notice is given by recording a document in the public record. Legally, constructive notice is as valid as actual notice; which is express or direct knowledge acquired in the course of a transaction.

When more than one lien is filed against a property, it is important to be able to prioritize the claims because the proceeds from the sale of the property may be insufficient to cover all claims. In most states, the lien for the construction of a building dates back to the commencement of the construction and all mechanic's liens are treated equally as if all work began at the same time. In some states, the priority date is the date each lienor began work, not the date the general construction began. In other states, lien priority is based upon the date that the lien is recorded.

JUDGMENT LIEN

A judgment lien differs from a mechanic's lien in that it is a claim on both personal and real property resulting from a lawsuit. Further, the cause of action for the lawsuit is not necessarily related to a transaction involving real estate. It could, for example, relate to liability for personal injuries suffered in an automobile accident. If a court decides that one party owes another money, a formal decree, or judgment, will be entered to that effect. The winning and losing parties then become judgment creditor and judgment debtor, respectively. However, winning a lawsuit and collecting the judgment are two separate matters. If the judgment debtor does not pay the obligation, and the proper procedure is followed, the court judgment is converted into a judgment lien. To collect the judgment, the judgment creditor must attach the debtor's property. The creditor can attach the debtor's bank accounts, wages, personal property, or the debtor's real property, except homestead property.

Judgment liens are general liens in that they may be applied against all real property the judgment debtor owns or may later acquire, but they are usually only valid against real property located in the county where the judgment was granted. In some states, it is possible to extend the lien to other counties by filing a notice of lien with each county. In most states, if the judgment is not paid, the judgment creditor may force the sale of the judgment debtor's real property, by securing a writ of execution that directs the county sheriff to seize and sell a sufficient amount of the debtor's property, to satisfy the debt. Even without this process, the lien is recorded against the property and title cannot be passed or insured until the judgment has been paid or otherwise resolved. Often, however, a judgment debtor will divest themselves of any real property ownership interest before the judgment is granted, and/or will refrain from acquiring an ownership interest in any additional real property while the judgment lien is in force. The priority of judgment liens is determined on the basis of the recording time. The claim of a judgment creditor is superior to mechanic's liens filed after the judgment lien attaches, and junior to those that became effective before the judgment lien.

Each state has a time period in which foreclosure proceedings may be taken before the judgment expires. For example, in Ohio a judgment lien has a legal life of seven years that may be extended another seven years if proof of potential collection is provided to the court. Judgment liens expire and are worthless if foreclosure proceedings are not started within the statutory time limit.

TAX LIEN

Taxing authorities may establish a tax lien against real property when the owner fails to pay taxes owed. Tax liens may result from a failure to pay several kinds of tax, including: state or federal income tax, federal estate taxes, and local property taxes. The first two types of tax give rise to general liens, the last a specific lien. As with other liens, the lienor may force the sale of the lienee's real property to satisfy the debt. Payment of the overdue tax, and possible penalties and interest, will eliminate these liens. Once established, tax liens have priority over all other types of liens regardless of when the other liens took force, and in the event the owner fails to pay the tax, ownership of the property may be lost for the price of the tax.

VENDOR'S LIEN

In some real property contracts the seller, or vendor, may help facilitate a sale by financing all, or a portion, of the sale price. In transactions where title to the property is conveyed, but less than the full purchase price is paid at the time of conveyance, several states allow the seller to reserve in the deed a lien on the property to secure full payment. Vendor's liens apply to installment sales (Chapter 7), but not to transactions where the seller provided financing using a second mortgage (Chapter 15). If the buyer subsequently defaults by not making full payment, the seller has a vendor's lien against the property for the unpaid balance. These liens have priority over subsequent liens and encumbrances and also over prior judgments against the purchaser.

A vendor's lien is often referred to as an equitable lien, or as an equitable mortgage. An equitable mortgage is anything a court would treat as a mortgage, although on its face it is not. The vendor's lien will be eliminated when the vendee makes full payment. Until that time, if the vendee defaults, the holder of a vendor's lien has the same right to foreclose on the lien as the mortgage holder (Chapter 15).

ENCROACHMENTS

An **encroachment** exists anytime improvements or fixtures of one property encroach on, or overlap, another property. Examples of encroachment would include tree branches that extend over a neighboring property, or a fence, building, or other improvement erected by one property owner on the land of another. The owner of the property being encroached is entitled to either force removal of the encroachment, or be awarded monetary damages. Failure to force removal of the encroachment may make the property more difficult to sell because it clouds the title. Eventually, if unchallenged, the owner of the encroaching property may be able to claim a legal right to continue the use.

Decision Point

Many years ago your neighbor planted a blue spruce sapling on her property six feet away from the property line. Within the last few years, the branches of the nearly 60 foot tall tree have extended across the property line. What steps would you take to cure the encroachment?

GOVERNMENTAL POWERS AFFECTING REAL ESTATE

When the government transfers land to private ownership it retains certain rights or powers that may limit the rights of individual real property owners. There are four basic public powers that may influence land ownership and use. One is the power of taxation. As described above, failure to pay taxes will result in a lien being placed on the property, and failure to satisfy the lien may result in loss of ownership. The other powers retained by the government include eminent domain, escheat and police power.

DOING BUSINESS
LEGAL ISSUES

A real estate law professor had an interesting experience involving encroachment that he related to his students. Hundreds of townhouses had been erected in a development. After all of the units had been sold, it was determined that none were built entirely on the land designated for the particular unit. Each unit was encroaching on one or more unit's land, and each was being encroached upon by one or more units. The professor was living in one of the units at the time of the discovery. Not wanting to get involved in what could become a legal nightmare, the professor found someone willing to purchase his unit, sold it, and moved into a single-family home. But, at the time the story was told the problem still existed and the professor had moved back into the same development. Student curiosity was naturally aroused. Why had he moved back?

There are a number of ways to cure an encroachment. If removal of the encroachment will not create great economic waste, the encroachment can be cured by removal. While this might be an appropriate cure for a tree with overhanging limbs, or a garage with overhanging eaves, it was clearly inappropriate in this case. Where great economic waste would occur with removal, such as a twenty-story building erected four inches onto the land of a neighboring property, a common solution is to require the encroacher to pay the landowner for his damages. This was not done in the townhouse example because it was determined that with the number of units involved the legal costs of correcting the problem would exceed the payments. Instead, everyone agreed that they would live with the problem until it corrected itself. The development was located in Nebraska, one of several states with a Marketable Title Act (some states call them Merchantable Title Act). In these states, such title problems become mute after a statutory time period. In this case, ownership of the land would legally change from what was legally owned to the land under each unit. A slow, but effective way to cure an encroachment. Oh yes, why did the professor move back? Because he decided he liked the lifestyle in the development and because encroachments can be cured.

Go to www.lexis-nexis.com/universe using your university computing system, click on "Legal Research," then click on "Area of Law by Topic," and use the keyword "encumbrance" to find the results of lawsuits involving encumbrances.

EMINENT DOMAIN

Eminent domain is the right of the government to take private property, without the owner's consent, for public use upon making just compensation. The right of eminent domain is based upon the principle that a private real property owner should sometimes have to give up his or her property to better society. The right is established in the Fifth and Fourteenth Amendments to the Constitution. The Fifth Amendment prohibits the federal government from depriving any person of "property, without due process of law," and also provides that, "private property shall not be taken for a public use, without just compensation." The Fourteenth Amendment has wording almost identical to the Fifth Amendment, but applies to state governments.

Eminent domain is an extensive public limitation on real property ownership. Governmental bodies possessing the right of eminent domain can delegate the power to others. Historically the power has been delegated to political subdivisions and various governmental units to acquire land for schools, roads, parks, and public buildings. The power has also been extended to quasi-public parties such as public utilities, airports, and railroads, or to private parties such as developers in urban renewal projects and private universities. Before exercising the right of eminent domain, most organizations will attempt to acquire the needed real estate through negotiation with the property owner. If these efforts fail, the property may be taken by eminent domain without the consent of the property owner.

To take property under eminent domain, the condemnor is obliged to prove the following: that the property is needed for a public use; that the condemnor is not acting out of malice to deprive the owner of the land; and that the amount of compensation being offered is the reasonable value of the property being taken. The first two points are rarely a major issue. Most disputes arise over the question of reasonable compensation. Reasonable, or just, compensation is almost universally defined as fair market value. Fair market value is defined as the price that a property would bring, given a reasonable amount of time on the market, a knowledgeable seller and knowledgeable buyer, neither of whom is under any pressure to complete the transaction.

Few condemnees are satisfied with the compensation they receive in an eminent domain proceeding. This dissatisfaction may be due, in part, to irreconcilable differences of opinion between the condemnor and condemnee regarding the fair market value of the property. The dissatisfaction is also likely due to the fact that compensation is not paid for all damages suffered by a condemnee. Examples of possible damages which are not factored into eminent domain awards are: the costs of locating and securing a replacement property, the loss of profits or goodwill associated with the condemned location, and the negative effects of having the improvement for a neighbor. If the improvement were a park, few would argue that it damaged the value of the adjoining properties. If, instead, the improvement is a waste disposal treatment plant, the possible negative effect on adjoining properties becomes more obvious. The cost of moving to the replacement property is another example of damage that may not be recovered in an eminent domain proceeding, however, the federal government and several state governments do pay this cost in some situations.

The timing of the valuation also causes dissatisfaction over the amount of compensation. If the public use is likely to drive up property values, for example, the construction of a major highway, condemnees would prefer that the property be valued based on its future value. Instead, compensation is based on the value at the time of the taking. At least this procedure protects those condemnees whose property value would decrease after the improvement is implemented.

The public good may be served by condemning only a portion of a property. In some cases, a partial condemnation will depress the value of the remaining property. To compensate owners for this loss, many states provide for severance damages. That is the amount paid in the condemnation will be the fair market value of the property actually taken plus an amount equal to the reduction in value of the remaining property.

In recent years it has become more common for the condemnor to acquire only an easement on privately owned real estate, rather than full title. Examples are scenic easements near recreation and public parks, and easements for flooding acquired on land located near large public reservoirs. There are several possible advantages to taking only an easement, compared to full title. Easements can be acquired for less money and, therefore, may be attractive to the taxpayers who ultimately pay the eminent domain bill. In addition, the affected property generally does not have to be removed from productive use. Finally, easements cause less disruption of the local real estate market because property owners seldom must relocate when only easements are taken.

Inverse Condemnation

Inverse condemnation occurs when a property owner attempts to force a governmental unit to purchase their property, claiming that an action of a government has destroyed or reduced the value of their property. Many property owners have used this type of action successfully. An example of inverse condemnation is a property owner with property near an airport who sues to force condemnation of his property and payment for damages caused by low-flying aircraft noise. Another example is when a governmental body announces plans for a new highway, but postpones acquiring the properties needed for the right-of-way. A property owner in the path of the planned highway could contend that the announcement has made it impossible to sell the property for private use and sue to force condemnation.

ESCHEAT

If a person dies without heirs and intestate (without a valid will), ownership of any real property owned by that person reverts to the state. This process, called **escheat,** is perhaps the most unusual method of acquiring title to real estate. The doctrine of escheat comes from the feudal concept that all land ultimately belonged to the king. Escheat is not really a restriction on ownership. Instead, it is intended to solve the problem of property becoming ownerless. Escheat generally does not greatly affect land values and land use patterns because the state sells the property to the highest bidder at a public sale and successful bidders usually do not change the use of the property.

Escheat rarely occurs with valuable tracts of real estate because, with few exceptions, long-lost relatives appear to claim the property. Whether the relatives will be successful in enforcing their claim depends upon the law that prevails in the state. For example, under the escheat provisions of the Uniform Probate Code (UPC) only littoral descendents (sons and daughters and their offspring) of the paternal or maternal grandparents of the deceased may inherit. States that have adopted some form of the UPC include: Alabama, Alaska, Arizona, Colorado, Florida, Hawaii, Idaho. Louisiana, Maine, Minnesota, Montana, Nebraska, New Jersey (in principle), New Mexico, North Dakota, Pennsylvania, Utah, and Wisconsin. In these states, property will escheat before collateral heirs (aunts, uncles, and cousins) inherit.

Decision Point

How can you ensure that property you own will not escheat to the state?

POLICE POWER

The term **police power** encompasses several kinds of land use controls, including: rent controls (Chapter 18), building codes, zoning, and subdivision regulations. The rationale for police power is that the government should be allowed to exercise control in order to protect the health, safety, morals, and welfare of the public. When a state legislature passes an enabling act, local governments receive the authority to control land use. Many regulations that control land use are made locally.

Master Plan

Local authorities are learning that to derive the most benefit from the various police powers at their disposal, these powers must be integrated into a coordinated **master plan.** Some communities call such plans comprehensive plans; others call them general plans. Regardless of the label, these plans are generally prepared by a city or regional planning commission for the purpose of providing direction for the orderly development of the community. The first step in the planning process is to conduct a study of physical and economic factors in the area. The planning commission then sets certain goals that they would like the area to achieve, for example, concentric growth around the city center, maintaining the vitality of the downtown shopping area, reserving a certain percentage of the area as "green space," or the preservation of historic structures. The plan usually contains the following elements: a land use plan, a transportation plan, a public facilities plan, and an analysis of projected population changes and economic development. Effective plans provide continuity in the long-term by including planning periods of fifteen to twenty-five years. The plan is not a static tool, however, and is subject to change as conditions warrant.

Building Codes

Many cities and towns have established extensive building codes. These codes limit private property rights by regulating the occupancy and construction of new buildings and the alteration of existing structures. Building codes are intended to help ensure that businesses and homes are safe places in which to work and live. The requirements, which specify minimum construction standards, cover such things as the number of windows required in each room, exits, sanitary requirements, structural load and stress, fireproofing, plumbing, heating, electrical systems, and the quality of construction material. Historically, the states have given local governments the authority to set building codes. A lack of uniformity among local jurisdictions has been the result, often leaving gaps in consumer protection and substantially increasing construction costs. To overcome these problems, there is a trend toward statewide or regional building codes.

Enforcement of building codes occurs at all stages of construction of the improvements. A building permit is required before construction can begin. The plans for each proposed structure must be submitted to the local building inspector's office, which verifies that the plan conforms to the code, before issuing a permit. If a property owner builds without a permit, he can be forced to tear down the building. During construction, inspectors visit the building site to ensure that the codes are being observed. When construction is complete, a certificate of occupancy is issued if the building conforms to the code. The structure cannot be legally occupied without this certificate, and financial institutions frequently require a certified copy of the certificate before they will close a mortgage loan.

Zoning Ordinances

Another method of governmental regulation of real estate involves zoning ordinances enacted by municipalities. **Zoning ordinances** are used to promote the orderly development of land and to protect property values by requiring incompatible land uses to occur in different areas. This type of regulation is not new, although early regulations focused on the prevention of nuisances rather than on a comprehensive plan. For example, in colonial America, many towns controlled the location of certain odorous activities, such as leather tanning. In the 1880s, several cities, including Baltimore, Boston, Indianapolis, and Washington D.C., enacted ordinances to limit the height of buildings. The first truly comprehensive zoning laws were enacted by the city of New York in 1916. Today, almost all communities have some zoning laws.

Modern zoning ordinances regulate land use by dividing communities into districts. Examples of these districts include: residential, commercial, industrial, agricultural, and public lands. Within a particular district the ordinance may specify subclassifications. For example, residential zoning often includes subclassifications for various types of single-family and multiple-family dwellings. Commercial and industrial zones also often include subclassifications based on the type of enterprise.

In addition to the general use to which the property may be put, zoning ordinances regulate the intensity of use by specifying regulations on structure height, area, and the placement of improvements upon the land. These regulations may include among other things, required setbacks from the front, rear, and side of the lot, minimum lot size, minimum usable floor area, minimum usable open space, and minimum parking area. Courts have found some zoning ordinances to be discriminatory. Exclusionary zoning is a term used to describe ordinances designed to prevent low and moderate income groups from locating in a particular area. In some cases, minimum floor space and minimum lot size requirements have been associated with exclusionary zoning.

Zoning influences land development patterns, and, to the extent that it channels demand to certain parcels and away from others, it has a powerful impact on property value. Zoning is often criticized and subject to controversy because different people have different ideas about what constitutes a community's orderly development. Zoning ordinances may harm some real property owners by denying them the opportunity to make more profitable use of their property than is allowed by the comprehensive plan adopted for the zoned area. Therefore, it is imperative to determine how a property is zoned before purchasing it so that you can determine whether or not your intended use is allowed.

Zoning can be either exclusive or cumulative. Exclusive zoning means that more restrictive uses are not permitted within the zone. Cumulative zoning means that more restrictive uses are permitted. If an area is zoned cumulatively for heavy industry, for example, both heavy industry and more restrictive uses such as light industry, or commercial uses are permitted. If the area is zoned exclusively for heavy industry, however, more restrictive property uses are not permitted within the area. Even when an area is zoned exclusively for a particular use, accessory uses are normally permitted. For example, if an area is zoned exclusively for single-family homes, owners are normally permitted to construct such things as a detached garage, a tool shed or a swimming pool.

A specialized zoning category that permits a mixture of land uses within a given parcel is known as overlay zoning. This type of zoning is required for planned unit developments (PUD) and residential planned developments (RPD). A PUD is a development in which a variety of uses are planned and developed as a unit. A PUD, for example, might contain a 700-acre tract with clusters of houses, apartments, or townhouses, a neighborhood shopping center, recreational facilities, and open spaces.

Exceptions to Zoning Real property owners are sometimes allowed to use their property in a manner that is inconsistent with the prevailing zoning. There are a number of ways in which this can happen. One, known as a **nonconforming use,** pertains to a use that predated the zoning ordinance. A property may have been used for one purpose when a zoning ordinance was enacted to make that use illegal. Most zoning ordinances provide that nonconforming uses may continue after the enactment of the ordinance. Buildings on the nonconforming property may be repaired, but the owner may not enlarge the structure, or raze and rebuild it. In many cases, the nonconforming use may continue indefinitely. However, some ordinances contain provisions that allow nonconforming uses to continue only for a specified time period. The time limitation for a nonconforming use is known as amortization. After the amortization period has expired the property must be used in a manner consistent with the zoning ordinance. Similarly, the exception to the zoning ordinance is lost if the owner abandons the nonconforming use. In the event of abandonment, or when the building is ultimately demolished, subsequent use of the property must conform to the ordinance.

It is also possible for an owner to legally use a property in a manner that violates a zoning ordinance although the ordinance predates the use. To do this the owner must obtain a variance from the zoning board. Generally, in order to obtain a **variance** the owner must demonstrate several things: that the variance will not change the economic nature of the neighborhood; that the land will not yield a reasonable rate of return if used as zoned; and that the hardship imposed by the ordinance adversely effects only the property on which the variance is sought, not other properties. For example, a variance might be granted to reduce the setback requirements slightly for an irregularly shaped building lot so that a house can be fit on it.

An owner who is unsuccessful in obtaining a variance may attempt to have the area rezoned through amendment. An amendment to the zoning laws can be initiated by either the government or by a local property owner. In either case, notice of the proposed change must be given to all property owners in and around the area affected by the proposed change, and a public meeting held so that all concerned have a chance to voice their opinions before the zoning board makes any zoning changes.

Many zoning ordinances contain provisions for floating zones and special exceptions that allow for variation without the need for formal amendment to the ordinances. Floating zones occur when the ordinance provides for a particular use but does not allocate land to this zone until a request is received by a landowner. An example of a special exception would be ordinances that allow parks, churches or schools to be located in areas zoned residential. When ordinances contain such special exceptions, the tests for a variance do not apply and the special use must be allowed.

Spot zoning offers another means to use a property differently than allowed by the zoning in the neighborhood. Spot zoning is the term used to describe the situation in which a single piece of real estate is classified for a use that is different from the zoning for the surrounding area. If the use permitted by the spot zone is not inconsistent with the surrounding zoning, spot zoning sometimes occurs. For example, a neighborhood shopping center might be allowed in a residential neighborhood. Spot zoning is not used if the use is inconsistent with the area.

Floor-Area Ratio Zoning A method used to regulate the intensity of use is floor-area ratio zoning. This is a formula approach to regulate structural density of commercial buildings and multi-family structures. Under this system, a single number describes the relationship between building height and the portion of the lot that may be covered by the structure. For example, a permissible ratio of five to one would allow a five-story building to occupy the entire lot, a ten-story building to occupy half the lot, and a twenty-story building to cover one forth the lot. Coverage ratios are established to meet planning, open space, and parking objectives. Some cities apply different ratios for different types of structures. Some apply different ratios for the same type of structure based on location. New York City, for example, to encourage development of the west side of Manhattan allows higher ratios compared to those that apply to the east side.

Transferable Development Rights   One of the objections some people have had with traditional zoning is that it restricts them from using their property as intensely as they would like. In some communities that have a comprehensive master plan, transferable development rights (TDRs) are an innovation that permits some property to be used more intensely than normally allowed. This is accomplished by separating the right to develop a tract of real estate from the tract itself. For example, the owner of a twenty-acre tract may wish to subdivide and build homes on the land, but minimum lot size requirements of five acres per lot restrict the development to four houses, which the owner determines is financially unsound. If the owner of the twenty-acre tract can convince the owners of nearby properties to sell to him their development rights, more houses could be built on the twenty-acre tract. Thus, the density requirements for the overall area are maintained, the owner of the twenty-acre tract can develop the property in the manner he wishes, and the owners who sold the development rights have been compensated for their agreement not to further develop their property.

TDRs have been used to protect environmentally sensitive areas, farmland, and open spaces in several states, including: Florida, Maryland, New Jersey, Pennsylvania, and Vermont. They have also been used in some large cities, such as Chicago and New York, to preserve privately owned historic buildings. Owners who agree not to raze their buildings are compensated by being given TDRs that they may sell to nearby landowners.

What if you buy a parcel of raw land for development in an area where TDRs are used and the development rights to the property have previously been sold? The answer is either you find someone willing to sell you development rights or you do not build. Therefore, the astute purchaser should first ascertain whether TDRs are used in the area, and if they are, ascertain that the rights to develop the property have not been sold, or that development rights can be obtained at a reasonable price from another property owner.

Subdivision Regulation

Chapter 8 includes a discussion of the plat maps prepared and submitted by developers to a planning commission. In preparing these maps, the developer must comply with the government subdivision regulations. These regulations, sometimes called mapping requirements, set standards for such things as: the placement of sewers, fire hydrants and street lights; the design and construction of streets, sidewalks and curbs, water and utility lines; and the grading of soil. In addition, some communities require the developer to set aside land in the development for parks or schools, or provide money so that nearby land may be purchased for that purpose. Mandatory dedication of land is controversial; some even consider it a violation of due process (although developers surely try to pass on this cost to lot purchasers). Courts are divided on the issue of mandatory dedication.

Other communities provide for set-aside land by requiring the developer to reserve the land only for a certain period of time during which the local government may purchase the property. If they do not do so in the stated time period, the developer is no longer bound by the reservation. In addition to land dedication, some communities also require the developer to pay impact fees to help raise the funds needed for the expansion of public facilities caused by the new development. While the use of impact fees is also controversial, their use is becoming widespread.

Environmental Regulations

Of increasing importance to real estate development is the proliferation of environmental regulations that are being enacted at all levels of government. Many communities now require that an environmental impact report, be included in the development package submitted to the planning commission. This document shows the expected impact of the development on the total environment, including air quality, employment, energy consumption, noise levels, vegetation, vehicular traffic, wildlife, and population density. The development of real property may be restricted because the land is in a designated flood-prone area. In addition, laws and regulations have been enacted to protect environmentally sensitive areas and endangered wildlife species.

Several uses of lead in products that could cause lead poisoning have been reduced or banned in recent years, including: lead in solder used in water pipes, and paint. A great deal of lead remains, however, in older homes. Title 10 of the Housing and Community Development Act of 1992, also known as the Residential Lead-Based Paint Hazard Reduction Act, addresses this issue. One of the objectives of the legislation is "to develop a national strategy to build the infrastructure necessary to eliminate lead-based paint hazards in all housing as expeditiously as possible." For sellers of homes containing lead-based paint, the removal or containment of the paint (paint dust, or contaminated soil) may prove costly. It is estimated that three of four homes built before 1978 contain lead, an estimated total of 3,000,000 tons of lead in the form of lead-based paint.

SUMMARY

The real property rights of the possessory interest holder are limited. Encroachments, nonpossessory interests, potential interests, and government regulations all limit property rights. Nonpossessory interests, such as easements, are active interests, which either entitle someone aside from the owner to use the property for a specific purpose, or prevent the owner from using the property in some way. Easements can be created in a number of ways, including by express grant, by reservation, by implied grant, by implied reservation, and by prescription. Easements, and other nonpossessory interests, especially profits and deed restrictions, act as an encumbrance on the property and may reduce the value of the possessory interest holder's title because they may limit the use to which the property can be put, or hamper title transfer.

A potential interest, such as a lien, is also an encumbrance on the possessory interest holder's title. There are various types of liens that may attach to real property, including mechanic's liens, judgment liens, tax liens, and vendor's liens. Potential interests complicate title transfer and may ultimately result in loss of ownership.

The property rights of the owner may also be limited by government regulations, including eminent domain, escheat, police power, and taxation. The police powers of the government give rise to several kinds of land-use controls, including building codes, zoning ordinances, and subdivision regulations.

KEY TERMS

appurtenance	inverse condemnation	potential interest in real
deed restriction	license	property
dominant tenement	lien	profit
easement	master plan	servient tenement
eminent domain	mechanic's lien	variance
encumbrance	nonconforming use	zoning ordinances
encroachment	nonpossessory land interest	
escheat	police power	

REVIEW QUESTIONS

1. How is an easement by prescription similar to taking title by adverse possession? How do they differ?

2. How is an easement similar to a license? How do they differ?

3. What is the difference between an appurtenant easement and an easement in gross?

4. How is a profit different from an easement?

5. What types of deed restrictions are legal? What types of restrictions are illegal?

6. What is the difference between a specific lien and a general lien?

7. Is the government's power of eminent domain a violation of your constitutional rights?

8. Why are many condemnees unhappy with the payment they receive in an eminent domain proceeding?

9. What is the difference between exclusive zoning and cumulative zoning? If you owned a home, would you prefer that the zoning be one type or the other?

10. Your neighbor's property is not in conformance with the zoning ordinance that regulates land use in the area. Under what circumstances is your neighbor not in violation of the law? If these circumstances do not exist, would you report your neighbor to the authorities?

11. What conditions must exist for escheat to occur?

12. What is your answer to the questions in the two "Decision Point" sections in this chapter?

13. What is your answer to the "Ethical Issue" in this chapter?

REAL ESTATE ON THE WEB

Use your favorite search engine to:

1. Discover how various entities have used easements to create or increase nature preserves using the key word "easement."

2. Learn how governmental units pass on some development costs to developers using the key words "encroachment permit."

3. Find an example of adverse possession.

4. Determine if local building codes, master plan, and zoning ordinances (or zoning maps), are available on the Internet.

5. Discover whether your state has a Marketable (Merchantable) Title Act.

6. Learn the requirements to file a mechanic's lien in your state.

Refer to the companion Web site at www.wiley.com/college/larsen for a variety of online activities including additional chapter content, review materials, assignments, and related links.

ADDITIONAL READINGS

Armentano, J. M. "Zoning and Land Use Planning." *Real Estate Law Journal* (Winter 2001): 256268.

Burby, R. J., P. J. May, E. E. Malizia and J. Levine. "Building Code Enforcement Burdens and Central City Decline." *Journal of the American Planning Association* (Spring 2000): 143–161.

Cordes, J., D. H. Gatzlaff and A. M. Yezer. "To the Water's Edge and Beyond: Effects of Shore Protection Projects on Beach Development." *The Journal of Real Estate Finance and Economics* (March, 2001): 287–302.

Duvall, R. O. and D. S. Black. "Dividing the Pie: Compensating Landlords and Tenants in Takings of Leased Real Property." *The Appraisal Journal* (January, 2001): 1–10.

Jennings, M. M. "A Potpourri of Cases: Landowners Haven't Been Busy Enough with Details." *Real Estate Law Journal* (Fall 1998): 199–206.

Shea, R. "Whose Tree is it Anyway? A Case of First Impression." *77 University of Detroit Mercy Law Review 579* (Spring 2000).

Titus, J. G. "Rising Seas, Coastal Erosion, and the Takings Clause: How to Save Wetlands and Beaches without Hurting Property Owners." 57 *Maryland Law Review* 1279 (1998).

Van Hefner, W. "Easements? We Don't Need No Stinking Easements!" *America's Network* (September 1, 2001): 14.

Womack, L. "Private Property and the Power of Eminent Domain." *Real Estate Law Journal* (Spring 2000): 307–318.

7

Income Taxes

Learning Objectives

After studying this chapter, you should be able to:

- Describe the classes of real property for income tax purposes.
- Explain the classes of income used to determine taxable income.
- Explain the various tax shelters to which real property owners are entitled.
- Calculate the gain or loss on the sale of real estate.
- Calculate the depreciation allowance for an investment property.
- Identify the quantitative factors that should be considered in a purchase/rent decision.
- Estimate the effective monthly cost of home ownership.

FROM THE WIRE

Want to build a new home or remodel an existing one? Perhaps you should do it in Hawaii. In June 2002, Governor Ben Cayetano announced that he planned to approve a one-year extension for a housing construction tax credit program launched in the fall of 2001 to address the state's economic downturn following September 11. About 4,000 tax credit claims had been filed by June totaling about $4 million, and another $4 million in claims were likely among those awaiting processing. That was far less than the amount the State Department of Taxation had estimated the program would cost. The program allows home owners and housing developers to claim a 4 percent income tax credit on new construction and remodeling work up to $250,000 per unit, but not for improvements that are not a part of the dwelling, such as swimming pools and landscaping. Cayetano said he was confident that the tax credits had helped strengthen Hawaii's economy and should continue. Lowell Kalapa, president of the independent Tax Foundation of Hawaii, questioned whether the tax credits remained necessary; citing the fact that home prices in Oahu had risen to their highest level in more than six years. "The demand is there anyway," Kalapa said. "We didn't like the bill to begin with, because it just skews the market."

Go to www.irs.gov, and enter the key words "real estate" in the Search the IRS Site box to learn about proposed changes to the federal tax code and more detailed information than is presented in this chapter.

INTRODUCTION

In this chapter, we present provisions of the United States income tax code (Code) that pertain to real property. An understanding of this information is important because these provisions may significantly affect the value and affordability of real estate. The information presented here should be considered only a starting point for learning more about how the Code interfaces with investment in real property.

Benjamin Franklin said, "In this world nothing can be said to be certain, except death and taxes." It is safe to add a third certainty of life to those offered by Mr. Franklin; the tax law will change. Therefore, before making any decision regarding the purchase, use, or disposition of real property, consultation with a real estate tax expert is recommended. The Code is complex; we review only major provisions here. In addition, as the chapter opener "From the Wire" suggests, periodically state (and local) governments provide tax benefits to stimulate home ownership.

One reason for the complexity of our federal tax system is the complex nature of our economic system. Another is the fact that the Code was developed piecemeal, over time. As it exists, our tax system can work to the benefit of real property owners. Property values may be enhanced to the extent a community employs taxes well. Most citizens value good school systems, efficient police and fire protection, and other public services. In addition, real property owners enjoy certain tax benefits. The exact benefits to which a real property owner is entitled depend, in part, on the classification of their property under the Code. For example, home ownership entitles owners to certain tax advantages, and additional tax advantages are associated with the ownership of income-producing property.

Congress has enacted numerous tax advantages to encourage people to invest in and develop real estate. Upon occasion, however, the system spurs activity that penalizes real property owners. In the 1980s, for example, much of the commercial property construction that took place was driven primarily by the desire to capture tax benefits; many investors ignored supply-and-demand factors. The focus on tax benefits helped contribute to overbuilding, which depressed real estate values in many areas for more than a decade. One of the chief successes of the Tax Reform Act of 1986 (TRA) was the elimination of real estate investments based solely on tax benefits, so-called abusive tax shelters. Today, real estate must compete with other assets for investment dollars on a more level playing field. However, despite TRA and other recent changes in the Code, real estate continues to be one of the most tax-favored sectors of our economy.

THE PURPOSE OF INCOME TAXES

The federal government, most state governments, and many local governments use income taxes to raise revenue to finance various activities, such as road construction, education, and national defense. Many provisions in the Code were designed to provide taxpayers with financial incentives to act in a socially desirable manner. Home ownership is encouraged, for example, by several provisions in the Code that enable homeowners to avoid income tax and reduce their federal income tax liability.

There is an important difference between tax avoidance and tax evasion. **Tax evasion** occurs when a party reduces their tax liability in violation of the Code. It is illegal to evade taxes and penalties for doing so include fines and prison time. **Tax avoidance** occurs when a party reduces their tax liability in accordance with the Code. Not only is tax avoidance legal, it is encouraged by the Code.

TAX RATES

One factor that affects a real property owner's income tax liability is the form of property ownership employed. Homeowners are subject to "individual rates" as are owners of income-producing property who are either sole proprietors, partners in a partnership, or shareholders in an S corporation. Individual tax brackets vary slightly according to a taxpayer's filing status (e.g., single, or married filing jointly with spouse). Corporate owners are subject to "corporate rates."

Ordinary income tax rate schedules for individuals and corporations in 2002 are shown in Exhibit 7.1. The marginal tax rates for the four highest individual brackets are

| EXHIBIT | 7.1 | FEDERAL INCOME TAX RATES |

	Individuals		
Taxpayer Status	Taxable Income	Base Amount of Tax	+ Rate on Income Above Base Amount
Single	$ 0–6,000	$ 0	10%
	6,000–27,950	600	15%
	27,950–67,700	3,892.50	27%
	67,700–141,250	14,625	30%
	141,250–307,050	36,690	35%
	>307,050	$94,720	38.6%
Head of Household	$ 0–10,000	$ 0	10%
	10,000–37,450	1,000	15%
	37,450–96,700	5,117.50	27%
	96,700–156,600	21,115	30%
	156,600–307,050	39,085	35%
	>307,050	91,742	38.6%
Married Filing Jointly and Surviving Spouse	$ 0–12,000	$ 0	10%
	12,000–46,700	1,200	15%
	46,700–112,850	6,405	27%
	112,850–171,950	24,265.50	30%
	171,950–307,050	41,995.50	35%
	>307,050	89,280.50	38.6%

| EXHIBIT | 7.1 | **2002 FEDERAL INCOME TAX RATES (CONTINUED)** |

Married Filing Separately			
	$ 0–6,000	$ 0	10%
	6,000–23,350	600	15%
	23,350–56,425	3,302.50	27%
	56,425–85,975	12,132.75	30%
	85,975–153,525	20,997.75	35%
	>153,525	44,640.25	38.6%

Capital Gains

Capital gains and losses are assigned to baskets. Four tax rates will apply to most capital gains and losses:

- Ordinary income rates (up to 38.6% in 2002) for gains on assets held one year or less.
- 28% rate on collectibles gains and Section 1202 gains.
- 20% rate on gains on assets held for more than one year but no more than five years (or acquired before January 1, 2001).
- 18% rate on gains on assets held more than five years (and acquired after December 31, 2001).

Corporate Rates

Taxable Income	Base Amount of Tax	+	Rate on Income Above Base Amount
$0–$50,000	$0		15%
50,000–75,000	7,500		25%
75,000–100,000	13,750		34%
100,000–335,000	22,250		39%
335,000–10,000,000	113,900		34%
10,000,000–15,000,000	3,400,000		35%
15,000,000–18,333,333	5,150,000		38%
>18,333,333	6,416,667		35%

scheduled to decrease in 2004 (to 26%, 29%, 34%, and 37.6%) and in 2006 (to 25%, 28%, 33%, and 35%). And the brackets used in 2002 will be adjusted in 2004 and 2006 to account for changes in the Consumer Price Index. Note in the exhibit, that a lower long-term capital gains rate applies to gains realized on the sale of most assets when the asset being sold was owned for the required time.

In reviewing the figures in Exhibit 7.1 you will note that our income tax system is progressive; the percentage of each dollar that is taxed is positively related to the taxpayer's taxable income. The theory behind a progressive tax is that each taxpayer's tax liability should be positively related to the taxpayer's ability to pay. Other taxes, such as a sales tax, are said to be regressive. Regressive taxes tend to fall more heavily on the poor; that is, they represent a larger share of lower-income taxpayer's income.w

TAXABLE INCOME

The tax rates described in the preceding section are applied to the taxpayer's taxable income to determine the amount of income tax owed. Taxable income will be less than the taxpayer's gross income to the extent that the taxpayer is able to utilize tax shelters. The term **tax shelter** is a phrase used to describe a tax advantage that allows a taxpayer to eliminate or postpone the payment of income tax. Some tax shelters come in the form of a **deduction,** so called because certain amounts may be deducted from the taxpayer's gross income in calculating taxable income. Examples of items that real property owners may be able to deduct from gross income include other taxes, mortgage interest paid during the tax year, and depreciation. Other tax shelters to which real property owners may be entitled are discussed later in this chapter.

CLASSIFICATION OF INCOME

Those with diversified sources of income may find it complicated to determine their taxable income. The Code requires that all income (or loss) be classified into one of three categories for tax purposes: active, passive, and portfolio. **Active income** is income derived from salaries, wages, fees for services, bonuses, and income from a trade or business in which the taxpayer materially participates. The Code defines material participation as "involvement in the operations of the activity on a regular, continuous, and substantial basis." As a general rule, if a taxpayer devotes at least 500 hours per year attending to a particular activity it will qualify as material participation. **Passive income** is income derived from a trade or business in which the taxpayer does not materially participate. However, even if a taxpayer materially participates, income from most real estate rental activity is classified as passive income. For example, income from activities in which the taxpayer is a landlord is classified as passive. **Portfolio income** is income derived from securities such as dividends on stocks and interest on bonds. Portfolio income derived from real estate activity includes dividends received on shares in a real estate investment trust, as well as income received on ground leases and long-term net leases (Chapter 18).

PASSIVE ACTIVITY LOSS LIMITATION (PALL)

TRA put the above income classifications in place to help eliminate some possibilities for abuse of the tax system. Prior to 1986, losses from real estate investments could be used to offset any type of income, and many limited partnerships intentionally acquired real estate that produced large tax losses because their wealthy limited partners (in high tax brackets) could use the losses to offset other taxable income. Such activity was the primary cause of the overbuilding mentioned in the chapter introduction. TRA addressed this problem with the **passive activity loss limitation,** which may prevent a taxpayer from using passive losses to offset either active or portfolio income in the year the passive loss is incurred. PALL requires that passive losses be used first to offset passive income, and only passive income, earned during the tax year. If any unused passive losses remain after all passive gains have been offset; the excess can be carried forward indefinitely to offset passive income in future years, or to offset any gain resulting from the sale of the investment. Given the time value of money (Chapter 17), the present value of passive losses as a tax shelter is reduced by any delay before a taxpayer can use them as an offset.

Exceptions to PALL

Exceptions to PALL exist for both real estate professionals and nonprofessionals. The Omnibus Budget Reconciliation Act of 1993 allows real estate professionals to offset real estate rental losses (excluding prior year losses) against other income if the following three conditions are met: more than 50 percent of the taxpayer's personal services are performed in real property trades or businesses in which the taxpayer is a "material" participant; the taxpayer spends at least 750 hours per year in real estate activities; and the taxpayer owns more than 5 percent of the activity if the personal services are performed as an employee.

For taxpayers who are not real estate professionals, real estate investment is generally considered to be a passive activity, but there is an exception to PALL that benefits many rental property owners (other than limited partners) who actively participate in the management of the property. Active participation requires less personal involvement than is required for material participation. An individual is deemed to be an active participant if the individual owns at least a 10 percent interest in the activity and is involved in management decisions, such as rent determination and tenant selection. If passive losses for the year exceed passive income from other activities, such individuals may use up to $25,000 of passive losses to offset active income. The $25,000 exception is reduced, however, by fifty percent of the amount of the individual's adjusted gross income in excess of $100,000. To illustrate, consider the table in Exhibit 7.2 that shows the maximum amount of passive losses an individual can use to offset active income.

Decision Point

Paul and Dave both work full-time as entertainers. They are interested in sheltering some of their income from income taxes, and are considering separate real estate investments. Paul, whose adjusted gross income is $85,000 a year, is thinking of purchasing a small office building. Dave has $8,000,000 in annual adjusted gross income, and is interested in purchasing an apartment complex. At the current time, neither property is showing a profit. Will either entertainer be able to use the losses to offset other income?

CLASSIFICATION OF REAL ESTATE FOR INCOME TAX PURPOSES

The tax owed by a real property owner is also influenced by the type of real property involved. For federal income tax purposes, real estate is classified into one of the following categories: personal residence, investment property, trade or business property, or dealer property. A personal residence is property used as the taxpayer's home. Investment property is real estate held as an investment for income production. Trade property or business property is real estate held for use in a trade or business, and dealer property is real estate held for sale to others. The information presented in this chapter focuses on the first two classifications, but some general information about all four classifications is presented in Exhibit 7.3. Examination of this exhibit should make it clear that while TRA targeted abusive real estate tax shelters, it did not eliminate real estate tax shelters.

PERSONAL RESIDENCE

Congress has provided several tax shelters to encourage home ownership. For individuals, interest paid on investment loans and home mortgage loans is the only type of deductible interest allowed by TRA. Previously, other types of consumer interest (e.g., auto loans and

EXHIBIT	7.2	EXAMPLES OF EXCEPTIONS TO THE PASSIVE ACTIVITY LOSS LIMITATION

Adjusted Gross Income	Active Income Allowable Offset
$ 100,000	$ 25,000
110,000	20,000
120,000	15,000
130,000	10,000
140,000	5,000
150,000	0

| EXHIBIT | 7.3 | SUMMARY OF REAL PROPERTY CLASSIFICATIONS FOR INCOME TAX PURPOSES |

Item	Personal Residence	Business Property	Dealer Property	Investment Property
Depreciation allowed	No*	Yes	No	Yes
Operating Expenses deductible	No*	Yes	Yes	Yes
Property tax deductible	Yes	Yes	Yes	Yes
Mortgage interest deductible	Yes	Yes	Yes	Yes
Selling Expenses Deductible	Yes**	Yes	Yes	Yes
Like-kind exchange allowed	No	Yes	No	Yes

* An exception occurs when one uses part of their home for business purposes.

** Effectively deductible if gain exceeds the limits described in the next section.

credit cards) were also deductible, but TRA mandated a phase out of their deductibility over a period of several years. This resulted in the popularity of home equity loans (Chapter 15).

Each year, homeowners may deduct any mortgage interest paid during the year for both their principal residence and second home. A homeowner in the 27 percent marginal tax bracket, for example, who paid $10,000 in mortgage interest during the year will pay $2,700 less in income tax. The federal government subsidizes the homeowner by effectively paying part of the mortgage interest. In addition, when purchasing a home, points representing interest are deductible in the year paid. Points representing interest charged on a home improvement loan or a refinance may not be deducted in full in the year in which the loan is obtained. Instead, for tax purposes, the cost of such points must be spread over the life of the loan.

Finally, each year, homeowners may deduct, in full, the amount of property taxes on their home paid during the year. Other tax shelters that apply at the time a personal residence is sold are examined in the following sections.

INCOME TAXES ON THE SALE OF A RESIDENCE

The Code is not perfectly balanced regarding the sale of a home. If the sale of a personal residence results in a loss, the loss is not tax deductible, but some of the gain resulting from a sale may be taxable. It is the seller's responsibility to determine if tax is due. To calculate the realized gain or loss on the sale of a personal residence, the owner's adjusted basis in the property is subtracted from the amount realized. Initially, an owner's **basis** in their home is the purchase price plus any closing costs associated with the purchase, paid for and not previously deducted by the owner. The basis may be increased by an amount equal to any expenditures made for improvements to the property. For this reason, it is important for homeowners to keep records of the cost of any major improvements made to the property. The amount realized is the gross sales price reduced by any selling expenses associated with the sale paid for by the owner/seller (e.g., brokerage commission, interest rate buydown, title insurance premium, recording fees).

An example of this calculation, based on the following assumptions, is summarized in Exhibit 7.4. Mary Martin just sold her home for $65,000. She paid the broker a commission of 6 percent, and paid $2,000 to buy the interest rate down for the purchaser. Other closing costs for which she was responsible amounted to $300. She purchased the home nine years ago for $45,000, and paid $640 in non-interest closing costs at that time. During her ownership she had a bedroom and garage added; which cost $7,870. Her gain on the transaction, therefore, is $5,290. At one time, Mary would have owed income tax on this gain, but the Code concerning gains on the disposition of a personal residence was modified in favor of homeowners in 1997. Today, a single person is exempt from tax on gains up to $250,000

EXHIBIT	7.4	**HOME SALE GAIN (LOSS) CALCULATION ILLUSTRATED**

Sale Price		$65,000
- Closing costs		6,200
Adjusted sale price		58,800
Purchase price	$45,000	
+ Closing costs	640	
+ Improvements	7,870	
Adjusted basis		53,510
Gain on sale		**$ 5,290**

resulting from the sale of a personal residence (for married couples filing jointly, up to $500,000). This exclusion can be taken every two years as long as the taxpayer has used the property as his or her principal residence at least two of the five years preceding the sale.

INSTALLMENT SALE METHOD

The **installment sale** method allows property owners who either use an installment land contract to convey their property (Chapter 11) or provide seller financing for a "regular" sale of their property to defer paying income tax on any gain until the year in which they receive payment. To calculate the tax due each year, the product of the amount of principal received during the year and the seller's gross profit margin is multiplied by the seller's marginal tax rate. For investment property, gross profit margin is the adjusted sales price (the gross sale price, less the selling and fixing-up expenses) less the seller's adjusted basis in the property, divided by the adjusted sale price. However, for a personal residence, any gain on the sale that is exempt from income tax is not included in calculating the gross profit margin.

The following example demonstrates how to calculate taxable income for an installment sale of a personal residence. In 2003, a house in which the seller's adjusted basis was $75,000 is sold. The adjusted sales price is $400,000. The seller agrees to finance the purchase, with the buyer paying $40,000 down and making monthly principal payments of $2,000 for thirty-six months beginning November 1, 2003. The unpaid balance is due with the last monthly payment.

Solution:

1. Payments toward principal will equal $44,000 in 2003, $24,000 in 2004 and 2005, and $308,000 in 2005 (interest on the loan is ignored in this example because it is all taxable in the year received).
2. The seller's gross profit margin is 18.75 percent [($400,000 - $75,000 - $250,000) ÷ $400,000]. (Remember, the first $250,000 of gain is not taxable)
3. Therefore, taxable income on the gain will be $8,250 in 2002 ($44,000 × .1875), $4,500 in 2003 and 2004 ($24,000 × .1875), and $57,750 in 2005 ($308,000 × .1875).
4. Each year's income tax will equal the taxable gain in step 3 multiplied by the seller's marginal ordinary or long-term capital gains rate (whichever is applicable).

INVESTMENT PROPERTY

To encourage the productive use of real property, the Code offers owners of investment property several tax shelters. Like homeowners, investment property owners may claim deductions for mortgage interest and property taxes paid. In addition, they may deduct expenditures for operating costs, property insurance premiums, and depreciation. Owners of investment property may also defer income taxes on gains resulting from the disposition of the property using the installment method, or by exchanging the property for other real property. In some cases, owners of investment property may be entitled to tax credits.

TAX CREDITS

A **tax credit** is an amount that directly reduces one's tax liability. Tax credits are generally more valuable to taxpayers than a deductible item. For example, if a taxpayer were in the 27.5 percent tax bracket, a $100 tax credit would reduce the taxpayer's tax bill by $100, but a $100 deduction would only reduce it by $27.50. Tax credits are designed to provide incentives for socially desirable private sector activities. Currently, federal income tax credits may be claimed for three real-estate-related reasons: for providing low income housing, for rehabilitating older and historic structures, and for business and commercial projects in low-income and moderate-income areas.

LOW-INCOME HOUSING TAX CREDIT

The Tax Reform Act of 1986 introduced the low-income housing tax credit. One who makes low-income housing available may claim the low-income housing credit annually for a period of ten years. The maximum annual credit is equal to either 4 percent of the acquisition cost of existing housing, or 9 percent of new construction or rehabilitation costs. Two special features are associated with the low-income housing credit. First, the credit may be used to offset taxes due on all types of income (passive, active, and portfolio) whether or not the owner materially participates in the management of the property. Second, taking the credits does not reduce the property's depreciable basis. To qualify for the credit the project must meet both a cost test and a use test. To pass the cost test, construction or rehabilitation expenditures must exceed $2,000 per low-income unit. The use test requires that either at least 25 percent of the units in the project be occupied by households with incomes no greater than 50 percent of the median income for the area (as determined by the U.S. Census), or at least 40 percent of the units be occupied by households with incomes no greater than 60 percent of the median income for the area.

Decision Point

An acquaintance asks for your help in analyzing two apartment buildings. The first has a purchase price of $400,000; the second $410,000. All operating cash flows associated with the properties are identical. The first property is located in an area where it will be nearly impossible to qualify for the low-income tax credit. Given the current tenant profile, the second property already qualifies for the credit. The hopeful investor only wishes to invest in one of the properties. Which property offers higher after-tax cash flows? What other factors would you suggest she consider before making the investment?

REHABILITATION TAX CREDIT

The rehabilitation tax credit was implemented to provide investors with a financial incentive to preserve architectural history. Two tax credit programs are available to encourage the preservation of older structures. One entitles the taxpayer to a credit equal to 10 percent of the rehabilitation expenditures on nonresidential structures constructed before 1936. The other entitles the taxpayer to a tax credit equal to 25 percent of the rehabilitation expenditures on residential or nonresidential structures that are either on the National Register of Historic Places or are nominated for placement on the register. The register is a list maintained by the United States

Department of Interior of properties and areas that are unique or have historic significance. Local historic properties committees nominate properties for placement on the register.

There are two important differences between this credit and the low-income housing credit. First, the depreciable basis of the historic property is reduced by the full amount of the credit in the year the credit is taken. This means that when the property is sold, a larger taxable gain will be realized. Second, the rehabilitation investment tax credit is taken in the year the rehabilitation expenditures occur, rather than being spread over several years.

To illustrate how the amount of the credit is determined, assume a developer purchases a national registry property for $250,000 and spends $600,000 on restoration or repairs approved by the Department of Interior. The tax credit is $150,000 ($600,000 × .25), which can be deducted from that portion of the developer's tax liability resulting from passive income for the year.

Because the tax credit was designed to encourage the preservation of still useful and historically significant structures, developers must comply with a number of restrictions including the use of materials, construction methods, and building redesign. For example, at least 75 percent of a historic building's internal structural framework and external walls must be retained as either interior or exterior walls, and at least 50 percent of the external walls must remain as external walls. In addition, the rehabilitation costs must exceed the greater of $5,000 or the adjusted basis of the property prior to the rehabilitation.

If the rehabilitation tax credit was taken and the property is disposed of within five years after the rehabilitation, the Code requires some of the credit to be recaptured. Continuing the above example, and using Exhibit 7.5, if the developer sold the property in the third year after the credit was taken, a payment of $90,000 ($150,000 × .60) would be due the Internal Revenue Service.

NEW MARKETS TAX CREDIT (NMTC)

The New Markets Tax Credit (NMTC) is the newest federal real-estate-related tax credit. It is designed to spur $15 billion in new capital for business development in economically underserved communities. It will give investors an income tax credit for new investments in eligible business and commercial projects in low-income and moderate-income areas. The credit is equal to 39 percent of the investment spread over seven years. Almost any type of business, community facility, or commercial real estate project located in nearly 40 percent of all census tracts in the country (containing one-third of the U. S. population), will qualify for the credit. The NMTC program is being administered by the U. S. Department of the Treasury.

DEPRECIATION

The benefits derived from many expenditures made by real property owners pertain to a single year (e.g., maintenance costs) and, therefore, the Code permits owners to deduct the

| EXHIBIT | 7.5 | REHABILITATION TAX CREDIT RECAPTURE PERCENTAGES |

Year of Disposition	Recapture Percent
First	100
Second	80
Third	60
Fourth	40
Fifth	20

entire cost in the year the expenditure is made. The benefits associated with other expenditures may span several years (e.g., the purchase price of the property, or the cost of major improvements). In recognition of this fact, the Code requires that the cost of a long-lived asset be written off over a time period that, theoretically, approximates the asset's useful life.

Unlike other deductions, the **depreciation allowance** requires no cash outlay in the year the allowance is taken. It is merely an allocation of the asset's cost over its estimated life. According to the theory upon which depreciation allowances were originated, the allowance serves two purposes. First, it results in a book value that approximates the property's market value, and second, it thereby encourages the asset owner to accumulate the tax savings provided by the allowance and eventually use them to replace the property. Neither rationale may be valid today. First, owners are likely to invest the tax savings generated from depreciation allowances on one property in other properties. In addition, since World War II, there has been little relationship between the market and book values of real property. In essence, the market value of many properties increases over time while the Code allows taxpayers to pretend that the property value is going down. For this reason, some refer to depreciation deductions taken under these circumstances as "illusory depreciation" or "phantom depreciation."

Regarding real property, only property held as an investment or for use in trade or business is depreciable; personal residences and dealer property may not be depreciated. The amount of the permissible depreciation deduction is prescribed in the Code, and depends on three factors: the method of depreciation, the life of the asset, and the asset's depreciable basis.

DEPRECIABLE BASIS

The total amount that may be depreciated by a property owner is referred to as the **depreciable basis.** It is important to note that only the original cost of improvements plus the cost of any additions to the improvements may be depreciated. Because land is virtually indestructible and will retain its value regardless of the value of any improvements upon it, land is not depreciable. The value of the land, therefore, is not included in the depreciable basis. The depreciable basis is usually determined in one of two ways. First, the relative values of the land and improvements as recorded in the property tax assessor's office can be used. For example, if you paid $300,000 for a small apartment complex, and the assessor's office has the property appraised at $50,000 land, $200,000 improvements, the depreciable basis of the property is $240,000 [$300,000 × ($200,000 ÷ $250,000)]. Second, if the property tax assessment is not current, an appraisal of the property, conducted by an independent real estate appraiser, may increase the amount allocated to the depreciable basis and, therefore, the tax shelter.

Appraisals are an ordinary part of most real estate transfers, but one could also be conducted subsequent to acquisition if a property that did not formerly qualify for the deduction becomes eligible. For example, assume you purchased your home fifteen years ago for $50,000. At that time it was appraised as 75 percent improvements and 25 percent land. Now you decide to lease the house to another party; for tax purposes you have converted the property from a personal residence to income property. The fifteen-year-old appraised value could be used to determine the depreciable basis of $37,500 ($50,000 × .75, assuming no additional improvements have been made). This is the depreciable basis regardless of either the extent to which borrowed funds were used to make the property acquisition, or the estimated dollar value of the property for property tax purposes. If, however, you believe that the value of the improvements has increased relative to the value of the land, a new appraisal may enable you to establish a higher depreciable basis. For example, if a new appraisal reveals that 85 percent of today's total property value of $220,000 is attributable to the improvements, $42,500 ($50,000 × .85) may be used as the depreciable basis.

For new acquisitions, determination of the depreciable basis may be facilitated if the purchase contract separates the purchase price into its component parts. Under most circumstances, each owner's depreciable basis is unaffected by the amount of depreciation the previous owners claimed. Instead, each owner's depreciable value depends on the cost of the property and the proportion of the total property value attributable to improvements.

METHODS OF DEPRECIATION

Historically, several methods of depreciation were available to real property owners. One was straight-line, wherein the depreciable basis is written off uniformly over the estimated life of the asset. Several accelerated depreciation methods, which allowed for faster write-offs than straight-line, were also available and, for tax purposes, owners of depreciable assets elected to use these methods whenever possible. A problem under the former system was that both real property owners and the government wasted resources as the IRS challenged many depreciation claims. In 1981, these disputes were eliminated with the introduction of the Accelerated Cost Recovery System (ACRS).

The ACRS system was modified in 1986, and today, depreciation allowances are governed by the **Modified Accelerated Cost Recovery System (MACRS).** Under MACRS, some (non-real estate) classes of depreciable property may be depreciated faster than straight-line. For owners of real property, however, the word "accelerated" is a misnomer. Nonresidential real estate, such as commercial office buildings, must be written off straight-line over 39 years, and residential rental property straight-line over 27.5 years. These time periods are longer than previously allowed, which decreases the depreciation tax shield enjoyed by owners of depreciable real property. One provision of MACRS offsets this disadvantage to some extent. In general, previous tax law required owners to reduce a property's depreciable basis by the amount of salvage value. Salvage value is the estimated market value of a depreciable asset at the conclusion of its useful life. Under MACRS, salvage value does not reduce the depreciable basis. In essence, the entire depreciable basis can be written off over time.

Regardless of when a real property is placed in service, the Code deems it to have been placed in service in the middle of the month. To illustrate the calculation of the depreciation allowance, assume an apartment building with a depreciable basis of $300,000 is purchased on September 1, year one. The owner will be entitled to 3.5 months depreciation in year one, or $3,181.82 [($300,000 ÷ 330 months) × 3.5 months]

TAX TREATMENT OF INVESTMENT PROPERTY DISPOSITIONS

The determination of the gain or loss on the sale of investment property is similar to that previously demonstrated for a personal residence. The primary difference is that the basis of an investment property will be reduced by an amount equal to any depreciation or rehabilitation tax credits the owner claims. Thus, a larger taxable gain (or smaller loss, which may be used to offset other passive income) results than if the owner had not claimed depreciation. Investment property owners may postpone the payment of income tax on gains by using the installment method (when applicable), or by exchanging the property for other real estate.

LIKE-KIND EXCHANGES

Owners of investment real property (or property held for use in a trade or business) are afforded a tax shelter, known as a **like-kind exchange,** if the property is traded for other real property. In essence, no gain is recognized upon the exchange, and under no circumstances may a loss resulting from an exchange be used as a deduction. For real property to qualify for a tax-free exchange, it must be traded for other real property, although not necessarily real property put to the same use as the original property. For example, an exchange of a shopping center for a golf course, or the exchange of an apartment building for a warehouse would both qualify as a like-kind exchange. The exchange of real property for any type of personal property does not satisfy the like-kind definition.

While an exchange may occur simultaneously (e.g., owner A trades property with owner B), it need not for the transaction to qualify as a like-kind exchange. To qualify as a like-kind exchange, the property to be received in the "trade" must be identified within forty-five days after the transfer of the relinquished property, and title to the second property must actually be acquired within 180 days after the transfer of the relinquished property (e.g., owner A sells the original property to owner C and subsequently purchases another property from Owner D). It is also important that the exchangor not use the proceeds from the sale of the original property, keeping it in a separate account earmarked for the acquisition of the second property. Part of the exchange may be taxable if other assets, referred to as **boot,** are included in the deal. For example, if one property is exchanged for another plus $10,000, the party receiving the cash will owe tax to the extent of the boot received up to the realized gain on the exchange.

AT-RISK RULE

In general, the loss from a particular investment that can be used to offset gains on other investments is limited to the amount that the investor could actually lose. In essence, the maximum offset is equal to the amount the investor has at risk. Under the right circumstances, however, the Code exempts real estate investors from the at-risk rule, and losses claimed may exceed the amount at risk. This exception is only applicable when non-recourse financing is provided by a disinterested third party. Non-recourse means that in the event the borrower/investor defaults, the lender may look only to the property for satisfaction of the debt.

To illustrate how a real estate investor might benefit from exception to the at-risk rule, assume that an individual invests $10,000 as a limited partner in a real estate limited partnership and that the individual's share of the partnership's non-recourse debt equals $90,000. In this case, the investor may use up to $100,000 in losses passed through by the partnership, but each loss recognized reduces the investor's basis in the investment which may result in greater taxes due at the time the investment is sold.

LIABILITY FOR TAX ADVICE

You now know the basics of the federal income tax law as it affects real property owners. You should, however, follow the same procedure competent brokers, appraisers, loan officers, and other real estate professionals follow; direct tax questions to a tax expert. Upon occasion, real estate practitioners are asked questions about the tax implications of a particular real estate transaction. If a client is damaged as a result of incorrect information supplied, a court may hold the party who gave the advice liable for the damage.

Decision Point

The previous Decision Points in this chapter called upon you to offer tax-related advice to others. What steps would you take to minimize your liability for such advice?

THE EFFECT OF INCOME TAX ON THE RENT VS. PURCHASE DECISION

As explained in Chapter 3, there are advantages and disadvantages associated with both home ownership and renting. Some factors, such as privacy, mobility, and the pride of ownership are qualitative in nature; others may be quantified. Informed decision-making requires that one consider both qualitative and quantitative factors when making a housing purchase/rental decision. To facilitate such analysis, in this section we present an analytical approach that one can use to make such a decision. The example demonstrates how to calculate the effective payments associated with each alternative. It also illustrates the different tax treatments for investment property and a personal residence.

RENTING VS. PURCHASE OF A SINGLE-FAMILY HOME

For discussion purposes, you currently rent, or are considering renting, an apartment for $600 per month. An alternative is to purchase a home that will cost $100,000. Assume the home is financed with an $80,000, thirty-year, 10-percent, fixed-interest-rate mortgage. Property taxes on the home are $3,600 per year, insurance on the home amounts to $360 per year, and your marginal income tax rate (both federal and state) is 40 percent. You should note in the calculations for the purchase alternative the effective (not actual) payment is determined. Specifically, it is assumed that various income tax benefits are realized each month, when in reality these are usually realized once each year (or four times per year for the self-employed).

Likewise, it is possible that property taxes and insurance premiums are paid less frequently than monthly. The effective payment is determined in order to more readily compare the alternatives. For the purpose of comparison, the monthly payment associated with renting is $600. One may question this figure based on the undisputed possibility that the renter's housing costs include some cost for maintenance and utilities. In comparing the alternatives, it is important to understand that it is the incremental amount (difference between alternatives) for such items that must be (and is, later) included in the analysis.

Calculation of the monthly mortgage payment is a first step in determining the effective monthly payment associated with ownership. Using the information from Chapter 17, the monthly payment of principal and interest is $702.06. This figure and those to follow are summarized in Exhibit 7.6. Next, the mortgage payment is adjusted for the income tax shield due to mortgage interest. To approximate this figure quickly for each month in the first year, multiply the loan amount by the monthly interest rate, and the purchaser's marginal tax rate; $266.67 [$80,000 × (.10 ÷ 12) × .40]. Property taxes have two effects on the effective monthly payment. First, payment of the tax increases the effective monthly payment, in this example by $300 ($3,600 ÷ 12). Second, property taxes present an income tax shield equal to the monthly tax amount multiplied by the marginal tax rate; $120 ($300 × .40).

Several expenditures incurred by homeowners are not tax deductible, including premiums for hazard insurance, utility costs, and maintenance expenditures. Premiums for property insurance raise the effective monthly payment, in this case by $30 ($360 ÷ 12). Finally, one must consider differences in maintenance and utility costs. A common rule of thumb suggests that owners should incur maintenance costs equal to approximately 1.5 percent of the purchase price per year. We assume that maintenance costs and utilities will be zero if you rent and $150 per month if you purchase.

Examination of Exhibit 7.6 reveals that for the first year, it would cost $195.39 more per month to own compared to rent. It is important to note that some of the amounts used in this analysis are likely to change over time. The income tax shield from mortgage interest will decline over the life of the loan, as tax-deductible interest becomes a smaller percentage of each payment. Premiums for property insurance, maintenance costs, utilities, and property taxes (and, therefore, the tax shield associated with property taxes) are all likely to increase over time. Combined, these changes will increase the effective monthly

| EXHIBIT | 7.6 | QUANTITATIVE FACTORS IN THE RENT/PURCHASE DECISION: AN EXAMPLE |

$600.00	Monthly rent
$702.06	Payment of principal and interest
-266.67	Income tax shield on mortgage interest
+300.00	Property tax
-120.00	Income tax shield on property tax
+ 30.00	Property insurance premiums
+150.00	Incremental utility and maintenance costs
$795.39	**Effective monthly payment for purchase of single-family dwelling**
-400.00	Rental income
+160.00	Income tax on rental income
- 6.00	Tax shield on property insurance premiums
- 51.52	Tax shield due to depreciation
- 30.00	Tax shield on maintenance and utility costs
$467.87	**Effective monthly payment for purchase of multi-unit dwelling**

cost of owning. Landlords are, however, likely to incur the same cost increases and to pass them on in the form of higher rents. For the purpose of decision making these costs increases are, therefore, deemed less important than the following points.

Difference in Up-front Cash Flows

For many people, the critical difference between the alternatives is the difference in the up-front cash flows. In most rental agreements the landlord will require no more than two months rent up front (rent for the first and last months), and a security deposit (usually equal to rent for one month). The minimum down payment required for a purchase may run as much as 20 percent if one employs conventional financing. In our example, this means that $1,800 is initially required to rent compared to $20,000 to purchase (ignore closing costs). There is an opportunity cost associated with the $18,200 difference. Prospective home owners who can invest the funds in something else and earn a higher after-tax return than the expected after-tax return associated with a home purchase have this additional factor to consider in making a housing decision. But, the use of a government-sponsored loan (Chapter 15) may greatly reduce the initial cash requirement associated with the decision to purchase.

The Effect of Reversion Value on Rent/Purchase Decision

It is possible for one to arrive at a rent/purchase decision based on the difference in each alternative's effective monthly payments and whether the difference is justified by differences in qualitative factors (e.g., size of living space and privacy). One could take the analysis a step further, however, if the would-be owner can estimate the period of time he or she will be in the property, and can estimate the annual increase in the home's value over that time. One could calculate the net present value (Chapter 17) of ownership if these are known factors.

Perhaps not surprisingly, very few people undertake such a detailed analysis prior to making housing decisions, and virtually nobody makes a housing decision based solely on net present value. If one did focus on net present value, no one would rent because renting always results in a negative net present value; the only type of cash flows associated with renting are outflows. Ownership, on the other hand, offers the possibility (but not the guarantee) of a positive net present value. In essence, the present value of the after-tax net reversion value (sale price adjusted for selling expenses and taxes) may exceed the present value of the down payment and monthly payments. The net present value of ownership will, of course, be affected by the extent to which one employs borrowed funds and how long the property is owned.

PURCHASING A MULTIPLE-FAMILY PROPERTY

Many experts suggest that an excellent way for first-time homeowners to enter the real estate market is to purchase a small, multi-unit, rental property, live in one unit and rent the rest to others. In this way, the renters help to pay the mortgage while the owner builds equity in the property. In addition, purchasers of such properties may qualify for larger loans if the lender considers the rental income in qualifying loan applicants. To demonstrate the soundness of this advice, the analysis, which is summarized in Exhibit 7.6, continues by examining the purchase of a $100,000 duplex.

Assume that you are contemplating the purchase of a duplex, and that all of the numbers given in the example for the single-family home purchase hold true for the duplex. This assumption introduces an important qualitative difference. It is unlikely that living in half of a $100,000 duplex will provide the same benefits as living in a $100,000 home. The assumption is made, however, only to facilitate the numerical example. All of the analysis needed for the single-family home purchase also applies for the purchase of a duplex. Therefore, we can continue the example where we left off. We assume that half of the property will be used as a personal residence and half as investment property.

Because investment property is treated differently than a personal residence for income-tax purposes, several additional items are pertinent in determining the effective monthly payment for the duplex. First, the rental income reduces the effective payment; we assume rental income of $400 per month. Taxes are, of course, due on the rental income, which increases the payment by the amount of the income multiplied by the owner's marginal tax rate, or $160 ($400 × .40).

The effective payment is also reduced because property insurance premiums paid on investment property are deductible. We have a mixed-use property, therefore, the reduction is equal to the product of the monthly premium and the proportion of the structure that is investment property, multiplied by the owner's marginal tax rate. In this case, property insurance premiums result in a deduction of $6 ($30 × .5 × .40).

Improvements on income property can be depreciated, resulting in an income tax shield. We assume that the property is appraised 85 percent improvements, 15 percent land (which is fairly typical for this type of property). This information can be obtained from the county assessor, or by hiring an independent appraiser. As explained earlier, residential investment property is depreciated over 27.5 years, or 330 months. The reduction in the effective monthly payment due to depreciation is, therefore, equal to the depreciable basis of the rental unit divided by the number of months over which the property is depreciated, multiplied by the owner's marginal tax rate. In this example, the depreciable basis is equal to $42,500 ($100,000 × .85 × .5), and the effective reduction in the monthly payment is $51.52 ($42,500 ÷ 330 × .40).

Finally, the portion of any utilities or maintenance that are attributable to the rental property offer an income tax shield equal to the cost of utilities and maintenance devoted to the rental property multiplied by the owner's marginal tax rate. Assuming half of the $150 cost, given earlier, is used for the rental unit; the effective monthly payment is reduced by $30 ($150 × .5 × .4). After all of these adjustments are made, we see that the effective monthly payment for the duplex is $467.87.

This example is not intended to suggest that ownership of a duplex will result in lower monthly payments compared to renting. It does, however, demonstrate the relative tax advantages of owning investment property or a home compared to renting. The expert's advice is not, however, universally applicable. Someone who is not handy at repairs, or does not have the time to perform them, could see much of the monthly savings lost by hiring repairpeople.

SUMMARY

Basic information about the federal income tax system was presented in this chapter; knowledge of this material is important for all real estate market participants. Income tax, however, is only one of many factors that market participants must consider when making real estate investment decisions. In following chapters, this information is integrated with other factors that should facilitate more informed decision-making.

The Code provides real property owners with several tax shelters. Homeowners may deduct mortgage interest and property taxes in calculating their income tax liability each year. They may also deduct points representing interest on a mortgage loan in the year paid, and postpone or avoid paying tax on the gain resulting from the sale of their home. The tax shelters available to owners of investment property are even greater. Owners of investment property may deduct mortgage interest, property taxes, operating costs, property insurance premiums, and depreciation. Owners of investment property may postpone taxes due to the disposition of the property at a gain, and may be entitled to tax credits.

KEY TERMS

active income	installment sale	passive income
adjusted sales price	like-kind exchange	portfolio income
basis	modified accelerated cost	tax avoidance
boot	recovery system	tax credit
deduction	(MACRS)	tax evasion
depreciable basis	passive activity loss limita-	tax shelter
depreciation allowance	tion	

REVIEW QUESTIONS

1. What is a progressive tax? What is a regressive tax? Give examples of both.
2. Are real property taxes progressive or regressive?
3. Why does Congress provide tax shelters to homeowners and to owners of investment property?
4. If income taxes are lowered (or raised), how might this affect your decision to purchase a home or buy investment real estate?
5. How do income tax laws subsidize home ownership?
6. In what ways may the owner of investment real estate postpone the payment of income tax resulting from the sale of the property?
7. What special tax shelter is provided to owners of low-income housing? Given that this shelter applies only to low-income housing, why would anyone choose not to own low-income housing?
8. How is depreciation different from other deductible items?
9. What is the difference between a tax deduction and a tax credit?
10. What is your answer to the questions in the three "Decision Point" sections in this chapter?

PROBLEMS

1. If a taxpayer's taxable income is $100,000, what amount of tax does the taxpayer owe assuming that the taxpayer is classified as:
   a. Single (not a surviving spouse)
   b. Married, filing a joint return
   c. Married, filing a separate return
   d. Head of household.

2. A taxpayer who actively participates in a real estate investment has adjusted gross income of $117,000. What amount of the $22,000 loss the property generated during the year can the taxpayer use to offset active income?

3. If, during the first month of the tax year, a taxpayer pays $250,000 for a residential real property that is appraised 80 percent improvements, 20 percent land:
   a. What is the annual depreciation tax shield for the first year?
   b. What is the annual depreciation tax shield for the second year?

4. If, during the first month of the tax year, a taxpayer pays $250,000 for a nonresidential real property that is appraised 80 percent improvements, 20 percent land:
   a. What is the annual depreciation tax shield for the first year?
   b. What is the annual depreciation tax shield for the second year?

5. Given the following facts that pertain to the sale of a personal residence, answer the following four questions:
   a. What is the adjusted sale price?
   b. What is the seller's basis in the property?
   c. What is the gain on the sale?
   d. What is the amount of tax due on the sale?

   Sale price = $122,000
   Brokerage Commission = 7 percent
   Closing costs for which the seller is responsible = $1,100
   Original purchase price = $77,700
   Noninterest closing costs at original purchase = $760
   Improvements made during seller's ownership = $14,450
   Fixing-up costs = $4,000

6. On July 27, an investor purchased an apartment building for $750,000, a house to be used as the investor's personal residence for $300,000, and a shopping center for $1,100,000. The apartment and house were appraised 80 percent improvements, 20 percent land, while the shopping center was appraised 90 percent improvements, 10 percent land.
   a. What amount of depreciation will the investor be allowed to claim in the first tax year for the apartment building?
   b. What amount of depreciation will the investor be allowed to claim in the first tax year for the house?
   c. What amount of depreciation will the investor be allowed to claim in the first tax year for the shopping center?

7. An investment property is sold for $145,500. The seller's basis in the property is $78,000. The buyer has agreed to make payments of $45,500, $50,000, and $50,000 in years one, two, and three, respectively. Assume all payments are made as agreed and the seller is in the 27.5 percent income tax bracket each year.
   a. What is the tax due from the sale in each year?
   b. How much tax would be due each year if the property were a personal residence?

REAL ESTATE ON THE WEB

Use your favorite search engine to:

1. Locate your state tax department's Web site.
2. Determine what, if any, real-estate-related tax credits are offered in your state, or community.
3. Locate a real estate dealer.

In addition, check out the Internal Revenue Service Web Site (www.irs.gov).

Refer to the companion Web site at www.wiley.com/college/larsen for a variety of online activities including additional chapter content, review materials, assignments, and related links.

ADDITIONAL READINGS

Auster, R. "Can a Homeowner Deduct the Garage?" *Real Estate Review* 30:4 (Winter 2001): 58–60.

Byrne, C. L. and L. S. Hall. "Conservation Easements Benefit Both the Taxpayer and the Environment." *Journal of Real Estate Taxation* 28:1 (Fall 2000): 49–56.

Cuff, T. F. "Tax-Free Real Estate Transactions." *Journal of Real Estate Taxation* 28:1 (Fall 2000): 68–74.

Fellows, J. A. "When is Real Estate a Capital Asset? And When is it Not? A reply from the Tax Court." *Real Estate Law Journal* 29:1 (Summer 2000): 43–52.

Howard, R. L. "The Effect of Recent Changes in the Tax Laws on the Residential Real Estate Market." *Real Estate Review* 30:1 (Spring 2000): 47–53.

Misey, R. J. Jr. "International Tax Issues for Real Estate Holdings." *Real Estate Law Journal* 29:2 (Fall 2000): 99–119.

Rosenfeld, J. "Section 1031—Tax Deferred Exchanges: Real Estates Best-kept Secret for Tax Relief." *Real Estate Issues* 25:4 (Winter 2001): 12–16.

Segal, M. A. "Tax Considerations in Related-Party Rentals of a Residence." *Real Estate Law Journal* 29:2 (Fall 2000): 120–125.

CHAPTER 8

Legal Descriptions

Learning Objectives

After studying this chapter you should be able to:

- Explain why informal property descriptions are unacceptable for transferring or leasing real property, and appreciate the need to describe real property accurately.
- Describe the methods used to legally describe real property.
- Calculate the acreage contained in a parcel described by the government survey system.
- Understand the importance of vertical land descriptions.
- Explain how property boundaries are determined when water borders the property.

FROM THE WIRE

Harrison County (Mississippi) Chancery Judge Tom Teel presided over a tough case. Alice Dauro had filed suit to protect a nineteenth century family cemetery from a development by Stone Investment Company. The city of Biloxi had already required Stone Investment to protect an area that encircled the marked graves and headstones in the cemetery, but Dauro had funeral home records that indicated that at least five people were buried in the cemetery in unmarked graves. She requested that the judge draw a one-acre boundary around the cemetery to prevent Stone from building homes next to, and possibly over, the cemetery on the North side of Biloxi's Back Bay. Stone Investment officials said the company did not want to give up any more land because it would encroach on two waterfront properties that were once advertised for $554,000. The judge concluded that he could not draw the boundary, in part because the deeds submitted by Dauro did not provide the exact location of the property. Based on a legal description of the property provided by Stone Investment, Teel discovered that the acre described in the original 1878 deed was not in the same location as the cemetery. Archeologists hired by Stone Investment did not find remains outside of the marked graves, but Dauro thinks that if families end up building homes there, they should be careful when they dig in their backyards.

Go to www.ngs.noaaa.gov, and click on "frequently Asked Questions" to learn the National Geodetic Survey's answers.

INTRODUCTION

Under our legal system, an individual cannot transfer legal title to real estate, or lease it, without some method of describing the property and the boundaries that separate it from others. In this chapter, we explain why informal references, such as a street address, are almost always inadequate for these purposes. To reduce such problems, a legal description is required. Although, as the chapter opener "From the Wire" indicates, mistakes in legal descriptions can be problematic as well. Several systems that provide legal descriptions are presented in the chapter. Two other aspects of real property descriptions are also addressed: vertical property descriptions, which are used to describe space above or below the surface of the land, and the determination of boundary lines when water borders a property.

INFORMAL PROPERTY DESCRIPTIONS

For a real property description to have legal effect, it should enable a competent surveyor to identify the particular tract of real property to the exclusion of all other tracts. Informal property descriptions, such as a street address, are inadequate for this purpose, and their use may result in confusion and costly legal proceedings. Therefore, informal descriptions are not recommended, and are almost never used in real property transactions. In isolated cases, informal descriptions have been found to be sufficient to pass title (e.g., a street address was found to be sufficient in Michigan (*Stamp* v. *Steele*, 209 Mich. 205,176 N.W. 464 [1920]) and a reference to a property by its popular name, "Commencement Plantation, consisting of 1330 acres," was judged sufficient in Mississippi (*Vaughn* v. *Swayzie*, 56 Miss. 704 [1879])). Although most improved real property can be identified in this manner, a street address is not a legal description and its use may result in confusion. To demonstrate this point, consider the following example.

Mr. Smith buys a home located at 111 Blue Street, on a single lot in Dayton, Ohio. He later builds an in-ground swimming pool, meeting local set-back requirements by purchasing the back ten feet of the lot directly behind his. (Most zoning ordinances contain set-back requirements that regulate, among other things, how close improvements may be located to a property boundary. Still later, he sells his property to Mr. Jones. The description Mr. Smith used to transfer the property to Mr. Jones is 111 Blue Street, Dayton, Ohio. What did Mr. Jones buy, the original lot, or the original lot plus the back ten feet of the adjoining lot? The use of a street address does not allow us to determine conclusively the answer to this question.

Other types of informal descriptions can result in similar problems. For example, Mr. Summer conveys to Mrs. Winter a property described as "out of the 80 acres that I own by deed from Mr. Spring, the house and five acres." What has been conveyed, the house and surrounding five acres, the house and an undivided 5/80 in the entire 80 acres, or the house and five acres located elsewhere on the 80 acres?

Incomplete descriptions may compound the problems that arise from the use of informal property descriptions. For example, consider a contract for the sale of land that uses only "222 Green Street" as the property description. The seller's intent to deliver this particular property is not conclusive evidence of which property is to be sold. Is it 222 Green Street in Green Bay, Wisconsin, or 222 Green Street in Amarillo, Texas? (People sometimes enter into contracts to deliver property they do not currently own, but to which they expect to acquire title in time to deliver as agreed.) To avoid these types of problems a legal description that enables a competent surveyor to identify the property boundary is required.

LEGAL PROPERTY DESCRIPTIONS

Several systems that provide a legal description are currently used to locate and identify land, including: the metes and bounds system; the United States government rectangular survey system; descriptions based on a recorded plat; and state plane coordinates. The particular system used to describe a tract of real estate is generally determined by the method used when the land was initially surveyed. One system is not inherently better than another. If the owner of a tract wishes to sell the entire tract, the owner is most likely to use the description under which title was acquired. If, however, the owner wishes to dispose of a portion of the tract, or to subdivide the tract, a new description must be created. The important thing to remember is that for a description to have legal effect it should allow a trained surveyor to locate precisely the boundaries of the subject property.

UNITED STATES RECTANGULAR GOVERNMENT SURVEY SYSTEM

One system used to describe real property is the United States **rectangular government survey system,** sometimes referred to as the government survey system. This system is employed in most states to describe rural and suburban land; the major exceptions to its use are the states that comprised the original thirteen colonies, Hawaii, and Texas. The federal government at one time owned much of the land in the United States. Congress recognized the importance of describing the public land in order to facilitate its management or transfer to private ownership. Therefore, starting with the Ordinance of 1785, Congress enacted several pieces of legislation that directed the surveying of public lands.

The Bureau of Land Management in the United States Department of the Interior was given the responsibility of surveying the public domain. Surveyors were instructed to locate and mark by monuments a series of thirty-five points. To date, 1.5 billion acres have been surveyed from the Florida Keys to Point Barrow, Alaska, and from East Liverpool, Ohio, to San Diego with 2.6 million section corners marked. For example, latitude 38 degrees, 28 minutes 27 seconds (38° 28' 27") North, longitude 89° 08' 54" West for central Illinois. From each such point the line of longitude was extended conceptually as a **principal meridian.** Each principal meridian was numbered or named for subsequent reference. For example, the Choctaw or Indian meridian for Oklahoma, and the Sixth meridian for Colorado. Each line of latitude was similarly extended from the point as a base line. Exhibit 8.1 indicates the base lines and principal meridians.

EXHIBIT	8.1	PRINCIPLE MERIDIANS AND BASE LINES

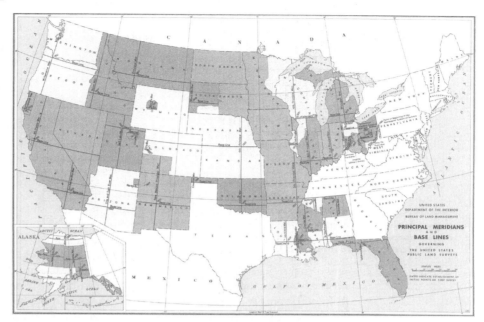

SOURCE: Bureau of Land Management, U.S. Department of Interior.

Townships and Sections

Using the base lines and meridians, surveyors were to map a grid of **townships,** each six miles square, and within each township, thirty-six **sections,** each one mile square and containing 640 acres. There is a standard numbering system for sections within a township that is illustrated in Exhibit 8.2. Section one is located in the northeast corner of a township, with subsequent sections numbered consecutively in a pattern that winds its way first from east to west, then west to east, and so on until ending in the southeast corner of a township with section thirty-six.

Surveyors marked townships, sections, and, sometimes, even quarter-section corners, with stakes, plates set into rocks, or cement markers. When the survey was complete, the surveying markers could be used for subsequent transfers of the surveyed land. Usually, one can refer to a particular section by using the rectangular description, know that the land is monumented to facilitate its location, know that it is squarely oriented north and south and that each section consists of 640 acres. Such certainty is not, however, always possible.

The townships were intended to consist of grids containing thirty-six square miles. However, due to the curvature of the earth and the convergence of longitudes toward the North Pole, a township can be squarely oriented north and south, or it can be six miles square, but it cannot be both. Deviations from the ideal occurred for a number of reasons and if you examine an actual survey map, you are likely to discover that townships and sections are not as neatly set out as the examples in this chapter. In addition to the curvature problem discussed in the body of the text, adjustments had to be made for surveying inaccuracies. There were several possible causes for inaccuracies including the fact that surveys were often made years apart and had to fit into monuments placed by previous surveys; terrain difficulties; variations in measurement instruments; the shifting or disappearance of monuments; and surveys conducted in a hasty manner due to the close proximity of hostile Indians.

EXHIBIT	8.2	SECTION NUMBERING WITHIN A TOWNSHIP

6	5	4	3	2	1
7	8	9	10	11	12
18	17	16	15	14	13
19	20	21	22	23	24
30	29	28	27	26	25
31	32	33	34	35	36

If one were to use the length of the northern boundary of one township as the length of the southern boundary for the next township, those townships at northern latitudes would contain considerably less than thirty-six square miles. The Bureau of Land Management addresses the problem of longitudinal convergence in two ways. One way is through the use of correction lines and guide meridians. **Correction lines** (or *standard parallels)* and guide meridians are generally used every fourth township line to adjust for convergence by expanding the length of the southern boundary of a township to six miles as illustrated in Exhibit 8.3. Each twenty-four by twenty-four mile area created by the correction lines and guide meridians is called a **check** and each check contains sixteen townships. However, correction lines and guide meridians do not completely solve the problem of longitudinal convergence.

A second way to correct for longitudinal convergence is through the use of government lots. A **government lot** is a section that contains less than 640 acres. When surveyors were unable to create a proper six-mile square township, they were instructed to normalize as many sections as possible by working from south to north and east to west to make each section contain 640 acres. Therefore, adjustments may have been made to sections 1 through 7 as well as sections 18, 19, 30 and 31. These adjustments are usually contained in the outside half of the involved sections.

Exhibit 8.4 shows how a particular principal meridian and a base line are used to identify a township. In this exhibit we ignore guide meridians and correction lines to simplify the presentation. The boundaries lying on the north and south sides of each township are called **township lines,** and are numbered consecutively from the base line. A row of townships lying in an east-west plane is sometimes called a **tier.** For example, tier four is located between township line number four and township line number three. If you stand on a township line facing the base line, the township immediately in front of you has the same number as the township line on which you are standing. Abbreviations are commonly used in government survey descriptions to shorten what can become quite lengthy descriptions. For example, the letters S or N following a township number in Exhibit 8.4 indicate whether the township is south or north of the base line.

The east and west boundaries of each township are called **range lines.** Range lines are numbered consecutively from the principal meridian. The area comprising range five is located between range line five and range line four. Again, if you stand on a range line facing the principal meridian, the range immediately in front of you would have the same number as the range line on which you are standing. The letters W and E that follow the range line indicate whether the range lies west or east of the principal meridian. Township and range lines are used in combination to determine the general location of a particular tract of land. In Exhibit 8.4, three townships are specifically identified. For example, the township in the upper-left corner of the figure is identified as T6N R6W (township 6 north, range 6 west). This means that the subject township is the sixth township north of the base line and is in the sixth range west of the principal meridian.

| EXHIBIT | 8.3 | CORRECTION LINES AND GUIDE MERIDIANS |

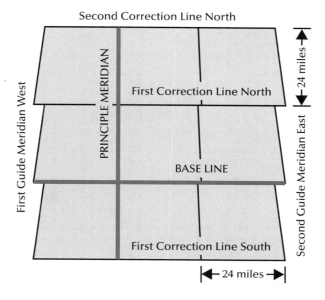

| EXHIBIT | 8.4 | TOWNSHIPS AND RANGES |

Can you formulate the designations for the townships marked A, B, C, and D?

A section may be divided into any number of parts, and one can use the government survey system to describe fractional parts of the section. If the fractional part of a section is irregular, however, and has boundaries that do not run north-south and east-west, a metes and bounds description (explained later in this chapter) is most likely to be used.

Exhibit 8.5, which represents section 10 (located south of the base line and west of the first principal meridian) illustrates how regular fractional parts of a section are described using the government survey system. The legal description of the quarter-section located in the northeast quadrant of the section in Exhibit 8.5 would be:

The Northeast Quarter (NE1/4) of Section 10, Township Two South, Range Four West of the First Principal Meridian, containing 160 acres.

Other regularly shaped tracts are also identified in Exhibit 8.5. In the upper left hand quarter of the figure is a parcel labeled: The Northeast quarter (NE1/4) of the Northwest quarter (NW1/4). Because the top of the section represents north, this parcel can easily be located by first finding the northwest quarter of the section and then following the remainder of the legal description.

The previous example highlights the procedure that should be followed in locating properties described by the government survey method. One should start at the end of the description and work backward through it. This procedure is especially helpful in locating properties with longer and more complicated descriptions. For example, to locate the tract of land described as the NE1/4 SW1/4 SW1/4 of the section, we start by locating the southwest quarter of the entire section, then find the southwest quarter of that quarter, and finally the northeast quarter of the quarter-quarter section.

The use of the rectangular survey system, or any other system providing a legal description, does not eliminate the need for care in formulating the description. Errors or misunderstandings similar to those arising from informal descriptions may also result from poorly worded descriptions that are based on a legal description. For example, Mr. White owns a quarter-quarter section of land. The legal description of the land is:

EXHIBIT | **8.5** | **RECTANGULAR SURVEY DESCRIPTIONS WITHIN A SECTION**

Can you give the legal description for the parcels labeled A, B, C, and D?

The Northeast quarter of the Northeast quarter of Section 3, Township 2
North, Range 3 West of the Second Principal Meridian, containing 40 acres.

Mr. White decides to sell ten acres to a neighbor and uses the following language: "The Northwest quarter of my land." What did Mr. White convey, a square in the corner of the tract, a tract marked off by a diagonal line between the west and north boundaries, or something else? Both Mr. White and the buyer probably intended to transfer a square tract, but the description used does not make that clear. To eliminate this ambiguity, the legal description of the entire tract should be modified to indicate exactly the portion being sold. For example:

The Northwest quarter of the Northeast quarter of the Northeast quarter of
Section 3, Township 2 North, Range 3 West of the Second Principal Meridian,
containing 10 acres.

DECISION POINT

Everything else constant, would you rather own the E 1/2 S 1/4, or the S 1/2 W 1/2 SE 1/4 of a section? Why?

METES AND BOUNDS DESCRIPTIONS

Another system that provides a legal description of real property is the **metes and bounds** system. In this system metes stands for distances and bounds represents boundaries. This system was used for surveying much of the land in the original thirteen colonies and is also used to describe irregular parcels of land originally described by the rectangular survey system.

A metes and bounds description starts with a point located somewhere on the perimeter of the tract. The beginning point is marked by a monument, either natural, such as a tree or rock, or artificial, such as a metal rod or stake. A good description will also reference the beginning point to two other easily located points using distances and directions. This provides a means of triangulation so that the beginning point can be relocated if the marker on the perimeter of the property is lost or destroyed.

The metes and bounds system is based on the fact that a complete circle contains 360 degrees. As illustrated in Exhibit 8.6, each degree contains 60 minutes and each minute contains 60 seconds. The precise direction, or course, of a property boundary line is determined by specifying the exact degrees, minutes and seconds that the line varies from the North, East, South, or West. In addition, the description specifies the exact distance for which the boundary line continues before it changes course. Once the line changes course, the exact direction and distance to the next change in course is specified. In a similar fashion the metes and bounds description continues to describe exactly how to trace the perimeter of the tract until it returns to the beginning point.

In older metes and bounds descriptions it is not uncommon to identify several points on the property's boundary by referencing such points to some permanent monument such as a stream, a large rock or a tree. Again, a good description will reference the exact location of these monuments to other easily located monuments because over time these monuments may be moved, destroyed, or grow.

Metes and bounds descriptions can be imposing. The description in Exhibit 8.7 is quite lengthy, but it is nothing more than a sequence of calls. A **call** is an operational instruction to the reader that explains how to trace the lines that bound the tract. When analyzed by each call, the description becomes less complex. The description in Exhibit 8.7 has nine calls. In this example, the first call is the anchor of the description.

| EXHIBIT | 8.6 | COURSE MEASUREMENTS FOR METES AND BOUNDS DESCRIPTIONS |

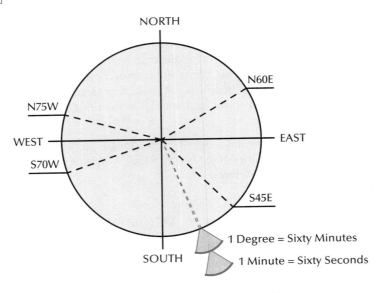

While directions similar to those shown in this exhibit are common, historic and current surveys also use directions measured from true north clockwise through 359°59′59″. Usage depends on local surveyors' conventions.

> Situate in Section 26, Township 3 North, Range 6 East, Butler Township, Montgomery County, Ohio and being a tract of land more particularly described as follows,

The **anchor** allows us to determine the general location of the property. Note that this anchor is expressed in terms of the government rectangular survey system.

> The second call,

> Beginning at an iron pin at the intersection of the north line of said Section 26 and the west line of the Baltimore and Ohio right-of-way, said point also being 100.00 feet west of the center line of the northbound tract of said railroad,

identifies the beginning point. An artificial monument, an iron pin, is specified as the point of beginning. The directions are given so that the beginning point can be relocated if the pin is lost.

> The third through eighth calls:

> thence from said Point of beginning South 3 degrees 21′ 2″ West with the West line of said railroad right-of-way a distance of 107.79 feet to an iron pin...

instruct us how to trace the property boundary. The third call Contains an adjoiner (property owned by the Miami Conservancy). An **adjoiner** is property owned by someone other than the owner of the subject parcel. Because a course and distance are given in this call, the monument and adjoiner are not needed to find the terminus of the first line. The record details about the Miami Conservancy property are not required in the description, but speed the search if one wishes to locate the document.

EXHIBIT	8.7	**EXAMPLE METES AND BOUNDS DESCRIPTION**

Situate in Section 26, Township 3 North, Range 6 East, Butler Township, Montgomery County, Ohio and being a tract of land more particularly described as follows: Beginning at an iron pin at the intersection of the north line of said Section 26 and the west line of the Baltimore and Ohio right-of-way, said point also being 100.00 feet west of the center line of the northbound tract of said railroad; thence from said point of beginning South 3 degrees 21' 20" West with the west line of said railroad right-of-way a distance of 107.79 feet to an iron pin at the northeast corner of a triangular shaped tract of land conveyed to the Miami Conservancy District by deed recorded in book 408, Page 127 of the Deed Records of Montgomery County, Ohio; thence South 76 degrees 22' 20" West with the north line of said Miami Conservancy tract and its westward extension a distance of 111.64 feet to an iron pin; thence South 26 degrees 34' 55" East a distance of 91.48 feet to a concrete monument, thence South 81 degrees 33' 30" West a distance of 644.33 feet to a concrete monument at the easterly angle point of the 0.14 acre tract of land conveyed to the Board of Montgomery Commissioners by deed recorded in Microfiche 71-94-D07 of the Deed Records of Montgomery County, Ohio; thence North 13 degrees 55' 10" East with a new division line a distance of 300.16 feet to an iron pin in the north line of said Section 26; thence North 88 degrees 18' 00" East of said Section line a distance of 639.29 feet passing a concrete monument at 460.06 feet to the place of beginning, containing 3.581 acres, more or less, subject, however, to all legal highways and easements of record.

The ninth, and last, call,

containing 3.581 acres, more or less, subject, however, to all legal highways and easements of record.

is a call for quantity; it indicates the size of the area enclosed by the boundary lines of the description.

Land Measurements

Sometimes land descriptions include forms of measurement that are not commonly used. For example, some uncommon measures result from use of the surveying chain, a device that was designed long ago to make surveys made over rough terrain more precise. The surveyor's chain, used in the United States Public Land Surveys, is a series of 100 links each of which is 7.92 inches long. This should not be confused with an engineer's chain that is also a series of 100 links, each of which is one foot long.

The surveying chain is still used today under special circumstances. The chain is comprised of one hundred links and totals sixty-six feet in length. One will occasionally see a property description that calls for distances in units of chains and links or other unusual units. A table of cross-references for various measurements used in land descriptions is provided in Exhibit 8.8.

PLAT DESCRIPTIONS

Individual parcels of land, or lots, in urban areas, suburban and rural residential subdivisions are usually described using a plat description, sometimes called lot and block description, lot-block-tract, recorded survey, or recorded map system. A **plat map** is a survey map on file at the County Recorder's office, which shows the boundaries and location of individual properties within a development or subdivision.

When a developer creates a subdivision, the land is surveyed and, after receiving the approval of local officials, the plat is filed with the office of public records in the county in which the property is located. In addition to showing the precise location, size and shape of each lot, plat maps show the name of the subdivision and provide some type of surveying anchor. Plat maps frequently indicate the exact sizes, locations and names of public streets, and the locations and sizes of utility easements. An example of a plat map is shown in Exhibit 8.9. Another document recorded with the map lists restrictions regarding the way in which the land may be used. Examples of such restrictions include the type and size of structures that may be erected on the lot, and set-back requirements.

Once the plat is recorded in the public records office, each property in the subdivision is identified in two ways. First, to precisely locate each lot, the surveys utilize either a metes and bounds description and/or a rectangular survey description. Second, either a letter or a number identifies each block within the subdivision, and a number identifies every lot in the subdivision. The following is an example of a plat description.

Lot 16, Block 1, in Linden Terrace, being a subdivision of a part of the Southeast 1/4 of Section 3, Township 7 North, Range 21 East, in the City of Dayton.

The first portion of the above property description gives the lot and block number as well as the subdivision name, Linden Terrace. The terms that follow the plat description are an anchor for the plat description and reveal that before the plat was developed the property was described by the government survey method.

The example involves only a single lot. In some cases, a transaction may involve all of one lot and parts of others. The following is an example of such a legal description.

Lot 16, Block 1, and the south ten feet of Lot 15, Block 1, Linden Terrace being a subdivision of a part of the Southeast 1/4 of Section 3, Township 7 North, Range 21 East, in the City of Dayton.

EXHIBIT	8.8	MEASUREMENT CROSS REFERENCES

Linear Measures

	Links	Feet	Yards	Rods	Chains	Miles
1 Link	1	66/100	22/100	4/100	1/100	1/8,000
1 Foot	1.2*	1	1/3	1/16.5	1/66	1/5,280
1 Yard	3.6*	3	1	1/5.5	1/22	1/1,760
1 Rod	25	16.5	5.5	1	¼	1/320
1 Chain	100	66	22	4	1	1/80
1 Mile	8,000	5,280	1,760	320	80	1

*approximate: 1 link = 7.92 inches.

Square Measures

	Square feet	Square yards	Square rods	Square chains	Square acres	Square miles
1 Sq. Foot	1	1/9	1/272.25	1/4,356	1/43,560	1/27,878,400
1 Sq. Yard	9	1	1/30.25	1/484	1/4840	1/3,097,600
1 Sq. Rod	272.25	30.25	1	1/16	1/160	1/102,400
1 Sq. Chain	4,356	484	16	1	1/10	1/6,400
1 Acre*	43,560	4,840	160	10	1	1/640
1 Sq. Mile (1 Section)	27,878,400	3,097,600	102,400	6,400	640	1

*Hectare = 2.471 acres = 100 ares, are = 100 square meters.

EXHIBIT | **8.9** | **PLAT MAP**

WALNUT GROVE
SECTION SEVEN
LOCATED IN SECTION 5, TOWN 2, RANGE 6 MRS
CITY OF BEAVERCREEK, GREENE CO., OHIO

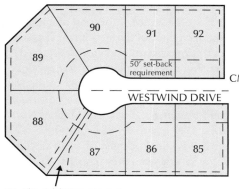

10' utility and drainage easement

DESCRIPTION

Situate in Section 5. Town 2. Range 6 MRS. City of Beavercreek. Greene County, Ohio and being a subdivision of 5.407 Acres; Being 5.407 Acres of a 9.791 Acre Tract (Tract II) as conveyed to John E. Rowland and Robert Arnold in Volume 387, Page 34 of the Official Records of Greene County, Ohio; Being 0.639 Acres in public street.

• C.M.—Denotes Concrete Monument
Basis of Bearings—Walnut Grove Section One

CERTIFICATION

I certified that this is a true and complete survey made under my direction. Iron pin monuments and concrete monuments (as shown) will be set at all lot corners upon completion of construction.

James Sorensen
Registered Surveyor
Ohio #8467

AUTHOR'S NOTE: Lot measurements have been eliminated from the drawing for the sake of clarity.

For discussion purposes, the street address of Lot 16, Block 1, Linden Terrace is 111 Blue Street, and Lot 15 adjoins the rear of Lot 16. Recall from the discussion of informal property descriptions that part of the lot adjoining the rear of 111 Blue Street had been acquired to meet set-back requirements for a pool installation, and the property was transferred to another using only the street address as the property description. Use of the street address did not indicate exactly what property was being transferred. Use of the above plat description solves this problem.

The advantage of the plat description system is that it allows one to conveniently refer to a particular lot by using its lot and block number, rather than the more lengthy description used by the surveyor. Yet, if questions arise as to exact boundary locations, the detailed survey instructions are available for public inspection. The county recorder assigns each plat map a book and page number and places it in the survey books, or map books, along with plats of other subdivisions in the county. In fact, sometimes the book and page reference is included in the legal description as in the following example.

Situate in the City of Kettering, County of Montgomery, State of Ohio, and being lot numbered One Hundred Eight (108) Wagner Hills Section Three, as recorded in Plat Book "105", Page 4 of the Plat Records of Montgomery County, Ohio.

HI-TECH SURVEY SYSTEMS

Two systems are currently available to provide a way to accurately identify tracts of land even if monuments, landmarks or other markers are obliterated. One is a land-based system, known as the state plane coordinate system (SPC). The other is a space-based system, known as the global positioning system (GPS).

Under the SPC, each state is flattened mathematically into a level plane. The United States Coast and Geodetic Survey has a series of stations in the United States. Any spot in the country can be described by reference to the conceptual grid of lines running east and west, north and south, from the stations. Location of any spot thus described can be quickly located by triangulation from three of the stations. This system is currently used to augment the other property description systems previously described. It is not likely that you will see a property description using this system, but its existence may prove invaluable if a natural disaster were to destroy many of the markers used in the traditional methods of property description. SPC descriptions give a reference to a particular survey on which the coordinates are based and call for points, such as: Coordinates North 1, 470, 588; East 416 239.

GPS, initiated in the 1980s, consists of twenty-four military satellites orbiting 12,500 miles above the Earth. The original purpose of these satellites was for tracking troops and weapons targeting, but in recent years they have also been used to plot accurate real property boundary lines. These satellites send radio signals that enable trained personnel to precisely locate any point on the Earth. The system has come in handy in many situations including western Maryland where the boundary descriptions in many deeds referenced "a chestnut tree." But, a chestnut tree blight in 1931 resulted in the removal of many of the trees. However, sometimes advances in technology has unexpected consequences. For example, boundary disputes, not a common event in the United States since the settlement of our country, are increasing in frequency due to improved surveying methods. The following Doing Business: Technology provides a case in point.

DECISION POINT

A volcanic eruption eliminates all real property boundary markers within fifty miles of a once dormant volcano. How would you go about locating the boundary for the properties in the affected area?

VERTICAL LAND DESCRIPTIONS

The description methods that have been discussed in this chapter are all used to describe property boundaries on the surface of the land. Real property owners may also have rights that extend above and below the surface of the land. Vertical measurements are necessary to describe these areas.

Every vertical land description refers to a datum. A **datum** is any line, point, or surface from which a distance, vertical depth, or height is measured. The United States Geological Survey (USGS) uses mean sea level at New York harbor for their datum, but a number of cities have established their own datum for use in local surveys. The USGS surveyors set out markers known as **benchmarks** at calculated intervals. The elevation of each benchmark relative to the datum is recorded, thus eliminating the need for a surveyor to travel to the original datum to determine the elevation for a particular tract. These benchmarks are often used as reference points in metes and bounds descriptions.

Vertical measurements are especially important for condominiums, an increasingly popular form of real property ownership, with the unique feature that the only property owned exclusively by any individual condominium owner is the airspace over a given tract

Consider the dilemma of eight residents of Hopkinton, Rhode Island who were surprised to learn recently that part of their property was actually in a different state! This fact came to light when North Stovington, Connecticut utilized the Global Positioning System (GPS) to determine that two boundary markers, located six miles apart, from an 1840 survey were inaccurate. Officials for North Stovington plan to add the 25 acres of affected property to its property tax roles, and officials for Hopkington plan to fight the move in court. They argue that the incorrect boundary line has been used for so long that it should constitute the actual border. This legal battle is not the first boundary dispute to result from a GPS survey; lawsuits in six other states have been filed due to similar circumstances.

Go to www.blm.gov/nhp/, click on FAQ, then click on one or more of the results to learn more about issues of importance to the Bureau of Land Management.

---

of land. This area is referred to as an **air lot.** To describe an air lot, both the tract of land beneath the air lot and the elevation of the air lot above the tract must be identified. The land beneath the air lot is usually described with a map similar to a plat map. A description of the air lots for three dwellings on building lot #5835 of University Woods Condominium appears in the upper left-hand corner of Exhibit 8.10. The elevations in this example refer to the number of feet above the USGS datum. In this example all three units have three floors. Hypothetically, each unit could be located on a single floor. If this were the case, the owner of the condominium on the upper level would own an air lot between 927.68 and 935.16 feet above sea level.

Another case in which vertical measurements are important is in the leasing or selling of subsurface mineral rights. In such cases, the datum is normally the surface of the property and extraction is allowed only up to or below a certain depth.

Vertical land measurements are also important in land development. A topographic map, or **contour map,** shows the elevation of a parcel in detail using contour lines. A contour line is a line connecting all points on the property that have the same elevation. A sample topographic map is shown in Exhibit 8.11. A developer can use a contour map to determine if and where soil must be moved to provide an acceptable surface for the construction of improvements.

BOUNDARY LOCATION ALONG WATER COURSES

When land is adjoined by water, confusion may result regarding the exact location of the property boundary. Complicating the problem is the possibility that the body of water may change its shape or course. In this section we explain concepts that govern real property boundaries when land borders water.

Natural forces may result in the acquisition, or loss, of title to real property. For example, if a stream or river is used as a boundary for two tracts of land, and the course of the water changes gradually, the property boundaries change with the course of the water. In this case, one owner loses property through erosion and the other gains property through accretion. **Accretion** is defined as the gradual addition to land through the operation of natural causes; the washing up of sand and soil to form firm ground. The terms alluvion and accretion are frequently used as synonyms. However, alluvion refers to the deposit itself and accretion denotes the act. Not all changes in a river or stream result in a boundary change. If a sudden change occurs in the course of a river, the property boundaries remain as were. Accretion also may occur on property located at the mouth of a river. Sediments may accumulate at such locations over time, forming firm ground and expand-

EXHIBIT 8.10 **DECLARATION OF CONDOMINIUM SHOWING AIR LOT**

LOT 5835

	Bsmt. FL. Elev.	Bsmt. Ceiling Elev.
Unit 2123	909.38	917.38
Unit 2125	909.38	917.38
Unit 2127	909.38	917.38
	First FL. Elev.	First FL. Ceiling Elev.
Unit 2123	918.36	925.98
Unit 2125	918.36	925.98
Unit 2127	918.36	925.98
	First FL. Elev.	First FL. Ceiling Elev.
Unit 2123	927.68	935.16
Unit 2125	927.68	935.16
Unit 2127	927.68	935.16

Declaration of Condominium Ownership
for the

**UNIVERSITY WOODS
CONDOMINIUM
PHASE IV**

SECOND FLOOR LEVEL

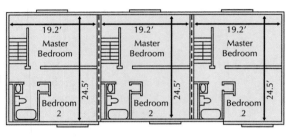

FIRST FLOOR LEVEL

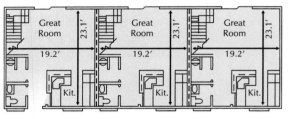

BASEMENT FLOOR LEVEL

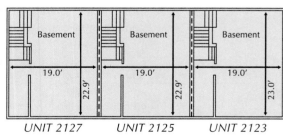

UNIT 2127   UNIT 2125   UNIT 2123

These exhibits to the University Woods Condominium Phase filing, accurately show the units as constructed and graphically show the particulars of the condominium units as intended by the exhibits.

By: _Landau_
Josh Landau
Registered Surveyor
No. 8767

By: _Landau_
Josh Landau
Registered Surveyor
No. 51939

ing the property. Another way real property may be expanded by natural causes is by **dereliction,** or reliction, which occurs when a body of water shrinks below its usual high water mark. A good example of man hastening reliction is the system of dikes used to expand the landmass of Holland.

Ownership of the land under the water depends upon the water body type. In the case of a navigable river or lake, the property owner's title runs only to the edge of the water; the government owns the land under the water. For non-navigable bodies of water, the owner of adjoining property has title to the land under the water to the middle of the water. For property bordering a large, non-flowing body of water, ownership of the land extends only to the average high-water mark of the body of water. All land under the water on the waterside of this watermark belongs to the government.

DECISION POINT

After purchasing an acreage, you plan to subdivide it into two building lots. You plan to build your home on one and sell the other. There is a non-navigable stream running through the middle of the property that could be used as a boundary line for the newly created lots. Would you use the stream as a boundary line or define the boundary in some other way? Why?

SUMMARY

For property owners to enforce the rights associated with real property ownership, they must be able to determine the boundaries of their property. This is best accomplished with the use of a legal description. A legal description is one that allows a trained surveyor to ascertain the exact location of property boundaries. Systems that provide a legal descrip-

| EXHIBIT | 8.11 | **CONTOUR MAP** |

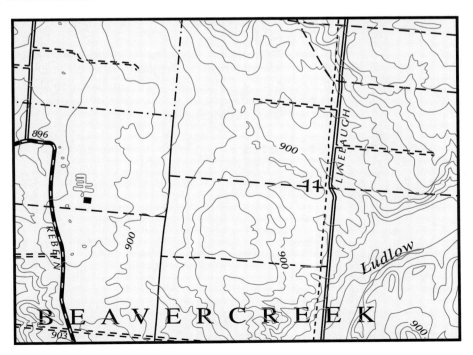

tion include the government rectangular survey, metes and bounds, plat descriptions, and state plane coordinate system. When conveying title to another party, a property owner will generally use the description under which title was acquired. Informal references, such as a street address, are not legal descriptions, and their use in the transfer of property ownership can result in confusion and costly legal disputes.

Two specialized topics were also examined: vertical property descriptions, and boundary lines along bodies of water. Vertical property descriptions are important because real property ownership rights are frequently three-dimensional. In many cases, it is particularly important to be able to define the area above and below the property surface. When water borders a property, the exact location of the property line depends on what type of water body borders the property.

KEY TERMS

accretion	correction line	rectangular government
adjoiner	datum	survey system
air lot	dereliction (or reliction)	section
anchor	government lot	state plane coordinate
base line	metes and bounds	system
benchmark	plat map	tier
call	principal meridian	township
check	range lines	township lines
contour map		

REVIEW QUESTIONS

1. Why are informal property descriptions almost always unacceptable for transferring or leasing real property?

2. Describe the rectangular government survey system that is used to provide a legal real property description. How is a quarter-quarter section of land described under this system?

3. Describe the metes and bounds system that is used to provide a legal real property description. How is a parcel of land described under this system?

4. Describe the plat description system that is used to provide a legal real property description. How is a parcel of land described under this system?

5. When are vertical land descriptions used?

6. What townships are located to the west, south, north, and east of Township 1 North, Range 1 West?

7. In a metes and bounds description, would it be better for a call to provide a course and distance to indicate the terminus of a line or simply specify: thence to the concrete marker? Why?

8. In a metes and bounds description, if instead of a distance, the call said: "to the property owned by Mr. Smith," (the next-door neighbor) how would you verify where Mr. Smith's property ends?

9. How many checks, townships, and sections are included in Exhibit 8.3?

10. A stream that is used as a boundary between two properties changes course. Does the boundary line change?

11. For a typical township, what sections are located to the west, south, north, and east of section 12?

12. Consider the following real property description: The Northwest quarter of the Northwest quarter of Section 6, Township 6 North, Range 3 West of the Second Principal Meridian, containing 40 acres. Do you see anything in the description that makes you question its accuracy? (Hint: Note the position of section 6 within any township, recall the discussion about adjustments to account for the curvature of the earth, and look again at the acreage claimed in the description).

13. What is your answer to the questions in the three "Decision Point" sections in this chapter?

PROBLEMS

1. Use a government survey description to identify the parcels labeled A, B, C, and D in Exhibit 8.5. How many acres are in each of these parcels?

2. Using Exhibit 8.5, describe the following parcels:
   a. The parcel to the northwest of parcel B;
   b. The parcel to the north of C; and
   c. The parcel to the east of parcel D.
   How many acres are in each of these parcels?

3. Formulate the designations for the townships marked A, B, C, and D shown in Exhibit 8.4.

4. Using Exhibit 8.4, formulate the designations for the following townships:
   a. The township to the north of the township marked A;
   b. The township to the east of the township marked B;
   c. The township to the northeast of the township marked C; and
   d. The township to the west of the township marked D.

REAL ESTATE ON THE WEB

Use your favorite search engine to:

1. Determine which of the formal property description methods are used in your area.

2. Determine the legal property description for your home or some other selected property.

3. Locate mortgage loan service providers that will provide real property legal descriptions.

Refer to the companion Web site at www.wiley.com/college/larsen for a variety of online activities including additional chapter content, review materials, assignments, and related links.

ADDITIONAL READINGS

Debole, P. L. "Verifying Property Descriptions in Deeds." *Practical Real Estate Lawyer* (May 1994): 77.

Heller, M. A. "The Boundaries of Private Property." 108 *Yale Law Journal* 1163 (April 1999).

Miller, B. S. "Working with Legal Descriptions." *Practical Real Estate Lawyer* (March 1997): 43–51.

Mooney, S. and L. M. Eisgruber. "The Influence of Riparian Protection Measures on Residential Property Values: The Case of the Oregon Plan for Salmon and Watersheds." *The Journal of Real Estate Finance and Economics* (March 2001): 273–286.

Sostek, Anya. "Remapping in the Wake of Disaster." *Governing* (December 2000): 54.

Real Estate Transactions

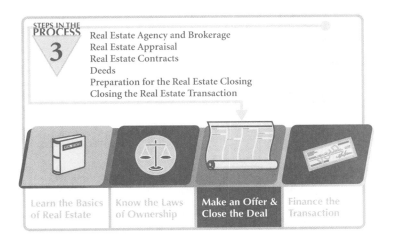

STEPS IN THE PROCESS
3

Real Estate Agency and Brokerage
Real Estate Appraisal
Real Estate Contracts
Deeds
Preparation for the Real Estate Closing
Closing the Real Estate Transaction

Learn the Basics of Real Estate

Know the Laws of Ownership

Make an Offer & Close the Deal

Finance the Transaction

Acquiring ownership of real property can be a time-consuming and complicated process involving a number of parties. In addition to the seller and buyer, transactions typically involve include brokers, appraisers, attorneys, title insurers, settlement agents, and lenders. Part III focuses on the relationship between buyers and sellers, and also examines the role of brokers, appraisers, title insurers, and settlement agents in real estate transactions.

Most people are unfamiliar with the details needed to complete a transaction. Therefore, they can benefit from the services provided by real estate specialists. In Chapter 9, the role played by brokers is explained, and the contracts between brokers and clients are described. An independently determined estimate of the value of real property is a frequent concern for sellers, buyers, and lenders. Each may employ an appraiser to provide them with a value estimate. Real estate appraisal is the topic examined in Chapter 10. Because of the high value of real estate, it is important that transactions involving the transfer of ownership satisfy all legal requirements. A basic understanding of the material presented in Chapter 11, real estate contracts, is essential. Chapter 12 examines the transfer of real property ownership by deed (or according to the provisions of a will). You will note that the promises made by the seller depend on the type of deed used. But, because we are unsure whether sellers will be able to honor their promises, most people will take additional steps to assure the quality of the title being acquired. Methods by which this can be accomplished are reviewed in Chapter 13. Finally, the actual transfer of property ownership may take place with or without a meeting of the seller and buyer, as described in Chapter 14.

9

Real Estate Agency And Brokerage

Learning Objectives

After studying this chapter, you should be able to:

- Differentiate between a broker and dealer.
- Explain the requirements that generally have to be met in order for one to be licensed as a real estate broker.
- Describe the types of agency relationships commonly used in real estate brokerage.
- Understand the duties of the agent to the client and customer.
- List the characteristics of successful agents

PRACTITIONER PROFILE

Real estate agent Jim Droz was formerly the number one agent for Century 21 Real Estate Corporation. As the top producing agent for the CENTURY 21 System, Droz averaged approximately 300 transactions per year with just one full-time and one part-time assistant. He earned more than $1 million in commissions four years in a row with an average sales price of only $125,000. During his selling career, Droz averaged nearly 20 listing contracts per month and lost only four listing opportunities while doing more than 1,500 presentations. He once sold nine homes in a single day and 40 homes in a single month.

Today, Droz focuses his energies on training other agents to duplicate his success systems. He shares his unique insight in his learning workshops titled "Releasing the Winner Within." Workshop attendees get "down-to-earth" techniques they can use daily to live successful lives, and to have phenomenal real estate careers. Droz has an appreciation for the advances in technology and its impact on the brokerage business, saying, "I used to spend between $5,000 and $10,000 monthly to maintain recognition with my clientele. You can now make contact repetitively with thousands of potential buyers and sellers for just $39.95 each month."

Go to www.realtor.org, click on "REALTOR® Directories," then click on "Find a REAL-TOR®" and determine how many REALTORs® there are in the country (and your state) with your name.

INTRODUCTION

Real estate brokers have specialized training that enables them to play a vital role in real property transactions. Most people have infrequent contact with the real estate market and, therefore, they can benefit from using the services of a trained specialist. Even knowledgeable people employ brokers when buying or selling real property so they can focus on other obligations. Sellers frequently employ brokers because they value the increased market exposure that may be gained by employing a specialist and, as the chapter opener "Practitioner Profile" suggests, some agents have developed unique marketing concepts.

Several aspects of the real estate brokerage industry are examined in this chapter. With few exceptions (e.g., attorneys and court-appointed estate administrators), only a party who is licensed to act as a real estate broker may legally accept compensation for engaging in real estate brokerage activities. Therefore, the licensing and regulation of real estate brokers is examined. After obtaining a brokerage license, the licensee may serve as an agent in real estate transactions. Hence, this chapter also examines various aspects of the broker-client relationship. The chapter concludes with a review of some of the professional associations that brokers may join. As a starting point, we compare the functions of a broker and a dealer.

BROKER DISTINGUISHED FROM A DEALER

The role of an intermediary, one who facilitates a transaction, can be accomplished by a broker or a dealer; but there are important differences between the two. A broker brings together sellers and buyers of a particular asset, and assists in negotiating an agreement between the parties in exchange for compensation. Brokers maintain no inventory of the asset, and are usually compensated by a fee charged to one of the transacting parties. A dealer, on the other hand, maintains an inventory and stands ready to sell to those who wish to purchase, and buy from those who wish to sell. Dealer compensation is equal to the difference between the amount the dealer pays for an asset and the amount for which the dealer sells it.

Either the broker or the dealer system tends to dominate a particular market. For example, most people have dealt with a car dealer, or a securities broker. The broker system dominates the real estate market, although real estate brokers sometimes act as dealers. For example, some national real estate franchises, discussed in more detail later in this chapter, have guaranteed sale programs whereby the firm promises property owners that the firm will purchase the property if it remains unsold for a certain period of time. In addition, individual brokers sometimes act as dealers, purchasing property on their own behalf for investment purposes.

REAL ESTATE AGENTS

Brokerage is one of the most visible occupational specializations within the real estate industry. Many people are employed in the real estate brokerage industry and most people employ a real estate agent when selling their home. In 2000, more than 2 million people in the United States held a real estate brokerage license. Exhibit 9.1 shows the number of real estate licensees by state.

| EXHIBIT | 9.1 | REAL ESTATE LICENSEES BY STATE |

Active Real Estate Licensees 2002			
State	Brokers	Salespersons	Firms
Alabama	3,337	8,024	1,774
Alaska	465	1,037	523
Arizona	1,198	27,209	3,541
Arkansas	3,640	4,779	2,200
California	89,938	204,990	17,062
Colorado	28,013	307	9,136
Connecticut	6,341	12,245	NA
Delaware	665	2,415	NA
District of Columbia	2,010	3,467	654
Florida	49,009	108,383	14,438
Georgia	8,528	30,368	8,851
Hawaii	2,309	5,016	930
Idaho	945	3,362	418
Illinois	27,296	38,223	4,658
Indiana	8,982	12,840	1,380
Iowa	2,272	5,354	1,054
Kansas	4,285	8,001	2,600
Kentucky	4,893	8,321	3,358
Louisiana	2,966	8,955	1,097
Maine	2,161	1,400	1,204
Maryland	4,117	24,156	4,117
Massachusetts	24,458	25,100	1,423
Michigan	11,988	40,336	4,563
Minnesota	23,963*	23,963*	4,883
Mississippi	3,471	3,361	1,440
Missouri	10,781	21,245	2,623
Montana	2,238	1,846	730
Nebraska	2,636	3,387	1,456
Nevada	2,232	8,890	NA
New Hampshire	5,142	6,699	2,132
New Jersey	3,183	62,143	4,648
New Mexico	4,005	3,436	NA

EXHIBIT 9.1	REAL ESTATE LICENSEES BY STATE (CONTINUED)		
New York	47,403	55,032	1,266
North Carolina	29,829	14,693	5,404
North Dakota	596	817	186
Ohio	7,794	30,989	2,216
Oklahoma	6,475	7,114	3,595
Oregon	5,835	9,406	1,962
Pennsylvania	7,936	29,579	NA
Rhode Island	2,230	2,914	NA
South Carolina	6,072	11,133	5,937
South Dakota	1,086	943	333
Tennessee	6,601	16,857	3,892
Texas	37,793	49,767	4,451
Utah	2,986	7,696	1,897
Vermont	1,274	898	375
Virginia	9,518	34,773	5,392
Washington	7,540	18,716	3,389
West Virginia	856	2,532	856
Wisconsin	13,025	9,795	2,102
Wyoming	672	914	666

NA = not available
* includes both brokers and salespeople
SOURCE: ARELLO, various state real estate commissions and state association of REALTORS®

A real estate broker is defined as any licensed person or business entity that, in exchange for valuable consideration, negotiates the sale, purchase, lease, or exchange of real property for others. Members of the general public often use the term "broker" to describe any person licensed to perform such activities, but there are actually several classes of agents in the real estate brokerage industry. Brokers have the power to act on their own behalf and employ others in their business. Salespeople (sometimes called sales associates or associate licensees) must work under the supervision of a broker. Some states have a real estate license classification called, alternatively: associate broker, affiliate broker, broker-associate, or broker-salesperson. This classification is used to describe a person who is qualified as a broker but still works for, and is supervised by, another broker. Most states require that each branch office of a real estate brokerage be registered and have a manager who is responsible for the operations of the branch. In most cases, the manager must be a broker, but some states only require a salesperson. For the remainder of the chapter, we refer to both brokers and salespersons collectively as agents. A real estate agent may assist in the sale or lease of any type of real property. Because each property type requires some specialized knowledge, however, many agents develop a specialization within the real estate brokerage industry. Some agents deal only with residential properties; others specialize in industrial, commercial, or agricultural property. Many real estate companies do not limit their service to brokerage. Some provide one or more additional services, including: property management, rental listing services, escrow services, auctioneering, and counseling.

LICENSING REAL ESTATE AGENTS

Every state requires that real estate agents be licensed. Generally, in order to obtain a real estate salesperson's license, individuals must first evidence good character, complete any educational or experience requirements, and pass a test that demonstrates their knowledge of various areas of real estate. Some states also require that a candidate for the salesperson's examination be sponsored by a broker who, in effect, agrees to hire the candidate upon successful completion of the test. In addition, many states require that licensees complete continuing education requirements in order to retain their license. The educational and experience requirements are more rigorous for brokers than for salespeople.

Several states have recently increased the educational requirements to sit for license examinations, and others are contemplating such action. The increased requirements are generally initiated, or supported, by practitioners in the industry. Increased educational requirements may be viewed as an effort to increase the professionalism of the industry. Alternatively, they may be viewed as barriers to entry erected by those already in the business.

Real estate agent licensing examinations vary by state. Many states use examinations prepared by private testing organizations, others use examinations prepared by a university, or by the state's real estate commission. While the exact nature of the license examinations also varies, similarities exist. The examinations are generally comprised of multiple choice questions, and consist of two parts. One part of the examination contains questions that require general knowledge of real estate principles and practices and real estate law. The second part of the examination contains questions that focus on real estate laws applicable to the state in which the examination is being taken. Sample tests may usually be acquired by contacting the state real estate commission. Because the licensing of real estate agents is controlled at the state level, acquisition of a license in one state does not automatically allow a licensee to operate in other states. It is possible, however, for a licensee in one state to obtain a license in another state without taking another examination if both states involved have entered into a reciprocity agreement. There is a growing trend toward reciprocity among states, especially between neighboring states. Even in cases where there is reciprocity, the licensee must still apply for, and obtain, permission from the other state before conducting brokerage activities in that state.

THE AGENCY RELATIONSHIP

When a person enters into a contract with a broker (or salesperson), an agency relationship is created. There are two parties in every agency: the principal, and the agent. The agent is the party hired to represent the interest of another, the principal, in dealing with third parties. Real estate agents rarely, however, refer to the party they represent as their "principal." Instead, they refer to the principal as their client, and parties with whom the agent negotiates on behalf of the principal are referred to as customers or prospects.

Two types of agency are common in real estate, a general agency, and a special agency. In a **general agency,** the agent is authorized by the principal to transact all business at a certain place, or to transact all matters in connection with a particular kind of business. This is the type of agency created when the owner of rental property hires a property manager to operate the rental property. A **special agency** is created when an agent is authorized to facilitate a particular business transaction, or to perform a certain act. An example of a special agency is when a broker is hired to sell a particular property. If an agent acts beyond the authority granted, the principal may sue for any damages incurred, or the principal may subsequently agree to be bound by the agent's actions. The latter case is known as ratification.

SERVICES PROVIDED BY THE REAL ESTATE BROKER

The exact relationship of an agent to the seller and buyer depends upon who employs the agent. A real estate agent usually works for the property owner/seller. Working for the seller, the agent usually performs a variety of functions. Agents use their knowledge of current market conditions to assist the seller in setting the list price. Agents also advertise the property and show it to qualified prospects. The task of qualifying the buyer, determining whether the prospect can afford the property before arranging a showing, can save time and effort for all parties concerned. Agents also negotiate with prospective buyers on behalf of the seller, offer sellers advice regarding the reasonableness of an offer, and assist them in formulating a counter-offer. In addition, agents may facilitate transactions by assisting the buyer in locating financing, property insurance, and title insurance. To help ensure that the transaction proceeds smoothly, agents monitor all of the details that must be completed between the time a purchase offer is accepted and closing, and attend the closing.

An important part of the sales process is the establishment of the list price, or asking price, the price at which the property is advertised to the public. Some sellers object to their agent using the phrase "asking price" because it implies a degree of flexibility in negotiations that the seller may not wish to convey. Agents usually advise property owners about the price at which the property should be listed, and formulate an opinion by analyzing sale prices of recently sold comparable properties. Owners are sometimes disappointed in the price suggested and seek the opinion of other agents. If owners search long enough, they are likely to find an agent who is willing to list the property at the owners' desired price. In an attempt to secure listings some real estate agents may practice highballing, listing at a price higher than can reasonably be expected to be attained. Other agents may resent highballers, or refuse to cooperate with them. In some cases, real estate agents have actually turned down business rather than list properties too high. Rather than waste the brokerage firms' time trying to market an overpriced property, and perhaps create ill will on the part of sellers disappointed with the eventual selling price, agents decline many listings.

OTHER CONTRACTUAL RELATIONSHIPS BETWEEN BROKERS AND SELLERS/BUYERS

The legal relationship between brokers, sellers, and real estate brokers has evolved over the last twenty years, and this evolutionary process continues today. There is a growing trend for purchasers of real estate to have representation. A **buyer's broker** is hired and paid by the buyer, and acts as the buyer's agent. Even though brokers usually represent the seller, most will represent a buyer at some point in their career. Some agents specialize in representing buyers and refer prospective sellers to other agents

It may also be possible for an agent to represent both the buyer and seller in the same transaction. In this case, a **dual agency** exists, and ethical questions may arise. As the agent of the buyer, the broker's duty is to locate real property meeting the buyer's requirements at the lowest possible price. At the same time, the broker's duty to the seller is to sell the property at the highest possible price. It is questionable whether a real estate agent can simultaneously fulfill both of these duties, but dual agency does occur. To help reduce subsequent problems, real estate agents are prohibited from acting as the agent for both parties without obtaining the written permission of both parties. Because of the potential problems associated with dual agency, at the time of this writing, several states are in the process of prohibiting it.

A trend in real estate brokerage is towards reduced broker liability in the form of non-agency client representation. Recently some states have authorized transactional brokers, who represent neither the buyer nor the seller. The transactional broker's duty is to provide neutral third-party real estate services to buyers and sellers. In essence, transactional brokers act as facilitators, making sure that the transaction progresses smoothly. Transactional brokerage is not without controversy. Some critics claim that transactional brokerage is just a disguise for dual agency with reduced liability for the broker. Others wonder if it is possible for a transactional broker to remain neutral when, for example, a seller's agent working in the same office listed the property. Proponents of this system assert that by avoiding advocacy the transactional broker may sidestep positions that could cause impasses in negotiations. It can also be argued that this is the way the industry has always really worked; but now it has a name.

Decision Point

If you were selling real property, would you object if the agent you employed asked for dual agency authorization? Under what circumstances would you hire a broker to represent you as a buyer?

DUTIES OF AN AGENT TO THE PRINCIPAL

An agent owes several duties to the principal. These duties include loyalty, honesty, obedience to instructions, properly accounting for money and property, attention to the delegation of authority, and the duty to avoid negligence.

Loyalty

The agency relationship between an agent and client requires that the agent always act in the client's best interest. Even the suggestion of improper conduct may be costly for the agent. To illustrate, suppose an agent were to present, and the seller were to accept, a less than full list price purchase offer. The seller later learns that the purchaser is related to the agent. The seller may be able to recover any commission paid plus the difference between the purchase price and the list price because the agent violated the duty of loyalty by not disclosing the relationship with the purchaser to the seller. Were the agent to have disclosed his or her relationship with the purchaser at the time the offer was made, the seller would not have such recourse.

During the 1980s, it became apparent that most prospective homebuyers were under the mistaken belief that the real estate agent who was assisting them in their search for a home was representing them; when, in fact, the broker was the agent of the seller. To protect such naïve shoppers, most states have adopted agency disclosure laws that require agents to provide prospective buyers (and sellers) with written notice of the exact nature of their agency relationship. In many cases, the agent meets this disclosure requirement if this notice is provided to the buyer as late as the time an offer is made, and it appears that many agents postpone notification as long as possible. A copy of the agency disclosure form that real estate agents in Ohio are required to use is presented in Exhibit 9.2

Honesty

Closely related to the duty of loyalty is the duty of honesty that requires the agent to disclose to the principal any information that might influence the principal's pricing or selling decisions. For example, the agent has a responsibility to explain how factors, such as the location of new roads or proposed zoning changes, might influence the value of the property. Likewise, if the agent knows that the prospective purchaser is acting for another party, the agent must make that fact known to the principal. Large companies often hire "straw buyers" when accumulating land in an attempt to hold prices down.

Avoiding Negligence

Failure to disclose such information, even if the facts were unknown to the agent, or failure to properly handle other facets of the transaction may constitute a violation of the agent's

EXHIBIT   9.2   AGENCY DISCLOSURE FORM

Disclosure of Agency Relationship
(THIS FORM IS NOT A CONTRACT)

The real estate agent who is providing you with this form is required to do so by Ohio law. It does not, by itself, obligate you to work with this agent or his/her brokerage; nor will you be bound to pay any compensation to the agent or the agent's brokerage by merely signing this form.

Instead, the purpose of this form is to make sure you have the necessary information you need to know about the role of this agent if you choose to work together. By signing, you acknowledge that you have been provided this information and agree to it. If you do not, you can consult with an attorney for further advice.

As a potential seller/landlord or buyer/tenant of real estate I understand and agree that

_____ and _____ will:
Agent(s)   Brokerage

☐ Represent the seller/landlord
☐ Represent the buyer/tenant

I also understand and agree that the following may also possibly occur in a real estate transaction in which I may be involved with this agent:

☐ The same agent who represents me could potentially represent the other party in a transaction involving me. The agent and brokerage would then both be **dual agents.**

☐ A different agent in the same brokerage could potentially represent the other party in a transaction involving me. Each agent would represent the interests of their separate client. The brokerage would be a **dual agent.** A management level licensee is also a dual agent if representing a client in an in-company transaction.

I have reviewed the information on the reverse side of this form and I have been given a completed copy of this Disclosure of Agency Relationship.

_____   _____   _____   _____
Buyer or Tenant   Date   Seller or Landlord   Date

_____   _____   _____   _____
Buyer or Tenant   Date   Seller or Landlord   Date

To be completed only in an in-company transaction involving two agents ("Split" Agency)

Both buyer/tenant and seller/landlord acknowledge and agree that in a contemplated transaction involving property located at

_____the buyer/ tenant is represented by _____

_____and the seller/landlord is represented by_____

By initialing below both parties acknowledge and agree that they are aware that both agents are affiliated with the same brokerage; that each agent will represent the separate interests of their separate client, (unless a management level licensee is one of the agents involved in the transaction); that it was previously disclosed that this could occur; and that they consent to the brokerage acting as a dual agent.

Buyer/Tenant's initials: _____   Seller/Landlord's initials: _____
Date: _____   Date: _____

Any questions regarding the role or responsiblities of the brokerage or its agents can be directed to an attorney or to:
Ohio Division of Real Estate and Professional Licensing
77 S. High Street, 20th Floor
Columbus, OH   43215-6133
(614)466-4100
Page 2 of 2

EQUAL HOUSING
OPPORTUNITY

duty to avoid negligence. Whether or not an act by the agent constitutes negligence depends upon what other qualified agents would do under the same circumstances. In essence, a real estate agent is required to exercise the same degree of skill as other agents would exercise. If negligent in this regard, the agent is liable for any loss incurred by the principal

Proper Accounting

As an ordinary part of their business, real estate agents are required to receive and hold money and papers for the benefit of a client. Agents are required to exercise care in handling and accounting for these items. Under no circumstances should the agent commingle money held for a client, such as earnest deposits, with personal funds. The licensing laws of each state stipulate that the commingling of funds may result in license suspension or revocation. To avoid this problem, agents should open a separate account at a financial institution to be used exclusively as a depository for funds belonging to clients.

Obedience to Instructions

Most listing agreements contain instructions that the agent must obey. For example, most states require that the agent obtain permission from the owner before placing a "for sale" sign on the property. In addition, the agent has a duty to follow any special instructions of the principal so long as they do not violate the law. For example, the owner may not wish the property to be shown to prospects without prior notice. The agent may be held liable for any damages suffered by the principal resulting from failure to follow instructions.

Responsibility for Delegation of Authority

Most listing agreements give the listing broker permission to delegate routine duties involving the agency to others (e.g., salespersons or other brokers), but the broker remains personally responsible for any errors or other problems resulting from the work of subagents. For example, suppose a broker hires a subagent to help sell a property that is listed for $100,000 and the subagent secures a buyer willing to pay $105,000, but colludes with another party and only reports an offer of $100,000 to the broker. The owner accepts the offer and the property is sold to the party conspiring with the subagent who subsequently sells the property to the party offering $105,000. The broker may be held personally liable for the actions of the subagent although the broker did not know of the deception.

DUTIES OF AN AGENT TO THIRD PARTIES

Real estate agents also have certain legal duties to third parties with whom they deal on behalf of the principal. The agent must disclose fully all knowledge about the real property that may materially affect a prospective purchaser's decision. In contract law, making a false statement or concealing a material fact known to one party that that party knows is not reasonably ascertainable by the other party is known as **misrepresentation.** In a real estate transaction, misrepresentation may result from an affirmative statement by the seller, or the seller's agent, such as, "there are no structural defects in this property," when in fact, the basement floods after every heavy rain. Failure to mention the condition, sometimes referred to as **negative fraud,** also constitutes misrepresentation. A buyer acting on misrepresentation may be able to have the purchase contract rescinded or sue for damages, and the license of an agent guilty of misrepresentation may be suspended or revoked.

In recent years, agents have been held to a higher standard and found liable for misrepresentation because they should have known about the falsity of a statement, even if they had no actual knowledge of the falsity. Usually, misrepresentation has to do with the physical condition of the property. However, stigmatized (or psychologically impacted) properties, and houses located in close proximity to the residence of sexual offenders are receiving increased attention. A stigmatized property is one that has been the site of a suicide, murder, some other felony, or was occupied by a person diagnosed with a disease that has been determined by medical evidence to be highly unlikely to be transmitted through occupancy (e.g., HIV/AIDS), or is reportedly haunted. Because some buyers may be put off by the events that have occurred on (or near) the property, sellers and agents are sometimes hesitant to disclose this information. Many states have enacted laws to specifically exempt agents from failing to inform buyers that a property is stigmatized. Regarding proximity of the subject house to the residence of sexual offenders, Federal and State legislation, enacted in the 1990s, has now made it easier to ascertain the residence of offenders. Some agents have encountered problems when the buyer learns the facts after a purchase offer is made or a sale is consummated. Such circumstances may be powerful reasons for buyers to hire an agent to represent them.

Not all non-truths, however, constitute misrepresentation. **Puffing,** which is a superlative or exaggerated comment or opinion, is not considered an illegal misrepresentation. Buyers expect that sellers and their agents may do this and seldom rely on such statements when making purchase decisions. For example, if an agent were to say, "This house has a tremendous view," prospects can certainly assess the quality of the view for themselves.

Real estate agents must also be careful to avoid misrepresentation in advertising properties. Advertising that contains misleading, or blatantly false, information is false advertising. An agent responsible for false advertising is subject to disciplinary action, and any misrepresentation gives the purchaser grounds for canceling the purchase contract. In addition, real estate agents are generally prohibited by state law from using a **blind ad,** which is an advertisement that does not include the name of the brokerage firm placing the advertisement. The purpose of laws that require the brokerage firm name be included in advertisements is to make it clear to prospects that a broker is involved in the transaction. Finally, as explained in the next section, brokers must not illegally discriminate in real estate transactions.

FAIR HOUSING LAWS AND REAL ESTATE AGENTS

In conducting their activities, real estate agents must be sure to abide by federal and state fair housing laws, which are designed to ensure minorities equal treatment by real estate brokers and owners. These laws include the Civil Rights Act of 1964, and the Federal Fair Housing Act of 1968 (with amendments). The first federal law that addressed fair housing was, however, enacted during the civil war era. The Civil Rights Act of 1866 prohibited owners of real property from racial discrimination in the sale or lease of real property. Real estate agents were not, however, covered by this act and, unfortunately, many people ignored this law until the civil rights movement in the 1960s.

In 1968, Congress passed the Civil Rights Act, Title VIII of which became known as the Federal Fair Housing Act. The Office of Equal Opportunity administers the Act under the direction of the Secretary of the Department of Housing and Urban Development (HUD). The 1968 Act expanded the definition of groups protected from housing discrimination,

AN ETHICAL ISSUE
AGENCY DISCLOSURE

From the broker's perspective, what do you think are the advantages and disadvantages of postponing agency disclosure until the customer is ready to write an offer? Do you think it would be more ethical to provide the agency disclosure sooner? If so, when? If not, why?

and covers both real property owners and real estate brokers. The amended Act makes illegal discrimination based on race, color, sex, religion, national origin, families with children, persons with HIV or AIDS, or the disabled in connection with the sale or lease of most dwellings and any vacant land offered for residential construction or use. The Act did not, however, prohibit discrimination in other types of real property transactions such as those involving industrial and commercial properties. Most states quickly replicated the 1968 federal law at the state level, and at least one, Colorado, has expanded coverage of the state statute to commercial property.

The impetus for the Act was a proliferation of steering and blockbusting, both of which the Act made illegal. **Blockbusting,** also called panic peddling, occurs when one party, the blockbuster, induces another to enter into a real estate transaction from which the first party may benefit financially. Typically, the blockbuster suggests to homeowners that a change in the neighborhood with respect to race, color, religion, or ancestry of the occupants may occur, and that such change will lower property values, increase the crime rate, or result in a decline in school quality. For example, a blockbuster might purchase a home, install a minority family in the dwelling and pass the word that other homeowners in the area are thinking of selling their homes to minorities. Some owners may panic and agree to sell their homes to the blockbuster at below-market prices. The blockbuster, in turn, sells the homes, at inflated prices, to minorities. **Steering** is the channeling of prospective home purchasers searching for equivalent properties to particular areas to either maintain the homogeneity of the area, or to create blockbusting opportunities.

The Act provides those subjected to housing discrimination with two remedies, both of which must be commenced within 180 days of the alleged infraction. The aggrieved party may file a complaint with the Fair Housing Section of HUD. Alternatively, they may take their complaint directly to court (state court if the state has antidiscriminatory laws, otherwise, the federal district court). HUD will provide legal council for the complainant and the court may either issue a permanent or temporary injunction, a temporary restraining order, or other appropriate relief, including actual and punitive damages. A real estate agent facing a discrimination charge is subject to civil penalties up to $50,000, and may also be liable for actual damages and unlimited punitive damages for the humiliation caused the aggrieved party by the discriminatory activity.

Discrimination in federally subsidized housing projects is also prohibited under Title VI of the Civil Rights Act of 1964. This Act states that "no person in the United States shall, on the ground of race, color, or national origin, be excluded from participation in, be denied from the benefits of, or be subject to discrimination under any program or activity receiving federal financial assistance."

AGENT COMPENSATION

In most areas, a particular commission level predominates (e.g., 7 percent of the sale price). To avoid a repeat of previous charges of price-fixing by consumer interest groups and the Federal Trade Commission, most real estate agents now make it clear that the commission is negotiable. Usually, the commission negotiation takes place at the time the parties sign the listing agreement. With increasing frequency, however, sellers presented with less than full price offers are successfully suggesting that agents reduce the agreed commission in order to close the deal. The commission is usually payable at the closing of a transaction. Other arrangements have been used. Some brokers obtain a nonrefundable advance fee before any services are rendered, which is used to cover advertising costs for the property. Because brokers do not guarantee that they can locate buyers, some authorities hold that advance fees are improper conduct. To reduce any suggestion of impropriety, brokers should maintain accurate records of expenditures. A broker may also agree to a deferred commission. For example, a broker may have earned a commission, but by prior agreement with the seller, not be paid until some event, such as the completion of construction occurs. Usually an agent may not receive a commission from anyone other than his or her present employer. A general exception to this is deferred commissions due an agent from a previous employer.

PERCENTAGE COMMISSION

Although several systems of agent compensation are available, the predominant system in the real estate brokerage market is the percentage commission. Under this system, the total commission for a particular transaction is equal to the property's selling price multiplied by the percentage commission rate agreed to by the agent and principal. For example, if a house that was listed for $110,000 eventually sells for $100,000 and the percentage commission is 7 percent; the commission is $7,000. Similarly, a 7 percent commission on a house sold for $40,000 results in a commission of $2,800. In transactions involving expensive properties, the percentage commission is often on a graduated basis such as 6 percent on the first $500,000, and 3 percent on the balance.

Decision Point

Consider the following unique commission system. For a full-price offer, 7 percent, adjusted downward in proportion to a less than full list price offer. For Example, the commission for an offer equal to 95 percent of the list price would be 6.65 percent (7 × .95). Do you think such a system would be fair to both the seller and the broker? Can you suggest an alternative system?

FLAT-FEE COMMISSION

For people who question the percentage commission system, some agents, known as **flat-fee brokers** or discount brokers, offer to perform their services for a fee that is independent of

DOING BUSINESS
CUSTOMER SERVICE

Real estate brokers must comply with a variety of regulations administered by their state real estate commission. But, one thing that is not subject to regulation is the transportation of the client to visit available houses. The phrase, different strokes for different folks, certainly applies to real estate brokerage. Compare the marketing style of Karen Santo to that of Real Estate B.O.S.S.

Santo became a real estate salesperson in 1988, shortly after graduating from Wright State University. She joined Irongate Realty in Dayton, Ohio, a firm that specializes in residential real estate and charges a percentage commission for their services. Karen quickly became one of their most successful agents. Her skills include the ability to think of, and implement, unique marketing tools. For example, Karen purchased a stretch limousine (she's now on her second) and when viewing properties she and prospects are transported in chauffeur-driven comfort. Karen is still with Irongate and is known locally as the "Limo Lady."

Real Estate B.O.S.S., a brokerage company in Boca Raton, Florida started a new program in 2001. Under this program, the company says that it will return (at the closing) at least half the commission paid by the seller in exchange for a $250 registration fee. Interesting concept. The company says that it will assist the client in all the ways that a normal brokerage would except one—they will not drive the client around!

Go to www.arello.com, and click on "regulatory agencies" to find contact information for real estate license law officials for every state and some foreign countries. In many cases, you can link directly to the state regulator's Web site.

the eventual selling price. For example, a flat-free broker may offer to sell any home for a flat-fee of $3,000. Flat-fee brokers have entered many local markets without significant success. Some suggest that their lack of success may be due to the poor incentives a flat-fee provides brokers compared to a percentage commission. In essence, the more expensive the home, the fewer the people that can afford it, and, therefore, the agent's buyer-search effort must be more intense. The material in the following section provides another possible explanation for the lack of success by discount brokers.

MULTIPLE LISTING SERVICES (MLS)

A **multiple listing service (MLS)** is an organization whose members agree to share listings. This system provides an advantage to both agents and property sellers. The seller benefits from the fact that all members of the MLS, not just the agent with whom the property was listed, may offer the property to prospective buyers. Agents benefit in that the inventory of properties available to sell is not limited to those listings secured by the firm, and agents are assured a portion of the commission if they either list or sell a property.

A broker who assists in locating a buyer is referred to as a cooperating broker. **Cooperating brokers** have no contractual relationship with the property seller and must look solely to the listing agent for their share of the commission. Under most multiple listing rules the cooperating broker is deemed to be a sub-agent of the listing agent and, therefore, owes all of the previously discussed duties to the principal. If the cooperating broker decides to represent the purchaser, then all parties must be given written notice of this fact.

Because one piece of information formerly included in MLS listings was the total commission to be paid upon the sale of a property, consumer groups and federal authorities charged various MLSs with restraint of trade. In essence, the authorities asserted that an MLS provides a means for agents to identify and sanction price-cutters. To illustrate how this may occur, suppose you are a real estate agent and have a prospect looking for a house that costs $100,000. Scanning the MLS book you find two suitable properties. The first has a total commission of 7 percent; the second (listed by a flat-fee broker) has a total commission of $3,000. On which property would you concentrate your sales effort?

LISTING CONTRACTS

A real estate agent's employment contract with a principal is called a listing contract. There are three types of contracts that are commonly used: open, exclusive agency, and exclusive right to sell. In most states, a fourth contractual arrangement is available, but seldom used—the net listing.

OPEN LISTING

Many brokers dislike open listing contracts because of the poor incentives they provide to the listing broker. With this type of arrangement the listing broker is entitled to a commission only if he or she locates the buyer. The owner is free to sign other open listing contracts with as many brokers as can be found. It is unlikely, however, that many residential real estate brokers will be willing to enter into such contracts because if anyone else (e.g., the property owner, one of the owner's relatives, friends, neighbors, or another broker) locates a buyer the listing broker does not receive a commission. In effect, the open listing broker competes to sell the property with everyone. The listing broker, therefore, has little incentive to locate a buyer, or spend money advertising the property. Despite the poor incentives, open listings are sometimes used for residential properties and are not uncommon for undeveloped land and also for commercial properties. Apparently brokers involved in open listing transactions either incur lower marketing costs, are less risk averse, or are more willing to compete for the sale.

EXCLUSIVE AGENCY LISTING

With an exclusive agency contract, the property owner may sign a contract with only one broker. From the perspective of the listing broker, however, this arrangement does not significantly increase the incentive to spend time or money attempting to sell the property. Such contracts allow the seller to locate a buyer resulting in no commission to the broker.

EXCLUSIVE RIGHT TO SELL LISTING

The listing contract residential real estate brokers are most likely to offer is an exclusive right to sell. Under this arrangement, the listing broker is entitled to the sales commission no matter who locates the buyer. A sample exclusive right to sell contract is shown in Exhibit 9.3. There are ten major provisions in the sample contract; and most (1-9) cover an area that should be contained somewhere in all exclusive right to sell contracts.

The first contract provision gives the listing broker "the exclusive right to sell." The second provision specifies the date on which the contract expires. Every listing contract should clearly define the beginning and ending date for the agreement. In this case, space for the beginning date is provided at the top of the form. Most states prohibit clauses that provide for an automatic extension of the contract.

The third provision specifies the terms of sale. On the sample contract, both the price the seller is willing to take for the property and the type of deed to be delivered are mentioned. If the owner has other terms upon which the sale is conditional (e.g., they wish to sell only to a buyer who has cash or conventional financing) they can specify these desires with an addendum to the contract. Other items that may be included in an addendum are any fixtures that will be removed by the seller, and any items of personal property to be included in the sale.

The fourth provision specifies the commission be paid to the broker if the property is sold. Many listing contracts specify that if the broker locates a buyer willing and able to purchase the property according to the terms set out in the listing contract, then the broker is entitled to a commission even if the owner changes his or her mind and refuses to sell. In addition, many contracts require the seller to pay the commission should the property sell within a reasonable length of time (e.g., ninety days) after the expiration of the contract if the buyer became aware of the property through the effort, of the broker during the listing period.

The fifth provision allows the broker to submit the listing to the local multiple listing service. In the sixth provision, the sellers' right to refuse (or agree) to have a dual agent involved in the transaction is spelled out. In the seventh provision, the seller asserts that he or she actually owns the property and has the authority to fulfill the contract. In addition, the owner promises not to discriminate against any potential buyers and stipulates that, unless specified, the property is free from environmental hazards and latent defects. In the eighth provision, the seller is notified of state and federal fair housing requirements. The ninth provision informs the seller of their responsibilities with regard to lead-based paint disclosure. The tenth provision is included because some cities in the area require housing inspections. Inclusion of this provision ensures that the seller will obtain an inspection if required. In this provision, the seller also agrees (or refuses to permit) the broker to install a lock box on the property. A lock box is a device put on the front door that contains a key to the property. This enables agents to show the property without the owner being present.

EXHIBIT 9.3 **EXCLUSIVE RIGHT TO SELL LISTING CONTRACT**

EXCLUSIVE RIGHT TO SELL CONTRACT
ADOPTED BY THE MULTIPLE LISTING SERVICE OF THE DAYTON AREA BOARD OF REALTORS®

Date: _____

This Exclusive Right to Sell Contract ("Contract") is made between _____ ("Owner," whether one or more), whose address is _____, and _____ ("Broker"), whose address is _____

1. **Exclusive Right to Sell.** In consideration for Broker's efforts to procure a purchaser, and for Broker's acceptance of the duties as Owner's exclusive agent, Owner grants to Broker the exclusive right to sell the real property (the "Property") located at and commonly known as (use street location and lot number or size): _____

The Property includes the features shown on the Profile Sheet attached to this Contract.

2. **Listing Period.** This Contract shall begin on the date first written above and shall expire at 12:00 Midnight on _____, _____ (the "Listing Period").

3. **Terms of Sale.** The Property will be offered for sale at a price of $_____. Owner agrees to convey marketable title to the Property by general warranty deed with release of dower.

4. **Brokerage Fee.** If the Property is sold during the Listing Period, Owner shall pay Broker a brokerage fee of (insert dollar amount or percentage of total sales price) _____. This right to a brokerage fee applies to any sale during the Listing Period, whether the Property is sold through Broker, by Owner's own efforts, or otherwise, and applies regardless of the amount of the sales price accepted by Owner. For purposes of this Contract, the Property is deemed "sold" when (a) Owner receives a written offer to purchase the Property for not less than the price stated in Paragraph 3, and otherwise upon the terms and conditions set forth in this Contract, from a ready, willing and able purchaser; or (b) Owner conveys or enters into a contract to convey the Property on any other terms and conditions acceptable to Owner. In addition, Broker shall be entitled to the same brokerage fee if the Property is sold within the _____ day period following the expiration of the Listing Period (the "Terminal Period"), to any person (or anyone acting on that person's behalf) with whom Broker had made contact relative to the sale of the Property before the expiration of the Listing Period. However, this right to a brokerage fee with respect to a sale during the Terminal Period shall not be operative if the Property is then listed with another real estate broker who will receive the brokerage fee.

5. **Other Brokers.** Owner authorizes Broker to list the Property in any Multiple Listing Service. Owner authorizes Broker to offer compensation in accordance with Broker's company policy, which is to offer compensation to (check if applicable):

_____ Subagents   Compensation amount _____
_____ Buyer Brokers   Compensation amount _____
                              (State compensation as dollar amount or percentage of sales price)

Owner (check one) _____ has _____ has not received Broker's written disclosure of its company policy on agency relationships.

6. **Dual Agency.** If a prospective buyer of the Property is represented by Broker, or any agent of Broker, or if the prospective buyer is an employee or agent of Broker, Broker will be considered a "dual agent" (that is, agent of both Owner and the buyer) in the transaction. If this situation arises, Owner is willing to permit Broker's dual agency role, subject to Owner's approval of a dual agency consent agreement in accordance with Ohio law setting forth the rights and obligations of the parties.

7. **Owner's Representations.** Owner represents to Broker that (a) Owner is the sole owner of and has exclusive control of the Property; (b) Owner is fully authorized and able to enter into and perform this Contract; (c) to the best of Owner's knowledge, no latent defects are present in the Property, no toxic, explosive or otherwise hazardous substances have been stored, disposed of, concealed within or released on or from the Property, and no other adverse environmental conditions affect the Property, except as set forth in the Residential Property Disclosure Form or as follows:

_____;
and (d) Owner has been advised of the requirement to provide to prospective purchasers a Residential Property Disclosure Form in accordance with Ohio law.

8. **Fair Housing Statement.** It is illegal, pursuant to the Ohio Fair Housing Law, Division (H) of Section 4112.02 of the Revised Code and the Federal Fair Housing Law, 42 U.S.C.A.3601, to refuse to sell, transfer, assign, rent, lease, sublease or finance housing accommodations, refuse to negotiate for the sale or rental of housing accommodations, or otherwise deny or make unavailable housing accommodations because of race, color, religion, sex, familial status as defined in Section 4112.01 of the Revised Code, ancestry, disability as defined in that section, or national origin or to so discriminate in advertising the sale or rental of housing, in the financing of housing, or in the provision of real estate brokerage services. It is also illegal, for profit, to induce or attempt to induce any person to sell or rent any dwelling by representations regarding the entry or respective entry into the neighborhood of a person or persons belonging to one of the protected classes.

9. **Lead-Based Paint Disclosure.** Owner has been advised that if the Property contains housing constructed before 1978, Owner is required (a) to provide to the purchaser a federally approved lead hazard information pamphlet; (b) to disclose to Broker and the purchaser the presence of any known lead-based paint and/or lead-based paint hazards on the Property; and (c) to provide to Broker and the purchaser any additional information, records or reports in Owner's possession or available to Owner pertaining to lead-based paint and/or lead-based paint hazards in the Property. In addition, Owner must provide to the purchaser a 10-day opportunity to conduct a risk assessment or inspection of the Property for the presence of lead-based paint and/or lead-based paint hazards, unless waived by the purchaser in writing. Finally, any contract for the sale of the Property shall include an attachment containing a Lead Warning Statement as well as the information and disclosures described above. Owner agrees to comply with these requirements and to indemnify, defend, and hold Broker harmless against any claims, damages, losses or expenses, including attorney's fees, arising from Owner's violation of these requirements.

10. **Miscellaneous.** (a) If the Property is located in a jurisdiction requiring a housing inspection before transfer (such as the City of Oakwood or the City of Huber Heights), Owner shall immediately make application for any required housing inspection and furnish Broker with a copy of the resulting certificate. (b) Owner agrees to make the Property available for showing at all reasonable times by Broker, its associates and other brokers designated by Broker. (c) During the Listing Period, Broker may place "For Sale" signs on the Property. (d) Owner (**please initial choice**) ____ authorizes ____ does not authorize the use of a lockbox. If a lockbox is used, Owner releases Broker and Broker's agents from any liability resulting from the use of the lockbox except any loss or damage resulting from the gross negligence or intentional acts of Broker or Broker's agents. (e) Broker is authorized to disclose all information pertaining to the Property to all parties involved with its marketing and/or sale, including all M.L.S. participants. Broker is further authorized to place information about the Property in any other informational service medium to advertise and promote the sale of the Property.

_____
_____
_____

Owner _____ Phone _____
Owner _____ Phone _____
The undersigned Broker accepts the exclusive right to sell agency for the Property on the terms stated above.
Broker _____ Phone _____
        By _____ Phone _____
Present encumbrance of $ _____ held by (Lender): _____
Lender's Address _____ Account No. _____
Other encumbrances/line of credit held by (Lender): _____
Lender's Address _____ Account No. _____
Owner's social security/taxpayer ID number(s): _____

WHITE - REALTOR'S COPY • CANARY - MLS COPY • PINK - OWNER'S COPY   Copyright © June, 2001 Dayton Area Board of REALTORS®

NET LISTING

In a net listing, the sellers specify a price they wish to net from the property, and the commission is equal to the selling price less the seller's reservation price. For example, if the sellers specify that they want $80,000 from the sale and the property sells for $85,000; the commission is $5,000, but if the property sells for only $84,000; the commission is $4,000. Net listings are legal in most states, but highly discouraged by state real estate commissions because of the bad incentives they provide to agents. As mentioned, sellers frequently rely on the agent's advice in setting the list price, and with a net listing; an agent may be tempted to suggest a low reservation price to increase the commission.

COMMISSION SPLITTING

There are several circumstances under which two or more licensees must share the commission on a real estate transaction. To illustrate this, consider the following three scenarios.

First, assume that a salesperson secured a listing and sold the property for $80,000 with a 7 percent commission. The salesperson and employing broker have an agreement to split all commissions generated by the salesperson on a 45/55 basis, with the larger share going to the broker. This arrangement is fairly typical, although the exact split is subject to negotiation. Continuing the example, the total commission owed by the seller would be $5,600 ($80,000 × .07) with the salesperson entitled to $2,520 ($5,600 × .45), and the balance to the broker.

Next, assume that a salesperson lists a property and another salesperson in the same office secures a buyer. The sales price was $80,000 and a 7 percent commission was paid. In this case, each salesperson was responsible for generating half the total commission of $5,600. If the listing and selling agent's agreements with the broker call for commissions to be shared on a 45/55 and a 40/60 basis, respectively; the listing agent is entitled to $1,260 [($5,600 ÷ 2) × .45], the selling agent's share is $1,120 [($5,600 ÷ 2) × .40], and the broker gets the remainder.

Finally, in areas with an MLS, properties are frequently listed by an agent of one firm and sold by an agent of another. In this case, the commission would first be split between the two firms and each broker would then split the firm's share of the total commission with the salesperson. Many MLSs stipulate that cooperating firms split the total commission evenly. Some suggest that an even split of the commission may lead firms to delay submitting a listing to the MLS in the hope that the property can be sold quickly. The listing firm can thereby retain the entire commission. Apparently, some MLSs recognize this possibility and, in an attempt to reduce it, stipulate commission splits that favor the listing firm such as 60/40.

Decision Point

If one is to be successful as a real estate agent, do you think it is more important for the person to sell properties or to obtain listings?

TERMINATING AN AGENCY RELATIONSHIP

An agency relationship may be terminated in several ways. Termination occurs automatically when the purpose for which the relationship was created is completed, or, if the purpose was not accomplished, upon the expiration date specified in the contract. Termination is also automatic in the event of either party's death or insanity, or if the principal declares bankruptcy. In addition, the principal may terminate the agency at any time unless it is an agency coupled with an interest, which means that the agent has an interest in the property itself and not merely the proceeds from its sale. For example, the principal cannot terminate the agency at will if the agent gave some consideration to the principal for the right to exercise the authority. Finally, if the agent has procured a buyer, ready willing and able to transact on the seller's terms, the owner may not avoid the commission by firing the broker.

CHARACTERISTICS OF SUCCESSFUL AGENTS

Successful agents tend to have certain common characteristics that customers value, including good time management, extraordinary effort, superior organizational skills, professionalism, superior knowledge of the market, and good personal communication skills. A number of researchers have attempted to explain variations in residential real estate agent income using the human capital theory, which holds that one's income is related to various human capital variables. The results of these studies are mixed, but, in general, conclude that agent income is positively related to educational levels, the agent's tenure in the real estate business, and the number of hours the agent works.

Not all agents enjoy the level of success enjoyed by Jim Droz (chapter opener); there is a wide range in agent earnings. One possible explanation for the earnings disparity is that the manner in which the residential real estate brokerage market operates allows brokers to pass most business costs on to their salespeople. Brokers therefore have the incentive to hire more salespeople than are required to cover the market efficiently. An issue that contributes to this problem is that, for income tax purposes, real estate salespeople are considered independent contractors as opposed to employees. This distinction is important because brokers are not required to withhold income taxes or the workers share of social security contributions, nor is the broker required to make the employer's share of social security contributions for independent contractors. It is the responsibility of the independent contractor to make these payments.

FRANCHISE OPERATIONS

The real estate brokerage industry can be characterized accurately as one that consists primarily of relatively small, local firms. There is a growing movement, however, toward larger nationally diversified firms. One form of business operation, long popular in other industries, such as fast food restaurants and automotive repair shops, is the franchise. Under a franchise, one party, the franchisor, in exchange for compensation agrees to let another, the franchisee, operate a business using the franchisor's trade name and operating procedures. Franchised operations on a national level in real estate brokerage represent a fairly recent innovation. The oldest such organization, Century 21, has been in operation less than 35 years. Other real estate brokerage franchises include ERA (Electronic Realty Associates), Coldwell Banker, and RE/MAX International Inc. With the possible exception of a few offices, the franchisor does not own or operate individual offices. Instead, the franchisor licenses its trade name, operating procedures, and referral services to independently owned brokerages.

PROFESSIONAL ASSOCIATIONS

Real estate brokerage licensees have the opportunity to join various professional associations. The National Association of REALTORS® (NAR) is the largest professional association for real estate agents in the United States with 760,000 members as of August 2001. A real estate broker who belongs to NAR is referred to as a REALTOR® and a member salesperson is called a REALTOR associate®. Both of these terms are copyrighted, and only members of NAR may refer to themselves as REALTORS®.

NAR provides a variety of opportunities for the professional development of its members. It has developed an education program through which members who demonstrate advanced levels of expertise may earn a GRI designation (Graduate, Realtor Institute). NAR also provides membership opportunities for several related groups (e.g., The American Chapter of the International Real Estate Federation, The American Society of Real Estate Counselors, the Realtors Land Institute, the Institute of Real Estate Management, Real Estate Securities and Syndication Institute, and the Society of Industrial & Office Realtors). In addition, NAR is actively involved in the legislative process. It has several legislative committees and the largest political action committee in the country. Members of NAR are subject to the organization's code of ethics that specifies how members are expected to conduct their affairs with other REALTORS®, and the public.

Another major professional association is the National Association of Real Estate Brokers. The Association's copyrighted trade name is Realtists. They have also been individually active in both political and legislative matters with equal opportunity in housing as their focus.

LICENSE SUSPENSION AND REVOCATION

Unfortunately, a few agents do not abide by the standards set forth in the NAR code of ethics, or the state regulations that govern their activities. State real estate commissions have the power to sanction a licensee who violates state regulations. Depending on the severity of the infraction the offender's license may either be revoked or suspended. **License revocation** bars the offender from any future practice of real estate brokerage in the state. **License suspension** prohibits the holder from engaging in real estate brokerage during the suspension period, but practice may be resumed after the suspension is served. Suspensions can run from a few days to several months. Causes for disciplinary actions frequently result from the mishandling of money. In some cases, licensees are disciplined because they commingled client's funds with their personal funds; in others, they fail to release funds that should have been released; and in others, they released funds that should not have been released.

RECOVERY FUNDS

Most states have established and maintain a real estate recovery fund that is used to indemnify members of the public who have suffered financial harm as a result of negligence or fraud by a licensed real estate person. Most states also require that the recovery funds contain a minimum balance. Fees levied on all licensees fund the recovery funds. An action by a licensee that results in a disbursement from the recovery fund may also result in license suspension or revocation. To remove a suspension the licensee may be required to reimburse the fund.

SUMMARY

Real estate brokerage is one of the most visible of the specializations within the real estate industry. In the conduct of their business, real estate brokers interact with a number of groups; clients, customers, other brokers, professional associations, and state real estate commissions. Through their police power, states have the right to license and regulate brokers. To help protect the public from unscrupulous activities in real estate brokerage, every state has enacted laws and regulations that govern the activities of real estate brokers. To be successful, and minimize conflicts with other parties, brokers should be familiar with these regulations. An agency relationship is created when a real property owner hires a broker to assist in the sale or lease of property, or when a buyer hires a broker to assist in a search for property. This relationship obligates a broker to act in the best interest of his or her client, but the broker must also treat other parties fairly.

Real estate brokerage can be a profitable career, but it is not an easy way to make a living. Residential brokers, in particular, must be willing to work long and irregular hours because some customers may only be able to view properties at night or on weekends. Licensees may enhance their professionalism through continuing education classes and participation in activates sponsored by any of several professional associations.

KEY TERMS

agency
blind ad
blockbusting
buyer's broker
cooperating broker
dual agency
flat-fee broker

general agency
license revocation
license suspension
misrepresentation
multiple listing service
 (MLS)
net listing

puffing
special agency
steering
transactional broker

REVIEW QUESTIONS

1. Who does a real estate broker usually represent? What are the duties of a real estate broker to his or her client? What duties does the broker owe to the customer?
2. What is a dual agency? What disadvantages and advantages do you think are related to this type of agency?
3. Why are net listings discouraged? Do you think they present a real problem?
4. How does a general agency differ from a special agency?
5. List the ways in which the agency relationship created in a real estate sales transaction may be terminated.
6. How are real estate brokers compensated?
7. To be successful in real estate brokerage, do you think it is more important to secure listings or to make sales?
8. What is the difference between license suspension and revocation?
9. What are the advantages and disadvantages of a real estate franchise from the perspective of the franchisee?
10. Successful brokers have several characteristics in common. Rank those listed in the chapter in order of importance and explain your ranking. What other qualities do you think are valuable for real estate brokers?
11. What is your answer to the questions in the three "Decision Point" sections in this chapter?
12. What is your answer to the "Ethical Issue" in this chapter?

REAL ESTATE ON THE WEB

Use your favorite search engine to:
1. Locate the Web sites of real estate firms or individual agents in your community.
2. Visit the Web site of your state's real estate commission to determine the pre-licensing and continuing education requirements for brokers and agents in your state.

3. Visit the Web site of your state's real estate commission to determine the agency disclosure provisions that apply to licensees in your state, and whether transactional brokers are allowed in your state.

4. Determine if there are any flat-fee (or discount) real estate brokers in your area.

5. Visit the Web site of your local Multiple Listing Service.

Refer to the companion Web site at www.wiley.com/college/larsen for a variety of online activities including additional chapter content, review materials, assignments, and related links.

ADDITIONAL READINGS

Anderson, R. I. and J. R Webb. "The Education of Real Estate Salespeople and the Value of the Firm." *The Journal of Real Estate Research* (July-October 2000): 143–152.

Benjamin, J. D., G. D. Jud and G. S. Sirmans. "Real Estate Brokerage and the Housing Market: An Annotated Bibliography." *The Journal of Real Estate Research* (July-October 2000): 217–278.

Finn, M. K. "Administrative Enforcement in the Real Estate Profession: A Nationwide Examination of Regulatory Ambushes and Pitfalls." *Real Estate Law Journal* (Summer 1999): 7–24.

Hardin, W. G. III. "Practical Experiences, Expectations, Hiring, Promotion and Tenure: A Real Estate Perspective." *Journal of Real Estate Practice and Education* (2000): 17–34.

Jud, G. D. and D. T. Winkler. "A Note on Licensing and the Market for Real Estate Agents." *The Journal of Real Estate Finance and Economics* (September 2000): 175–184.

Larsen, J. E. and J. W. Coleman. "Psychologically Impacted Houses: Broker Disclosure Behavior and Perceived Market Effects in an Unregulated Environment." *Journal of Real Estate Practice and Education* (2001): 1–16.

Lewis, D., R. I. Anderson and L.V. Zumpano. "An Analysis of Affinity Programs: The Case of Real Estate Brokerage Participation." *Financial Services Review* (1999): 183–197.

Linnell, J. "Enhancing Search Capabilities on Real Estate Web Sites." *Real Estate Review* (Fall 2000): 49–50.

Moore, G. S. "The Buyer's Agent and the "As Is" Clause: A Liability Trap." *Real Estate Law Journal* (Spring 1999): 374–389.

Moore, G. S. and G. Smolen. "Real Estate Disclosure Forms and Information Transfer." *Real Estate Law Journal* (Spring 2000): 319–336.

Muhanna, W. A. "E-Commerce in the Real Estate Brokerage Industry." *Journal of Real Estate Practice and Education* (2000): 1–16.

Sirmans, G. S. and P. G. Swicegood. "Determining Real Estate Licensee Income." *The Journal of Real Estate Research* (July-October 2000): 189–204.

Real Estate Appraisal

Learning Objectives

After studying this chapter, you should be able to:

- Describe the minimum requirements for appraiser licensing and certification.
- Explain the basic principles of value used in real estate appraisal.
- List the steps in the appraisal process.
- Describe the various methods used in the appraisal process.
- Identify the major real estate appraisal professional organizations.

FROM THE WIRE

In October 2001, Rob MacGregor decided to refinance his mortgage. He searched the Internet and located a mortgage broker in Southern California. The broker said, "I can have somebody come out and do an appraisal of your house, and this is the one thing you'll have to pay for—$300." The lender said that he could use the appraisal elsewhere if he decided to go with another lender, and that sounded fair to MacGregor.

When the appraiser showed up, MacGregor gave him a $300 check. Later, he called the lender and asked for a receipt and a copy of the report. The receipt arrived, but no report. MacGregor ended up switching lenders and asked the first lender to forward the appraisal report to the second lender. It didn't happen. So, MacGregor convinced the appraiser to send him a copy—cost $50. MacGregor made two copies of the report at a supermarket—cost much less than $50. Then, he switched to a third lender and had to pay the appraiser $30 to change the name of the lender on the cover of the report.

There is a federal regulation that requires lenders to provide a copy of the appraisal report to loan applicants. The lender must disclose this fact in the paperwork that accompanies the good-faith estimate. The typical disclosure says: "You have the right to a copy of the appraisal report used in connection with your application for credit." Despite this regulation, sometimes lenders will use the appraisal as leverage to prevent a customer from switching lenders, and this is apparently what happened to MacGregor, twice.

Go to www.appraisalinstitute.org and click on one or more of the "Headlines from Appraiser News Online" to learn about an issue of present concern to the appraisal industry.

INTRODUCTION

Good decision-making requires that the decision maker know the value of the assets involved in a transaction. However, reasonable people may disagree on the worth of a particular asset. This problem can be reduced in real estate transactions by using the services of a professional **appraiser** who is trained in estimating real property value.

Several parties may desire estimates of real property value. The value judgment an appraiser renders may provide prospective purchasers or investors with some assurance that they are not paying too much for a property. Current owners, contemplating the sale, exchange, or refinancing of their real property, may be interested in an independent estimate of their property's worth. The value of real property is also important to insurance companies, which must know the value of insured property—both at the time the policy originates and at the time of any loss—in order to calculate premium amounts and claims on policies. As the chapter opener "From the Wire" suggests, most mortgage lenders need to know the value of real property pledged as collateral for a loan because they must comply with regulatory restrictions regarding the maximum loan amount as a percentage of the property's value. Governmental units also require estimates of property value to determine compensation amounts in condemnation proceedings, and in assessing property taxes.

The appraisal of real property is a complicated and evolving art. For those considering a career in real property appraisal, the information presented in this chapter serves as a starting point for further study, and it should assist others in making informed decisions when using the services of appraisers. Parties who employ the services of an appraiser should understand how the appraiser arrives at a value estimate and the estimate's implications. Toward this end, we present basic appraisal concepts, terminology, and value estimation methods. To facilitate the presentation of this material, we begin by introducing the report appraisers use to present their estimate of property value.

UNIFORM RESIDENTIAL APPRAISAL REPORT

An **appraisal** is an unbiased written estimate of the fair market value of a property at a particular time. The **appraisal report** is the document the appraiser submits to the client, which, if prepared properly, should enable the client to understand the appraiser's estimate of value. The report contains the appraiser's final estimate of value, the data on which the estimate is based, and the calculations the appraiser used to arrive at the estimate.

Periodically, the appraisal industry is the subject of criticism. In the 1980s, poorly prepared appraisal reports and inflated appraised values were blamed as a contributing cause for high loan delinquency rates and resulting losses to mortgage investors and the private mortgage insurance industry. It is unlikely, however, that the appraisal industry was solely to blame for the problems. Changes in the income tax code in the early 1980s provided investors with an incentive to overbuild, and deregulation of financial institutions in the early 1980s contributed to the problem. As the twenty-first century begins, some appraisers are being accused of contributing to another wave of mortgage loan fraud. The following "Consumer Checklist" suggests that there are some problems in the appraisal process. As of this writing, the jury is still out regarding the responsibility of appraisers in the more recent debacle.

Responding to the earlier criticism, several appraisal organizations worked with federal government agencies (Farmers Home Administration, Federal Home Loan Mortgage Corporation, Federal Housing Administration, Federal National Mortgage Association, Veterans Administration) to develop an appraisal report that would be acceptable to all the government agencies. An example of the uniform report that is a product of these meetings is shown in Exhibit 10.1. Residential appraisal reports should also include a location map that shows comparables used in the appraisal, a floor plan showing rooms with doorways, an exterior sketch of the dwelling with measurements, and two sets of original 35-millimeter photos showing the property front, rear, and street scene. Note that the uniform report in Exhibit 10.1 was designed to be used in appraising single-family houses. Other uniform reports were designed to account for the unique characteristics of other property types such as condominiums and small residential income properties.

Since 1987, uniform appraisal reports have been required for mortgage loan documentation purposes for all single-family homes. The uniform report, which is designed for use with computers with a programmable format, resolved some of the criticism directed at the appraisal industry. The use of computers alone does not, however, guarantee a good appraisal report.

In conjunction with the development of the uniform report, a series of professional standards, known as the Uniform Standards of Professional Appraisal Practice, were designed to assist appraisers in preparing the report. This effort was important because these were the first uniform standards ever adopted by the various appraisal organizations. Unfortunately, the Uniform Report and Standards did not eliminate all appraisal problems, and the level of skill within the industry varied widely.

LICENSING REAL ESTATE APPRAISERS

Parts of the Financial Reform, Recovery, and Enforcement Act of 1989 (FIRREA), popularly known as the savings and loan bail-out bill, directly address the quality control problem in the appraisal industry. As with real estate brokers, the licensing of real estate appraisers is done at the state level, and before passage of FIRREA, not all states required appraisers to be licensed. To improve the overall quality of the appraisal industry, FIRREA specifies minimum quality standards for appraisers, requires that an appraisal be conducted for all federally related mortgage loans, and requires that a qualified appraiser conduct these appraisals. FIRREA provides minimum standards for two classes of appraisers: licensed appraisers and certified appraisers (although some states have expanded the number of categories).

CONSUMER CHECKLIST

COMMON ERRORS IN APPRAISAL REPORTS

In a 2001 report, the National Association of Real Estate Appraisers found the following errors the most common in residential appraisal reports. The survey results provide a valuable list of items today's consumers of appraisal services might check for accuracy. It should be noted that results are not in order of frequency as the "errors" varied depending on the type of property and report being made.

1. Contract specifications not followed
2. Typing, grammatical and punctuation errors
3. Mathematical errors
4. Poorly reproduced copies of supporting data and reports
5. Poor exhibits-quality and relevance
6. Poor overall format
7. Appraisers failing to understand the client's requirements or procedures
8. Loading the appraisal with "chamber of commerce" type data without relating factual data to subject
9. Inadequate history of property
10. Errors in land area or building size
11. Failure to properly consider zoning or potential zoning
12. Failure to properly consider easements on property
13. Inadequate discussion of "highest and best use"
14. Not adequately searching market for sales and leases
15. Using comparables too far afield in size and use
16. Failure to fully analyze and adjust all comparable data
17. Abundant sales or rental data with little or no discussion relating it to the subject
18. Not using the same methods of measurement between comparables and subject
19. Inconsistent adjustment patterns
20. Relying on mathematical exercises, formulas, curves, etc., without relating them to the subject
21. Failure to follow through in the analysis of data in the factual presentation
22. Values derived on assumptions not consistent with the "highest and best use" statement
23. Inconsistencies among cost, market and income approaches remaining, economic life, depreciation, net returns
24. Making unsupported adjustments for time
25. Using techniques and procedures not appropriate to the problem
26. Capitalization rates not current or adequately supported from the market
27. Lack of clarity or explanation of the appraiser's reasoning or procedures
28. Photographs of the subject do not adequately show the property
29. Report missing neighborhood data trends of the subject area
30. Appraiser utilizing inexperienced staff personnel without adequate supervision
31. Failure to state why an approach to value has not been used
32. Overall report is too short to adequately cover the property
33. Positive or negative features of property not mentioned
34. Failure to deliver report in a reasonable time or meet deadlines

SOURCE: National Association of Real Estate Appraisers, 1224 North Nokomis NE, Alexandria, Minnesota 56308

EXHIBIT 10.1 SAMPLE UNIFORM RESIDENTIAL APPRAISAL REPORT (PAGE 1)

UNIFORM RESIDENTIAL APPRAISAL REPORT

Property Description & Analysis   File No.

SUBJECT

Property Address	415 Cape Avenue Census Tract 3653.01
City	Metropolis County Greene State OH Zip Code 11111
Legal Description	In lot #1003 City of Metropolis
Owner/Occupant	Kent Map Reference 42-D-4
Sale Price $ 56,000 Date of Sale 11/02	PROPERTY RIGHTS APPRAISED
Loan charges/concessions to be paid by seller $ -0-	[X] Fee Simple
R.E. Taxes $ 385.20 Tax Year 2002 HOA $/Mo.	[ ] Leasehold
Lender/Client	Daily Planet Mortgage Co. [ ] Condominium (HUD/VA)
	Luther [ ] De Minimis PUD

LENDER DISCRETIONARY USE

Sale Price	$
Date	
Mortgage Amount	$
Mortgage Type	
Discount Points and Other Concessions Paid by Seller	$
Source	

NEIGHBORHOOD

	Urban	Suburban	Rural
LOCATION	[X] Urban	[ ] Suburban	[ ] Rural
BUILT UP	[X] Over 75%	[ ] 25-75%	[ ] Under 25%
GROWTH RATE	[ ] Rapid	[X] Stable	[ ] Slow
PROPERTY VALUES	[ ] Increasing	[X] Stable	[ ] Declining
DEMAND/SUPPLY	[ ] Shortage	[X] In Balance	[ ] Over Supply
MARKETING TIME	[X] Under 3 Mos.	[ ] 3-6 Mos.	[ ] Over 6 Mos.

PRESENT LAND USE	%	LAND USE CHANGE		PREDOMINANT
Single Family	100	Not Likely	[X]	OCCUPANCY
2-4 Family		Likely	[ ]	Owner [X]
Multi-family		In process	[ ]	Tenant [ ]
Commercial		To:		Vacant (0-5%) [X]
Industrial				Vacant (over 5%) [ ]
Vacant				

SINGLE FAMILY HOUSING

PRICE $ (000)	AGE (yrs)
30 Low	60
75 High	120
52.5 Predominant 90	

NEIGHBORHOOD ANALYSIS

	Good	Avg.	Fair	Poor
Employment Stability		[X]		
Convenience to Employment		[X]		
Convenience to Shopping	[X]			
Convenience to Schools	[X]			
Adequacy of Public Transportation		[X]		
Recreation Facilities		[X]		
Adequacy of Utilities		[X]		
Property Compatibility		[X]		
Protection from Detrimental Cond.		[X]		
Police & Fire Protection		[X]		
General Appearance of Properties		[X]		
Appeal to Market		[X]		

Note: Race or the racial composition of the neighborhood are not considered reliable appraisal factors.

COMMENTS: The subject neighborhood is located within the City of Metropolis west of the Farmer's Market Business District. This older urban area of single family homes is convenient to many amenities. A few homes are currently for sale and values have remained stable.

SITE

Dimensions	55.37 x 100	Topography	Level
Site Area	5,537 Sq. Ft. Corner Lot No	Size	Typical
Zoning Classification	Residential Zoning Compliance Yes	Shape	Rectangular
HIGHEST & BEST USE: Present Use X Other Use		Drainage	Adequate

UTILITIES	Public	Other	SITE IMPROVEMENTS	Type	Public	Private
Electricity	[X]		Street	Asphalt	[X]	[ ]
Gas	[X]		Curb/Gutter	Concrete	[X]	[ ]
Water	[X]		Sidewalk	Concrete	[X]	[ ]
Sanitary Sewer	[X]		Street Lights	Overhead	[X]	[ ]
Storm Sewer	[X]		Alley	Asphalt	[X]	[ ]

View	Typical
Landscaping	Average
Driveway	Gravel
Apparent Easements	None
FEMA Flood Hazard	Yes* [ ] No [X]
FEMA* Map/Zone	

COMMENTS (Apparent adverse easements, encroachments, special assessments, slide areas, etc.): An alley runs along the rear lot line. The subject site is generally typical of other sites in the area. No adverse conditions were apparent. Traffic is minimal.

IMPROVEMENTS

GENERAL DESCRIPTION		EXTERIOR DESCRIPTION		FOUNDATION	
Units	One	Foundation	Stone	Slab	
Stories	One	Exterior Walls	Aluminum	Crawl Space	79%
Type (Det./Att.)	Det.	Roof Surface	Shingle	Basement	21%
Design (Style)	1 Story	Gutters & Dwnspts.	Aluminum	Sump Pump	None
Existing	X	Window Type	Vinyl	Dampness	None
Proposed		Storm Sash	Insulated	Settlement	None
Under Construction		Screens	X	Infestation	None
Age (Yrs.)	92	Manufactured House	No		
Effective Age (Yrs.)	23				

BASEMENT		INSULATION	
Area Sq. Ft.	196	Roof	[ ]
% Finished	0	Ceiling	[X]
Ceiling		Walls	[X]
Walls		Floor	[ ]
Floor		None	[ ]
Outside Entry	None	Adequacy	[ ]
		Energy Efficient Items: Windows	

ROOM LIST

ROOMS	Foyer	Living	Dining	Kitchen	Den	Family Rm.	Rec. Rm.	Bedrooms	# Baths	Laundry	Other	Area Sq. Ft.
Basement												
Level 1		X	X	x				2	1		Bkfst.	926
Level 2												

Finished area **above** grade contains: 5 Rooms; 2 Bedroom(s); 1 Bath(s); 926 Square Feet of Gross Living Area

INTERIOR

SURFACES	Materials/Condition
Floors	Carpet/Tile/Avg.
Walls	Plaster/Avg.
Trim/Finish	Wood/Avg.
Bath Floor	Tile/Avg.
Bath Wainscot	Marlite/Avg.
Doors	Wood/Avg.
Fireplace(s)	None #

HEATING	
Type	FA
Fuel	Gas
Condition	Avg.
Adequacy	Avg.
COOLING	
Central	X
Other	
Condition	Good
Adequacy	Avg.

KITCHEN EQUIP.	
Refrigerator	[ ]
Range/Oven	[ ]
Disposal	[X]
Dishwasher	[X]
Fan/Hood	[X]
Compactor	[ ]
Washer/Dryer	[ ]
Microwave	[ ]
Intercom	[ ]

ATTIC	
None	[ ]
Stairs	[ ]
Drop Stair	[ ]
Scuttle	[X]
Floor	[ ]
Heated	[ ]
Finished	[ ]

IMPROVEMENT ANALYSIS	Good	Avg.	Fair	Poor
Quality of Construction		[X]		
Condition of Improvements	[X]			
Room Sizes/Layout Misc.		[X]		
Closets and Storage		[X]		
Energy Efficiency	[X]			
Plumbing-Adequacy & Condition		[X]		
Electrical-Adequacy & Condition		[X]		
Kitchen Cabinets-Adequacy & Cond.	[X]			
Compatibility to Neighborhood		[X]		
Appeal & Marketability		[X]		
Estimated Remaining Economic Life			37	Yrs.
Estimated Remaining Physical Life			58	Yrs.

AUTOS

CAR STORAGE:		
Garage	[X]	Attached [X] Adequate [X] House Entry [X]
No. Cars 2	Carport [ ]	Detached [X] Inadequate [ ] Outside Entry [X]
Condition Avg.	None [ ]	Built-In [ ] Electric Door [ ] Basement Entry [ ]

Additional features: The subject home features new replacement windows and new central air. The exterior is considered to be mostly maintenance-free. Porch 11 x 6; Enclosed porch 11 x 5. The interior is very clean.

Depreciation (Physical, functional and external inadequacies, repairs needed, modernization, etc.): The kitchen has been remodeled. Access to the bathroom is through the bedroom. Two-bedroom homes are common within the subject market area. As of the date of inspection, no needed repairs were noted for the subject.

COMMENTS

General market conditions and prevalence and impact in subject/market area regarding loan discounts, interest buydowns and concessions: General market conditions are considered to be good with most homes selling in less than three months. Sales concessions are not widespread and their impact is considered to be minimal.

EXHIBIT 10.1 SAMPLE UNIFORM RESIDENTIAL APPRAISAL REPORT (PAGE 2)

Valuation Section **UNIFORM RESIDENTIAL APPRAISAL REPORT** File No. _____

Purpose of Appraisal is to estimate Market Value as defined in the Certification & Statement of Limiting Conditions.

COST APPROACH

BUILDING SKETCH (SHOW GROSS LIVING AREA ABOVE GRADE)
If for Freddie Mac or Fannie Mae, show only square foot calculations and cost approach comments in this space.

```
     2 x 19 =    38
    12 x 30 =   360
    14 x 37 =   518
     2 x  5 =    10

     TOTAL     926 Sq. Ft.
```

Functional: Bathroom located off bedroom.

(Not Required by Freddie Mac and Fannie Mae)
Does property conform to applicable HUD/VA property standards? [X] Yes [ ] No
If No, explain: _____

ESTIMATED REPRODUCTION COST – NEW – OF IMPROVEMENTS:

Dwelling 926 Sq. Ft. @ $ 68.00	= $	63,000
_____ Sq. Ft. @ $ _____	= $	
Extras Central air, Kit. Appl.	=	2,300
	=	
Special Energy Efficient Items Windows	=	1,900
Porches, Patios, etc. Encl. Porch	=	1,000
Garage/Carport 396 Sq. Ft. @ $ 10.00	=	4,000
Total Estimated Cost New	= $	72,200

	Physical	Functional	External		
Less Depreciation	27,400	500	---	= $	27,900
Depreciated Value of Improvements				= $	44,300
Site Imp. "as is" (driveway, landscaping, etc.)				= $	2,400
ESTIMATED SITE VALUE				= $	9,500
(If leasehold, show only leasehold value.)					
INDICATED VALUE BY COST APPROACH				= $	56,200

Construction Warranty [ ] Yes [X] No
Name of Warranty Program _____
Warranty Coverage Expires _____

SALES COMPARISON ANALYSIS

The undersigned has recited three recent sales of properties most similar and proximate to subject and has considered these in the market analysis. The description includes a dollar adjustment, reflecting market reaction to those items of significant variation between the subject and comparable properties. If a significant item in the comparable property is superior to, or more favorable than, the subject property, a minus (–) adjustment is made, thus reducing the indicated value of subject; if a significant item in the comparable is inferior to, or less favorable than, the subject property, a plus (+) adjustment is made, thus increasing the indicated value of the subject.

ITEM	SUBJECT	COMPARABLE NO. 1	+ (–) $ Adjustment	COMPARABLE NO. 2	+ (–) $ Adjustment	COMPARABLE NO. 3	+ (–) $ Adjustment
Address	415 Cape Ave.	429 Super Way		1112 Krypton Blvd.		809 Jimmy Street	
Proximity to Subject		1 Mile S. E.		1 Mile S. E.		1½ Mile East	
Sales Price	$ 56,000	$ 56,500		$ 55,000		$ 53,000	
Price/Gross Liv. Area	$ 60.48	$ 48.71		$ 47.74		$ 47.45	
Data Source	Inspection	MLS/PACE		MLS/PACE		Files/PACE	
VALUE ADJUSTMENTS	DESCRIPTION	DESCRIPTION	+ (–) $ Adjustment	DESCRIPTION	+ (–) $ Adjustment	DESCRIPTION	+ (–) $ Adjustment
Sales or Financing Concessions		Conv.		FHA	–1000	FHA	–900
Date of Sale/Time	11/02	7/02		8/02		7/02	
Location	Metropolis	Metropolis		Metropolis		Metropolis	
Site/View	55x100/Typ.	42x120/Typ.		50x150/Typ.	–1000	.2 Ac/typ.	–2000
Design and Appeal	1 Story/Avg.	1 Story/Avg.		1 Story/Avg.		1 Story/Avg.	
Quality of Construction	Alum./Avg.	Vinyl/Avg.		Alum./Avg.		Alum./Avg.	
Age	92 years	62 years		69 years		92 years	
Condition	Good	Good		Good		Good	
Above Grade Room Count	Total 5 | Bdrms 2 | Baths 1	Total 5 | Bdrms 2 | Baths 1		Total 4 | Bdrms 2 | Baths 1		Total 4 | Bdrms 2 | Baths 1	
Gross Living Area	926 Sq. Ft.	1160 Sq. Ft.	–3000	1152 Sq. Ft.	–2500	1117 Sq. Ft.	–2500
Basement & Finished Rooms Below Grade	Pt. Bsmt. Unfinished	Pt. Bsmt. Unfinished		Full Bsmt. Unfinished	–2000	Pt. Bsmt. Unfinished	
Functional Utility	Avg./Misc.	Average	–500	Average	–500	Average	–500
Heating/Cooling	FA/AC	FA/AC		FA/AC		FA/None	+1000
Garage/Carport	2 car	2 car(larger)	–500	1 car plus	+500	1 car plus	+500
Porches, Patio, Pools, etc.	Porch Encl. Porch	Porch	+500	Porch	+500	Porch	+500
Special Energy Efficient Items	Replacement windows	Storm windows	+1000	Storm windows	+1000	Storm windows	+1000
Fireplace(s)	None	None		None		None	
Other (e.g. kitchen equip., remodeling)	Extras & Updating	Sim. Extras Less Remod.	+3000	Sim. Extras Less Remod.	+3000	Sim. Extras Less Remod.	+2500
Net Adj. (total)		[X] + [ ] – $ 500		[ ] + [X] – $ 2,000		[ ] + [X] – $ 400	
Indicated Value of Subject		$ 57,000		$ 53,000		$ 52,600	

Comments on Sales Comparison: Comparable One was an estate sale. All three comparables are 2-Bedroom homes from the subject market area. They offer similar utility as the subject and are reliable indicators of value.

INDICATED VALUE BY SALES COMPARISON APPROACH .... $ 56,000

INDICATED VALUE BY INCOME APPROACH (If Applicable) Estimated Market Rent $ _____ /Mo. x Gross Rent Multiplier _____ = $ N/A

This appraisal is made [X] "as is" [ ] subject to the repairs, alterations, inspections or conditions listed below [ ] completion per plans and specifications.

Comments and Conditions of Appraisal: Based upon the subjects overall good condition, a value estimate near the top of the value range is justified.

Final Reconciliation: The Sales Comparison Approach most closely reflects the thinking of the typical purchaser and is considered the best indication of value. The Cost Approach is demonstrated and is used primarily as a check for the Sales Comparison Approach.

RECONCILIATION

This appraisal is based upon the above requirements, the certification, contingent and limiting conditions, and Market Value definition that are stated in

[ ] FmHA, HUD &/or VA instructions.
[X] Freddie Mac Form 439 (Rev. 7/86)/Fannie Mae Form 1004B (Rev. 7/86) filed with client _____ 20____ [X] attached.

I (WE) ESTIMATE THE MARKET VALUE, AS DEFINED, OF THE SUBJECT PROPERTY AS OF December 2, 2002 to be $ 56,000

I (We) certify: that to the best of my (our) knowledge and belief the facts and data used herein are true and correct; that I (we) personally inspected the subject property, both inside and out, and have made an exterior inspection of all comparable sales cited in this report; and that I (we) have no undisclosed interest, present or prospective therein.

APPRAISER(S)
Signature Karil S. This
Name Karil S. This, SRA

REVIEW APPRAISER
(if applicable) Signature _____
Name _____
[ ] Did [ ] Did Not Inspect Property

FIRREA allows licensed appraisers for transactions involving residential, one-to-four-unit properties valued up to $1 million. FIRREA requires a licensed appraiser to have at least two years of appraisal experience (using a standard of 1,000 hours per year), and seventy-five hours of education (most states require that fifteen of the hours cover professional appraisal practice and ethics). In addition, appraisers must pass a uniform state examination in order to be licensed. FIRREA also requires appraisers to take a minimum of ten classroom hours of continuing education for license renewal.

FIRREA allows certified appraisers to appraise all types of real estate. Because these can include more complex transactions than those in which a licensed appraiser may be involved, minimum certification standards are more stringent than licensing requirements. In addition to two years of appraisal experience, FIRREA mandates that a certified appraiser have at least one year of the experience in nonresidential appraisal practice. The minimum education requirement for certification is 165 hours (under certain circumstances, a college degree may substitute for the 165 hours). FIRREA also requires appraisers to pass a uniform state examination for certification. Although the certification examination is more rigorous than the licensing examination, both exams cover: appraisal topics, real estate instruments, real estate law, real estate financing, and an appraisal code of ethics. Minimum continuing education requirements, identical to those for a licensed appraiser, are also required for certification renewal. All states have enacted legislation that meets FIRREA minimums and some have enacted legislation that extends coverage to transactions not covered by FIRREA such as for insurance or estate purposes.

Decision Point

You are contemplating paying $900,000 for a twenty-unit apartment building. To gain some assurance that you do not offer too much for the property you decide to hire an appraiser. The financial institution you have contacted informs you that they may be able to use the appraisal in processing your loan application. Assuming that this is your wish, what type of appraiser should you employ?

MARKET VALUE AND MARKET PRICE

Value is usually defined in terms of the relationship between an asset and the person who desires it. Value can also be thought of as the ability of one commodity to command another in exchange, or as the worth or importance of an object. In the Uniform Standards **market value** is defined as "the most probable price that a property should bring in a competitive open market under all conditions requisite to a fair sale, the buyer and seller each acting prudently and knowledgeably, and assuming the price is not affected by undue stimulus." Note that the word "price" is used in the definition of market value. An important point to remember, however, is that market value does not necessarily equal **market price,** which is the price for which the property actually sells. Theoretically, the two should be identical; differences between the two, however, are not unusual. If, for example, a seller decides that time is more valuable than the difference between an offer and market value, the seller may decide to accept a price lower than market value to facilitate the transaction.

BASIC PRINCIPLES OF VALUE

In formulating their estimate of market value, appraisers use the valuation principles described in the following sections. Some of these principles stem from observation and analysis of real estate investment experience; others are simply basic economic principles appropriate for the appraisal of real property.

SUBSTITUTION PRINCIPLE

In most real estate markets, one property may provide similar income or utility compared to another property. This fact is captured in the substitution principle, which holds that the maximum value of a property is equal to the cost of acquiring an equally desirable substitute property, assuming one would not encounter costly delays in acquiring the substitute. In essence, the substitution principle recognizes that real estate consumers have options, and that a prudent party will pay no more for a property than would be paid for an existing substitute, or the cost of building a like structure. The substitution principle dictates, for example, that a house with a market value of $80,000 is not worth $86,000 because buyers have the option to purchase a house with slightly more desirable features for $82,000, or slightly less desirable features for $79,000.

The substitutability of real estate is an important element in analyzing market data and in estimating market value. In fact, substitutability gives appraisers another way in which to define a particular market. Assuming that prices reflect differences in utility accurately, if buyers are not willing to substitute one property for the other, then the properties are in different submarkets. A house in Lincoln, Nebraska, for example, may not be a good substitute for one located in Omaha. Therefore, the houses are in different submarkets. Within either city, however, a house in one neighborhood may be deemed a good substitute for another house located in a different neighborhood.

PRINCIPLE OF ANTICIPATION

The principle of anticipation holds that the current market value of a property is based on the present value of the future benefits of ownership. This principle is especially important in valuing income property, where the value of the property is determined by discounting the future cash flows the property is expected to generate by an appropriate rate to arrive at the present value of those cash flows. Of course, the value that individuals attach to a particular property may vary, either because the individuals estimate different benefits, discount future benefits at different rates, or because they would put the property to different uses.

A thorough appraisal will include an estimate of value based on the current use and an estimate based on the highest and best use if it differs from the current use. The **highest and best use** can be defined as the use that results in the highest present value of the property (Chapter 17). In an efficient market all property is put to its highest and best use. Recognizing that real estate markets are not perfectly efficient, however, the Uniform Standards state: two separate highest and best uses exist: one for the site as though vacant, and one for the site as though improved. The first looks through the building as though it did not exist and estimates the best use of the site as though it were vacant. The second estimates the best use of the site and building(s) with all improvements together.

PRINCIPLE OF CONTRIBUTION

Appraisers must be skilled in estimating how much the buildings or other improvements contribute to a property's market value. In making such evaluations, appraisers follow the principle of contribution that holds that the component parts of real property assume value according to how much they contribute to the market value of the entire property. The value of a component is not necessarily equal to its cost. To illustrate, consider a homeowner who adds a sauna room that costs $25,000. The addition of the sauna does not necessarily increase the market value of the home by $25,000. Instead, the value of the sauna depends on the additional amount buyers are willing to pay for a house with a sauna. An addition may increase the value of the property by an amount equal to or greater than its cost, but in many cases the value added by an addition is less than its cost. It is possible that an addition may even reduce property value. For example, the addition of a swimming pool to a home site may reduce the property value, especially if the lot is located in a neighborhood populated by families with small children.

PRINCIPLE OF DIMINISHING RETURNS

Related to the principle of contribution is the principle of diminishing returns, which recognizes that, after a certain point, additional improvements to a property will increase the value of the property by smaller and smaller amounts. To illustrate this principle, consider a single-family home without any garage. The addition of a one-car garage is likely to increase the value of the property. The addition of a two-car garage may increase the property value even more, however, the incremental value of the second space may be less than the incremental value of adding the one-car garage. Continuing the example, assume that the owner continues to add garages; imagine the contribution to property value that results from the addition of the seventeenth garage!

PRINCIPLE OF COMPETITION

The principle of competition recognizes the fact that, over time, competitive forces tend to reduce abnormally high profits. The principle of competition applies to all competitive markets, including real estate markets. Competition takes place at two levels—existing properties compete with each other, and existing properties compete with newly developed properties. If a particular type of property earns unusually high profits, these profits will attract new entries into the market, thereby increasing the supply, and driving profits down to equilibrium levels. New constructions will include the features currently desired by consumers and may incorporate state-of-the-art technology that tends to put older properties at a disadvantage. In estimating the value of new or existing properties, appraisers must recognize this fact and adjust for unusually high temporary profits. Appraisers should, however, support such adjustments by evidence of market trends.

PRINCIPLE OF PROPORTIONALITY

The principle of proportionality, sometimes called the principle of balance, states that for each property there is an optimum combination of improvements and land that maximizes value. The value of a particular property may suffer because the owner does not follow this principle. In essence, real estate can be under- or over-improved. It would not be appropriate, for example, to construct a one-story, eight-unit apartment if the site could be developed and rented as a 100-unit apartment building. Similarly, it would not make good financial sense to invest large sums building a 4,000-unit self-storage facility when demand for such facilities over the foreseeable future is only a small fraction of that amount.

The principle of proportionality suggests that there is some optimum proportion of elements that meets consumer preferences in land use and building design. In estimating the value of a property, the appraiser must make judgments on the ideal use of the property. For example, demand is likely to be low for a one-bedroom, 1,000-square-foot, single-family home with five bathrooms. Demand is also likely to be low for the hypothetical single-family home surrounded by seventeen garages. Appraisers might describe such properties by stating that the elements of the property are not in balance, and the value estimate of such properties would be lowered to account for the imbalance.

PRINCIPLE OF CONFORMITY

Related to the principle of proportionality is the principle of conformity, which holds that the value of a property is positively related to the degree of harmony between it and surrounding properties. For example, as a dwelling, a single-family home is more valuable if located in a neighborhood of other single-family homes rather than in an area dominated by industrial or commercial properties. Similarly, an expensive home is likely to have less value if it is located in a neighborhood of modest homes.

PRINCIPLE OF CHANGE

The principle of change recognizes that real estate values are subject to supply and demand factors that are in a continual state of evolution. Like most assets, the value of real estate is positively related to the level of demand for it, and negatively related to its supply. The demand for real estate for a particular use depends on factors such as: population, income, employment, family size, age of head of household, savings levels, and real property prices. The supply of real property is also affected by numerous factors, including: the number and size of the existing units, the number of similar (or substitute) units being constructed, zoning ordinances, building codes, the type and availability of financing, and real property prices. Appraisers must estimate both the direction and degree of any change in such factors, and the impact of these changes on market value. To accomplish this, appraisers must conduct, or update, a market analysis as described in Chapter 20.

STEPS IN THE APPRAISAL PROCESS

The appraisal of real property is facilitated if the appraiser follows a systematic approach. Because planning facilitates most tasks, the first step in the appraisal process is to plan the appraisal. To plan the appraisal, the appraiser must identify several factors: the reason for the appraisal, the character of the subject property (the particular property being appraised), the character of the market in which the subject property is located, and the data that will be needed to complete the appraisal. In addition, the appraiser should estimate the time and expense required to complete the appraisal. An appraiser requires a clear statement of the type of value being sought because this may affect the value estimate. For example, the value of a particular property may be quite different for an eminent domain condemnation proceeding compared with a value derived for insurance purposes. The character of the property includes not only the type of property and the use to which it is put, but also the property rights to which the owner is entitled. Identifying the character of the market requires the appraiser to identify both the submarket in which the subject property belongs, and the relevant economic, environmental, and social factors mentioned earlier.

A physical inspection of the property enables the appraiser to verify the number and quality of various characteristics (e.g., number of rooms, type of building materials, and condition of the property) present in the subject property. It may also reinforce or modify the appraiser's opinion regarding the necessary market data that must be assembled to make the appraisal. Market data may be secured from a number of sources, including: public records, real estate agents, other appraisers, mortgage lenders, the local chamber of commerce, planning and zoning authorities, and suppliers of building materials and equipment.

Once the appraiser assembles and studies all the data, he or she must reach a value decision. The approaches appraisers use to make a value decision are the subject of the following section. Finally, the appraiser presents the value estimate on the appraisal report, and submits the report to his or her client.

APPROACHES USED IN APPRAISING REAL PROPERTY

Real estate appraisers use three basic approaches to estimate value: the sales comparison approach, the cost approach, and the income approach. The Uniform Standards dictate that appraisers use at least two of the three approaches to support their final value estimate. The value estimate the appraiser derives from each approach is based on unique information. The approaches are similar, however, in that the information used in each is market-derived. With the cost approach, current market costs of the components comprising the property are a key element. Under the sales comparison approach, the value estimate stems from the value of similar properties as determined by recent market transactions. The "income" used in the income approach is based on the market demand for the product or service provided by the real property as reflected by current or potential market rents.

SALES COMPARISON APPROACH

Several steps are involved in the **sales comparison approach,** also known as the market approach or the direct sales comparison approach. First, the appraiser identifies several (at least three for residential appraisals) recently sold properties that are similar in character and utility to the subject property. These are referred to as **comparables,** or "comps." Appraisers frequently identify comparables using data they obtain from individual real estate brokers or multiple listing services, but a number of other sources are also available. Sources of data for all three appraisal approaches are shown in Exhibit 10.2.

Next, the appraiser adjusts the sale price of each comparable to account for differences between it and the subject property. If a comparable has a more desirable feature than the subject property, such as an extra room or a fireplace, the appraiser adjusts the comparable sale price downward by the value of the feature. If the subject property has a more desirable feature than the comparable, the appraiser increases the comparable sale price by the value of the feature. Finally, the appraiser uses the adjusted sale prices of the comparables as a guide to estimate the value of the subject property.

The importance of the substitution principle in the sales comparison approach should be obvious. In essence, the approach holds that the market value of the subject property should closely approximate the market value of a comparable property plus or minus any adjustments. Evidence of a comp's market value is provided by its recent sale price.

The middle portion of the second page of the appraisal report in Exhibit 10.1 illustrates the sales comparison approach. Note that the adjusted sale prices for the three comparables are not identical, and that the appraiser's estimate of value based on the sales comparison is not simply an arithmetic exercise [i.e., $56,000 does not equal ($57,000 + $53,000 + $52,600) ÷ 3]. Instead, the appraiser exercises his or her best judgment to reconcile the adjusted comparable sale prices.

Adjustments to the comparable sale price can be based on the cost of the feature or on market-determined values, which are now widely used by property tax assessors and are increasingly being used by independent appraisers. These values are determined by loading recent transaction information into a computer and using regression analysis. Specifically, sale prices are regressed against various property characteristics, such as: lot size, living area, number of rooms, structure design, construction materials, number of garage stalls, fireplaces, and location. The estimated coefficients for each characteristic show the implied value of the characteristic. Appraisers generally place great reliance on the sales comparison approach, especially when valuing residential properties. Sometimes, however, lack of good comps makes it difficult or impossible for appraisers to use this approach. Similar properties may be scarce, or unavailable, for properties such as a truly unique home, or for special purpose properties like a school, or a fire station. In other cases, either slow markets or a remote property location may force the appraiser to use comps that are not in close proximity to the subject property or ones that sold some time ago. In these cases, an appraiser may have to make adjustments to account for locational differences or inflation, thereby diminishing his or her reliance on the approach.

Financing concessions can also complicate the appraiser's task because they may distort the selling price. Examples of situations that could result in an increased sales price include a transaction where: part or all of the closing costs are paid by the seller, a low interest rate loan is used, or the buyer makes a lower than usual downpayment. The type of financing a purchaser uses to acquire the property can also affect the sales price. Mortgage lenders should assist appraisers by providing them with as much information about the transaction as possible, including information about any financing concessions and the type of financing to be employed. Note, on page one of the appraisal report in Exhibit 10.1, that in this case the appraiser did receive some financing information.

COST APPROACH

Under the **cost approach,** the appraiser must determine the total cost required to produce a property that provides the same utility as the subject property. This does not necessarily mean reproduction of an exact replica of the existing structure. For older structures it may not be feasible to reproduce a property. The materials and design used in many older buildings may be more costly and/or less efficient than what is available or required today. There are four basic steps involved in the cost approach. First, the appraiser must estimate the value of the land. Second, the appraiser must estimate the current cost to produce the improvements on the land. In calculating these costs, the appraiser must include both direct costs, such as labor, supplies, and profits, and indirect costs such as fees, financing costs, and taxes. Third, the appraiser must determine any loss in value, or **depreciation,** of the subject property and subtract it from the current production cost. Finally, the appraiser determines the appraised value of the subject property by adding the value of the land to the adjusted production cost.

The upper right-hand portion of the second page of the appraisal report in Exhibit 10.1 shows the estimate of value for the subject property based on the cost method.

Estimating the Cost of Improvements

Appraisers may select from a number of methods to estimate production costs, including quantity survey, unit-in-place, comparative unit, construction-cost manuals, and cost indexing. The appraiser selects a particular method based on the value and type of property, common practice in the area, or the client's preference. Those clients with a preference should express it before the appraisal begins.

The most detailed, accurate, and expensive manner by which an appraiser may estimate costs is known as the quantity survey method. With this method, the appraiser bases the cost estimate on a list of prices for materials and their cost, labor cost, and the contractor's overhead and profit. Contractors use this method extensively to prepare bids for proposed construction projects. The quantity survey does, however, require a great deal of skill, and the expense involved in generating the estimate is not justified for most appraisal assignments.

The unit-in-place method, also known as the segregated cost method, requires less time, detail, and expense compared to the quantity survey. Under this method, the appraiser classifies the subject property into components, such as parking areas, floors, walls, roofs, electrical systems, and plumbing systems. Next, the appraiser calculates the unit price for each component on either a square, linear, or cubic footage basis. The appraiser then estimates total production cost by multiplying the quantity of each component in the subject property by its unit price.

A third method, the comparative unit method, provides reasonably accurate production cost estimates, and requires less technical knowledge of construction practices compared with the methods discussed previously. For these reasons, the comparative unit method is the most widely used by appraisers. Under this method, an appraiser estimates production cost by determining the cost (or, keeping the principle of substitution in mind, the sale price) of recently constructed buildings, similar in nature, and located in the same market as the subject, expressed as a unit cost such as cost per square foot. For example, suppose an appraiser must estimate the production cost of a 10,000 square foot commercial property the appraiser has identified three recently constructed (or sold) properties that are similar to the subject property.

Estimating Construction Cost with the Comparative Unit Method

Property	Square Feet	Cost/Square Foot
Subject	10,000	?
Comp1	9,000	$15.00
Comp 2	10,000	15.50
Comp 3	10,600	14.75

Based on the comparable properties cost per square foot, the appraiser decides that $15.08 represents the average cost per square foot of such properties and, therefore, concludes that the production cost of the subject property is $150,800 ($15.08 × 10,000).

Cost Manuals   Appraisers can secure production cost estimates by using cost data from published manuals. Several organizations publish current construction cost data for different types of properties in selected cities. A partial list of these organizations is shown in Exhibit 10.2. Appraisers must exercise care when using cost manuals because the costs in them represent the average cost for standard building types. Regardless, appraisers have found several uses for the information. They use cost manuals frequently to estimate costs for complex, special-purpose buildings for which comparable properties are scarce or nonexistent. Appraisers also use the data in the manuals to verify the reasonableness of cost estimates derived by another method. Finally, the information contained in a construction cost manual may assist the appraiser in using the cost indexing method of estimating reproduction costs.

Cost Indexing   If the appraiser knows the date and original construction cost of the subject property, the appraiser may employ the cost indexing method. Under this method, the appraiser estimates current production cost by multiplying the original construction costs by a cost index reflecting the change in construction costs since the original construction occurred. To illustrate, consider the task of estimating reproduction costs in 2003 for a 20,000-square-foot building that cost $11.25 per square foot to build in 1989. A cost manual lists construction costs for this size and type of building as $11 per square foot in 1989, and $24 in 2003. Therefore, the 1989/2003 cost index is 2.182 (1 + [($24 − $11) ÷ $11]). The appraiser could use the $24 figure from the 2003 manual to estimate current total production cost at $480,000 ($24 × 20,000). However, the cost indexing method enables the appraiser to assume that cost differentials that existed at the time of construction persist. Using the cost indexing method, the cost is estimated at $490,950 ($11.25 × 2.182 × 20,000).

Decision Point

Using the cost indexing method, estimate 2003 reproduction costs in the above example assuming that the 1989 construction cost of the subject property was $10.75 instead of $11.25.

| EXHIBIT | 10.2 | **SOURCES OF APPRAISAL INFORMATION** |

Sales Comparison Approach

Residential dwellings:

- Residential real estate brokers and MLS
- Property developers and subdividers
- Mortgage loan originators
- Registrar of deeds
- Tax assessors

Commercial property:

- Commercial real estate brokers and MLS
- Chambers of commerce
- Mortgage originators
- Tax assessors

Industrial property:

- Industrial real estate brokers and MLS
- Chambers of commerce
- City planning departments
- Industrial development departments
- State development departments
- Tax assessors

Cost Approach

Marshall Valuation Service. Marshall and Swift Publication Company. Los Angeles, California.
Residential Cost Handbook. Marshall and Swift Publication Company. Los Angeles, California

Income Approach

Statements supplied by the current owner
Property management companies
Utility companies
Dollars & Cents of Shopping Centers. Urban Land Institute. Washington, D.C.
Downtown and Suburban Office Building Experience Exchange Report. Building Owners and Managers Association International. Washington, D.C.

Estimating Depreciation

For all but the newest of structures, an appraiser must ordinarily adjust production costs downward for one or more types of depreciation: physical, functional, or external. Physical depreciation is a reduction in property value due to an impairment of the physical condition of the property. Such depreciation may be caused by ordinary wear and tear, by the action of physical elements such as wind and rain, or by a catastrophic event. Examples of physical depreciation would include: worn carpeting, cracks in walls or ceilings, or an old leaky roof. Functional depreciation describes decreases in property value that may be caused by changes in technology, design, or consumer preferences. Examples of functional depreciation include: an outdated floor plan, unusually small rooms, inadequate insulation, obsolete electrical wiring, and poor window placement. External depreciation, also known as economic depreciation, environmental obsolescence, or locational obsolescence, is a loss of value caused by factors outside of the property itself. Examples of situations in which external obsolescence is likely to occur include: a zoning change that adversely affects the subject property value, a residence with a commercial property built next to it, a commercial property where new highway construction results in more difficult access, or a well-maintained house in a deteriorating neighborhood.

Physical and functional depreciation can be further classified into one of two categories: curable and incurable. Curable depreciation describes any loss in value that can be corrected at a reasonable cost. Examples of curable depreciation are a leaky roof that may be fixed with new shingles or a high ceiling that may be lowered to a more energy efficient height. If depreciation is curable, appraisers usually use the cost of curing it as their estimate of depreciation. Incurable depreciation is the deterioration or functional obsolescence of an improvement that is economically infeasible to repair. An example of incurable depreciation is the inability to justify the cost needed to correct an outdated architectural design. The amount of incurable depreciation is calculated by the present value of the loss in rental income due to the incurable item. Because a property owner may have little, or no, control over nearby negative influences on the value of the subject property, external depreciation is almost always incurable.

The major weakness of the cost approach is the fact that cost does not necessarily equal value. A prime example of cost not being equal to value is the Phoenician Hotel in Arizona. The hotel is a beautiful facility, and it should be—it cost more than $500,000 per room to construct. Federal regulators, who confiscated the hotel from a failed savings and loan company, estimate that to break-even, rooms would have to be occupied more than 70 percent of the time at $500 per night.

Another weakness of the cost approach concerns the estimation of depreciation. Because the estimation is subjective and estimation of the replacement cost of older structures may be difficult, the cost approach is best suited for the appraisal of relatively new buildings.

There are, however, cases in which the cost approach is the most appropriate appraisal method. For example, for existing special purpose buildings, such as a school or a church, that do not produce income, the income approach (discussed next) may not work well. Likewise, these types of properties are not sold frequently so it may be difficult or impossible to locate comparable sales needed for the sales comparison approach.

INCOME APPROACH

The **income approach** is based on the idea that a property's worth is largely a function of the present value of any future income the property generates. The income approach is most appropriate for properties that can, or do, produce predictable annual income, such as apartment complexes, office buildings, and shopping centers. As suggested above, appraisers may also be forced to use this approach for other property types if there are few comparable sales, or if the cost method is inappropriate because it would not be economically feasible to replace the current structure.

Several basic steps are involved in the income approach. First, the appraiser must estimate annual potential gross income. Depending on conditions, the estimate may not be the same as present or past annual gross income, and the appraiser must adjust the estimate to account for estimated vacancies. Second, the appraiser must estimate annual operating expenses. Again, this estimate may be different from past or present expenses. Third, the appraiser subtracts expenses from income to determine **net operating income.** Finally, the appraiser converts estimated net operating income into an estimate of property value through a process known as capitalization.

To illustrate the income approach, assume an apartment building contains ten units that rent for $500 per month, and that over the last several years, the vacancy rate for this and similar apartment buildings has averaged 5 percent. After analyzing the market, the appraiser determines that rents and vacancies are not expected to change. **Potential gross income** is the income that the property would generate if it were rented completely. In this case, annual potential gross income equals $60,000 ($500 × 10 units × 12 months). Subtracting a $3,000 allowance for vacancies ($60,000 × .05) from potential gross income yields **effective gross income** of $57,000. Based on the appraiser's analysis, this is the amount of income that the property should generate if competently managed.

The appraiser estimates annual operating expenses (not including debt service and income taxes) to be $27,000. The appraiser may obtain information about operating expenses from several sources; some are listed in Exhibit 10.2. The appraiser then subtracts operating expenses from effective gross income to yield **net operating income** (NOI) of $30,000. A simplified statement of net operating income for the subject property, therefore, looks like the following.

Potential Gross Income	$60,000
Less: Vacancy allowance	3,000
Effective gross income	$57,000
Operating expenses	27,000
Net Operating Income	$30,000

Once the subject property's NOI has been estimated, the appraiser estimates the property's value by capitalizing NOI, that is dividing NOI by a **capitalization rate.** While a number of definitions exist for the capitalization rate, we prefer to define it as the rate of return required to attract investment dollars to a real estate project. Assume that ten percent is the appropriate rate of return in this case. Therefore, the value of the property is $300,000.

$$\text{Estimated property value} = \text{NOI} \div \text{capitalization rate}$$
$$\$300,000 = \$30,000 \div .10$$

Before demonstrating how appraisers calculate a capitalization rate, we stress two points. First, appraisers use the capitalization technique just demonstrated most frequently, and it is known as direct capitalization. Implicit in this technique is the assumption that the return generated by the property is attributed proportionately to the land (a nondepreciating asset) and the improvements (a depreciating asset). While this assumption is valid in many cases, it is not always appropriate. When such an assumption is not justified, other capitalization techniques, which consider the value of the land and improvements separately, are available. These techniques, which are beyond the scope of this text, include the building residual technique, and the mortgage residual technique. Second, by capitalizing the estimated NOI for a single year, as is done under direct capitalization and other techniques, the appraiser is assuming that NOI is a perpetuity. In essence, the appraiser assumes that the estimated NOI will repeat year after year, however, this may be an invalid assumption.

DETERMINING THE CAPITALIZATION RATE

Selection of the capitalization rate, or "cap rate," to be used in appraising a particular property is critical because small differences in the rate may result in dramatically different estimates of property value. To illustrate, consider the values in the following highlighted material. In examining these figures, you will also note the inverse relationship between the cap rate and estimated value.

Sensitivity of Estimated Property to The Capitalization Rate

(Assuming Net operating income equals $30,000)

Cap Rate	Value Estimate	Cap Rate	Value Estimate
8.5	$352,941	10.0	$300,000
9.0	333,333	10.5	285,714
9.5	315,789	11.0	272,727

Appraisers can use several methods to determine the cap rate. Some of the more popular methods to determine the cap rate are: band-of-investment, market comparison, and the debt coverage ratio.

Band-of-Investment

Using the band-of-investment method, the capitalization rate is a weighted average of the yield earned by all suppliers of funds used to acquire the property. To illustrate the method, assume that a property will be financed with an 80 percent loan-to-value, thirty-year, 9 percent mortgage loan, and the investor's required return is 18 percent. Given this information, the appropriate capitalization rate is 11.324 percent.

Calculating the Cap Rate Using the Band-of-Investment Method

Share Interest	Weight	×	Yield	=	Weighted yield
Lender	.80		.0965		.07724
Equity owner	.20		.18		.036
Overall capitalization rate					.11324 = 11.324%

The weights used in the above calculation are straightforward; the lender is supplying 80 percent of the funds, and the purchaser 20 percent. The lender's yield, .0965, is equal to the annual mortgage constant (AMC) associated with the loan. One can calculate the AMC by multiplying the monthly mortgage constant by twelve. The monthly mortgage constant (MMC), .008046, is simply the reciprocal of the appropriate present value of an annuity interest factor (1 ÷ 124.28187, see Chapter 17).

$$Lenders\ yield = AMC$$
$$Where:$$
$$AMC = MMC \times 12$$
$$= (1 \div PVIFA) \times 12$$
$$= (1 \div 124.28187) \times 12$$
$$= .008046 \times 12$$
$$= .0965$$

The equity holder's yield is based on the return a prudent investor would require given the risk associated with the investment. Note that the equity holder's yield is higher than the lender's in the above example. This should always be the case because the equity holder's risk is greater than the lender's. The investor is only entitled to the residual cash flows after he or she makes payments to the lender.

Finally, each capital supplier's yield is multiplied by the appropriate weight, and the combination of the weighted yields results in the overall capitalization rate of 11.324 percent. Note that this capitalization rate is independent of the dollar amount borrowed, and could be used to capitalize any property's NOI as long as it is being financed with an 80 percent loan-to-value, thirty-year, 9 percent interest rate loan.

AN ETHICAL ISSUE
APPRAISALS

A financial institution that will be providing most of the money for the purchase of a house has asked an appraiser to appraise the house. As it turns out, the house is owned by a relative of the appraiser. Do you think the appraiser should reveal this fact to the financial institution? If so, when? If not, why? Do you think such an omission is really important if the mortgage originator plans to sell the loan to an unknown company located in another state?

Market Comparison

Using the market comparison method, the appraiser first identifies recently sold properties that are similar to the subject property with regard to location, property characteristics, and net operating income generated. The appraiser can then calculate the capitalization rate to be used in valuing the subject property by dividing the sale price of the comparable by the comparable's net operating income. Assume, for example, that a comparable property that generates $29,000 in net operating income, recently sold for $285,000. The capitalization rate implied by this transaction is 10.18 percent ($29,000 ÷ $285,000).

Debt Coverage Ratio

Under the debt coverage ratio method, the capitalization rate shows the relationship of net operating income to annual debt service. Specifically, the capitalization rate is calculated using the following formula.

$$\text{Capitalization rate} = \text{DCR} \times \text{AMC} \times \text{LVR}$$
Where:
$$\text{DCR} = \text{debt coverage ratio}$$
$$\text{AMC} = \text{annual mortgage constant, and}$$
$$\text{LVR} = \text{loan-to-value ratio.}$$

The debt coverage ratio is derived by dividing net operating income by the debt service.

To illustrate the debt coverage ratio method, continue to assume that the subject property will be financed with an 80 percent loan-to-value ratio, thirty-year, 9 percent, fixed-rate mortgage loan; and that $300,000 is being paid for the property. Therefore, we know that the annual mortgage constant is .09655 (calculated above). With an 80-percent loan-to-value- ratio, the loan amount is $240,000, and the annual debt service equals $23,173.13 [($240,000 ÷ 124.281866) × 12]. The debt coverage ratio, therefore, is 1.2946.

$$\text{DCR} = \text{NOI} \div \text{debt service}$$
$$1.2946 = \$30,000 \div \$23,173.13 \text{ and the capitalization rate}$$
Based on the debt coverage ratio method the capitalization rate equals 10 percent.
$$\text{Capitalization rate} = \text{DCR} \times \text{AMC} \times \text{LVR}$$
$$.10 = 1.2946 \times .09655 \times .80$$

RECONCILIATION OF VALUE

The appraiser's final task in estimating property value is to consolidate the estimated values derived under the sales comparison, cost, and income approaches into a single number. This process, known as reconciliation of value, or correlation of value, is not a simple mathematical exercise; it involves the exercise of judgment and analysis. In most cases, the estimates of value derived by the three approaches should be similar. If substantial differences exist, the appraiser must review the data gathering method and analysis for each approach. If the estimates remain widely divergent, the appraiser must consider the purpose of the appraisal. For example, the appraiser may deem the cost approach most important and, therefore, give it more weight in the reconciliation process if the appraisal was made for insurance purposes. If, instead, the appraisal was for the purpose of estimating value in a condemnation suit, the appraiser may consider the market approach more important.

Like most other areas of real estate, the introduction of the personal computer has impacted the way appraisers conduct their business. For example, for more than a decade, most appraisers have used computer programs to generate their final reports. A more recent innovation is the automated valuation model (AVM). An AVM is a database that consists of selling price and information about a variety of property characteristics for thousands of residential properties. AVM providers obtain this information from a number of sources including public records, financial institutions, appraisers, and the Appraisal Institute. AVM systems have been developed by the Federal National Mortgage Corporation (Freddie Mac) and dozens of privately owned companies and appraisers, or others, can use this information for valuation purposes.

AVM systems are experiencing a mixed reception. An attractive feature of AVM systems is that they can produce information faster and at a lower cost than sending an appraiser out in the field to look at a property. This could cut costs and shorten turnaround time for lenders and borrowers. Lenders could also use it as a tool to double-check a transaction where the valuation of the property is suspect. A potential problem, from the perspective of the appraisal industry, is that AVM systems may be viewed by some as an appraisal substitute. Some appraisers fear that AVMs will eventually lead to the elimination of their role, and some are likely to be forced from the market because AVM systems will provide appraisers with an additional tool that will make them more efficient. On a more positive note, these systems may increase appraiser profitability and reduce the time required for drive-by and desktop appraisals for low-risk loans (e.g., home equity loans) allowing appraisers to focus more effort on full appraisals.

Go To www.appraisaltoday.com, click on Search and use "avm" as your search term, then click on one or more of the results to learn more about this topic.

The reconciliation process used in the example in Exhibit 10.1 is explained on the second page of the exhibit. Note that in this case, the appraiser based the final estimate of value solely on the sales comparison approach. Because the example involves a single-family home that will be owner-occupied, the appraiser did not use the income approach. The appraiser also states that the cost approach was used primarily as a means to verify the reasonableness of the sales comparison estimate.

APPRAISAL ORGANIZATIONS

To increase their professional competence, appraisers may become members of numerous organizations. These organizations provide various designations to members who meet qualifications set by the organization. In general, the requirements to earn such designations include the documentation of appraisal experience, passing one or more examinations, and submitting demonstration appraisal reports for review. In addition, several appraisal organizations provide educational programs, support appraisal research, and publish textbooks, journals, and reference studies. The largest national appraisal organization, with a membership of more than 35,000 is the Appraisal Institute (formed in 1990 when the Society of Real Estate Appraisers and the American Institute of Real Estate Appraisers merged).

Qualified members may hold either the designation "Member Appraisal Institute" (MAI) for those specializing in the appraisal of income-producing properties, or "Senior Residential Appraiser" (SRA) for those specializing in the appraisal of residential properties. Other appraisal organizations are listed at the Web site for this text (www.wiley.com/college/larsen).

SUMMARY

Real property buyers and sellers, mortgage lenders, insurance companies, and others, rely on the services appraisers perform. To derive the most benefit from an appraisal, each decision-maker should be aware of how an appraiser conducts an appraisal. The estimate of market value the appraiser provides is only as good as the quality of the data used and the skill of the appraiser.

Each of the major approaches to value has some limitations. The sales comparison approach works best for properties that are similar to others in the area, but a lack of recently sold comparables will reduce the ability of an appraiser to rely on this approach. The cost approach works well when improvements on the subject property are relatively new. Older structures require the appraiser to estimate depreciation, which can be a difficult process. It is also important to remember that cost does not necessarily equal value. The income approach requires the appraiser to estimate a number of factors, including the income the property will generate, the expenses needed to operate the property, and the correct capitalization rate. The market value estimate the appraiser derives from the income approach can be thought of as a generic estimate of value because it ignores debt service and income taxes. These excluded cash flows are likely of critical importance to investors as is shown in Chapter 21.

Appraisers interested in their professional development may join a number of professional associations. These organizations offer members a variety of services, including educational programs, research support, and professional designations.

KEY TERMS

appraisal	cost approach	market price
appraisal report	depreciation	market value
appraiser	effective gross income	net operating income
capitalization rate	highest and best use	potential gross income
comparable (comp)	income approach	sales comparison approach

REVIEW QUESTIONS

1. What is an appraisal report?
2. Why were uniform appraisal reports developed for various types of residential properties?
3. What are the steps in the real estate appraisal process?
4. List and describe the three valuation approaches used in real property appraisal.
5. What are the strengths and weaknesses of each of the three valuation approaches?
6. What is a capitalization rate?
7. Describe three ways an appraiser may derive a capitalization rate?
8. Explain and give examples of the three different types of depreciation that are recognized under the cost method of appraisal.
9. Give at least three examples of curable and incurable depreciation.
10. In estimating market value, appraisers must consider the principles of value reviewed in the chapter. Which of these principles do you think are particularly important for the sales comparison approach? The cost approach? The income approach?
11. What is market price? What is market value? Under what conditions could the market price of a property be higher than its market value?
12. When using the cost approach, an appraiser must estimate the cost to reproduce the improvements. What are the disadvantages and advantages of each of the various ways this may be accomplished?

13. Explain the reconciliation process an appraiser uses to arrive at a final value estimate.

14. What are your answers to the questions in the two "Decision Point" sections in this chapter?

15. What is your answer to the Ethical Issue in this chapter?

PROBLEMS

1. Given: annual gross income of $100,000; expenses of $59,000 including $12,000 for income taxes; and occupancy levels expected to remain constant at 93 percent.

   a. What is effective gross income?

   b. What is net operating income?

   c. By what amount does effective gross income and net operating income change if operating expenses increase by 10 percent?

2. An investor is considering purchasing a retail store for $1,000,000. A lender is willing to write a 25-year, 10 percent fixed-rate loan in the amount of $750,000. The investor's required rate of return on equity is 25 percent, and the property is expected to generate $95,000 in annual net operating income.

   a. What is the indicated value of the property using the band of investment method?

   b. What is the indicated value of the property using the debt coverage method?

   c. Does the investment seem feasible?

   d. What factors does the income approach ignore and how might these factors influence your answer to question c?

3. An investor anticipates obtaining a 25-year fully amortized loan with a loan-to-value ratio of 80 percent. The fixed interest rate on the loan is 10 percent and the investors required rate of return on equity is 15 percent. What is the capitalization rate the investor should use based on the band of investment technique?

4. Use the debt coverage method to calculate the capitalization rate and property value in each of the following five independent cases.

   a. Seventy-five percent loan to value ratio, 10 percent mortgage interest rate, 25-year loan, 1.2 debt coverage ratio, and $50,000 net operating income.

   b. Same facts as in a, but loan to value ratio of 80 percent.

   c. Same facts as in a, but mortgage interest rate is 12 percent.

   d. Same facts as in a, but mortgage amortization period is 30 years.

   e. Same facts as in a, but debt coverage ratio is only 1.1

REAL ESTATE ON THE WEB

Use your favorite search engine to:

1. Determine which local appraisers have Web sites.

2. Determine the requirements for being certified as a qualified appraiser in your state.

3. Learn what role inflated appraisals have played in recent years in mortgage loan fraud.

4. Learn what actions the appraisal industry has taken to insulate itself from the mortgage loan fraud debacle.

5. Discover what other issues currently concern appraisers.

6. Determine the membership requirements of appraisal trade organizations and the designations they offer to qualified members.

Refer to the companion Web site at www.wiley.com/college/larsen for a variety of online activities including additional chapter content, review materials, assignments, and related links.

ADDITIONAL READINGS

Champagne, D. M. "Interim Highest and Best Use: Condemnation Appraising." *The Appraisal Journal* 69:1 (January 2001): 19–25.

De Reza, C. "Appraiser Identity Theft on the Rise." *Real Estate Finance Today* 18:26 (July 2, 2001): 5.

Edge, J. A. "The Globalization of Real Estate Appraisal: A European Perspective." *The Appraisal Journal* 69:1 (January 2001): 84–94.

Frederick, M. "The Appraiser on Trial: Expert Reports and Expert Witnesses." *Canadian Appraiser* 44:4 (Winter 2000): 10–11.

McGovern, J. J. and R. Kellelliher. "Bringing Value Back to Contaminated Property." *Real Estate Finance Journal* 16:3 (Winter 2001): 65–70.

Roe, C. E. "Land Use: The Second Battle of Gettysburg." *The Appraisal Journal* 68:4 (October 2000): 441–449.

Waller, B. D. "A Survey of the Technology Astuteness of the Appraisal Industry." *The Appraisal Journal* 68:4 (October 2000): 469–473.

Wolverton, M. L. and D. Epley. "National Survey of Residential Appraisers Shows: SRAs Have More Earning Power." *The Appraisal Journal* 68:4 (October 2000): 395–405.

CHAPTER

11

Real Estate Contracts

Learning Objectives

After studying this chapter you should be able to:

- Explain the essential elements of a contract.
- Describe the important provisions of a real estate purchase contract.
- Compare and contrast a purchase contract and an installment land contract.
- Understand why and how options are used to acquire real property.
- List the possible remedies if one party fails to honor their contractual obligations.

FROM THE WIRE

In August 2001, a three-judge Arizona Court of Appeals upheld a $3.7 million jury award to two companies that had paid $15 million for two apartment buildings. The problem was that the buildings had plastic pipes that fail in a relatively short period. The buyers said they would have paid $5 million to $6 million less if they had known of the defect. The pipes were inside walls and not visible during the pre-purchase inspections. The sellers argued that the "as is" clause in the purchase contract shifted the burden of discovering the pipes to the buyers. The Court, in a two-to-one vote, disagreed. "The buyer-beware rule remains intact if the defect is reasonably noticeable or if the buyer has a reasonable ability to discover it," said Judge William F. Garbarino. But, since this was not so in this case, the court concluded that the seller had a duty to disclose the defect under Arizona laws requiring good-faith dealing in contracts.

Go to www.realtor.org/realtormag, and search "latent defects," then click on one or more of the search results to learn more about this topic.

INTRODUCTION

It is important for everyone involved in real estate transactions to have at least a basic knowledge of contracts. In order to know their responsibilities and to protect their rights, brokers, sellers, and buyers should understand contracts. The material presented in this chapter will enable you to converse with an attorney and to better understand the advice that is offered. Perhaps the most important lesson to learn from this chapter is that the time to seek competent legal advice is before, not after, you sign a contract. Generally, the signature on a contract makes the agreement binding regardless of whether the signatory actually read the contract or understood its terms.

We begin by presenting the essential elements that must be present in any contract (not just those involving real estate) if it is to be enforceable in court. The chapter then focuses on contracts that govern several specific types of real estate transactions: listing property for sale with a broker, selling and buying property, and options to purchase real property.

CONTRACTS

A **contract** is a legally enforceable agreement between competent parties who, for a consideration, agree to perform, or refrain from performing, certain acts. The contract governs the rights and responsibilities of the parties to the contract. If either party fails to honor their contractual obligations, the contract is said to be breached, or broken, and the party harmed by a **breach of contract** can bring legal action to enforce his or her contractual rights.

In many cases, a contract may be either written or oral. As a practical matter, however, the terms of a written contract are easier to prove in a legal action should the parties disagree after entering into the contract. Certain contracts, including most used in conjunction with real property transactions, must be written to be enforceable. It is also important to note that a written contract cannot be amended orally. The only way to validly change a written contract is in writing, and both parties must sign the amended contract.

Contract law allows either party to sell, or assign, their contract rights to a third party unless explicitly prohibited by the contract. In many cases, the possibility of an **assignment** does not concern either party, but in other cases, one or both of the parties may wish to prevent it. The parties may do so by including a clause in the contract that prevents assignment.

The five essential elements of a contract that must be present in order for the contract to be legally enforceable are competent parties, an offer, acceptance, consideration, and a legal and proper objective.

COMPETENT PARTIES

The element of **competent parties** requires that both parties be of legal age to enter into a contract and that both are sane and not under the influence of a mind-altering substance such as alcohol or drugs. This requirement helps ensure that one party will not take unfair advantage of another party who does not have either the maturity or mental capacity to exercise good judgment. If someone who is intoxicated agrees to purchase your home for a certain price, the agreement is not enforceable because the buyer was not competent at the time the offer was made. Upon regaining sobriety the party making the offer could ratify, or reaffirm, his or her intention to purchase the property, and if the other essential elements of a contract are present, then an enforceable contract is created. Similarly, if a minor enters into a contract, the contract is unenforceable because the requirement of competent parties has not been met. Upon reaching the age of majority, however, the individual could ratify the contract.

Decision Point

What would you do if the person with whom you were negotiating a contract did not appear to have full mental capacity when it was time to enter into the contract?

OFFER

An **offer** is a conditional promise to perform some act, such as transferring title to real estate, provided that another party performs in the manner requested. Making an offer demonstrates an intention to enter into a contract. The party making an offer is the offeror, and the party to whom the offer is made is the offeree. An offer is conditional upon the offeree's acceptance of the offer and can be revoked, or withdrawn, by the offeror anytime before receiving notice of the offeree's acceptance.

ACCEPTANCE

A third essential element of a contract is **acceptance** of the offer. When an offeree accepts the offer in all material respects it is said that the parties have reached **mutual assent,** sometimes called "a meeting of the minds." Mutual assent is missing from a contract if either the acceptance or the offer was obtained by fraud, undue influence, or duress. For mutual assent to occur, the offeree must communicate the acceptance to the offeror. This communication must occur within the time limit specified in the offer and be in the proper form. A favorable response to an offer after the time limit to accept has passed is not an acceptance; at best it is a **counter-offer.** If the offeror does not specify a time limit to respond, an acceptance is valid only if it is made within a reasonable time. What constitutes a "reasonable" time is determined on a case-by-case basis. Generally, communication of the acceptance need not be in writing, but if the offer is in writing and the contract pertains to real property, the acceptance must also be in writing.

For a contract to be created there must be mutual assent between the offeror and offeree. To illustrate: a potential buyer offers $112,000 for a property and the owner responds that she will sell the property for $120,000. The seller's price is a new offer, or counter-offer. A counter-offer indicates that there is no mutual assent and a contract does not exist. The buyer has three possible responses to the counter-offer: acceptance, rejection, or making a counter-offer to the seller's counter-offer. In real estate transactions many counter-offers may be made before the parties reach mutually agreeable terms and price. A contract does not exist until one of the parties accepts the other's offer.

CONSIDERATION

Perhaps the most misunderstood of the essential elements of a contract is "consideration." **Consideration** means that something of value must be given in exchange for each promise in a contract. Money, personal services, or property, as well as the promise to deliver any of them, may serve as consideration in a contract. In a real estate sales contract, consideration usually consists of two valuable promises—the seller's promise to transfer title to the purchaser and the purchaser's promise to pay the purchase price to the seller. As long as consideration exists, the contract will be enforceable even if the money and property exchanged are of unequal value.

LEGAL OR PROPER OBJECTIVE

The requirement of a **legal or proper objective** means that agreements to perform acts which are either illegal or against public policy are not enforceable contracts. Contract law cannot be used to force one to perform an illegal act. For example, a contract to have someone killed is unenforceable because murder is illegal. Similarly, a real property sales contract with a clause that requires that a property located in a city center be used only as a nudist colony is not likely to be enforceable because its objective is illegal or improper.

Additional Contract Terminology

- **Bilateral contract**—Contract in which both parties make valuable promises. Example: Contract to purchase real estate.
- **Executed contract**—A contract where both parties have performed all that is required of them by the contract. Actually a misnomer because once both parties have completely performed, the instrument is merely evidence of an executed agreement rather than a contract. The distinction between an executed and executory contract can be important. For example, a seller cannot be forced to convey a deed under an executory oral contract because of the Statute of Frauds. However, The Statute of Frauds does not generally apply to executed oral contracts. So, a seller who conveys a deed in accordance with an oral contract cannot later regain title by asserting the Statute of Frauds.
- **Executory contract**—A contract where one or more parties have not performed all that is required of them.
- **Express contract**—A contract to which the parties have actually agreed.
- **Implied contract**—Sometimes called a quasi contract, may exist even if the parties have not entered into an actual agreement, if the parties behave as if there is a contract.
- **Unilateral contract**—Contract in which one party gives a promise in exchange for an act, but the first party is not obligated to perform on the promise unless the second party decides to act. Example: An option to purchase real estate.
- **Valid contract**—Contract that a court would enforce because it has all of the essential elements.
- **Void contract**—Unenforceable contract because one, or more, of the essential elements of a contract is missing. A void contract is not enforceable, because it is arguably not even a contract. Example: An agreement to perform an illegal act.
- **Voidable contract**—Contract in which one of the parties has the right to rescind, or require that the contract not be carried out. Example: Minor who enters into a contract to purchase real estate.

REAL ESTATE CONTRACTS

To be legally binding, any contract that involves real estate must contain all of the essential elements described earlier. In addition, most contracts concerning real estate must be written and signed according to laws known as the **Statute of Frauds.** Derived from the Statute of Frauds enacted in England in 1677, every state has such laws that require that certain agreements be evidenced by a signed writing to be enforceable in court. In several states, the Statute of Frauds may be satisfied if there is some written memorandum recognizing the existence of a contract and the memorandum is signed by the party who would be the defendant if a lawsuit is filed. The typical Statute of Frauds requires signed writings for any conveyance of title to real estate as well as any real estate lease lasting longer than one year. Even for a real estate transaction not covered by the Statute of Frauds, attorneys recommend a written contract that clearly details the rights and responsibilities of each party because a written contract can help avoid subsequent misunderstandings between the contracting parties.

There are several types of transactions in real estate for which contracts are commonly used: when a property owner hires a broker to assist in the sale or purchase of property; when a buyer agrees to purchase and an owner agrees to sell real estate; and when a property owner sells a prospective buyer an option to purchase real estate at some time in the future. Other real estate contracts include leases (Chapter 18) and mortgages (Chapter 15), as well as loan commitments and escrow agreements (Chapter 14).

LISTING CONTRACTS

The **listing contract** is the real estate broker's employment contract with a real property owner. Most states require that the broker's right to receive a commission for negotiating the sale of a parcel of real estate be based on a written agreement signed by both the property seller and the real estate broker. For a discussion of the type of listing contracts available see Chapter 9. Even in states where the listing agreement does not have to be written, good business practice dictates that they almost always are.

As the following "Ethical Issue" demonstrates, in all but one state, listing contracts are considered mere advertisements. Therefore, owners who list property with a broker are under no obligation to accept an offer regardless of the offer amount. However, if the hopeful buyer is willing and able to pay a price greater than or equal to the list price and is also willing to meet all other terms in the listing, the owner owes the broker a commission.

PURCHASE CONTRACT

The final agreement between a buyer to purchase and an owner to sell a parcel of real estate usually involves a **purchase contract,** sometimes called a contract for the sale of land, a contract to purchase real estate, a sales contract, or a purchase and sale contract. Purchase contracts specify a relatively short period of time, usually thirty to ninety days, in which the contract will be completed and title conveyed to the buyer. Some refer to this type of contract

AN ETHICAL ISSUE
LIST PRICE: AN OFFER OR AN ADVERTISEMENT?

In every state except Vermont the listing agreement is considered an advertisement, not an offer to sell. In essence, the listing contract creates no power of acceptance in the buyer. Many people have discovered this fact first-hand. In "hot" housing markets, consumer complaints about unfair bidding practices surge. In 1986, the Vermont legislature responded to such complaints with a rule that defines the list price as an offer instead of an advertisement. The rule, in effect, forces a seller to accept the first full asking price offer or risk litigation.

You receive a full list price offer on the first day your property is on the market which makes you suspicious that you listed the property too low. Under what circumstances would you refuse the offer and relist the property at a higher price?

as an earnest money contract because the buyer deposits a sum of money at the time an agreement is reached and the contract signed. The specific amount of the deposit is subject to negotiation but often determined by local custom. The deposit, called **earnest money,** is used, in part, to show the buyer's intention to fulfill the contract. If both parties carry out the contract, the earnest money deposit is usually deducted from the purchase price at the time of closing.

An earnest money deposit is supposed to make it costly for the buyer not to finalize the deal. This is generally done by specifying in the contract that the deposit will serve as **liquidated damages** if the buyer fails to close the deal. In essence, the buyer forfeits the deposit to the seller to, at least partially, compensate the seller for expenses incurred in the failed transaction. Some states have statutory guidelines as to what constitutes a reasonable amount for liquidated damages. In California, for example, if the deposit is more than 3 percent of the sales price, the seller must prove that the excess is reasonable or return the excess to the buyer.

The extent to which an earnest money deposit is effective in preventing buyers from walking away from transactions depends to a large extent on the size of the deposit. In the Midwest, earnest deposits, by custom, are a very small percentage of the value of the property. For example, an earnest deposit of $1,000 on a $250,000 property is not unusual. In some areas in the eastern part of the country, it is customary for earnest deposits to be 10 percent of the purchase price. The larger the earnest deposit, the less likely a buyer is to walk away from the transaction. What if the buyer has a good reason for failing to close? Suppose his employer transferred the buyer across the country after making the deposit. Under such circumstances courts have generally found that the buyer is entitled to a refund of the earnest money. A cautious purchaser will include inspection and financing contingencies in the offer that make it easier for the buyer to walk away with the earnest money even if he or she wishes to cancel the contract for other reasons.

Important Provisions of a Purchase Contract

A typical purchase contract for residential property is shown in Exhibit 11.1. Preprinted or form contracts similar to the one shown in the exhibit are used by most residential brokers to speed the contracting process. A purchaser may, however, draft his or her own contract or have an attorney do so. Most contracts for commercial properties are individualized and can be twenty or more pages in length.

There are eleven provisions in the sample contract; any well-drafted purchase contract should include these provisions. The property is described in the first provision. Space is provided for both a street address and a legal description. The contract also specifies the

| DOING BUSINESS |
| LEGAL/FINANCIAL |

There have been a lot of news stories recently on the growing number of unjustified fees being included in home sale transaction settlement forms (Chapter 14). These fees, sometimes called "junk fees," must be paid by the home seller or buyer unless they are waived at the last minute by the party levying the fee. In most cases, these fees are charged by the broker or lender. For example, lenders have charged an "attorney's review fee" even though in some cases there was never an attorney review. Some brokers are charging a "transaction fee" over and above their standard commission. The issue has flared up since the Department of Housing and Urban Development (HUD) issued a policy statement suggesting that some fees may be duplicative of other fees, or simply not justified by the service provided. The best time to spot a junk fee is not at the settlement table. To avoid paying junk fees, consumers should carefully read their listing contract and purchase contract, including the fine print. If you see a fee you do not understand, question it. If it is not justified, request that it be deleted. It will probably be quickly removed.

Go to www.mtgprofessor.com, click on Public Policy Issues, and then click on one or more of the results to learn more about this and related topics.

EXHIBIT | **11.1** | **PURCHASE CONTRACT**

CONTRACT TO PURCHASE REAL ESTATE

(Form approved by the Dayton Area Board of REALTORS®. This is a legally binding contract.
If the provisions are not understood, legal advice should be obtained.)

Dayton, Ohio _____ , _____ (Date)

1.
2. **OFFER.** The undersigned Purchaser offers to buy through _____ , Broker(s), on
3. the terms and conditions set forth below, the real property (the "Property") located in _____
   (City or Township)
4. County of _____ , State of Ohio, described as follows:
5. _____
   (Street and Number, Zip Code, Legal Description)
6. The Property shall include the land, all appurtenant rights, privileges and easements, and all buildings, improvements and fixtures, including, but not limited to, such
7. of the following as are now on the Property: all electrical, heating, plumbing and bathroom fixtures; all window and door shades, blinds, awnings and screens; storm
8. windows and doors; television antennae; curtain rods; garage door opener and control(s); all landscaping; and
9.
10.
11. Any personal property items listed above are owned by Seller and will be free and clear of liens and security interests at closing.
12. **2. PRICE.** Purchaser agrees to pay for the Property the sum of $
13. payable in cash at closing. Purchaser's obligations under this Contract are conditioned upon Purchaser's ability to obtain prior to closing a mortgage loan of
14. $ _____ (Conventional) (FHA) (VA) at rates and terms generally prevail-
15. ing in the Dayton, Ohio area.
16. Mortgage discount points/origination fees/prepaid items permitted by lender/Purchaser's closing costs not to exceed _____ are to be paid by Seller.
17. Seller shall have the option to cancel this Contract if Purchaser fails to either (a) make a complete mortgage loan application, including ordering an appraisal, within
18. _____ days after the date of acceptance of this offer, or (b) obtain mortgage loan approval within _____ days after the date of acceptance of this offer.
19. **3. DEED.** Seller shall furnish a transferable and recordable general warranty deed conveying to Purchaser, or nominee, a marketable title to the Property (as determined
20. with reference to the Ohio State Bar Association Standards of Title Examination) with dower rights, if any, released, free and clear of all liens, rights to take liens,
21. and encumbrances whatsoever, except (a) legal highways, (b) any mortgage assumed by Purchaser, (c) all installments of taxes and assessments becoming due and
22. payable after closing, (d) rights of tenants in possession, (e) zoning and other laws and (f) easements and restrictions of record which would not prevent Purchaser
23. from using the Property for the following purpose: _____ If title to all or part
24. of the Property is unmarketable or is subject to matters not excepted as provided above, Seller at Seller's sole cost shall cure any title defects and/or remove such
25. matters within 10 days after receipt of written notice from Purchaser, and if necessary the closing date may be extended to permit Seller the full 10 days to clear title.
26. **TITLE INSURANCE.** Purchasers are encouraged to inquire about the benefits of title insurance from the closing agent or other title insurance provider. A lender's pol-
27. icy of title insurance does not provide protection to the purchaser. It is recommended that purchasers obtain an owner's policy of title insurance to insure their own interests.
28. **4. TAXES.** At closing, Seller shall pay or credit on the purchase price (a) all real estate taxes and assessments, including penalties and interest, which became
29. due and payable prior to the closing, (b) a pro rata share, calculated as of the closing date in the manner set forth below, of the taxes and assessments becoming
30. due and payable after the closing, and (c) the amount of any agricultural tax savings accrued as of the closing date which would be subject to recoupment if the
31. Property were converted to a non-agricultural use (whether or not such conversion actually occurs), unless Purchaser has indicated in paragraph 3 that Purchaser
32. is acquiring the Property for agricultural purposes. If the Property is located in Montgomery County, the tax proration shall be made in accordance with the
33. Montgomery County "short proration" method, in which Seller's share is based upon the number of days from the date of the immediately preceding semi-
34. annual installment to the date of closing. If the Property is located outside of Montgomery County, the tax proration shall be made in accordance with (check one):
35. _____ the Montgomery County "short proration" method or _____ the "long proration" method, in which Seller's share is based upon the taxes and assessments
36. which are a lien for the year of the closing. (If neither method is checked, the short proration shall apply.) If the short proration method is used, any special assessments
37. which are payable in a single annual installment shall nevertheless be prorated on the long proration method. All prorations shall be based upon the most recent avail-
38. able tax rates, assessments and valuations.
39. **5. SELLER'S REPRESENTATIONS.** Seller represents that those signing this Contract constitute all of the owners of the title to the Property, together with their
40. respective spouses. Seller further represents that with respect to the Property (a) no orders of any public authority are pending, (b) no work has been performed or
41. improvements constructed that may result in future assessments, (c) no notices have been received from any public agency with respect to condemnation or appropria-
42. tion, change in zoning, proposed future assessments, correction of conditions, or other similar matters, and (d) to the best of Seller's knowledge, no toxic, explosive
43. or other hazardous substances having been stored, disposed of, concealed within or released on or from the Property and no other adverse environmental conditions
44. affect the Property. These representations shall survive the closing.
45. **6. POSSESSION.** Rentals, interest on any assumed mortgages, water and other utility bills, and any current operating expenses shall be prorated as of the date of
46. closing. If the Property is owner-occupied, possession is to be given _____ days after closing at _____ A.M./P.M. and utilities shall not be prorated as above but
47. paid for by Seller until delivery of possession. Seller shall be responsible to Purchaser for any damages caused by Seller's failure to deliver possession on the stated date.
48. **7. DAMAGE TO BUILDINGS.** If any buildings or other improvements are substantially damaged or destroyed prior to the closing, Purchaser shall have the option
49. (a) to proceed with the closing and receive the proceeds of any insurance payable in connection therewith, or (b) to terminate this Contract. Seller shall keep the
50. Property adequately insured against fire and extended coverage perils prior to closing. Seller agrees to maintain the Property in its present condition until delivery
51. of possession, subject to ordinary wear and tear and the provisions of this paragraph.
52. **8. ACCEPTANCE; CLOSING.** This offer shall remain open for acceptance until _____ (Date), at 11:59 p.m. The closing for delivery of the deed
53. and payment of the balance of the purchase price shall be held on or before _____ (Date), at a time and place mutually agreed upon by Seller and
54. Purchaser. In the event of a failure of both parties to agree, the closing shall be held on the last day designated in this paragraph and the Selling Broker shall designate
55. the time and place of closing.
56. **9. EARNEST MONEY; DEFAULT.** Upon presentation of this offer, Purchaser has delivered to _____ , Broker,
57. the sum of $ _____ as earnest money, to be (1) deposited in the Broker's trust account promptly after acceptance of this offer or (2)
58. returned to Purchaser upon request if this offer is not accepted. The earnest money shall be paid to Purchaser or applied on the purchase price at closing. If the
59. closing does not occur because of Seller's default or because any condition of this Contract is not satisfied or waived, Purchaser shall be entitled to the earnest money.
60. The parties acknowledge, however, that the Broker will not make a determination as to which party is entitled to the earnest money. Instead, the Broker shall release the
61. earnest money from the trust account only (a) in accordance with the joint written instructions of Seller and Purchaser, or (b) in accordance with the following proce-
62. dure: if the closing does not occur for any reason (including the default of either party), the Broker holding the earnest money may notify Seller in writing that the earnest
63. money will be returned to Purchaser unless Seller makes a written demand for the earnest money within 20 days after the date of the Broker's notice. If the Broker does
64. not receive a written demand from the Seller within the 20-day period, the Broker shall return the earnest money to Purchaser. If a written demand from Seller is received
65. by the Broker within the 20-day period, the Broker shall retain the earnest money until (i) Seller and Purchaser have settled the dispute; (ii) disposition has been ordered
66. by a final court order; or (iii) the Broker deposits the earnest money with the court pursuant to applicable court procedures. Payment or refund of the earnest money
67. shall not prejudice the rights of the Broker(s) or the non-defaulting party in an action for damages or specific performance against the defaulting party.
68. **10. GENERAL PROVISIONS.** Upon acceptance, this offer shall become a complete agreement binding upon and inuring to the benefit of Purchaser and Seller and
69. their respective heirs, personal representatives, successors, and assigns, and shall be deemed to contain all the terms and conditions agreed upon, there being no oral
70. conditions, representations, warranties or agreements. Any subsequent conditions, representations, warranties or agreements shall not be valid and binding upon the
71. parties unless in writing signed by both parties. Purchaser has examined the Property and, except as otherwise provided in this Contract, is purchasing it "as is"
72. in its present condition, relying upon such examination as to the condition, character, size, utility and zoning of the Property. Time is of the essence of all provisions
73. of this Contract. Any word used in this Contract shall be construed to mean either singular or plural as indicated by the number of signatures below.
74. **11. INSPECTIONS AND OTHER ADDENDA.** The following Addenda and attachments are attached to and shall be considered an integral part of this Contract:
75. ❑ Inspection Addendum ❑ Land Contract Addendum ❑ Other (Describe) _____

76. **WITNESS:** _____   **Purchaser** _____

77. **MAKE DEED TO (Print):** _____   **Purchaser** _____

78. _____   **Address** _____

---

79. **ACCEPTANCE** Date: _____

80. The undersigned Seller (_____) accepts the foregoing offer; or (_____) counteroffers according to the initialled changes set forth above or in the attached Addenda,
81. which counteroffer shall remain open for acceptance until _____ (Date), at 11:59 P.M.

82. **WITNESS** _____   **Seller** _____

83. Not accepted at this time. Thank you for your offer.   **Print** _____

84. **Seller** _____   **Seller** _____

85. **Seller** _____   **Print** _____

---

86. **DEPOSIT RECEIPT** Date: _____

87. Receipt is acknowledged of $ _____ earnest money, to be deposited in the undersigned Broker's trust account upon acceptance of this
88. offer and to be applied as provided in paragraph 9 above.

89. _____   By _____ , REALTOR®
    (Firm Name)   (Agent's Sign.)
    Phone _____

Copyright ©08/99 Dayton Area Board of REALTORS®

fixtures to be included in the sale. It may seem overly cautious to specify that, for example, the plumbing and bathroom fixtures are included, but it is important that the contract terms be as clear as possible. If one of the fixtures on the preprinted form is not to be sold with the property, a garage door opener, for example, the item can be removed from the contract by lining it out. The party that strikes out a clause should place his or her initials next to the change to signify their approval. Space is also provided in the contract so the parties can specify other items. For example, the buyer might specify that the purchase is to include fireplace tools or a satellite dish.

In the second contract provision, the price the buyer is willing to pay is specified. The form contract includes a clause that makes the offer a contingent offer. A **contingency** allows one of the parties to withdraw from the contract if a stated event occurs, or fails to occur. In this case, the contingency is a common one; the offer is contingent on the ability of the buyer to secure financing at terms prevailing in the area. If the buyer were paying cash, this clause could be struck from the contract. Other common contingencies to purchase offers include the approval of the offer by a spouse, business partner, or attorney.

The third contract provision calls for the seller to provide a marketable title by a general warranty deed. Real estate contracts that involve title transfer almost always specify the quality of title that the seller is required to deliver to the buyer, and most buyers want a title that is marketable. A **marketable title** is one that is reasonably free from risk of litigation over possible defects.

The fourth contract provision specifies that the seller must pay any overdue property taxes or existing assessments, and that property taxes for the current installment are to be split, or prorated, between the seller and buyer. Prorations are usually based on the proportion of time the seller has owned the property during the billing period (Chapter 14).

The fifth contract provision requires several warranties by the seller. Among others, the warranties include: that all owners will sign the contract; that the owner(s) has no knowledge of any work that has or will be done that will result in charges to the property; and that no adverse environmental conditions affect the property.

The sixth contract provision calls for the proration of additional items such as interest on any mortgages on the property the buyer assumes, or rental income the property generates.

The seventh contract provision requires that, until closing when title actually is conveyed, the seller keep the property adequately insured and maintain it in the same condition as existed when the purchase contract was signed. In this contract, if the building is damaged before closing, either the seller must repair it, or the buyer is entitled to any insurance proceeds, or the buyer can rescind the contract. This provision may be especially important because without it, under common law, the buyer may be forced to proceed with the transaction even though the improvements were destroyed before title is conveyed.

Two important time limits are included in the eighth contract provision. The first specifies how long the seller has to respond, in writing, to the offer. The second specifies the closing date. If all the buyer's terms are acceptable to the seller, they will be the effective dates. If, instead, the seller decides to counter-offer, new dates must be inserted in the contract. Should the seller decide to counter-offer, the parties could use an entirely new form, but in most cases changes will be made to the original contract. After several rounds of counter-offers the original document may become cluttered and then it may be beneficial to use a new contract.

The ninth contract provision specifies that any earnest money is to serve as liquidated damages, and the circumstances under which the seller will, or will not, refund the deposit to the buyer.

There are several important points contained in the tenth contract provision. It begins with a statement that makes it clear that the parties intend the agreement to be a contract. The provision also makes it clear that either party can assign the contract to another, and that any modifications to the contract must be in writing. The phrase "time is of the essence" emphasizes that punctual performance is an essential element of the contract and makes it easier to determine damages. If either party does not perform within the specified time period they are in default, and damages may be assessed from that point.

The eleventh and last contract provision makes any additions to the contract a part of the contract. If, for example, the buyer elects to have inspections conducted, the inspection addendum shown in Exhibit 11.2 must be completed and signed. The addendum makes it clear that if the buyer discovers defects, the seller must correct them or supply funds to an escrow account so the buyer can have them corrected. If the seller is unwilling to repair the defects, the buyer may choose to back-out of the contract and require the seller to return any earnest money.

Decision Point

In selling or purchasing real property, what factors would influence your decision to use either the form contract normally used by real estate brokers in your area or a specially prepared contract?

INSTALLMENT LAND CONTRACT

Another contract that can be used in real estate sales transactions is an **installment land contract,** also known as a land contract, installment contract, contract for deed, or as a conditional sales contract. There are similarities between installment land contracts and purchase contracts. The buyer gets possession of the property, and is responsible for its maintenance and the payment of property taxes and premiums on any property insurance policy. The contracts differ, however, in several respects. One important difference between the contracts is when legal title is conveyed to the buyer. In a purchase contract, title is conveyed when the grantee takes possession and before any periodic mortgage payments are made (most real estate transfers involve a third-party lender). In an installment land contract, the seller (usually) finances the property and title does not pass until the buyer pays the entire purchase price. However, in several states, executing an installment land contract gives the buyer equitable title, although the deed conveying legal title will be executed only after all payments are received. Because no grant of legal title occurs until some time in the future in an installment land contract, the seller and buyer in a land contract are referred to as the vendor and the vendee, respectively, instead of grantor and grantee. Another difference between the contracts concerns the length of the financing term. While the typical mortgage loan has a term of fifteen or thirty years, most installment land contracts have much shorter terms, usually five to ten years.

Land contracts have been used for some time. They were used in the Midwest during settlement times, and by the railroads in disposing of their land grants. In the Great Depression of the 1930s, land contracts were used by lenders to dispose of properties they acquired through foreclosure. The word "land" in land contract does not mean that a vendee acquires only unimproved land using this instrument. While much unimproved land is so acquired, land contracts are also used in connection with improved properties.

Risks for Land Contract Vendees

There are potential hazards for the purchaser who uses a land contract. The danger lies in the fact that many states do not require land contracts to be recorded. When a land contract is not recorded, record title to the property is in the vendor's name. Many things can occur to make it difficult or impossible for the vendee to obtain title although he or she performs as contracted. The vendor could die, go bankrupt, become mentally incompetent, fail to make mortgage payments, further mortgage the property, have a judgment rendered against him or her, fail to pay income tax, move to another state, fail to pay the people who

EXHIBIT | **11.2** | **ADDENDUM TO A PURCHASE CONTRACT**

CONTRACT TO PURCHASE REAL ESTATE
INSPECTION ADDENDUM
(Form approved by the Dayton Area Board of REALTORS®)

PURCHASER: _____

PROPERTY: _____

1. Inspection Period. Purchaser shall have the right for a period of _____ calendar days after the date of Seller's acceptance (the "Inspection Period") to obtain inspections of the Property at Purchaser's expense in each of the following areas:

_____ Structural	_____ Roof	_____ Air Conditioning	_____ Radon
_____ Basement	_____ Electrical	_____ Appliances	_____ Whole House
_____ Fireplace	_____ Plumbing	_____ Termite or Wood	_____ Other (specify)
_____ Chimney	_____ Well (quality and quantity)	Boring Insects	_____
_____ Lead-Based Paint and/or Lead-Based Paint Hazards	_____ Heating & Furnace	_____ Septic System	_____

Inspections shall be made by qualified contractors and inspectors (duly licensed and certified where applicable) selected by Purchaser.

During the Inspection Period, Purchaser and Purchaser's inspectors and contractors shall be permitted access to the Property at reasonable times. Unless seller otherwise agrees, Purchaser shall not be present at inspections unaccompanied by Purchaser's Agent. Purchaser shall be responsible for any damage to the Property caused by Purchaser or Purchaser's inspectors or contractors.

If the inspections disclose any defects in the Property, Purchaser shall notify Seller in writing of the defects prior to the expiration of the Inspection Period. For purposes of this Addendum, "defects" do not include minor, routine maintenance and repair items not affecting habitability. Items shall not be considered defective merely because of their age. Seller shall have no obligation to repair any such items unless specifically agreed in writing. FAILURE TO NOTIFY SELLER OF ANY DEFECTS BEFORE EXPIRATION OF THE INSPECTION PERIOD SHALL CONSTITUTE A WAIVER OF SUCH DEFECTS, AND PURCHASER SHALL TAKE THE PROPERTY "AS IS" WITH RESPECT TO SUCH DEFECTS.

Inspections required by FHA/VA or local municipalities do not necessarily eliminate the need for other inspections.

2. Lead-Based Paint. If the item "Lead-Based Paint and/or Lead-Based Paint Hazards" is checked in Section 1 above, the Inspection Period represents the agreed upon period for Purchaser to conduct an assessment or inspection of the Property to determine the presence of lead-based paint and/or lead-based paint hazards. Except as provided in this Inspection Addendum, Purchaser waives any right or opportunity to conduct an assessment or inspection for these purposes.

3. Repair Period. In the event Purchaser's inspections disclose any defects in the Property which are timely reported to Seller, Seller shall have the right, for a period of 10 calendar days after expiration of the Inspection Period (the "Repair Period"), to either (a) repair the defect in a good and workmanlike manner, using contractors reasonably acceptable to Purchaser or (b) provide other assurances reasonably acceptable to Purchaser, by means of an escrow of funds at closing for the repairs or otherwise, that the defects will be repaired with due diligence and in a good and workmanlike manner.

4. Right to Cancel. If Seller is unwilling or unable to repair any defect or to provide the assurances described above during the Repair Period, Purchaser shall have the right, at Purchaser's sole option, to cancel this Contract, in which event the earnest money shall be returned to Purchaser in accordance with the procedures set forth in Paragraph 9 on the first page of this Contract and the parties shall be released from all further obligations under this Contract. This right of cancellation shall be exercised, if at all, by giving written notice to Seller within 5 calendar days after the earlier of (a) receipt of a written notice from Seller stating that Seller is unwilling to make the repairs or provide the assurances described above or (b) expiration of the Repair Period. FAILURE BY PURCHASER TO CANCEL THIS CONTRACT WITHIN SUCH 5 CALENDAR DAY PERIOD SHALL CONSTITUTE A WAIVER BY PURCHASER OF ANY UNCURED DEFECTS AND PURCHASER SHALL TAKE THE PROPERTY "AS IS" WITH RESPECT TO SUCH DEFECTS.

5. Release. Seller and Purchaser release the Broker(s) from any and all liability arising from (a) any action by the Broker(s) in obtaining or recommending an inspector or contractor, (b) the contents of any inspection report or the work of any contractor, (c) any advice concerning the necessity of any inspections, (d) and defect or deficiency in the Property and (e) the failure to deliver any notice within the time periods provided herein unless specifically requested to do so. This waiver shall survive the closing.

6. Homeowner's Warranty Disclosure. If a homeowner's warranty is being provided under the terms of this Contract, the party furnishing the warranty may select any reputable company to issue the warranty, unless a specific warranty company has been specified. The parties acknowledge that a fee may be paid by the warranty company to one of the Brokers involved in this transaction. The amount of this fee will be disclosed to Seller and Purchaser upon request after the warranty company has been specified.

7. Residential Property Disclosure Form. Purchaser _____ has _____ has not (check one) received a State of Ohio "Residential Property Disclosure Form" before signing this offer.

OTHER ADDENDA

_____

_____

_____

_____

_____

_____

_____

_____

_____

_____

_____

_____

_____

Purchaser _____	**Seller** _____
Purchaser _____	**Seller** _____
Date _____	**Date** _____

built or repaired improvements, or even sell the property to another party. Because of these risks most title insurance companies will not insure title to be received under an installment land contract.

To protect land contract vendees, some states require vendors to place the property deed with an escrow agent. This system has advantages for both parties. The vendee benefits from the fact that delivery of the deed to the escrow agent effectively divests the seller of title so that the quality of the title will not be affected by any subsequent financial difficulties incurred by the vendor. The escrow arrangement, therefore, provides the vendee with an insurable title. An advantage for the vendor is that the vendee places a signed quit-claim deed in escrow at the time of closing which can minimize title imperfections if the vendee defaults.

Some states specify what a land contract must contain and require that they be recorded. The degree to which land contracts are recorded in states where recordation is not mandatory varies greatly. The recordation of land contracts minimizes the potential problems described earlier. Buyers should still use great care when contemplating the use of a land contract because such contracts often include provisions that are slanted in favor of the seller.

Who Uses Land Contracts?

In many cases, those who use land contracts are property owners who want to sell, and buyers who cannot qualify for a mortgage loan from an institutional lender. Land contracts are generally considered to be a creative financing device, attractive to buyers because they require little or no down payment. In addition, they may carry a below-market interest rate. The seller sometimes recoups the difference by inflating the selling price. In some instances, the people who use land contracts are not sophisticated buyers and may sign the contract before an attorney reviews it. In other cases, particularly where land prices are rising rapidly, sophisticated buyers may use land contracts because it is one of the few ways they can afford the purchase.

Decision Point

You are extremely interested in acquiring a particular parcel of real property and have agreed to enter into a land contract with the property owner. What would you do if the owner informs you that the deal is off unless you sign the contract today?

OPTION CONTRACTS

Option contracts involve an arrangement whereby one party pays another a sum of money in exchange for the second party's promise to keep open an offer for a specific period of time. The party who bought the option, the optionee, has the right, but not the duty, to exercise the option within the allotted time. The party who sold the option, the optionor, has the duty to hold the offer open and deliver ownership of the optioned property to the optionee if the option is exercised.

Options are used in a number of ways in real estate. For example, a lease may give the tenant the option to purchase the leased property or the option to extend the term of the lease. Another common use of options in real estate occurs in the development process, to secure the right to purchase property at a particular price.

An option to purchase real estate is similar to a call option in securities trading in that it gives the optionee the right to purchase, on or before a particular date (the expiration date), a particular parcel of real estate at a particular price (the exercise price). In exchange

CONSUMER CHECKLIST

INSTALLMENT LAND CONTRACTS

Because of the disreputable practices previously associated with land contracts, many states have enacted laws that govern them. If you plan to enter into a land contract, first you should determine if the state in which the property is located has such a law and ensure that all provisions of the law are followed. In addition, whether required by law or not, the following list contains suggestions to be included for the protection of both the vendor and the vendee.

1. Both parties should receive a copy of the contract.
2. The contract should include:
    a. The full names and address of all parties to the contract
    b. The date each party signed the contract
    c. A legal description of the property involved
    d. The contract price of the property
    e. Any fees or charges that are included in the contract but separate from the contract price
    f. The amount of the downpayment
    g. The balance owed
    h. The due date and amount of each payment
    i. The interest rate that applies to the unpaid balance and the method of computing the payment
    j. A statement regarding whether prepayments are allowed without penalty
    k. A statement regarding how the balance owed will be determined in the event of early payoff
    l. A statement of any encumbrances against the property
    m. A statement regarding any pending order of any public agency against the property
    n. A provision that the vendor supply evidence of title in accordance with the prevailing custom for the area in which the property is located
    o. A provision that requires the vendor to deliver a warranty deed (or whatever deed is available if the vendor is unable to deliver a warranty deed) upon completion of the contract
    p. A statement that the vendor will not mortgage the property for more than the amount owed on the land contract
    q. A statement that should the vendor default on any mortgage on the property, the vendee may make the payments and deduct such payments from the balance owed
    r. A provision that, unless otherwise agreed, the vendee is responsible for the payment of property taxes and any other charges against the property from the contract date
    s. A provision requiring the vendor to have the contract recorded within a certain time period (e.g., twenty days) of the date it is signed

---

for the promise to deliver upon demand, the optionor receives some compensation: the option price. Once the option contract is signed there are only a few possible outcomes. One possibility is that the option is never exercised. In this case, the option expires worthless and the optionor keeps the money received for the option. A second possibility is that the optionee decides to exercise the option. In this case, the optionee pays the optionor the exercise price and the optionor conveys title to the property. Like any other contract, an option may be sold, or assigned, to a third party unless this is forbidden in the contract. Therefore, a third possibility is that the option is sold to a third party, who, in turn, can either let it expire, sell it to another, or exercise it.

The value of an option is a function of both the amount of time that remains before it expires (time value) and the relationship of the exercise price to the market price of the property (in the money value). The longer the time until the option expires, the more valuable the option. If the exercise price of the option is higher than the market price of the property, the option is said to be "out of the money." If the exercise price is equal to the market price of the property, the option is "at the money." Initially, it is likely that an option to purchase real estate will be out of or at the money. In either case, the option has no "in the money" value. However, over time the market price of the property may increase and exceed the exercise price of the option. In this case, the option is "in the money," and the option has value because it allows the optionee to acquire the property at less than its current market price (or sell the option at a profit).

Why Do People Sell Options?

Some property owners sell options as a way to generate income from a property. If they do not actually wish to sell the property, selling an option is a gamble that the option will not be exercised. Others may wish to sell property to a particular buyer who, for one reason or another, is not ready to proceed with the transaction. Some may view options as a way to effectively increase the selling price of the property, a view that is not recommended. To illustrate this point, assume an owner is willing to sell a piece of property for $100,000 and someone has offered $2,000 for the right to purchase it for that price sometime in the next year. At worst, the owner reasons, the buyer will not exercise the option and both the land and option price will be retained. Even if the option is exercised the owner reasons that he or she effectively sold a $100,000 property for $102,000. The owner is likely to regret selling the option, however, if the optionee locates a buyer willing to pay $125,000 for the property. Therefore, every option should be supported by actual consideration because the option entitles the optionee to a valuable right—the right to purchase the property at a set price.

Why Do People Purchase Options?

One reason a person may purchase an option is if the purchaser finds the sale price attractive, but wishes more time to evaluate the property and is afraid that it will be sold to another in the time it would take to conduct the analysis. As the above example demonstrates, another reason to acquire an option is that it affords the optionee the opportunity to make a profit.

If an investor is convinced that a property is going to increase in value, the property itself rather than an option to purchase could be acquired. If this were done, given the facts in the above example, a profit of $25,000 could have been earned, resulting in a holding period return of 25 percent [($125,000 − $100,000) ÷ $100,000]. By acquiring an option, however, the investor can employ leverage that may increase his or her return. **Leverage** is generally defined as using borrowed funds to make an investment, but in this case the investor effectively borrowed the property. Given the above facts, use of the option would result in a holding period return of 1,250 percent [$125,000 − $100,000) ÷ $2,000]. This profit can be realized in one of two ways: the option can be exercised and the property then sold to a third party, or the option can be sold to another. Assuming that the option is exercised just before it expires, it will have little, if any, time value. But, because the option entitles the holder to acquire property for $25,000 less than its current market price, the option should sell for approximately this amount.

The above example is not meant to imply that options are a sure way to riches. The price of real property, like the price of any other asset, can go down as well as up. If the price of the property in our example had decreased, the option would have lost value as time passed and the option would have either been allowed to expire or sold at a loss.

Decision Point

A property is for sale by owner for $100,000. The owner has expressed an interest in selling you an option on the property that would allow you to purchase it at that price. One alternative is a 30-day option costing $1,000; the second is a 90-day option costing $3,000. You make the following estimates:

Locating a buyer willing to pay	Probability
$110,000 within 30 days	50 percent
$100,000 within 30 days	50 percent
$110,000 within 90 days	70 percent
$100,000 within 90 days	30 percent

Which, if either, option contract would you purchase?

REMEDIES FOR NONPERFORMANCE

Sometimes one of the parties to a contract fails to perform as agreed. To illustrate the possible remedies to which either party may be entitled in the event of a breach, consider a purchase contract. If a real property seller fails to perform as agreed, the remedies available to the purchaser include an action for specific performance, and an action for damages. **Specific performance** means that a court will order the party in breach of the contract to perform according to the contract. Courts are generally not reluctant to order sellers to specifically perform because of the unique nature of real estate. There may be no other similar property, and there certainly is no property that is identical to the property the seller is unwilling to deliver. **Damages** refer to any monetary loss caused by the breach. The court may award any costs incurred by the buyer in negotiating the purchase of the property or in acquiring financing for the property.

When a buyer fails to perform as agreed, sellers have three possible remedies: action for specific performance, action for damages, and liquidated damages. Specific performance is, however, seldom granted as a seller's remedy because courts are reluctant to force a party to purchase a property they no longer wish to purchase. Unlike properties, which are unique, the courts generally consider one buyer just as good as another. Of course, another buyer may pay a lower price, and the seller may incur costs in securing another buyer that can be recovered in a suit for damages. A seller who seeks a remedy may avoid a lawsuit for either specific performance or damages by settling for the liquidated damages specified in the sales contract.

SUMMARY

To make sound decisions regarding real estate one must have a basic understanding of contracts. A contract governs the rights and responsibilities of the involved parties. The five essential elements of a contract that must be present in order for the contract to be legally enforceable are competent parties, an offer, acceptance, consideration, and a legal and proper objective.

Contracts are commonly used in several types of real estate transactions, including listing property with a broker, purchase agreements between a buyer and seller, and options to purchase. One may acquire property by using a purchase contract similar to the form provided in Exhibit 11.1 which contains provisions that should be included in all such contracts, although special circumstances may necessitate additional provisions. As an alternative to the purchase contract, title to real property may be acquired with an installment land contract. Installment land contracts do, however, present special hazards to the buyer.

KEY TERMS

acceptance	damages	mutual assent
assignment	earnest money	offer
breach of contract	installment land contract	option contract
competent party	legal or proper objective	purchase contract
consideration	leverage	specific performance
contingency	liquidated damages	Statute of Frauds
contract	listing contract	
counter-offer	marketable title	

REVIEW QUESTIONS

1. What are the five essential elements of a contract? Locate each element in the purchase contract in Exhibit 11.1.
2. What are the buyer's remedies if the seller breaches a real estate purchase contract by failing to deliver marketable title? Does the seller have different remedies if the buyer defaults?
3. What happens if an offeror revokes an offer to purchase real property after the offeree has accepted it, but before the acceptance has been communicated to the offeror?
4. How does an installment land contract differ from a contract for the sale of land?
5. What is the difference between a voidable contract and a void contract?
6. What motivates people to buy and sell options to purchase land?
7. What is the difference between a unilateral contract and a bilateral contract? Give examples of both.
8. Identify and explain at least five important provisions of a real estate purchase contract.
9. What are your answers to the questions in the four "Decision Point" sections in this chapter?
10. What is your answer to the "Ethical Issue" in this chapter?

REAL ESTATE ON THE WEB

Use your favorite search engine to:

1. Locate a Web site from which preprinted real estate purchase contracts may be downloaded.
2. Research the use of option contracts in real estate development and investing.
3. Discover if installment land contracts must be recorded in your state.
4. Learn the size of earnest money deposits normally required in your area.

Refer to the companion Web site at www.wiley.com/college/larsen for a variety of online activities including additional chapter content, review materials, assignments, and related links.

ADDITIONAL READINGS

Knight, J.R., T. Miceli and C. F. Sirmans. "Repair Expenses, Selling Contracts, and House Prices." *The Journal of Real Estate Research* (Nov./Dec. 2000): 323–336.

Newman, J. H. "Impairing the Remedy of Stipulated Damages." *Real Estate Review* (Spring 1999): 63–67.

Seiders, D. F. "What's in a House Price?" *Builder* (August 2000): 104–106.

Valachi, D. J. "Installment Sales." *Commercial Investment Real Estate Journal* (Sept./Oct. 1997): 34–37.

12 Deeds

Learning Objectives

After studying this chapter you should be able to:

- Explain the elements essential to a valid deed.
- Compare the various types of deeds and explain the covenants contained in each.
- Describe the circumstances that may result in a deed being declared void.
- Understand why it is important to record a deed in the public record.
- Understand how a person may use a will to specify the distribution of real property.

FROM THE WIRE

In May 2002. Manatee, Florida authorities began a criminal investigation after receiving a complaint from a local resident. The resident, whose home is located adjacent to the Manatee River, had been approached by a man who said that he had purchased the small lot adjoining the resident's property, and that unless the resident gave him $20,000 he was going to park junk cars on the lot. In related transactions, the authorities discovered that the same person had previously tried to parlay careful research and cheap tax deed purchases into huge profits. In Pinellas County, he built a fence between the water and the pricey homes around it and told homeowners they would have to pay $30,000 each to get back their views. And in South Pasadena, he purchased a tax deed for the submerged lands under Boca Ciega Bay and told homeowners they would have to pay him to keep their docks from being fenced off. Unfortunately for the culprit, in the Manatee case, the lot that he claimed to have purchased was owned by a company that went out of business fourteen years ago, and authorities could find no record of the individual whose signature appears on the deed that "transferred ownership" to him.

Go to www.hillsclerk.com, click on "search," then search "tax deeds" and read one or more of the 27 records to learn more about tax deeds in Florida.

INTRODUCTION

You should have a basic understanding of deeds and wills to make good decisions concerning the acquisition or disposal of real estate. If you are acquiring real estate, you should be aware of the type of deed employed because it influences the quality of the title you possess which, in turn, may affect the property's value. The type of deed is also important when you convey title because it can affect both your current obligations and your future liability should a title defect become apparent. Some knowledge of wills is important to ensure that, upon one's death, property is distributed according to one's wishes.

It is possible to hold title to real property without a deed. Examples of such cases include title acquired through adverse possession, and title acquired through a legal life estate such as dower or curtesy. In these relatively rare cases, ownership is deemed to exist as an operation of the law, so a deed is not needed. However, most real estate transactions require a documentary act to transfer ownership, and the document used is a deed. Therefore, in this chapter, we explain the important elements of a deed, which, as the chapter opener "From the Wire" implies, includes a valid signature. We also explain the various types of deeds that can be used, as well as the use of a will to specify one's real property distribution wishes. As in many other areas of real estate, state laws concerning deeds and wills vary greatly. It is, therefore, important to consult with an attorney who specializes in real estate when structuring a transaction.

VOLUNTARY AND INVOLUNTARY OWNERSHIP TRANSFERS

In previous chapters we discussed how ownership of real property might be lost to the government under the power of eminent domain, escheat, or confiscation, or to a nongovernmental party through adverse possession. Each of these means of transferring title is an example of an involuntary transfer of ownership. The majority of real property transfers, however, occur with the consent of the owner. A consensual transfer is referred to as a voluntary transfer, and is the focus of this chapter. Voluntary transfers of title are accomplished with a deed executed either by the grantor or, if the property owner is no longer living, by the executor of the owner's estate as prescribed in the owner's will. Both types of documents must be drafted carefully to ensure that they, in fact, transfer the desired ownership interest and amount of real estate.

DEEDS

A **deed** is a written instrument, or document, that serves two purposes: evidence of real property ownership, and as a vehicle to transfer title, a conveyance. Basically, a deed states that the holder of the deed is, in fact, the legitimate real property owner. It is important to understand that the deed is merely evidence of title and not title itself. Therefore, if a deed is lost or destroyed the property owner does not lose ownership or the rights associated with ownership. The deed is simply a tangible piece of paper that reflects the intangible rights of real property ownership.

When properly executed, delivered, and accepted a deed conveys title. Deeds are normally used for this purpose during the property owner's lifetime, whereas wills are used to specify the transfer of ownership after the owner's death. The party transferring title is called the **grantor,** and the party receiving title is referred to as the **grantee.** The grantee and buyer are usually, but not always, the same individual or entity. It is possible, for example, that one party may purchase real estate and put it in another individual's name, as a gift.

In previous chapters, we explained that a property owner is not required to transfer all property rights in a single conveyance. If, for example, the grantor wishes to retain road access across the transferred property, or wishes to retain a life estate in the property, the grantor's desire can be accomplished by placing a specific type of clause in the deed called a **reservation.** A reservation, therefore, creates an independent right that did not exist before the conveyance. A reservation can also be used to limit the manner in which a property is used, and an interesting example of this is provided in the following "Doing Business."

ESSENTIAL ELEMENTS FOR A VALID DEED

A deed need not contain any formal or technical wording to be valid. However, according to the Statute of Frauds, a deed must be in writing to be enforceable. Additionally, the following six items are essential for a deed to be valid.

1. Both the grantor and grantee must be named.
2. There must be a legal description of the subject property.
3. In most states, there must be some mention of consideration.
4. Words that make clear the grantor's intention to transfer an interest in the property must be included.
5. The grantor's, and possibly the grantee's, signature must be on the document.
6. The grantor must deliver the deed to the grantee, and the grantee must accept it.

DOING BUSINESS
LEGAL ISSUE

A sign outside Captain Sid's Subs and Sandwiches in Fredericksburg, Virginia announces that the restaurant is now selling hamburgers again. The restaurant's owner, Teresa Nagy, said her business began leasing its present site in 1997 after moving there from a nearby location. But, a clause in her lease prevented use of the property as "a fast food operation specializing in the sale of hamburgers, chicken and/or breakfast biscuits until March 23, 2002." The reason for the restriction resulted from a land swap that occurred in 1982. At that time, the property where Captain Sid's now sits was owned by the hamburger chain Hardee's, and the land where the local Hardee's is now located was owned by the (former) owner of the Captain Sid's property. To protect itself from competition, Hardee's placed the above restriction in the deed used to accomplish the swap. Over the next 20 years, a couple of restaurants, a used car business and a furniture store occupied the space; none of which were allowed to sell hamburgers. Nagy thought the restriction was ludicrous, and in 2000 hired a lawyer to try to get her out of the lease. She lost, but now the restriction has lapsed, Captain Sid's is selling Burgers, and according to Nagy, "Everybody loves them."

Go to www.realtor.org/realtormag, use "deed restrictions" as your search term, then click on one or more of the search results to learn more about this topic.

Named Grantor and Grantee

The named grantor(s) must be competent (of legal age and of sound mind). This requirement is to ensure that those who do not have the mental capacity or maturity to understand the consequences of executing a deed will not be deprived of their property. If a deed is executed without this requirement, the grantor can take legal action to have the transfer set aside and title restored. In cases with more than one grantor, it is customary to have each named in a single deed, although each grantor may convey his or her interest with a separate deed.

The grantee must be named in the deed. In some cases, a void deed results although this requirement is satisfied. For example, a deed delivered to the estate of a deceased grantee is void for lack of an actual grantee. Likewise, a deed to a fictitious party is void. A deed to a party using a fictitious name is, however, valid. For example, if a deed names Morgan Fairchild as the grantee, the deed is valid although her real name is Patsy McKinney. While a competent grantor is required, naming an incompetent or minor grantee will not necessarily invalidate the deed.

Legal Description of the Property

Inclusion of a description that results in the unquestionable identification of the property must also be included in the deed. Any of the legal description methods described in Chapter 8 can be used for property identification. A common exception to this requirement is a condominium deed, where the unit designation and a post office address are generally sufficient because the full legal description is included in the recorded condominium declaration. Usually, to avoid confusion, it is advisable to use the same legal description contained in previous deeds to convey a property. In some instances, for example, in the case of land that has been subdivided, using an earlier description may not be appropriate. If an error occurs in a legal description that purports to convey more than the grantor owns, the deed is usually valid for the portion of the description the grantor actually owns. Sometimes, following the legal description, there is a **recital clause** that states all, or part, of the title chain to indicate how the grantor acquired title.

Consideration

State laws vary regarding the recital of the consideration the grantee offers in exchange for the property. Some statutes require that the actual amount paid for the property, **actual consideration,** be included in the deed (deeds granted by corporations and fiduciaries must state the actual consideration). Most states only require the citation of **nominal consideration,** which need not be related to the actual amount paid. For example, for a house that sold for $250,000, the recital might state: "for $10 and other good and valuable consideration." Some states do not require a recital of consideration in the deed. Even in these states, however, some mention of consideration is usually included in the deed

Grantees may prefer a recitation of nominal consideration for at least two reasons. First, to keep the actual consideration confidential, although as we showed in Chapter 3 this objective can be defeated by anyone with a knowledge of the public records. Second, to make clear that the grantee is a purchaser and not a recipient of a gift. The distinction between purchasing the property or acquiring it by gift may be important, and is discussed in a following section titled "Deeds Which May Be Declared Void."

A monetary value is stated for both actual and nominal consideration, both of which are types of valuable consideration. The recital of good consideration in a deed may also be acceptable. An example of good consideration is "for love and affection." This, or a similar phrase, is sometimes used in a gift deed where, for example, one party wishes to hold title jointly with a spouse property that was previously owned in severalty.

Operative Words of Conveyance

To make clear the grantor's intent to convey title to the grantee, each deed must contain operative words of conveyance. These words are commonly called the granting clause, and they must be carefully chosen because, as shown in the following table, they reflect the type of deed being used.

Listed below are some of the phrases commonly used as the operative words of conveyance in the deeds discussed in this chapter.

Type of Deed	Operative Words of Conveyance
General warranty	"grant and convey"
	"convey and warrant"
	"warrant generally"
Special warranty	"warrant specially"
Bargain and sale	"grant bargain and sell"
	"conveys"
	"grant and release"
Quitclaim	"remise, release, and quitclaim"
	"release and quitclaim"

Signatures

A deed is executed when it is signed by the grantor, sealed (a more formal method of acknowledgement required in some states), and delivered to the grantee. Most states require a corporate seal if the grantor is a corporation. The corporate seal serves as evidence that the proper corporate officer, with control of the corporate seal and the power to convey property, has executed the deed. For a deed to be properly executed, each grantor must sign it, or make a mark if he or she cannot write. In most states, a signature by grantor's mark must be witnessed. With a **power of attorney** deeds are sometimes legally executed by someone other than the grantor. Some states require that the marital status of the grantor(s) be stated and, if married, require the spouse to sign the deed to release any community property, dower, curtesy, or homestead rights. It is important that deeds be accurate, however, a mistake in the spelling of the grantor's name or signature does not affect the validity of the deed if the grantor's identity is otherwise clear. These types of mistakes may be corrected by filing a correction deed. If such a correction is not made the error may cause problems in subsequent transfers of the property.

Some states require that deeds be acknowledged. An **acknowledgement** is a formal declaration, before a notary public or another duly authorized official, by the person who has executed an instrument that such execution was one's own free and voluntary act. An unacknowledged deed is valid for the purpose of transferring title, but an unacknowledged deed cannot be recorded in many states.

The grantee's signature on the deed is usually not required. However, the grantee's signature is required if the grantee assumes an existing mortgage or agrees to comply with a restrictive covenant in the deed. When title to real estate is conveyed it is assumed to be made free of any restrictions and encumbrances except those expressly stated. Restrictive covenants that are binding on future owners are sometimes referred to as covenants running with the land. Examples include limitations on the height of improvements, and whether livestock may be kept on the property. To be enforceable, such a covenant must: "touch and concern" the land, be included in the deed, have been the intention of the original parties that it would run with the land, and subsequent grantees must have notice of its existence.

Deeds have been used to transfer land title for several centuries. Some early deeds were known as indenture deeds. Two copies of such deeds were drawn on a single sheepskin, signed by both the grantor and grantee, then torn into two pieces with the grantor and grantee each receiving a copy. In this way grantees could prove that their half of the deed was legitimate by matching the indentations, or indentures with those on the other half. Today some deeds (and other documents) still begin with the words "By this indenture." Unlike the indenture deed, a deed poll required only the signature of the grantor, and had a clean-shaven edge. Although the terms indenture deed and deed poll are infrequently used today, when used, they imply deeds that are signed by both parties or only by the grantor, respectively.

Delivery and Acceptance

The final act of the grantor, which signifies that the deed shall take effect, is the delivery of the deed to the grantee. Usually, title to real property transfers when the deed is delivered to, and accepted by, the grantee (under the Torrens registration system, which is explained in Chapter 13, title is conveyed at the time of registration, not at the time of delivery and acceptance of the deed). Delivery can be actual, as during closings attended by both the grantor and grantee, or in escrow by agents of the parties (Chapter 14). Once the deed is

DOING BUSINESS

ESTATE PLANNING

Ivan Mean* is a bitter person who feels that none of his children give him the respect that he deserves. To retaliate, whenever possible, he finds ways to hurt them and he would like to continue doing so after his death. He owns a piece of real estate that he knows his children would love to purchase or inherit. So, Ivan drafts a deed transferring the property to his niece, Denise, who has always treated him well. Because he wants to retain control of the property until his death, he does not inform her about the deed. Instead, after signing the deed he gives it to Hal, an old school friend. Ivan instructs Hal to deliver the deed to Denise at Ivan's funeral. This part of Mr. Mean's venture into estate planning is likely to be unsuccessful because, after his death, if his children challenge the deed in court they will win. Before reading the next paragraph can you explain why?

One reason the deed can be successfully challenged is because it was never delivered to the grantee or her agent. It is highly unlikely that Hal was acting as Denise's agent because she knew nothing of the deed. Given the facts, it appears that Hal was acting as Ivan's agent and Ivan's death automatically terminates the agency relationship, so Hal no longer has the authority to deliver the deed after Ivan's death.

Delivery is a question of intent by the grantor, and usually must be made during the life of the grantor. Mr. Mean could have accomplished his objective if he acted in any one of several different ways. 1.) He could have inserted a clause in the deed specifying that the deed takes effect upon his death and delivered the deed to his niece. This would have met the delivery requirement, because it makes clear his intent to deliver now the right to the property upon his death. 2.) Ivan could have specified in his will that Denise was to receive the property. 3.) Ivan could have delivered the deed to a third person, in trust for the grantee. In a trust arrangement, however, the grantor must surrender all rights to control or recover the deed, which Mr. Mean was unwilling to do. For this reason he also would not elect 4.) to give Denise the property with a gift deed.

Go to www.lexis-nexis.com/universe, using your university computer system, click on Legal Research, then click on Area of Law by Topic and search "deed delivery" to find other cases involving the delivery of a deed.

*names changed to protect the guilty

delivered and accepted, the destruction of the deed has no effect on title because the deed is only evidence of title, not the title itself. If the deed is lost, the grantee does not have to be concerned with the possibility that title will revert to the grantor. In fact, if a grantee wished to transfer title back to the grantor, returning the deed to the grantor or destroying it would be ineffective for this purpose. The only way to accomplish such a transfer is to prepare a new deed that satisfies all the requirements just presented.

Recording a Deed

In most states, deeds do not have to be recorded to be valid between the grantor and grantee, but they usually are recorded to protect the grantee from claims made by third parties. In addition, if a deed is lost or destroyed, a property owner may have difficulty proving title if the deed was not recorded.

Recording a deed at the County Recorder's Office in which the property is located gives constructive notice that the grantee has acquired an interest in the property. Unless third parties have either constructive or actual notice of the ownership of the property, the grantee is not protected against their claims. For example, if Sam conveys title to his tavern to Woody, who does not record the deed, and subsequently Sam conveys the same property to Cliff, who does record the deed; Cliff would have legal title to the property if he had no knowledge of the previous unrecorded transaction.

Deeds Which May Be Declared Void

Under certain circumstances, a court may declare a deed void although it meets all of the legal requirements discussed above. A court would declare a deed void if undue influence was exerted on the grantor to induce the transfer of title. Often, such transfers occur with little or no consideration. Relatives of the grantor who would have inherited the property had ownership been retained by the grantor until death usually initiate lawsuits to have a deed set aside. Frequently, the grantee is alleged to have exerted undue influence on the grantor, although real estate brokers and other professionals are not immune.

A court is also likely to declare a deed void in any case in which the conveyance constitutes a fraud on the grantor's creditors. For creditors to be defrauded, a deed must be executed in exchange for less than the fair market value of the property, and the remaining assets of the grantor must be insufficient to satisfy all outstanding debts owed at the time of the transfer. If both of these conditions do not exist, then the real estate transfer did not harm the creditors. Frequently, deeds that defraud creditors involve transfer of title to a relative or close friend of the grantor. Imagine, for example, a person who is about to lose a large lawsuit and whose assets are in real property. The person might convey the property to a relative with a gift deed to avoid paying the judgment creditor. Under these circumstances, a creditor is likely to have a court set aside the transfer as a fraud. If, instead, the person sold the property to a stranger with a deed of purchase, it would be difficult for the creditor to convince a court to set aside the conveyance. The recitation of valuable consideration in such a deed helps protect the grantee as a good-faith purchaser under the state's recording acts.

Parts of a Deed

The following is a brief description of the three major parts of a deed:

■ **Premises**—Contains the terms upon which the transfer of title is to be made. The elements usually contained in the premises include: names of the grantor and grantee, recital of consideration, legal description of the property, operative words of conveyance, any exceptions and restrictions, and the date. The last two items are not essential elements for a valid deed. A date is, however, recommended to help prevent future questions concerning the time of the transfer.

- **Habendum**—Part of the deed in which the extent of the interest (quantum of estate) being conveyed by the grantor is defined (e.g., fee simple, easement, life estate). The habendum follows the granting clause, and usually begins with the words "to have and to hold" and then describes the estate being conveyed. The habendum may include an appurtenance clause. Recall that an appurtenance is a right that runs with the land. The inclusion of such a clause, which describes any improvements on the land and all the additional rights that are necessary to the proper use and enjoyment of the property, is optional. If an appurtenance clause is included in the habendum, it must be consistent with the granting clause in the premises. Inconsistency between the two may result in unwanted legal costs to resolve the problem.

- **Testimonium**—Contains any covenants of warranty, the signatures, and the acknowledgement.

TYPES OF DEEDS

In voluntary transfers, parties may employ any one of several types of deeds. The two most commonly used deeds are the general warranty and the quitclaim. Other types are sometimes employed, including bargain and sale, and special warranty. The primary difference between deed types is the number of promises, or warranties, made by the grantor.

General Warranty Deed

The deed most commonly used to satisfy purchase agreements is the **general warranty deed,** also referred to as a warranty deed, or full warranty deed. An example of a general warranty deed is shown in Exhibit 12.1. The name of this deed is descriptive because in using it the grantor makes several warranties to the grantee. From the purchaser's perspective, this is the most desirable type of deed because the grantor fully warrants the title to the property.

Occasionally, a grantor conveys property to which the grantor, either knowingly or unknowingly, does not own title. There is a legal doctrine known as estoppel by deed, also called title by estoppel, which applies to general warranty deeds, and not others, such as a quitclaim. Under this doctrine, should the grantor subsequently obtain the interest claimed, but not possessed at the time of the deed delivery, the interest is automatically vested in the grantee.

Various versions of the general warranty deed are sometimes used. For example, a grant deed is commonly used in California and other states. In these deeds, the grantor normally warrants only three things: that the grantor has not encumbered the title except as noted in the deed, that the interest currently being conveyed has not previously been conveyed by the grantor, and that any title to the property later acquired by the grantor will be conveyed to the grantee.

The general warranty deed covenants bind not only the grantor, but also the grantor's heirs and assigns. There is no time limit concerning the enforcement of the promises made by the grantor in a general warranty deed. Therefore, the grantor, the grantor's administrator, executor, or heirs can be liable to defend a dispute over the quality of the title, and to compensate the grantee for any losses incurred should the title later be found to be other than the character represented in the deed.

There are five standard covenants in a general warranty deed: the covenant of seisen, the covenant against encumbrances, the covenant of quiet enjoyment, the covenant of further assurance, and the covenant of warranty forever. The first two concern the present character of the title while the others make guarantees about the future goodness of the title.

EXHIBIT 12.1 **GENERAL WARRENTY DEED**

GENERAL WARRANTY DEED, Statutory Form No. 22-S   (Reprinted 10/91)   **apco** Registered in U.S. Patent and Trademark Office
anderson publishing co. cincinnati, ohio 45201

General Warranty Deed*

[1], of   County,

for valuable consideration paid, grant(s) with general warranty covenants, to

, *whose tax-mailing address is*

the following **REAL PROPERTY:** *Situated in the County of*   *in the State*

of Ohio and in the   of   :[2]

Prior Instrument Reference: Volume   *Page*   *of the Deed Records of*

County, Ohio.

[3] *wife (husband) of the*

Grantor, releases all rights of dower therein. Witness   *hand(s) this*   *day*

of   , 19

Signed and acknowledged in presence of:

_____   _____ [4]

_____   _____

State of Ohio   *County of*   ss.

BE IT REMEMBERED, *That on this*   *day of*   , 19   , *before me,*

the subscriber, a   *in and for said state, personally came,*

                                                          the Grantor(s) in the

foregoing deed, and acknowledged the signing thereof to be   *voluntary act and deed.*

IN TESTIMONY THEREOF, *I have hereunto subscribed my name and affixed my*   *seal*

on the day and year last aforesaid.

_____

This instrument was prepared by _____

(1) **Name of Grantor(s) and marital status.**
(2) **Description of land or interest therein, and encumbrances, reservations, and exceptions, taxes and assessments, if any.**
(3) **Delete whichever does not apply.**
(4) **Execution in accordance with Chapter 5301 Ohio Revised Code.**

Auditor's and Recorder's Stamps

*See Sections 5302.05 and 5302.06 Ohio Revised Code.

Covenant of Seisen   With this covenant, the grantor warrants possession of good title to the real property at the time of the transfer. The term "seisen" derives from the ancient custom whereby a landowner signified the intention to transfer ownership by grabbing a handful of the land and handing it to the new owner. If, at the time of delivery, the grantor does not hold the interest claimed in the deed, this clause entitles the grantee to recover the price paid for the property.

Covenant Against Encumbrances   With this covenant, the grantor warrants that there are no encumbrances, such as liens or easements, against the title other than those disclosed in the deed. From the perspective of the grantor, it is important to have all existing encumbrances listed in the deed, because the grantee can usually recover from the grantor any expenses incurred in extinguishing unlisted encumbrances. Even if the encumbrance was unknown by the grantor at the time of the conveyance, the grantee can recover such expenses. An exception to recovering expenses would be where there was an open and visible physical encumbrance such as an easement for a power line.

Covenant of Quiet Enjoyment   Surprisingly, for many beginning real estate students, this covenant has nothing to do with noise. With this covenant, the grantor promises that the grantee, as well as the grantee's heirs and assigns will have the right to the property free from interference by third parties. Thus, innocent grantees are protected from disputes arising between former claimants and the grantor.

Covenant of Further Assurance   With this covenant, sometimes called the covenant of further assistance, the grantor promises to take, and pay for, whatever action is required after delivery of the deed to perfect the title delivered to the buyer. Examples of such actions include securing releases for unrecorded interests in the property, or recording a satisfaction of the grantor's mortgage.

Covenant of Warranty Forever   With this covenant, sometimes called the covenant of warranty of title, the grantor promises to pay for the defense of the grantee's title, should it ever be challenged by a third party. Under this covenant, the grantor is also liable to the grantee for the value of the property should the grantee be evicted by a third party with a superior title.

Special Warranty Deed

The covenants in a **special warranty deed** are far less extensive than those of a general warranty deed. These deeds make no warranty concerning title defects arising prior to the grantor's ownership. They make only the single promise that the title has not been impaired by the grantor. The clause in the deed where this promise is contained is sometimes referred to as the covenant against grantor's acts. To illustrate the difference between a special warranty and general warranty deed consider the following case. Fred deeded land to Barnie. The land was subject to a mortgage given to the Bedrock Bank by the party who sold the land to Fred. The deed Fred used to convey title to Barnie contained no mention of the fact that the title was subject to a mortgage. Later, the Bedrock Bank foreclosed. If Fred gave a special warranty deed, he would not be liable for damages resulting from foreclosure of the preexisting mortgage, or any other defect created before he took title. If, instead, Fred gave a general warranty deed, he would be liable despite the fact that the mortgage was placed on the property before he took title.

Although a special warranty deed could be used to satisfy a purchase agreement, they seldom are. From the grantee's perspective, there are many disadvantages that stem from the fact that the grantor is only required to defend the title against claims arising during the grantor's period of ownership. Special warranty deeds do, however, serve a useful purpose in cases where a general warranty deed is unneeded or inappropriate. Special warranty deeds are sometimes used in divorce settlements, when one spouse conveys real property to the other, and the Federal Housing Administration currently uses them to deed property the agency has acquired through foreclosure. Additionally, people who act in a fiduciary capacity such as estate executors, trustees and court officers, frequently convey the property under their control using a special warranty deed, or a bargain and sale deed, because they do not have the authority to make warranties against their predecessors in title.

Bargain and Sale Deed

A **bargain and sale deed** is a deed that was formerly in the form of a contract between the buyer and seller that recites a consideration and transfers all of the grantor's interest in the property to the grantee. Synonyms for such a deed include deed without warranty, and bargain and sale deed without warranty. The synonyms are descriptive in that such deeds usually do not include a warranty of title to the property conveyed. The bargain and sale grantor asserts by implication that ownership is possessed, but makes no other claims, unless included in the deed. These deeds are similar to, but offer the grantee even less protection than, special warranty deeds. In effect, the grantor promises only that the grantor has done nothing to cause a defect in the title and is, therefore, not liable for unknown defects. Thus, if the grantee later learns of defects in the title, the grantor cannot be forced to clear up the defects because the grantor did not promise to do so.

If the parties agree, covenants against liens and other encumbrances may be included in the deed, and in this case the deed is a bargain and sale deed with covenants. Fiduciaries, estate executors, trustees and court officers frequently convey the property under their control using a bargain and sale deed, sometimes with a covenant against the grantor's acts.

Quitclaim Deed

For a deed to be valid, it is not necessary that it contain any warranties. The simplest form of deed, the **quitclaim,** or release deed does not contain any warranties. An examination of the sample quitclaim in Exhibit 12.2 will reveal that quitclaims provide grantees the least title protection of all deed types. Quitclaims convey only the interest the grantor holds at the time the deed is delivered, which may include full title. If, however, the grantor has some lesser interest, including no interest in the property at the time the quitclaim is delivered, that is exactly what the grantee receives, and the grantee has no recourse against the grantor because no warranty of ownership is made in a quitclaim. Due to the lack of protection afforded grantees, quitclaims are not recommended for transfers of fee interests.

You may question whether quitclaims have any legitimate use. The answer is yes; quitclaims do have a number of legitimate uses. They are frequently used to remove a title cloud, or to remove a name from a deed (e.g., partitioned property among tenants in common, divorce settlements, or a deceased co-owner). They can also be used to remove restrictive covenants in a prior deed, although this may be impractical because quitclaims must be secured from all beneficial owners.

Decision Point

You are purchasing some real property from your brother. He has owned the property for more than a decade, having acquired ownership shortly before entering the ministry. Would you accept a quitclaim deed as a conveyance?

If you were interested in obtaining a clear title, would you accept a quitclaim deed from a complete stranger?

EXHIBIT 12.2 | **QUITCLAIM DEED**

QUIT CLAIM DEED, Short Form, Statutory Form No. 27-S   (Reprinted 2/89)   [apco] Registered in U.S. Patent and Trademark Office
                                                                                   anderson publishing co. cincinnati, ohio 45201

QUIT-CLAIM DEED *

(1), of   County,

for valuable consideration paid, grants(s) to

, whose tax-mailing address is

the following **REAL PROPERTY:** Situated in the County of   in the State

of Ohio and in the   of   : (2)

Prior Instrument Reference: Vol.   Page   of the Deed Records of

County, Ohio.   (3) wife (husband) of the

Grantor releases all rights of dower therein. Witness   hand(s) this   day

of   , 19   .

Signed and acknowledged in the presence of:

_____   _____(4)

WITNESS

_____   _____

WITNESS

State of Ohio   County of   ss.

    BE IT REMEMBERED, That on this   day of   , 19   , before me,

the subscriber, a   in and for said county, personally came,

                                        the Grantor(s) in the

foregoing Deed, and acknowledged the signing thereof to be   voluntary act and deed.

IN TESTIMONY THEREOF, I have hereunto subscribed my name and affixed my seal on this day

and year aforesaid. _____

This instrument was prepared by _____

1. Name of Grantor(s) and marital status.
2. Description of land or interest therein, and encumbrances, reservations, exceptions, taxes and assessments, if any.
3. Delete whichever does not apply.
4. Execution in accordance with Chapter 5301 of the Revised Code of Ohio.

Auditor's and Recorder's Stamps

* See Section 5302.11 Ohio Revised Code

Special Use Deeds

Deeds are sometimes used in special circumstances, and people frequently refer to these deeds as if they are additional deed types—*they are not.* In fact, they frequently take the form of a bargain and sale deed, or a quitclaim.

- **Administrator's deed**—Used to convey the property of one who dies intestate
- **Cession deed**—Used to convey the rights to land designated for a public use, such as a neighborhood park, and streets to the government. Also, a subdivider who dedicates streets to the municipal government would use a cession deed.
- **Committee's deed**—Used by a court appointed committee to transfer the real property of an incompetent or otherwise legally impaired person
- **Correction deed** (also known as confirmation deed, confirmatory deed, or reformation deed)—Used to correct mistakes such as a misspelled name, or an inaccurate property description in a prior deed
- **Deed in lieu of foreclosure** (also known as voluntary deed)—Given by a property owner/borrower to a lender transferring ownership of a mortgaged property in which the mortgage is in default as an alternative to a foreclosure action
- **Deed in trust**—Used when real property is conveyed to a trustee, usually to establish a land trust
- **Deed of release**—Employed to release property from a blanket deed of trust or a blanket mortgage that encumbers more than one parcel
- **Deed of trust** (also known as trust deed)—Used to convey title to a third party trustee as security for a debt owed by the trustor (borrower) to the beneficiary (lender)
- **Executor's deed**—Used by the person with responsibility for distributing the property of one who died testate
- **Gift deed**—One in which good, rather than valuable, consideration is recited
- **Guardian's deed**—Used by a court appointed guardian to convey the property of a minor
- **Partition deed**—Used when concurrent owners of real property wish to divide their property into individually owned tracts
- **Reconveyance deed**—Used by a trustee to reconvey title to a borrower after the borrower satisfies his or her debt with the lender
- **Sheriff's deed**—Used by a court to convey title to real property acquired through a foreclosure sale conducted to satisfy a judgment
- **Statutory deed**—A condensed deed written in plain English that state legislatures permit parties to use instead of having an attorney draft the deed
- **Support deed**—Employed to convey property, usually to a younger family member, in exchange for the grantee's promise to support financially the grantor for the rest of the grantor's life
- **Tax deed**—Used to convey title to property sold by the government for nonpayment of taxes
- **Wild deed**—One in which the grantor has no recorded interest in the subject property. Wild deeds may be the result of fraud, or the grantor may have a legitimate interest in the property under an unrecorded deed.

DEDICATIONS OF REAL PROPERTY

A dedication is a voluntary transfer that involves a gift of real property to the public for public use. Dedications may be motivated by a number of factors, including the largess of the donor or tax benefits associated with the dedication. Dedication is usually accomplished by the method that is specified by state statute. Most state laws require that the donor sign and deliver a deed to the appropriate public body.

A rarely used dedication method is to follow the common law procedure. Two requirements must be met to dedicate real property under this method: the grantor must intend for the public to use the property, and the public must actually make some use of the property. A common law dedication does not require the use of a formal document and no extended period of public use is required to create use rights for the general public. Full

CONSUMER CHECKLIST
AVOIDING DEED PROBLEMS

Listed below are several things that you can do to protect your interest in a real estate transaction, and avoid problems that sometimes occur in deeds. Of course, it is always a good idea to have a competent attorney review the documents used in a real estate transaction.

1. Inspect the purchase agreement before you sign it to determine the type of deed the grantor is to deliver. A warranty deed is preferred, but in most states if the agreement is silent on this matter the grantor may use a quitclaim.

2. If a preprinted deed form is used, make sure that it is one that was printed in the state where the land is located. Almost all deed forms include waivers of dower and homestead rights that vary by state.

3. The prepared deed should not contain any alterations or erasures. Such items may result in objections by title examiners in the future.

4. Check the deed by which the grantor acquired title to ensure that the grantor's name is spelled the same way in the deed by which title is being conveyed. If title is to be granted under a different name than the one used to acquire title, both should be used. For example, if a woman acquires title under her maiden name and then marries, the deed should show both names (e.g., Joan Rivers, formerly Joan Burns).

5. Ensure that all grantee's names are on the deed. Each grantee's full legal name should be used. Avoid the use of initials. For example, John Quincy Adams should be used instead of John Q. Adams. Similarly, a married woman should not be named as Mrs. John Adams, but rather by her own name, Mary Evans Adams.

6. If survivorship is desired, ensure that the grantee's names are followed by the appropriate phrase.

7. Make sure a monetary consideration that conforms with the governing state statute is stated in the deed.

8. Double-check the legal description in the deed for accuracy.

9. To avoid personal liability, the grantor should be certain that all title defects are listed in the deed. They cannot, however, be in addition to what the grantee agreed to accept in the purchase agreement.

10. All parties should sign the deed exactly as the names are printed on the deed. Again, any variation may result in objections by title examiners in the future. The signatures should be witnessed and acknowledged.

11. Grantees should file the deed in the proper public office immediately after it has been delivered.

title to real property, or an easement, can be transferred using either statutory dedication or the common law dedication method.

Decision Point

The following deed, after being sealed and acknowledged, was recorded in the deed records of Cass County, Illinois. What type of deed is it?

I, J. Henry Shaw, the grantor, herein

Who lives at Beardstown the county within,

For seven hundred dollars to me paid today

By Charles E. Wyman, do sell and convey

Lot two (2) in Block forty (40), said county and town,

Where Illinois River flows placidly down,

And Warrant the title forever and aye,

Waiving homestead and mansion to both a goodbye,

And pledging this deed is valid in law

I add here my signature, J. Henry Shaw

Dated July 25, 1881

WILLS

A **will** is a document that specifies to whom both real and personal property should be distributed after the property owner's death. The will itself does not convey real property ownership, but directs the executor of the estate to whom transfers should be made. The transfer of real property according to the terms of a will differs from a normal transfer by deed in at least two ways. First, title does not pass until the person making the will, the testator, dies (see "Doing Business: Estate Planning" for an exception). Second, because a will is not effective until the death of the testator, it can be revoked during the lifetime of the testator.

Most states have several, easily met requirements for a valid will. In most cases, wills must be in writing. Most wills are typed; a handwritten will is called a **holographic will.** To be valid, most state require that a will be signed by the testator, as well as by two or more credible witnesses. In addition, the testator must be of sound mind, have achieved the age of majority, and the intention of the testator to create a will must be made clear by the language in the will.

Because state laws concerning the requirements for a valid will vary, it is advisable to consult an attorney to draft a will, although a number of computer software packages are available for those who wish to draft their own will. More than one state's laws may be applicable to a single will. With regard to real property, the requirements of the state in which the real property is located must be met. For personal property, the requirements of the state of the testator's residence govern.

Upon the death of the testator, the will is filed with the probate court that reviews it to ensure that all of the formal requirements have been met. Then, under probate supervision, the executor is responsible for: assembling and managing the assets of the testator, paying any taxes due and other claims, distributing the assets in accordance with the directions in the will, and presenting a final accounting to the probate court.

Many people do not realize that wills may need to be revised periodically. To ensure that one's wishes are carried out, it is necessary to revise a will any time a material life change occurs. Examples of such events would include: a divorce, marriage, birth or death of a beneficiary; the acquisition of assets; change in value or dispossession of assets named in the will; the death or removal of a named guardian or executor. Revisions to a will may be accomplished with a supplement to the existing will, known as a codicil, which must be executed with the same formalities as a will, or with a completely new will. When a person dies without a will (intestate), as do more than half of the people in this country, or when one dies with a defective will, an individual's real property is distributed according to the intestacy statutes of the state in which the real property is located. These laws specify the order to be used in distributing property to the relatives of the decedent. If the decedent has no will or heirs, title to his or her real property will escheat to the state.

SUMMARY

It is important to have a basic knowledge of both deeds and wills when making decisions concerning the acquisition or conveyance of real estate. Both documents need to be constructed carefully to ensure that the desired ownership interest in, and amount of, real estate is transferred to the intended party. Some knowledge of wills is important to ensure that, after death, an individual's property is distributed according to his or her wishes. The type of deed employed is important to those acquiring real estate because it affects the quality of the title received, and, therefore, the value of the property. The type of deed is also important to those conveying title because it affects both their current and future liability should a defect in the title become apparent.

One may employ several types of deeds. The deed most commonly used to satisfy purchase agreements is the general warranty deed. From the perspective of the purchaser, this is the most desirable type of deed because the grantor fully warrants the title to the property. Other types of deeds—the special warranty and the bargain and sale—contain fewer warranties compared with the general warranty deed. The quitclaim deed does not contain any warranties. Regardless of the type of deed used, to be valid, it must be in writing and contain: the names of the grantor and grantee, a legal description of the subject property, consideration, a granting clause and the grantor's signature. In addition, the grantor must deliver the deed to the grantee, and the grantee must accept it.

CONSUMER CHECKLIST
DRAFTING A WILL

Although not required by law, most wills follow a standard format, and contain the provisions listed below.

1. A publication clause which is a statement of the testator's name and capacity (i.e., "being of sound mind"), and the intention to make a will
2. A revocation clause which revokes all previously drawn wills
3. Instructions regarding burial or cremation
4. Instructions regarding the payment of debts, including specification of what property is to be used to pay the debts
5. Bequests, or gifts of personal property or money. The gift itself is referred to as a legacy and the recipient is called a legatee.
6. Devises, or gifts of real property
7. A residuary clause which governs the disposition of all property not included by a specific devise or bequest
8. A penalty clause that specifies a punishment to be enforced against anyone named in the will who contests the will. Generally, such a clause states that if one contests the will they are to receive nothing from the decedent's estate
9. Name of the guardian for any minor children
10. Name of the executor (party responsible for carrying out the instructions in the will)

KEY TERMS

acknowledgement

actual consideration

bargain and sale deed

deed

general warranty deed

grantee

grantor

holographic will

nominal consideration

power of attorney

quitclaim deed

recital clause

reservation

special warranty deed

will

REVIEW QUESTIONS

1. What is the difference between a general warranty deed and a special warranty deed?
2. What is the difference between a special warranty deed and a bargain and sale deed?
3. What interest does the grantee receive when the grantor delivers a quitclaim deed?
4. List and explain the essential elements of a valid deed.
5. What type of deed would you prefer to use as a grantee? Why?
6. What type of deed would you prefer to use as a grantor? Why?
7. If a grantor asserts that he or she holds a fee simple interest in land being conveyed, but really only has a life estate, what covenant in a general warranty deed has been breached?
8. When does title to real property pass from grantor to grantee? If, prior to closing, the grantor gives the deed to the grantee's attorney, has delivery occurred?
9. Why is it important to state at least nominal consideration in a purchase deed?
10. Explain the covenants normally contained in a general warranty deed.
11. Describe the circumstances that may result in a deed being declared void.
12. How does a deed differ from a will?
13. What are your answers to the questions in the two "Decision Point" sections in this chapter?

REAL ESTATE ON THE WEB

Use your favorite search engine to:

1. Determine whether your county recorder's office has a Web site and, if so, what information is available on it.
2. Locate a company that will prepare a deed over the Internet.
3. Locate a company that provides a software package so that you can prepare your own will.
4. Discover whether tax deeds can be purchased on properties located in your state.

Refer to the companion Web site at www.wiley.com/college/larsen for a variety of online activities including additional chapter content, review materials, assignments, and related links.

ADDITIONAL READINGS

Huffaker, J. B. "No Marital Deduction under Will or Family Settlement Agreement." *Journal of Taxation* (September 1995): 158–159.

13 Preparation for the Real Estate Closing

Learning Objectives

After studying this chapter you should be able to:

- Understand the need to assure good title.
- Explain the title search process.
- List and explain the methods that can be used to protect title.
- Distinguish between the various types of title insurance policies.
- Explain how Torrens registration streamlines the title search.

FROM THE WIRE

In April 2002, the American Land Title Association (ALTA) released the results of a survey of 420 member companies that showed that the public perception that title insurers pay little in the way of claims is incorrect. ALTA says that in 2000, title insurers paid approximately $350 million in claims. The survey also showed that title problems occur in about 25 percent of all transactions, which would equal about 1.6 million of the 6.5 million residential transactions that closed in 2001. However, in many cases, buyers are never aware of these problems because the title insurer has resolved them, without bothering the buyer, before the transaction closes. For the industry, the percentage of operating revenue expended on losses and loss adjustment expenses was 5.3 percent in 2000, which was up from previous years. Much of the rise in the industry loss ratio was attributed to a drop off in revenue coupled with a larger dollar amount of losses due to a large increase in business written during 1998 and 1999. Title insurance policies have no termination date on filing claims, but the only charge for a policy is the one-time fee collected at the time the policy is issued. Most title losses are reported and paid within the first five to seven years after policy issuance.

Go to www.alta.org, and click on "Industry News" to see what issues are of current concern in the title insurance industry.

INTRODUCTION

In the last chapter, you learned that a general warranty deed grantor makes several strongly worded promises designed to assure the quality of the title being conveyed. However, there is no guarantee that the grantor will be financially capable of backing up those warranties in the future. Therefore, when you acquire title to real property you should secure additional assurance of the title quality because of the potentially large loss that can occur if the title is defective.

The focus of this chapter is on the methods that may be employed to obtain additional assurance of the title quality: an opinion of title rendered by an attorney, title insurance, and registration of title under the Torrens system. To employ any of these title assurance methods, the party providing the assurance examines a number of public records to determine the title's quality. The title examination process can be quite cumbersome, but it is not critical that you be able to conduct such an examination. To make good real estate decisions, it is important that you have a general understanding of: the examination process, the types of notice for which purchasers are responsible, and the types of title defects covered by the various means of title assurance. To begin, we briefly review the duties to which the parties must attend and comment on the time usually required to accomplish these tasks.

PRELIMINARY REQUIREMENTS FOR CLOSING

A well-written real estate purchase contract specifies the steps that must be taken by the seller and the buyer, and who is responsible for paying for various items. After both parties sign the contract, each must perform as agreed before the closing may be held. Steps that are usually required as a prerequisite to closing include: verification of the goodness of the seller's title, the buyer securing a loan commitment, surveying the property, having inspections conducted, and preparation of the new deed and other documents. As we show in this chapter, verification of the title may be accomplished in one of several ways. Any encumbrances discovered in the process must be removed by the seller, or be accepted by the buyer.

Physical inspections of the property are an ordinary part of the pre-closing process, and they may serve a number of purposes. In locations where pest damage is a potential problem, lenders generally require termite inspections. Even where lenders do not require inspections, it is a good idea for the buyer to require such an inspection. In purchasing a home, many buyers require professional inspections of the property to ascertain the condition of such things as the roof, electrical, and plumbing systems. Who pays for such inspections and any needed repairs is a matter of negotiation between the buyer and seller and should be set out in the purchase contract. Inspection of the property may reveal that the party in possession is not the owner. In such cases, the party in possession should be identified and the extent of their property rights determined.

In some instances, a survey may be required to determine both the precise boundaries of the property, and if there are any encroachments. Surveys are commonplace for large commercial properties, but less common for single-family homes.

Several documents must be prepared before the closing. The seller must prepare a deed as specified in the purchase contract. When financing is required, the buyer must secure a loan commitment from a lender. Before granting the loan request, the lender will conduct a credit check on the buyer and order an appraisal of the property. In addition, the lender will require that the buyer either obtain new hazard insurance on the property, or have the unused portion of the seller's hazard insurance policy transferred to the buyer. The lender must prepare the promissory note and the mortgage to be signed by the buyer at the closing. If the buyer is assuming an existing mortgage loan, arrangements must be made with the lender to transfer responsibility for the mortgage loan to the buyer.

TIME REQUIRED TO CLOSE

Although both the buyer and seller may want to close immediately, the pre-closing procedures take time, and therefore, the closing date is usually four to six weeks after the parties sign the purchase contract. If the contract makes no mention of a closing date, closing within a reasonable time period is implied. Parties may disagree as to what time period is reasonable. Therefore, it is good practice to specify a closing date in the purchase contract. The real estate broker often suggests a date far enough in the future to ensure that both seller and buyer may attend to the details necessary to consummate the transaction.

Such details, however, are not common to all transactions. For example, when an installment land contract is used, the processing time is usually shorter because third party lenders are not involved. In addition, advances in technology are shortening the time necessary to prepare for a closing. Mortgage networking is being developed in several areas. At its simplest, mortgage networking involves local lenders submitting their current mortgage interest rate and loan origination charges into a computer database. Real estate brokers can access this data to assist buyers in selecting a lender. More extensive networks enable lenders to take loan applications, and convey tentative decisions, through the computer network.

TITLE EVIDENCE

There are two ways by which a party can give notice of an interest in real property: by physically occupying the property, or by recording documents concerning the interest in the public records. The proper recording of a document gives constructive, or legal, notice to the world of the documents' existence and contents. **Constructive notice** is the notice of certain facts that one may discover by examining the public records. There is a legal presumption that any person is responsible for knowing these facts. The owner of real property as shown by the records is called the record owner. Conversely, the record owner is the one having record title, where record title is the title that appears in the public records.

The American recording system began in 1640 when the colony of Massachusetts enacted a "Registry Act" that provided for the public recording of documents affecting title to real property. Today, every state has statutes, referred to as **recording acts,** which are fundamental to title protection in the United States. These statutes provide for the recording of documents by which an interest or right in real property is created, transferred, or encumbered. These records are maintained by each county recorder of deeds, or equivalent public office, and establish priorities among successive purchasers of real property interests. Although they differ in detail, all recording acts provide for the following:

1. Centralized filing of documents that create or transfer real property interests;
2. Maintenance of public records systems, which consist primarily of copies of the filed documents; and
3. Priority for those interests that appear in the public records, as opposed to those that do not.

The last point implies that records kept pursuant to the recording acts are not the only sources of information about real property titles.

One who is interested in a property is also responsible for making further inquiry of anyone giving visible notice. This type of inquiry is referred to as **inquiry notice.** For example, anytime one purchases rental property, the purchaser should inquire as to the occupants' rights. An occupant might hold important rights that the purchaser would not know about without asking. For example, the occupant might have the right to occupy the premises for a substantial period of time, or the option to buy the property.

Finally, everyone is responsible for actual notice. **Actual notice** is knowledge that one obtains based upon what has been seen, heard, read, or observed. For example, if you saw a deed from Smith to Myers, you have actual notice of the deed and Myers' claim to the property. Similarly, if you see someone in possession of the land, you have actual notice of his or her claim to be there. Examples of rights of parties in possession, other than the record owner, would include rights acquired by: an unrecorded deed or installment land contract, a lease-option, and rights acquired by adverse possession.

REQUIREMENTS FOR RECORDATION

A primary goal of recording acts is to reduce the possibility that forged, or fraudulently induced, documents enter the public record. To accomplish this purpose, recording laws specify that, before a document may be recorded, a third party observe the document signing to ensure that the signatory is the same as the one named in the document and that the signing was a voluntary act. Exactly who must observe such document signatures varies by state. In many states, a document must be acknowledged (signed and sworn to in the presence of a notary public) before it may be recorded; others permit proper witnessing as a substitute. In states that permit witnessing, the person(s) signing the document must do so in the presence of at least two or three witnesses, who, in turn, place their signatures on the document. If needed, the witnesses may later be summoned to a court to testify as to the authenticity of the signature. In such cases, therefore, it is important that the witnesses know the person named in the document. Some states require that a document be both witnessed and acknowledged before it can be recorded.

Every document brought to the recorder's office for recordation is marked with the date and time received, photocopied, and the original returned to its owner. The copy is placed in chronological order with copies of similar documents. Each copy is stamped with a consecutive page number and bound in a book; these books are available for public inspection. A current trend is toward paperless systems whereby documents are recorded directly onto microfilm. In this case, each is assigned a reel and frame number. Filing documents in chronological order establishes their chronological priority, but it does not provide an easy method to locate all documents for a given property. Consequently, recording offices have developed indexing systems, which are described in the following section.

TITLE SEARCH AND EXAMINATION

Before title to property is conveyed, it is common practice to have the property's title history examined. Title examination can be a laborious task. When examining title, one must visit several offices, including the registrar of deeds, the county clerk, the county treasurer, the city clerk and collector, and the clerk's office of various courts. The records that one must search include: all recorded title transfers, mortgages, deeds of trust, taxes, assessments, judgments, liens, probate proceedings, and quiet title or other judicial decisions.

An **abstractor** usually conducts the task of title examination. An attorney, an employee of a title insurance company, or an independent professional abstractor may serve in this capacity. The document created by the abstractor, an abstract of title, or **title abstract,** condenses information from all public records and shows in brief form the content of all recorded documents affecting the title to a particular parcel of real property.

The process of conducting the title search is sometimes referred to as running the chain of title, and the ownership history of the property is called the chain of title, or **title chain.** Most title chains in this country date back to the time a patent was issued by the United States government. However, in some states such as Texas, Louisiana, and former colonial states, title chains originate before the acquisition of land by the federal government.

An unbroken chain of title is one that can be traced through linking conveyances from the present owner back through successive owners to the original source of title. In practice, however, title searches are rarely conducted back more than sixty years. If any conveyance is not properly linked, a gap, or break, exists in the title chain. Discovery of a title gap results in a cloud on the title and a court action is usually needed to establish ownership. In essence, any broken link in a property's chain of title means that the current owner does not have valid title to the property. For example, titles derived from a forged deed somewhere in the title chain means that no subsequent grantee acquired legal title to the property.

To avoid apparent problems in the chain of title, the parties' names should be consistent and be spelled out properly in all documents. Other problems arise when a party acquires title using one name then conveys the property under another. In such cases, the conveyance should indicate the name by which title was acquired. For example, "Christine Jones, who acquired title as Christine Smith." Apparent gaps in the title may also occur because the grantor is an administrator, a judge, a sheriff (because a mortgage against the property was foreclosed), or an executor (because the owner died). To fill the gap, the abstractor must check other public records outside the recorder's office. For example, civil court actions in the event of a foreclosure, or, in the case of a death, the probate court records.

Decision Point

1. The record owner of a property is shown as Donna Boyer, but the person about to present you with a deed is named Donna Bishop. Does this necessarily represent a break in the chain of title?

2. Roy Caudill is about to deed a property to you and Roy Caudill is listed as the record owner. Does this mean you receive a valid title?

INDEXING SYSTEMS

Two systems are used to facilitate the title search. All states use grantor and grantee indexes, and a few (Iowa, Louisiana, Nebraska, North Dakota, Oklahoma, South Dakota, Utah, Wisconsin, and Wyoming) use a tract index. A **tract index** is simple to use. Under this system, one page is allocated to each property, or group of properties, called a tract. This page lists all the recorded documents at the recorders office related to the tract. Each document is briefly described and the volume and page reference for the photocopy is given. It is a mystery why such a handy system is used in relatively few states. State lawmakers may, in part, be concerned with the cost of implementing and maintaining such a system at public expense.

Both the **grantor index** and the **grantee index** are kept in alphabetical order for each calendar year. The grantor index lists all grantors named in the documents recorded that year. An example is shown in Exhibit 13.1. The name of the grantee for the particular conveyance is shown next to the grantor's name along with a book and page reference for the photocopy of the document and perhaps a brief description of the document. The grantee index contains the same information as the grantor index, except that it is organized according to the names of the grantees.

Running the Chain of Title: An Example

To illustrate how an abstractor would use the grantor and grantee indexes in a title search, consider the following sequence of events.

1. After obtaining a patent from the government in 1882, Ben First began farming a tract of land;
2. In 1918, Ben First sold the farm to Robert Second;
3. In 1950, Mr. Second sold the farm to Betty Third;
4. In 1990, Betty Third sold the farm to Bill Fourth; and
5. Now, you have entered into a contract to buy the property from Mr. Fourth.

The title abstractor begins the search knowing only the property description and the name of the party who claims ownership. The formulation of a title abstract is, therefore, similar to putting a puzzle together. The first step is to determine if Mr. Fourth is the record owner and if there are any breaks in the chain of title for the subject property. To do this, the abstractor begins by looking at the grantee index found in the County Recorder's Office

EXHIBIT   13.1   SAMPLE GRANTOR INDEX

BROWN COUNTY RECORDERS OFFICE OFFICIAL RECORDS INDEX

Microfiche Parcel Number

Page Grantor	Grantee	Date Filed	Vol	Page	Are BK	No.
CAREY, JANE	Roberts, Beverly	04/01/03	695	0776	M400129	324
CAUDILL, EVELYN	Luedecke, Shirly	04/01/03	696	0122	L320215	047
DATTE, RAJ	Stiltner, Nicole	04/01/03	696	0122	L320215	047
EMERY, SANDRA	Nickell, Terrence	04/01/03	696	0036	B420307	057
EMERSON, DAVID	Adams, Nathaniel	04/01/03	696	0036	B420307	057
GALAGAN, ERIC	Thoman, Dawn	04/01/03	696	0243	L320102	035
GANTT, THOMAS	Porter, Kyle	04/01/03	696	0243	L320102	035
GUILES, MELINDA	Tankersley Solomon Earl	04/01/03	695	0882	B420216	197
	Kalishman Jerome	04/01/03	686	0164	B420216	197
HITT, MARY	Carlson, Majoa	04/01/03	696	0266	L320103	160
HITT, MARY	Sunset Devlpmt-Sugar, CK	04/01/03	696	0290	L320103	160
HITT, MARY	Sunset Devlpmt-Sugar, CK	04/01/03	696	0296	L320103	160
HITT, MARY	Sunset Devlpmt-Sugar, CK	04/01/03	696	0317	L320103	160
KNIGHT, ELEIN	Meyer, Carl	04/01/03	696	0266	L320103	160
KNIGHT, ELEIN	Dirkmen, Tarnian	04/01/03	696	0290	L320103	160
KNIGHT, ELEIN	Shannon, Doug	04/01/03	696	0296	L320103	160

in which the property is located (remember that when Mr. Fourth took title he was a grantee). Initially, the abstractor does not need to know when Fourth, or anyone else, took title. The abstractor examines the grantee index for the name Fourth from the present back to 1990, where a notation of the deed to Fourth from Third is found. The backward search of the grantee index continues with the abstractor looking as follows: 1.) for Third's name from 1990 back to 1950, where the notation of the deed from Second to Third appears; 2.) under Second's name back to 1918, where the deed from First to Second is noted; and 3.) for First's name from 1918 to 1882 where the patent is discovered. The abstractor must also verify the quantum of estate conveyed by each transfer. This is simple if the interest conveyed by each transfer was noted in the index, otherwise, using the book and page references given in the index, each deed must be located and inspected separately.

The abstractor's next task is to determine that multiple title chains do not exist (i.e., that each grantor conveyed title only once). To do this, the abstractor examines the grantor index as follows: 1.) for First's name from 1882 to 1918; 2.) under Second's name from 1918 to 1950; 3.) for Third's name from 1950 to 1990, and finally, 4.) under Fourth's name from 1990 to the present.

Finally, the abstractor must check all of the other above mentioned sources to ensure that there are no other claims on the property. Any existing judgments that would affect the title may be found in the judgment rolls and information about pending lawsuits in the lis pendens index, both located in the office of the clerk of the county court. In some states, mortgages are recorded in the grantee index. In other states, the abstractor must search separate index books: the mortgagor index, and the mortgagee index. The process involves looking for the record owner's name in each annual mortgagor index. When a mortgage is found an additional check will reveal whether it has been satisfied and released. If it has been, the recorder's office will have placed a notation of the book and page where the release is located on the margin of the recorded mortgage. If the lender's name is known, the abstractor could also find the photocopy of the mortgage and its subsequent release by searching the mortgagee index.

TITLE ASSURANCE PROVIDED BY ABSTRACTORS

There is no guarantee that the abstract accurately reflects the true condition of the title. What was no doubt a good system when title histories were short and searches relatively easy has become a cumbersome procedure. Mistakes can occur in abstracts for a number of reasons: inefficiently maintained public records, errors by recorders, failure of the abstractor to adequately search both on and off record to ascertain the condition of the title, and the risk of outstanding title interests that cannot be determined by any reasonable search.

Although the title abstract itself is not intended as a title assurance vehicle, abstractors do certify their work. If there is either an omission from the abstract, or if the abstract contains an error, and this results in a loss to the client, the abstractor is liable for that loss. Therefore, most abstractors are bonded and/or carry an errors-and-omissions insurance policy to indemnify those who suffer a loss because of an abstracting error.

ATTORNEY'S OPINION OF TITLE

Purchasers of real property may seek title assurance in the form of an **opinion of title** rendered by an attorney. In fact, until fairly recently this was the primary method of title assurance. Under this method, an attorney reviews the title abstract and provides the client with a written opinion of title. Specifically, in this document, the attorney states an opinion concerning the marketability of the seller's title. Almost all purchase agreements require the seller to deliver marketable, or merchantable, title.

A **marketable title** is one that is reasonably free from risk of litigation over possible defects. A marketable title is not necessarily a title that is completely free of defects, just one that is free from reasonable objections. If a title is deemed to be unmarketable, the property may still be transferred but there may be defects that limit the owner's rights. The buyer cannot, however, be forced to accept a title that is materially different from the one specified in the purchase contract. An example of an attorney's opinion of title is shown in Exhibit 13.2.

EXHIBIT	13.2	ATTORNEY'S OPINION OF TITLE

January 15, 2003

Ms. Jane Russell

1234 Main Street

Hanover, Indiana

In Re: Abstract of title to a tract of land located in the southeast quarter (SE1/4) of the Northeast quarter (NE1/4) of the Southwest quarter (SW1/4) of Section 8, Township 2 North, Range 6, West of the 3rd Principal Meridian in Hypothetical County, Indiana, being that part of the previously described property lying South of State Highway 84.

Dear Ms. Russell,

At your request, I have examined Abstract 11,567 prepared, extended and certified by Ace Abstract Company, Inc., to the 10th day of January 2003, at 9:00 a.m., containing sheets 1 to 77, both inclusive, and covering the above described real estate.

It is my opinion that title, as shown by this abstract, is vested in Lois L. Kent and Clark S. Kent her husband, as shown at sheet 75, subject to the following:

1. At sheet 76 is shown a mortgage dated August 1, 1992, given to Crypton Savings and Loan Association of Hypothetical, Indiana, a corporation, to secure payment of a note of even date in the amount of $98,000.00 payable upon terms and at a rate of interest therein stated, with the final payment being due and payable on September 31, 2007. This mortgage is an outstanding lien on the property.

2. The abstract shows state and county taxes for years 2001 and 2002 due and unpaid and they are delinquent. The taxes for 2003 are now a lien. The liens for delinquent taxes should be removed.

3. The abstract shows no special assessments against the property. However, at sheet 76 it does show that the property is within Water supply District No. 5.

4. The certificate attached to the abstract shows that a divorce and partition suit between Clark S. Kent and Lois L. Kent is now pending in The District Court of Hypothetical County, Indiana. Thus, you should verify that the person(s) granting title to you do in fact have full title to the above described property.

5. The certificate attached to the abstract shows no Federal judgment liens or bankruptcy proceedings affecting the property.

6. You should verify by survey or otherwise the location of boundaries on the land and the location of any improvements with regard to the boundaries, to determine that there are no encroachments on the property.

7. You should verify that there have been no recent improvements for which mechanic's liens may be filed. In the state of Indiana, mechanics liens may be filed up to ninety days after the last materials are furnished to or the last labor is performed on the property.

8. The property is subject to the rights of any tenants or other parties in possession of or using the property.

Assuming the abstract to be complete and correct, it is my opinion that marketable title is vested in Lois L. Kent and Clark S. Kent, her husband, subject only to the mortgage, the lien for delinquent taxes which should be removed, the lien for current taxes, any mechanic's liens which may be outstanding if the time for filing has not elapsed, and the rights of parties in possession.

Sincerely,

Ima Lawyer

Attorney at Law

As is the case with abstractors, there is no guarantee that the opinion of title rendered by the attorney is completely accurate. With an opinion of title, property owners are protected against errors in title examination, and attorneys can be sued if their negligence results in a loss to a client. There are, however, many types of mistakes that can occur for which neither the abstractor nor the attorney are liable such as a deed executed by an incompetent grantor, a deed containing an incorrect land description, or confusion resulting from similar names on documents. Other cases that could result in a substantial loss to a property owner without attorney or abstractor liability include a recorded forged deed, a married person representing themselves as a single person on a deed resulting in an unextinguished dower right, a misfiled document, or a missing will later discovered. Title insurance, which is described next, offers property owners an opportunity to transfer the loss associated with these risks to privately owned insurance companies.

Eliminating Title Defects

There are a variety of ways in which title defects can be eliminated. Sometimes the title holder need not take any action because the defects will expire with the passage of time. Occasionally, changes in the law eliminate present or potential title defects, for example, statutes abolishing dower. In other cases, the party who wishes to clear title must take action. A common means is a **quiet title suit** that can result in a court decree clearing the title of some, or all, of its defects. In this type of action, parties with claims against the title are notified of a hearing date by personal service or by publication. Those claims not represented at the hearing are extinguished. Only a small percentage of such suits are contested, either because the other party deems that the value of their claim is not worth the trouble or, when notice is by publication, because they never learned of the suit. The holder of a defective title has additional options for clearing the title: liens or encumbrance claims may be paid off; an outstanding title interest may be purchased; land description uncertainties may be eliminated by surveying the property and recording a correction document; and affidavits may be secured to resolve questions concerning lawful heirs, and the identity or marital status of parties in the chain of title. None of these actions are without cost, and each may require a substantial amount of time.

Decision Point

Assume that you have been approached by an attorney to sign a quitclaim to a parcel of real property that is valued at $500. You were asked to do so because your name is the same as one that appears on the record making the title unmarketable. You are absolutely certain that you have no legitimate claim to the property. How much compensation would you require to sign the deed? How would your answer change if the property were worth $10,000,000? Why?

TITLE INSURANCE

Title insurance is similar to other types of insurance. In general, insurance allows parties desiring a certain amount of financial protection from a hazard to contract with an insurance company for this purpose. The contract between the insured and the insurance company is called a policy, the payment made by the insured party is called the premium, and the maximum amount of protection called for in the policy is referred to as the coverage amount. The insurance company places premiums in a fund that is invested in various securities. When a hazard occurs and results in financial loss to the insured, money from the fund is paid to the beneficiary named in the policy, which could be the insured or another party.

A title insurance policy may be purchased at any time, although one usually purchases a policy when an interest in real property is acquired. Policies are written under a number of circumstances. For example, title companies issue policies to cover a lender under a leasehold mortgage, a vendee under an installment land contract, or the leasehold interest of a lessee.

Title insurance is, however, different from other forms of insurance in two important respects. First, as mentioned in the chapter opener "From the Wire," coverage is obtained with a one-time premium that is generally paid when the policy goes into effect. Almost all other forms of insurance require premiums to be paid at regular intervals over the term of the coverage. Second, unlike other types of insurance that cover future hazards, title insurance covers hazards that have already occurred.

GROWTH OF THE TITLE INSURANCE INDUSTRY

The title insurance industry has grown rapidly because of the benefits it provides to grantors, grantees, and mortgage lenders. Even with a general warranty deed, grantees desire title insurance because there is the possibility that the grantor will not be financially capable of backing up the promises made in the deed. In addition, title insurance usually provides the grantee with broader assurances than a warranty deed. For example, physical dispossession of the grantee resulting from the claim of an outsider must occur before a court considers the covenant of quiet enjoyment contained in a deed broken. The same claim would, however, be covered by title insurance before dispossession occurs. In addition, in the event an outsider asserts a superior claim, a title insurance company will pay the legal cost to defend the policy holder's interest.

From the lender's perspective, the use of title insurance has made mortgage lending more attractive because title insurance has removed the risk of loss due to title defects. As a consequence, borrowers may benefit in that lenders can charge a lower rate of interest because the risk of loss has been transferred to the title insurance company. Title insurance also provides a means for grantors to transfer the liability for title defects to the insurance company.

The growth of the title insurance industry can also be attributed to the fact that it provides more economic accountability than is available with an attorney's opinion of title. Insurance companies have more funds dedicated to paying claims and they tend to die less frequently than do attorneys. Title insurance also covers a number of risks for which an attorney would not be liable because they were not disclosed in the title search. Finally, title insurance has increased the marketability of titles. An **insurable title** is one that a title insurance company will insure. While a title may not be marketable in a strict sense, a title company may elect to insure it anyway, and insurable titles are generally considered to be the functional equivalent of marketable titles.

TITLE REPORT

When a title insurance company receives a request for a policy, a title search is conducted to identify any existing claims on the property. The search may be done either by an employee of the title company or by an independent attorney or title abstractor. To speed the examination process, larger title companies have duplicated the public records pertaining to all parcels of real property in a particular county and maintain them on their own premises in what is known as a title plant.

After the records examination, a title company attorney reviews the information and renders an opinion as to who is the fee owner and lists any other current legitimate interest in the property (e.g., easements, mortgages, liens). This becomes the title report; an example of which is shown in Exhibit 13.3. Synonyms for title report include title commitment, preliminary title report, certificate of title, and interim binder. A title report differs from a title

| EXHIBIT | 13.3 | **PRELIMINARY TITLE REPORT** |

The following is a report of the title to the land described in your application for a policy of title insurance.

LAND DESCRIPTION: LOT 11, Block 4, Golf Park Addition, Lancaster County, State of Nebraska

DATE AND TIME OF SEARCH: September 10, 2002 at 10:00 A.M.

VESTEE: Christine Skeslock, a single woman.

ESTATE OR INTEREST: Fee simple.

EXCEPTIONS:

PART I

1. A lien in favor of Lancaster County for property taxes, in the amount of $930, due on or before October 31, 2002.
2. A mortgage in favor of Gem Savings and Loan Association in the amount of $45,455, recorded August 12, 1991, in Book 1134, page 122 of the Official County Records.
3. An easement in favor of Lincoln Telephone Company along the western six feet of said land for underground utility lines. Recorded on June 15, 1977, in Book 784, Page 98 of the Official County Records.
4. An easement in favor of Lincoln Power and Light Company along the south ten feet of said land for underground pipes. Recorded of June 18, 1977, in Book 784, Page 102 of the Official County Records.

PART II

1. Taxes or assessments not shown by the records of any taxing authority or by the public records.
2. Any facts, rights, interests, or claims that, although not shown by the public records, could be determined by inspection of the land and inquiry of persons in possession.
3. Discrepancies or conflicts in boundary lines or area or encroachments that would be shown by a survey, but which are not shown by the public records.
4. Easements, liens, or encumbrances not shown by the public records.
5. Zoning and governmental restrictions.
6. Unpatented mining claims and water rights or claims.

abstract. Remember that an abstract summarizes all recorded events that have affected the title to a given piece of real property. A **title report** can be thought of as a photograph that shows the condition of the title at a particular time. Examination of the following sample title report will show that it does not state who previous owners were, or list all mortgage loans ever made against the property, it lists only those mortgages that have not been removed.

Examination of the title report in Exhibit 13.3 will reveal that it does not guarantee clear title to the property. Part 1 of the report lists all recorded objections that could be found. In Part 2, the insurance company states that there may be unrecorded items that either were not researched, or could not be researched in preparing the report. For example, title companies generally do not conduct a visual inspection or survey of the property. So, when the policy is issued it will not cover items that could be determined by actual notice, and the party seeking the insurance is responsible for employing a surveyor if he wishes to verify the property's boundaries. Lenders generally consider title insurance commitments good for up to thirty days; after that time they may require an update.

It is important to understand that the title report is not the same as a title insurance policy. The title report can be used to verify that the seller is in fact the owner of the property, and it informs the lender, seller, and buyer of the state of the title before the transaction is closed. Therefore, the title report identifies what needs to be done to bring the title to the condition specified in the sales contract. The title report does not guarantee title, it does not offer protection against unrecorded items such as the rights of parties in possession and undisclosed liens, nor does it offer protection against **hidden defects** in the records. Examples of hidden defects include: grantor's lack of competency, lack of delivery, fraud, forgery, unrecorded mechanic's, tax, and miscellaneous liens; encumbrances, easements, encroachments, and rights of parties in possession.

TYPES OF TITLE INSURANCE POLICIES

In this section, we focus on the two basic types of policies issued in conjunction with the transfer of a fee interest: the owner's policy, sometimes called the fee policy, and the mortgagee's policy, sometimes called the loan policy, or lender's policy. These policies are classified according to the named beneficiary.

Owner's Policy

With an owner's policy, coverage is equal to the sale price, and the policy remains in force as long as the owner (or the owner's heirs) has an interest in the property. An owner's policy is not assignable; each time the property is sold a new policy must be purchased. However, if you refinance your property, the owner's policy obtained in conjunction with the initial mortgage loan remains in force; a new owner's policy need not be acquired. Two types of owner's policies are available: the standard policy, and the extended coverage policy. As shown in the following highlighted material, the standard policy covers losses arising from a variety of title defects, but hidden defects are excluded from coverage. Some lenders require that borrowers obtain an extended coverage policy that, for an added premium, also covers hidden defects.

Prudent owners of real property will acquire a title insurance policy although they are not required to do so by any governmental unit. Lending institutions, however, almost always require the borrower to purchase a mortgagee's policy. They may even require title insurance where title is registered under the Torrens System (explained later) to protect against items, such as federal tax liens that are not shown on the transfer certificate of title.

Coverage of Title Defects

The following title defects are covered under the standard policy:

- Confusion resulting from similarity of names
- Forgeries (deeds, mortgages, or other documents)
- Incorrectly given marital status
- Grantor's lack of capacity (e.g., deeds granted by minors or those who are mentally incompetent)
- Misfiled documents
- Unauthorized acknowledgements
- Mistaken legal interpretation of wills and undisclosed heirs

Hidden title defects generally not covered by standard policy:

- Any facts that an accurate survey would reveal incude:
  - Encroachments
  - Certain water rights
- Rights of parties in possession not reflected in the public records are:
  - Unrecorded easements
  - Taxes and assessments not yet due
  - Unpatented mining claims
  - Zoning or other governmental restrictions

Mortgagee's Policy

There are several important differences between an owner's and a mortgagee's policy besides the named beneficiary. The mortgagee's policy covers only the amount owed on the loan. Therefore, as the loan amount is repaid over time, coverage on the mortgagee's policy decreases, and ends when the loan is paid in full. In addition, the mortgagee's policy does not contain the exceptions shown on the owner's policy regarding claims to ownership that could be revealed by a physical inspection of the property. Finally, the mortgagee's policy can be assigned to subsequent holders of the mortgage loan.

The insurance company assumes increased risk by eliminating some of the exceptions found in the owner's policy, but some of this risk is offset by the fact that the insurance company's liability decreases as the loan is repaid. Upon foreclosure and purchase by the mortgagee, the mortgagee's policy automatically becomes an owner's policy and insures the mortgagee against any loss arising out of matters existing before the effective date of the policy. In the event of a loss under a mortgagee's policy the insurance company pays the mortgagee the balance due on the loan, and thus extinguishes the owner's debt. The owner can, however, still lose the property and for this reason it is generally sound practice to obtain an owner's policy even when the lender only requires a mortgagee's policy.

Additional Coverage Available

If an insured property increases in value, it is possible and recommended that the amount of coverage on the owner's policy be increased. Of course, this will require an additional premium at the time the mortgagee obtains added coverage. In recent years many owner's policies have an inflation guard endorsement to automatically cover appreciation in property value. Additionally, both lenders and owners may obtain a closing protection letter, which is a form of additional coverage not arising out of the basic policy. It is given by the title insurance company to cover losses resulting from errors or infidelity committed by the company's agent or approved attorney in the handling of the transaction or closing.

TITLE INSURANCE COST

Compared to the cost of other types of insurance, title insurance is a bargain. The charge for a title report and title insurance is approximately one-half of one percent of the coverage amount. Premiums are based on the type of policy and the amount of coverage.

The rates charged by title insurance companies do not differ significantly within a geographic market. Some would argue that this is because of the nature of the industry. There are approximately 2,000 title companies that are members of the American Land Title Association (ALTA), but only about ninety write title insurance, and the six largest title insurers write more than half of all policies. In many states, lack of price competition is the result of state regulations that set permissible premiums. In others, title insurers have formed state-sanctioned rating bureaus that set uniform state rates.

There are ways to reduce the cost of title insurance. Some companies offer policies at re-issue rates that are lower than the rate they usually charge. Re-issue rates are used when the company issued the policy held by the seller. In addition, title companies will frequently issue both a mortgagee's policy and an owner's policy for less than what the two would cost if purchased separately.

TITLE INSURANCE AND TECHNOLOGY

For decades there was little change in the way the title insurance industry conducted business; it was one of the last segments of the real estate industry to incorporate technology into its operations. In recent years, however, with the rise in the Internet and the amount of information available to title companies, technology has become a significant issue in the title industry. The primary emphasis to increase electronic efficiency in the industry came from the residential side rather than the commercial side of the business for at least two reasons. First, the volume of residential transactions is much greater than commercial transactions. Second, most commercial transactions are more complex than residential transactions.

Even though the title industry's use of this technology is in its infancy, greater efficiencies are already being observed. The Internet allows lenders to place orders and select services (e.g., appraisals or flood certifications) directly from the title insurer's Web site. It also gives insurers the ability to link to other sources of electronic information (e.g., county records and tax liens), and to e-mail important documents (e.g., title commitments and statements) to customers and lenders. Finally, with 24-hour a day access, it is more convenient for buyers, sellers and their attorneys to view documents before the closing.

The use of e-technology has interesting implications for the title industry. Some industry insiders suggest that by the year 2005 every piece of information needed to close a real estate transaction will be available online. This will enable paperless closings that may be performed with the parties in multiple locations. The availability of electronic information is also predicted to reduce costs because fewer "brick and mortar" offices and fewer people will be required to do the work. Finally, some experts predict that the use of technology will result in consolidation in the industry with fewer and larger title insurers in the future.

Decision Point

You just inherited a parcel of real property from your aunt. When she acquired title to the property, fifty years ago, an attorney had written an acceptable opinion of title. In pricing alternative title assurance vehicles, you have discovered that an attorney's opinion of title currently costs $150 less than an owner's title insurance policy. Which form of title assurance will you choose? Why?

TORRENS REGISTRATION

The process of searching a title can be time consuming and redundant because it must be repeated every time title to real property is transferred. Several states have attempted to streamline the process of land title record keeping and examination by allowing for registration of titles under a Torrens system. In the United States, the term "Torrens" is commonly used to designate any land title registration system in which a public official makes a binding title determination of each registered title. Such systems basically operate as follows. The owners of a parcel of real property electing to register their title notify the appropriate government official. Where the Torrens systems are in effect, registration is administered at the county level. The official has a title search conducted, and gives the required notice of a court hearing where any and all must attend to defend any claim on the property. At the hearing, the court decides the legitimacy of the defended claims and removes other clouds on the title. A public official then issues a **Torrens certificate** stating the condition of the title at that time. Subsequent transfers of the property require only an update of the certificate. Updating the certificate of registration requires another title search, but the major benefit of the Torrens system is that the records only have to be searched back to the date of the last certificate update.

Torrens registration is not widely used in the United States; only ten states have statutes that provide for Torrens registration (Colorado, Georgia, Hawaii, Illinois,

Massachusetts, Minnesota, New York, North Carolina, Virginia, and Washington). Registration is fairly substantial around Boston, Chicago, Honolulu, and Minneapolis, but registration is not mandatory in any state and no community has a majority of its parcels registered. However, in some states, once land has been registered it cannot be withdrawn from registration. The system had its greatest support in the twentieth century, but interest in it faded and ten states that had Torrens systems (California, Ohio, Mississippi, Nebraska, North Dakota, Oregon, South Carolina, South Dakota, Tennessee, and Utah) either let them expire or repealed them.

Advocates of the Torrens system assert that it is potentially the least cumbersome of title assurance systems and would result in faster, less expensive, and more certain means of title assurance. Additionally, American Torrens laws generally provide that an owner of a registered land title may not lose title by adverse possession. As land title records become more massive, and as advances in computers make dealing with storage and retrieval of records easier, a shift to Torrens may be desirable and necessary. Support for more comprehensive Torrens systems occasionally surfaces, giving title insurers concern about the threat to their business.

As with the title assurance systems previously examined, mistakes may occur under the Torrens system. Valid off-certificate interests may exist, and it is possible that the registered interests may be invalid. Therefore, each county Torrens system has a fund established to indemnify any party damaged by an error in the registration process. The indemnification fund is funded by contributions required when property is originally registered and when an updated certificate is issued. Compared to the usual fees associated with title insurance, the initial Torrens fees are high, but fees to have the certificate updated are low.

Unfortunately, when only a few properties are registered, a single error may be enough to completely deplete the fund. The problem of off-certificate risks is similar to off-record risks under the recording acts previously described. You can protect yourself from these risks to some extent by searching other public records, questioning knowledgeable parties, and by examining the premises. Private title insurance companies also insure Torrens titles. In some areas, Chicago for example, such coverage is common.

MARKETABLE TITLE ACTS

Some states have truncated the title search process by adopting a Marketable Title Act. These acts dramatically reform the impact of recording under the recording acts by eliminating from a title search most interests in land that are not recorded for a particular

DOING BUSINESS
INTERNATIONAL ISSUES

In much of the rest of the world, Torrens registration prevails as the principal form of title assurance, particularly in countries that were once a part of the British Empire. Title insurance is an American innovation. The first title insurance company was formed in 1876. Initially, such coverage was designed primarily for the benefit of attorneys who wanted protection from errors that they might make in interpreting abstracts, but, in time, title insurance became available to anyone who wished to purchase it. Although title insurance is the major form of title protection in most parts of the United States, little of it is written outside this country. Some title insurance is written in England, Canada, Mexico, and several Caribbean countries, and much of this coverage is written by United States' companies or their subsidiaries.

Go To www.worldbank.org, and search the key words "real property title registration" to learn about activities in which the World Bank has participated in order to improve real property registration in various developing countries.

number of years. Therefore, the title search need cover only the statutory time period. Recording one's interest, or re-recording it, is the usual means of preserving old interests under marketable title acts, rather than bringing a quiet title suit. States with marketable title acts include: Connecticut, Florida, Illinois, Indiana, Iowa, Kansas, Michigan, Minnesota, Nebraska, North Carolina, North Dakota, Ohio, Oklahoma, South Dakota, Utah, Vermont, Wisconsin, and Wyoming.

SUMMARY

Before a real estate transaction can be completed both the seller and buyer must complete several tasks. Of paramount importance for buyers is the determination of the quality of the seller's title. Claims by others on the title may limit ownership rights. In the worst case, funds may be expended acquiring a title that later proves to be worthless. Because such claims may also affect the value of the property as loan collateral, lenders also seek to assure that borrowers will acquire title that is reasonably free from risk of litigation over possible defects. To help avoid these kinds of problems, purchasers of real property should secure, and lenders will require, assurance of the title's quality.

Claims on real property may be disclosed by visibly occupying or making use of the land, or by recording documents in the public records. Purchasers are responsible for investigating the rights of all parties who do either. Examination of the public records can be a cumbersome process that requires some expertise. Most purchasers do, therefore, employ the services of a professional abstractor for this purpose. The title abstract the abstractor prepares is a necessary prerequisite for all of the title assurance methods discussed in this chapter. There is, however, no guarantee that the abstract accurately reflects the true condition of the title, or that any title assurance method will cover all types of risk. The risk of incurring an uncompensated loss is reduced when one obtains some type of title assurance beyond that offered by the grantor. In most cases, title insurance appears to offer the best protection against a potential loss.

KEY TERMS

abstractor	inquiry notice	title abstract
actual notice	insurable title	title chain
constructive notice	marketable title	title insurance
grantee index	opinion of title	title report
grantor index	quiet title suit	Torrens certificate
hidden defect	recording acts	tract index

REVIEW QUESTIONS

1. If one acquires title with a general warranty deed, why waste money securing additional assurance of title?

2. Real estate transactions are a relatively rare occurrence for most people and they know little about title insurance. Therefore, many decide to leave the selection of a title insurance company up to their attorney or real estate broker. Comment on the wisdom of this decision.

3. What is the amount of coverage on an owner's title insurance policy? What would be the consequences of having coverage set higher or lower than this amount?

4. List three important differences between a mortgagee's title insurance policy and an owner's title insurance policy. Who pays for these policies?

5. How does the Torrens system affect the title search process?

6. For what types of notice is a prospective purchaser of real property responsible?

7. Does a title search that reveals no breaks in the chain of title mean the current owner has clear title?

8. What are the basic steps in a title search? How are the grantee index and the grantor index used in this process?

9. What types of risks are not eliminated by: Torrens registration, an attorney's opinion of title, and title insurance?

10. What are your answers to the questions in the three "Decision Point" sections in this chapter?

REAL ESTATE ON THE WEB

Use your favorite search engine to:

1. Determine which of the public record's offices in your area have Web sites and discover what information they make available on their sites.

2. Locate the Web sites of title insurance companies, and discover how much they charge for a title insurance policy.

3. Locate the Web site of local title abstractors.

Refer to the companion web site at www.wiley.com/college/larsen for a variety of online activities including additional chapter content, review materials, assignments, and related links.

ADDITIONAL READINGS

Bell, J. "Technology and the Title Insurance Industry: A New Chapter." *National Real Estate Investor* (March 2000): 70–74.

Mattson-Teig, B. "Engineering a New Title Machine." *National Real Estate Investor* (December 1999): 94–98.

Midkiff, L. "The Automation of the Title Industry." *Mortgage Banking* (October 2000): 193–194.

Richards, G. "Rating Title Firms: A Trend that Keeps Going." *National Real Estate Investor* (May 1998): 102–110.

Rush, A. "Why Title Insurance?" *Mortgage Banking* (August, 2000): 66–69.

14 Closing the Real Estate Transaction

Learning Objectives

After studying this chapter, you should be able to:

- Describe the seller's rights and the borrower's rights under the Real Estate Settlement Procedures Act.
- Explain the basic provisions of the Federal Truth-in-Lending Law.
- Describe what occurs at a closing.
- Understand a closing statement.
- Calculate the proration of a closing cost.

FROM THE WIRE

In June 2002, the Bush administration proposed a "homebuyer bill of rights" in what was said to be an effort to overhaul the Real Estate Settlement Procedures Act of 1974 and make it easier for Americans to own a home. The proposal was the latest in a series of administrative initiatives intended to build affordable housing in low-income areas and increase home ownership, especially among minorities. Housing and Urban Development Secretary, Mel Martinez, said, "Americans enter into mortgage loans, the largest single investment most families ever make, without the clear and useful information that they receive with every other major purchase. We're taking the most meaningful and comprehensive step in years to clarify a settlement process that is cloaked in confusion and uncertainty." Among the buyer's rights included in the proposal are receiving settlement costs information early in the buying process, knowing they are protected through the enforcement of real estate regulations, benefiting from high-tech innovations such as online credit reports and information about competing lenders that could lower settlement costs, and having disclosed costs be as firm as possible to avoid surprises at settlement. In addition, the proposal would simplify the form that lenders provide to buyers to detail the costs they will incur.

Go to www.hud.gov, click "Search/Index," then use "homebuyers bill of rights" as your search term to learn the current status of this proposal.

INTRODUCTION

The term **closing,** or settlement, is used to describe the final step in a real estate transaction. This is the time when documents are signed, the buyer pays the agreed purchase price, and the seller delivers title to the buyer. To familiarize you with the closing process, several important aspects of it are reviewed in this chapter. To begin, two of the most important laws that apply to the process, the Federal Truth-in-Lending Law, and the Real Estate Settlement Procedures Act (RESPA), are highlighted. Such laws help assure that the trust placed in mortgage lenders and other parties is not misplaced. However, as the chapter opener "From the Wire" suggests, changes to RESPA are on the horizon or may have been implemented by the time you read this.

The settlement statement, which shows the financial details of the transaction and is used by the parties to settle at the closing, is also examined. The terms of the purchase contract control how specific items should be handled at the closing, and frequently the parties agree to share, or prorate, the cost of certain items. Therefore, we show how the division of such costs may be calculated.

The material presented in this chapter may be of value to you for at least two reasons. First, transactions tend to proceed more smoothly when all parties involved have an understanding of what is required of them. To assist their clients, real estate agents, in particular, must be knowledgeable in this area. Second, the closing process has certain costs; the people who assist in closings do so for a fee. Compared to the cost of a home, most closing costs are relatively minor, but they can add up. Knowledge of the information presented here should enable you to recognize these costs and factor them into real estate purchase and disposition decisions.

THE CLOSING

The procedures used at a closing usually follow local custom and are not controlled by statute. As we see in the next section, however, law may regulate certain aspects of the closing. The buyer and seller alone may handle a closing, but usually a third party, the settlement agent, coordinates the closing. A settlement agent can be an attorney, lending institution, real estate broker, or title insurance company. The closing is usually held at the settlement agent's office, but it could be held anywhere. Anyone with an interest in the transaction may attend. The seller(s), the buyer(s), and their respective attorneys usually attend the closing. It is also common for the real estate broker(s) involved in the transaction to attend, as well as representatives of the title insurance company and perhaps a representative from the lending institution.

At the closing, the settlement agent acts as a master of ceremonies, distributing, and explaining each document that the parties must sign, and then collecting the signed documents and distributing copies to the appropriate parties. In addition, the settlement agent keeps a copy of each document for the agent's own file that may prove useful should questions arise after the closing. After all documents have been signed (e.g., the buyer signs the note and mortgage, and the seller signs the deed), the settlement agent distributes checks. Two checks are usually distributed at the closing table: the real estate brokers receive their commission checks, and the seller receives a check for the net proceeds. Once the parties sign all the documents and receive their respective checks, the closing is complete.

The settlement agent's duties do not end with the conclusion of the meeting. The agent may be responsible for having certain documents recorded, and is responsible for mailing other monies due, such as inspection fees. To help ensure collection of any income tax due on the sale or exchange of residences with four or fewer units, the Internal Revenue Service (IRS) requires that the settlement agent report the details of the closing to the IRS.

REAL ESTATE SETTLEMENT PROCEDURES ACT OF 1974 (RESPA)

We described the settlement agent's role at the closing to that of a master of ceremonies. In playing this role, the agent may not ad-lib. The proceedings must follow the "script" laid out in the purchase agreement, and the settlement agent is subject to the direction of the **Real Estate Settlement Procedures Act** (RESPA). RESPA was specifically designed to eliminate several abuses that had occurred too frequently in real estate transactions. The Act covers the following three major areas:

1. It limits the amount of money that home buyers/borrowers may be required to place in escrow to partially cover the costs of future expenses such as hazard insurance premiums and property taxes.
2. It makes illegal the payment of kickbacks that increase the cost of some settlement services.
3. It requires lenders to disclose closing costs to both the buyer and seller in advance of the closing.

CLOSING COST DISCLOSURE

Real estate **closing costs** are frequently substantial and, until passage of RESPA, often an unpleasant surprise that the principals did not discover until the closing. Perhaps the primary benefit of RESPA is that it requires lenders writing federally related mortgage loans to fully disclose closing costs in advance of the closing. By RESPA definition, a federally related mortgage loan is any mortgage loan made by a lender regulated or insured by the federal government or covered by the Consumer Protection Act, and who makes or invests in more than $1,000,000 per year in residential real estate loans; or any mortgage loan that is eligible to be purchased by various organizations (e.g., Federal National Mortgage Association, Federal Home Loan Mortgage Corporation) in the secondary mortgage market (Chapter 16).

Closing costs may be disclosed in two ways. First, lenders are required to prepare, free of charge, a **good faith estimate** of closing costs at the time of the loan application using the standard, or uniform, **settlement statement.** In many cases, this estimate is presented to the loan applicant on the day of the application, but the law allows delivery of the estimate up to three days after the application date. A "good faith" estimate means that the estimate does not have to reflect the actual amounts that will be charged on the day of the closing, but the estimate must be a reasonable approximation based on the conditions that exist at the time of the application. When prepared by a qualified loan officer, these estimates are usually very close to the figures actually used at closing. RESPA also requires that within the same three-day period, lenders present the loan applicant with a copy of "Settlement Costs and You," a booklet prepared by the U.S. Department of Housing and Urban Development (HUD). The booklet is designed to assist borrowers in understanding the costs and nature of real estate closing services. Some mortgage originators have, with the approval of HUD, developed their own booklet for the same purpose. The good faith estimate and the information booklet received by the loan applicant should enable the borrower to make better judgments regarding the reasonableness of the closing costs.

RESPA also requires lenders to make available, on the (business) day before the closing, a copy of the actual settlement statement that will be used at the closing. In addition to showing the precise amounts for items that were estimated earlier, the statement will include closing costs that were not on the original good faith estimate because previous disclosure was not required. For example, the statement will include any required deposits to an escrow, or impound account. To secure a copy of the statement, the party requesting the information must do so in writing at least two (business) days before the closing. If no request is received, the lender is not obligated to provide the advance disclosure statement.

LIMITS ON ESCROW DEPOSITS

Most, but not all, home mortgage loans made today require escrow accounts because lenders wish to reduce the possibility that borrowers will be unable to make the full hazard insurance premium payment or property tax payment when due. So, lenders require borrowers to make these payments in installments together with their regular payment of principal and interest. This type of mortgage is known as a budget mortgage.

Some lenders do not require escrow balances, perhaps because they deem that the cost of maintaining the escrow accounts exceeds the benefit of reduced problems resulting from nonpayment of the above items. A few lenders even pay interest on loan escrow balances. They can do so because they are not subject to RESPA. For example, interest may be paid on escrow amounts for a loan written by a state-chartered institution that will be held in the originator's portfolio.

People with good savings habits may resent being required to place funds in a noninterest-bearing account. They may prefer a loan with an interest-bearing escrow account, or a loan without escrow requirements so that they can invest and earn a return on the funds that otherwise would be paid into a noninterest bearing account. Mortgage loan escrow accounts were designed to protect people with poor savings habits. People who do not fit this description may find it worth their time to shop for a mortgage lender that does not require noninterest bearing escrow deposits.

According to RESPA, the maximum initial deposit that a lender may require to be placed into an escrow account is one-sixth of the annual amount due. For example, if the lender is to make the payment of the premiums on the borrower's hazard insurance, or to pay the property taxes (from funds supplied by the borrower), the initial escrow deposit may equal the amount necessary to cover these charges for two months. This does not mean, however, that the buyer's initial costs will be limited to this amount; only the amount of money to be placed in the escrow account is limited. Many lenders require the borrower to show proof of payment for a one-year hazard insurance policy at the closing. For this item, the buyer's up-front costs could equal fourteen months of premiums; the premium for the first year policy and an escrow deposit equal to one-sixth of the premium for the second year. RESPA also prohibits lenders from earning or paying interest on amounts in escrow.

PROHIBITION OF KICKBACKS

Under RESPA, no party can give or receive a kickback, or fee, as a result of a referral. If any party refers a buyer/borrower to a particular party involved in the closing (e.g., attorney, appraiser, lender, real estate broker, title company) and receives a fee for the referral, they are in violation of the Act, and subject to treble damages (three times the amount of damage suffered by the buyer). Fee splitting by parties associated with the closing is also prohibited unless the fees are paid for services actually performed. This part of RESPA has resulted in some confusion because of the vagueness of the term "services actually performed." The intent was to prevent parties from paying or receiving referral fees under the guise of fee splitting.

Under RESPA, a seller may not require a buyer to use a particular title insurance company as a condition of the sale. Therefore, RESPA ensures that buyers have the freedom to select the title insurance company of their choice. However, many buyers delegate the selection to someone else. This regulation was designed primarily to prevent a practice employed by some land developers who would obtain a favorable rate on title insurance for undeveloped land with the understanding that buyers of the developed property would be required to secure title insurance with the same company.

EXCEPTIONS TO RESPA COVERAGE

Not all mortgage loans are covered by RESPA. The basic coverage is for loans secured by a first lien on one-to-four family dwellings. Construction loans and other temporary financing for such properties, and first lien loans on other types of property, are not covered by the Act based on the theory that borrowers involved in such loans are more sophisticated and do not need the same level of protection. In addition, it is important to note that RESPA does not regulate the amount of the fees that may be charged for providing settlement services.

Decision Point

As a loan officer at a commercial bank subject to RESPA, you have received requests for disclosure of the exact closing costs to be incurred on three separate loans. The first involves a verbal request on a first mortgage home loan. The second is a written request on a home construction loan. The third is a verbal request on a commercial mortgage loan.

On which of the loans are you required by RESPA to provide the closing costs? If you are not legally required to disclose the information, will you do so anyway? Why?

DOING BUSINESS
LEGAL ISSUES

While RESPA has certainly reduced the incidence of the problems it addresses, it has not completely eliminated them. As the following examples suggest, the alleged violations that do occur can happen just about anywhere. In the 1990s, for example, two large commercial banks in Massachusetts and Georgia were accused of requiring mortgage loan applicants to place too large an amount into their escrow accounts, and a bank in Minnesota was charged with paying illegal referral fees to real estate brokers. In 2001, a prominent Mississippi title insurance company had a $6 million lawsuit filed against it charging that it paid illegal referral fees to real estate agents. And in 2002, a California title company agreed to pay $2 million to settle allegations that it had lavished gifts on real estate agents in exchange for them directing business to the company.

Go to www.homes.wsj.com, use "closing costs" as your search term and click on one or more of the results to learn more about this subject.

FEDERAL TRUTH-IN-LENDING LAW OF 1968

In dealing with loan applicants and in preparing figures for the closing statement, mortgage lenders must also comply with the **Federal Truth-in-Lending Law** (FTL). The primary purpose of FTL, which applies to a variety of lenders not just those that write mortgage loans, is to help enable borrowers to compare the cost of different loan terms. FTL requires lenders to make full disclosure when advertising loan terms, and to fully disclose to loan applicants, in a uniform manner, financial information contained in loan agreements. As can be observed in the following material, the information that FTL requires lenders to disclose to loan applicants depends upon the type of loan.

Mortgage loans that require RESPA disclosure also usually require FTL disclosure. Similar to the initial disclosure requirements of RESPA, the disclosures required by FTL must be made no later than three days after the loan application is made. Unlike the initial RESPA disclosures that need only be reasonable estimates, the disclosures required under FTL must be accurate. Under certain circumstances, it is possible for a mortgage transaction to be covered by either FTL or RESPA, but not both. For example, when an individual applies for a mortgage to refinance a residence or to assume another individual's mortgage, FTL disclosure would be required but RESPA would not. If the borrower in a mortgage transaction is a business, or the transaction involves one-to-four family residential rental property, FTL disclosure is not required, but the lender must comply with RESPA requirements.

FTL DISCLOSURE REQUIREMENTS

Constant Payment Mortgages:

1. The amount financed, which is the mortgage amount less any finance charges that are paid at the closing.
2. The dollar amount of each payment. If the payment will vary, for example, when a graduated payment mortgage is used all payment amounts must be disclosed. If the payment varies because of the cost of mortgage insurance, usually the highest and the lowest payment amounts are disclosed.
3. The annual percentage rate, which is the borrower's effective cost of credit expressed on an annual basis as determined by a method prescribed by FTL. Usually the lender will commit to a particular interest rate, but if it does not and interest rates change before the closing, the lender must make additional disclosures prior to the closing.
4. Whether or not the loan may be assumed, and if so, whether the loan terms may be changed at the time of the assumption.
5. Total finance charges, which is the sum of all interest paid over the term of the loan, premiums for required insurance policies (mortgage, hazard, disability, and credit life), loan origination fees, discount points, prepaid mortgage interest, assumption fees, escrow charges made for establishing an escrow account, and fees for the preparation of a loan amortization schedule when paid for by the borrower.
6. Total payment amount, which is the amount of principal reduction, interest, and fees for required credit life and mortgage insurance to be paid over the entire loan term.
7. The total number of payments.
8. Any assets that will be used as collateral for the loan and the nature of any interest the lender will require in the borrower's property should the loan be granted.
9. Any statutory fees for filing liens against assets securing the loan.
10. The amount of any late charge, if applicable.

11. The payment due date after which the lender may charge a late fee.

12. Whether or not the borrower may repay the loan ahead of schedule without a penalty. The dollar amount of any penalty need not be disclosed. Prepayment penalties are usually expressed as a percentage of the remaining unpaid principal at the time of the prepayment.

13. The amount of the mortgage insurance premium if the lender offers it for sale or requires that the borrower obtain it.

14. Whether or not hazard insurance is required as a condition of the loan.

Adjustable Rate Mortgages:

1. All of the above.

2. The index to which changes in the mortgage interest rate are to be tied.

3. The margin, or percentage, that will be added to the index value to determine the mortgage interest rate at subsequent adjustment dates.

4. The composite rate at the time of origination. The composite rate is the combination of the index value and the margin.

5. The adjustment period, which specifies how frequently the mortgage interest rate or payment may be adjusted.

6. Interest rate caps at each adjustment period, if any, which limits the interest rate that may be used to adjust payments at each adjustment date.

7. Life of loan interest rate caps, if any, which limit increases in the interest rate that may be used in calculating payments over the entire repayment period.

8. Payment caps at each adjustment period, if any, which limit the dollar amount that a mortgage payment may be increased at each adjustment date.

9. Life-of-loan payment caps, if any, which limit the dollar amount of payment increases allowed over the entire repayment period.

10. Whether composite rate increases will affect the loan balance, or the payment amount, or both and, if so, an example of the effect.

CLOSING COSTS

In the typical real estate transaction, both the buyer and seller incur a number of costs that are paid for at the closing. Closing costs include both expenses that the buyer must pay in addition to the purchase price and expenses that are deducted from the sale proceeds if the seller is responsible for paying them. As previously mentioned, the party responsible for paying a particular closing cost is often determined by local custom. But, responsibility for closing costs is subject to negotiation. For example, despite the fact that local custom dictates the buyer pay for any inspections, the buyer may include in the offer the demand that the seller cover this cost.

Certain closing costs are fixed in amount regardless of the eventual closing date. The typical fixed closing costs that a buyer and seller might incur are listed in the following material.

Who Is Normally Responsible for Fixed Closing Costs?

Buyer's Closing Costs	Seller's Closing Costs
Appraisal fee	Abstract of title
Buyer's attorney's fee	Broker's commission
Condominium transfer fee	Certificate of title
Escrow fee*	Conveyance tax
Hazard insurance premium	Cost of clearing title
Inspection fees	Escrow fee*
Loan fees (either new or assumption)	Inspection fee (termite)

Buyer's Closing Costs	Seller's Closing Costs
Prepaid interest on a new loan	Interest in arrears on existing loan
Prepaid taxes reimbursed to seller	Prepayment penalty on existing loan
Recording fees for the deed and the mortgage	Seller's attorney's fee
Title insurance premium	Survey cost

* The buyer and seller usually share escrow fees. Purchasers using Veterans Administration financing are not permitted to pay any escrow fees, and the amount of escrow fees that a purchaser using an FHA loan can pay are limited, so that the seller may have to pay for more than half of this item.

PRORATION OF EXPENSES AND INCOME

In addition to the fixed closing costs listed above, there are other items that vary in amount because they are directly related to property ownership. The cost for items such as property taxes, accrued interest on assumed obligations, and prepaid insurance premiums are usually shared by the buyer and seller. The process of splitting these items between the parties is known as proration, and the item itself is referred to as a **prorated item.** Some operating expenses and rents are also prorated for income-producing properties.

Methods of proration vary. The preferred proration method is to divide the cost of the item to be prorated by the actual number of days in the year to arrive at a daily figure. Then, each party's share of the total cost is determined by multiplying the daily amount by the number of days that the party has ownership. The party who is assigned the cost or income for the closing date usually depends on local custom, but again this is subject to negotiation. In many areas, it is customary to assign costs and income for the closing day to the buyer. Examples of such calculations are shown in Exhibit 14.1. In other areas, such as Ohio, responsibility for costs and income for the closing day are assigned to the seller. Even the date to be used as the cutoff in the proration is subject to negotiation. Usually, the cutoff date is the closing date, but the parties may mutually agree to another date. For example, the sales contract could specify proration as of the date of occupancy, which could be a month, or more, after the closing.

The parties sometimes use alternative methods that result in solutions similar to those that would result from using the preferred method. Sometimes the total cost is divided by 360 to arrive at the daily cost, or by twelve to determine a monthly cost. When the latter method is used, the monthly amount is further divided by 30 to arrive at the daily amount when needed. These alternative calculations are holdovers from the days before hand-held calculators, when it was common to simplify calculations by assuming a 360-day year comprised of twelve months each with thirty days. Using the alternative method may not significantly affect the solution, but if large amounts are involved, the difference may be significant to the parties. In prorating any item at closing, the parties have the right to agree to use any method of proration, or to impose the liability for an item solely on one of the parties.

Decision Point

A first-time homebuyer has exactly $20,000 and plans to use all of it as a down payment on a $100,000 home. Do you think the buyer considered all the costs? What additional expenditures are likely to be involved in the transaction? How would you council the buyer to proceed?

THE SETTLEMENT STATEMENT

The settlement statement, also known as a closing statement or adjustment sheet, provides an accounting of the real estate transaction, and is prepared either by an attorney, an escrow agent, a real estate broker, or other designated party. The closing statement itemizes

| EXHIBIT | 14.1 | **SAMPLE PRORATION CALCULATIONS** |

Example One: property taxes
Assume:

1. That tax is due the first day of each January,
2. The next tax payment is $1,095,
3. That closing is on August 15, and
4. Buyer is responsible for the date of closing.

Therefore:
The daily cost = $3.00 ($1095/365),
The seller's share = $678 ($3 x 226), and
The buyer's share = $417 ($3 x 139).

Example Two: rental income
Assume:

1. Property rents for $600 per month,
2. Rents are prorated on the basis of the actual number of days in the month,
3. Closing is on September 11, and
4. Buyer is responsible for the date of closing.

Whether the buyer or seller is credited or charged with their share at the closing depends when the rent is paid. If the rent was paid to the seller before closing: seller must pay buyer $400 [($600 ÷ 30) x 20]. If the tenant is to pay the rent to the buyer after the closing: buyer must pay the seller $200 [($600 ÷ 30) x 10)].

closing costs, indicates how they are allocated between the seller and buyer, and all the cash received and paid out in the transaction. For some transactions, settlement statements may be individually drafted documents, but preprinted forms are widely used. The settlement statement, required by RESPA, is shown in Exhibit 14.2

SAMPLE CLOSING

The settlement statement contained in Exhibit 14.2 reflects a fairly typical residential transaction, although each will have unique features. Administrative information, the identification of the parties involved in the transaction, and the location of the subject property are disclosed in the upper portion of the first page. The lower portion of the first page is divided into two sections. The left-hand side, section J, summarizes the transaction from the buyer's perspective, and the right-hand side, section K, summarizes the transaction from the seller's perspective. Both sections begin with the sale price and then work toward the amount owed by the borrower and the amount to be received by the seller. Note that the sale price was $102,000, and that the buyer must deliver $23,281.33, while the seller leaves the closing with $42,890.37.

SECTION J, SUMMARY OF THE BORROWER'S TRANSACTION

The amount owed by the borrower includes not only the sale price of $102,000, but also settlement charges equaling $1,726.21 which are detailed on the second page of the statement. This results in a gross amount due of $103,726.21. In this case, the gross amount is reduced by three items; an $80,000 loan provided by National City Bank, a $270 refundable loan application fee, and $174.88 credit from the seller for property taxes due but not yet paid.

The seller made the last semi-annual property tax payment on June 30 and the newly issued tax bill shows that $560 will be due for the second half of the year, so the $560 was prorated, with the seller paying for the fifty-eight days she owned the property. Usually, the gross amount would also be reduced by the amount of the earnest money tendered by the buyer when the offer was made. It is possible that no earnest money was involved in this transaction; sometimes buyers sign a promissory note instead of making a cash deposit. It is also possible that the real estate company simply returned the funds to the buyer separately at the closing.

SECTION K, SUMMARY OF THE SELLER'S TRANSACTION

Note that three items reduce the amount payable to the seller: $5,939 of settlement charges which are detailed on the second page, $52,995.75 needed to payoff the existing mortgage on the property, and the credit to the buyer for property taxes.

SETTLEMENT STATEMENT: PAGE 2

The settlement charges detailed on the second page of the statement are comprised of fees charged by a number of parties, including: brokerage firm(s), mortgage lender(s), the settlement agent, and the government.

Charges to the Seller

Note that the brokerage commission of $5,650 is paid entirely by the seller. As we saw in Chapter 9, the seller usually pays the commission because the broker was hired as the agent of the seller. In this situation, two firms were involved in selling the property; Cardboard Box Realty listed the property, and Bridge Realty located the buyer.

Other charges to the seller total $289. The settlement agent charged the seller $35 for preparing the deed and other documents and $50 for processing the closing. The State levies a transfer tax on deeds of $1 per $500 of sales price. The seller was charged $204 to pay the transfer tax.

Charges to the Buyer

The mortgage lender levies several of the charges to the borrower. In this example, they include: $190 for an appraisal of the property, $80 for a credit report on the buyer, and an additional $106.50 for other services associated with originating the loan. The buyer's first mortgage payment is not due until the end of September and it will include interest on the amount borrowed for September only. Therefore, $115.07 of prepaid interest is charged to the buyer to cover five days worth of interest on the loan through the end of August. The lender also requires the buyer to deposit certain amounts to help cover future property tax payments and insurance premiums. The deposit of $35.50 represents one-sixth of the annual hazard insurance premium, $369.48 represents one-third of the annual property taxes, and $48.16 represents one-sixth of the annual flood insurance premium.

Occasionally, one, or both, parties may pay directly some item that could be handled at the closing. Our sample closing statement contains two such items: the buyer secured a one-year hazard insurance policy costing $213 and, because the property is located in a flood plain, a required one-year flood insurance policy costing $289. The initials P.O.C. (for paid outside of closing) are shown in the amount column to make it clear that these items were not mistakenly omitted from the statement.

Additional charges to the buyer included: $150 to the settlement agent, $125 for title examination, $25 for a title insurance binder, $280 for title insurance policies covering both

EXHIBIT 14.2 SAMPLE SETTLEMENT STATEMENT

A. Settlement Statement

U.S. Department of Housing
and Urban Development

OMB No. 2502-0265

B. Type of Loan		
1. ☐ FHA 2. ☐ FmHA 3. ☒ Conv. Unins.	6. File Number 91-0001	7. Loan Number 0000000001
4. ☐ VA 5. ☐ Conv. Ins.	8. Mortgage Insurance Case Number	

C. Note: This form is furnished to give you a statement of actual settlement costs. Amounts paid to and by the settlement agent are shown. Items marked "(p.o.c.)" were paid outside the closing; they are shown here for information purposes and are not included in the totals.

D. Name and Address of Borrower	E. Name and Address of Seller	F. Name and Address of Lender
Melvin H. Buyer 203 Forrer Blvd. Mythical, MO 12345	Christine Marie Seller 3013 Meadow Park Drive Mythical, MO 12345	National City Mortgage Co. 3232 Newmark Drive Mythical, MO 12345

G. Property Location	H. Settlement Agent	
3013 Meadow Park Drive Mythical, MO 12345 Fictitious County, Missouri Hollywood Hills Lot 108 Section 3	Fidelity Land Title Agency, Inc. TIN-82-8389204	
	Place of Settlement 116 E. Thirteenth Street Mythical, MO 12345	I. Settlement Date 8/27/03

J. SUMMARY OF BORROWER'S TRANSACTION:		K. SUMMARY OF SELLER'S TRANSACTION:	
100. GROSS AMOUNT DUE FROM BORROWER		**400. GROSS AMOUNT DUE TO SELLER:**	
101. Contract sales price	102,000.00	401. Contract sales price	102,000.00
102. Personal property		402. Personal property	
103. Settlement charges to borrower (line 1400)	1,726.21	403.	
104.		404.	
105.		405.	
Adjustments for items paid by seller in advance		*Adjustments for items paid by seller in advance*	
106. City/town taxes to		406. City/town taxes to	
107. County taxes to		407. County taxes to	
108. Assessments to		408. Assessments to	
109.		409.	
110.		410.	
111.		411.	
112.		412.	
120. GROSS AMOUNT DUE FROM BORROWER	103,726.21	**420. GROSS AMOUNT DUE TO SELLER**	102,000.00
200. AMOUNTS PAID BY OR IN BEHALF OF BORROWER		**500. REDUCTIONS IN AMOUNT DUE TO SELLER**	
201. Deposit or earnest money		501. Excess Deposit (see instructions)	
202. Principal amount of new loan(s)	80,000.00	502. Settlement charges to seller (line 1400)	5,939.00
203. Existing loan(s) taken subject to		503. Existing loan(s) taken subject to	
204. Application Fee Paid	270.00	504. Payoff of first mortgage loan	52,995.75
205.		505. Payoff of second mortgage loan	
206.		506.	
207.		507.	
208.		508.	
209.		509.	
Adjustments for items unpaid by seller		*Adjustments for items unpaid by seller*	
210. City/town taxes to		510. City/town taxes to	
211. County taxes 7/1/03 to 8/27/03	174.88	511. County taxes 7/1/03 to 8/27/03	174.88
212. Assessments to		512. Assessments to	
213.		513.	
214.		514.	
215.		515.	
216.		516.	
217.		517.	
218.		518.	
219.		519.	
220. TOTAL PAID BY/FOR BORROWER	80,444.88	**520. TOTAL REDUCTION AMOUNT DUE SELLER**	59,109.63
300. CASH AT SETTLEMENT FOR OR TO BORROWER		**600. CASH AT SETTLEMENT TO OR FROM SELLER**	
301. Gross amount due from borrower (line 120)	103,726.21	601. Gross amount due to seller (line 420)	102,000.00
302. Less amounts paid by/for borrower (line 220)	80,444.88	602. Less reduction amount due seller (line 520)	59,109.63
303. CASH From BORROWER	23,281.33	**603. CASH To SELLER**	42,890.37

EXHIBIT | 14.2 | SAMPLE SETTLEMENT STATEMENT (CONTINUED)

U.S DEPARTMENT OF HOUSING AND URBAN DEVELOPMENT
SETTLEMENT STATEMENT
PAGE 2

			PAID FROM BORROWER'S FUNDS AT SETTLEMENT	PAID FROM SELLER'S FUNDS AT SETTLEMENT
L.	**SETTLEMENT CHARGES:**			
700.	TOTAL SALES/BROKER'S COMMISSION based on price $ 102,000.00			
	Division of commission (line 700) as follows:			
701.	$ 2,590.00 to Cardboard Box Realty			
702.	$ 3,060.00 to Bridge REalty			
703.	Commission paid at Settlement			5,650.00
704.				
800.	**ITEMS PAYABLE IN CONNECTION WITH LOAN**			
801.	Loan Origination Fee 0.0%			
802.	Loan Discount 0.0%			
803.	Appraisal Fee to National City Mortgage Co.		190.00	
804.	Credit Report to National City Mortgage Co.		80.00	
805.	Lender's Inspection Fee to			
806.	Mortgage Insurance Application Fee to			
807.	Assumption Fee to			
808.	Underwriting fee to: National City Mortgage Co.		50.00	
809.				
810.	Tax Service FEe to National City Mortgage Co.		56.50	
811.				
900.	**ITEMS REQUIRED BY LENDER TO BE PAID IN ADVANCE**			
901.	Interest from 8/27/03 to 9/1/03 @$23.0137 /day 5 days		115.07	
902.	Mortgage Insurance Premium for to			
903.	Hazard Insurance Premium for 1 yrs. to Calamity Ins. Inc. 213.00		P.O.C.	
904.	Flood Insurance Premium for 1 yrs. to Catastrophe Inc. 289.00		P.O.C.	
905.				
1000.	**RESERVES DEPOSITED WITH LENDER FOR**			
1001.	Hazard Insurance 2 mo. @ $17.75 /mo.		35.50	
1002.	Mortgage insurance mo. @ $ /mo.			
1003.	City property taxes mo. @ $ /mo.			
1004.	County property taxes 4 mo. @ $92.37 /mo.		369.48	
1005.	Annual assessments mo. @ $ /mo.			
1006.	Flood Insurance 2 mo. @ $24.08 /mo.		48.16	
1007.	mo. @ $ /mo.			
1008.	mo. @ $ /mo.			
1100.	**TITLE CHARGES**			
1101.	Settlement or closing fee to Fidelity Land Title Agency, Inc.		150.00	
1102.	Abstract or title search to			
1103.	Title examination to Fidelity Land Title Agency, Inc.		125.00	
1104.	Title insurance binder to Fidelity Land Title Agency, Inc.		25.00	
1105.	Document preparation to This & Larsen, Inc.			35.00
1106.	Notary fees to			
1107.	Attorney's fees to			
	(includes above items No:)			
1108.	Title insurance to Fidelity Land Title Agency, Inc.		280.00	
	(includes above items No:)			
1109.	Lender's coverage $ 280.00 for $80,000.00			
1110.	Owner's coverage $ for $102,000.00			
1111.	EPA Endorsement		75.00	
1112.	Processing Fee			50.00
1113.				
1200.	**GOVERNMENT RECORDING AND TRANSFER CHARGES**			
1201.	Recording fees: Deed $ 10.50 ; Mortgage $ 16.00 ; Releases $		26.50	
1202.	City/county tax/stamps: Deed $ 204.00 ; Mortgage $			204.00
1203.	State tax/stamps: Deed $; Mortgage $			
1204.				
1205.				
1300.	**ADDITIONAL SETTLEMENT CHARGES**			
1301.	Survey to Lewis & Clark		100.00	
1302.	Pest inspection to			
1303.				
1304.				
1305.				
1400.	**TOTAL SETTLEMENT CHARGES (enter on lines 103 and 502, Sections J and K)**		1,726.21	5,939.00

I have carefully reviewed the HUD-1 Settlement Statement and to the best of my knowledge and belief, it is a true and accurate statement of all receipts and disbursements made on my account or by me in this transaction. I further certify that I have received a copy of the HUD-1 Settlement Statement.

Borrower _____ Date _____ Seller _____ Date _____
Borrower _____ Date _____ Seller _____ Date _____

To the best of my knowledge, the HUD-1 Settlement Statement which I have prepared is a true and accurate account of this transaction. I have caused, or will cause, the funds to be disbursed in accordance with this statement.

If marked, the following riders are attached: (For use when one or more parties are not present at closing.)

☐ Certification of Buyer(s)
☐ Certification of Seller(s)

Settlement Agent _____ Date _____

WARNING: It is a crime to knowingly make false statements to the United States on this or any other similar form. Penalties upon conviction can include a fine and imprisonment. For details see: Title 18 U.S. Code Section 1001 and Section 1010.

REV. HUD

the lender and the buyer, and $75 for an EPA endorsement. The buyer was also charged $26.50 to record the deed and mortgage. Finally, the buyers had the property surveyed at a cost of $100. This is not always done with residential properties and probably was in this case because the property is located in a flood zone.

ESCROW ARRANGEMENTS

An alternative to the closing meeting discussed above is an **escrow arrangement,** or escrow closing. In an escrow closing the buyer and seller perform separately, rather than have a joint meeting. Both parties execute and deliver all documents and monies to an independent third party, the **escrow agent** (who is compensated with a fee that is usually split equally between the seller and buyer). In a few states, real estate brokers have authority to handle an escrow closing, but it is more common to have a title company, a lending institution, or a licensed escrow company perform this function.

The duties of an escrow agent are similar, but perhaps more diverse, than those of a settlement agent. The escrow agent performs such duties as ordering title evidence, clearing encumbrances from the title, calculating prorations, preparing the settlement statement, obtaining needed signatures, and recording documents. The escrow agent holds the funds and documents until all the terms and conditions specified by the parties have been satisfied. Then the agent distributes all funds and documents according to either the escrow instructions contained in the purchase contract, or according to the instructions given under a separate document known either as an escrow agreement, or escrow instructions.

Escrow instructions detail the steps necessary to close a transaction and direct the escrow agent how to proceed. To be valid, both the seller and buyer must sign the escrow agreement, although sometimes both prepare separate instructions. Care must be exercised in preparing the purchase contract or separate escrow instructions; otherwise delays may occur in finalizing the transaction. For example, the document must specify who is to pay the various expenses, and the proration date and method. In the event of a disagreement, escrow can only be revoked, or changed, by mutual agreement. To ensure that they receive their commission, brokers need to be parties to the escrow agreement. Otherwise, the seller may successfully order the escrow agent not to pay any commission.

To avoid wasted effort, escrows are usually not established until after any major contingencies in the purchase contract are satisfied (e.g., arranging new financing, obtaining a building permit, loan assumption approval, securing a zoning change). Minor contract contingencies that generally do not threaten the transaction, such as termite and property inspections, or the signing of condominium bylaws can be performed after the escrow is opened.

Whether a closing meeting or escrow closing is used depends on several factors. Escrow closings are common practice in some states. They are also used in cases when it is inconvenient for both parties to attend the closing, for example, if either party is living in a different state, or, as in one case, where the seller had treated the buyers rudely

AN ETHICAL ISSUE
MISTAKE IN CLOSING COSTS

Assume you have exercised your right under the Real Estate Settlement Procedures Act and the day before closing obtained a copy of the exact figures to be used at the closing for a property you are purchasing. In reviewing the figures you notice a mistake, which, if undetected, will result in a $30 savings to you. Why will you, or will you not, call the mistake to the attention of other parties to the transaction? Would your answer change based on the amount of the mistake, or based upon who will be financially injured by the mistake? Why?

during negotiations and did not wish to face them at closing. An escrow arrangement is required for some transactions. For example, in closing an entire condominium project, some state laws require the developer to escrow the funds received from each condominium unit purchaser.

ESCROW MAY PROVIDE INCREASED CONVENIENCE

In some cases, escrow arrangements provide increased convenience or flexibility. A **back-to-back escrow,** or double escrow, is an escrow established to facilitate the concurrent sale of one property and the purchase of another. For example, if one needed the proceeds from the sale of one property as the down payment for another, the escrow agent could easily do this. Of course, the same thing could be accomplished by holding back-to-back closings attended by the parties; in fact, this is not uncommon. A potential drawback of back-to-back closings is the possibility that the two closings will be held at different locations. Investors sometimes use a double-escrow to generate a profit without long-term ownership of the property. In essence, the buyer's money in the second escrow is used to purchase the property in the first escrow. For example, a party might have a contract in escrow to purchase a property for $50,000. Then the party contracts with another to sell the same property for $62,000. Finally, escrow arrangements are also used to simplify transactions involving several lenders.

SUMMARY

Closing is the final step in the purchase or exchange of real estate. At the closing, documents are signed, and funds are transferred to the seller and other parties as dictated by the terms of the purchase agreement. For the closing to proceed smoothly, it is important that the purchase agreement specify each party's responsibilities, and that each party understand their responsibilities.

Throughout the closing process all legal requirements must be met. Two laws in particular are important in this regard. The Federal Truth-in-Lending Law provides unsophisticated borrowers with some protection against unscrupulous lenders, and enables knowledgeable borrowers a ready means of comparing alternative loan terms. The Real Estate Settlement Procedures Act specifies regulations to be followed by the lender and any other party assigned the duty of preparing the closing statement.

In many locations, it is customary for both the seller and buyer to attend the closing. It is possible, however, to close in escrow. In this manner, both parties deliver any needed documents or funds to an independent third party who acts as the agent of both in consummating the transaction. Regardless of how the transaction is consummated, sellers and

DOING BUSINESS

TECHNOLOGY

A number of firms are introducing automated systems to speed up the closing process. These systems include transactions for traditional mortgage loans and for home-equity loans. One example of the latter is offered by Ellie Mae, a leading Internet technology provider based in California that, in June 2002, announced they had formed a partnership with Ohio's DeepGreen Bank to offer paperless home equity loan origination. Mortgage brokers can upload all the information needed for loans of up to $200,000 and within five minutes receive an approval and schedule the closing with no "paper chase" in between. Another possible benefit of the system—24/7 loan closings at the customer's home.

Go to www.realtytimes.com, and use "electronic closing" as your search term, then click on one or more titles to learn more about this topic.

buyers should be aware of the costs involved. The growing use of e-technology by the title insurance industry should help reduce (or hold down increases in) these costs.

KEY TERMS

back-to-back escrow
closing
closing costs
escrow arrangement
escrow agent

escrow instructions
Federal Truth-in-Lending Law
good faith estimate
mortgage networking

prorated item
Real Estate Settlement Procedures Act (RESPA)
settlement statement

REVIEW QUESTIONS

1. This chapter makes it clear that both buyers and sellers may incur a number of closing costs in a typical real estate transaction. How could you reduce these costs? Comment on the wisdom of each of your suggestions.
2. Why are some closing costs prorated and others not?
3. Explain how escrow closings are handled.
4. What is RESPA and what are the major requirements?
5. What types of transactions are and are not covered by RESPA?
6. What is mortgage networking?
7. Why do you think noninterest bearing escrow accounts are a good or bad idea?
8. How can the use of e-technology reduce the cost of doing business for a title insurance company?
9. What are your answers to the questions in the two "Decision Point" sections in this chapter?
10. What is your answer to the "Ethical Issue" in this chapter?

PROBLEMS

Use the settlement statement in Exhibit 14.2 to answer problems 1 and 2.

1. What amount would appear on lines 211 and 511 if the closing were not held until September 10?
2. Assuming a closing date of August 27, how would the statement change in the unlikely event that property taxes were paid in advance?
3. Given the following information, calculate the seller's and buyer's share of property tax.

   Closing date is February 28, 2004.

   Annual property taxes are $2,124.

   Taxes due on December 15, 2004.

   Use the proration method described in the text as the preferred method.

   Cost for closing date is assigned to seller.

REAL ESTATE ON THE WEB

Use your favorite search engine to:

1. Learn where real estate closings are usually held in your area.
2. Determine if any companies in your state have encountered difficulty complying with RESPA or the Truth in Lending Law.
3. Investigate whether physical real estate closings or escrow closings are used in your area.
4. Discover Internet systems available to speed up the closing process.

Refer to the companion Web site at www.wiley.com/college/larsen for a variety of online activities including additional chapter content, review materials, assignments, and related links.

ADDITIONAL READINGS

Abella-Austriaco, A. N. "Title Defects." *ABA Journal* (July 1998): 56.

Black, R. T. and H. O. Nourse. "The Effect of Different Brokerage Modes on Closing Costs and House Prices." *The Journal of Real Estate Research* (1995): 87–98.

Cobert, B. F. and C. Kenworthy. "Reinventing Real Estate Closings." *The McKinsey Quarterly* (1997): 133–137.

Colmery, N. "Meeting the Challenges of Multiple Recording Requirements." *Mortgage Banking* (November 1998): 75–76.

Stein, J. "After the Closing." *Practical Real Estate Lawyer* (March 2000): 9–17.

Stein, J. "Title Closings: Step by Step." *Practical Lawyer* (October 1999): 77–88.

Stein, J. "How to Streamline, Simplify, and Save Money in the Loan Closing Process." *Real Estate Review* (Fall 1998): 27–44.

Real Estate Financing

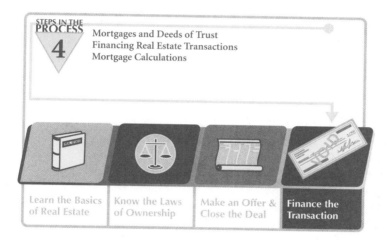

STEPS IN THE
PROCESS
4

Mortgages and Deeds of Trust
Financing Real Estate Transactions
Mortgage Calculations

Learn the Basics
of Real Estate

Know the Laws
of Ownership

Make an Offer &
Close the Deal

Finance the
Transaction

The relatively high cost of real estate forces purchasers in most real estate transactions to use some borrowed funds. Therefore, in Part IV, several aspects of financing real estate transactions are examined. If you are to make sound real estate decisions, it is essential that you have an understanding of the material presented. Lenders require borrowers to sign a number of documents, including a promissory note and either a mortgage or a deed of trust. The note personally obligates the borrower to repay the debt, while the mortgage (deed of trust) pledges the borrower's interest in real property as collateral for the loan. These documents are described in Chapter 15. Also included in Chapter 15 is a description of the various types of mortgage contracts you can use and, in case things go badly, an explanation of the mortgage foreclosure process. You will see that borrowers are faced with a variety of mortgage loan products and lending institutions. In Chapter 16, basic information about mortgage lenders and products is presented. In Chapter 17, the math skills required to calculate solutions to a variety of mortgage-related problems are reviewed.

CHAPTER

15

Mortgages and Deeds of Trust

Learning Objectives

After studying this chapter you should be able to:

- Compare and contrast conventional, Federal Housing Administration, and Veterans Administration mortgage loans.
- Explain the essential elements of a mortgage and describe various mortgage clauses.
- Differentiate between the mortgage theories employed by the states.
- Describe the events related to a mortgage foreclosure.
- Explain the difference between a first and second mortgage.
- Distinguish a mortgage from a deed of trust.

FROM THE WIRE

The Nehemiah Corporation of California, the nation's leading privately funded, non-profit provider of down payment assistance, is recognized as an industry pioneer. Founded in 1994, it operates programs nationwide, including the Nehemiah Program launched in 1997, which "gifts" home buyers funds required to meet the down payment and closing costs of a home purchase. As of the beginning of 2002, the Nehemiah Program had enabled more than 100,000 families to realize the American dream of home ownership. The company's direct impact on the building, real estate, and mortgage industries is evident in the $11 billion of national real estate sales the organization has helped to generate. Nehemiah publicly supported the January 2002 HUD position that disallows the use of down payment assistance grants to pay off installment loans, credit cards, collections, judgments, and similar debts in order to improve the individual's debt-to-income ratio. "We are concerned that newcomers to our industry who enable home buyers to pay off bad or outstanding debt with gift funds are doing the buyers, as well as the entire real estate industry, a real disservice. Not only does this practice prevent lenders from accurately analyzing a borrower's debt to income ratio, but it inevitably leads buyers to assume and accept higher risk and higher interest rate loans that they cannot manage on a monthly basis," said Scott Syphax, president and chief executive of Nehemiah Corporation.

Go to www.hud.gov, click on Search/Index, then search "down payment assistance" to learn more about this topic.

INTRODUCTION

Most real property acquisitions involve some borrowed funds wherein the arrangement between the borrower and lender is formalized in a written contract known as a promissory note. The note specifies the rights and responsibilities of both parties, and you should understand its terms in order to make intelligent decisions. In addition, you must decide what type of loan to use. Knowledge of the different types of loans is critical in the decision-making process because the loan terms (e.g., down payment requirement) can affect, among other things, how much property you can afford to purchase. However, as the chapter opener "From the Wire" suggests, there are ways that borrowers may be able to qualify for a loan even if they do not have the down payment themselves.

Institutional lenders, such as a savings and loan association or commercial bank, almost always require that borrowers pledge their interest in the acquired property as loan collateral, and for this purpose they employ one of two types of security instruments, a mortgage or a deed of trust. State law generally determines which instrument the lender uses. Many of the provisions in these contracts are negotiable, but state law controls others, including the lender's interest in the property while the loan is in force, and both the lender's and borrower's rights in the event of a loan default.

THE MORTGAGE AND PROMISSORY NOTE

Many documents are involved in a typical mortgage loan. Two primary documents are a promissory note and a mortgage (or a deed of trust). The borrower assumes a personal obligation to repay the loan by signing a **promissory note.** The **mortgage** creates a right, or security interest, in the real property for the lender. Specifically, a mortgage is used to pledge the borrower's interest in the real property as security for a loan. The word mortgage is derived from two French words: "mort" which means dead, and "gage" meaning pledge. The word mortgage, therefore, is descriptive of the relationship between the parties to the loan because the borrower's pledge is extinguished when the debt is paid in full. When a mortgage is used, the party loaning the funds is referred to as the **mortgagee,** and the party receiving the loan is known as the **mortgagor.**

In theory, a lender could lend money using only a note, or the note and mortgage could be contained in the same document. From the lender's perspective, however, there are important reasons for having two separate documents. First, by using both documents, the lender has two possible courses of action in the event the borrower does not perform as agreed: sue on the note, or repossess the property serving as collateral. Second, separate documents allow the lender to record the mortgage to give constructive notice of its security interest in the property without recording the note. Once a mortgage is recorded, it acts as a cloud on the owner's title (preventing a subsequent transfer). Therefore, once the debt has been paid, it is important that a **satisfaction of mortgage,** a document that signifies that a mortgage debt has been satisfied (or forgiven) also be recorded in the same office as was the mortgage. Recording the promissory note would make the specifics of the loan agreement available to the lender's competitors who may search the public records to locate potential clients for refinancing on more attractive terms. Lenders who search the public records in such a manner are **raiding.**

When the mortgage and note appear as separate documents, it is important that they refer to each other to make it clear that they are parts of the same transaction. It is equally important that the terms of the two documents do not conflict. If the terms do conflict, costly disputes between the parties are more likely to occur.

PROVISIONS IN THE PROMISSORY NOTE

Exhibit 15.1 contains a promissory note developed by the Federal National Mortgage Association and the Federal Home Loan Mortgage Corporation. This note was designed to be used for fixed-interest-rate loans secured by single-family dwellings. It contains ten provisions; one (Paragraph 4) specifies the rights of the borrower, but the rest are designed for the lender's protection.

Paragraph 1 of the note contains the borrower's promise to pay both the loan principal and interest. Notice that the borrower's promise applies regardless of who holds the mortgage. Some lenders hold mortgages that they originate in their own portfolio, but, today, most mortgages are sold to a third party soon after they are originated.

Paragraph 2 indicates the fixed interest rate to be charged on the loan. If a note carries an adjustable interest rate, the initial interest rate and the manner in which the rate could be adjusted are specified.

Paragraph 3 specifies the amount of each payment, the date each payment is due, and the place payments are to be made.

Paragraph 4 gives the borrower the right to make prepayments. Sometimes borrowers make payments larger than the amount owed but less than the remaining balance of the loan in order to reduce the principal faster than scheduled. Borrowers can greatly reduce the total amount of interest they must pay on a mortgage loan by making such payments. Astute borrowers will also completely pay off a loan when interest rates drop and refinance to lock in a lower rate. Not all mortgages allow prepayments without the borrower incurring an extra charge. Some contain a clause that imposes a monetary prepayment penalty, usually stated as a percentage of the loan balance at the time of prepayment. The prepayment penalty is intended to compensate lenders that planned to earn the original rate, but must now lend the prepaid amounts at a new, lower rate. Because a prepayment penalty may work to the disadvantage of the borrower, a loan with a prepayment penalty should carry a lower rate of interest compared with a loan with no prepayment penalty.

Paragraph 5 allows the lender to make adjustments to loan charges and interest on the note should a court subsequently interpret any law such that the contract terms become illegal. Should such a court interpretation occur, inclusion of this paragraph prevents the borrower from later disaffirming the note by claiming that the contract is illegal.

| EXHIBIT | 15.1 | PROMISSORY NOTE |

NOTE

_____, _____   _____, ____   _____
[Date]   [City]   [State]

_____
[Property Address]

1. BORROWER'S PROMISE TO PAY

In return for a loan that I have received, I promise to pay U.S. $_____ (this amount is called "Principal"), plus interest, to the order of the Lender. The Lender is _____. I will make all payments under this Note in the form of cash, check or money order.

I understand that the Lender may transfer this Note. The Lender or anyone who takes this Note by transfer and who is entitled to receive payments under this Note is called the "Note Holder."

2. INTEREST

Interest will be charged on unpaid principal until the full amount of Principal has been paid. I will pay interest at a yearly rate of _____%.

The interest rate required by this Section 2 is the rate I will pay both before and after any default described in Section 6(B) of this Note.

3. PAYMENTS

(A) Time and Place of Payments

I will pay principal and interest by making a payment every month.

I will make my monthly payment on the _____ day of each month beginning on _____, _____. I will make these payments every month until I have paid all of the principal and interest and any other charges described below that I may owe under this Note. Each monthly payment will be applied as of its scheduled due date and will be applied to interest before Principal. If, on _____, 20____, I still owe amounts under this Note, I will pay those amounts in full on that date, which is called the "Maturity Date."

I will make my monthly payments at _____ or at a different place if required by the Note Holder.

(B) Amount of Monthly Payments

My monthly payment will be in the amount of U.S. $_____.

4. BORROWER'S RIGHT TO PREPAY

I have the right to make payments of Principal at any time before they are due. A payment of Principal only is known as a "Prepayment." When I make a Prepayment, I will tell the Note Holder in writing that I am doing so. I may not designate a payment as a Prepayment if I have not made all the monthly payments due under the Note.

I may make a full Prepayment or partial Prepayments without paying a Prepayment charge. The Note Holder will use my Prepayments to reduce the amount of Principal that I owe under this Note. However, the Note Holder may apply my Prepayment to the accrued and unpaid interest on the Prepayment amount, before applying my Prepayment to reduce the Principal amount of the Note. If I make a partial Prepayment, there will be no changes in the due date or in the amount of my monthly payment unless the Note Holder agrees in writing to those changes.

5. LOAN CHARGES

If a law, which applies to this loan and which sets maximum loan charges, is finally interpreted so that the interest or other loan charges collected or to be collected in connection with this loan exceed the permitted limits, then: (a) any such loan charge shall be reduced by the amount necessary to reduce the charge to the permitted limit; and (b) any sums already collected from me which exceeded permitted limits will be refunded to me. The Note Holder may choose to make this refund by reducing the Principal I owe under this Note or by making a direct payment to me. If a refund reduces Principal, the reduction will be treated as a partial Prepayment.

MULTISTATE FIXED RATE NOTE--Single Family--**Fannie Mae/Freddie Mac UNIFORM INSTRUMENT**   Form 3200   1/01   _(page 1 of 3 pages)_

EXHIBIT | 15.1 | **PROMISSORY NOTE (CONTINUED)**

6. BORROWER'S FAILURE TO PAY AS REQUIRED

(A) Late Charge for Overdue Payments

If the Note Holder has not received the full amount of any monthly payment by the end of _____ calendar days after the date it is due, I will pay a late charge to the Note Holder. The amount of the charge will be _____% of my overdue payment of principal and interest. I will pay this late charge promptly but only once on each late payment.

(B) Default

If I do not pay the full amount of each monthly payment on the date it is due, I will be in default.

(C) Notice of Default

If I am in default, the Note Holder may send me a written notice telling me that if I do not pay the overdue amount by a certain date, the Note Holder may require me to pay immediately the full amount of Principal which has not been paid and all the interest that I owe on that amount. That date must be at least 30 days after the date on which the notice is mailed to me or delivered by other means.

(D) No Waiver By Note Holder

Even if, at a time when I am in default, the Note Holder does not require me to pay immediately in full as described above, the Note Holder will still have the right to do so if I am in default at a later time.

(E) Payment of Note Holder's Costs and Expenses

If the Note Holder has required me to pay immediately in full as described above, the Note Holder will have the right to be paid back by me for all of its costs and expenses in enforcing this Note to the extent not prohibited by applicable law. Those expenses include, for example, reasonable attorneys' fees.

7. GIVING OF NOTICES

Unless applicable law requires a different method, any notice that must be given to me under this Note will be given by delivering it or by mailing it by first class mail to me at the Property Address above or at a different address if I give the Note Holder a notice of my different address.

Any notice that must be given to the Note Holder under this Note will be given by delivering it or by mailing it by first class mail to the Note Holder at the address stated in Section 3(A) above or at a different address if I am given a notice of that different address.

8. OBLIGATIONS OF PERSONS UNDER THIS NOTE

If more than one person signs this Note, each person is fully and personally obligated to keep all of the promises made in this Note, including the promise to pay the full amount owed. Any person who is a guarantor, surety or endorser of this Note is also obligated to do these things. Any person who takes over these obligations, including the obligations of a guarantor, surety or endorser of this Note, is also obligated to keep all of the promises made in this Note. The Note Holder may enforce its rights under this Note against each person individually or against all of us together. This means that any one of us may be required to pay all of the amounts owed under this Note.

9. WAIVERS

I and any other person who has obligations under this Note waive the rights of Presentment and Notice of Dishonor. "Presentment" means the right to require the Note Holder to demand payment of amounts due. "Notice of Dishonor" means the right to require the Note Holder to give notice to other persons that amounts due have not been paid.

10. UNIFORM SECURED NOTE

This Note is a uniform instrument with limited variations in some jurisdictions. In addition to the protections given to the Note Holder under this Note, a Mortgage, Deed of Trust, or Security Deed (the "Security Instrument"), dated the same date as this Note, protects the Note Holder from possible losses which might result if I do not keep the promises which I make in this Note. That Security Instrument describes how and under what conditions I may be required to make immediate payment in full of all amounts I owe under this Note. Some of those conditions are described as follows:

If all or any part of the Property or any Interest in the Property is sold or transferred (or if Borrower is not a natural person and a beneficial interest in Borrower is sold or transferred) without Lender's prior written consent, Lender may require immediate payment in full of all sums secured by this Security Instrument. However, this option shall not be exercised by Lender if such exercise is prohibited by Applicable Law.

EXHIBIT   15.1   **PROMISSORY NOTE (CONTINUED)**

If Lender exercises this option, Lender shall give Borrower notice of acceleration. The notice shall provide a period of not less than 30 days from the date the notice is given in accordance with Section 15 within which Borrower must pay all sums secured by this Security Instrument. If Borrower fails to pay these sums prior to the expiration of this period, Lender may invoke any remedies permitted by this Security Instrument without further notice or demand on Borrower.

WITNESS THE HAND(S) AND SEAL(S) OF THE UNDERSIGNED

_____(Seal)
                                                    - Borrower

_____(Seal)
                                                    - Borrower

_____(Seal)
                                                    - Borrower

[Sign Original Only]

Paragraph 6 defines what constitutes default, and specifies the rights of the lender in the event of either an overdue payment or loan default. Notice, in Part A, that a borrower may make a payment after the due date specified in paragraph 3 and not be assessed a late charge. Grace periods of fifteen days for overdue payments are not uncommon. Often a lender will not take immediate action when the borrower defaults. The lack of action by the lender is referred to as **forbearance.** Part D of the paragraph prevents the borrower from claiming that forbearance constitutes a waiver of the lender's right to subsequently demand that the borrower comply with the terms of the note.

Paragraph 7 specifies how either party is to contact the other if notice is required, written notice is standard.

Paragraph 8 is particularly important if more than one party signs the note. It specifies that each person signing the note is individually responsible for the entire debt, termed joint and several liability. If, for example, you and two other people sign a note that includes such a clause and the other two become unwilling or unable to pay, you could be held fully responsible.

Paragraph 9 becomes effective in the event of default. This clause enables the lender to commence foreclosure proceedings without giving notice to the borrower or other parties who might have an interest in the property, such as a second mortgage holder. Lenders will usually attempt to give such notice, but this paragraph is included to protect them in case they try to give notice and fail, or inadvertently fail to notify all interested parties.

Paragraph 10 gives the lender the right (but not the duty) to demand payment in full if the subject property is sold. This provision is frequently referred to as the due on sale clause. Whether a lender exercises this option depends, in part, upon what has happened to interest rates since the loan was originated. If interest rates have increased, the lender is quite likely to demand full payment. If, instead the rates have decreased, the lender may be willing to let another party assume the payments, especially if the lender can obtain some assurance as to the credit worthiness of the new party.

Decision Point

You are a mortgage lender and have been informed that a borrower whose payment is based on a 9 percent rate is selling the property serving as collateral for the loan. Under what conditions would you enforce the due on sale clause if interest rates are now 8 percent? Why might a person be willing to take over the payments on the 9 percent mortgage if interest rates are 8 percent?

ESSENTIALS OF A MORTGAGE

The elements essential for a valid mortgage are straightforward. The Statute of Frauds requires that a mortgage be in writing, and the rules of contract law (Chapter 11) apply. Specifically, in the mortgage: the competent parties must be named; the subject property must be legally described; the amount of the debt must be stated; there must be some mention of consideration; and a mortgaging clause, which pledges the borrower's interest in the subject property as collateral for the loan, must be included. In addition, the mortgage must be signed by the borrower(s).

MORTGAGE COVENANTS

Mortgage contracts can be quite lengthy (the uniform mortgage developed by Fannie Mae and Freddie Mac is fifteen pages in length) and contain many clauses that are known as **mortgage covenants** or provisions. As with the promissory note, some provisions specify the rights of the borrower, but most protect the lender. Some provisions, referred to as uniform covenants, are applicable to all transactions; other non-uniform covenants are used only in special cases. While the covenants contained in most mortgages are reasonable, all are subject to negotiation and if the parties agree, one or more covenants may be eliminated, or added, before the document is signed. It would be highly unusual, however, for a lender to agree to eliminate any of the uniform covenants. It is more common to see one or more of the nonuniform clauses struck from the mortgage simply because it does not apply.

Uniform Mortgage Covenants

There are twenty-one uniform covenants in a residential mortgage. In reading the following list (**Titles** followed by a brief explanation), you should notice that several of them duplicate provisions in the promissory note.

Payment of Principle, Interest, Escrow Items, Prepayment Charges, and Late Charges   This is sometimes called the covenant to pay indebtedness. By signing a mortgage with this clause included the borrower agrees to pay the mortgage debt and any prepayment and late charges in accordance with the terms of the promissory note.

Application of Payments and Proceeds   This covenant details the manner in which payments are to be applied. Typically, they are applied first to interest due under the note; second, to principal due under the note; third, to any shortfall in the escrow balance; fourth, to any late charges or other amounts due under the note.

Funds for Escrow Items   This covenant requires the borrower to pay the amounts needed to cover mortgage insurance premiums (if required by the mortgagee), property taxes, and property insurance. These payments are to be made in monthly installments in advance of when the items are due. This requirement enables the lender to better protect its security interest in the property by paying the charges directly out of the advances provided by the borrower. Lenders fear that some borrowers might fail to make timely tax and insurance payments. Advances for such purposes are usually held in a noninterest bearing escrow or trust account.

Charges; Liens   This is sometimes called the covenant to pay taxes. This covenant requires the borrower to keep the property taxes current, and to pay any assessments, charges, or fines that could take priority over the lender's security agreement.

Property Insurance   This is sometimes called the covenant of insurance. This covenant requires the borrower to keep the property adequately insured. Under this covenant, and also the previous one, the lender is empowered to make such payments and add them to the amount of the loan if the mortgagor fails to honor the covenants. Remember that the mortgage is the document that pledges the borrower's interest in the subject property as collateral for the loan. Without these clauses, if the property were destroyed or if the government took possession due to nonpayment of property taxes, the collateral would be of little, or no, value.

Occupancy   This covenant requires that the borrower use the property as their principal residence. It is included because lenders are concerned that if the property is leased to an unknown third party, the tenant may not keep the property in as good a condition as would an owner-occupant.

Preservation, Maintenance and Protection Of the Property: Inspections   These are sometimes called the covenant of good repair and the covenant against removal. The former requires the borrower to keep the property in good condition, and the latter prevents the borrower from destroying any improvements on the land. Again, if the borrower violates these provisions the lender's security interest would be damaged. This covenant also gives the lender the right to inspect the property, after giving prior notice, to verify that these covenants are not being violated.

Borrower's Loan Application This covenant states that the borrower shall be in default if the borrower or anyone acting at the direction of the borrower provides false, misleading, or inaccurate information to the lender during the loan application process.

Protection of Lender's Interest in the Property and Rights Under this Security Instrument This covenant provides that if the borrower fails to pay any insurance premiums, taxes, assessments, or other charges required under the mortgage, the lender has the right to make such payments and add them to the balance owed. Furthermore, if the mortgagor fails to protect the property against legal actions involving such things as building code enforcement and eminent domain, the lender has the right to take such actions.

Mortgage Insurance This covenant requires that the borrower maintain adequate mortgage insurance if required to do so by the lender as a condition of making the loan.

Assignment of Miscellaneous Proceeds; Forfeiture This covenant specifies that any awards or payments made in connection with any condemnation are to be applied toward the loan.

Borrower Not Released; Forbearance By Lender Not a Waiver This covenant states that forbearance by the lender does not constitute a waiver of any future right or remedy.

Joint and Several Liability; Co-signers; Successors and Assigns Bound This covenant specifies that if more than one party signs the contract, each is potentially personally liable for the entire debt. In addition, it is stipulated that the mortgage contract is binding on the successors and assigns of both parties.

Loan Charges This covenant stipulates that the lender may charge the borrower for costs incurred by the lender in protecting the lender's security interest (e.g., inspection fees, attorney's fees).

Notices This covenant spells out the details concerning how either party is to give notice to the other concerning the security instrument.

Governing Law; Severability; Rules of Construction Under this covenant, it is specified that the mortgage contract is subject to federal laws and the appropriate state laws. If one provision of the promissory note or the mortgage is deemed to be illegal, it does not effect the other provisions.

Borrower's Copy The borrower is to receive one copy of the note and the mortgage.

Transfer of the Property or a Beneficial Interest in the Borrower This is sometimes called an acceleration clause because it specifies the conditions that allow the lender to accelerate the original payment terms. This covenant stipulates that if the borrower transfers his or her interest in the property to another, the lender may require immediate payment in full of all sums secured by the mortgage. Conditions that may trigger an acceleration clause include the borrower's failure to keep the property in good repair, or adequately insured.

A missed payment can also trigger the acceleration clause. In the case of a missed payment, an acceleration clause is particularly important for lenders; without the clause a lender would be forced to bring a separate lawsuit to collect amounts in default. Theoretically, that could mean one lawsuit for each missed payment, which would be expensive. When the condition that triggers the acceleration is the sale of the property, a synonym for the acceleration clause is due on sale clause. Note, however, that the actions that can trigger this provision include more than just a sale. Therefore, a better description of the provision is an (non) alienation clause because if the borrower alienates (transfers his or her interest) in any way, not just by sale, the acceleration feature becomes active. It is important to understand that the provision gives the lender the option, but not the duty, to require payment in full.

Borrower's Right to Reinstate After Acceleration   This covenant stipulates that the borrower can stop an acceleration by paying all sums that would have been due up to the present time if an acceleration had not occurred, plus paying any expenses incurred by the lender in enforcing the security agreement, and curing any default of any other covenant or agreement.

Sale of Note; Change of Loan Servicer; Notice of Grievance   With the increased trading of mortgages in the secondary market, a common provision calls for the borrower to provide, at the request of the lender, a written statement of the amount remaining unpaid on the mortgage as of a particular date. The statement of the remaining unpaid amount is called an **estoppel certificate,** or certificate of no defense. Both certificate terms are descriptive. The certificate is based on the legal doctrine by which a party is prevented (estopped) from asserting facts that are inconsistent with a previous representation. Therefore, by signing the certificate, the mortgagor certifies the amount owed and is prevented from later claiming that a smaller amount was actually owed at the time the certificate was issued. The certificate enables the mortgagee to prove the amount owed to a secondary market investor.

Hazardous Substances   Specifies that the borrower shall not allow the presence, use, disposal, storage, or release of any hazardous substances on or in the property. Lenders have become more sensitive to environmental issues due to a 1986 federal court ruling that held the Maryland Bank and Trust Company liable for the hazardous waste cleanup costs on a property it acquired through foreclosure. As a result of this decision, many lenders now work with environmental consultants and will not make loans without an environmental clearance. Some lenders will not foreclose when they estimate potential clean up costs are high.

Mortgage Types

Mortgages can be classified based on a number of criteria, including whether the loan is supported by a government agency, by the priority of the mortgagee's claim, and according to the manner in which the loan is to be repaid. The focus in this chapter is limited to the first two criteria; classification based on loan repayment patterns is the focus of Chapter 16. In following sections, we review two government-sponsored mortgages: Federal Housing Administration, and Veterans Administration. Mortgages that are not supported by the government are referred to as conventional loans and, as explained in the following sections, there are several different types. Which type of mortgage is most suitable for a particular transaction depends on a number of factors; the cost of the property, and the desired amount of financing are the primary determinants.

Conventional Mortgage Loan   A **conventional mortgage,** so called because it conforms to conventional lending standards, is used for real estate loans in which the government is not participating either as an insurer or guarantor of the debt. The conventional loan mortgagee can be either a private party or an institutional lender. For example, if you had the money to lend, you could write a conventional mortgage loan. This is not true, however, for a government-sponsored loan, which must be written by an institutional lender approved by the appropriate governmental agency. Institutional lenders write most conventional mortgage loans. The mortgage loan activities of conventional lenders are examined in Chapter 16.

Conventional loans lack government sponsorship and, therefore, present more risk to the lender. To reduce the level of risk, down payment requirements on conventional loans tend to be higher than on government-sponsored loans. Currently, almost all conventional home loan mortgage originators require that borrowers make a minimum down payment of 20 percent of the purchase price, or require the borrower to purchase private mortgage insurance (described later) because the loan originator does not intend to hold the mortgages in its own portfolio. Instead, the mortgage is sold on the secondary mortgage market, and for a mortgage to qualify for secondary trading either the 20 percent down payment or private mortgage insurance is required.

While conventional loans are subject to state and/or federal regulation, these regulations are not as stringent as those that apply to government-sponsored loans. Therefore, conventional loans are more flexible with respect to lending terms compared with government-sponsored loans. Several of the more popular special-use conventional loans are described here.

- *Open-End Mortgage*—Mortgage funds are usually advanced all at one time, but this is not always the case. An **open-end mortgage** is an expandable loan in which a credit limit is offered to the borrower, with each incremental advance secured by the same mortgage. An open-end mortgage may be attractive to one acquiring property and planning substantial renovations, because the use of an open-end loan reduces future appraisal and refinancing costs. The interest rate the lender charges on future advances against the credit limit are subject to negotiation. The lender may agree to charge the prevailing rate at the time the mortgage was signed, but it is more common to charge the market rate at the time of the future disbursement. Lenders must be particularly cautious when using an open-end mortgage because it is possible that liens recorded between advances on the mortgage may take priority over the advances.

- *Package Mortgage*—A **package mortgage** is often used in the original sale of condominiums and new subdivision homes. Under this arrangement, the loan proceeds are used to finance not only the purchase of the home, but also the purchase of personal property such as a refrigerator, washer, dryer, and other appliances. These items are listed in the mortgage and declared to be fixtures (although they have not been installed at the time of the loan) and are, therefore, part of the mortgaged property.

  Both the mortgagor and mortgagee derive benefits from a package mortgage. Some lenders believe that fewer defaults occur with package mortgages. The mortgagor benefits in that essential items can be acquired with no additional down payment, and financed over a longer period than is available through the typical consumer installment loan. In addition, unlike interest paid on a consumer loan, mortgage interest is deductible in calculating personal income tax. Of course, when personal assets are financed with a long-term loan, it is likely that the borrower will still be paying for them long after their useful life expires.

- *Blanket Mortgage*—When several properties are used to secure a single mortgage, the mortgage is referred to as a **blanket mortgage.** Blanket mortgages are frequently used to obtain construction financing for condominium development projects and proposed housing subdivisions. Blanket mortgages can also be used when the equity in one property does not meet the lender's requirements, or when one buys a house and adjacent vacant property.

  Blanket mortgages usually contain a partial release clause that enables the mortgagor to obtain a release from the mortgage for each unit according to a specified release schedule. To illustrate, assume a developer finances the purchase of land that will be developed into 100 lots with a blanket mortgage of $1,000,000. The release schedule might require the developer to pay off $15,000 of principal in order to release each lot from the mortgage. The astute reader would notice that this example implies that the developer must pay $1,500,000 to release all lots when he or she borrowed only $1,000,000. Actually, once the developer repays the full principal, all remaining lots are released from the mortgage. Lenders intentionally set a high release schedule to prevent the developer from selling the choice lots and walking away from the rest.

  Sometimes developers have a special recognition clause placed in the blanket mortgage. A special recognition clause forces the lender to recognize the rights of each individual lot owner, even if the developer defaults and there is a foreclosure.

- *Budget Mortgage*—Many lenders require that each payment cover not only principal and interest, but also a portion of the next property tax payment and casualty insurance premium for the subject property. The theory of this requirement is that it is easier for the borrower to make these payments in installments rather than pay the full amount annually or semiannually. This arrangement forces the mortgagor to include these sums in his or her monthly budget and is, therefore, referred to as a **budget mortgage.** Because private lenders originate virtually all government sponsored mortgage loans (described next), they may also be budget mortgages.

FEDERAL HOUSING ADMINISTRATION (FHA) INSURED LOAN

To help facilitate homeownership, the federal government created agencies that have programs that enable lenders to write mortgage loans carrying more attractive terms than those available on conventional loans; one of these is the **FHA-insured mortgage.** The FHA was established as a part of the National Housing Act of 1934 to address problems in the housing industry that developed during the Great Depression.

Prior to the creation of the FHA, the terms on the typical home loan were dramatically different from what prevails today. For instance, down payment requirements of 50 percent were not uncommon. In addition, mortgage loans were nonamortizing, that is, periodic payments consisted of interest only; the principal had to be repaid in full at the end of the loan period. Further, most home loans had terms to maturity of approximately five years. During the Great Depression, many people were unable to repay their mortgage loans and lost their homes through foreclosure. High default rates made lenders reluctant to write additional home mortgage loans. As a result, Congress empowered the FHA to provide lenders with insurance against default losses to encourage them to make home loans and to stimulate the economy by encouraging the construction of new housing. The term to maturity on FHA loans was increased to twenty-five or thirty years, and the loans were paid on a fully amortized basis. An **amortized loan** is one in which each payment consists of both interest and principal reduction. A fully amortized loan is one in which the principal reduction included in all periodic payments completely eliminates the debt.

FHA loans have had an important influence on home financing. The terms that now prevail in the conventional mortgage loan market mirror those the FHA implemented. As we will explain in Chapter 17, increasing the repayment period makes housing more affordable, and the possibility of defaults decreases with amortized loans.

The FHA, which is a part of the Department of Housing and Urban Development (HUD), does not make mortgage loans. The FHA only provides insurance against losses incurred on loans originated by private lenders. Therefore, technically, these mortgages are called FHA-insured mortgage loans; many people refer to them simply as FHA loans. The FHA offers its insurance under a number of programs that are summarized in Exhibit 15.2.

The manner in which borrowers pay the FHA insurance premium has changed over time. Currently, federal legislation requires an initial premium equal to 2.25 percent of the loan amount plus an annual premium equal to 0.5 percent of the remaining insured principal balance. FHA mortgage insurance is generally available only on owner-occupied dwellings with from one to four living units. Exceptions to these requirements are set forth in Exhibit 15.2.

The size of an FHA mortgage is limited, with the limits dependent upon both the number of living units in the dwelling and the location of the property. The "standard limit" for a single-family dwelling under the most widely used FHA program, 203(b), is $132,000. However, as shown in the following table, the FHA increases the maximum loan amount above the "standard limit" on an area-by-area basis in order to meet local differences in housing costs.

Example FHA 203(b) Mortgage Limits (Effective August 2001)

City/Dwelling	1-Family	2-Family	3-Family	4-Family
Anchorage, AL	$203,700	$229,431	$278,747	$321,632
Columbus, OH	$191,425	$215,605	$261,950	$302,250
Jackson, MS	$138,700	$168,936	$204,192	$253,776
Los Angeles, CA	$228,000	$256,800	$312,000	$379,842
Newark, NJ	$239,250	$274,134	$333,060	$384,300

The low down payment required on FHA loans is attractive to many borrowers. Because the FHA insures 97 percent of the first $50,000 of appraised value and closing costs, plus 95 percent of the remainder (up to the appropriate limit), lenders will suffer no default losses if borrowers make down payments equal to at least 3 percent of the first $50,000 of property value and closing costs, plus 5 percent of the property's value exceeding $50,000.

The use of an FHA mortgage does not eliminate the need for a down payment, but the amount of the required down payment may be significantly less than that required for a conventional loan. To illustrate this point, consider a $100,000 property financed with a conventional loan. As mentioned earlier, most lenders will require a down payment of $20,000. Financing the same property with an FHA loan will, however, require a down payment of only $4,000 [$100,000 − ($50,000 × .97) − ($50,000 × .95)] assuming no closing costs.

There are possible drawbacks for borrowers who wish to use FHA financing. At the time an FHA loan is made, no secondary financing is permitted. At closing, therefore, the borrower must pay the difference between the purchase price and the amount of the insured commitment in cash. Borrowers are, however, not prohibited from adding secondary financing after the FHA mortgage is in place. For lenders, low down payments may potentially create a problem because borrowers are more likely to default on loans if property values fall below the loan balance. The lower the amount of the down payment, the less property values must fall for borrowers to view default as a palatable option. Even though the loan is insured, the foreclosure process, described later in this chapter, is a headache for the lender.

EXHIBIT 15.2	FHA LOAN PROGRAMS

Section	Provides mortgage insurance for:
203(b)	Loans for the construction, purchase or refinancing of a single-family to four-family dwelling. The most commonly used HUD program. Special terms are available for qualified veterans purchasing a single-family home.
203(h)	Loans financing the purchase of a single family dwelling by a person whose previous home was damaged or destroyed by catastrophe in an area the president declares a major disaster area..
203(i)	Loans financing the purchase of single-family housing in rural areas.
203(k)	Loans to purchase or refinance and rehabilitate housing that is at least one year old. May also be used to convert nonresidential buildings to residential or to change the number of family units in the dwelling. Available to profit-motivated investors, but cannot be used for condominiums or cooperatives.
203(n)	Loans used to acquire stock certificate or membership certificate in a cooperative covered by a blanket mortgage insured under the National Housing Act.
220	Loans financing the rehabilitation of existing single-family to eleven-family dwellings in urban renewal areas. (Mortgage limits are the same for single-family to four-family dwellings as they are under section 203(b). The limit is increased by $9,165 for each additional unit in the building.)
220(h)	Loans used to finance alterations, repairs, or improvements to existing single-family to eleven-family dwellings located in a redevelopment area as defined under section 220.
221(d)(2)	Loans used to finance the purchase of low cost single-family to four-family dwellings for low- or moderate-income families, or families displaced by government action (e.g., urban renewal), or as a result of the president's declaration of a disaster area.
222	Loans financing the purchase of a single-family dwelling or condominium unit by members on active duty in the Coast Guard or the National Oceanic and Atmospheric Administration.
223(e)	Allows HUD to insure a property that would not be eligible under a different program, but can qualify under this higher-risk program. Individuals cannot apply for mortgage insurance under this program. The determination of the use of Section 223(e) is at the discretion of HUD.
234(c)	The purchase of individual units in a condominium project.
237	Loans financing the purchase of a single-family dwelling or condominium unit by a low- or moderate-income family that is unable to meet the credit requirements under sections 203, 221, or 234.
238(c)	Loans financing the construction, repair, rehabilitation, or purchase of properties located near any military installation in federally impacted areas.
240	Loans used by homeowners to finance the purchase of fee simple title to the leased land on which their homes are located.
245	Loans for which the borrower elects a graduated payment mortgage (see Chapter 16).
245(a)	Loans for which the borrower elects a growing equity mortgage (see Chapter 16).
251	Loans for which the borrower elects an adjustable rate mortgage (see Chapter 16).

FHA Loan Assumptions

When interest rates rise subsequent to the issuance of a fixed interest rate mortgage, assumable mortgages are attractive to buyers because they allow for monthly payments that are lower than they can obtain with a new mortgage. Subject to certain restrictions, any FHA loan may be assumed using one of two methods. Under either method, the interest rate charged on the loan remains the same as the original rate. One assumption method is a simple assumption that allows the loan to be assumed without notification to the FHA.

Under this method, the original borrower remains liable for payment of the debt in the event that the party that assumes the loan defaults. The FHA does not allow simple assumptions during the first two years of a loan. Under the second assumption method, called a formal assumption, FHA notification is required. If the loan is current, the new buyer meets FHA qualification standards for credit worthiness, and agrees to the assumption, the FHA will approve the formal assumption. In the case of a formal assumption, the original borrower is not liable for a subsequent loan default.

FHA Loan Process

There are two methods used for processing FHA loans. The faster loan processing method is called direct endorsement processing. Under this method, lenders are authorized by HUD to issue loan commitments without prior submission of paperwork to HUD. The second loan processing method is called HUD processing. Under this method the lender is required to submit paperwork to HUD prior to approval of the property and, in a separate step, prior to HUD approval of the individual.

An applicant for an FHA loan initiates the loan procedure by making a loan application, with an FHA-approved lending institution, for an FHA appraisal of the subject property. The appraisal report specifies the appraised value and details any physical deficiencies in the property that must be corrected before FHA approval is granted. For properties that meet the eligibility standards, the FHA issues a conditional commitment that sets forth the appraised value of the property and the amount the FHA is prepared to insure. The applicant then formally applies for a mortgage loan with an FHA-approved lender, who transmits the application and financial information about the borrower to the FHA. If the FHA approves the application, it will issue a commitment of insurance to the lending institution, which then makes the loan in the usual manner.

VETERANS ADMINISTRATION (VA) GUARANTEED LOAN

As a part of the Serviceman's Readjustment Act of 1944 (sometimes called "The G.I. Bill of Rights") the VA was given the authority to partially guarantee loans made by qualified lenders to eligible veterans. To be eligible for a VA loan a person must meet several eligibility requirements. For example, the prospective borrower must have had over 180 days of active service, and other than a dishonorable discharge. The primary purpose of the VA home loan program is to help veterans finance the purchase of homes on more favorable terms than are available on other types of mortgage loans. A veteran can also use a VA loan to repair or improve a home, or to refinance an existing loan.

There are similarities and some important differences between the FHA and VA programs. Unlike the FHA, the VA can, and infrequently does, make loans in areas where funds are otherwise unavailable. Another difference between the FHA and VA programs is that in the VA program government sponsorship takes the form of a guarantee rather than insurance. For this reason, this type of mortgage, technically, should be referred to as a **VA-guaranteed mortgage loan.** But, they are frequently called simply VA loans. Similar to FHA loans, VA loans may be used for properties that contain up to four living units, one of which must be occupied by the borrower. In many cases, VA loans do not require a down payment. Most lenders require that a combination of the guarantee and any cash down payment equal 25 percent of the value of the property or sales price, whichever is less. Given regulations in effect in 2001, this would allow a veteran to purchase a home valued up to $144,000 with no down payment. Although there is no maximum VA loan amount, lenders generally limit the maximum loan to $203,000 so that the loans qualify for trading on the secondary market (Chapter 16).

Until recently, no fee was charged to veterans for the VA's guarantee because Congress underwrites losses incurred under the program. However, recent changes in the regulations now require the veteran to pay a "funding fee" that ranges from 1.25 to 3 percent of the loan amount, payable at the time of closing. However, this fee need not increase the down payment requirement because it can be included in the loan amount. Another difference between the FHA and VA programs is that anyone may finance a home purchase with an FHA loan, but only veterans may obtain a new VA loan. Three repayment plans are available: the traditional fixed interest rate, a graduated payment, and a growing equity mortgage (Chapter 16).

The terms associated with VA loans are quite favorable compared with those on other mortgage types. No prepayment penalties are allowed on any VA loan, and all are assumable. At one time, HUD and the Veterans Administration regulated the interest rate that lenders could charge on FHA and VA loans, respectively. Today, the interest rate charged on these loans is subject to negotiation between the borrower and the lender, just as for conventional loans. In the past, regulated interest rates frequently were below the rate prevailing in the conventional loan market. To encourage lenders to write FHA and VA loans, lenders were allowed to charge points for the loans (a point equals 1 percent of the loan amount). In the case of VA loans, the seller had to pay these points. This requirement was intended to enable lenders to earn the market rate while allowing the veteran/buyer to pay the lower regulated rate. However, many well-intended regulations result in unintended effects. In this case, several studies found that sellers were able to effectively transfer at least half of the points to buyers in the form of higher selling prices.

The amount of the VA guarantee is affected by both the loan amount and the amount of the veteran's unused entitlement. For loans of up to $45,000, the VA will guarantee up to 40 percent of the loan. For loans over $45,000, the guarantee is 40 percent of the loan amount up to a maximum guarantee (entitlement) of $36,000. The full guarantee may be used in a single transaction, or spread over two or more transactions. For example, if a veteran uses a guarantee of $25,000 to acquire her first home, she would still have $11,000 to help finance a replacement home. A veteran's full entitlement may be restored if the subject property is sold and the loan is paid in full, or if the buyer is a qualified veteran who assumes the loan and agrees to substitute his entitlement for that of the seller. In either case, the restoration of entitlement is not automatic; the veteran must apply to the VA to have it restored.

VA Loan Process

There are two methods used for processing VA loans: prior approval processing and automatic processing. Under the prior approval loan processing method, the lender takes the loan application, requests VA to appraise the property, and verifies the applicant's income and credit record. All of this information is put together in a loan package and sent to the VA for review. If the VA approves the loan, a commitment to guarantee the loan is sent to the lender. The lender then closes the loan in the usual fashion and sends a report of the closing to the VA. If the loan complies with VA requirements, the VA issues the lender a certificate of guaranty. The faster VA loan processing method is automatic processing. Under this method, the lender orders a property appraisal from the VA, but has the authority to make the credit decision without the VA's approval.

Under either method, one of the first things the applicant must do is prove that he or she is eligible for the VA program. This is accomplished by securing a "Request for Determination of Eligibility and Available Loan Guarantee Entitlement," available through the VA or most mortgage lenders. The completed form is submitted to the VA with the applicant's separation papers; the VA then issues a certificate of eligibility.

PRIVATE MORTGAGE INSURANCE (PMI)

FHA mortgage insurance became so popular that mortgage insurance is now offered on conventional mortgages. In 1957, Mortgage Guarantee Insurance Corporation of Milwaukee (www.mgic.com) was the first company to offer such coverage. The company was highly profitable and attracted numerous competitors over the years. High mortgage default rates in the 1980s, however, caused several of these companies to fail. Today, private insurance companies insure more mortgages than the FHA insures and the VA guarantees combined. PMI enables lenders to offer conventional loans with loan-to-value ratios that are more competitive with FHA and VA mortgages and, therefore, enables buyers to purchase homes with conventional loans requiring lower down payments than uninsured loans. The premiums charged by PMI companies depend upon a number of factors, including the amount of coverage, the relative size of the borrower's down payment, the initial term of the mortgage, and whether the mortgage payment is fixed in amount.

Decision Point

A friend has asked for your advice concerning the type of mortgage loan to use in acquiring her first house. She recently left the United State Air Force (with an honorable discharge) after a twenty-year career and has $20,000 available for a down payment on the $220,000 house she hopes to purchase. Given these circumstances, comment on the appropriateness of an FHA loan, a VA loan, an uninsured conventional loan, and an insured conventional loan.

SECOND (JUNIOR) MORTGAGES

A single parcel of real property can serve as collateral for more than one mortgage loan. In fact, any number of mortgages could be placed on a single property if a willing lender can be found and such additional financing is not prohibited by the terms of an existing mortgage loan. It is highly unusual, however, to have a single property simultaneously encumbered by more than two mortgages.

When more than one mortgage is in place, the priority of the mortgagees' claims is generally determined by the date each mortgage was recorded. The **first mortgage** recorded has the first, or senior, claim. Mortgages recorded later have a junior claim, and such a mortgage is commonly called a **second mortgage.** The time of recording does not, however, always determine mortgage seniority. A mortgage may contain a subordination clause that states that the lender's claim will be junior to certain other loans that the borrower may subsequently incur. For example, mortgage holders on undeveloped land are often asked to subordinate their interest so that construction financing can be obtained, and subsequently permanent financing.

From the lender's perspective, a second mortgage is generally considered more risky than a first mortgage. If the borrower defaults, the proceeds from the foreclosure sale are first applied toward the claim of the first mortgage holder, and this claim must be paid in full before any of the proceeds can be used to satisfy the claims of junior creditors. Second mortgage loans carry a higher interest rate than first mortgage loans because of the increased risk. Under certain circumstances, however, a second mortgage could, in fact, be less risky than the first mortgage loan. Consider, for example, a five-year second mortgage on a new office building (second mortgages tend to have original maturities of five to ten years, much shorter than the original maturity on most first mortgage loans). The office building is fully leased to high-quality tenants who all have lease terms of five years. If the lease payments exceed the payments of both the first and second mortgage loans, it could be argued that the second mortgage is actually safer than the first because it will be paid off before the leases must be renegotiated.

PURCHASE MONEY MORTGAGE

Sometimes, to facilitate a sale, the seller finances a portion of the sale price. For example, suppose a buyer wishes to purchase a $100,000 house, but has only $12,000 and a commitment from an institutional lender for $80,000. The seller may agree to finance the remaining $8,000 of the purchase price. To avoid disturbing the arrangement with the institutional lender, the seller and buyer agree to enter into a second mortgage. If the seller makes the loan to facilitate the sale, the mortgage is frequently referred to as a purchase money mortgage. In such transactions the seller is said to be "taking back a second." Like other second mortgages, the original maturity on most purchase money mortgages is relatively short.

HOME EQUITY LOAN

A **home equity loan** is another form of second mortgage. Home equity loans became popular due primarily to the Tax Reform Act of 1986 that eliminated the deductibility of interest payments on consumer loans. Interest on most mortgage loans is still fully deductible for income tax purposes, and interest on home equity loans up to $100,000 may be deducted in full for federal and many state income tax returns. Traditionally, borrowers used home equity loans to finance home improvements, but they have become all-purpose loans (used to finance not only home loans, but to pay for other purchases and vacations, among other things).

While home equity loans offer an important source of financing, they can cause problems for homeowners. For many years, steeply climbing home prices offset the drain on equity created by home equity loans. With declining home prices in many areas, however, households burdened with both first and second mortgage debt risk financial catastrophe. Falling real estate values combined with prolonged unemployment, for example, may mean that a homeowner will suffer a mortgage foreclosure, or be forced to sell his or her home for less than the amount owed on the mortgages.

There are two forms of home equity loans. A closed-end loan is made in a fixed amount that is borrowed all at once and repaid in monthly installments over a set period, such as ten years. An open-end loan, or line of credit, allows the borrower to draw, as needed, against the maximum amount that is established when the loan is originated. Open-end loans generally carry an adjustable interest rate with interest paid on the outstanding balance just as with a credit card. The borrower often has a choice of an amortized payment schedule or paying only interest for the first several years. Lenders frequently provide special checks that allow the borrower to draw on the line of credit, others allow borrowing through a regular checking account, and some even allow advances through automated teller machines.

WRAPAROUND MORTGAGE

A **wraparound loan,** sometimes referred to simply as a wrap, is usually used by a property owner who wishes to convert some of their equity in a property into cash without disturbing an existing mortgage. A wrap is created when a lender different from the one who originated the existing first mortgage writes a second mortgage loan. The wrap lender takes over the payments on the first loan. The face amount of the wrap equals the total funds advanced by the wrap lender and the remaining balance of the first loan. In effect, the new loan wraps around the old loan, and the borrower makes payments to the wrap lender only, who forwards the payment on the first mortgage loan and retains the balance.

Although wraps are a form of second mortgage, they frequently carry an interest rate below prevailing first mortgage loan rates. The following case illustrates how this can occur. Mr. Frumpp acquired a property financed in part with a 10-percent, fixed-rate first mortgage originated by City Bank. There is a remaining balance of $1,000,000 on this loan, but because a gambling casino has recently opened near the property, its value has doubled. Mr. Frumpp would like to convert $500,000 of the equity into cash but first mortgage interest rates have risen to 15 percent. He approaches State Bank that is willing to advance the $500,000 if Mr. Frumpp signs a wraparound mortgage carrying a 13 percent interest rate. How can State Bank afford to offer this wraparound mortgage? Easily—remember it is charging 13 percent on $1,500,000 but it only has to disperse $500,000. Therefore, it is earning 3 percent (the 13 percent it is collecting minus the 10 percent it is paying to City Bank) on $1,000,000 that it did not loan. The short-cut method presented here ignores the fact that interest charges will drop throughout the term of the loan. We show how to more precisely calculate the effective cost of a wrap in Chapter 17.

To approximate the effective rate of interest on the $500,000 use the following calculation.

Amount	@ Rate	= Interest
$500,000	13 percent	$65,000
$1,000,000	3 percent	$30,000
		$95,000

Rate of return = $95,000 ÷ $500,000 = 19 percent

This represents the effective return for State Bank and also Mr. Frumpp's effective cost. Before entering into the wrap he should investigate other possibilities to determine if a better price is available, for example, a $500,000 second mortgage may carry an interest rate lower than 19 percent.

BLENDED RATE MORTGAGE

Sometimes when a loan assumption is involved in the sale of a property, or when a loan is refinanced, the borrower and lender will compromise on the interest rate. A blended rate mortgage is one in which the interest rate charged on a newly refinanced loan is higher than the rate on the existing mortgage, but lower than the current market rate. Wraparounds use a blended rate, but a wrap is not synonymous with a blended rate mortgage because the same lender may provide both the old and new financing in a

CONSUMER CHECKLIST
HOME EQUITY LOANS

Homeowners should consider the following points before entering into a home equity loan:

- Base the amount of the loan on your ability to repay, not on the amount of equity in your home. A rule of thumb is that the first mortgage and home equity mortgage payments should not exceed 35 percent of gross monthly income. Most lenders will generally not make home equity loans in excess of an 80 percent loan-to-value ratio, including the first mortgage loan. For example, the maximum home equity loan on a $100,000 house with an existing $50,000 mortgage is $30,000.

- Beware of loans carrying a teaser rate. A teaser rate is one set below the current market rate. Many loans carrying these provide for rate increases after a year or two and, over time, the cost of such loans may exceed that on loans carrying the market rate.

- Home equity loans should be used primarily for home improvements, starting a business, or financing an education. Using home equity loans to finance vacations or to purchase luxury items is not recommended. Home equity loans should be used cautiously to cover emergency expenses and consolidate debts with non-tax-deductible interest.

- To reduce total interest payments, avoid loans with the interest-only option, and schedule installments that enable you to comfortably retire the debt as quickly as possible.

- Use close-end loans for refinancing and other one-time needs. Use open-end loans to cover deferred costs such as college tuition. In this way you avoid the inconvenience of multiple loan applications and pay interest only on the amount you need.

blended rate mortgage. It is, therefore, appropriate to think of wraps as a subset of blended rate mortgages.

MORTGAGE THEORIES

In previous sections of this chapter we used the word "claim" in reference to the mortgagee's interest in the property. Exactly what form this claim takes depends on the mortgage theory that prevails in the state where the property is located. Some states, located mostly on the East Coast, follow the title theory. Under this theory, the mortgagee is recognized as the owner of the mortgaged property, and this interest is extinguished only when the mortgagor has made payment in full. The title theory was imported from England where, under common law, it prevailed at the time the eastern part of the United States was settled. In the event of default, repossession of the subject property in title theory states is less cumbersome because the mortgagee already has legal title to the property.

Some states follow the lien theory. Under this theory, the mortgage is viewed purely as a lien on the real property. In the event of default the mortgagee must foreclose on the mortgage, offer the property for sale, and apply the sale proceeds to reduce the debt. Other states combine the title and lien theories. In general, states that follow the intermediate theory view the mortgage as a lien on the property until default occurs and then title is transferred to the mortgagee.

MORTGAGE FORECLOSURE

Foreclosure is the procedure whereby real property used as collateral for a debt is sold to satisfy the debt in the event of default. Most people think a mortgage default results from the borrower's failure to make payments on the loan. While this is certainly an important cause of mortgage default, technically, if the mortgagor fails to honor any of the clauses contained in the mortgage, the loan is in default. For example, failure to pay property taxes, keep the property adequately insured, or maintain it in good repair, all constitute a default.

In the event of default, the mortgagee's first action is likely to be an attempt to get the borrower to correct the default as simply as possible. That is, pay the property tax,

AN ETHICAL ISSUE
WRAPAROUND MORTGAGES

As previously mentioned, an assumable loan with an interest rate below the current market rate is valuable. Upon occasion, parties may use a wraparound loan to capture this value from a nonassumable loan. In such cases, the seller usually provides the wrap loan to avoid triggering the due-on-sale clause on an existing low-interest-rate loan. Such a strategy is risky for the parties involved because the first mortgage lender may become aware of the deal and demand payment in full. Assume that you were selling a property on which you have a nonassumable mortgage loan with an interest rate substantially lower than the prevailing rate. You can sell the property for $20,000 more, compared with the case where the buyer arranges entirely new financing, if a wrap is arranged for the buyer.

- If there were absolutely no chance of the first mortgage lender discovering the wrap loan, would you participate in the arrangement? If your answer is yes, why? If your answer is no, why? How much more than an additional $20,000 would the deal have to net you for your answer to change?

- Regardless of how you answered question 1, would your answer change if it were not a certainty that the transaction would go undetected?

insurance premium, or loan payment with a penalty, or repair the property. If the borrower fails to take the necessary action, the lender has the power to start a foreclosure proceeding. Lenders generally prefer to use foreclosure as a last resort. After all, lenders are in business to make loans and collect payments, not to maintain an inventory of real properties. Foreclosure proceedings can usually be avoided if the borrower demonstrates concern about the default and a willingness to correct it. Lenders cannot exercise forbearance indefinitely, however. State statutes of limitations specify how much time may elapse from the time of the default to the time the foreclosure action is commenced; lenders who do not begin the action in the allotted time are precluded from doing so afterward.

TYPES OF FORECLOSURE PROCEEDINGS

Mortgagee's use several types of mortgage foreclosure proceedings, the most prevalent are the judicial and power of sale. Regardless of which of the two is used, the mortgagee usually conducts a title search to determine if any other parties have an interest in the property, such as tax or mechanic's lien holders, and other mortgage creditors. The mortgagee will join these parties in the foreclosure proceeding, otherwise their claim on the property will not be erased with the foreclosure sale. Mortgagees go to this expense because they are frequently the winning bidder at the foreclosure auction. Exhibit 15.3 contains a summary of the proceedings each state follows.

Judicial Foreclosure

Judicial foreclosure enables the property to be sold by court order after sufficient public notice. The procedure starts with the mortgagee accelerating the due date of all remaining payments. Then the mortgagee files a lawsuit to foreclose the mortgage lien. Upon presentation of the facts in court, the court will order the property sold at a public auction. The court ordered sale is advertised, held, and the property sold to the highest bidder. The court subsequently reviews the sale to determine if the property was sold at a fair price. If the court decides the price is fair it will confirm the sale; if not, it will order that the mortgagee advertise and conduct another sale.

Power of Sale Foreclosure

Some states allow power of sale foreclosure if a **power of sale** clause is contained in the security instrument. Such a clause gives the mortgagee, or trustee in a deed of trust, the right to sell the property without court supervision. The mortgagee initiates the action by filing a notice of default at the county recorder's office. After filing the notice of default, the mortgagee places newspaper advertisements of the public sale of the property. The property is awarded to the highest bidder, and the procedure is finished when the mortgagee files an affidavit of foreclosure or notice of sale.

Strict Foreclosure

A few states allow mortgagees to acquire property through strict foreclosure. Under this procedure, after notice has been given to the delinquent mortgagor, and the appropriate papers filed, the court will establish a specific time by which the balance of the debt must be paid in full. If payment is not made, the mortgagor's redemption rights are waived and the court awards legal title to the mortgagee. This type of foreclosure can be dangerous for the mortgagee because they will obtain ownership of the property and any other unsatisfied claims on the property.

Foreclosure by Entry and Possession

Foreclosure by entry and possession, also called foreclosure by writ of entry, is used only in a few New England states. Under this method, the mortgagee actually takes physical possession of the property, with or without the permission of the mortgagor, if entry can be made peaceably or under court order. Under this procedure, the mortgagee's right to redeem his interest in the property by correcting whatever default resulted in foreclosure expires automatically after the mortgagee has been in possession for the time period specified by state statute.

Deed in Lieu of Foreclosure

One way a borrower in default may avoid foreclosure proceedings is to deed the mortgaged property to the mortgagee. In this situation, the deed is referred to as a deed in lieu of foreclosure. As in any other transfer, to be valid, the grantee must accept the deed. One reason the mortgagee may be reluctant or unwilling to accept a deed in lieu of foreclosure is that the deed will not eliminate other claims on the property, as would a foreclosure proceeding. Assume, for example, that a second mortgage had been placed on the property, as well as a couple of mechanic's liens. By accepting a deed in lieu of foreclosure, the mortgagee will be the owner of the property encumbered by these claims.

DEFICIENCY JUDGMENTS

It is unlikely that the foreclosure sale price will exactly match the amounts owed to creditors. If the proceeds from the sale exceed the amount owed to creditors plus court expenses, the excess is paid to the former mortgagor. It is uncommon, however, for the property to bring more at a foreclosure sale than the amounts owed to creditors. Usually the sales proceeds are less than the amounts owed. In such cases, under a judicial foreclosure, the court can enter a personal judgment against the mortgagor called a **deficiency judgment.** The judgment will be equal to the difference between the sale price and the amounts owed plus court costs. A deficiency judgment acts as a general lien on the debtor's assets. With a power of sale foreclosure, the mortgagee must institute a new court proceeding to obtain a deficiency judgment. In recent times, lenders appear to be reluctant to spend the resources necessary to obtain such judgments, as many have determined they are not likely to collect on them. To illustrate this, consider the experience of one national mortgage lender. During a single year, the company had $50,000,000 of potentially collectable deficiencies. The company decided to pursue $10,000,000 and wrote off the rest. Of the amount they pursued, they collected $900,000.

Deficiency judgments are not always available to a lender. Deficiency judgments are not allowed when a lender uses strict foreclosure, and several states have passed antideficiency legislation that prohibits deficiency judgments on purchase money mortgages. In addition, deficiency judgments are not permitted for FHA loans and are highly discouraged for VA loans.

TAX CONSEQUENCES OF MORTGAGE FORECLOSURE FOR THE BORROWER

When faced with financial difficulty, some real property owners may elect to walk away from mortgaged property. Before making such a decision, one should consider the tax consequences of the action. The potential income tax on a mortgage foreclosure may be so severe that the borrower may find other alternatives such as restructuring the loan preferable. The borrower's tax liability depends, in part, on the use of the property; property used for income purposes is treated differently than property used as a principal residence.

The IRS considers foreclosure as two taxable events: the sale of the property and retirement of the mortgage. Usually retiring a mortgage at face value has no tax consequences. But if the borrower is solvent and personally liable for the debt, debt cancellation (which often occurs in foreclosure) results in taxable ordinary income. Because the borrower received money when the loan was originated, it becomes taxable in the year the loan is forgiven. A mortgage foreclosure is generally deemed a sale of the property with loss or gain measured as the difference between the selling price realized at the foreclosure auction and the adjusted tax basis of the property. A borrower will realize a taxable gain on foreclosure to the extent that the sale price exceeds the adjusted tax basis, with the gain determined as if the lender paid cash to the borrower in exchange for the property.

LOAN ASSUMPTION VS. PURCHASING SUBJECT TO A MORTGAGE

There is an important difference, regarding deficiency judgments, between assuming a mortgage loan and purchasing a property subject to a mortgage. When a purchaser assumes a mortgage the purchaser accepts personal liability for the mortgage, but the seller remains contingently liable. In the event of a default, the lender first looks to the buyer to remedy the problem. If the buyer does not cure the default, however, the lender may require the seller to pay the balance due. With a mortgage assumption, either party may have a deficiency judgment levied against them. If, however, the buyer qualifies for the assumed loan with the lender, a seller can eliminate their responsibility by obtaining a release of liability. When a buyer purchases property subject to a mortgage, the buyer only acknowledges that there is a mortgage against the property, but does not agree to assume personal liability for it. In this case, the purchaser's liability extends only to the loss of the property. When property is acquired subject to a mortgage, the mortgagee can only seek remedy from the seller.

Decision Point

Assume that you purchased a property ten years ago financed with a mortgage that does not contain a due on sale clause. A prospective buyer approaches you with a full list price offer of $100,000. The prospect wants to purchase your property subject to the existing loan, which has a balance of $75,000. Under what conditions would you accept the offer? What kind of counter-offer might you formulate?

MORTGAGE REDEMPTION

Through time the relative legal advantage of mortgagors and mortgagees has varied. In feudal Europe, the mortgagee/landlord definitely had the legal advantage. At one time, only nobility could hold title to land. As commoners gained the right to own land, the typical arrangement required the prospective owner (tenant) to work the land for a number of years until "law day." On law day, payment for the land was due. If the tenant was unable to make complete payment, the landlord had the right to remove the tenant from the land; the landlord's exercise of this right marked the beginning of strict foreclosure. English courts of equity decided that this was not always a just solution, and instituted the **equitable right of redemption** whereby the hopeful landowner could redeem his or her interest in the property by paying in full after law day.

The right of equitable redemption fostered the concept of mortgage foreclosure. In fact, what is really being foreclosed in a foreclosure action is the borrower's right of equitable redemption. The initiation of a foreclosure action starts the clock that limits the borrower's right to redeem his or her interest. Today, the right of equitable redemption applies in all fifty states. This right ends with the sale of the property under a power of sale proceeding. In judicial foreclosures, it ends a few days after the sale, when a judge affirms the sale.

Some states, listed in Exhibit 15.3, carry the concept of redemption a step further by allowing the borrower to redeem his or her interest up to a year after the foreclosure sale. Redemption periods created by state statutes are known as statutory redemption periods. A party exercising the right of **statutory redemption** must pay the successful bidder at auction not only the price paid but also interest at a rate specified by statute, and all court costs associated with the foreclosure.

EXHIBIT 15.3 FORECLOSURE KEY FACTORS CHART

State ID	Security Instrument	Foreclosure Method	Initial Action	Months to Completion	Statutory Redemption Period	Deficiency Provision
AL	Mortgage	Non-Judicial	Publication	1 month	12 months	Allowed
AK	Deed of Trust	Non-Judicial	Notice of Default	3 months	None	Allowed[1]
AZ	Deed of Trust	Non-Judicial	Notice of Sale	3 months	None	Allowed[2]
AR	Mortgage	Judicial[3]	Complaint	4 months	None	Allowed
CA	Deed of Trust	Non-Judicial	Notice of Default	4 months	None	Prohibited
CO	Deed of Trust	Non-Judicial	Notice of Election	2 months	75 days[4]	Allowed
CT	Mortgage	Strict[5]	Complaint	5 months	None	Allowed
DE	Mortgage	Judicial	Complaint	3 months	None	Allowed
DC	Deed of Trust	Non-Judicial	Notice of Default	2 months	None	Allowed
FL	Mortgage	Judicial	Complaint	5 months	None	Allowed
GA	Security Deed	Non-Judicial	Publication	2 months	None	Allowed
HI	Mortgage	Non-Judicial[6]	Publication	3 months	None	Allowed
ID	Trust Deed	Non-Judicial	Notice of Default	5 months	None	Allowed
IL	Mortgage	Judicial	Complaint	7 months	None[7]	Allowed
IN	Mortgage	Judicial	Complaint	5 months	3 months[8]	Allowed
IA	Mortgage	Judicial	Petition of F/C	5 months	6 months[9]	Allowed
KS	Mortgage	Judicial	Complaint	4 months	6–12 months[10]	Allowed
KY	Mortgage	Judicial	Complaint	6 months	None[11]	Allowed
LA	Mortgage	Executory Process	Petition for Process	2 months	None	Allowed
ME	Mortgage	Judicial	Complaint	6 months	None[12]	Allowed
MD	Trust Deed	Non-Judicial	Notice	2 months	None	Allowed
MA	Mortgage	Judicial[13]	Complaint	3 months	None	Allowed
MI	Mortgage	Non-Judicial	Publication	2 months	6 months[14]	Allowed
MN	Mortgage	Non-Judicial	Publication	2 months	6 months[15]	Prohibited[16]
MS	Deed of Trust	Non-Judicial[17]	Publication	2 months	None	Allowed
MO	Deed of Trust	Non-Judicial	Publication	2 months	None	Allowed
MT	Trust Deed	Non-Judicial	Notice	5 months	None	Prohibited[16]
NE	Mortgage[18]	Judicial[18]	Petition[18]	5 months	None	Allowed
NV	Deed of Trust	Non-Judicial	Notice of Default	4 months	None	Allowed
NH	Mortgage	Non-Judicial	Notice of Sale	2 months	None	Allowed
NJ	Mortgage	Judicial	Complaint	3 months	None	Allowed
NM	Mortgage	Judicial	Complaint	4 months[19]	None[19]	Allowed
NY	Mortgage	Judicial	Complaint	4 months	None	Allowed
NC	Deed of Trust	Non-Judicial	Notice of Hearing	2 months	None	Allowed
ND	Mortgage	Judicial	Complaint	3 months	60 days[20]	Prohibited
OH	Mortgage	Judicial	Complaint	5 months	None	Allowed
OK	Mortgage	Judicial[21]	Complaint	4 months	None	Allowed

| EXHIBIT | 15.3 | **FORECLOSURE KEY FACTORS CHART (CONTINUED)** |

State ID	Security Instrument	Foreclosure Method	Initial Action	Months to Completion	Statutory Redemption Period	Deficiency Provision
OR	Trust Deed	Non-Judicial	Notice of Default	5 months	None	Allowed
PA	Mortgage	Judicial	Complaint	3 months	None	Allowed
RI	Mortgage	Non-Judicial	Publication	2 months	None	Allowed
SC	Mortgage	Judicial	Complaint	6 months	12 months	Allowed
SD	Mortgage	Judicial	Complaint	3 months	180 days[22]	Allowed
TN	Deed of Trust	Non-Judicial	Publication	2 months	None	Allowed
TX	Deed of Trust	Non-Judicial	Publication	2 months	None	Allowed
UT	Deed of Trust	Non-Judicially	Notice of Default	4 months	None	Allowed
VT	Mortgage	Judicial	Complaint	7 months[23]	None	Allowed
VA	Deed of Trust	Non-Judicial	Publication	2 months	None	Allowed
WA	Deed of Trust	Non-Judicial	Notice of Default	4 months	None	Prohibited[24]
WV	Trust Deed	Non-Judicial	Publication	2 months	None	Allowed
WI	Mortgage	Judicial	Complaint	Varies[25]	None	Allowed
WY	Mortgage	Non-Judicial	Publication	2 months	3 months[26]	Allowed

Footnotes:

1 Must foreclose judicially in order to preserve right to pursue recovery through a deficiency judgment
2 Deficiency judgments not allowed on one or two family homes situated on less than 2.5 acres
3 If the mortgage contains authorizing language, or if a deed of trust is used, foreclosure may be by non-judicial process
4 The redemption period following the sale is 6 months if the property is used for agricultural purposes
5 Judgment of Foreclosure by Sale may be ordered by the judge if the mortgagor has substantial equity in the property
6 Many foreclosures in Hawaii are still foreclosed via the Judicial method
7 Recent changes to Illinois law place the redemption period prior to the sale date
8 If the mortgage is dated prior to July 1, 1975, there is a six month redemption period
9 Iowa has substantial exceptions to the redemption periods for agricultural property and non owner occupied property
10 Length of redemption period following the sale depends on mortgagor's equity
11 Redemption period of 12 months follows the sale if the bid amount is less than $2/3$ of the appraised value
12 If the mortgage is prior to 10/1/75 and silent on the redemption period, a 1 year redemption period will exist
13 Massachusetts law also allows for alternate forms of foreclosure including Entry and Possession
14 Redemption period is increased to 12 months if property is in excess of three acres and 33% equity. Vacant 3 months
15 The redemption period will be 12 months if the mortgage is dated prior to 7/1/67 or if agricultural property
16 A deficiency judgment may be pursued if foreclosure is conducted judicially
17 Foreclosure may also be conducted judicially if a deficiency judgment is desired
18 Nebraska also allows for deeds of trust which can be foreclosed non-judicially if provided in the security instrument
19 Redemption period precedes sale. Mortgages after 1965 have 1 month redemption. Prior to 1965 period is 3 months
20 Redemption period following sale for mortgages after 7/1/81 is the later of 6 months from complaint or 60 days from sale
21 Oklahoma Power of Sale provides for foreclosure by publication if power is granted in the security instrument
22 Redemption period is one year if limited language is not included in the security instrument
23 The redemption period precedes the final action. If the mortgage is dated prior to 4/1/68, the redemption period is 12 months
24 A deficiency judgment may be awarded if the foreclosure is conducted judicially. Most VA guaranteed loans are judicially foreclosed
25 Redemption period precedes the sale. Length of redemption varies from 2 months to 12 months depending on the mortgage and occupancy
26 Agricultural property will have a 12 month redemption period following the sale

Prepared by: Dennis A. Jankowski: First American, 1500 Surveyor Blvd., Addison, TX, 75001

DEED OF TRUST

Another type of security instrument is a **deed of trust,** also known as a trust deed. Functionally, a deed of trust is identical to a mortgage. For example, senior and junior trust deeds can be used, subordination and partial releases are possible, trust deeds can be assumed, and property can be purchased subject to a trust deed. There are, however, important legal differences between trust deeds and mortgages.

The primary difference between a mortgage and a trust deed is that there are three parties to a trust deed. The trust deed is a document used to transfer title to a (third party) trustee as security for the obligation owed by the trustor (borrower) to the beneficiary (lender). The title that the borrower grants to the trustee is sometimes referred to as a "bare title" or a "naked title" because the borrower retains the usual rights of ownership. The trustee merely holds the trust deed until the trustor either pays off the loan or defaults. If the loan is paid off, the trustee is responsible for reconveying title to the trustor. A release deed or deed of reconveyance is used to reconvey title. If a default does occur, the trustor usually has the "power of sale."

Although noninstitutional trustees may be used, locating them to perform a needed function, such as performing a reconveyance, is sometimes a problem. For example, a church minister may be a very trustworthy person, but if he is overseas on missionary duty, he will be unavailable to perform his duties as trustee. Institutional lenders prefer institutional trustees, such as the trust department of a commercial bank.

SUMMARY

Knowledge of the material presented in this chapter is essential if you are to make informed decisions regarding the type of loan to use in acquiring, improving, or refinancing real

DOING BUSINESS

LEGAL ISSUES

In states that permit trust deeds, lenders prefer to use them to make residential property loans for a number of reasons, including the following:

1. Deeds of trust can be used to secure more than one note.

2. If a lender wishes to remain anonymous, he or she may do so because the lender need not be named in a deed of trust.

3. Unlike a mortgage where an action on the note is subject to the statute of limitations, the trustor has legal title to the property and can, therefore, sell the property at any time following default.

4. The judicial foreclosure process, which may be quite time consuming, can be avoided if the trustee is given the authority to sell the property after default. Most states that allow trust deeds prescribe redemption periods that allow borrowers in default to reinstate their position so the trustee cannot immediately accelerate the note. It is often easier, however, to foreclose on a deed of trust compared with a mortgage. In Nebraska, for example, where both documents are available, use of the deed of trust predominates. A likely reason for this is that with a deed of trust property can be repossessed in approximately five months, with a mortgage the foreclosure process takes at least a year.

5. The defaulted borrower usually has no statutory right of redemption after a sale by the power of sale. Offsetting this benefit is the fact that many states restrict or prohibit the use of deficiency judgments when the security instrument used is a deed of trust.

Go to www.lexis-nexis.com/universe, using your university computer system and click on Legal Research, then click on Area of Law by Topic, and use "deed of trust" as your search term to learn the results of legal cases concerning this topic.

property. The security instrument used (mortgage or deed of trust) and the promissory note, which personally obligates the borrower for the debt, contain many clauses that detail the rights and responsibilities of all parties to the contract. Borrowers should read and understand these documents before signing them.

A variety of mortgage types are available. While VA and FHA loans are not used as frequently as conventional mortgages, they enable purchasers to borrow with smaller down payments. However, the loan application process for these types of loans is more cumbersome and they can only be used to finance property in which the borrower intends to reside. The different conventional mortgages available offer borrowers some flexibility. A package mortgage, for example, enables the borrower to finance items usually considered personal property along with the real property. A blanket mortgage enables the borrower to finance more than one parcel with a single mortgage. Several types of second mortgage loans are also available to borrowers. Home equity loans, for example, enable homeowners to convert some of the equity in their home into cash. The interest rate on second mortgages, however, tends to be higher than on first mortgage loans to compensate the lender for additional risk.

If a mortgagor defaults, the lender may begin a mortgage foreclosure proceeding. Several different types of foreclosure proceedings may be followed, but the effect on the defaulting borrower is the same regardless of which type is used—the borrower may lose ownership of the property. Borrowers in default may redeem their interest in the property by exercising their right of equitable redemption, and in some states through statutory redemption.

KEY TERMS

amortized loan	first mortgage	package mortgage
blanket mortgage	forbearance	power of sale foreclosure
budget mortgage	foreclosure	promissory note
conventional mortgage	home equity loan	raiding
deed of trust	judicial foreclosure	satisfaction of mortgage
deficiency judgment	mortgage	second mortgage
equitable right of redemp-	mortgage covenants	statutory redemption
tion	mortgagee	VA-guaranteed mortgage
estoppel certificate	mortgagor	loan
FHA-insured mortgage	open-end mortgage	wraparound loan

REVIEW QUESTIONS

1. What factors would you consider in choosing between a conventional, FHA and VA mortgage loan?

2. As a borrower, what would you consider to be the five most important clauses in a mortgage contract? Why?

3. One could think of a pendulum on a clock as representing the advantage enjoyed by either the mortgagor or mortgagee in the event of mortgage default. Describe at least three developments that have caused the pendulum to swing in one direction of the other.

4. Why do you think the FHA imposes limits on the maximum amount of mortgage loan that it will insure?

5. What is the maximum FHA loan that can be obtained on single-family homes, located in a "standard limit" area, that cost (a) $89,000, (b) $120,000, and (c) $200,000?

6. What are the differences between a judicial foreclosure and a power of sale foreclosure?

7. Why are home equity loans popular? What are the disadvantages of these loans?

8. What incentives does the loan guarantee system used by the VA offer borrowers and lenders?

9. What is the difference between equitable redemption and statutory redemption?

10. What is the difference between a closed-end loan and an open-end loan? Under what circumstances would you prefer one loan to the other?

11. What is your answer to the questions in the three "Decision Point" sections in this Chapter?

12. What is your answer to the Ethical Issue in this chapter?

REAL ESTATE ON THE WEB

Use your favorite search engine to:

1. Determine the FHA and VA home loan limits in your area.

2. Learn the rate of interest that lenders in your area are charging for first and second mortgage loans.

3. Discover where and when foreclosure sales are held in your area.

4. Discover the cost of private mortgage insurance issued by MGIC and other private mortgage insurers.

Refer to the companion Web site at www.wiley.com/college/larsen for a variety of online activities including additional chapter content, review materials, assignments, and related links.

ADDITIONAL READINGS

Curtin, R. T. "National Survey of Home Equity Loans." Survey Research Center, The University of Michigan, WP51, October 1998.

Gauthier, L. "Another Look at Home Equity Loan Prepayments." *Journal of Fixed Income* (March 2000): 51–57.

Lee, J. and J. M. Hogarth. "Consumer Information Search for Home Mortgages: Who, What, How Much, and What Else?" *Financial Services Review* (Fall 2000): 277–293.

Smith, T. S. "Taking the Stress Out of Distressed Property." *Real Estate Issues* (Winter 2001): 49–53.

Van Order, R. and P. Zorn. "Income, Location and Default: Some Implications for Community Lending." *Real Estate Economics* (Fall 2000): 385–404.

CHAPTER 16

Financing Real Estate Transactions

Learning Objectives

After studying this chapter you should be able to:

- Explain the reasons why people borrow money to purchase real estate.
- Identify the financial institutions that originate loans in the primary mortgage market, and those that purchase mortgage-related securities in the secondary mortgage market.
- Describe the various mortgage loan contracts that have been developed as alternatives to the traditional thirty-year, fixed-rate mortgage.
- Understand how the secondary mortgage market operates and the benefits it provides.

PRACTIONER PROFILE

Donald Parrott, a branch manager and mortgage originator for Crossman Mortgage, headquartered in Indianapolis, Indiana has been in the mortgage business for more than 25 years. Initially, Donald was in the private mortgage insurance business. One day, when calling on a mortgage company to try and get their business it was he who was sold instead of the client. The loan originator he was talking with convinced Donald that he should be in the loan origination end of the business. He has been ever since. Prior to joining Crossman, Donald worked in several mortgage origination positions including 14 years as an originator for National City Mortgage Company. In his current position, which he began in 1998, Donald helps obtain mortgage funds for people purchasing a new Crossman home. One thing he likes about his job is that he does not have to solicit real estate agents for business. With new homes, the business 'walks in the door.' The job, however, is not always easy. "It's difficult to qualify applicants for a mortgage loan when they have large amounts of existing debt," says Donald, who is frequently amazed by the level of debt some loan applicants bring to the loan table. To decrease the odds that this would happen to you, he recommends taking a course in personal finance.

Go to www.mbaa.org, and click on one or more of "Today's Headlines" to learn what is new in the mortgage lending industry.

INTRODUCTION

An important decision you must make regarding most real property acquisitions is the amount of borrowed funds to be used. There are several reasons why you might seek financing for the acquisition of real estate. One is its relatively high cost. If prospective homeowners, real estate developers, and investors had to first accumulate the entire amount necessary to acquire real property, most purchases would not take place. A second reason you might use borrowed funds for the acquisition of real property is to maximize your consumption of all goods. For most individuals, interest paid on home mortgages is the only type of interest payment that is deductible under the current United States income tax code. Therefore, even if you have the full home purchase price available, it may be beneficial to borrow money for the home purchase and pay cash for other items. This way, nondeductible interest charges that would be incurred if borrowed funds were used for consumer purchases can be avoided. Finally, real property investors frequently use borrowed funds to increase the rate of return on their own funds (Chapter 21).

Additional decisions must be made if you decide to employ borrowed funds to acquire or refinance real property, including the selection of a lender and the type of mortgage contract to use. In the last chapter, we explained the importance of the downpayment because it can affect how much property a buyer can afford. Assessing the payment pattern required by a mortgage is important for the same reason. In this chapter, we review the various institutional mortgage lenders and discuss the payment pattern associated with several types of mortgages. This material should help enable you to select a lender that offers the mortgage with the best combination of downpayment requirement and payment pattern.

The chapter concludes with a brief description of the secondary mortgage market. The development of this market has enabled mortgage originators to raise funds more efficiently that can then be used to make additional mortgage loans. The development of the secondary mortgage market also gives investors an opportunity to diversify their investment portfolios by placing some of their funds in mortgages.

MORTGAGE LENDERS

While mortgage funds may be obtained from a friend, relative, or other private party, institutional lenders supply most mortgage funds. A variety of institutions participate in the **primary**

mortgage market, a term used to describe the origination of mortgage loans. These institutions include: savings and loan associations, commercial banks, mutual savings banks, life insurance companies, credit unions, finance companies, real estate investment trusts, pension funds, and mortgage companies. Certain institutions tend to specialize in particular types of mortgage lending. For example, savings and loan associations tend to specialize in home loans, whereas life insurance companies tend to specialize in commercial loans. The financial institutions examined in this chapter have evolved over time, however, in recent years, technological advances and relaxed regulations that previously prevented competition among different types of institutions have quickened the evolutionary process.

SAVINGS AND LOAN ASSOCIATIONS

A savings and loan association (S&L) is a financial institution that accepts deposits that it uses primarily to make loans. Early commercial banks specialized in serving the needs of business enterprises. Therefore, S&Ls were created to serve the financial needs of individuals; their principal function is to promote thrift and home ownership. For this reason S&Ls (together with mutual savings banks and credit unions) are sometimes referred to as thrifts or thrift institutions. Additionally, thrifts and commercial banks are collectively referred to as depository institutions because they accept deposits.

S&Ls are the most active participant in the home loan mortgage market. They write all types of mortgage loans, including FHA, VA, conventional, mobile home, and home equity loans. They may write conventional loans with a loan-to-value ratio as high as 90 percent. The **loan-to-value ratio** expresses the relationship between the loan amount and the lesser of the sales price or appraised value of the property. These loans must be amortized on a monthly basis with a maximum amortization period of forty years.

As is the case for most other types of depository institutions, an S&L must obtain permission before it can begin operations. Organizers secure a charter from the appropriate state or federal government authority. The amount of mortgage loans that an S&L can or must make is subject to regulation. Historically, the exact lending requirements depended on the type of charter the institution held. While state-chartered S&Ls' lending activity may still be influenced by state statutes, all S&Ls must comply with the provisions of the Financial Institutions Reform, Recovery and Enforcement Act of 1989 (FIRREA). This Act, some-times referred to as the S&L Bail-Out Bill, regulates a number of S&L operational areas.

DOING BUSINESS
TECHNOLOGY

The use of technology in the mortgage business is dramatically reducing the time and cost involved in originating and servicing loans. Consider, for example, First American Real Estate Solutions (RES), a member of the First American Corporation (NYSE: FAF). RES is the nation's largest supplier of data and decision-support products to the mortgage industry. In September 2001, they launched Lien Release Information Services (LRIS), a customized data fulfillment service that quickly and cost-effectively provides information to mortgage lenders. The service enables lenders to electronically update mortgage records using information abstracted from deeds, mortgages, assignments and other documents in more than 1,370 counties across the United States. The service is designed to reduce the number of files that require data research and to streamline lender's lien release preparation. Companies that participated in an LRIS pilot program realized cost savings of up to 75 percent per loan. George S. Livermore, president of RES, said, "Lenders who use this service tell us that they're saving millions of dollars by reducing the number of loans requiring manual research."

Go to www.internetoriginator.com, click on News, next click on Technology, or Computer News, and then click on one or more of the results to learn about similar innovations.

Financial Institutions Reform, Recovery and Enforcement Act (FIRREA)

Three important provisions of FIRREA focus on S&L real estate lending activities. First, each S&L is required to have at least 70 percent of its portfolio assets in housing-related investments. This provision is intended to return S&Ls to their original purpose of making home loans. Earlier legislation, in particular the Garn-St. Germain Act of 1982, permitted S&Ls to enter areas from which they were previously excluded, including commercial mortgage lending. Many S&Ls were attracted to this type of lending but lacked necessary expertise. Losses resulted and S&Ls failed in large numbers. As with many pieces of legislation, Congress attempted to direct S&L loan activity in a socially desirable direction; so in calculating the 70-percent requirement, S&Ls may double-count loans made for low-income housing, churches, schools, and small businesses located in low-income areas.

A second provision of FIRREA was specifically designed to limit S&L non-residential mortgage lending. Prior to FIRREA, S&Ls could make such loans up to 40 percent of total assets; under FIRREA the limit was set at 400 percent of capital (the owners' investment in the firm). A simple example demonstrates the extent to which these regulations could affect an S&L. Assume an S&L has total assets of $100, which are financed with $94 in liabilities (basically deposits) and $6 of capital. Under the old law its non-residential real estate loans could be $40 ($100 × .4); under FIRREA the limit is $24 ($6 × 4). The low level of capital (as a percentage of assets) in this example is not an exaggeration. Most financial institutions operate on capital investments close to the regulatory minimum, and FIRREA requires a minimum capital requirement of 6 percent of assets for S&Ls. Other types of financial institutions operate on similar capital contributions; on average, commercial banks have capital approximately equal to 6 percent of assets, and credit unions operate at approximately 9 percent capital.

FIRREA also requires that licensed or certified appraisers perform most real property appraisals. This provision was included in FIRREA because it was believed that a substantial portion of the losses incurred by S&Ls during the 1980s involved loans justified by bad appraisals (Chapter 10).

COMMERCIAL BANKS

A commercial bank is a financial institution designed to act as a depository and lender for many business activities. Commercial banks rely heavily on short-term sources of funds. Therefore, commercial banks tend to write short-term loans in an attempt to balance the maturity of their assets with the maturity of their liabilities. By doing so, if their cost of funds increases, they can cover the increase fairly quickly by charging higher rates on new loans.

Commercial banks are involved, however, in a number of real estate lending activities. Some own mortgage companies directly or through holding companies, and a few own real estate investment trusts through holding companies, both of which are described later in this chapter. Many banks provide lines of credit to other financial institutions that, in turn, make real estate loans. Commercial banks prefer to make short-term loans to finance construction, or to finance mortgage company operations. Construction loans made by commercial banks typically have maturities ranging from six months to two years. When providing such temporary, or **interim financing,** bankers usually require a **takeout loan** from another lender, who agrees to issue a permanent loan (long-term) when the construction project is complete. Construction loans are riskier than long-term mortgages and, therefore, usually carry a higher rate of interest. In addition, commercial banks offer the full spectrum of residential mortgage loans. They can write fully amortized, uninsured conventional loans with loan-to-value ratios up to 80 percent, and with a maximum amortization period of thirty years. Insured conventional loans can be written up to a 95 percent loan-to-value ratio.

The proportion of mortgage loans held by individual banks varies greatly and depends on the bank's geographic location, economic conditions, regulation, and bank policy. Historically, commercial banks tend to decrease their mortgage lending activity when business loan demand is strong. The development of the secondary mortgage market, which is described later in this chapter, does, however, enable commercial banks to continue writing mortgage loans during such periods because the mortgage loans can be sold quickly to generate the cash needed by their business customers.

MUTUAL SAVINGS BANKS (MSB)

Mutual savings banks (MSBs) are depository institutions that were originally developed to meet the financial needs of blue-collar workers. Unlike the other types of institutions reviewed in this chapter, which are located in every state, MSBs operate in only seventeen states, most in New England and the Middle Atlantic States. From the mortgage borrower's viewpoint, the difference between an MSB and a savings and loan association is insignificant. MSBs also offer a full spectrum of mortgage loans, including FHA and VA loans. MSBs may write insured conventional loans with a maximum loan-to-value ratio of 95 percent and maximum amortization period of thirty years. They may write uninsured conventional loans with a loan-to-value ratio up to 80 and, in some states, 90 percent.

CREDIT UNIONS

Like other depository financial institutions, a credit union can be chartered at either the state or federal level, but credit unions are unique in a couple of respects. One distinction is that credit unions are the only privately owned mortgage originators that are not subject to income taxes. Congress granted this exception to encourage the growth of credit unions. Without the burden of income taxes, credit unions should be able to offer higher interest rates on deposits, and lower rates on loans. With the deregulation that has occurred in the financial industry in recent years, however, Congress has considered subjecting credit unions to the same tax rules as other financial institutions.

A second difference between credit unions and other mortgage originators is that credit unions do not make loans or accept deposits from the general public. Membership in the credit union is a prerequisite for obtaining a loan from a credit union. To qualify as a member of a credit union one must meet the common bond requirement specified in the credit union's charter. Common bond requirements are based on some factor that the members have in common, such as employment. For example, the largest credit union is the United States Navy Credit Union, where membership is limited to current and former members of the United States Navy and their families.

Historically, credit unions specialized in making consumer loans. Legislation dating from 1977, however, has allowed federally chartered credit unions to expand their operations into a number of new areas including real estate loans. In recent years, credit unions have substantially increased their participation in real estate lending. Credit unions make first and second home mortgage loans and home equity loans. Most credit unions are prohibited from offering mortgage loans on commercial properties.

LIFE INSURANCE COMPANIES

Life insurance companies are primarily involved in writing insurance policies (contracts) which entitle them to receive periodic premiums (payments) from the insured party in exchange for the company's promise to pay a third party (beneficiary) a certain amount should the insured die while the policy is in force. The company invests the premiums to help accumulate the amount needed for future payoffs and to generate a profit. Compared to the other institutions reviewed in this chapter, life insurance companies are particularly well suited to invest in mortgage loans due to the long-term nature of their policy obligations, the cash requirements of which can be fairly accurately predicted by actuaries. Life insurance companies can select mortgages with appropriate terms to match their investment requirements.

Life insurance companies prefer to invest in large-scale projects such as multifamily dwellings and commercial properties, and most do not originate single-family home mortgages. Instead, they underwrite mortgages originated by a mortgage banker or mortgage broker. Life insurance companies have been subject to fewer regulatory restrictions concerning permissible investments compared with depository institutions, and they tend to shift among different types of investments to secure the highest return possible. During periods of tight money, life insurance companies tend to move away from mortgages to investments with a higher yield.

MORTGAGE COMPANIES

A mortgage company is a business firm that originates mortgages that are usually quickly sold to other parties. Many mortgage companies are subsidiaries of commercial banks or bank holding companies, although some are independent organizations. Mortgage companies can operate in one of two ways, either as a mortgage banker or as a mortgage broker. Both **mortgage bankers** and **mortgage brokers** originate loans that are placed with an investor. The investor pays for this service with a **loan origination fee,** which is typically 1 percent of the loan amount. There are, however, two differences between a mortgage banker and a mortgage broker. First, a mortgage bank may elect to hold some mortgages in its own portfolio. Second, mortgage bankers, unlike mortgage brokers, for an additional **servicing fee** (typically three-eighths of 1 percent of the outstanding loan balance), will continue to service the loan (collect payments, pay property taxes and insurance premiums, and attend to delinquencies) after origination.

For loans to be held in their own portfolio, some mortgage banks supply permanent long-term financing, but most specialize in short-term and interim financing, using either their own funds or by borrowing from commercial sources. Mortgage banks are a major source of construction loans, and are active in lending money on commercial properties such as office buildings and shopping centers. They also specialize in originating FHA and VA loans in areas where mortgage money is scarce. Mortgage banks sell these mortgages to financial institutions in other areas where loanable funds are available. In this respect, mortgage bankers help correct imbalances in regional mortgage demand by providing a mechanism to move funds from surplus to deficit areas.

From the perspective of their correspondents, mortgage companies serve another important function. Because the quality of individual real properties tends to vary greatly, knowledge of local markets is essential to properly assess the risk factors in mortgage loans. Large financial institutions, such as life insurance companies that wish to diversify their portfolios over a wide geographic area, are unlikely to have the knowledge possessed by a local mortgage company.

FINANCE COMPANIES

Finance companies raise money to make loans by selling securities and borrowing from commercial banks. They are organized either as a division of a corporation (such as General Motors Acceptance Corporation, which is a finance company subsidiary of General Motors) or as a private company. Historically, finance companies have been involved in both commercial and consumer lending. In recent years, however, finance companies have begun to originate second mortgage loans because they face less regulation in this area compared with consumer loans.

PENSION FUNDS

A pension fund is an organization that acts in a fiduciary capacity. Pension funds collect contributions from workers, invest these contributions, and make payments to qualified retirees. Pension funds have predictable cash needs, therefore, investment in both mortgages and mortgage-related securities are excellent investment choices for them. Historically, however, pension funds have concentrated their investments in corporate and government securities with little investment being applied to finance real estate.

With assets of more than 1 billion dollars, some view pension funds as having the potential to become a significant source of mortgage funds. However, some pension fund managers avoid mortgage-related securities because they are concerned about prepayments on the underlying mortgages. Prepayments make the cash flows of mortgage-related securities less predictable, and borrowers tend to prepay when it is least desirable for investors—when interest rates are low. Collateralized mortgage obligations, described later in this chapter, offer investors some protection against prepayments.

REAL ESTATE INVESTMENT TRUSTS (REITS)

Real estate investment trusts (REITs) were described in some detail in Chapter 5. Not all REITs originate mortgages and those that do specialize in large commercial transactions. Most REITs invest in home mortgages indirectly, by investing in mortgage-related securities in the secondary mortgage market.

Decision Point

Your church is considering a major building project and, being aware of your training in real estate, the Board of Trustees has asked you to assist in obtaining a mortgage loan. What type of lenders would you recommend that they approach? Can you suggest why one particular type of lender may have added incentive to provide such a loan?

LOAN REPAYMENT PLANS

The terms of a mortgage loan are often of critical importance in making decisions that concern the acquisition, or refinancing, of real property. Different loan types (e.g., conventional, FHA, VA) require different down payments (Chapter 15) that can affect the quantity of real property one can afford. The terms of repayment are just as critical to the decision-making process because they affect the size of the individual payments, and the total amount of interest the borrower must pay. The mathematics involved in such calculations is the subject of the next chapter. At this point, our objective is to introduce you to the available payment patterns. Several mortgage loans offer the borrower the opportunity to lower the monthly payment, at least during the early stages of the loan.

AMORTIZED LOAN

An **amortized loan** is one characterized by periodic payments that consist of both principal and interest. Today most mortgage loans are fully amortized. With a fully amortized loan, when the last payment is made the principal is paid in full. Further, with the traditional fixed-rate, fully amortized mortgage, the periodic payment remains constant over the life of the loan, but the portion of each payment representing interest and the portion representing repayment of principal change over time. Early payments consist largely of interest while later payments consist largely of principal repayment. In general, the periodic payment on an amortized loan could be set at any interval, but monthly payments are common for most types of real estate loans.

Occasionally a loan will be amortized so that the last payment must be substantially larger than the previous ones in order to pay off the principal. Such a loan is known as a partially amortized loan, or as a balloon loan, and the last payment is called a balloon payment. From the borrower's perspective, the advantage of a balloon loan compared to a fully amortized loan is a lower (except for the last) payment; the disadvantage is that the borrower must somehow come up with the large balloon payment. One of the attractions for borrowers of the fully amortized, fixed-interest-rate mortgage is that the mortgage payment pattern is constant. This type of lending arrangement does not, however, fully meet all borrowers' needs and has resulted in financial difficulties for some lenders.

ALTERNATIVE PAYMENT PATTERNS

Mortgage originators operated profitably for several decades writing the long-term, fully amortized, fixed-rate mortgage introduced by the FHA. High and volatile interest rates in the late 1970s, however, reduced the profitability of such loans. Most depository financial institutions fund long-term mortgages with short-term money, and they will incur losses if they pay higher rates on their short-term funds than they are earning on their long-term mortgage commitments. Mortgage originators incurred losses this way in the late 1970s. As a result, many mortgage originators, in particular S&Ls, failed and many others were brought to the brink of failure. In an attempt to alleviate the problem, the Comptroller of the Currency, the Federal Home Loan Bank Board, and the Federal National Mortgage Association authorized alternative mortgage instruments designed to enable lenders to pass on increases in their cost of funds to borrowers. These include the adjustable rate mortgage and the renegotiable rate mortgage.

Other alternative mortgage instruments are designed to make borrowing more affordable. Increased affordability is accomplished either by requiring (at least initially) lower payments—the graduated payment mortgage, the growing equity mortgage, and the shared appreciation mortgage—or by enabling the borrower to reduce the total amount of interest that must be paid over the life of the loan—the fast-pay mortgage. Still other mortgage instruments offer the borrower greater financial flexibility, including the wrap-around mortgage (Chapter 15) and the reverse annuity mortgage.

Adjustable Rate Mortgage (ARM)

The **adjustable rate mortgage (ARM),** which enables the lender to periodically adjust the interest rate on an existing mortgage, is one of the most significant innovations in residential real estate financing. Adjustments to the interest rate are based on changes in an index, specified in the loan agreement, which generally reflects the lender's cost of funds. In this way, lenders are able to transfer some, but not all, interest rate risk to the borrower. Interest rate risk results from the inverse relationship between interest rates and the market value of any fixed-income security (such as a corporate bond or a fixed-rate mortgage loan). If interest rates rise subsequent to the issue of the fixed-income security, its market value will fall.

Less than the full interest rate risk is transferred for several reasons. One is that lenders can adjust the interest rate only at the permitted adjustment time, usually once a year. Therefore, the lender must absorb the cost of rapid increases in interest rates between adjustment dates. A second reason is that adjustments to the mortgage rate must be based on the change in the index to which the mortgage rate is tied. Lenders may select from a number of permissible indices, but if the index chosen increases at a slower rate than the lender's cost of funds, again the lender must absorb the difference. The most popular index that lenders use today is the one-year Treasury Bill rate. Another reason the lender retains some interest rate risk is that almost all ARMs have a self-imposed annual rate cap and a life-of-loan rate cap. An **interest rate cap** places an upper limit on the adjustment that can be made to the mortgage interest rate. If interest rates increase above the cap, again the lender must absorb the loss.

Sometimes, but not often, lenders specify a **payment cap** instead of a rate cap. A payment cap differs from a rate cap in that it specifies the maximum dollar amount by which the monthly payment can be increased. ARMs with payment caps present a special risk to borrowers, **negative amortization,** which occurs when the amount the borrower owes increases, instead of decreases, with each payment. Because the payment cap limits only increases in the amount of the payment and not the rate at which interest is calculated, if interest rates increase enough, the adjustment permitted by the cap may result in a payment too small to cover the interest due. In such cases, the borrower is effectively borrowing the difference between the payment amount and the interest due. This difference is added to the amount the borrower previously owed, thereby increasing the principal.

A number of factors affect the extent to which ARMs are used. Rational borrowers demand compensation, in the form of a lower initial interest rate than is available on a fixed-rate loan, in exchange for assuming some interest rate risk. Therefore, one factor that affects the demand for ARMs is the difference, or spread, between the interest rate being offered on new fixed-rate mortgages and the rate being offered on ARMs. Lenders for income property almost always use ARMs. The demand for ARMs is also affected by other factors, including how long borrowers intend to own the property and their expectations about future interest rate levels. If borrowers perceive that interest rates are likely to increase enough over their intended ownership tenure to make the fixed-rate loan less expensive compared to an ARM, demand for ARMs will decrease. If borrowers do not perceive such a rate increase, demand for ARMs will increase.

Renegotiable Rate Mortgage (RRM)

A **renegotiable rate mortgage** (RRM, pronounced "rim") is similar to the term loans used in mortgage lending in the United States prior to the mid-1930s because the parties must renegotiate the loan on a regular basis. In effect, a RRM amounts to a series of short-term (three- to five-year) loans, but the differences between today's RRMs and the term loans used more than half a century ago include amortized payments and payments based on a long-term (twenty-five or thirty-year) amortization schedule. The interest rate on a RRM is fixed for the short-term, and can only be changed at the renegotiation date. Even at that time, lenders cannot change the rate to any level they choose because, when they originate the loan, the lender must specify an index to which changes in the RRM rate will be tied.

Like ARMs, RRMs were introduced to give mortgage lenders a way to transfer to borrowers some of the interest rate risk associated with fixed-rate mortgage loans. While this type of lending arrangement is popular in some other countries, lenders in the United

AN ETHICAL ISSUE

TRANSFERENCE OF INTEREST RATE

As explained above, adjustable rate mortgages were developed so that lenders could transfer interest rate risk to borrowers. It can be argued that this type of arrangement transfers risk from the party better capable of managing it to one less capable. With the financial acumen that financial institution managers should possess, and with mortgages worth millions of dollars in their portfolios, financial institutions could use relatively sophisticated financial tools such as futures contracts or interest rate swaps to eliminate most of the risk. It does not, however, make good financial sense for most mortgage borrowers to attempt to do the same. Do you think that adjustable rate mortgages represent an ethical solution to the problem of interest rate risk?

States considered the original regulations associated with RRMs too restrictive and, therefore, failed to offer the loan widely. Instead, once the ARM was introduced it became the major alternative to the fixed-rate mortgage.

The RRM is an exception to the other mortgage types reviewed here in that the names of the other mortgages are fairly descriptive of the arrangement entered into by the borrower and lender. The word "renegotiable" is a misnomer because the parties generally do not have equal bargaining power. Few borrowers would define "negotiation" as listening to the lender tell them what rate will be charged on the loan for the next period, as is the usual case. Each time renegotiation takes place, the borrower's options are to accept the terms proposed by the lender, or secure the funds elsewhere and pay off the RRM.

Graduated Payment Mortgage (GPM)

A **graduated payment mortgage (GPM)** loan provides for low initial payments, compared with a constant-payment, fully amortized loan. As the name implies, it provides for regular increases in the payments for several years until a level is reached that will fully amortize the loan over its remaining term. As shown in Exhibit 16.1, payment increases for GPMs, approved by HUD, range from 2.5 to 7.5 percent each year. From the borrower's perspective, a disadvantage of a GPM is negative amortization because with a GPM the early payments are not large enough to cover the interest on the loan.

GPMs were designed for people whose income levels are likely to rise by at least the same rate as the scheduled increases in the mortgage payments. The interest rate on GPMs is usually fixed for the term of the loan, but an adjustable rate can be used. Such a loan is known as a graduated payment adjustable mortgage or GPAM.

Growing Equity Mortgage (GEM)

Growing equity mortgage (GEM) loans are a type of graduated payment mortgage, but unlike a GPM there is no interest deferral or negative amortization with a GEM. Scheduled increases in monthly payments are tied to the borrower's ability to pay, and are applied directly to principal reduction and, therefore, dramatically reduce the total cost of the mortgage by reducing the period of mortgage payoff to approximately one-half the original term. Also, unlike the GPM, increases in GEM payments are not according to a fixed schedule. Instead, payments are adjusted annually to reflect 75 percent of the rate of change in a national index of per capita disposable personal income. GEM loans are most likely to be made to borrowers with rising income expectations.

Shared Appreciation Mortgage (SAM)

A **shared appreciation mortgage (SAM)** loan carries an interest rate that is below the current market rate of interest on a traditional fixed-rate loan. The borrower employing a

EXHIBIT	16.1	**GRADUATED PAYMENT MORTGAGE PLANS**

The Department of Housing and Urban Development and the Federal Housing Administration have developed five basic GPM plans. These plans vary by the number of years over which the payments increase, as well as the rate of payment increases. The longer the time over which payment increases occur or the greater the rate of increase, the lower the mortgage payments are in the early years.

Plan I	Monthly payments increase 2.5 percent each year for five years
Plan II	Monthly payments increase 5 percent each year for five years
Plan III	Monthly payments increase 7.5 percent each year for five years
Plan IV	Monthly payments increase 2 percent each year for ten years
Plan V	Monthly payments increase 3 percent each year for ten years

SAM may, therefore, be able to afford a more expensive property, or finance a larger share of the property than he or she could with a traditional loan. Lenders are willing to write SAMs because the borrower agrees to share any increase in value of the subject property with the lender. For example, if the conventional loan rate is 10 percent, a lender may be willing to write a SAM with a rate of 8 percent, in exchange for 20 percent of the appreciation in the property. However, lenders are not willing to wait forever to capture their share of appreciation, and SAMs usually have shorter maturities than other first mortgage loans.

The standard term to maturity for a SAM is ten years. If the property is sold before the maturity date, the lender can easily determine the increase in value. If the property has not been sold by the maturity date, an appraiser is employed to value the property and determine the appreciation in value. For properties not sold before the expiration of the loan, the lender's share of appreciation may be paid in cash by the borrower or the amount may be added to any unpaid principal and refinanced. A standard provision in a SAM is the lender's guarantee to refinance the entire property (including the lender's share of any increase in value) at the interest rate prevailing at the specified future date.

SAMs present unique risk for both the borrower and lender. Borrowers may be unable to afford the payment after the refinancing because a large increase in value may require a much larger loan at a rate higher than could be obtained currently. Lenders must be very selective about the properties financed with SAMs. If a property does not appreciate sufficiently, lenders will lose money compared with writing a traditional mortgage loan.

Reverse Annuity Mortgage (RAM)

The **reverse annuity mortgage (RAM)** was designed to enable homeowners to convert some of the equity in their homes into cash to meet living expenses. Again, the name is descriptive in that the cash flows associated with a RAM are the reverse of those associated with other mortgage types. Under this type of loan agreement, the borrower continues to live in the property and receives a one-time, lump-sum payment, or more likely, a series of annuity payments. The amount borrowed plus interest is repayable upon the occurrence of a specific event—the death of the borrower, the sale of the property, or another specified date. The interest rate on a RAM can be fixed or adjustable.

Most mortgage originators do not offer RAMs, but they are available from both public and private sector lenders. In many areas, government agencies have sponsored RAM loan programs for medium- and low-income homeowners. Some local governments have made them available to cover the cost of home improvement or repairs. Many states (California, Colorado, Connecticut, Florida, Georgia, Illinois, Massachusetts, Maine, New Hampshire, Oregon, Texas, Utah, Virginia, Washington, and Wisconsin) have RAM programs to assist owners in the payment of property taxes. Private sector lenders write three basic types of RAMs: uninsured, lender-insured, and FHA-insured. The cash advances from all RAMs originated in the private sector may be used for any purpose and there are no upper-bound borrower income restrictions. Uninsured RAMs provide the borrower with monthly cash advances, and the loan must be paid in full when it matures. The maximum maturity on these loans is ten years.

Many elderly people who might benefit from the funds provided by a RAM have not accepted this type of mortgage; they resist mortgaging property for which they spent years paying. Some elderly also fear that they might outlive the RAM term and become a burden on their family. Lender-insured and FHA-insured RAMs may have more appeal for elderly borrowers. With a lender-insured RAM, cash advances continue for as long as the borrower lives in the property, and no repayment is required until the borrower sells the property, permanently moves out, or dies. Cash advances on FHA-insured RAMs may be structured over a specific term, or for as long as the borrower lives in the home. In either case, no repayment is required as long as the borrower resides in the property.

Fast-Pay Mortgage

The fast-pay mortgage, sometimes called an accelerated payment mortgage (APM), enables a borrower to payoff the loan principal more quickly than the traditional thirty-year mortgage. Several types of fast-pay mortgages are available; the most popular of which are the biweekly payment mortgage (BPM), and the fifteen-year mortgage. With a BPM, the borrower makes payments every two weeks, or twenty-six payments a year. The biweekly payment amount is equal to fifty percent of what the monthly payment would be; the twenty-six biweekly payments are the equivalent of thirteen monthly payments per year. Therefore, a larger percentage of each BPM payment is credited to principal reduction. As a result, the BPM is paid off more rapidly, and the total interest cost of the BPM is significantly lower compared with a loan with monthly payments.

The fifteen-year mortgage is gaining wide acceptance. In addition to providing the borrower with more rapid principal reduction, fifteen-year mortgages generally carry an interest rate twenty-five to fifty basis points below that of a thirty-year mortgage. To illustrate the potential savings offered by a fast-pay mortgage, consider a $100,000 loan carrying an 11 percent interest rate. With a thirty-year mortgage the total interest paid over the life of the loan would be $242,835. With a fifteen-year mortgage or a BPM total interest would amount to only $104,588, and $147,603, respectively. For further explanation of such calculations see Chapter 17.

A potential drawback of the APM is higher payments compared with the standard thirty-year, monthly payment loan. Continuing the above example; with a fifteen-year mortgage the monthly payment would be $1,136.60 compared with $952.32 on the thirty-year loan, and the BPM would require an additional payment of $952.32 each year for the life of the loan.

Studies concerning the desirability of fast-pay mortgages have yielded conflicting results. Some suggest that the traditional thirty-year mortgage is the appropriate choice for most homebuyers, while others find the fifteen-year mortgage superior. Perhaps the most important lesson these studies provide is that, in deciding what type of mortgage to select, a borrower must consider several factors, not only the interest rate on the loans, but also the borrower's marginal income tax rate and the rate of interest that could be earned on other investments.

Borrowers can obtain roughly the same benefits of a fast-pay mortgage by making extra payments on a thirty-year mortgage. In fact, if prepayments are allowed without penalty, making one extra payment per year on a thirty-year mortgage will reduce the life of the loan to slightly less than twenty years, and reduce the total interest charge to approximately that of a BPM. If, however, prepayment penalties apply, they may wipe out much of the savings. Borrowers who make prepayments should realize that prepayments cannot be substituted for future scheduled payments. Thus, if a borrower were to have financial difficulties and be unable to meet a scheduled payment, late fees or more serious repercussions will not be avoided as a result of previous extra payments.

THE SECONDARY MORTGAGE MARKET

The development of the secondary mortgage market was an important step in the evolution of real estate finance. The term **secondary mortgage market** is used to describe the trading of mortgages that occurs subsequent to their origination. Like the secondary securities market, the secondary mortgage market provides increased liquidity for investors. In secondary trading of securities, investors do not have to be concerned with quality differences within a single issue; one share of IBM common stock is the same as every other share of IBM common stock, and this is true regardless of the location of the party selling the shares. Unlike corporate securities, however, each mortgage represents a loan made to a borrower with unique household and income characteristics. Without some type of standardization, therefore, parties who consider investing in mortgages may have serious concerns about the safety of the investment and be forced to evaluate each mortgage individually. Many investors may lack the expertise to conduct an adequate examination and others might deem the process too time consuming, so they will channel investment funds into segments of the economy where information costs are lower. Recognizing this problem, Congress has established a number of organizations, including the Federal National Mortgage Association, the Government National Mortgage Association, and the Federal Home Loan Mortgage Corporation, and charged each with fostering the development of a secondary mortgage market.

GOVERNMENT NATIONAL MORTGAGE ASSOCIATION (GNMA)

GNMA, popularly known as Ginnie Mae, was created in 1968 as a division of the United States Department of Housing and Urban Development. Congress charged GNMA with administering various federal mortgage-subsidy programs and facilitating the secondary trading of government-sponsored mortgages. In response to the second charge, GNMA initiated, in 1970, a program designed to create a mortgage-backed investment that could compete with government and corporate securities for investment funds. GNMA pass-through securities have become an important investment vehicle. These securities have provided funds used for financing more than half of all FHA and VA originations. GNMA, however, issues no securities itself; it simply acts as a guarantor for securities issued by others. In exchange for a fee, GNMA guarantees the timely payment of principal and interest to the pass-through investors.

A GNMA pass-through is secured by a pool of FHA, VA, or Farmer's Home Administration mortgages. A **mortgage pool** is created when lenders place mortgages in a pool, or package, and sell securities that represent shares in the pool. In exchange for a service fee, the mortgage originator continues to collect the regular payments, and any prepayments, from the borrowers. These payments are distributed, or passed through, to the investors in the **pass-through security.** Mortgage originators, such as savings and loan associations, and commercial banks, sell GNMA pass-throughs. As shown in Exhibit 16.2, there were over 1 trillion dollars in outstanding GNMA pass-throughs as of year-end 2000.

FEDERAL NATIONAL MORTGAGE ASSOCIATION (FNMA)

The Federal National Mortgage Association (FNMA), popularly known as Fannie Mae, is the oldest organization involved in the secondary mortgage market. It was established as a federal agency in 1938 to purchase FHA loans from mortgage originators. In 1944, VA loans were added to FNMA's purchase program, and in 1972 conventional loans were also added. FNMA was converted into a private corporation in 1968 and its stock is traded on the New York Stock Exchange. FNMA did, however, retain certain ties to the federal government; the President appoints five of its eighteen directors, and it can borrow some of

EXHIBIT	16.2	MORTGAGE POOLS—FOURTH QUARTER 2002 (IN MILLIONS OF DOLLARS)		
	Organization	1-4 Family	Multifamily	Total
	GNMA	$ 589,458	$567,559	$1,157,017
	FNMA	1,238,125	52,226	1,290,351
	FHLMC	940,933	7,476	948,409
	Private Mortgage Conduits	574,500	60,158	634,658

Source: Federal Reserve Bulletin, June 2002, Table A35

the funds used in its operation at the interest rate that usually applies to government agencies. Today, FNMA continues to purchase FHA and VA loans from loan originators, but the majority of its business is in conventional loans. FNMA is a major source of funds for mortgage brokers that hold no assets and must sell their loans quickly to replenish their available cash.

FNMA fulfills its duties by committing funds, at a set interest rate, to lenders who intend to make mortgage loans. These commitments can be made on a firm basis, in which case the lender must exchange the pledged mortgages for the commitment amount, or lenders can use FNMA's optional delivery market, in which case the commitment is advanced and the mortgages delivered to FNMA at the option of the lender. Lenders using the optional market will elect not to deliver if interest rates have moved in their favor before the optional delivery date arrives. Prior to 1981, FNMA pooled acquired mortgages and used them as collateral for GNMA pass-throughs. In 1981, attracted by the success of mortgage-backed securities issued by other organizations, FNMA began to issue its own pass-through security called a mortgage-backed security. These work very much like GNMA pass-throughs with FNMA providing the guarantee of principal and interest payments.

Federal Home Loan Mortgage Corporation (FHLMC)

The Federal Home Loan Mortgage Corporation (FHLMC), popularly known as Freddie Mac, was established in 1970 as a federally chartered corporation charged with the responsibility of purchasing mortgages in the secondary market. The common shares of FHLMC are owned by the Federal Home Loan Bank, and although it may purchase loans from any source, it was primarily designed to meet the needs of savings and loan associations by purchasing existing mortgages from their portfolios. Since 1971, FHLMC has issued its own mortgage-backed security, a mortgage participation certificate. As with other mortgage-backed securities, each investor (certificate holder) has an undivided interest in a pool of residential mortgages. Such an arrangement is not attractive to some investors and FHLMC made a pioneering effort to remedy this problem.

Collateralized Mortgage Obligation (CMO)

In 1983, FHLMC introduced the **collateralized mortgage obligation (CMO),** which is a variation of the mortgage-backed security. The CMO segments the cash flows from the underlying mortgage pool into several classes with different maturities. CMOs were designed to enable investors to select a security with a maturity that closely matches their investment needs, and to attract funds from investors that had not invested in mortgage-backed securities before. For example, money market funds that invest in short-term corporate and government (non-real-estate related) securities may achieve diversification benefits by investing in the shortest maturity class CMO.

BENEFITS OF THE SECONDARY MORTGAGE MARKET

Investors, borrowers, and mortgage originators have all benefited as a result of the development of the secondary mortgage market. The guarantees made by GNMA, FNMA, or FHLMC make mortgages a more attractive investment because the risk of default shifts to the organization making the guarantee. Therefore, investors who did not previously commit funds to mortgages can diversify their portfolios, and others can more easily diversify their mortgage portfolio geographically. The increased investment benefits both lenders and borrowers because more funds are available for additional mortgage loans. GNMA and the others give the "timely payment" guarantee because each mortgage serving as collateral for the pass-through security must meet certain required minimum standards. Because the

DOING BUSINESS

FINANCE

In 1997, Bob and Becky Walker obtained a $100,000 mortgage loan from a savings and loan located twelve miles from their suburban Indianapolis home. Each month the Walkers mail a payment check to the S&L, but upon arrival the payment has just begun its journey. Shortly after the Walkers' loan was written, the local S&L sold it, along with $50 million in other mortgage loans, to Freddie Mac. At Freddie Mac, the Walkers' mortgage became a part of Freddie Mac Pool No. 360018, which includes $443 million of fixed-rate loans from all over the United States. Pool No. 360018 was purchased by First Boston, a bank holding company, which combined it with other mortgages and issued a $550 million CMO. Among others, investors in First Boston's CMO included: an insurance company in Connecticut, S&Ls in Pittsburgh and Florida, and banks in Oklahoma and London. Each month the CMO investors receive a payment from First Boston that includes a portion of the Walkers' mortgage payment.

Go to www.fanniemae.com, click on "Investor Relations" and then select a "Headline" to learn about recent events in the secondary mortgage market.

---

issuance of pass-throughs enables lenders to transfer interest rate risk to investors willing to accept it, lenders are generally careful to write mortgages that conform to GNMA standards. Therefore, mortgage loan procedures have become more standardized. Borrowers benefit in that lenders may also be able to make mortgage loans at lower rates because the increased liquidity the market provides reduces the originator's risk. Finally, the development of the secondary mortgage market is credited with facilitating the interregional flow of funds, which in turn reduces regional interest rate differentials.

SUMMARY

Borrowed funds are used in most real property acquisitions and, from the borrower's perspective, the decision regarding the particular type of financing to be used may be just as important as the selection of the property to be purchased. Knowledge of the various sources of mortgage funds and alternative loan arrangements will help ensure that you secure funds at the most advantageous terms available. In addition, you can expedite the acquisition process by knowing the right institutions to approach for the type of loan that you desire. Many, but not all, credit unions originate a variety of residential mortgage loans, but none write commercial mortgage loans. Savings and loan associations, mutual savings banks, mortgage companies, and commercial banks all originate both commercial mortgage loans and mortgage loans to finance home purchases. Life insurance companies, real estate investment trusts, and pension funds tend to specialize in large commercial loans, but may, and infrequently do, originate home loans.

You can select from a variety of mortgage loans to finance the purchase of real property. Some mortgages, including the adjustable rate, the graduated payment, the shared appreciation, and the renegotiable rate, allow for (at least initially) lower payments compared with the traditional thirty-year, fixed-rate, fully amortized loan. Each type of mortgage presents the borrower with certain risks that must be factored into the decision process. Other types of mortgages have been designed to meet the needs of borrowers in nonpurchase situations. The reverse annuity mortgage enables real property owners to convert the equity in their real property into cash.

Claims on existing mortgages are traded in the secondary mortgage market. This market is particularly important because it channels money into the primary mortgage market, therefore, enabling the origination of additional mortgage loans. Lenders, investors, and borrowers all benefit from the operation of the secondary mortgage market.

KEY TERMS

adjustable rate mortgage
amortized loan
collateralized mortgage
   obligation
fast-pay mortgage
graduated payment mort-
   gage
growing equity mortgage
interest rate cap

interim financing
loan origination fee
loan-to-value ratio
mortgage banker
mortgage broker
mortgage pool
negative amortization
pass-through security
payment cap

primary mortgage market
renegotiable rate mortgage
reverse annuity mortgage
secondary mortgage market
servicing fee
shared appreciation mort-
   gage
takeout loan

REVIEW QUESTIONS

1. What factors would you consider in selecting a mortgage lender?

2. What factors would you consider in choosing among the various types of mortgages?

3. Why do people borrow money to purchase real property?

4. What type of mortgages were designed to enable lenders to pass on increases in their cost of funds to borrowers?

5. What type of mortgages were designed to make mortgages more affordable?

6. What type of mortgages provide the borrower greater financial flexibility?

7. What is negative amortization? On what types of loans is negative amortization possible?

8. Why are mortgage loans better suited for the portfolio of a pension fund or a life insurance company than for the portfolio of a commercial bank? If this is so, why do commercial banks originate more mortgage loans than the other two?

9. How are credit unions different than other mortgage originators?

10. What is the difference between a mortgage broker and a mortgage banker?

11. What is the difference between a payment cap and an interest rate cap?

12. Why do you think lenders self-impose rate caps on ARMs?

13. What are the advantages and disadvantages of a fast-pay mortgage from the perspective of the borrower?

14. How does the operation of the GNMA differ from that of the FNMA and the FHLMC?

15. What are the benefits of the secondary mortgage market?

16. What is your answer to the questions in the "Decision Point" section in this Chapter?

17. What is your answer to the questions in the "Ethical Issue" in this chapter?

REAL ESTATE ON THE WEB

Use your favorite search engine to:

1. Determine the types (e.g., ARMs, GPMs) of mortgage loans being offered by financial institutions in your area.

2. Learn what interest rates are being charged on mortgage loans today, and whether the rate is affected by the term of the loan, and/or the type of loan.

3. Find a lender that is currently originating a reverse annuity mortgage.

4. Discover companies providing Web-based data services to mortgage originators.

Refer to the companion Web site at www.wiley.com/college/larsen for a variety of online activities including additional chapter content, review materials, assignments, and related links.

ADDITIONAL READINGS

Avery, E. I., R. W. Bostic, P. S. Calem and G. B. Canner. "Credit Scoring: Statistical Issues and Evidence from Credit Bureau Files." Real Estate Economics (Fall 2000): 523–547.

Calderon, Jeanne A. "Mezzanine Financing and Land Banks: Two Unconventional Methods of Financing Residential Real Estate Projects in the 21st Century." *Real Estate Law Journal* (Spring 2001): 283–298.

Joshua, B. and K. Rhoda. "Mortgage Web Sites: Presenting Loan Information." *Real Estate Finance* (Winter 2001): 46–51.

LaCour-Little, M. "A Note on Identification in Mortgage Lending." *Real Estate Economics* (Summer 2001): 329–335.

Sprecher, C. R. and E. Willman. "The Role of the Initial Discount in the Pricing of Adjustable-Rate Mortgages." *Journal of Housing Economics* (March/June 2000): 64–75.

17

Mortgage Calculations

Learning Objectives

After studying this chapter you should be able to:

- Explain the concept of the time value of money.
- Calculate a loan payment amount.
- Formulate an amortization schedule.
- Calculate an outstanding loan balance.
- Evaluate alternative new loans and refinancing possibilities

FROM THE WIRE

In 2001, potential and current homeowners took advantage of low interest rates searching the real estate market for new purchases or refinancing options. In that year, Americans refinanced $1.2 trillion in mortgages. By refinancing, the average American reduced his or her monthly mortgage payment by $180, or took $23,000 in a lump sum from the cash-out option. To illustrate these savings for a hypothetical individual, consider a person who refinanced a $150,000 mortgage. Assume the originally loan carried an interest rate of 8.5 percent, requiring a payment of $1,150 per month. After refinancing at a rate of 6.75 percent, the monthly payment drops to $973, saving the borrower $177 per month, or approximately $2,100 per year.

But all is not rosy. As the refinancing activity of homeowners continued in this country during 2002, home foreclosures were on a steady increase. According to Lois

Maljak, a foreclosure specialist at Home Savers, Inc in Warren, Michigan: "Over the past ten years, the foreclosure rate in America has reached epidemic proportions, and today 4 percent of all homes in America are currently either in foreclosure or threatened by foreclosure because owners are 60 days or more behind in their mortgage payment." In addition, Maljak observes that 10 to 15 percent of homeowners nationwide are barely able to make their monthly payments as they struggle to make ends meet through credit cards and loans and, in turn, set themselves up as a prime candidate for foreclosure.

Go to www.bankrate.com, click "calculators," then click "Should You Refinance Your Mortgage" and enter values to analyze a hypothetical mortgage refinance.

INTRODUCTION

While the legal and technical differences between the various mortgages presented in the two preceding chapters are important, a key question for many borrowers concerns the periodic payment amount. The size of the payment is important to the borrower because it affects the affordability of the purchase. The payment amount is influenced by a combination of several factors: the loan amount, the interest rate, and the frequency and number of payments. When borrowers shop for mortgage funds they are often faced with an array of loans, each with a unique set of these factors. Good decision making, however, requires a comparison of not only payment amounts, but also the effective interest rate of each loan alternative. The information presented in this chapter will enable you to calculate both the periodic payment and the effective cost of a mortgage loan.

The same tools used to calculate mortgage payments provide a systematic means to evaluate a variety of problems that confront various participants in the real estate market. Appraisers use these tools to estimate property value. Lenders use similar calculations to determine the annual percentage rate (APR) that they must disclose to borrowers. Real property investors and consumers also use these tools to evaluate the feasibility of assuming a mortgage loan. As the chapter opener "From the Wire" suggests, individuals can also use these tools to evaluate refinancing alternatives that they may undertake to obtain a lower interest rate or to convert some of the equity in a property into cash. Finally, real estate brokers need to be familiar with the tools presented in this chapter in order to assist their clients. The calculations needed to solve problems like these are based on the principle of the time value of money, and are not used exclusively in real estate finance. In fact, these calculations are sometimes referred to as the "math of finance." We begin with a review of the time value of money.

TIME VALUE OF MONEY

The economic principle known as the time value of money holds that a dollar received today has greater worth than a dollar to be received in the future. There are several reasons for the validity of this principle. First, a dollar in your possession is certain, while there is some risk that you may not receive the future dollar. The fact that you can spend the dollar in your possession today also gives it value compared with the dollar to be received at a later date because inflation may erode the purchasing power of the future dollar. Finally, those with a dollar today have the option to invest (rather than spend) the funds and earn a return so that they will have more than a dollar at some future date.

SIMPLE VS. COMPOUND INTEREST

Interest on a deposit or loan may be calculated based on either the simple interest method or the compound interest method. The terms "simple" and "compound" are fairly descriptive. With **simple interest** only the original principal earns interest. With **compound interest,** interest is earned on both the original principal and on accrued interest. To illustrate the difference, consider the two $1,000 deposits in Exhibit 17.1. One is made to an account that pays 10 percent simple interest, the other to an account that pays 10 percent interest compounded annually. After the first year, each account has a balance of $1,100. But, in all subsequent years, the year-end balance of the account earning compound interest exceeds the balance of the account drawing simple interest. Today, virtually all interest computations are made on a compound interest basis, and all of the time value of money factors presented in this chapter are based on compound interest.

Decision Point

If you have $10,000 to invest for three years, would you prefer that it earn 10 percent interest compounded annually or 11 percent simple interest? If you had a different investment horizon, would this affect your answer?

TIME VALUE OF MONEY FACTORS

The relationship between interest rates and time is captured in the formulas presented in Exhibit 17.2. Given the needed information (e.g., interest rate and time), each formula can be solved, resulting in a time value of money factor (also known as an interest factor). As shown in the remainder of this chapter, many problems can be solved using one, or more, of these factors. Examination of Exhibit 17.2 reveals that there are four basic formulas that yield, respectively:

1. The future value interest factor of a single amount (FV$)
2. The present value interest factor of a single amount (PV$)

EXHIBIT 17.1	SIMPLE VS. COMPOUND INTEREST			
Time	Account Balance	10 Percent Simple Interest	Account Balance	10 Percent Annual Compound Interest
0	$1,000		$1,000	
1	1,100	(1,000 + 1,000 • .10)	1,100	(1,000 + 1,000 • .10)
2	1,200	(1,100 + 1,000 • .10)	1,210	(1,100 + 1,100 • .10)
3	1,300	(1,200 + 1,000 • .10)	1,331	(1,210 + 1,210 • .10)
4	1,400	(1,300 + 1,000 • .10)	1,464	(1,331 + 1,331 • .10)

| EXHIBIT | 17.2 | **TIME VALUE FACTORS** |

Operation (symbol)	Annual Compounding Factor	Multi-year Compounding Factor
Future Value Interest Factor of a Single Amount (FV$)	$(1 + i)^n$	$(1 + i/m)^{nm}$
Present Value Interest Factor of a Single Amount (PV$)	$1/(1 + i)^n$	$1/(1 + i/m)^{nm}$
Future Value Interest Factor of an Annuity (FVA)	$\dfrac{(1 + i)^n - 1}{i}$	$\dfrac{(1 + [i/m])^{nm} - 1}{i/m}$
Present Value Interest Factor of an Annuity (PVA)	$\dfrac{1 - [1/(1 + i)^n]}{i}$	$\dfrac{1 - [1/(1 + i/m)^{nm}]}{i/m}$

Where: i = interest rate, n = number of years, and m = the number of payments per year

3. The future value interest factor of an annuity (FVA)
4. The present value interest factor of an annuity (PVA)

A **future value,** sometimes called a compound value, is the value of a sum after investing it over one or more time periods. Study of the formulas in Exhibit 17.2 reveals that the formula for the **present value** of a single amount and the present value of an annuity are the reciprocal, or inverse, of the corresponding future value formula. The inverse relationship implies that in a present value calculation we simply reverse the compounding process used in future value calculations. The reverse process is called discounting. Therefore, a present value is the value of a future sum discounted at the appropriate interest rate **(discount rate).** When any positive rate of interest applies, the future value of a given amount will be larger, and the present value smaller, than the given amount. An **annuity** describes a series of equal cash flows paid, or received, over uniform time periods. One example of an annuity is the payments on a traditional fixed interest rate mortgage.

MULTI-YEAR COMPOUNDING

The value of a particular interest factor depends, in part, upon the frequency of compounding. The middle column of Exhibit 17.2 shows the formulas used in problems where interest is compounded annually. It is not uncommon, however, especially in real estate, to have situations where interest is compounded more frequently than once each year. In mortgage lending, for example, compounding usually occurs monthly.

The right-hand column of Exhibit 17.2 indicates the time value of money formulas adjusted to account for cases where interest is compounded more (or less) frequently than annually (e.g., semi-annually, quarterly, or monthly). Note that only two adjustments must be made to the formulas. Specifically, anytime an interest rate (i) appears in a formula it must be divided by the number of compounding (or discounting) periods per year (m), and anytime the number of years (n) appears in a formula, it must be multiplied by "m."

To demonstrate the effect of multi-year compounding let us continue the example in Exhibit 17.1 and assume that a third account pays 10 percent interest compounded quarterly. As the following calculations show, under this assumption, there would be $1,103.81 in the account at the end of the first year, and after four years the account would have a balance of $1,484.51.

Using Interest Factors	Or Using a Financial Calculator with $\boxed{\text{P/YR}}$ set at 4	
FV = PV • (FV$: 10%, 1n, 4m)	1000	$\boxed{\text{PV}}$
$\quad$ = \$1,000 • $(1 + .10/4)^{1 \cdot 4}$	0	$\boxed{\text{PMT}}$
$\quad$ = \$1,000 • 1.10381	10	$\boxed{\text{I/YR}}$
$\quad$ = \$1,103.81	4	$\boxed{\text{N}}$
	$\boxed{\text{FV}}$	(and calculator displays)
		1,103.81
FV = PV • (FV$: 10%, 4n, 4m)	1000	$\boxed{\text{PV}}$
$\quad$ = \$1,000 • $(1 + .10/4)^{4 \cdot 4}$	0	$\boxed{\text{PMT}}$
$\quad$ = \$1,000 • 1.48451	10	$\boxed{\text{I/YR}}$
$\quad$ = \$1,484.51	16	$\boxed{\text{N}}$
	$\boxed{\text{FV}}$	(and calculator displays)
		1,484.51

Comparison of these amounts with those shown in Exhibit 17.1 demonstrates that, other things constant, the greater the frequency of compounding, the greater the future value. Further, notice that by using "n = 4" in calculating the future value factor (N = 16 in the calculator solution), it was unnecessary to calculate the year-end account balance for either year two or three in order to calculate the account balance for year-end four.

SOLUTION ALTERNATIVES: FORMULAS, TABLES, CALCULATORS, COMPUTERS

Determining the value of any of the formulas shown in Exhibit 17.2 is not difficult mathematically, but the calculations can be time-consuming. Tables of interest factors (assuming annual and monthly compounding for selected time periods and interest rates) are shown in the appendix at the end of the text. These can be used to speed many of the calculations you may need to perform. Knowledge of the basic formulas is still important, however, because the tables shown in the appendix do not include all possible combinations of interest rates, compounding assumptions, and amortization periods. For example, the tables in the appendix would be of no value for a problem involving an interest rate of 8.875 percent and/or a time period of 4.75 years.

One can make time value of money calculations rapidly with a calculator (as in the above example) or a computer. Relatively inexpensive calculators, preprogrammed to solve many types of time value problems, are available, and more expensive calculators, or computers, may be programmed to solve complicated problems. In this chapter, we solve most problems two ways. We use time value of money factors. This should facilitate your understanding of the relationship between the variables in these types of problems. We also show the calculator entries needed to solve each problem. It is important to note that you may arrive at slightly different solutions (due to a rounding error) to a particular problem by using the formulas, tables, or a calculator.

CALCULATING THE FUTURE VALUE OF A SINGLE AMOUNT

The examples in the preceding sections involved the determination of the value to which a known amount would grow over a particular time at a given rate of interest. In essence, this determination requires calculation of the future value. More specifically, because the amounts used in the examples were not an annuity, we calculated the future value of a single amount, multiplying the known amount by the appropriate future value interest factor.

RELATIONSHIP OF TIME, INTEREST RATE, AND COMPOUNDING FREQUENCY TO FUTURE VALUE

The variables involved in a future value calculation (of a single amount or an annuity) are related to the future value in a particular manner. There is a positive relationship between the number of compounding periods per year and the future value, as already demonstrated. The future value is also positively related to the size of the given amount(s), and the interest rate. To demonstrate these relationships, consider the following example.

Two investors, Able and Baker, are contemplating the purchase of some undeveloped land. Being cautious, and unfamiliar with the market, they decide to study it for two years before making a purchase. Both agree to deposit $10,000 into a savings account that pays 12 percent interest compounded annually. Able deposits $10,000 today, while Baker deposits $4,000 now and deposits another $6,000 one year from now. In two years, how much will each have available in the account? The solution is straightforward.

The future value (FV) of Able's account is calculated by multiplying the deposit (D_0) by the appropriate future value interest factor of a single amount (FV$), or:

	Or Using a Financial Calculator with
Using Interest Factors	**P/YR** set at 1

$FV = D_0 \cdot (FV\$: 12\%, 2n, 1m)$ 10,000   PV

$\quad = \$10,000 \cdot (1 + .12)^2$ 0   PMT

$\quad = \$10,000 \cdot 1.2544$ 12   I/YR

$\quad = \$12,544$ 2   N

                                                FV   (and calculator displays)

                                                   12,544

To determine the future value of Baker's account an additional calculation is required because of the deposit at time 1.

	Or Using a Financial Calculator with
Using Interest Factors	**P/YR** set at 1

$FV = D_0 \cdot (FV\$: 12\%, 2n, 1m) + D_1 \cdot (FV\$: 12\%, 1n, 1m)$ 4,000   PV

$\quad = \$4,000 \cdot (1 + .12)^2 + \$6,000 \cdot (1 + .12)$ 6,000   PMT

$\quad = \$4,000 \cdot 1.2544 + \$6,000 \cdot 1.12$ 12   I/YR

$\quad = \$11,737.60$ 2   N

                                                  FV   (and calculator displays)

                                                  17,737.60

                                               −   6,000 (because the payment really is only made once)

                                               (and calculator displays)

                                               11,737.60

The timeline for the Able/Baker future value problem is as follows:

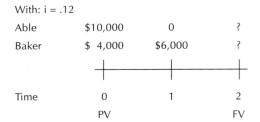

With: i = .12

Able	$10,000	0	?
Baker	$ 4,000	$6,000	?

Time   0   1   2

PV   FV

In two years, Able will have $12,544 and Baker $11,737.60. While both deposited $10,000, only Able had the full $10,000 earning interest for a full two years. This example further illustrates how the future value is positively related to the given amount. Finally, using this example, you can easily prove the positive relationship between future values and interest rates. Just consider what the future value of each investor's account would be if the deposits earned no interest (i.e., if i = 0).

Decision Point

You are saving money for a down payment on a home that you hope to purchase in six years. You will need $10,000 at that time. If you can earn 12 percent on your savings compounded quarterly, and have $5,500 now, will you meet your savings goal? What if you only have $4,000 now?

CALCULATING THE PRESENT VALUE OF A SINGLE AMOUNT

Suppose a real property owner knows that the next property tax payment of $1,100 is due one year from today and wishes to make a deposit so that amount will be available when due. If the owner can earn 10 percent interest compounded annually, how much must be deposited today?

In this case, we know the future value, $1,100; the interest rate, 10 percent; and the time period, one year. To solve for the present value (PV), we simply multiply the future value (FV) by the appropriate present value interest factor for a single amount (PV$):

Using Interest Factors	**Or Using a Financial Calculator with** $\boxed{\text{P/YR}}$ **set at 1**

PV = FV • (PV$: 10%, 1n, 1m)	1,100 $\boxed{\text{FV}}$
= $1,100 • (1/(1 + .10)^1)	0 $\boxed{\text{PMT}}$
= $1,100 • .90909	10 $\boxed{\text{I/YR}}$
= $1,000	1 $\boxed{\text{N}}$
	$\boxed{\text{PV}}$ (and calculator displays)
	1,000.00

RELATIONSHIP OF TIME, INTEREST RATE, AND COMPOUNDING FREQUENCY TO PRESENT VALUE

Recall that the present value formula is the inverse of the future value formula. Therefore, the relationship of the present value (of a single amount or an annuity) to the variables (time, interest rate, and the frequency at which interest is compounded) is the opposite of the variables' relationship to the future value. In essence, the variables are all negatively related to the present value. To demonstrate this, consider how much the property owner would have to deposit into an account to pay the property tax in one year under the following three independent variations of the above example.

1. The deposit earns 10 percent interest compounded quarterly, instead of annually:

Using Interest Factors	**Or Using a Financial Calculator with** P/YR **set at 4**	
PV = FV • (PV$: 10%, 1n, 4m)	1,100	FV
= $1,100 • (1/(1 + .10/4)^4)	0	PMT
= $1,100 • .90590	10	I/YR
= $996.55	4	N
	PV	(and calculator displays)
		996.55

2. The deposit earns 15 percent interest compounded annually, instead of 10 percent compounded annually:

Using Interest Factors	**Or Using a Financial Calculator with** P/YR **set at 1**	
PV = FV • (PV$: 15%, 1n, 1m)	1,100	FV
= $1,100 • (1/(1 + .15)^1)	0	PMT
= $1,100 • .86957	15	I/YR
= $956.53	1	N
	PV	(and calculator displays)
		956.52

3. The deposit earns the same rate of interest and compounded annually, as in the original example, but the tax is not due for two years:

Using Interest Factors	**Or Using a Financial Calculator with** P/YR **set at 1**	
PV = FV • (PV$: 10%, 2n, 1m)	1,100	FV
= $1,100 • (1/(1 + .10)^2)	0	PMT
= $1,100 • .82645	10	I/YR
= $909.10	2	N
	PV	(and calculator displays)
		909.09

CALCULATING THE FUTURE VALUE OF AN ANNUITY

Consider a self-employed real estate agent who wishes to provide for her retirement. She plans to deposit $2,000 into an Individual Retirement Account (IRA) one year from today and to make an identical deposit on this date each year for the next nineteen years ($40,000 from a total of 20 deposits). Assuming the account earns a return of 12 percent compounded annually, how much will be in the IRA after twenty years?

To determine the future value of an annuity one could multiply each cash flow by the appropriate future value interest factor of a single amount, and then sum the twenty products. When numerous payments are involved, however, this can be quite cumbersome. The calculation is simplified by multiplying the annuity amount by the appropriate future value of an annuity factor. For this case, the answer is easily determined to be $144,104.88 by multiplying the annuity payment (ANN) by the appropriate future value interest factor of an annuity (FVA), or:

Using Interest Factors	Or Using a Financial Calculator with P/YR set at 1	
$FV = ANN \bullet (FVA: 12\%, 20n, 1m)$	2,000	PMT
$= \$2,000 \bullet ((1 + .12)^{20} - 1)/.12$	0	PV
$= \$2,000 \bullet 72.05244$	12	I/YR
$= \$144,104.88$	20	N
	FV	(and calculator displays)
		144,104.88

CALCULATING THE PRESENT VALUE OF AN ANNUITY

A prospective buyer offers a landowner a series of fifteen annual $5,000 payments ($75,000 in total). According to the buyer's offer the first payment will be made one year from today and subsequent payments at the end of each of the next fourteen years. The owner would prefer a one-time, up-front payment. What amount should the owner suggest?

Present value calculations can also be cumbersome when many cash flows are involved, but when the cash flows resemble an annuity the determination of their present value is simplified by multiplying the annuity amount by the appropriate present value interest factor. To answer the above question the owner must select an interest rate with which to discount the installments. Assuming the owner can earn an 11 percent annual return on similar risk investments, she would be equally well off by accepting $35,954.35 now.

Using Interest Factors	Or Using a Financial Calculator with P/YR set at 1	
$PV = ANN \bullet (PVA: 11\%, 15n, 1m)$	5,000	PMT
$= \$5,000 \bullet 1 - (1/(1 + .11)^{15})/.11$	0	FV
$= \$5,000 \bullet 7.19087$	11	I/YR
$= \$35,954.35$	15	N
	PV	(and calculator displays)
		35,954.35

Decision Point

Assuming that the buyer in the previous example has the necessary funds now, would it be in the buyer's best interest to pay $35,954.35 now if the buyer has the opportunity to earn 10 percent interest compounded annually somewhere else? What if the buyer's opportunity interest rate were 12 percent?

OTHER APPLICATIONS OF INTEREST RATE FACTORS

As previously explained, time value of money problems involve several variables, and as long as all but one is known, one can calculate the value of the unknown variable using a financial calculator, or interest factors. In the preceding examples, we solved problems to determine present and future values. In this section we show how to determine unknown time periods and interest rates.

Suppose you are offered the choice of receiving $3,169.87 now, or $1,000 at the end of each of the next four years, which should you choose? To arrive at a solution, you must calculate and compare the rate of return implicit in the annuity to the rate of interest you could earn on the funds to be received now (the opportunity rate). To do this, first divide the present value by the annuity, which yields a target factor (TF), then determine the rate of interest implied by the annuity by comparing the target factor to factors in the appropriate time value of money factor table, and, finally, compare the implied rate to the opportunity rate. For this example:

Using Interest Factors	Or Using a Financial Calculator with P/YR set at 1		
TF = PV/ANN	3,169.87	PV	
= $3,169.87/$1,000	1,000	+/–	PMT
= 3.16987	0	FV	
	4	N	
	I/YR	(calculator displays)	
	10.0		

Scanning across the fourth time period line under the present value of an annuity factor column (in the appendix) we find 3.16987 under the 10 percent column. Therefore, the implied interest rate is 10 percent. So, if you can earn 10 percent, you would be indifferent between receiving the lump sum or the annuity (assuming the amounts to be received in the future are risk-free and that you have no pressing need for the cash now). If your opportunity rate is greater than 10 percent, you would prefer the lump sum, and if your opportunity rate is less than 10 percent, you would prefer the annuity.

Suppose, instead, that you know the present value, the interest rate, and the annuity amount, but not how many payments were included in the annuity. The solution to this problem is nearly identical to solving for an unknown interest rate. First, you must calculate the target factor, then compare the target factor to the factors under the applicable interest rate in the appropriate table (in this case, 10 percent, and the present value of an annuity). In this case, we find the target factor on the fourth time period line, which means that the annuity involves four payments. Similar techniques can be used to solve for an unknown time period or interest rate when single amounts are involved. For example, a target factor can be calculated by either dividing the present value by the future value or vice versa. In the former case the target factors should be compared to the present value tables, in the latter case to the future value tables.

Finally, division of the present, or future, value by the appropriate factor yields the annuity amount. Continuing the example, given a discount rate of 10 percent, the annuity amount is found to be $1,000 (based either upon the present value or the future value).

Using Interest Factors	Or Using a Financial Calculator with P/YR set at 1	
ANN = PV/(PVA: 10%, 4n, 1m)	3,169.87	PV
= $3,169.87/3.16987	4	N
= $1,000	0	FV
	10	I/YR
	PMT	(calculator displays)
		1,000
ANN = FV/(FVA: 10%, 4n, 1m)	4,641	FV
= $4,641/4.641	4	N
= $1,000	0	PV
	10	I/YR
	PMT	(calculator displays)
		1,000

Unlike the examples used so far, for most problems, it is unlikely that you will find the exact target factor in a table. Instead, the target will lie between table factors. To illustrate, assume that a real estate agent just sold a house and is now entitled to a $3,000 commission. The agent's broker offers an alternative compensation plan: a four-year annuity of $1,000 per year with the first payment one year from now. To make a decision regarding a compensation plan, the agent must determine the rate of interest implied by the annuity and compare this to his or her opportunity rate. The target factor is 3.00000 ($3,000 ÷ $1,000). Scanning the time period four line under the present value of an annuity column, we see 3.03735 (12 percent), and 2.97447 (13 percent). Therefore, the interest rate implied by the annuity is 12.59 percent (using linear interpolation), which the agent must compare to his or her opportunity rate in order to select a compensation alternative.

ORDINARY ANNUITIES VS. ANNUITY DUE

Annuities may be classified into one of two categories—ordinary and due. An **ordinary annuity** is an annuity in which the periodic payment (annuity) occurs at the end of each time period. The annuity problems in the preceding sections were ordinary annuities

CONSUMER CHECKLIST
PICKING THE CORRECT INTEREST FACTOR

By now many students have decided that determining the solutions to these types of problems is more easily accomplished using a financial calculator. For those who prefer using tables, note that people frequently have trouble determining which interest factor they should use to solve a particular problem. Here are three tips that may prove useful.

1. The choice of interest factor will be clearer if you diagram the cash flows as we did for the Able-Baker problem. If the cash flows resemble an annuity, an annuity factor is appropriate. If the cash flows do not resemble an annuity, you should use a single amount factor.

2. If the problem requires you to determine a present value, use a present value factor. If the problem requires the determination of a future value, use a future value factor.

3. To reduce the possibility of an error, check to ensure that your answer makes sense. For example, if the problem is to determine how much money one should deposit in an interest bearing account in order to have $1.000 at some point in the future, and your (present value) solution is greater than $1,000, there is a high probability that you have used an incorrect factor, or used the appropriate factor incorrectly.

because, in each case, the payments started at the end of the first time period. The interest factor tables in the appendix are for ordinary annuities. Sometimes, however, the annuity payments occur at the beginning of each time period; such an annuity is known as an **annuity due.** One common example of an annuity due is apartment rental payments (which are usually payable in advance). When the cash flows resemble an annuity due rather than an ordinary annuity, using ordinary annuity factors will result in an inaccurate solution. Fortunately, it is easy to convert an ordinary annuity factor into an annuity due factor; simply multiply the ordinary factor by (one plus the appropriate interest rate). Those who use a financial calculator must be careful when calculating this conversion; some inexpensive calculators are programmed to solve ordinary annuity problems only. More sophisticated models allow the user to specify a "begin" or "end" mode to solve annuity due and ordinary annuity problems, respectively.

While the basic difference between an ordinary annuity and an annuity due is the timing of the annuity payments, this difference results in other important differences. Other things constant, an annuity due will have a higher present value and a higher future value compared with an ordinary annuity. The annuity due must have a higher future value because the first payment occurs right away (time = 0) compared with the final payment occurring one time period in the future for an ordinary annuity (i.e., an annuity due has one additional compounding period). Likewise, the annuity due must have a higher present value because the payment occurring now does not have to be discounted while all payments in an ordinary annuity must be reduced. To demonstrate, consider the two annuities diagrammed in Exhibit 17.3. Each is a four-year annuity with a payment (A) of $1,000; the first is an ordinary annuity, the second is an annuity due. Assuming an interest rate of 10 percent, compounded annually, the future value of the annuity due is $464.10 more than the future value of the ordinary annuity, and the present value of the annuity due is $316.99 more than the present value of the ordinary annuity.

EXHIBIT	**17.3**	**A COMPARISON OF AN ORDINARY ANNUITY AND AN ANNUITY DUE**

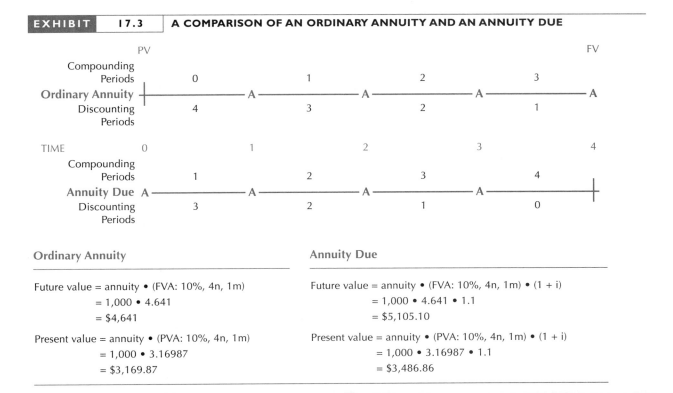

Ordinary Annuity

Future value = annuity • (FVA: 10%, 4n, 1m)
= 1,000 • 4.641
= $4,641

Present value = annuity • (PVA: 10%, 4n, 1m)
= 1,000 • 3.16987
= $3,169.87

Annuity Due

Future value = annuity • (FVA: 10%, 4n, 1m) • (1 + i)
= 1,000 • 4.641 • 1.1
= $5,105.10

Present value = annuity • (PVA: 10%, 4n, 1m) • (1 + i)
= 1,000 • 3.16987 • 1.1
= $3,486.86

CALCULATING MORTGAGE PAYMENTS

Every prospective borrower must know the loan payment amount. The payment amount is affected by several factors: the amount borrowed, the interest rate, the frequency of the payments, and the amortization period. As shown in Exhibit 17.4, the payment amount will increase the higher the amount borrowed, the higher the interest rate, the shorter the amortization period, or the less frequently payments are made.

A traditional fixed-interest rate, constant-payment mortgage is an ordinary annuity To illustrate how to calculate the payment on a fixed rate mortgage consider the purchase of a $100,000 house financed with an $80,000 conventional, 10-percent fixed-rate, thirty-year mortgage loan with monthly payments. The payment amount (ANN) of $702.06 is determined by dividing the loan amount (PV) by the appropriate present value factor (PVA).

Using Interest Factors	**Or Using a Financial Calculator with** $\boxed{\text{P/YR}}$ **set at 12**

$$\begin{aligned}
\text{ANN} &= \text{PV/(PVA: 10\%, 30n, 12m)} \\
&= \$80{,}000/(1 - (1/(.10/12)^{30 \bullet 12})/(.10/12) \\
&= \$80{,}000/113.95082 \\
&= \$702.06
\end{aligned}$$

80,000	$\boxed{\text{PV}}$
0	$\boxed{\text{FV}}$
12	$\boxed{\text{I/YR}}$
360	$\boxed{\text{N}}$
$\boxed{\text{PMT}}$	(calculator displays) 702.06

Some borrowers are shocked to realize the amount of the total payments to be made over the life of a loan. In this case, total payments equal $252,741.60 ($702.06 × 360), consisting of the $80,000 borrowed and $172,741.60 in interest. As discussed in Chapter 7, borrowers get some financial relief because mortgage interest is usually deductible when calculating income taxes.

EXHIBIT	17.4	THE EFFECT OF LOAN TERMS ON THE PAYMENT AMOUNT

Loan Terms	Present Value Interest Factor	Periodic Payment	Total Payment
$80,000 loan 10% interest rate 30 year term monthly payments	113.95082	702.06	252,741.60
$80,000 loan **12% interest rate** 30 year term monthly payments	97.218331	822.89	296,240.40
$80,000 loan 10% interest rate **25 year term** monthly payments	110.04723	726.96	218,088.00
$80,000 loan 10% interest rate 30 year term **quarterly payments**	37.93369	2,108.94	253,072.80

LOAN AMORTIZATION SCHEDULE

A loan **amortization schedule** shows the breakdown of each loan payment into components that represent interest and the amount by which the loan principal is reduced. A partial amortization schedule for the $80,000 loan introduced in the preceding section is shown in Exhibit 17.5. Note that interest payments, rather than principal reduction, constitute most of the early payments, and that the interest component decreases with each payment. This is always the case with a fully amortized, fixed-interest-rate loan.

The interest portion of each payment is calculated by multiplying the unpaid loan balance by the appropriate interest rate. With monthly payments, this is equal to the annual interest rate divided by twelve, in this case .008333 (.10÷12). The difference between the interest portion of each payment and the total payment is the amount by which the loan balance is reduced. For example, in Exhibit 17.5, $666.37 of the second payment is interest ($79,964.61 × .10/12), and the second payment reduces the loan balance by $35.69 ($702.06 – $666.37).

DETERMINING A MORTGAGE LOAN BALANCE

For any number of reasons, it may be important to know the remaining balance of a mortgage loan (BAL) at a particular time. Reference to the loan's amortization schedule provides a ready means of accomplishing this, if a schedule is available. Fortunately, one can determine a loan balance almost as easily if an amortization schedule is unavailable.

At any time, the value of an asset (including a mortgage, which is an asset to the mortgagee) is equal to the remaining cash flows associated with it, discounted by the appropriate interest rate. Therefore, determining the remaining balance on a loan is equivalent to calculating the present value of an annuity. To illustrate, assume that the mortgagor for the loan depicted in Exhibit 17.5 decides to pay off the loan immediately following the

EXHIBIT 17.5 **PARTIAL LOAN AMORTIZATION SCHEDULE**

Payment Number	Beginning Balance	Payment Amount	Interest	Principal Repayment	Ending Balance
1	80,000	702.06	666.67	35.39	79,964.61
2	79,964.61	702.06	666.37	35.69	79,928.92
3	79,928.92	702.06	666.07	35.99	79,892.93
4	79,892.93	702.06	665.77	36.29	79,856.64
5	79,856.64	702.06	665.47	36.59	79,820.05
356	3,418.80	702.06	28.49	673.57	2,745.67
357	2,744.67	702.06	22.87	679.19	2,065.48
358	2,065.48	702.06	17.21	684.85	1,380.63
359	1,380.63	702.06	11.51	690.55	690.08
360	690.08	695.83*	5.75	690.08	0.00

* to adjust for rounding error

120th payment (i.e., 20 years of payments remain). One can calculate that the mortgagor must pay $72,750.42 to eliminate the debt.

Using Interest Factors

Or Using a Financial Calculator with P/YR set at 12

BAL = ANN • (PVA: 10%, 20n, 12m)
= 702.06 • $1 - (1/ (1 + .10/12)^{20 \cdot 12})/(.10/12)$
= 702.06 • 103.62462
= $72,750.70

80,000	PV
0	FV
10	I/YR
360	N
PMT	(calculator displays) 702.06
N	240
PV	(calculator displays) 72,750.42

The above calculation requires that the payment amount be known. It is also possible to calculate the remaining balance on a mortgage loan without knowing the payment amount. Using interest factors, one can calculate the loan balance by multiplying the original balance by the ratio of the present value interest factor for the remaining amortization period and the present value interest factor for the original amortization period. Using the $80,000 loan example, we see this approach results in the same solution derived previously (ignoring small rounding errors).

BAL = original balance • [(PVA: 10%, 20n, 12m)/(PVA: 10%, 30n, 12m)]
= $80,000 • (103.62462/113.95082)
= $80,000 • .90938
= $72,750.40

The last term on the right hand side of the above calculation can be used to calculate the remaining balance for any mortgage loan with the appropriate interest rate, original and remaining term to maturity. For example, a 10-percent, thirty-year loan with twenty years remaining, and an original balance of $200,000, would be $181,876 ($200,000 × .90938).

ANNUAL PERCENTAGE RATE (APR)

Mortgage lenders often charge points to increase their effective yield above the stated interest rate on the mortgage contract (one point equals 1 percent of the loan amount). When borrowers pay points, their effective cost also exceeds the stated, or nominal, rate. In the past, lenders offering loans with different combinations of nominal rates and points made it difficult for borrowers to make an intelligent loan selection. To provide borrowers with a standard of comparison, the Consumer Credit Protection Act of 1968 (often referred to as the Truth in Lending Law) requires lenders to disclose, among other things, the **annual percentage rate** to loan applicants. The APR is an interest rate calculated according to procedures set out by the Federal Reserve Board. In general, regulations require mortgage lenders to subtract any points, prepaid interest, mortgage insurance, and origination fees from the loan amount in calculating the APR.

Some people confuse the APR with the borrower's effective (or true) interest rate. For at least two reasons, these rates may not be the same. First, in calculating the APR, mortgage lenders are allowed to assume that the borrower will not pay off the loan early. As we demonstrate shortly, when a borrower pays off a loan early, with either points or a prepayment penalty, the borrower's effective rate will be higher than the APR the lender is required to disclose. Second, the regulations allow the APR disclosed to mortgage loan applicants to be off by as much as one-eighth of a percent. Therefore, even when no points or prepayment penalties are involved, the APR may differ from the effective rate. In the following section we show how the APR is calculated for a fixed-rate mortgage loan.

CALCULATING THE APR FOR A FIXED-RATE MORTGAGE LOAN

The relationship of the APR to the nominal interest rate depends upon whether the lender charges points. If the lender does not charge points, the APR will closely approximate the nominal rate, but if the borrower is required to pay points, the APR may be significantly higher than the nominal rate. A rule of thumb suggests that for a thirty-year loan, the effective rate will increase by one-eighth of one percent for every point paid.

To demonstrate the APR calculation for a fixed-rate mortgage loan, we modify the terms of the thirty-year, $80,000 mortgage introduced previously and assume that the lender charges six points to be paid by the borrower. This means that although the monthly payment ($702.06) is based on $80,000, only $75,200 (94 percent of the loan amount) is actually disbursed (AD). As shown below, to calculate the APR, one can determine the target factor and locate the target factor in the present value of an annuity table to determine the implied rate.

Using Interest Factors	Or Using a Financial Calculator with P/YR set at 12		
TF = AD/A	75,200	PV	
= $75,200/$702.06	0	FV	
= 107.11335	702.06	+/−	PMT
	360	N	
Using linear interpolation, the APR is found to be 10.75 percent.	I/YR	(calculator displays) 10.75	

In this case, the rule of thumb regarding the effect of points on the effective rate worked well.

PREPAYMENTS AND EFFECTIVE RATES OF INTEREST

In comparing mortgage loans, borrowers should factor their intended holding period, if known, into the decision. When borrowers make payments faster than originally agreed, any points paid by the buyer result in an increased effective interest rate because they are spread over a shorter time. Recall that the effective rate of interest on the $80,000 fixed-interest-rate mortgage with six points was 10.75 percent, assuming that the loan was not paid early. What is the effective rate if the borrower intends to pay off the mortgage after ten years? To answer this question, one must determine the interest rate that equates the amount disbursed with the present value of both the payment stream and the early payoff amount. Above we determined that after ten years the remaining balance of the loan is about $72,750 and that the monthly payment is $702.06. The effective interest rate, of 11.02 percent, can easily be determined using

A fairly recent (and bad) development in mortgage origination is known as "predatory lending," the practice of loaning money with terms that make it difficult or impossible for the borrower to repay the loan. To appreciate how predatory lending can play havoc with your financial situation consider the following. When Priscilla Eva refinanced her Cleveland, Ohio, bungalow, she thought she was getting a lower interest rate and a deal to pay off her student loans without increasing her mortgage payment. Predatory lending often begins with an unsolicited appeal door to door or by mail, email, or telemarketer, suggesting the home owner use the equity in their home to pay off other loans. The poor, minorities, the elderly, and single women are frequent targets. Eva got a call from a Cincinnati lender who offered to reduce her 7.1 percent interest rate so that her mortgage payment of $785 would include her student loan and credit card payments. She was also promised that there would be no fees. Eva signed the agreement without reading it, which is definitely not a good idea. Unfortunately, for her, the student loan bills kept arriving in the mail, and later she discovered that she had been charged $8,700 in fees and the loan had an interest rate of 11.99 percent. If you do not wish the same to happen to you, take a lesson from this story, read and understand all contracts before you sign them (and read the next section).

Go to www.aarp.org, and search "predatory lending" to learn more about this subject.

your financial calculator. Earlier, or later, payoff assumptions would result in a higher, or lower, effective rate, respectively.

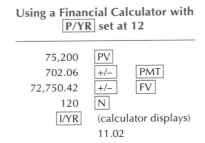

In a similar fashion, prepayment penalties increase the borrower's effective interest rate. Prepayment penalties can be stated in a number of ways, but are generally specified as a percentage of the mortgage loan balance at the time of the prepayment. Prepayment penalties may be on a sliding scale and disappear in three to five years after loan origination. We will assume, continuing the previous example, that the mortgage contains a prepayment penalty of 3 percent of the remaining loan balance. This means that, immediately following the 120th payment, the borrower must pay a total of $74,933.93 ($72,750.42 loan balance and $2,182.51 penalty) to eliminate the debt. The determination of the effective interest rate in this case is nearly identical to that shown above. The only difference is that the lump sum payment now includes the penalty. In this example, the effective interest rate increases to 11.18 percent. Here again, the nearer the prepayment date to the loan origination date; the greater will be the effect of the prepayment penalty on the effective rate.

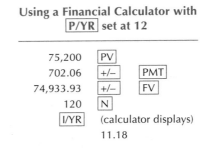

REFINANCING A MORTGAGE

There are two basic motivations for refinancing an existing mortgage: to reduce the size of the payment by locking in a lower interest rate, or to convert some of the equity in a property into cash. Astute real property owners should periodically determine whether they can save money by refinancing. When interest rates fall, substantial reductions in the payment amount may be obtained by replacing one mortgage with another carrying a lower interest rate. When refinancing, however, most lenders require the borrower to pay some finance charges up front. For refinancing to be feasible, the present value of the payment savings must more than offset the finance charges. To illustrate how this is determined, consider the following example.

Ten years ago Mary Brown financed the purchase of her $100,000 home with an $80,000, ten-percent, thirty-year mortgage loan. She has located a lender who is willing to write a twenty-year, 9 percent mortgage loan equal to the unpaid balance on the original loan. But, the lender requires the borrower to pay five points on such loans as an origination fee. Should Mary refinance? We know that the remaining balance on her existing loan is $72,750.42. Therefore, the finance charge on the new loan would equal $3,637.52 ($72,750.42 × .05). We also know that the monthly payment on the original loan is $702.06. Using your financial calculator, the payment on the new loan is found to be $654.55 ($72,750.70 ÷ 111.14495), resulting in monthly savings of $47.51 for twenty years.

There are at least two ways to evaluate this decision. One simple method is based on how long Mary plans to stay in the home. In this case, if she plans on staying less than 6.38 years, the savings will not be enough to cover the refinancing costs ($3,637.52÷$47.51 = 76.56 months). However, this technique ignores the time value of money. To overcome this shortcoming, determine the effective interest rate associated with the savings and compare this rate to the rate that could be earned if the $3,637.52 were invested elsewhere. Assuming Mary intends to stay in the house twenty years, we can evaluate the situation as follows.

Using Interest Factors	Or Using a Financial Calculator with P/YR set at 12	
TF = Refinance Charge/Monthly Savings	3,637.52	PV
= $3,637.52/$47.51	47.51	+/− PMT
= 76.57979	0	FV
Scanning the twenty year line under the present value of an annuity column, we note that the interest rate implied by the equation is between fourteen and fifteen percent (linear interpolation yields 14.85 percent).	240	N
	I/YR	(calculator displays)
		14.85

In this case, refinancing is the equivalent of earning a 14.85 percent return on the finance charges. This interest rate is then compared with the rate of return available on other investments. If Mary cannot earn this amount on investments of similar risk, she should refinance.

The second motivation for an owner to refinance a property is the desire to convert equity in the property into cash. An owner's equity in real property increases in one or both of two ways, either the amount of the mortgage debt on the property is reduced, or the value of the property increases. As mentioned in Chapter 16, several types of mortgages are available which may enable an owner to draw on their equity. An owner could refinance the property with a new first mortgage, or a lender may be willing to write a second mortgage loan, a home equity loan, or a wraparound mortgage loan.

The same techniques and equations discussed previously will enable the owner/borrower to determine the best alternative by comparing the effective interest rates of the loan alternatives. For example, assume a homeowner financed the purchase of her $125,000 house five years ago with a $100,000, fifteen-year, 8-percent first mortgage loan (monthly payment of $955.65). The value of the house has increased to $160,000 and the homeowner would like to convert $25,000 of the equity into cash. The owner is perplexed to find that current rates on first mortgages and second mortgages are 12 and 15 percent, respectively. One lender is, however, willing to write an 11-percent, ten-year, wraparound loan. Assuming (for simplicity) that the lender is not charging points, the wrap may appear to be the preferred alternative; but it is not. Remember, with a wrap, the lender charges interest on the face amount of the wrap loan (the amount disbursed plus original loan balance).

To determine which loan the owner should use one must calculate and compare the effective interest rates of the alternatives. The wrap loan amount is $103,766.30 ($78,766.30 remaining balance on the first mortgage, plus the $25,000 desired), and the monthly payment on the wrap is $1,429.38 ($103,766.30 ÷ 72.59528). In effect, the wrap loan requires the borrower to pay $473.73 more (wrap payment less original payment: $1,429.38 − $955.65) per month for ten years in exchange for $25,000 now. To determine the effective rate on the wraparound loan we proceed as follows:

Using Interest Factors	Or Using a Financial Calculator with P/YR set at 12	
TF = AD/A	25,000	PV
= $25,000/$473.73	473.73	PMT
= 52.77267	0	FV
which implies an effective rate of 19.4 percent on the wrap loan	120	N
	I/YR	(calculator displays) 19.4

AN ETHICAL ISSUE
IGNORANCE OF THE TIME VALUE OF MONEY

One scheme offered by purveyors of get-rich-quick seminars suggests that buyers offer to pay a combination of a small cash down payment plus an existing mortgage, which the buyer purchases on the secondary market. To illustrate, consider the following scenario. If a seller were not pressed for cash, he or she might be persuaded to accept $5,000 in cash and a mortgage with a remaining balance of $95,000 for a $100,000 home. One mortgage that would have a balance of approximately $95,000 would be one with an original balance of $100,000; an 8 percent interest rate; and an original term of thirty years with twenty-five years remaining. This mortgage would entitle the seller to a monthly annuity of $733.76 for the next twenty-five years, and the buyer is likely to point out that this means the total amount being offered for the property is not $100,000 but $225,128 [$5,000 + ($733.76 × 300)]. If the seller is reluctant to accept the offer because the he or she needs cash, the buyer can suggest that the mortgage could be converted into cash by selling it on the secondary mortgage market.

The catch is that the market value of the loan may be significantly less than the remaining loan balance if interest rates are currently higher than the rate on the existing mortgage. For example, if rates are currently at 10 percent, the buyer will only pay $80,748 for the mortgage. This fact is not made clear to the seller (nor is the fact that that is all the seller would be able to sell the loan for if he or she accepts the buyer's offer). In effect, if the seller accepts the offer, he will sell his $100,000 home for only $85,748. Clearly only ignorant or desperate sellers would accept such an offer. Assuming you could find a seller willing to accept such a "deal," do you think it is ethical to take advantage of such a person? Why?

Therefore, the owner would be better served with either a new first or second mortgage compared with the wrap loan.

LOAN ASSUMPTIONS

An assumable loan carrying an interest rate that is below the current market rate has value. Whether the assumption of such a loan will be beneficial to a particular purchaser, however, depends on both the difference between the assumable and current interest rates and the amount of the assumable loan compared with the total amount of needed financing. To illustrate, suppose that current first and second mortgage rates are 12 and 15 percent, respectively, that a buyer has $20,000 for a down payment and has been prequalified for a twenty-year, first mortgage loan in the amount of $80,000. The buyer locates a house costing $100,000. The existing mortgage on the home is assumable. The original amount of this mortgage was $80,000 and it has a 10 percent interest rate. Twenty years of the original thirty-year amortization period remain. From a previous example, we know that the remaining balance of such a loan is $72,750.42. The buyer must decide whether to use a new $80,000 first mortgage, or assume the existing loan and secure a second mortgage of $7,249.58 ($80,000 − $72,750.42). Determining which mortgage to select is straightforward. We know that the payment on the existing loan is $702.06, and can calculate the payment on the other two loans.

$880.87 = new first mortgage payment = $80,000 ÷ 90.81942

$95.46 = second mortgage payment = $7,249.30 ÷ 75.94228

In this case, the buyer would benefit by assuming the loan because his or her total payments would equal $797.42 ($702.06 + $95.46) compared to $880.87 for a new first mortgage. In fact, loan assumption will be preferred whenever the effective rate on new first mortgages is greater than the weighted average of the assumable mortgage and the second mortgage; in this case, 10.44 percent.

SUMMARY

In this chapter we reviewed the economic principle of the time value of money, and demonstrated how one can solve a variety of problems confronting real estate market participants. Such problems have a number of variables: present value, future value, any periodic cash flows, an interest rate, and time. As long as all but one of the variables is known, the value of the missing variable can be calculated.

An understanding of the material in this chapter is critical if you are to make informed real estate decisions. In some instances, this knowledge might result in trivial benefits, such as being able to file for an income tax refund early because you can calculate the amount of mortgage interest paid during the year rather than waiting for a statement of the amount from the lender. In other cases, such as comparing the effective cost of loan alternatives, this knowledge could save you thousands of dollars.

Several useful tips for resolving a variety of real estate financing issues were demonstrated. For example, visualizing a problem using a timeline is a good way to begin many calculations. In this way, it should become apparent how to go about solving the problem. In particular, it is important to determine if the periodic cash flows resemble an ordinary annuity or an annuity due. We used interest factors to enable you to grasp the relationship between the variables in these types of problems. While an understanding of interest factors is important, in most cases, these types of problems can be solved more quickly with a financial calculator or computer.

KEY TERMS

amortization schedule	compound interest	present value
annual percentage rate	discount rate	simple interest
annuity	future value	
annuity due	ordinary annuity	

REVIEW QUESTIONS

1. Why does money have time value?

2. Assume your instructor has promised to pay you either $10 now or another amount one year from now. What future amount would make you indifferent in choosing between the alternatives? Why? What interest rate is implied by your answer?

3. How is a future value related to: the payment amount, the interest rate, the manner in which interest is compounded, and time? How is a present value related to these factors?

4. Distinguish an ordinary annuity from an annuity due.

5. Under what conditions is the APR the same as the borrower's effective interest rate for a fixed rate loan?

6. What is the relationship of the principal reduction and interest components of a fully amortized mortgage loan payment over time?

7. In mortgage lending, what is a point?

8. How do points paid by the borrower influence both the effective rate of interest paid by the borrower on a mortgage loan and the effective rate earned by the lender?

9. How do points paid by the seller influence the effective rate of interest paid by the borrower on a mortgage loan and the effective rate earned by the lender?

10. What is your answer to the questions in the three "Decision Point" sections in this chapter?

11. What is your answer to the questions in the "Ethical Issue" in this chapter?

PROBLEMS

1. Assume an investment of $10,000 will earn a return of 20 percent interest compounded quarterly. How much will the investment be worth after five years?

2. What simple rate of interest would have to be earned to equal a 12 percent rate compounded monthly over one year? Two years? Three years?

3. In demonstrating the future value of a dollar we showed that Able's $10,000 invested for two years at 12 percent (compounded annually) would have a future value of $12,544 compared to Baker's future value of $11,738 (initial deposit of $6,000 and a $4,000 deposit one year later). Assuming that Baker's account earns only 10 percent in the first year, what rate of interest would it have to earn in year two to result in a future value of $12,544?

4. What is the present value of a twelve-year, $10,000 ordinary annuity given a discount rate of 8 percent? What is the present value of a similar annuity due?

5. If you can earn 6 percent, what is the future value of a seven-year, $7,000 ordinary annuity? What is the future value of a similar annuity due?

6. What is the remaining balance of a $100,000, thirty-year, 11-percent fixed-rate mortgage after the 240th payment? After the 246th?

7. What is the effective interest rate on a fifteen-year, 10-percent fixed-rate mortgage on which four points are charged and the loan will be paid off after the 60th payment? What is the APR on this loan?

8. What is the monthly payment on a $100,000, 13-percent fixed-rate, twenty-five year mortgage? How much of the first, second, and third payments represents interest?

9. You are considering two thirty-year mortgage loans, each in the amount of $90,000. One has an 8 percent interest rate, requires you to pay five points and has a prepayment penalty equal to 5 percent of the remaining balance. The other carries an interest rate of 9.25 percent, has no prepayment penalty, but requires you to pay one point. If you only plan to live in the property for five years and payoff the loan at that time, what is the APR of each loan? What is the effective rate of interest on both loans?

REAL ESTATE ON THE WEB

Use your favorite search engine to:

1. Learn more about predatory lending and what federal, state, and local authorities are doing to eliminate it.

2. Check the mortgage rate quotes from one or more lenders and determine (with calculations) if the effective rate for loans with and without points is the same.

3. Check the mortgage rate quotes from one or more lenders and determine how much lower the rate on the lender's adjustable rate loans is compared with the lender's fixed rate loans.

4. Check the mortgage rate quotes from one or more lenders and determine how much lower the rate for fifteen-year loans is compared to the lender's thirty-year loans.

5. Find the Federal Reserve APR regulations

Refer to the companion Web site at www.wiley.com/college/larsen for a variety of online activities including additional chapter content, review materials, assignments, and related links.

ADDITIONAL READINGS

Brueggeman, W. and Fisher, J. *Real Estate Finance & Investments.* 11th edition. McGraw-Hill Irwin Publishers. Homewood, Illinois. (2001).

Real Estate Development And Investment

V

Part V of this text contains four chapters that should be of interest to those who own real estate, as well as to those who want to create improvements or invest in real estate. Chapter 18, Property Management and Leasing, provides a description of the responsibilities of real property managers. Leasing is an integral part of the property manager's job and information concerning lease transactions and the landlord-tenant relationship is also presented. Real property ownership entails the risk that fire or some other catastrophe may damage the property, or that someone may be injured while on the property. In the worst case, the financial burden associated with these events could result in the loss of ownership. Therefore, in Chapter 19, Property Insurance, we explain the types of contracts that real property owners can enter into in order to manage these risks. In Chapter 20, Property Development and Market Analysis, we examine important regulations and issues faced by real estate developers, and explain the steps in the development process. Finally, in Chapter 21, Investment Analysis, we describe the advantages, disadvantages, and risk factors associated with direct investments in real estate, and demonstrate how to determine whether such an investment makes good financial sense. We also review a number of indirect real estate investment possibilities. The material presented should enable you to make more informed real estate investment decisions.

18 Property Management And Leasing

Learning Objectives

After studying this chapter you should be able to:

- Describe the duties of real estate managers.
- List and explain the essential elements of a lease.
- Explain the different tenancies that a tenant may hold.
- Describe the various rental payment arrangements.
- Distinguish a sublease from an assignment of lease.
- Be aware of the responsibilities of both landlords and tenants under the Uniform Residential Landlord and Tenant Act.
- Understand rent control and fair housing laws.

FROM THE WIRE

What do the Fiesta Mall in Mesa, Arizona; The Hanover Mall in Hanover, Massachusetts; the Stratford Square Mall in Bloomingdale, Illinois; the Garden City Center in Cranston, Rhode Island; the Sandburg Mall in Galesburg, Illinois; the Marquette Mall in Michigan City, Indiana; the Auburn Mall in Auburn, Maine; the Adrian Mall in Adrian, Michigan; and the Ford City Mall in Chicago have in common? Do they all have the same owner? No, each is owned by a different institutional investor. Does each have a food court available for hungry shoppers and mall employees? Well, maybe, but that is not the answer we are looking for. The answer—owners of each facility signed a property management agreement with the Third Party Management Division of General Growth Properties (GGP) during the first half of 2002.

GGP is a good example of specialization within the real property management industry; many property management companies specialize in managing a particular type of property. The nine malls mentioned here brings the total number of malls owned by others and managed by GGP to forty-nine. GGP is the country's second largest owner, developer and manager of regional shopping malls. They currently have an ownership interest in, or management responsibility for, 146 shopping malls in forty states. Libby Lassiter, GGP Senior Vice President, said, "We're looking forward to working with the current mall teams in enhancing each mall's merchandise mix, customer traffic, and overall retail sales. We will capitalize on our experience as we formulate new strategies for these centers."

Go to www.boma.org, and click on one or more of the Latest BOMA Headline News items to learn about issues of current interest to building owners and managers.

INTRODUCTION

This chapter begins with a brief description of another type of real estate service provider, real property managers, such as GGP's Third Party Management Division mentioned in the chapter opener, From The Wire. Two of the duties they perform are selecting tenants and negotiating lease terms. Because leasing is an integral part of the property manager's job, and because the topic may be of interest to you personally, important information concerning lease transactions and the landlord-tenant relationship is also presented. All parties that enter into a lease should understand this information. Our focus is on residential property, although we include some important issues concerning commercial property. Leases can be categorized based upon various criteria. One way to classify them is according to the type of tenancy created; another is by the manner in which the rent is computed and paid.

As explained in previous chapters, the owner of real property is entitled to the rights of: possession, enjoyment, control, and disposition. Usually, when an owner enters into a lease, he or she transfers the rights of possession and enjoyment to the tenant for the lease term. In essence, tenants gain the right to occupy the premises and the right to preclude others from interfering with their occupancy. In some cases, tenants may also gain the right to control (physically alter the property), and/or a right of disposition (the right to convey the leasehold estate to others). At the expiration of the lease, however, all rights revert to the landlord. Both landlords and tenants sometimes view leases as a creative financing device. For example, the lease agreement may give the tenant the option to purchase the property during the term of the lease or at its expiration. In any event, when real property is leased, the tenant enjoys the use of the property and avoids the substantial up-front costs associated with ownership acquisition. Perhaps this helps explain why many businesses conduct their operations in leased premises and why more than 30 percent of all households in the United States rent their residences.

REAL ESTATE MANAGEMENT

Specialized skills are needed to make the day-to-day decisions required to properly operate almost all income-producing properties. Many owners do not possess these skills, and some that do are busy attending to other activities. In either case, these owners can benefit by employing a professional property manager. Real estate management usually involves the administration, operation, marketing, and maintenance of real property in order to achieve the objectives of the real property owner. To clearly identify the responsibilities of both parties, a written management agreement is recommended. This document should specify the scope of the manager's authority, the duties the manager is expected to perform, and the compensation to be received for performing these duties. The management fee is usually set equal to a percentage of the property's gross income (Chapter 21). The management fee is a function of the duties assigned to the manager and the size of the property. The duties of a real property manager vary depending upon the type of real estate being managed, the organization the manager works for, and the position the manager holds. For large properties, such as a regional shopping mall or a high-rise apartment building, the fee tends to be around 4 percent. For smaller properties the fee can increase to around 10 percent.

Among the types of organizations that employ real estate managers are property management firms and full-service real estate companies. A property management firm is a company that specializes in providing management services to institutional and individual real estate owners. A full-service real estate company offers a full range of real estate services (e.g., brokerage, appraisal, etc.), with real estate management being one of the services provided. Real property owners may employ either of these types of firms, but many institutional owners have real estate managers on staff. Such institutions include commercial banks that have asset managers to manage properties owned by the bank's customers and held in trust by the bank, as well as properties the bank has acquired through foreclosure. Development companies use real estate managers to assist in renovation projects and in marketing properties to prospective investors. Real estate investment trusts use real estate managers to evaluate the profitability of properties they are contemplating adding to their investment portfolios. Property managers also manage investment properties owned by insurance companies, pension funds, and other large institutional investors. Many large corporations have real estate divisions that manage the real property used in conducting the firm's business. Corporate real estate managers help determine the best use of the firm's real property and also help in negotiating the terms of property sales and acquisitions. Other consumers of real property management services include the federal, state, and local governments; religious and charitable organizations; and colleges and universities.

Specific jobs within the real estate management field include site manager, property manager, and asset manager. A **site manager** usually deals with residential properties, and when the manager lives at the property being managed, he or she is known as a resident manager. When your textbook author was a college undergraduate, he worked as the resident manager of a small (six-unit) apartment building in exchange for free rent. This was a great way to help hold down living expenses during those years. Resident managers for larger properties may receive a stipend in addition to free rent, and for very large developments a salary large enough to live on, although this would leave little time to study and attend class because in this case the managerial duties require a significant amount of time. Site managers basically perform a caretaker role. They oversee the daily operation of a property and provide a critical link between tenants and the property manager. They may be responsible for distributing and collecting lease applications and collecting rent, and attending to tenant complaints. Site managers may also perform maintenance and make minor repairs or arrange for others to perform these and a variety of other services on the property. In addition, the site manager may be responsible for maintaining accurate records of the property's expenses and income that will enable the property manager to track the property's financial performance.

The **property manager** is in charge of the operation of the property and is directly responsible for maintaining or increasing its market value by developing and following an owner-approved management plan. This plan should cover all aspects of the physical plant, tenant relations, market positioning, community image building, and the financial operation of the property. The market value of almost all income-producing properties is strongly associated with the net operating income (Chapter 21) produced by the property, and net operating income is enhanced when the property manager follows efficient operating procedures that control expenses and optimize rental income.

The revenue a property will generate is positively related to both occupancy rates and rent levels; the higher both are, the greater the income the property will generate. But, other factors being constant, the higher the rent the greater the possibility that vacancies will occur as tenants move to less-expensive facilities. Therefore, managers must be aware of market conditions and use this information to fine-tune the amount of rent being charged. For example, in a neighborhood shopping center, the manager may determine that the property's effective gross income (Chapter 21) will be maximized by setting rents at a level slightly below the going rate in order to lower tenant turnover and the property's vacancy rate. Similarly, the manager of an apartment building might decide that offering tenants a discount for the early payment of rent, rather than (or in combination with) penalties for late payment will ensure the timely payment of rent. The property manager's duties include overseeing the daily operations of the property site manager and other site personnel and serving as a conduit between site personnel and the property owner or the owner's agent, frequently an asset manager.

The responsibilities of an **asset manager** may differ from one professional setting to the next, and it is possible that, in some cases, the job responsibilities of the asset manager and property manager overlap. In general, however, it is the asset manager who is at the top of the decision-making hierarchy, and it is the asset manager who is ultimately responsible for enhancing the value of the subject property. The asset manager focuses on managing the real property and making decisions that govern the financial performance of the property. In many cases, it is the asset manager who establishes the operating procedures that are carried out by the property manager. The asset manager must pay careful attention to financial developments, economic factors, and changing market opportunities because these may suggest changes that should be made to the physical or financial structure of the property. An asset manager's role can cover the entire life cycle of a real property investment; the manager's advice may be sought at the time of acquisition and sale of the property. In between, overseeing the tasks of marketing the property and securing tenants is a critical element of the asset manager's duties. Therefore, we next examine various aspects of leasing.

ESSENTIALS OF A VALID LEASE

A lease is a conveyance in that it conveys certain rights to the tenant. Therefore, the usual legal requirements for a real estate conveyance must usually be present for a lease to be enforceable. For example, in most states, the Statute of Frauds requires that any lease lasting longer than one year must be in writing in order to be enforceable. When the legal requirements for a lease are present and the lease term is one year or less, an oral lease is as enforceable as a written lease.

A renter holds a leasehold estate, so called because the agreement between the property owner (landlord) and the renter (tenant) is called a **lease.** The interest the landlord holds is called a leased fee estate. To protect both parties to the lease, good business practice dictates that all leases be in writing and cover all reasonable contingencies, regardless of the rental period. A written lease tends to minimize disputes between the landlord and tenant that arise subsequent to the agreement. While no special wording is required to create the landlord-tenant relationship, the following elements are essential to a valid lease.

CAPACITY TO CONTRACT

For a valid lease to be created, both parties to the lease agreement must have the legal capacity to contract (Chapter 11). In essence, there must be a grantor, known as either the landlord or **lessor,** having legal capacity to grant possession; and there must be a grantee, known either as the tenant or **lessee,** legally capable of receiving possession. If a written lease is employed, both parties should be named in the agreement.

DESCRIPTION OF THE PREMISES

A lease must contain a description of the leased property, but the type of description required depends upon the property. A legal description is generally unnecessary for residential and small commercial properties. For such properties, a street address and/or apartment number is usually an adequate description. Descriptions for large commercial sites tend to be more detailed and include such things as a floor plan, total square footage, and parking areas. A legal description should be used, however, if a lease is for land (as with a ground lease, which is described later in the chapter).

A sample residential lease is shown in Exhibit 18.1. In the sample lease, the description of the leased premises would be inserted about a third of the way down the first page below the agency disclosure portion of the lease.

POSSESSION OF THE LEASED PREMISES

For a valid lease to exist, the landlord must deliver possession of the leased premises to the tenant. At a minimum, constructive delivery of possession must occur. By giving the keys to the premises to the tenant, the landlord satisfies the constructive delivery of possession requirement. Constructive delivery, however, does not guarantee the tenant actual possession because the leased property may be occupied by another party, such as a previous tenant or a trespasser. Most states require that the landlord give the tenant actual possession of the leased premises, and if the leased property is occupied by another, it is the landlord's obligation to bring any necessary court action to secure actual possession for the tenant. In a few states, however, the landlord is only required to give the tenant the right of possession and the tenant is responsible for taking any legal action necessary to secure actual possession. Note that in Exhibit 18.1, the provision marked [13] addresses this issue.

USE OF THE PREMISES

In Chapter 11, we explained how the objective of a contract must be legal for a valid contract to exist; this requirement also applies to lease agreements. It would be illegal, for example, to lease a building as a crack cocaine factory, and a lease for such a purpose would be void. If a lease does not state a specified purpose for which the property will be used, the tenant may use the property for any legal purpose. The lessor can restrict the legal uses of a property through certain lease provisions. Examples of such restrictions are shown in Exhibit 18.1 in the provisions marked [4-6]. These provisions specify that the property be used as a residence, limit the number of inhabitants, prohibit pets, and require that the property be used in compliance with federal, state, and local law. Provisions that restrict use are just as important, if not more so, for commercial space leases. Imagine, for example, the dismay of a shopping center developer who secured leases with forty different retail companies so that a wide range of products would be offered, only to find out that each sells only cellophane tape.

EXHIBIT 18.1 | **SAMPLE LEASE**

NCR (No Carbon Required)

RESIDENTIAL LEASE WITH OPTION TO PURCHASE

AGENCY RELATIONSHIP CONFIRMATION. The following agency relationship is hereby confirmed for this transaction and supersedes any prior agency election (if no agent, insert "NONE"):

LISTING AGENT: _____ is the agent of (check one):
(Print Firm Name)

☐ the Owner exclusively; or ☐ both the Tenant and the Owner.

SELLING AGENT: _____ (if not the same as the Listing Agent) is the agent of (check one):
(Print Firm Name)

☐ the Tenant exclusively; or ☐ the Owner exclusively; or ☐ both the Tenant and the Owner.

Note: This confirmation DOES NOT take the place of the AGENCY DISCLOSURE form which may be required by law.

RECEIVED FROM _____, hereinafter referred to as Tenant,
the sum of $_____ (_____ dollars),
evidenced by _____, as a deposit which, upon acceptance of this Lease, the Owner of the premises,
hereinafter referred to as "Owner", will apply as follows:

		RECEIVED	BALANCE DUE PRIOR TO OCCUPANCY
Non-refundable option consideration	$ _____	$ _____	$ _____
Rent for the period from _____ to _____ ..	$ _____	$ _____	$ _____
Security deposit	$ _____	$ _____	$ _____
Other	$ _____	$ _____	$ _____
TOTAL	$ _____	$ _____	$ _____

In the event that this Agreement is not accepted by the Owner or his or her authorized agent, **within** _____ **days**, the total deposit received will be refunded.

Tenant hereby offers to lease from the Owner the premises situated in the City of _____ _____
County of _____
State of _____, commonly known as _____,
upon the following TERMS and CONDITIONS:

1. TERM. The term will commence on _____, 20_____, and continue for a period of _____ months thereafter.

2. RENT. Rent will be $_____, per month, payable in advance, upon the _____ day of each calendar month to Owner or his or her authorized agent, at the following address: _____
or at such other places as may be designated by Owner from time to time. In the event rent is not paid in full and received by Owner **within** _____ **days** after due date, Tenant agrees that it would be impracticable or extremely difficult to fix the actual damages to Owner caused by that failure, and Tenant agrees to pay a **late charge** of $_____. Tenant further agrees to pay $ _____ for each dishonored bank check. The late charge period is **not** a grace period, and Owner is entitled to make written demand for any rent if not paid when due and to collect interest on said sum. Any unpaid balance including late charges, will bear interest at 10% per annum, or the maximum rate allowed by law, whichever is less.

3. UTILITIES. Tenant will be responsible for the payment of all utilities and services, except: _____,
which will be paid by Owner.

4. USE. The premises will be used exclusively as a residence for no more than _____ persons. Guests staying more than a total of _____ days in a calendar year without written consent of Owner will constitute a violation of this Agreement.

5. ANIMALS. No animals will be brought on the premises without the prior consent of the Owner; except _____.

6. ORDINANCES AND STATUTES. Tenant will comply with all statutes, ordinances, and requirements of all municipal, state and federal authorities now in force, or which may later be in force. If the premises is located in a rent control area, the Tenant should contact the Rent and Arbitration Board for his or her legal rights.

7. ASSIGNMENT AND SUBLETTING. Tenant will not assign this Agreement or sublet any portion of the premises without prior written consent of the Owner. Any such assignment or subletting without consent will be void and, at the option of Owner, will terminate this Lease.

8. MAINTENANCE, REPAIRS, OR ALTERATIONS. Tenant acknowledges that the premises are in good working order and repair, unless otherwise indicated. Tenant will, at his or her own expense, maintain the premises in good working order and repair, including all equipment, appliances, and smoke detectors, plumbing, heating and air conditioning, will keep the premises in a clean and sanitary condition, and will surrender the same, at termination, in as good condition as received, normal wear and tear excepted. Tenant will be responsible for damages caused by his or her negligence and that of his or her family, invitees, and guests. Tenant will not paint, paper or otherwise redecorate or make alterations to the premises without the prior written consent of the Owner. Tenant will irrigate and maintain any surrounding grounds, including lawns and shrubbery. Tenant will not commit any waste upon the premises.

9. INVENTORY. Any furnishings and/or equipment to be furnished by Owner will be listed in a separate inventory. The inventory will be signed by both Tenant and Owner concurrently with this Agreement. Tenant will keep the furnishings and equipment in good condition and repair, and will be responsible for any damage to them other than normal wear and tear.

Tenant [_____] [_____] has read this page.

| **EXHIBIT** | **18.1** | **SAMPLE LEASE (CONTINUED)** |

Property Address

10. **DAMAGES TO PREMISES.** If the premises are damaged by fire or from any other cause which renders the premises untenantable, either party will have the right to terminate this Agreement as of the date on which the damage occurs. Written notice of termination will be given to the other party **within fifteen (15) days after occurrence** of such damage. Should such damage or destruction occur as the result of the negligence of Tenant, or his or her invitees, then only the Owner will have the right to terminate. Should this right be exercised by either Owner or Tenant, then rent for the current month will be prorated between the parties as of the date the damage occurred. Any prepaid rent and unused security deposit will be refunded to Tenant. If this Agreement is not terminated, then Owner will promptly repair the premises and there will be a proportionate reduction of rent until the premises are repaired and ready for Tenant's occupancy. The proportionate reduction will be based on the extent which repairs interfere with Tenant's reasonable use of the premises.

11. **ENTRY AND INSPECTION.** Owner and owner's agent will have the right to enter the premises: (a) in case of emergency; (b) to make necessary or agreed repairs, decorations, alterations, improvements, supply necessary or agreed services, show the premises to prospective or actual buyers, lenders, tenants, workers, or contractors; (c) when tenant has abandoned or surrendered the premises. Except under (a) and (c), entry may be made only during normal business hours, and with at least 24 hours prior notice to Tenant.

12. **INDEMNIFICATION.** Owner will not be liable for any damage or injury to Tenant, or any other person, or to any property, occurring on the premises, or in common areas, unless such damage is the legal result of the negligence or willful misconduct of Owner, his or her agents or employees. Tenant agrees to hold Owner harmless from any claims for damages, no matter how caused, except for injury or damages caused by negligence or willful misconduct of Owner, his or her agents or employees. It is understood that Owner's insurance does not cover Tenant's personal property. To the maximum extent permitted by insurance policies which may be owned by the parties, Owner and Tenant waive any and all rights of subrogation against each other which might otherwise exist.

13. **PHYSICAL POSSESSION.** If Owner is unable to deliver possession of the premises at the commencement date set forth above, Owner will not be liable for any damage caused, nor will this Agreement be void or voidable, but Tenant will not be liable for any rent until possession is delivered. Tenant may terminate this Agreement if possession is not delivered **within _____ days** of the commencement of the term in Item 1.

14. **DEFAULT.** If Tenant fails to pay rent when due, or perform any provision of this Agreement, after not less than **three (3) days (or longer if required by local law)** written notice of such default given in the manner required by law, the Owner, at his or her option, may terminate all rights of Tenant, unless Tenant, within said time, cures such default. If Tenant abandons or vacates the property while in default of the payment of rent, Owner may consider any property left on the premises to be abandoned and may dispose of the same in any manner allowed by law. In the event the Owner reasonably believes that such abandoned property has no value, it may be discarded. All property on the premises will be subject to a lien for the benefit of Owner securing the payment of all sums due, to the maximum extent allowed by law.

In the event of a default by Tenant, Owner may elect to: (a) continue the lease in effect and enforce all his or her rights and remedies, including the right to recover the rent as it becomes due; or (b) at any time, terminate all of Tenant's rights and recover from Tenant all damages he or she may incur by reason of the breach of the lease, including the cost of recovering the premises, and including the worth at the time of such termination, or at the time of an award if suit be instituted to enforce this provision, of the amount by which the unpaid rent for the balance of the term exceeds the amount of such rental loss which the Tenant proves could be reasonably avoided.

15. **SECURITY.** The security deposit will secure the performance of Tenant's obligations. Owner may, but will not be obligated to, apply all portions of said deposit on account of Tenant's obligations. Any balance remaining will be returned to Tenant, together with an accounting of any disbursements, **no later than three (3) weeks** after termination, or earlier if required by law. Tenant will not have the right to apply the security deposit in payment of the last month's rent. No interest will be paid to Tenant on account of the security deposit, unless required by local ordinance.

16. **WAIVER.** Failure of Owner to enforce any provision of this Agreement will not be deemed a waiver. The acceptance of rent by Owner will not waive his or her right to enforce any provision of this Agreement.

17. **NOTICES.** Unless otherwise provided, any notice which either party may give or is required to give, may be given by mailing the same, postage prepaid, to Tenant at the premises or to Owner at the address shown in Item 2, or at such other places as may be designated by the parties from time to time. Unless otherwise provided, notice will be deemed effective three (3) days after mailing, or on personal delivery, or when receipt is acknowledged in writing, whichever is earlier.

18. **HEIRS, ASSIGNS, SUCCESSORS.** This Agreement is binding upon and inures to the benefit of the heirs, assigns, and successors in interest to the parties.

19. **TIME.** Time is of the essence of this Agreement and of the right to exercise the Option to Purchase.

20. **HOLDING OVER.** Any holding over after expiration of this Agreement, with the consent of Owner, will be construed as a month-to-month tenancy in accordance with the applicable terms of this Agreement. No such holding over or extension of this Agreement will extend the time for the exercise of the Option to Purchase unless agreed upon in writing by Owner.

21. **ATTORNEY'S FEES.** In any action or proceeding involving a dispute between Tenant and Owner arising out of the execution of this Agreement or the sale, whether for tort or for breach of contract, and whether or not brought to trial or final judgment, the prevailing

Tenant [_____] [_____] has read this page.

FORM 106.2 (07-2002)   COPYRIGHT © 1993–2002 BY PROFESSIONAL PUBLISHING, 365 BEL MARIN KEYS BLVD., SUITE 100, NOVATO, CA 94949   (415) 884-2164

PROFESSIONAL PUBLISHING

| EXHIBIT | 18.1 | SAMPLE LEASE (CONTINUED) |

Property Address _____

party will be entitled to receive from the other party a reasonable attorney fee, expert witness fees, and costs to be determined by the court or arbitrator(s).

22. FAIR HOUSING. Owner and Tenant understand that the state and federal housing laws prohibit discrimination in the sale, rental, appraisal, financing or advertising of housing on the basis of race, color, religion, sex, sexual orientation, marital status, national origin, ancestry, familial status, source of income, age, mental or physical disability.

23. OPTION. So long as Tenant is not in default in the performance of any term of this Agreement, Tenant will have the option to purchase the real property described herein for a PURCHASE PRICE OF$_____(_____dollars), upon the following TERMS and CONDITIONS:

_____
_____
_____
_____
_____
_____
_____

24. DISCLAIMER. The parties acknowledge that the availability of financing and other purchase costs can not be ascertained with certainty. The parties agree that these items will not be conditions of performance of this Agreement, and the parties agree they have not relied upon any representations or warranties by Brokers, Owner, or other parties which are not set forth in this Agreement.

25. DISCLOSURES. Within _____ days after acceptance, or earlier if required by law, Owner will provide the following or comparable disclosures to Tenant:
- ▢ SELLERS REAL PROPERTY DISCLOSURE STMT. ▢ NATURAL HAZARD REPORT BY _____
- ▢ EARTHQUAKE HAZARDS DISCLOSURE ▢ MEGAN'S LAW DISCLOSURE _____
- ▢ NOTICE RE SEPTIC SYSTEMS ▢ OTHER _____
- ▢ LEAD-BASED PAINT DISCLOSURE (for dwellings constructed prior to 1978 - must be delivered prior to acceptance.)

26. FIXTURES. All items permanently attached to the property, including light fixtures and bulbs, attached floor coverings, all attached window coverings, including window hardware, windows and door screens, storm sash, combination doors, awnings, TV antennas, burglar, fire and smoke alarms (except leased systems), pool and spa equipment, solar systems, attached fireplace screens, electric garage door openers with controls, outdoor plants and trees (other than in movable containers), are included in the purchase price free of liens, EXCLUDING: _____

27. PERSONAL PROPERTY. The following personal property, on the premises when inspected by Tenant, is included in the purchase price and will be transferred to Tenant free of liens and properly identified by a Bill of Sale **at close of escrow. Unless itemized here personal property is not included in the sale. No warranty is made as to the condition of the personal property.**

_____

28. EXAMINATION OF TITLE. Owner will convey title to the property subject only to: [1] real estate taxes not yet due; and [2] covenants, conditions, restrictions, rights of way and easements of record, if any, which do not materially affect the value or intended use of the property.

   Within three (3) days from exercise of the Option to Purchase, Tenant will order a Preliminary Title Report and copies of CC&Rs if applicable. **Within ten (10) days of receipt,** Tenant will report to Owner in writing any valid objections to title contained in such report (other than monetary liens to be paid upon close of escrow). If Tenant objects to any exceptions to the title, Owner will use due diligence to remove such exceptions at his or her own expense **before close of escrow.** If such exceptions cannot be reasonably removed before close of escrow, this Agreement will terminate, unless Tenant elects to purchase the property subject to such exceptions. In the event there is a bond or assessment which has an outstanding principal balance and is a lien upon the property, such principal will be assumed by tenant without credit toward the purchase price, EXCEPT AS FOLLOWS:

_____

29. EVIDENCE OF TITLE, will be in the form of a policy of title insurance, issued by _____,
paid by _____.NOTE: In addition to coverage under a standard CLTA policy, the ALTA Owner's Policy, or CLTA Homeowner's Policy of Title Insurance, may offer additional coverage for a number of unrecorded matters. Tenant/Buyer should discuss the type of policy with the title company of their choice at the time escrow is opened.

30. CLOSING COSTS. Escrow fees, if any, and other closing costs will be paid in accordance with local custom and practice, except as otherwise provided herein.

31. CLOSE OF ESCROW. Within _____ days from exercise of the Option to Purchase, both parties will deposit with an authorized escrow holder, to be selected by the Tenant, all funds and instruments necessary to complete the sale in accordance with the terms of this Agreement.

32. PRORATIONS. Rents, real estate taxes, and other expenses of the property will be prorated as of the date of recordation of the deed. Security deposits, advance rentals or considerations involving future lease credits will be credited to Tenant.

33. EXPIRATION OF OPTION. This Option to Purchase may be exercised at any time after (date) _____, and will expire at midnight (date) _____. Upon expiration Owner will be released from any obligation to sell property to Tenant.

Tenant [_____] [_____] has read this page.

Page 3 of 4
FORM 106.3 (07-2002)   COPYRIGHT © 1993–2002 BY PROFESSIONAL PUBLISHING, 365 BEL MARIN KEYS BLVD., SUITE 100, NOVATO, CA 94949 (415) 884-2164

PROFESSIONAL PUBLISHING

EXHIBIT 18.1 SAMPLE LEASE (CONTINUED)

Property Address _____

34. EXERCISE OF OPTION. The Option to Purchase will be exercised by mailing or delivering written notice to the Owner prior to the expiration of this Option and by an additional payment, on account of the purchase price, in the amount of: $_____
_____ dollars) for account of Owner to the authorized escrow holder **within 10 days after the exercise of the Option to Purchase.**

Notice, if mailed, will be by certified mail, return receipt requested, to the Owner at the address set forth in Item 2, and will be deemed to have been given on the date shown on receipt or upon the fifth day following deposit in the U.S. Mail, whichever is earlier.

In the event the Option to Purchase is exercised, the consideration paid for the Option and _____ % from the rent paid by Tenant prior to the exercise of the Option to Purchase will be credited toward the purchase price.

NOTICE: Some states require that residential leases contain language which notifies the parties as to how to access the convicted sex offenders data base ("Megan's Law"). If such a notice is required, an appropriate addendum should be attached to this form.

LIMITATION OF AGENCY: A real estate broker or agent is qualified to advise on real estate. If you have any questions concerning the legal sufficiency, legal effect, insurance, or tax consequences of this document or the related transactions, consult with your attorney, accountant or insurance advisor.

The undersigned Tenant hereby acknowledges that he or she has thoroughly read and approved each of the provisions contained in this Offer, and agrees to the terms and conditions specified.

Tenant _____ Date _____ Owner _____ Date _____

Tenant _____ Date _____ Owner's Address _____

Tenant's Address _____ _____

Tenant's Telephone _____ Owner's Telephone _____

Receipt for deposit acknowledged by _____ Date _____

ACCEPTANCE

The undersigned Owner accepts the foregoing Offer.

NOTICE: The amount or rate of real estate commissions is not fixed by law. They are set by each broker individually and may be negotiable between the owner and broker.

COMMISSION. Upon execution, the Owner agrees to pay to _____,
the Broker in this transaction, _____% of the option consideration for securing the Option plus the sum of $(_____ dollars) for leasing services rendered and authorizes Broker to deduct this sum from the deposit received from Tenant. In the event the option is exercised at any time during the term of the lease or any extension of the term or **within 180 days after termination of occupancy,** the Owner agrees to pay Broker the additional sum of $_____ (_____ dollars) upon close of escrow. This Agreement will not limit the rights of Broker provided for in any listing or other agreement which may be in effect between Owner and Broker.

In any action for commission the prevailing party will be entitled to reasonable attorney fees.

Owner acknowledges that he or she has read and understands the provisions of this Agreement, agrees to the terms and conditions specified, and acknowledges receipt of a copy.

Owner _____ Date _____

Owner _____ Date _____

Rev. by _____
Date _____

PROFESSIONAL PUBLISHING

LEASE TERM

The period for which the lease will run should be precisely stated. You will note that in Exhibit 18.1, the provision marked [1] contains space for a starting date and lease term. In some states, lease terms are limited by statute. In practice, the maximum long-term lease is ninety-nine years (including renewals) because several early state court decisions held that a lease of 100 years or more conveyed a fee simple interest to the lessee.

CONSIDERATION

Rent is the consideration the tenant grants for the right to occupy the leased premises. Usually, rent is a monetary amount, but any good and valuable consideration will satisfy this requirement. For example, the owner of agricultural land may lease the property in exchange for half the crop harvested by the tenant. The amount of rent, and the date each payment is due, should be clearly stated in the lease. In Exhibit 18.1, these items are included in the provision marked [2]. You will note that the provision in the sample lease requires the tenant to pay rent in advance, as do most leases. It is important for landlords to include this point in the lease because common law dictates that rent is payable at the end of the lease term unless otherwise stated in the lease.

SIGNATURES

To be valid, a written lease must be signed by the landlord, and most states also require the landlord's spouse to sign if there is any dower interest. It is good business practice to also secure the lessee's signature on the lease, although courts have held that this is not required because the tenant's acceptance of the lease terms is implied by taking possession and paying rent. Generally, when two or more tenants sign a lease, they become jointly and severally liable to the landlord (although some states require that this be stated in the contract). Joint and several liability means, for example, that if you and two friends sign an apartment lease, you may be held solely responsible for the rent payment if your friends decide not to contribute their share. The only way to avoid joint and several liability is to have each tenant sign a separate lease that specifies their separate obligations. You will note, in Exhibit 18.1, that space is provided for both the landlord's and tenant's signatures on the fourth page of the lease.

OTHER LEASE PROVISIONS

Typically, a lease contains numerous provisions that cover items beyond the essential elements discussed in the preceding section. Many leases contain clauses that specify the obligations of both the landlord and tenant in the event of special circumstances, such as if either party dies, or if the property is damaged by fire or some natural disaster. Other common clauses specify how the landlord should handle security deposits (provision [15]), the tenant's right to lease the premises to a third party (provision [7]), and under what conditions the landlord may enter the premises (provision [11]).

DEATH OF A PARTY TO THE LEASE

A clause that obligates the tenant, landlord, and their heirs and assigns to fulfill the lease terms clearly indicates that the death of a principal will not terminate the lease agreement. The provision marked [18] on the lease in Exhibit 18.1 is an example of such a clause. Without such a clause, the death of either party to the lease would terminate the agreement.

LANDLORD'S RIGHT TO ENTER THE PREMISES

Although possession of the leased premises is given to the tenant, most residential leases contain a clause that allows the landlord to enter the premises periodically. From the tenant's perspective, it is important to review this clause to ensure that such entry will not be obtrusive. Typically, a lease will state when, and for what purpose, the landlord may enter. Reasons for entry usually include for the purpose of making repairs or to inspect the property. Except in the case of emergencies, such clauses usually require prior notice of entry by the landlord.

DAMAGE TO THE PROPERTY

Tenants can be held responsible for damage they cause to the leased premises, as covered by the provision marked [10] in the sample lease. In some areas, tenants may even be obligated to continue paying rent if the leased premises are damaged, or completely destroyed, through no fault of their own. In such areas, a clause that permits the tenant to stop paying rent and terminate the lease if the premises are substantially damaged is important to tenants.

SECURITY DEPOSITS

A security deposit is money the tenant deposits with the landlord to offset a number of contingent expenses. In general, the landlord can use the security deposit for a number of purposes, including:

1. To pay for accidental or intentional damage to the property by the tenant;
2. For failure to pay rent, although this is prohibited in some states;
3. For damages caused by a tenant who wrongfully quits the premises; and
4. To clean the premises and thereby return it to the same condition as when the tenant's possession began (allowing for normal wear and tear).

If the deposit is not required for any of these conditions upon the expiration of the lease, the landlord must return the deposit to the tenant. In the sample lease, space is provided at the top of the first page to insert the security deposit amount, and provision [15] pertains to the security deposit.

The term "security" is a bit of a misnomer in that security deposits provide the landlord with relatively little monetary security. For residential leases, most states limit security deposits to one month's rent, but it is quite easy for the damages incurred by the landlord (either in the form of property damage or lost rent) to exceed the security deposit amount. The landlord may offset this risk by collecting the rent for the last month in advance. Perhaps the security deposit is more valuable to landlords as a screening device to identify tenants with the financial capacity to meet the scheduled rent payments. A prospective tenant who can pay the rent for the first and last month plus a security deposit provides a solid cushion against future unpaid rent and damage, and is less likely to default on future rent payments compared with a prospective tenant who cannot.

Security deposits are also used in commercial leases, but not with the frequency seen in residential leases. If a property has been vacant for some time, or if a tenant agrees to lease property "as is," many commercial property landlords will not require a security deposit. Increasingly, institutional lenders require that leases include security deposits before they will advance funds secured by a leased fee estate. As the following highlighted material demonstrates, security deposits may provide landlords with relatively little security.

DOING BUSINESS
SECURITY DEPOSITS

John Skeslock owned two general-purpose warehouses in Columbus, Ohio. Early in 1999, he leased the warehouses to a married couple who stated that they were starting a tire recycling business. On April 15, he telephoned the tenants to find out why the rent check due on April 1 had not arrived. He feared he had trouble when he discovered that his tenants' telephone was disconnected. His fears were confirmed when he visited the property. Inspection of the warehouses revealed that the couple had disappeared, but they left behind two warehouses full of badly worn tires; one warehouse was so full that the door had to be pried open. Because the couple had leased the property "as is," he had not required a security deposit, but even if he had the deposit would have amounted to only a few thousand dollars, to properly dispose of the tires it cost Mr. Skeslock approximately $35,000.

Go to www.realtytimes.com, use "security deposit" as your search term, and then click on one or more of the titles to learn more about this topic.

The Internal Revenue Service treats security deposits differently than rental payments. Unlike rental payments, security deposits are not taxable to the landlord until they are applied to remedy a tenant default. In addition, business tenants may not claim security deposits as a tax deduction as they can payments of rent. Finally, if a landlord were to declare bankruptcy, tenant's claims to security deposits are superior to most claims of the landlord's creditors, and any deposit not returned can be written off as a tax-deductible loss.

TENANT'S RIGHT TO LEASE THE PROPERTY TO OTHERS

In most states, either party to a lease may transfer their interest to another party at any time unless prohibited from doing so in the lease agreement. Two circumstances may motivate lessees to transfer their leasehold interest before the contract rental period expires. First, for any number of reasons, lessees may simply desire to move out; perhaps because the premises no longer meet their needs, or because they are experiencing financial difficulties. It is also possible that lessees may profit by transferring their interest to another, especially if the lease is long-term and contains favorable provisions. In the industry, tenants refer to such a lease as a sweetheart lease. Although in some states, by law, leasehold interests may not be transferred unless the tenant first obtains the permission of the landlord.

One situation that may create a sweetheart lease is when economic rent exceeds contract rent. **Contract rent** is the rental amount actually due under a lease agreement. **Economic rent** is the rental amount that the real estate commands in an open, competitive market. For example, assume that you just signed a lease that entitles you to 1,000 square feet of office space for $12 per square foot, per year, for three years. If your leasehold interest is transferable and market office space rents suddenly increase to $15 per square foot, your leasehold is of obvious value. Knowing this, you might decide to purchase and use a different property, in part, because you could effectively sell your leasehold interest for a $250 profit per month.

Sublease Vs. Assignment of Lease

The two terms used to describe the transfer of a leasehold interest are: sublease, and assignment of lease. A **sublease** refers to the situation in which the original tenant either transfers a portion of the leased property to another, or transfers all of the leased property for a portion of the lease term. With a sublease, the original tenant retains an interest in the property and the third party, the sublessee, pays rent to the original tenant, who in turn remains liable to the landlord for the rent stipulated in the original lease. An **assignment of lease** occurs when all of a tenant's rights are transferred to another for the entire lease term. With a lease assignment, the assignee pays rent directly to the landlord.

Good business practice dictates that landlords specify the lessee's right (or lack thereof) to assign or sublease the premises in a written lease. Provisions preventing assignments and subleases are common because while landlords may consider the tenant with whom they negotiated to be responsible, they may have legitimate concerns about an unknown sublessee or assignee. These concerns include the sublessee's or assignee's ability to pay the rent in a timely fashion, and the manner in which the property will be maintained, both of which may affect the value of the property. Note that the provision marked [7] in Exhibit 18.1 precludes the tenant from assigning or subletting the premises without the landlord's permission.

OPTION CLAUSES

Some leases contain a provision, called an option clause, which provides the tenant with the right, but not the duty to do something at a future time. Typical option clauses empower the tenant to extend the term of the lease, or renew it at a preset price. Other options clauses may entitle the tenant to more space, or give the tenant the right to buy the property at a predetermined price. A lease that contains the last type of option is referred to as a lease with an option to purchase. Note that this is the type of lease shown in Exhibit 18.1; much of the third and fourth pages of the lease are devoted to the purchase option.

LEASE TERMINATION

The lease agreement between landlord and tenant may be terminated in a number of ways. Unless renewed, a lease automatically terminates at the expiration of the lease term (the tenant's possession may not end, but the legal relationship between the parties changes as described below). A lease may also be terminated before the expiration of the lease term by mutual agreement of the parties. If a written lease was employed, the agreement to terminate should also be in writing. Abandonment of the leased premises also terminates the leasehold interest. Abandonment occurs when the tenant vacates the property with no intention to perform under the terms of the lease. When abandonment occurs, the landlord regains full possession and control, but the tenant remains liable for the remaining rent. Several other circumstances may also terminate a lease agreement, including breach of the leasing terms and conditions, destruction or condemnation of the leased premises, and commercial frustration of purpose. An example of the latter would be a case in which the tenant's use of the property is precluded by a zoning ordinance.

EVICTION

In some cases, a tenant may violate the terms of the lease. In other cases, a tenant may, for one reason or another, decide not to vacate the premises when the lease terminates. In either case, the tenant is in wrongful possession and a landlord may take both informal and formal action to remove the tenant. If the party in wrongful possession cannot be convinced to quit the premises, the landlord can file a lawsuit to remove the party from the premises. This process, called **eviction** (also known as ejectment, forcible detainer, or forcible detainer and entry) begins when the landlord serves the tenant with a notice to vacate, a sample of which appears in Exhibit 18.2. Eviction can be a time-consuming and costly process because courts attempt to protect the rights of both landlords and tenants. Delays required for legal notices may cause the eviction process to extend over a protracted time period, and in some cases the landlord may lose rental income for several months if the tenant is unwilling or unable to pay.

EXHIBIT   **18.2**   **NOTICE TO VACATE**

LANDLORD'S FIVE DAYS' NOTICE

To _____

You are hereby notified that there is now due the undersigned landlord the sum of _____ Dollars and _____ Cents, being rent for the premises situated in the _____, County of _____ and State of _____ described as follows:

_____

together with all buildings, sheds, out-buildings, barns and garages used in connection with said premises.

And you are also notified that payment of said sum is hereby demanded of you, and that unless payment is made on or before the expiration of five days after service of this notice you lease of said premises will be terminated. Acting as the landlord's agent _____ is hereby authorized to receive said rent for the undersigned.

Unless the landlord agrees in writing to continue the lease in exchange for receiving partial payment, only **FULL PAYMENT** of the rent demanded in this notice will waive the landlord's right to terminate the lease under this notice.

Dated this _____ day of _____, 19_____

_____

Landlord

Source: Author (Caution: Consult an attorney before using or acting under this form.)

CONSTRUCTIVE EVICTION

Not all evictions are legal. One type of illegal eviction is **constructive eviction,** which occurs when the landlord so disturbs the tenant's enjoyment of the leased property that the tenant is effectively forced to move. Imagine a tenant in a situation where the landlord cuts off the water, heat, or electricity. Any of these actions may result in constructive eviction. However, the tenant must vacate the premises within a reasonable time of the landlord's act. Constructive eviction might also occur in cases where the landlord makes extensive repairs to the property, fails to control pest infestations, or fails to provide elevator service in a high-rise apartment building. When constructive eviction occurs, a tenant may sue for damages and/or to recover possession. If, however, the tenant does not vacate the premises, the tenant's duty to pay rent is not terminated.

In the event the premises become uninhabitable, a tenant may be able to avoid the inconvenience of moving out by taking other actions. As Exhibit 18.3 shows, some states permit tenants to make necessary repairs and deduct the expense from their rent payment. Other states permit tenants to withhold rent until the landlord makes needed repairs. Also included in Exhibit 18.3 is a list of the states that have enacted legislation that requires landlords to provide premises that are in habitable condition before a tenant is required to pay rent. Reasonable people can disagree as to what constitutes habitability. Therefore, insertion of a clause that enables the tenant to place disputed lease payments into an escrow account may be beneficial to the tenant. If a court later finds that the premises were habitable, a tenant who otherwise refused to pay rent would be in violation of the lease.

RETALIATORY EVICTION

Another type of illegal eviction is **retaliatory eviction.** This occurs when a landlord evicts a tenant, increases the tenant's rent, or decreases services rendered to the tenant, in response to some action taken by the tenant. A landlord can raise the rent if it can be demonstrated that increased taxes or other costs have forced the increase, but the Uniform

EXHIBIT 18.3	STATE-BY-STATE LAWS

	URLTA Adopted	Statutory Warranty of Habitability	Rent Withholding	Repair & Deduct
Alabama	No	No	No	No
Alaska	Yes	Yes	Yes	Yes
Arizona	Yes	Yes	Yes	Yes
Arkansas	No	No	No	No
California	No	Yes	No	Yes
Colorado	No	No	No	No
Connecticut	No	Yes	Yes	Yes
Delaware	No	Yes	Yes	No
Florida	Yes	Yes	Yes	No
Georgia	No	Yes	No	No
Hawaii	Yes	Yes	No	No
Idaho	No	Yes	No	No
Illinois	No	No	No	Yes
Indiana	No	No	Yes	No
Iowa	Yes	No	Yes	No
Kansas	Yes	Yes	Yes	No
Kentucky	Yes	Yes	Yes	Yes
Louisiana	No	Yes	No	Yes
Maine	No	Yes	No	No
Maryland	No	Yes	Yes	No
Massachusetts	No	Yes	Yes	No
Michigan	No	Yes	Yes	No
Minnesota	No	Yes	Yes	No
Mississippi	No	No	No	No
Missouri	No	No	Yes	No
Montana	Yes	Yes	No	Yes
Nebraska	Yes	Yes	Yes	Yes
Nevada	No	Yes	Yes	Yes
New Hampshire	No	Yes	No	No
New Jersey	No	No	Yes	No
New Mexico	Yes	Yes	Yes	No
New York	No	Yes	Yes	Yes
N. Carolina	No	Yes	Yes	Yes
N. Dakota	No	Yes	No	Yes
Ohio	No	Yes	Yes	Yes
Oklahoma	No	Yes	No	Yes
Oregon	Yes	Yes	Yes	Yes
Pennsylvania	No	No	Yes	No
Rhode Island	Yes	Yes	Yes	No
S. Carolina	No	Yes	Yes	Yes
S. Dakota	No	Yes	No	Yes
Tennessee	Yes	Yes	Yes	Yes
Texas	No	Yes	Yes	Yes
Utah	No	No	No	No
Vermont	No	No	Yes	No
Virginia	Yes	Yes	Yes	Yes
Washington	No	Yes	Yes	Yes
West Virginia	No	Yes	No	No
Wisconsin	No	Yes	Yes	No
Wyoming	No	No	No	No

Source: various state statutes

Residential Landlord and Tenant Act (URTLA)and many state laws provide that a landlord may not retaliate against the following actions:

1. Request for necessary repairs;
2. Organizing or attending tenants' meetings;
3. Forming a tenants' union;
4. Good faith complaint to the authorities of conditions that constitute a violation of a health regulation or building code; and
5. Lawful withholding of rent.

Proving that a landlord's action constitutes retaliatory eviction is not always easy. Some states have statutes that set a time to determine the motivation behind an eviction. For example, in California, if a landlord acts against a tenant within sixty days after a tenant made a complaint, it is assumed that the landlord is trying to retaliate. Even with such time guidelines, it is not always possible to identify retaliatory evictions. If, for example, a tenant's rent was doubled one month after the tenant complained about a building code violation, the landlord's intention is fairly clear-cut. But how does one assess a rent increase that does not occur until six months after the complaint? Tenants who suffer retaliatory eviction are generally entitled to damages.

TYPES OF TENANCIES

In this section we describe four kinds of tenancies, or leasehold estates, that a tenant may hold: tenancy for years, periodic tenancy, tenancy at will, and tenancy at sufferance. In reading the material on these estates, you will note that the basic factor that distinguishes one from another is the term of the tenancy.

TENANCY FOR YEARS

A **tenancy for years** is created with a lease where both the beginning and expiration dates of the lease term are specified. Synonyms for tenancy for years include term for years and estate for years. Sometimes the terminology "tenancy for years" is confusing, particularly when such a lease is for less than one year. As long as the term of the lease is known and definite, a "tenancy for years " applies regardless of whether the lease will terminate at the end of five years, one year, three months, or one week. Most commercial leases and ground leases are tenancies for years.

A tenancy for years ends on the expiration date of the lease, and neither party is required to give notice of termination. Unless a tenancy for years is renewed, when a tenant continues possession after the lease term, a different tenancy is created, either a periodic tenancy or a tenancy at sufferance.

PERIODIC TENANCY

A **periodic tenancy,** also called a tenancy from period to period, is created when the parties agree to a rent for specific rental periods on a period-by-period basis. The two most common rental periods are one year, and one month. Leases that create periodic tenancies never have a term of more than one year, but occupancy by the tenant may extend over several years. This is because a periodic tenancy automatically continues for another period if the lease is not terminated by proper notice. Either the lessee or the lessor can terminate a periodic tenancy by giving the other party notice prior to the expiration of the lease (one month notice is common). To avoid later problems, the termination notice should be in writing. A periodic tenancy is common for farm and ranch property, but may be used for any kind of property.

TENANCY AT WILL

A **tenancy at will** is used to describe the situation in which a tenant is in possession of a property with the permission of the owner, but without any agreement as to the term of the lease, or the rent amount. A tenancy at will may be created when the parties are negotiating the purchase or lease of the property, or by a void contract for sale, or oral lease. Such tenancies may also be created when a tenancy for years or periodic tenancy expires, the tenant holds over, and the landlord continues to accept rent. As the name of this leasehold suggests, the tenant is in possession at the will of the landlord. A tenant cannot assign such leaseholds, but may usually sublease the premises. Under common law, either party may terminate a tenancy at will at any time, but many state laws require prior notice. Georgia, for example, requires that landlords and tenants give sixty- and thirty-days notice, respectively. Unlike other tenancies, a tenancy at will is terminated upon the death of either the landlord or the tenant.

TENANCY AT SUFFERANCE

A **tenancy at sufferance** is created when a tenant who lawfully acquired possession of real property remains in possession without the landlord's permission for a longer time period than that which was agreed upon. By remaining in possession after a lease expires, the tenant converts the lease into a tenancy at sufferance, and the tenant becomes a **holdover tenant.** If the landlord subsequently accepts rent from the tenant, a periodic tenancy is created. Until that time, the tenant at sufferance may be evicted by the landlord at any time.

The tenancy at sufferance is the lowest interest one may hold in land. This tenancy does, however, offer some protection to both parties. A tenancy at sufferance prevents the tenant from being classified as a trespasser. Likewise, the landlord is afforded some protection by this tenancy because tenants at sufferance may not acquire title through adverse possession.

LEASES CLASSIFIED BY RENTAL PAYMENT

Real estate leases are frequently categorized by the manner in which the rent is calculated and paid. Based on these criteria, some of the more common types of leases are described in the following paragraphs. It is not uncommon for a lease to involve a combination of two or more of the general categories described here.

GROSS LEASE

A **gross lease,** also known as a flat lease, straight lease, or fixed lease, is one that calls for a constant rental payment to be made at stipulated intervals. Under a gross lease, the landlord is responsible for paying property taxes, special assessments, property hazard insurance premiums, and for major repairs. The major advantage of a gross lease for either party is that the rental amount is predictable; under other arrangements the rent can increase or decrease which may work to the disadvantage of either the tenant or landlord. Gross leases are commonly used for residential property and are sometimes used in leasing commercial property, but net leases are more common for commercial property.

NET LEASES

There are several variations of the **net lease** that are used for many commercial properties: the net lease, the net-net lease, and the net-net-net lease. As the following highlighted material shows, each of these arrangements makes the tenant financially responsible for expenses that would ordinarily be paid by the landlord under a gross lease. Most people have a net-net-net, or triple net, lease in mind when they refer to a net lease. The term "net," therefore, is descriptive in that the rent received by the landlord represents a net return. Responsibility for each of these items, and others, is, however, subject to negotiation and variations of the arrangements shown in the highlighted material are not uncommon. A net lease rent payment may be fixed or it may take one of the forms described here.

Lease Type	Tenant Responsible for Payment of:
Net	Rent and property taxes for the leased premises.
Net-net	Rent, property taxes, and the premium for hazard insurance on the leased premises.
Net-net-net	Rent, property taxes, hazard insurance, and maintenance.

Decision Point

You are negotiating the lease of retail space you plan to use as a store. The landlord has offered you the following alternatives: 1.) a gross lease of $1,000 per month; 2.) a net lease with a rental payment of $900 per month; 3.) a net-net lease with rent equal to $840 per month; or 4.) a triple net lease with rent of $775 per month. Property taxes on the space are $1,200 per year and the insurance premium is $600 per year. Maintenance costs are expected to run $50 per month. Which lease would you choose?

PERCENTAGE LEASE

A **percentage lease,** in which rent is based on a percentage of the tenant's sales, is commonly used with commercial properties such as retail establishments in a shopping center. Sometimes such leases take on a hybrid form; requiring payment of a flat sum plus a percentage of the tenant's sales. From the tenant's perspective, percentage leases have two advantages. First, a percentage lease will result in rental payments that fluctuate in accordance with the tenant's ability to pay. Second, a percentage lease provides the landlord with an incentive to keep the leased property in attractive condition because it may lead to both increased sales and rent earned by the landlord. To illustrate how the rent on such a lease is determined, consider a three-year lease that requires rent of $1,500 per year, plus 5 percent of the tenant's gross sales. If the tenant's sales in years one, two, and three are $10,000, $20,000, and $15,000 respectively; annual rent will be $2,000 [($10,000 × .05) + $1,500] for year one, $2,500 for year two, and $2,250 for year three.

GRADUATED LEASE

Landlords may prefer to use a **graduated lease,** or step-up lease, in an attempt to protect the purchasing power of rent received during inflationary periods. With a graduated lease, the rent payments increase by stated amounts over time. For example, if a three-year lease calls for initial rent of $20 per square foot, to be increased 10 percent per year; rent would be $22 [($20 × .10) + $20] and $24.20 [($22 × .10) + $22] for years two and three, respectively.

During inflationary periods, a graduated lease should allow for lower initial rent compared with other lease types that require the landlord to factor inflation into a fixed rent amount. The lower early payments of a graduated lease should benefit tenants. A graduated lease does, however, require both parties to forecast what will happen to rents over the lease period. If market rents rise more or less rapidly than forecast, one of the parties will be worse off than if they arranged a fixed rental amount.

INDEX LEASE

An **index lease** calls for a rental payment that fluctuates in direct proportion to some general economic indicator, such as the Consumer Price Index. Index leases are increasing in popularity because they offer protection not only to landlords in case of inflation, but also to tenants in case deflation occurs. To illustrate how the rent payment on such a lease is determined, consider a three-year lease with the rent tied to the Mythical Price Index. Assume that rent for the first year is set at $2,000, and that the index stood at 100 at the time the lease was signed. Further assume that the index was 110, and 95 at the end of the first and second year, respectively. Rent for year two would equal $2,200 [($110 ÷ 100) × $2,000], and for year three $1,900 [($95 ÷ 100) × $2,000].

Decision Point

You are negotiating a five-year lease for some retail space you plan to use as a store. The landlord has offered you the following alternatives: 1.) a gross lease of $1,000 per month; 2.) an indexed lease with annual rent adjustments. The index to which rents are to be tied has risen at an average annual rate of 7 percent for the last five years, and you estimate it will continue to increase at this rate in the future. What is the maximum initial rent you would pay on the index lease?

REAPPRAISAL LEASE

A lease that calls for periodic changes in the amount of rent based on future appraised valuations of the leased property is called a **reappraisal lease.** In effect, a reappraisal lease is closely related to an index lease, but instead of rent tied to a market basket of goods, it is tied to the value of a single good, the leased premises. Landlords use reappraisal leases to protect against decreases in the purchasing power of the rent that occurs with inflation. To illustrate how such a lease might work, consider a property currently valued at $120,000. With annual rent specified at 5 percent of appraised value, current rent would be $6,000. If the property were appraised at $135,000 next year, the annual rent would increase to $6,750.

LEASES CLASSIFIED BY FUNCTIONAL FORM

When most people think of a lease arrangement for improved real property, they imagine a tenant renting a preexisting structure, or a structure that the owner erects. These are not,

CONSUMER CHECKLIST
REAPPRAISAL LEASES

To avoid confusion, those who use reappraisal leases should examine the lease to ensure that the following information is clearly specified:

1. When and how often appraisals should be made,
2. How the appraisers are to be chosen,
3. What shall trigger a rent adjustment and the formula for making the adjustment,
4. The assumptions on which appraisals are to be made, and
5. How any disputes are to be handled.

Item four may be of particular importance to lessees because, unless otherwise instructed, appraisers base value estimates on the concept of highest and best use of the land. If the highest and best use is something other than the current use, the tenant could be stuck paying rent based on a use that is unavailable.

however, the only two possibilities. In this section we review lease arrangements in which the tenant constructs the improvements.

SALE AND LEASEBACK

A **sale and leaseback** usually begins when the potential tenant owns, or purchases, land on which he or she constructs improvements that will be used in a business. The property is next sold to another party, often an institutional investor (e.g., life insurance company or pension fund) and then leased from the buyer under a long-term lease. Buyers are usually available for these types of transactions, and they benefit from the fact that the property is already leased when acquired.

A sale and leaseback also offers benefits to the tenant. First, they are one way to acquire money to operate the tenant's business. Sale and leaseback arrangements may also provide tax advantages. In calculating income tax liability, for example, only the portion of each mortgage payment that represents interest is tax deductible. The tenant may, however, deduct lease payments in full. Finally, the tenant may have the option to purchase the property at the end of the lease, which provides the tenant the opportunity to regain ownership if it is desirable to do so.

A sale and leaseback is sometimes thought of as a creative financing device for existing structures. It can be used to create cash for the owner-turned-tenant, especially if the property has been completely depreciated. Whether a sale and leaseback is more desirable than mortgaging the property depends on the cost of obtaining funds in this manner. An obvious cost associated with a sale and leaseback is the lease payments. Another consideration in a sale and leaseback arrangement is the opportunity cost associated with any appreciation in the value of the property. In undertaking a sale and leaseback without a purchase option the opportunity to sell the property at the end of the lease is forgone.

GROUND LEASE

The **ground lease** is a unique lease that is used when a property owner conveys land or air rights to a lessee who develops the property through new construction or substantial improvements. Ground leases are used primarily in urban areas. Rockefeller Plaza, the Pan Am Building, the New York Hilton, the Waldorf-Astoria, many cooperative residential and office buildings, and expensive single-family homes on choice Pacific oceanfront lots were erected on ground lease property.

As with other leases, ownership of any leasehold improvements reverts to the property owner at the termination of the lease. Despite this, ground lease tenants are willing to invest considerable amounts of money constructing improvements on the leased property because of the benefits they realize. Ground leases enable the tenant to erect and use a structure on land that is otherwise unavailable, and the improvements are customized to meet the tenant's needs. In addition, by using a ground lease tenants can employ financial leverage. A ground lease requires a small down payment compared with a land purchase. Finally, when income-producing improvements are involved, the tenant may effectively depreciate the entire investment; the improvements are depreciated and the ground lease expensed.

Ground leases are long-term in nature. Commonly, twenty-one years, excluding renewal options, is the shortest period for a ground lease; most are renewable. The length of the lease alone, however, does not distinguish a ground lease from a long term lease of office space. Ground leases are invariably triple net leases with the lessee assuming the managerial roles of developing and operating the property. They also frequently contain provisions for reappraisal rental payments.

Ground leases also offer advantages to the lessor. The Astors, Duponts, Rockefellers, other wealthy families, and institutional owners such as the Roman Catholic Church,

Columbia University, New York Life Insurance Company, and John Hancock Mutual Life Insurance Company have used ground leases to generate secure long-term income from real property without selling their ownership interest. In addition, the development of the land by the lessee under a ground lease enables the lessor to obtain substantial mortgage funds if needed. The underlying value of the land increases as a result of the improvements. Therefore, the landlord is able to borrow against the improved property for a larger amount than could be obtained for a mortgage on the raw land. The loan is not subject to tax in the year received, and interest on the loan is tax deductible. Finally, the lessor has no property management duties. Several municipalities are also resorting to the ground lease as a community planning aid and a source of new revenue.

VERTICAL LEASES

When a ground lease conveys an interest above or below the land surface the lease is sometimes referred to as a vertical lease. Previously, we learned that owners of real property generally have property rights at three levels that may be sold separately: the land surface, the subsurface, and air space above the property. Rights to the three levels may also be leased separately, and this may benefit both the property owner and society. From the owner's perspective, income generated by the property may be enhanced, and from a societal viewpoint, more effective use of limited space may be achieved. For example, it is possible for a property owner to lease the surface to a farmer and, at the same time, the right to extract minerals from the subsurface could be leased to a mining company. Leasing of air space in cities allows real property to be used more intensively. In several cities, including New York, Cleveland, and Chicago, railroad companies have leased surface and air space above their tracks on which office buildings have been constructed.

LAWS AFFECTING LEASED PROPERTY

The owners of leased residential property are, in general, subject to the same laws that affect other types of real property. Federal, state, and local housing laws apply to leased real property. At the federal level, the Civil Rights Act of 1866 prohibits discrimination in housing based on race, and the Fair Housing Act of 1968 prohibits discrimination based on race, color, sex, religion, or national origin. Most states enacted similar laws, therefore, making such discrimination a violation of both federal and state law. Some states and local communities have extended protection to other groups, making it illegal to discriminate based on marital status, age, welfare status, physical handicaps, or sexual orientation. With regard to rental property, these laws cover various forms of discrimination, including refusing to rent, choice of apartment unit, and the size of the security deposit. For example, it would be illegal to charge different security deposits based on the prospective tenant's race.

Additional laws apply specifically to residential rental property and we close the chapter with a review of two of the most important types: landlord-tenant laws, and rent controls.

LANDLORD-TENANT LAWS

State laws govern the landlord-tenant relationship. While state laws vary, some uniformity is provided by the Uniform Residential Landlord and Tenant Act (URLTA), which fourteen states have adopted, with some modification (Exhibit 18.3). URLTA governs rental agreements, condition of the premises, security deposits, uses of the property, termination of the tenancy, and both the landlord's and tenant's rights and obligations. Provisions of URLTA are summarized in Exhibit 18.4. It may be instructive to compare these provisions with the terms of the lease in Exhibit 18.1. In reviewing the information in Exhibit 18.4, you will note that not all types of residential leases are covered by URLTA.

EXHIBIT | **18.4** | **URTLA SUMMARY**

Landlord's Rights and Obligations

1. Must disclose in writing the name and address of the party authorized to manage the property, as well as the party who is to receive legal notices for the landlord at or before commencement of the tenancy.

2. To make all repairs needed to keep the premises fit for habitation.

3. Must comply with local housing and building codes and maintain in good operating condition all electrical, plumbing, heating, and other appliances and facilities such as elevators, which are supplied by the landlord.

4. To provide for the maintenance of common areas, for trash and garbage receptacles, running water, a reasonable amount of hot water, and heat during the required months unless the tenant has control over the installations supplying these.

5. The landlord may enter the premises during reasonable hours to inspect the unit, supply services, make necessary repairs or improvements, or show the unit to prospective tenants or buyers after giving reasonable notice.

6. The landlord may enter without prior permission from the tenant only in cases of extreme emergency.

7. The duties of landlord do not apply if compliance is prevented by conditions beyond the landlord's control.

8. A landlord is prohibited from decreasing the services provided to a tenant who has made a complaint to the landlord or to a governmental agency, or who has joined a tenants union.

9. When the property is sold: The landlord is relieved of these obligations as of the sale date, with the exception of the duty to return security deposits, and the previous landlord's liabilities and duties are assigned to and assumed by the new owner.

Tenant's Rights and Obligations

1. Must not willfully damage or destroy the premises, or allow others to do so, and must not disturb the neighbors quiet enjoyment of the premises.

2. The tenant must comply with local housing and building codes affecting health and safety such as disposing of trash and garbage and keeping the premises clean and safe for habitation.

3. The tenant must use in a reasonable manner all facilities provided by the landlord, such as elevators, plumbing, electrical, heating, and cooling systems.

4. Tenants may also terminate the lease if the landlord fails to perform his or her duties. Thirty days notice is required prior to termination. The landlord can stop termination by beginning a good faith effort to correct the problem within the time specified by the notice. Alternatively, tenants can obtain a court injunction requiring the landlord to correct the problem or they can sue for damages and recover reasonable attorney's fees if the landlord's noncompliance is willful.

5. The tenant is entitled to recover any prepaid rent and security deposit whenever a lease is terminated because of the landlord's noncompliance.

6. If the landlord willfully fails to deliver possession of the premises, the tenant's obligation to pay rent ceases until possession is delivered. The tenant may either terminate the lease, or sue for performance, reasonable damages, and attorney's fees.

7. If fire or some other catastrophe destroys the unit or damages it to an extent where the tenant's enjoyment of the premises is impaired, the tenant may vacate the premises at once and give the landlord written notice of the intention to terminate the lease as of the day of vacating. Where portions of the dwelling are still habitable that tenant may vacate the damaged part with rent reduction in proportion to the decrease in the fair rental value of the unit.

8. If the landlord illegally excludes the tenant from the premises or diminishes services to the tenant, the tenant has the right to either recover possession or terminate the lease.

9. The tenant may also recover reasonable damages and attorney's fees if the landlord fails to supply some essential service, such as running water or heat. The tenant may give written notice of the contract breach to the landlord and then take appropriate actions to obtain the services and deduct the cost from rent payments. Alternatively, the tenant may find substitute housing. If the tenant finds alternative housing, he or she has no obligation to pay rent until the problem is corrected.

10. The successful eviction of the tenant by a third party whose title is superior to that of the landlord relieves the tenant of the obligation to pay rent.

EXHIBIT	18.4	URTLA SUMMARY (CONTINUED)

Exceptions to URTLA

URTLA does not apply to all leases. The following leases/living arrangements are specifically excluded from coverage by the Act.

1. Commercial, industrial, agricultural, or any other nonresidential lease.
2. Mobile home lots, unless the landlord also provides the mobile home.
3. Occupancy of a structure operated for the benefit of a fraternal organization by a member of the organization.
4. Residence at a private or public institution for the purpose of receiving health care, counseling, education, or a similar service.
5. Residence under an installment land contract.
6. Transient occupancy in a motel or hotel.
7. Occupancy by an employee of the landlord when the employee's right to reside in the property is conditioned upon his or her employment.
8. Occupancy by the holder of a proprietary lease in a cooperative, or by the owner of a condominium unit.

RENT CONTROL

Some state and local governments restrict the amount of rent that landlords can charge. Various courts have determined that these **rent control** regulations are a legitimate exercise of the state's police power. Two basic motivations lie behind the implementation of such controls. In some cases, rent controls are applied to all properties to remedy high rents caused by an imbalance between demand and supply of housing. For example, rent controls in communities in California and Massachusetts were implemented for this reason. In other cases, New York City for example, rent controls are used to regulate the quality of rental properties. In such cases, controls are implemented only against those properties that do not conform to applicable building codes. Sometimes the two motives for rent control are used simultaneously. In New Jersey, for example, the enabling statute stresses quality control, but some New Jersey communities located close to New York City have implemented rent control ordinances to restrain inflated rents caused by housing shortages.

In many situations, the imposition of regulations result in unintended effects, and this is true regarding rent controls. For example, a "key market" (a form of black market) tends to develop in rent-controlled areas. In these markets, the exiting tenant "sells" the new tenant the keys to the rent-controlled unit for an amount equal to the discounted value of the difference between economic rent and the rent-controlled amount. In addition, rent controls may depress new construction of rent-controlled units because builders cannot realize acceptable rates of return. Similarly, rent controls may provide landlords with an incentive to defer maintenance.

Other solutions to housing problems are available such as: subsidies paid to tenants, landlords, or builders; and improving mass transit systems so that more remote locations have easier access to urban centers. Most solutions do, however, require expenditures that may increase a city's already heavy tax burden. The motivation of politicians for votes may outweigh better long-term solutions to the housing problem. Because there are more tenants than landlords and builders, politicians may be inclined to vote for inexpensive, immediate rent control measures.

SUMMARY

An understanding of the material presented in this chapter should enable both landlords and tenants to make more well-informed decisions. Owners of income-producing real property may find it advantageous to use the services of a real property manager. However, for small properties the cost of this service may be prohibitive. For both parties, the lease agreement is central to understanding real property leasing. A lease involves a transfer of an interest in real estate. Therefore, a valid lease can be created only if it satisfies the general legal requirements for a real estate conveyance. Both the lessor and lessee must be competent, the real estate being leased must be described with adequate certainty, and the landlord must deliver possession of the real property to the tenant. Leases usually contain many provisions beyond those necessary to create a valid agreement. Because these provisions may affect the use of the property, they should be fully understood before entering into a lease agreement.

Leases may be classified according to the terms under which a tenant is entitled to remain in possession. A tenancy for years lease is one that terminates on a certain date. A periodic tenancy has an indefinite termination date, but a known rental period. A tenancy at will does not have a definite time period, definite rental period, or expiration date. A tenancy at sufferance exists if a tenant remains in possession longer than he or she has a right to be in possession. Leases may also be classified according to the manner in which rent is calculated and paid. A constant rent amount is usually used in leasing residential property. For commercial leases, variable rents, tied either to the tenant's sales or some price index, are more common.

Federal and state regulations control certain aspects of leasing. Commercial leases tend to be less regulated than residential leases because commercial tenants are assumed to be more knowledgeable than residential tenants. For landlords and tenants to protect their

CONSUMER CHECKLIST
FACTORS TO CONSIDER IN A RESIDENTIAL LEASE

A written lease agreement that sets forth the duties and responsibilities of the landlord and tenant is in the best interests of both parties. Before either party enters into a lease they should verify that its terms are as negotiated. While the following checklist may not be complete in all circumstances, it should assist in this process:

1. Any items that need repair or replacement should be fixed, or at least noted so the tenant is not later charged for the cost.

2. Is the lease term correct?

3. Are the rent amount and the due date correct?

4. Are subleases and/or assignments allowed?

5. What is the amount of any deposit and its purpose? Is it refundable?

6. Who pays for utilities?

7. Are the appropriate options, if any, included in the lease?

8. Are children, pets, waterbeds, permitted?

9. What provision is made for the installation and removal of fixtures?

10. Are there regulations regarding things such as pool use or noise?

11. Which party is responsible for maintenance of common areas?

12. Under what conditions may the landlord enter the premises without permission?

13. Are there any penalties for late rent payments?

14. How much notice must either party give to terminate the lease?

> **AN ETHICAL ISSUE**
>
> ## REPORTING VIOLATIONS OF LEASE TERMS
>
> With some frequency, tenants either intentionally or unintentionally violate one or more provisions of their lease agreement. In contemplating your answers to the following questions, does the type, or severity, of the violation (e.g., presence of a pet, or illegal drug trafficking), or your relationship to the other tenants or the landlord affect your decision?
>
> 1. Under what conditions, if any, would you report a violation of your lease to the landlord? Why?
> 2. Under what conditions would you report another party's violation of their lease agreement to their landlord? Why?
> 3. If you were the landlord, under what conditions would you wish to be informed of lease violations? Why?
> 4. If your answer to question three differs from your previous answers, why?

own interests, each should be aware of Fair Housing Laws, landlord-tenant laws, and rent control regulations.

KEY TERMS

asset manager	index lease	rent control
assignment of lease	lease	retaliatory eviction
constructive eviction	lessee	sale and leaseback
contract rent	lessor	site manager
economic rent	net lease	sublease
eviction	percentage lease	tenancy at sufferance
graduated lease	periodic tenancy	tenancy at will
gross lease	property manager	tenancy for years
ground lease	rent	
holdover tenant	reappraisal lease	

REVIEW QUESTIONS

1. How do the duties of a site manager differ from those of a property manager?
2. When, in most states, must a lease be written in order to be enforceable?
3. List the legal requirements that must be met to create a valid real estate lease.
4. Distinguish an assignment of lease from a sublease.
5. What is the difference between a tenancy for years and a periodic tenancy?
6. What is the difference between a gross lease and a net lease? As a landlord, under what conditions would you prefer one more than the other? As a tenant, under what conditions would you prefer one more than the other?
7. What are the similarities of, and differences between, an index lease and a graduated payment lease?
8. Holding other factors constant, how should an option to purchase affect the rent amount? Why?
9. What must the landlord and tenant do to terminate each of the following types of leases?
   a. Tenancy at will
   b. Tenancy from month to month
   c. Tenancy from year to year
   d. Tenancy for years

10. Consider your living arrangement. Are you covered by URLTA? If not, why?

11. What is the most likely relationship between economic rent and contract rent in rent-controlled markets?

12. What is your answer to the questions in the two "Decision Point" sections in this chapter?

13. What is your answer to the questions in the "Ethical Issue" section in this chapter?

PROBLEMS

1. Hal Sweetheart is a tenant with four years remaining on a commercial lease. He is required to pay rent of $1,500 per month, but observes that similar property is currently being rented for $2,000 per month. Subleasing is not prohibited in his lease and Hal no longer requires the property, so he has decided to do so. If he can earn 10 percent on investments, what is the lowest one-time, up-front amount that he could accept in order to make him no worse off than netting $500 each month ($2,000 – $1,500) for the next four years? (hint: Chapter 17)

2. You are about to enter into a four-year lease for a commercial property. The landlord has offered you a choice of either a flat rental amount or a percentage lease equal to 8 percent of your annual gross sales. You estimate, with a high degree of certainty, that your sales will be equal to $100,000 in year one, $110,000 in year two, $121,000 in year three, and $133,000 in year four. What rent will be due each year under the percentage lease? What flat rent amount would make you prefer the flat lease alternative? How would your answer change if your certainty about future sales were reduced?

3. As part of your new job, you have been assigned the task of evaluating two, five-year lease alternatives. Rent on the first alternative is tied to an index that is expected to increase by 5 percent per year over the life of the lease. Rent for the first year is $10,000, and adjustments are to be made at the beginning of each year. Rent on the second lease is equal to 10 percent of the value of the leased premises. For the first two years, rent will equal $10,500. An appraisal of the property will be made at the end of year two and rent for the last three years will be based on this value. Under what conditions would you prefer the indexed lease instead of the reappraisal lease?

4. Assume that you own a commercial building that is fully depreciated and have the opportunity to enter into a sale and leaseback arrangement. Given the following information, would you enter into the sale and leaseback? You need the money and could earn a 12 percent return on it. The sale price is $100,000. The monthly rent on the ten-year lease is $1,000. The lease does not contain a repurchase clause. The property value is expected to increase 5 percent per year, and your marginal tax rate is 30 percent.

REAL ESTATE ON THE WEB

Use your favorite search engine to:

1. Locate property management firms in your area.
2. Determine what kind of residential units are available for rent in your area.
3. Determine current apartment and office vacancy rates.
4. Discover if there are rent controls in your community or state.

Refer to the companion Web site at www.wiley.com/college/larsen for a variety of online activities including additional chapter content, review materials, assignments, and related links.

ADDITIONAL READINGS

Arnott, R. and M. Igarashi. "Rent Controls, Mismatch Costs and Search Efficiency." *Regional Science & Urban Economics* (May 2000): 249–288.

Basu, K., P. M. Emerson and B. Diane. "The Economics to Tenancy Rent Control." *Economic Journal* (October 2000): 939–962.

Blumenfeld, G. D. and J. F. Rowe II. "Consider A Counteroffer They Can't Refuse—An Alternative to Options, Rights of First Refusal, and Rights of First Offer." *Real Estate Review,* (Summer 2000): 40–45.

Horn, J. S. "Elusive Sources of Capital Forcing Corporations to Re-focus on Benefits of Sale-leaseback Financing." *Real Estate Issues* (Summer 2000): 34–41.

Manley, P.M. "Its all in a Name." *Practical Real Estate Lawyer* (May 1999): 7, 60+.

Saltz, S. G. "Nonresidential Security Deposits." *Real Estate Law Journal* (Winter 1999): 225–286.

Segal, M. A. "Tax Considerations in Related Party Rentals of a Residence." *Real Estate Law Journal* (Fall 2000): 120–125.

Senterfitt, D. B. and J. Thanhauser. "Behind Every Successful Office Lease is a Vigilant Lender." *Real Estate Finance Journal* (Winter 2001): 60–64.

19

Property Insurance

Learning Objectives

After studying this chapter you should be able to:

- Explain the important terms associated with real property insurance policies.
- Describe the types of insurance policies available for commercial properties.
- Describe the perils that are, and are not, covered in a homeowner's policy.
- Calculate the amount that an insurance company will pay on a claim if the coinsurance clause is, or is not, met.
- Explain the factors that one should consider in selecting an insurance company.

FROM THE WIRE

2001 was not a good year for the nation's property and casualty insurers. They reported losing $9 billion that year compared with a $27 billion profit in 2000. The industry was hit hard by a number of factors including an extraordinary number of claims from catastrophic events (e.g., storms, wild fires), rising repair costs, inadequate premiums, and staggering claims from the September 11 terrorist attacks. In addition, sagging securities markets resulted in reduced investment income for insurers. By year-end, total claims reached $381 billion, an increase of 86 percent over claims made in 2000. Companies writing homeowner's policies also had to cover large jury awards for the latest environmental concern—black mold. Mold claims, virtually unheard of just a few years ago, cost insurers more than $1 billion in 2001. The experience of property and casualty insurers directly affects real property owners. To illustrate this point, consider the situation at State Farm, the country's largest home insurer with policies on more than 15 million homes nationwide. In 2001, State Farm reported a $5 billion loss. In an attempt to stabilize its financial condition, the company announced that it would stop writing new homeowner's policies in 20 states, and it applied to state insurance regulators for (in many cases double-digit) rate increases for existing policies. For example, in West Virginia where loss experiences were particularly bad, a 27.5 percent rate increase was requested. Owners of commercial property face similar or even higher rate increases.

Go to: www.statefarm.com, to learn what insurance products they are currently offering in your state.

INTRODUCTION

Real property ownership entails the risk that fire or some other catastrophe may damage the property. In the worst case, this could mean that the owner suffers a loss equal to the value of the improvements and their contents. In addition, owners can be held liable for injuries suffered by others while on the property, and this liability could amount to many times the value of the property. In either event, the financial burden could result in the owner losing title to the property. Therefore, most owners have some kind of insurance on their property to (at least partially) protect themselves from financial losses resulting from these types of risks. This is so, in no small part, because mortgage lenders routinely require that borrowers keep the property serving as loan collateral adequately insured, but astute owners will secure and maintain insurance regardless of whether a lender requires it.

In this chapter, we present some basic information about real property insurance. We begin by explaining important terminology included in insurance policies. Then we examine the types of policies real property owners may obtain (or as the chapter opener "From the Wire" suggests, may, at least temporarily, find difficult to obtain). Because most readers of this text have an interest in home ownership, our focus is on homeowner's policies.

INSURANCE BASICS

Insurance is a device by which one party through a contract (policy) and for consideration (premium) assumes financial responsibility for another party for certain types of risks of loss. The parties to an insurance contract are the insurer (insurance company) and the insured (property owner). As with other forms of insurance, the insurer promises to indemnify (restore financially) the insured in the event a risk covered by the policy occurs and results in a financial loss. Before a company issues a policy, the insured will be required to prove an **insurable interest** in the property. For an insurable interest to exist there must be a relationship between the insured and the event insured against so that the occurrence of the event will cause the insured some injury or loss. From a social standpoint, the requirement of an insurable interest is particularly important. For example, fire departments would likely be extremely busy if people without an insurable interest could take out policies.

Similar undesirable outcomes would be likely if the insured could collect more than the value of the damage. This is prevented because most property and liability insurance contracts contain a provision, based on the **principle of indemnity,** which states that the insured may not be compensated in an amount exceeding the economic loss. Therefore, even if a $50,000 home, insured for $1,000,000, were completely destroyed; the most the owner could collect for the home would be $50,000. This principle also applies when the same risk is covered by multiple policies. Most policies contain a pro rata liability clause which provides that when multiple policies are in force, the insurer is only responsible for a portion of any loss equal to its policy amount as a percentage of the total insurance carried on the property against the peril involved. To illustrate, suppose a $50,000 home is insured by one company for $45,000, and by a second company for $40,000. If the home is completely destroyed by a covered risk, the owner will only collect $50,000: $26,471 [$50,000 × ($45,000 ÷ $85,000)] from the first company, and $23,529 [$50,000 × ($40,000 ÷ $85,000)] from the second company.

DEDUCTIBLES AND CO-INSURANCE

Similar to some other forms of insurance, real property owners are required to bear part of any covered loss in one, or both, of two ways specified in the policy: deductibles, and co-insurance. The amount the insured is required to pay toward each loss is called the **deductible.** A deductible amount, in essence, makes the insured a limited co-insurer. One way that you can reduce your premium is to select a large deductible amount. The larger the deductible, the lower the premium should be because when the insured is required to pay a large amount for each loss, the insurance company can anticipate paying out fewer dollars on each claim.

Co-insurance clauses are designed to encourage owners to insure their property near market value. Most co-insurance clauses require the company to pay the entire insured loss (up to the policy amount) if the policy holder has paid premiums on the basis of the co-insurance rate; usually 80 percent of the property's market value. Under some co-insurance clauses, however, lower and higher co-insurance rates may apply.

When a property is insured for less than the required level, the company is only required to pay a fraction of any loss. To illustrate, consider a $90,000 home, insured with a policy containing an 80 percent co-insurance clause. The middle column of Exhibit 19.1 shows the amount of various losses for which the insurer would be responsible assuming that the home is insured for the minimum amount required to fully indemnify partial losses: $72,000 ($90,000 × .80).

Total losses are relatively rare, therefore, the co-insurance clause is more important for partial losses. Owners who wish to economize on premium payments might insure the property for less than the required co-insurance rate, provided this does not violate lender requirements. In doing so, however, owners risk paying for the premium savings many times over in the event of a loss. This is illustrated in the third column of Exhibit 19.1, which shows the amount of reimbursement to be made assuming that the sample property was insured for only $63,000. In this case, only 70 percent of any loss would be covered because the policy amount is only 70 percent of the property's market value.

TYPES OF POLICIES

Fire is the most common cause of property damage in the United States, but real property owners are also exposed to other **perils,** (also called risks, or hazards) including: building

| EXHIBIT | 19.1 | **EXAMPLE OF LOSS PAYOFFS FOR A $90,000 HOME WITH AN 80 PERCENT CO-INSURANCE CLAUSE** |

Loss Amount	With $72,000 Policy	With a $63,000 Policy
$15,000	$15,000	$10,500
$30,000	$30,000	$21,000
$45,000	$45,000	$31,500
$60,000	$60,000	$42,000
$75,000	$72,000	$52,500
$90,000	$72,000	$63,000

collapse, earthquakes, explosions, freezing, glass breakage, hail, riots, smoke damage, tornados, vandalism, waterpipe leaks, and windstorms. Two basic types of policies are available to cover these risks: named perils and package policies.

As the title implies, a named perils policy only insures against the specific cause(s) of loss named in the policy. The most common named perils policy covers fire damage. Property owners with a fire policy can obtain coverage for other risks either by purchasing separate named perils policies, or by adding an endorsement to the fire policy. With an **endorsement** (also called an attachment, or rider) the insurer agrees to extend coverage to losses not included in the basic policy in exchange for an additional premium. Named perils policies are widely used for commercial and industrial properties where owners can employ them to cover specific risks economically which may be particular to the business or location. Homeowners use them less frequently; they prefer package policies that cover an assortment of common perils.

Package policies have several benefits compared with named perils policies. They reduce the confusion that can result when owners are forced to buy insurance on a piecemeal basis. In addition, by buying a package policy, an owner can obtain coverage at a lower cost compared with purchasing separate individual policies with identical total coverage. The most widely used package policy is the homeowner's policy. These policies also cover certain liability and property losses that occur away from the homeowner's premises.

COMMERCIAL PROPERTY INSURANCE

Commercial property insurance is fairly complex, and largely beyond the scope of an introductory real estate course. Therefore, in this section we simply present some information about the type of policies available to commercial property owners. Owners of commercial real estate face a wide assortment of risks that can be individually insured, or the owner can obtain an all-risks policy. Available policies include:

1. Standard fire insurance—covers all direct damage to the real property by fire, but other perils are specifically excluded in the policy (e.g., explosion, hail, windstorm, riot, aircraft, civil disturbance, vehicles, and other miscellaneous causes).
2. Extended coverage—covers losses due to fire, as well as many perils that are excluded from the standard fire policy. However, as you will see in the following section, not all perils are necessarily covered.
3. Business interruption insurance—compensates the owner for losses resulting from the suspension of business operations as a result of damage to or destruction of the property.
4. General liability—covers liability for injuries to people or damage to the property of others that occurs on the insured's property or off site in the conduct of the insured's business.

5. Casualty insurance—covers losses due to theft, burglary, plate glass breakage, and the breakdown of machinery, elevators, boilers, and other systems.

6. Business owner's policy—designed for small and medium-sized retail stores, office buildings, and similar businesses. This policy is similar to a homeowner's policy (discussed later) in that it provides for coverage of the building, personal property in the building, business income losses resulting from a covered peril, and liability insurance.

Terrorism—A New Industry Concern

Terrorism was not a major insurance issue before September 11. Prior to that date, "all risks" policies included terrorism protections, or at least they did not specifically exclude them. But, as those annual policies expired, insurers almost uniformly excluded coverage for terrorist acts. As a result, the United States House of Representatives passed "The Terrorism Risk Protection Act" in an attempt to provide a temporary industry risk-sharing program to allow for the continued availability of commercial property and casualty insurance. But, the Bill hit a roadblock in the United States Senate. As a result of the legislative stalemate, forty-three states have followed the recommendation of the National Association of Insurance Commissioners that individual states adopt "terrorism exclusions" in order to protect insurer solvency. A majority of states have adopted the exclusion language offered by Insurance Services Office, Inc. (ISO). The ISO terrorism exclusion for liability insurance coverage is subject to the following limitations:

- Exclusions for acts of terrorism only apply if the acts result in industry-wide insured losses that exceed $25 million for related incidents that occur within a 72 hour period: or
- Fifty or more people sustain death or serious physical injury; and
- The $25 million threshold does not apply in cases of terrorism using nuclear, chemical or biological materials.

Two major states that have not accepted the terrorism exclusions are California and New York. Among other reasons, the insurance commissioners in those states believe that the $25 million threshold is too low. The $25 million threshold, for example, would exclude virtually every building in lower Manhattan around the World Trade Center site.

HOMEOWNER'S POLICIES

There are several standardized **homeowner's policies,** most designed for single-family dwellings (HO-1, HO-2, HO-3, HO-15, and HO-8) one for condominiums (HO-6), and one for leased dwellings (HO-4). Information concerning covered perils and coverage amounts for the major forms of homeowner's policies is summarized in Exhibit 19.2.

DOING BUSINESS
COMMERCIAL PROPERTY INSURANCE

At the time of this writing, only four insurers (American International Group, Berkshire Hathaway, Lloyds of London, and Ace Group of Companies) offer stand-alone terrorism policies, and the premiums greatly exceed the normal cost of property insurance. Typically, the policies cover no more than $100 million in losses and require high deductibles on any claim. In addition, coverage is usually limited to damage from bombs and airplane crashes, but not from nuclear, chemical or biological attacks. And these insurers often retain the right to cancel the policies at any time for any reason. Go to www.iso.com, use "terrorism" as your search term, then click on one or more of the results to learn the current status of terror exclusion clauses.

EXHIBIT 19.2 SUMMARY OF HOMEOWNER'S POLICIES

Coverage	HO-1 (Basic Form)	HO-2 (Broad Form)	HO-3 (Special Form)
A. Dwelling (minimum)	$15,000	$15,000	$20,000
B. Other Structures	10% of A	10% of A	10% of A
C. Personal Property	50% of A	50% of A	50% of A
D. Loss of Use	10% of A	20% of A	20% of A
E. Personal Liability (minimum)	$100,000	$100,000	$100,000
F. Medical payments to others (minimum)	$1,000 per person	$1,000 per person	$1,000 per person
Perils Covered	1. Fire or lightning 2. Aircraft 3. Breakage of glass 4. Explosion 5. Riot or civil commotion 6. Smoke 7. Theft 8. Windstorm or hail 9. Vehicles 10. Volcanic Eruption 11. Vandalism and malicious mischief	Same as HO-1 plus: Accidental discharge or overflow of water or steam Falling objects Freezing Sudden & accidental damage for artificially generated electrical current Weight of ice, snow, or sleet Sudden & accidental tearing, cracking, burning, or bulging of steam, hot water, air conditioning, automatic fire protective sprinkler system, or appliance for heating water	Same perils covered as HO-2 except losses specifically excluded

Coverage	HO-4 (Renters' Form)	HO-6 (Condominium Unit Owners' Form)	HO-8 (Older House Form)
A. Dwelling (minimum)	NA	$1,000	$15,000
B. Other Structures	NA	NA	10% of A
C. Personal Property	$6,000 minimum	$6,000 minimum	50% of A
D. Loss of Use	20% of C	40% of C	10% of A
E. Personal Liability (minimum)	$100,000	$100,000	$100,000
F. Medical payments to others (minimum)	$1,000 per person	$1,000 per person	$1,000 per person
Perils Covered	Same perils covered as HO-2 for personal property	Same perils covered as HO-2 for personal property	Same perils covered as HO-1: losses are paid based on actual cash value, theft coverage limited to $1,000 and applies only to losses on the residence premises

Focusing on the single-family forms, note that each form covers both damage to, or loss of, the insured property, and liability of the insured and the insured's family. Each form also provides for other areas of coverage, the extent of which varies by policy form. The single-family forms also cover other structures (excluding those that are used for business purposes or leased to others) such as a detached garage or a tool shed. Personal property is also covered, including all household contents and other personal belongings that the insured or the insured's family owns, uses, carries, or wears, whether at home or elsewhere (automobiles, pets, and business property are excluded). Temporary living expenses incurred as a result of loss of use of the insured dwelling are also covered.

The list of covered perils also varies by policy form. Homeowners 1 (HO-1), also called the basic form, insures against eleven perils. Homeowners 2 (HO-2), also called the broad form, insures against the same perils as (HO-1) plus six additional perils. Homeowners 3 (HO-3), or the special form, provides HO-2 coverage on the dwelling and other structures, but may contain some specific exceptions. HO-3, which is generally considered to provide the most coverage for the premium cost is the most popular of the single-family home policies.

An all-risks policy (not shown in the exhibit) covers all risks other than damage from flood, vermine, war, earthquakes, and nuclear hazards. At one time, all risk policies were known as HO-5; they are currently designated as HO-15. Coverage for most risks not covered in a particular policy can be obtained using riders or separate policies, but increasingly, states have gotten involved to help lower the cost for protection against particular hazards. The California Earthquake Authority, for example, has more than 840,000 policies in force in the quake-prone state. Florida, which has been vulnerable to hurricanes, has a special Windstorm Underwriting Association to ensure coverage for coastal residents.

ACTUAL CASH VALUE VS. REPLACEMENT COST

Insurers may use one of two methods to determine the amount of the claim that will be paid when a loss occurs. One is the **actual cash value,** which is the new price minus accumulated depreciation. The other method of determining the amount of the claim is **replacement cost** wherein coverage is based on the actual amount a builder would charge to replace the damaged property at the time of loss. To illustrate the use of actual cash value, suppose a twenty-five-year-old home is damaged. The timbers and material are twenty-five years old and therefore do not have the same value as new material. The amount of the loss, according to the actual cash method, would equal the cost of new materials, say $10,000, reduced by the estimated depreciation of $2,500 suffered by the old material. If the owner rebuilds, he or she must pay the $2,500 difference between actual cash value and the cost of the repairs. Claims based on the actual cash basis result in lower loss exposure for the insurer and, therefore, such policies should be associated with lower premiums. For example, the premium on an HO-8 policy should be less than on an HO-1. Both cover the same perils, but claims for damage to the structure on an HO-8 are calculated on actual cash value while claims on the HO-1 are based on replacement cost.

A relatively new development in homeowner's insurance, which some mortgage lenders now require, are policies that provide for automatic coverage adjustments tied to the inflation rate. Similar protection may be obtained on other policies with an inflation guard endorsement.

Decision Point

A friend of yours has decided to buy a 100-year-old house and is now in the market for homeowners insurance She has narrowed the choice of policies down to an HO-8 and an HO-1, but favors the HO-8 because the annual premium is $45 less. What advice would you offer her before she secures the policy?

INSURANCE FOR MOBILE HOMES

Package insurance policies are also available to the several million households residing in mobile homes (manufactured homes). The coverage offered to mobile homeowners is similar to that provided by the HO-2 form. Premium rates are higher for mobile homes because total losses on mobile homes occur much more frequently compared with more permanent structures. Mobile homes are particularly susceptible to fire and wind damage; some sarcastically refer to them as "tornado magnets."

POLICY CANCELLATION

Either party can cancel an insurance policy. The insured can cancel at any time without prior notice, and because premiums are paid in advance, will be entitled to a partial refund for any unused coverage. The manner in which refunds are to be calculated is explained in the policy; short rates which result in higher charges for the period of coverage compared to a pro rata charge are usually employed. For example, a one-year policy holder who cancels after four months may be entitled to only a 56 percent refund using short rates instead of a 66.66 percent refund.

Although unlikely to occur, the insurer also has the right not to renew a policy or to cancel a policy, but must give the insured prior written notice and calculate any refund on a pro rata basis. For example, insurance companies may consider people who filed more than one claim within the past few years as potentially bad risks. On average, a homeowner files a claim once every 8 to 10 years. If you file a couple of claims for losses that are only $50 to $100 above the deductible, it may increase the probability that your coverage won't be continued with your present company.

Under certain circumstances, however, the insurer may suspend coverage without written notice. Some policies cause insurance coverage to lapse if the home is not occupied for long periods of time (e.g., sixty days, in some states thirty days) because there is a greater probability of loss occurrence in vacant properties. Therefore, continuous occupancy clauses can be especially undesirable for homeowners who travel a great deal. Coverage may also be suspended if the insured allows a risk exposure to the insurer to increase beyond the level usually associated with the type of property being insured. For example, converting a home into a place of business.

Finally, insurance offers homeowners an opportunity to be penny-wise and pound-foolish. One might be tempted to reduce premium expense by failing to mention a pertinent fact (e.g., part of the property is used for business purposes). In such a case, however, one may waste any money paid for insurance because any misrepresentation or concealment of a material fact or circumstance concerning the property, the policy, or the insured, either before or after a loss, will void the policy.

FLOOD INSURANCE

Damage from floods is not covered under any homeowner's policy because of a problem in the insurance industry known as **adverse selection.** In essence, if one knows that the probability they will suffer loss is relatively high, they are more likely to purchase a policy compared with those with only a small chance of suffering the same loss. This problem is why many life insurance companies require a physical exam before they will issue a life insurance policy. In the case of flood insurance, the only people who would buy insurance would be those who own property in a flood plain.

The National Flood Insurance Act of 1968 was designed to improve the management of the flood plain areas through land use controls and also to assist owners of real property in flood-prone areas by subsidizing flood insurance. Flood insurance is required on all types of building on properties located in flood plains if the property is financed by mortgages or other loans, guarantees or grants obtained from federal agencies, or by loans from federally insured or regulated lending institutions. Policies can be obtained from the National Flood Insurance Program, which is part of the Federal Emergency Management Agency, or from any licensed property insurance broker. The amount of coverage is equal to either the amount of the mortgage loan or the value of the property subject to the maximum limits available. The National Flood Insurance Program currently makes $100,000 worth of coverage available for $352 a year. Owners of property in flood plains who do not secure flood insurance are ineligible to obtain federally related financial assistance in the event of flood damage.

CHOOSING AN INSURANCE COMPANY

Many companies write insurance policies for homeowners and, as we have seen, there are several types of policies from which homeowners may choose. Some experts recommend that premium savings may be available if insurance is purchased through an independent agent as opposed to one who represents a particular company, because the independent agent can shop for the best deal. While there is merit to this advice, you should recognize that factors other than price are also important in selecting an insurer. The insurance company's financial stability and claim payment record are critical. Many insurance companies have recently experienced severe financial difficulties. It would be comforting to have some assurance that the company a homeowner selects will still be in business if he or she must file a claim. While no guarantees are available, information about the financial strength of individual companies, claims payment record, and possible rates charged, is available through your state insurance regulator or private rating agencies such as A. M. Best.

When choosing an insurance company, it would be wise to compare not only premium amounts, but also any differences in a number of key clauses, including: deductible amounts, co-insurance rates, the manner in which claim amounts will be calculated, conditions that will cause coverage to lapse automatically, and the manner in which the company will calculate refunds.

CONSUMER CHECKLIST
LOWERING HOMEOWNER'S INSURANCE PREMIUMS

1. Maintain a good credit rating. Many insurers are using credit-based insurance scores to determine homeowner's premiums. Other things being equal, a person with a good score will have much lower premiums compared with someone with a poor score.

2. Purchasing your homeowner's and auto policies from the same company can reduce your premium by 5 to 15 percent.

3. Selecting a high deductible can reduce your premium by 15 to 30 percent.

4. Improve your home security by installing smoke detectors, dead-bolts locks, and burglar alarms. You may be able to reduce your premium from 15 to 20 percent by installing a sprinkler system, or burglar and fire alarms that ring at fire, police or other monitoring stations.

5. Improving the disaster resistance of your home may result in reduced premiums. For example, retrofitting older homes to make them more earthquake resistant, adding storm shutters, or reinforcing your roof can reduce the probability that you will have to file a claim.

Go to: www.ambest.com, to learn the rating of several insurance companies that operate in your area.

SUMMARY

A potential disadvantage of real property ownership is the possibility that either the property will be damaged by some catastrophe, or that the owner will be held liable for injuries suffered by a third party while on the property. In either case, the owner's resulting financial burden could result in loss of ownership. You should transfer most of the financial responsibility for these risks through insurance. The material presented in the chapter suggests that you should spend perhaps as much effort in selecting an insurance company, and policy type, as in selecting the property to purchase.

KEY TERMS

actual cash value	endorsement	perils
adverse selection	homeowner's policy	principle of indemnity
deductible	insurable interest	replacement cost

REVIEW QUESTIONS

1. What is meant by the term "insurable interest"?
2. What is a co-insurance clause? Why are co-insurance clauses in homeowner's policies?
3. Why do mortgage lenders require evidence of complete insurance coverage at the time of closing?
4. Why do you think certain perils, such as war, are excluded from homeowner's policies?
5. What is an insurable interest? Why is an insurable interest important?
6. What is a deductible? How should the size of the deductible affect the premium amount?
7. In settling insurance claims, what is the difference between actual cash value and replacement value? Lower premiums should be associated with policies that have which of these two settlement clauses?
8. What factors should you consider in selecting an insurance company?

PROBLEMS

1. A homeowner's policy in the amount of $75,000 that has an 80 percent co-insurance clause is in force on a $110,000 home. If the structure suffers $50,000 damage from an insured risk, what is the most the insurance company will pay for this damage?
2. A homeowner's policy in the amount of $90,000 that has an 80 percent co-insurance clause is in force on a $110,000 home. If the structure suffers $60,000 damage from an insured risk, what is the most the insurance company will pay for this damage?
3. A homeowner's policy in the amount of $90,000 that has an 80 percent co-insurance clause is in force on a $110,000 home. If the structure suffers $95,000 damage from an insured risk, what is the most the insurance company will pay for this damage?
4. A windstorm flattened a personal residence (nobody suffered any personal injuries, but no hint of any portion of the improvements or contents has been found). Assuming that the co-insurance requirement of an HO-2 policy was met, what is the maximum amount the insured could collect on a $100,000 policy (be sure to consider coverage items A, B, C, and D from Exhibit 19.2)?
5. Suppose a $200,000 home is insured for $160,000 by one company and $180,000 by another company (both have an 80 percent coinsurance clause). If the home suffers $80,000 in damage, how much will each company pay the insured?

REAL ESTATE ON THE WEB

Use your favorite search engine to:

1. Locate real property insurance companies and agents in your area.
2. Determine the premium that several different insurers would charge to insure your home.
3. Find companies, other than A. M. Best, that rate insurance companies.

Refer to the companion Web site at www.wiley.com/college/larsen for a variety of online activities including additional chapter content, review materials, assignments, and related links.

ADDITIONAL READINGS

Cox, M. D. and C. Siskos. "Weather Beaters." *Kiplinger's Personal Finance* (August 2002): 56, 18.
Hillman, B. "The Case of the Disappeared Sign." *Property & Casualty Risk & Benefits* (April 29, 2002): 106, 20.
Loomis, C. J. "Insurance After 9/11." *Fortune* (June 10, 2002): 145, 62.
Razzi, E. and C. Pulfrey. "Three Strikes and You're Out." *Kiplinger's Personal Finance* (July 2002): 56, 87.
Silverstein, L. "Building Castles in the Clouds." *Newsweek* (July 29, 2002): 160, 54.

20

Property Development and Market Analysis

Learning Objectives

After studying this chapter you should be able to:

- Describe regulatory and environmental issues of concern to real estate developers.
- Explain the importance of a market study in the real estate decision-making process.
- List the steps in a market study.
- Describe the factors of supply and demand that influence real property value.
- Explain how supply and demand interact to determine real property prices.

PRACTIONER PROFILE

Maxine Mitchell is president of Applied Real Estate Analysis (AREA), headquartered in Chicago, and current president of the Counselors of Real Estate (CRE), an honorary organization of real estate counselors. She earned a master's degree in city planning from the Massachusetts Institute of Technology and a bachelor's degree in economics from Northwestern University. She is currently a member of the board of trustees of the Chicago Architecture Foundation, and a member and past president of the Ely Chapter of Lambda Alpha International, an honorary land economics society. She has more than 25 years of experience in real estate market analysis and public policy planning, and has completed a wide range of economic and financial feasibility studies for residential, commercial, institutional, and industrial development for both public and private sector clients. Ms. Mitchell's work in public policy planning encompasses such subjects as urban growth patterns, property taxation, low- and moderate-income housing development, central area revitalization, residential rehabilitation financing, and the development and implementation of neighborhood revitalization strategies.

Early in her career, Ms. Mitchell was retained by the City of Milwaukee to assess the market demand for alternative new development opportunities and adaptive reuses in the Schlitz Brewery area and to prepare a redevelopment strategy for this district. The Schlitz Brewery area is an older industrial, commercial, and residential area north of Milwaukee's downtown. The property consisted of several hundred thousand square feet of space, some of which contained huge copper vats that had been used for beer production. The result of this assignment was an implementation strategy that defined specific roles for the public and private sectors in the development process, identified specific projects with immediate development potential, and provided time frames for carrying out the revitalization strategy.

Go to www.cre.org, click on News & Publications, then click on Market Information, then click on one or more of the titles to learn about issues of current interest to Counselors of Real Estate.

INTRODUCTION

In this chapter, we briefly review some of the issues and regulations that real estate developers (and investors) must address and present the steps in the development process. One of the most important steps in real estate development is the determination of whether or not a proposed development makes good financial sense. This is accomplished, in part, by conducting a market study. Therefore, our focus is an explanation of this process.

To be successful, real estate market participants need reliable and timely market information upon which to base decisions. Gathering such information requires some expense and effort, which tends to discourage many novice investors. In addition, relatively few novices know what to look for, or where to locate the market information necessary to make real estate decisions. This explains why most people rely on experts like Maxine Mitchell, described in the chapter opener "Practitioner Profile."

In this chapter, we present the important types of information used to analyze real estate markets. The accumulation of market information alone does not ensure a project's success. Once the pertinent market information is obtained (via a market study), it must be analyzed to determine both the current and future investment climates. Basically, this requires the determination of current supply and demand for the property type in question, and a prediction of future supply-and-demand levels. It is possible to make correct real estate decisions without first conducting a market study, but most people who do so are lucky and few people who rely on luck are likely to make good decisions consistently.

REAL PROPERTY DEVELOPMENT

A real estate developer is an individual or firm that converts raw land into an operating property by adding improvements (e.g., buildings, roads, utilities, and landscaping) to the land. Developers may also be involved in rehabilitation or redevelopment projects by which an improved property is restored, modernized, and/or converted to another use. The land development process, which is regulated at all (but, in particular, local) levels of government, starts with land planning by the developer, who must get approval from the local government planning body before proceeding with the project. To ensure the orderly progress of a project, developers must have a command of local regulations such as zoning regulations, building codes, and any local master plan (Chapter 6).

In the case of a housing subdivision, the land planning process usually starts with a pre-application conference where the developer meets informally with the local planning board (city planning department) before preparing a formal plat. One purpose of this meeting is to ensure that the developer's plans conform to applicable subdivision regulations, which are local laws governing the conversion of raw land into building sites. These regulations may govern additional factors, but usually cover:

- Rights of way for streets, with specific location, alignment, width, grade, surfacing material, and possible dedication to the community;
- Minimum dimensions and building setback lines for lots and blocks;
- Easements for utilities and disposal of wastes; and
- Reserved areas for public uses.

The developer then prepares a preliminary plat. After the authorities approve the preliminary plat, a final plat is recorded with the county, and work on the project is started. Plats must be drawn that provide a detailed map that has been surveyed by a professional surveyor. The plat map includes topographic data with existing boundary lines, utilities, and ground elevations, and the layout of the proposed development.

Local communities may provide additional infrastructure required by the project, such as roads, utilities, and schools. But, with increasing frequency, the developer is likely to be charged an impact fee to help pay for these infrastructure needs. Many local communities are also requiring a mandatory dedication, a requirement that the developer cede a piece of the land for public use such as a park or school. However, this is a controversial issue that is being decided in the courts. (Is the developer being deprived of property without compensation?)

Finally, a developer's plans must be consistent with any local Smart Growth regulations. The phrase "Smart Growth" may be considered simply a new label for what was formerly referred to as a "master plan," although many Smart Growth regulations place more emphasis on environmentally sensitive property than did master plans. Smart Growth regulations are land-use plans that identify land to be used for residential, commercial, recreational and industrial uses and provide for projected infrastructure needs (e.g., schools, roads and other facilities), as well as land to be set aside for meaningful open space. Ideally, such regulations should protect environmentally sensitive areas, but also allow for the orderly development of property in sufficient quantity to accommodate a community's projected need for increased housing and other real property uses. Critics of Smart Growth regulations argue that the regulations may actually be used as a tool to slow or stop growth. In some cases, they are probably correct. An objective of many of these regulations is to limit urban sprawl. But, well-designed regulations will allow for the construction of higher density housing in some areas as well as provide for infill developments in suburban and inner-city neighborhoods.

ENVIRONMENTAL ISSUES

Today, developers must also be concerned with a variety of environmental issues. Numerous projects have been stalled or abandoned in recent decades because of concerns about the impact of new developments on the ecology (shorelines, plant life, or the habitat of an endangered species). In addition, to protect people from environmental hazards (see highlighted material later in the chapter), in most cases, lenders will demand a satisfactory environmental assessment of the site to be developed as a condition of providing funding for the project.

There are two types of environmental assessments. A Phase I environmental assessment identifies the potential for environmental problems on the site. If the Phase I report indicates a potential problem (and sometimes even if it does not), a Phase II environmental assessment will also be required. The Phase II assessment involves taking samples of soil, groundwater, and air and analyzing them for contaminants. If a problem is discovered, as the next paragraph indicates, the developer must fix it.

An important piece of federal legislation that addresses the problems caused by environmental hazards is the Comprehensive Environmental Response, Compensation, and Liability Act (CERCLA), which was passed by Congress in 1980. According to CERCLA, the current landowners are responsible for cleaning up any environmental hazards on their property, regardless of who was responsible for the presence of the hazard. Further, CERCLA specifies joint and several liability, which means that all owners are responsible but if only one can afford to pay the bill, that owner will pay the entire bill. However, if the current owners are financially incapable of cleaning up the site, CERCLA assigns retroactive liability—previous owners are also responsible for the clean up. Finally, CERCLA established the Superfund to pay for cleanups in cases where no financially responsible party can be identified. CERCLA is administered by the Environmental Protection Agency (EPA). Several states have also created their own Environmental Protection Agency to deal with environmental laws. In addition, many states have enacted Brownfield legislation that allows for voluntary agreements between the owner and the state to reuse urban land. Typically, under these agreements, the owner cleans up most of the pollution and the state certifies that the property has been cleaned up. The owner can then build or renovate the property with protection from future liability.

Environmental Hazards

- **Asbestos**—Asbestos is a mineral that was once commonly used in insulation because it contains heat. Unfortunately, it has been found to be a carcinogen and usually becomes hazardous when it gets old and crumbles or is disturbed by remodeling. In the redevelopment of older existing properties, developers must pay to have asbestos safely removed, and for properties in use, removal may be necessary because the property will become impossible to lease or insure if asbestos fibers reach a dangerous level.

- **Lead-based paint**—Lead was once used as a drying agent and pigment in alkyd oil-based paint. Again, unfortunately, it has been determined that high levels of lead in humans can cause damage to the brain, kidneys, nervous system, and red blood cells. Therefore, in rehabilitation projects, developers must pay to have it safely removed. For homes built before 1978, it is estimated that 75 percent have had lead-based paint used in them.

- **Radon**—Radon is an odorless and tasteless gas that is produced by decaying of radioactive substances that occur naturally in the ground. It has been determined that protracted exposure to Radon can lead to the development of cancer.

- **Urea-formaldehyde**—Urea-formaldehyde is a type of insulation that may be harmful. Exposure to the vapors it emits may cause respiratory problems, or eye and skin irritations.

- **Contaminated ground water**—Groundwater is present in spaces in geological formations under the earth's surface. It forms the water table that many communities use as their source of drinking water. Any contamination can threaten private and public water. Contamination can come from waste disposal sites, pesticides, herbicides, and underground storage tanks. Numerous state and federal laws are designed to preserve and protect the water supply.

- **Underground storage tanks**—Commonly used to store petroleum products and chemicals. Problems arise when the tank leaks and contaminates the surrounding area. The Resource Conservation and Recovery Act (RCRA) as amended in 1984 set up a program called Leaking Underground Storage Tanks (LUST). It sets regulations for installation, maintenance, monitoring of leaks, and specifies record-keeping procedures. It also requires the landowner to have sufficient financial resources to cover damages resulting from leaks.

- **Waste disposal sites**—A landfill begins as a huge hole in the ground that is lined with a synthetic material or clay. Garbage is layered with dirt until the hole is full and a layer of topsoil is used as a capping. Test wells are installed around the site to monitor the water in the surrounding area. Hazardous waste sites (paint, toxic chemicals, medical, and scientific) and radioactive waste sites (where waste material from nuclear power plants is put in containers that are buried) are subject to stringent federal regulations.

Additional information about environmental hazards is available from the Occupational Safety and Health Administration (www.osha.gov) as well as state and local authorities.

MARKET STUDY BASICS

To determine whether a proposed real estate project makes financial sense, most developers conduct (or commission another to conduct) a **feasibility study.** Such a study may be divided into two parts: market study and financial analysis. A **market study** is the study of factors external to a property that influence the property's value, utilization, ability to generate rent, and/or its sales potential. For example, a market study enables the decision maker to determine if there are any physical or legal factors that would hinder or preclude the project, such as: access problems, or zoning restrictions. In addition, the information acquired in conducting a market study (such as rent and absorption levels, discussed later in the chapter), should facilitate subsequent financial analysis.

If the results of a market study are favorable, the second step, financial analysis of the project, is warranted. In this step, the analyst examines the profit potential of the proposed project. This involves estimating the project's revenues and expenses, and determining whether the required investment is justified. In this chapter, we focus on market analysis. In Chapter 21, we examine financial analysis.

While the knowledge gained by performing a market study helps determine if, where, and when an investment should be made, it is important to realize that real estate market analysis is not an exact science. Unlike a physicist who can predict accurately how far, and in which direction, an object will move if propelled by a certain force; a real estate market analyst must make predictions based on factors not subject to physical laws. The factors the analyst must consider include economic conditions at all levels (in particular the local level), demographic information, and the existing and potential supply of similar projects.

The value of real estate, like other assets, is a function of the interaction of supply and demand. Therefore, market analysis involves the gathering of data, and the translation of that data into usable information regarding the supply and demand for specific kinds of real property uses. A well-designed market study develops specific conclusions about why, and the degree to which, market factors affect the value of the property. In addition, because the factors that affect the real property market are less predictable than those in the physical sciences a good market analysis should result in a plan with some flexibility.

TYPES OF MARKET STUDIES

Market studies may be classified into one of two categories: general, and site specific. A **general market study** is one conducted to determine the potential for a particular type of development without reference to a specific property. For example, a general market study might be used to determine the best location for a regional shopping mall. The best location for a particular project is influenced by the nature of the project. A business may find it beneficial to be located in close proximity to its customers. Some amusement park operations, however, have determined that it is best to split the difference between metropolitan areas such as Chicago and Milwaukee, or Cincinnati and Dayton so that the facility may draw customers from both cities. In addition, land costs may be minimized by locating the parks in fairly remote areas.

A **site-specific study** is used to determine the strength of the market for a project at a particular location. In most cases, the way in which the land will be used is predetermined. A sporting goods retailer, for example, would be interested to know how many people will be willing to travel to the site to shop. In some cases, however, a developer has a site and wishes to determine what type of use will be the most profitable (e.g., a sporting goods store, a health food store, or a bookstore). In such cases, the study is referred to as a highest and best use study.

Decision Point

Do you think a market study is important if one is considering investing in an existing project? If not, why? If yes, what if a satisfactory market study was conducted six years ago when the project was developed? Would the type of project influence your decision? If no, why? If yes, give an example.

MARKET STUDY USERS

Experienced real estate market participants realize that the probability of success in any real estate venture is increased if a market study is conducted prior to investment. Conducting market research does, however, have a cost, and the more detailed the study, the more costly it is to produce. Each decision-maker must weigh the benefits associated with a market study against the cost and time needed for its preparation. Some small, locally based developers, for example, may not consider a formal market analysis to be of central importance to their decision-making process. Their familiarity with the area, and the relatively small amounts of money involved in a particular project, may allow for such behavior.

Virtually all real estate market participants do, however, benefit from market analysis. For developers and builders contemplating a major development or redevelopment project, market analysis is critical to determining whether to initiate a project. Builders and developers realize that under favorable market conditions a particular project may be profitable, but that the same project may be a disappointment under more adverse conditions. Investors also use market information to estimate the profitability of alternative investment opportunities. Governmental units may conduct market studies when a project involves public funding. They also use market studies to analyze the feasibility of bond financing for proposed new projects and in the creation of tax incentive districts. Regional and local planning agencies occasionally commission studies to convince prospective developers of the value of a particular location. Mortgage lenders and insurers are discovering that market analysis helps them to manage the risk associated with their business more effectively. Mortgage Guarantee Insurance Corporation, for example, has adopted standard underwriting guidelines that depend on how a regional market is classified. Tenants, involved in negotiating a new lease or renegotiating an existing lease may also benefit from a comprehensive study of market conditions. When rental properties are in abundant supply, tenants may be able to negotiate more favorable lease terms.

Market studies are most likely to be beneficial when conducted by an experienced party who is familiar with the local market. For major projects, some developers conduct the market study themselves; others hire an economist or market research firm for this purpose. Less experienced individuals may hire third parties to conduct the study, including privately owned firms, or university research departments. In recent years, advances in computer technology and the decreasing price of software for such applications have enabled market analysts to use personal computers to perform analysis. Available programs include historical and projected demographic data, base maps, and econometric models. Regardless of who prepares the market study, several steps are required. These steps are detailed in the following sections.

STEPS IN MARKET ANALYSIS

Every market study should include: evaluation of any physical, legal, and social constraints; definition of the market area; estimation of demand for the project; identification of supply conditions; correlation of supply and demand; and a recommendation based on the preceding steps.

EVALUATION OF PROJECT CONSTRAINTS

To avoid wasted effort, the analyst should first investigate the physical, legal, and social factors which may make it difficult, or impossible, to implement an otherwise acceptable project. An example of a potential legal constraint is restrictive zoning. If the proposed site is not zoned in a manner that allows for the planned use, the analyst must estimate the likelihood and cost of a zoning change. Because all zoning changes require public hearings, the analyst must also gauge the reaction of the community to the planned development. A project can be doomed to failure if local residents are negative toward it, regardless of whether their protests are successful in preventing a zoning change. In one case, a developer completed a neighborhood shopping center despite negative reaction by the surrounding residents, who were concerned about the increased traffic congestion the facility would cause. Before the project was completed, however, the anchor tenant (a national grocery chain) bowed to the pressure and withdrew from the lease. Without an anchor tenant to draw customers to the center, most of the shops remained empty for several years.

The analyst must also investigate numerous physical factors that might have an impact on a project. For example, the analyst must determine if the developer will encounter any difficulty in securing utilities and other services for the site. In some remote areas, the cost of extending such services to the site must be completely borne by the developer, which can be costly. In areas where utilities already operate at full capacity, obtaining service for a new project may also present difficulties.

The analyst must also investigate the possibility of environmental hazards on the property. Regardless of whether such hazards were caused by a former owner of the site or a contaminant leached onto the site from a nearby property, toxic hazard clean-up costs can be astronomical. The presence of environmental hazards on a project site are both literally and figuratively poison. For most commercial and industrial projects, and some residential projects, lenders require testing for environmental hazards before they will make a loan commitment.

Topographic and soil problems can complicate or ruin a project. Sharply contoured land may be ideal for a ski slope, but unacceptable for other purposes. The analyst must, therefore, determine whether the cost of modifying unacceptable topography is reasonable, Likewise, the analyst must ensure that the property has, or at a reasonable cost can have, adequate drainage, especially in areas that use septic systems. In areas without city water, authorities generally require a residential developer to prove that a development has adequate ground water to support the development.

Finally, a project may be unacceptable if there is limited access to the site. Examples of such limitations would include congested traffic patterns, restrictions on the number of curb-cuts allowed for adequate driveways to serve the project, or inadequate space for parking. The material in the following Doing Business section illustrates a rather severe access problem and a solution to it.

DOING BUSINESS
ASSEMBLAGE

In the 1980s, as Lake Erie made a comeback from severe pollution problems, the demand for recreational boat slips soared. So, Mr. Green, driving a highway along the northeastern Ohio shoreline was surprised to observe a marina virtually deserted. As it turned out, there was a good reason for the lack of business at the marina. The channel from the marina to the lake ran under a bridge on an access road and because the lake was several feet higher than in previous years, no boat larger than a rowboat could pass under the bridge without suffering structural damage. The marina owner was anxious to sell. The "land" next to the marina was a swamp owned by another individual who was also willing to sell his property for what he thought was a handsome price.

With a little market research, Mr. Green developed a better vision of the properties than either owner. Prior to acquiring the properties, he approached the local authorities and obtained permission to remove the obstructing bridge if the access road to the highway was rerouted through the property adjacent to the marina. In talking with many boaters and recreational fishermen, Mr. Green also discovered that many of their families were unhappy being left at home while the boaters/fishermen were out having fun. Housing at the lake would provide the families a mini-vacation while the boaters/fishermen pursued their hobbies. After acquiring title to both properties, Mr. Green proceeded to construct residential condominiums on the marina property. The purchase of a condominium conveyed title to both a residential unit and a boat slip. The project sold more quickly than the condominiums could be built. Mr. Green solved the marina's access problem by employing **plottage,** or assemblage, increasing the value of real property by combining two or more parcels into a single parcel.

Go to www.nreionline.com, use "development" as your search term, then click on one or more of the titles under Magazine Rack to learn more about this topic.

DEFINITION OF THE MARKET AREA

The task of defining the relevant market for a proposed project is necessary because, as first explained in Chapter 1, the real estate market actually consists of many markets. A proper definition of a market area requires the analyst to consider a number of factors, including: the quality and uniqueness of a project, the distance and time people are willing to travel to reach the site, and transportation barriers that inhibit travel to the project site. Such transportation barriers may be physical or psychological. Examples of physical barriers include rivers with few bridges and major highways that are difficult to cross. Consumer (or employee) reluctance to travel into, or through, high-crime areas is an example of a psychological barrier.

The use to which the property will be put influences the size of the relevant market area. For certain uses, such as industrial plant locations, the market may range from regional to international in scope. Managers of industrial firms consider a number of factors in making a plant location decision, including: the availability and cost of transportation, workforce, and utilities; the quality of living conditions in the surrounding area; and tax incentives offered by local governments. In addition, depending on the weight or bulk of their raw materials, and/or finished goods, some industrial firms prefer to locate close to their customers, others prefer to locate close to their suppliers, and some attempt to locate centrally between the two groups.

Compared with industrial properties, the relevant market for other types of property is much smaller. Food stores, for example, typically have small market areas because most people do not travel very far to buy groceries. The relevant market area for housing is usually community-wide. This means that the amount of land available for residential development in one city has little impact on the value of real property being developed residentially in another city 100 miles away. In some larger metropolitan areas, the relevant market area for residential property may be even smaller; residential property values on one side of a city will be unaffected by the availability of residential property on the other side of the city. The cost of energy and the availability of mass transportation systems may influence the size of residential market areas in the future. Higher energy costs tend to narrow the geographical range of acceptable housing alternatives, while improved mass transportation systems tend to widen them.

Real Property Submarkets

Real property markets are frequently classified according to the type of property use. Seven common classifications are residential, commercial, industrial, institutional, hotel, motel, and recreational. Recreational real estate is usually put to a very specialized use such as a country club, fitness center, or marina. Institutional real estate also tends to be designed for a specific purpose and is not easily adaptable to other uses. Examples of institutional real estate include university buildings, fire stations, and hospitals. Residential real estate is property used as residences by individuals and families. Included in this classification are single-family houses, multi-family properties, condominiums, cooperatives, and townhouses. Despite the fact that hotels and motels provide shelter they are classified separately because the residences provided are temporary. Motels are primarily used for overnight dwellings; they tend to be located close to major highways and have few amenities. Hotels are designed for those who plan more extended stays and provide numerous amenities such as swimming pools, meeting rooms, dining facilities, and limousine service. Hotels tend to be located near tourist attractions.

Commercial real estate includes a wide range of both retail space and office buildings. Examples of retail space use include: small single-tenant stores, shopping centers, parking lots, restaurants, and regional shopping malls. Office buildings range from multi-tenant skyscrapers in major cities to single-tenant buildings built to tenant specifications (e.g., dental offices and medical office buildings). Industrial real estate is property used for heavy or light manufacturing or as warehouse space. Also included in this classification are older buildings that were initially used as office buildings. Sometimes a combination of uses is housed in a single structure. Such properties are called mixed use properties. For example, a single building could contain commercial, retail, and residential space.

Decision Point

An established brewing company intends to expand into a new regional market. You are conducting the general market study to locate a site for a new brewery. What factors would you consider critical in determining the location?

ESTIMATION OF DEMAND FOR THE PROJECT

Once the analyst defines the market area, he or she must estimate demand for the project. An analyst can use two types of data for this purpose: primary, and secondary. **Primary data** is obtained directly from prospective renters or purchasers using written questionnaires, telephone, or face-to-face interviews. The questions are customized for the project and, therefore, this type of data can be extremely valuable to measure the opinions, preferences, attitudes, and current and future behavior of renters or buyers. Analysts also use primary data for commercial projects to determine the area from which consumers will be drawn to the products or services offered by the business that will occupy the site. A major disadvantage of primary data is that it is expensive to gather and, therefore, generally unavailable in a form that can measure changes in opinion.

Individuals other than an analyst collect and tabulate **secondary data,** which is usually aggregated and, therefore, does not provide the individualized information available with primary data. The two primary benefits of secondary data are that much of it is available in time series and it is relatively inexpensive. With unlimited resources, analysts would prefer to base market studies on primary data gathered in the same manner over multiple time periods. Due to cost constraints, analysts usually employ more secondary data than primary data

Despite several decades of modeling real estate markets, analysts still have difficulty assessing demand accurately. Economic models that work well to predict demand for other goods ignore many of the unique characteristics of real estate (e.g., durability, immobility, heterogeneity, and expense). Another factor that complicates the process of demand estimation is the fact that real estate demand is a **derived demand.** The demand for real estate is a function of the demand for the goods or services to be provided by the project. In general, neoclassical economic models assert that rational consumers attempt to maximize their utility with respect to goods and services subject to constraints imposed by market prices and the consumer's income. The utility consumers derive from housing consumption, for example, is also influenced by personal preferences. Because personal preferences are difficult to measure, market analysts attempt to determine differences in preferences by using proxies, including demographic information (e.g., age, marital status, and income) and household composition.

Analysis of the Economy

National and regional economic conditions influence the real estate investment climate and, therefore, a market study should include an examination of these factors. For example, a growing Gross Domestic Product, low unemployment rates, and increasing real (inflation adjusted) wages, contribute to the demand for real property. However, local factors are critical to most projects because of the immobility of real property. The value of real property is, therefore, largely determined by local government policies and local economic conditions.

Some analysts use base industry analysis to measure local economic conditions. This type of analysis requires that all area business firms be classified into one of two categories: a base industry or a service industry. A **base industry,** also known as a primary industry, or export industry, is one that brings in money from outside the local area. Base industries are considered essential to the maintenance and growth of real estate values, and analysts gauge the strength of a local economy by examining the financial strength of its base industry employers. If base industries invest in new equipment, hire new employees, or expand their facilities, the local economy is likely to benefit. Retail sales and service expenditures are likely to increase, and more people are likely to seek new or better housing. Likewise, demand for commercial and residential property is likely to increase as small companies emerge to serve the base industries. For every base industry job, it is estimated that three service industry jobs are created.

A **service industry,** also known as a secondary industry, filler industry, or non-base industry, produces goods and services that are used within the market area. The classification of firms into service and base categories is not always easy. For example, restaurants and gasoline service stations are ordinarily classified as service industries. How should they be classified if they are located on an interstate highway on the border of the community?

The economic stability of an area can be inferred from the nature of employment within the area. In general, diversity in local employment increases the ability of the locality to withstand lulls in the national or regional economy. Some industries have more stable employment patterns than others. For example, firms that manufacture capital goods such as machine tools, tend to be cyclical. In essence, their sales, and employment, vary with the general business cycle. Other industries, such as clothing manufacturers, and food processors, tend to have more stable operations. Analysts who produce long-term regional economic forecasts use local industry mix as the key factor to convert national macroeconomic forecasts to subnational areas.

Demographics

Demographics is the term used to refer to studies of the size, density, distribution, and other vital statistics of human population. Knowledge of demographics is a prerequisite if one is to anticipate correctly the demand for a particular real property use because the demand for all types of real estate depends upon the number of consumers and their purchasing power.

Population Other factors constant, the larger the population, the greater the demand for real property. Exhibit 20.1 shows some historical information about the population of the United States. In examining the exhibit, consider at least two noteworthy points. First, the population of the United States continues to grow. During the 1990s the population grew at a rate of 13 percent, up from the 11 percent growth rate of the 1980s. Second, note the aging of our population. This fact is particularly important to consider when making decisions regarding real property uses because the demand for retail stores and housing is influenced strongly by the age of the population. For example, older people tend to prefer low-maintenance dwellings, such as apartments and condominiums, as opposed to the traditional single-family house.

Real estate market analysts must be aware of one of our nation's distinguishing characteristics—the mobility of the population. In recent decades, roughly 20 percent of our population moved once every five years. For more than twenty years, the populations of many large cities have been decreasing, resulting in a major population shift from the cities to the suburbs. Many people who still live inside central cities tend to be elderly, or poor, and in need of public social services. In addition, childless working couples and single people may live in the central city to be close to their place of employment and cultural and entertainment opportunities. All of these factors suggest that the design of residential units within cities should differ from those in suburban areas.

Population growth does not occur uniformly throughout the country. Information gathered by the United States Bureau of the Census (Census Bureau) indicates that since 1970, the population of southern and western states has generally been growing at a more rapid rate than other states. This is primarily due to population migration from northern states (rather than from disparate birth and death rates). For example, during the 1990s, the population of Connecticut decreased by 0.2 percent (the only state to decrease in population over the decade) while the populations of Arizona and Nevada grew at rates of 30.4 and 50.6 percent, respectively.

Information about population and migration patterns is available from several sources. The data collected by the Census Bureau is generally considered to be the best single information source on population mobility. Among other things, each year, the Census Bureau estimates births, deaths, and net migration, for states, counties, and metropolitan areas. Demographic and migratory information is also available from a number of sources in the private sector. Demographic services can provide customized current and forecast data for markets as small as a neighborhood. Moving companies, utility companies, and financial institutions are other potential information sources.

Households Population alone may be inadequate as a demand measure, especially for housing. A better indicator for housing demand may be the number of households. The Census Bureau defines a **household** as a group of people living in one dwelling unit where there is one head of household. Numerous factors determine the number of households in existence at any time. The number of households will increase as a result of children moving out of their parents' homes, and divorces (because divorced people rarely return to live with their parents). Marriages, joint living arrangements, and children moving back into their parents' homes decrease the number of households. The size and type of household affects the demand for both the size, and kind, of housing. For example, the larger the household, the more bedrooms and bathrooms a household will require in a dwelling. Households with children may prefer to live away from busy streets and on lots large enough to give the children room to play.

Income The demand for real property (and other goods and services) is also a function of the population's purchasing power. Two measures of purchasing power are available, nominal income and real income. Nominal income is income unadjusted for the effect of inflation. **Nominal income** figures may, however, be misleading during inflationary periods because they will increase although there may be no increase in purchasing power. Therefore, most market analysts prefer to use **real income figures,** those that have been adjusted to account for inflation. Real household income has increased by 34.2 percent since 1967 when the Census Bureau first started calculating this figure. In general, the higher a population's income, the higher the demand for real estate. In 2000, median household real income in the United States was $42,148, but this varies by region, as can be observed in Exhibit 20.2. The percentage change figures in the last column of the exhibit reflect the fact that the Consumer Price Index (the index now used by the Census Bureau as an inflation measure) was 3.4 percent during 1999.

EXHIBIT   20.1   POPULATION OF THE UNITED STATES

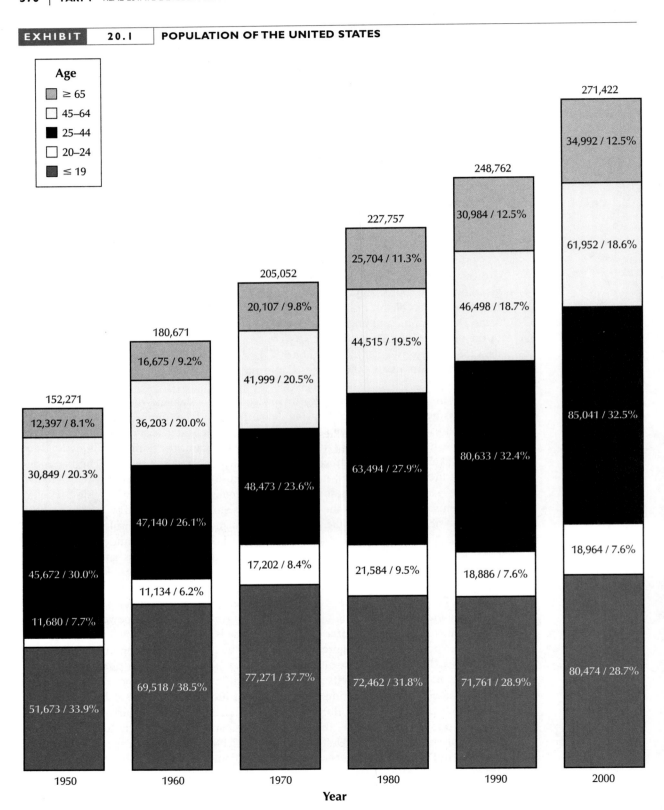

SOURCE: U.S. Census Bureau. Table DP-1 Profile of General Demographic Characteristics for the United States. May 15, 2001.

As we have previously emphasized, analysts must be aware of local conditions. Fortunately, localized demographic data is also available from the Census Bureau. They provide this information, including income levels, by census tract (dozens of which may be contained within a large city). Analysts should also consider the type of employment in the area, especially if the local economy is heavily dependent on a particular industry, because wage rates vary by industry.

IDENTIFICATION OF SUPPLY CONDITIONS

It is relatively easy for analysts to determine the current supply of improved real properties. Such information may be available at a modest cost from a number of sources, including; chambers of commerce, multiple listing services, industrial development commissions, financial institutions, local boards of realtors, and state universities and colleges. Many local planning commissions and/or county assessors have implemented **Geographic Information Systems** (GIS), which include a complete inventory of all real property within a jurisdiction. GIS data is stored in a computer and can be retrieved to provide detailed information about the number, size, and location of various property types. GIS is a relatively recent innovation that is growing in importance. Many local authorities use GIS to help attract development projects to their area.

While information about current supply may be readily available, predicting the future supply of a particular type of real estate may be more difficult than predicting demand because fewer people influence supply. In particular, real estate developers and public sector regulators of development have a major influence on the supply and location of real estate projects. Several variables affect the supply of real estate. One important variable is the willingness of developers, investors, lenders, and builders to accept the risks associated with such projects (Chapter 21). Other factors include the cost and availability of construction materials, labor, land, utilities, and mortgage credit. Supply conditions are usually estimated by using several indicators, including building permits, vacancy rates, absorption rates, mortgage defaults and foreclosures, and construction activity.

Construction Activity

An analyst can estimate the amount of any type of real property that will be available in the future by combining existing supply with the amount of current construction activity. Under ordinary conditions, new construction will result in a net gain of 65 to 75 percent of useable space; the difference is due to existing buildings that are demolished or abandoned. Care must be exercised, however, in analyzing construction data. Many historic buildings are being converted to office space in order to receive the special tax treatment described in Chapter 7. Such rehabilitation expenditures are often classified separately

EXHIBIT	20.2	UNITED STATES HOUSEHOLD INCOME BY REGION		
Region		2000 Median Income	1999 Median Income	Percentage Change in Real Income: 1999–2000
All households		$42,148	$40,816	-0.1
Northeast		45,106	41,984	3.9
Midwest		44,646	42,679	1.2
South		38,410	37,442	-0.7
West		44,744	42,720	1.3

Source: U.S. Census Bureau

from construction figures. As the inventory of available properties approaches the saturation point for the market, profit margins begin to decrease and astute builders will slow down or cease building new projects.

Analysts can obtain information about planned construction at little or no cost because lenders regularly report amounts committed to construction loans to federal authorities. Regional planning commissions are another good source of data on area land use and construction activity. They collect such information to assist in making policy decisions and usually have a bibliography of available reports. The local building inspectors' office can provide information about building permits granted. In gauging future market activity these figures may be misleading. Some developers obtain loan commitments or building permits but do not actually build. In addition, loan commitments are usually reported in dollar amounts, and these amounts are often not adjusted for inflation. Therefore, as construction costs rise the amounts reported also increase without any real increase in activity. Information about construction costs may be obtained from local builders or appraisers.

Vacancy Rates

A **vacancy rate** expresses the number of empty units as a percentage of total units on the market. Regardless of what type of real property is being analyzed, high vacancy rates indicate (at least temporary) excess supply, and low vacancy rates indicate under-supply. When vacancy rates are low, landlords have an incentive to raise rents, and investors may decide to build new rental units. High vacancy rates may mean that real property owners must reduce rents to avoid losing tenants.

Using rent levels to gauge relative supply and demand may be misleading, however, because landlords may use rent concessions to attract or retain tenants rather than reduce rent levels when vacancy rates are high. For example, landlords may be unable to attract tenants at a monthly rent of $1,200, but may be able to attract tenants by offering free rent for the first month. Effective monthly rents in this case are $1,100, not $1,200. The extent of rent concessions relates directly to the imbalance between supply and demand for space. An analyst may also use real estate prices to gauge supply conditions. Stable or falling prices suggest an abundant supply. Increasing prices suggest that supply is low relative to demand.

Vacancy rates vary with property type and location, and they do not necessarily remain constant over time. Vacancy rates of 4 to 5 percent for single-family homes, for example, are common. However, in some areas, New York City, for example, such a "high" vacancy rate would concern investors. Vacancy data is available from a number of sources. Analysts can obtain information about residential unit vacancies from the Census Bureau, regional housing reports published by the Department of Commerce, local utility companies, boards of realtors, and multiple listing services. Commercial and industrial property brokers and owners maintain vacancy rate information for potential investors. Vacancy rates, however, only provide part of the supply picture. They are more informative when combined with the absorption rate.

Absorption Rates

An important factor that affects project feasibility is the **absorption rate,** the time that may elapse between a project's completion and its eventual sale, or lease. Consequently, analysts attempt to determine the absorption rate for the market. The typical absorption study includes the number of units already on the market, the number of units expected to come on the market, the projected annual increase in market area income or population, and the number of units demanded each year based upon income and/or population projections. Many analysts also incorporate time-on-market data, which is available from local brokers or multiple listing services, into the absorption study. Time-on-market is the term used to describe the amount of time between the date that an owner lists a new or existing property for sale and the date that the owner accepts a purchase offer.

While it is difficult to estimate accurately the number of competing units that may come into the market over an extended period (two to five years) experience and good judgment tend to result in reasonable estimates. A thorough absorption study may, for example, indicate that although an over supply of units exists at the current time a shortage may occur in the future.

Mortgage Defaults and Foreclosures

High levels of mortgage defaults and foreclosures indicate excess supply, whereas a low level of defaults and foreclosures is consistent with adequate or insufficient supply. Analysts may obtain information concerning the number of mortgage defaults and foreclosures from local lenders or their regulators.

CORRELATION OF SUPPLY AND DEMAND

The amount of real estate provided for any particular use (e.g., residential, office space) and the value of that real estate are a result of the interaction of supply-and-demand factors. To depict this interaction visually, economists construct charts containing supply-and-demand curves (referred to as curves although in simplified analysis, such as that presented here, the lines are straight).

Both the short-run and long-run supply and demand curves for real estate are shown in Exhibit 20.3, where the quantity of real estate is measured on the horizontal axis, and price is measured on the vertical axis. At any point, the amount of real estate provided is determined where the supply curve (S) and demand curve (D) cross (i.e., where supply equals demand) the price that equates the two is referred to as the **equilibrium price.**

In examining Exhibit 20.3, you will note that in both the short-run and long-run, the demand curve slopes downward. This demand curve characteristic is true for almost all goods and services and signifies that the higher (lower) the price, the less (more) of the good consumers will desire. You will also note that the slope of the long-run supply curve differs from the short-run supply curve. The short-run supply curve is shown as a vertical line, which signifies that in the near-term the supply of real estate available for any particular use is fixed. This is so because it is impossible to add instantaneously to supply by construction, or by converting property originally designed for one type of use to another use. Likewise, it is highly unlikely that it is feasible to reduce supply in the short-run through demolition. The inability to reduce supply in such a way is a characteristic that distinguishes the real estate market from most others.

In the long-run, the supply of real property more closely resembles other markets; supply may be adjusted either up or down to meet demand. If the demand for a particular use increases, over time, developers will build new properties, or properties originally constructed for one use for which demand has decreased may be converted to another use with increased demand. In addition, long-run supply may be reduced by allowing properties to wear out, or by demolition. The upward-sloping long-run supply curve signifies that the higher (lower) the price, the more (less) of the product that will be made available.

To illustrate how a change in demand affects the market for a particular real property use, consider the housing market in Mythic, Montana. The existing equilibrium price for homes in Mythic is shown in Exhibit 20.4 as P_0. When a new manufacturing facility begins operation in Mythic it creates new jobs, which attracts workers to the area and, consequently, the demand for housing increases above existing supply. In essence, the demand curve shifts from D_0 to D_1. It takes time to develop and construct new housing. Therefore,

| EXHIBIT | 20.3 | SUPPLY AND DEMAND |

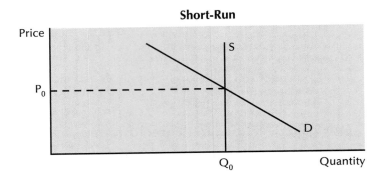

Short-Run

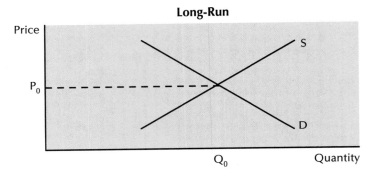

Long-Run

the short-run effect of the increased demand is an increase in the price of housing from P_0 to P^*. Builders and investors will note (or anticipate) the higher price and, assuming the price is high enough to justify new construction, they will construct new housing. In our example, the quantity of housing increases from Q_0 to Q_1. In the long-run, the plant opening drives the price of housing to P_1. The exact amount of P_1 depends on the slope of the demand curve and the extent of the shift in the supply curve.

The previous example also demonstrates how the long-run supply curve shown in Exhibit 20.4 is derived; it actually consists of a series of points representing short-run market equilibriums. In addition, the example serves to demonstrate that the term "equilibrium" is not a static concept. In most real estate markets, supply-and-demand factors change constantly. In the housing market, for example, individuals must make housing decisions as they leave their parents, change jobs, marry, have children, divorce, retire, or move for some other reason.

Decision Point

The football stadium at Maine State University can seat 40,000 people; but demand for tickets, priced at $20 each, is 60,000. What short-run and long-run solutions to this dilemma are possible? Which do you recommend?

RECOMMENDATION

The last step in a market study requires the analyst to draw a conclusion regarding the proposed project. In a general market study, the analyst recommends the best site (if any) for the project, and ranks alternative sites. In a site-specific study, the analyst either recommends, or fails to recommend, the proposal. If the study is a highest and best use study, the analyst ranks alternative property uses. Regardless of the type of study, the analyst should clearly set forth

| EXHIBIT | 20.4 | **EQUILIBRIUM LEVELS ARE NOT CONSTANT** |

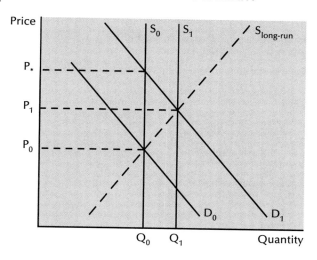

the findings of all steps involved in the analysis, and explain the reason for the decision (rankings). For example, a good market study explains the reasons for demographic trends, and how the trends might affect a particular project. In addition, a positive finding requires a recommendation as to the size of the project and when the builder should start the project. Users of market studies must keep two points in mind. First, a positive recommendation does not guarantee the success of the project. The conclusion the analyst reaches is based on the analyst's judgment regarding the market for a specific project. Second, market studies have a limited shelf life. The best market analysis is only good for a few years.

SUMMARY

In evaluating a real estate investment opportunity, the decision maker must determine if the proposed project makes good financial sense. Most decision makers, therefore, conduct (or commission) a feasibility study; the first portion of which is a market study. A market study involves the systematic gathering and analysis of data, and translating the data into usable information regarding the supply of and demand for a particular type of real estate project. The knowledge gained by performing market analysis enables builders, lenders, investors, and others to determine if, where, and when to make an investment.

Market analysis involves five steps; evaluation of physical, legal, and social constraints; definition of the market area; estimation of demand for the project; identification of supply conditions, correlation of supply and demand, and finally, a recommendation. While it is impossible to predict accurately changes in supply and demand; following such a systematic approach makes it possible to make reasonable estimates of trends in supply and demand factors and future market conditions.

KEY TERMS

absorption rate
base industry
demographics
derived demand
equilibrium price
feasibilty study
general market study

geographic information
  system
household
market study
nominal income
plottage
primary data

real income
secondary data
service industry
site-specific study
vacancy rate

REVIEW QUESTIONS

1. What is the purpose of a real estate market study?
2. What is primary data? Secondary data? What are the advantages and disadvantages of using either in a market study?
3. What are the steps involved in a market study? Do you think one step is more important than the others? Why?
4. Explain how a market area can be delineated.
5. Assume that the world can be divided into two markets: Mythic, Montana and everywhere else. Using the Mythic example on page 373 and assuming all else constant, what happened to the long-run equilibrium price and quantity of housing everywhere else after the plant opened in Mythic?
6. What is economic base analysis? Why is it important in predicting future real estate price trends in a particular market area?
7. What (tentative) conclusion about a proposed development would you draw if you discovered that the local absorption rate has been increasing?
8. Distinguish between a site-specific and a general market study.
9. Is nominal or real income a better measure of purchasing power?
10. Why is the number of households in a market area relevant to real estate developers?
11. A developer is thinking of building an 80,000-square-foot office building. Currently, there is 1,000,000 square feet of similar space on the market and the vacancy rate is 15 percent. Another 300,000 square feet of office space is under construction. What is the likely amount of office space that will be available after the 300,000 square feet are completed? If the market is absorbing 50,000 square feet per year, how long might it be before the proposed 80,000-square-foot project is fully rented?
12. What types of environmental hazards must developers be aware?
13. According to CERCLA, who is responsible for paying for environmental hazard site cleanup costs?
14. What is your answer to the questions in the three "Decision Point" sections in this chapter?

REAL ESTATE ON THE WEB

Use your favorite search engine to:

1. Find real property developers in your area.
2. Determine the population and number of households in your state and local area and the percentage change in these numbers over the last ten years.
3. Find an example where a development was cancelled or modified because it would impact an endangered species.
4. Discover what environmental issues are of the most concern to developers in your state.
5. Learn about a successful urban rehabilitation project in your state.
6. Determine if your community has smart growth regulations.

Refer to the companion Web site at www.wiley.com/college/larsen for a variety of online activities including additional chapter content, review materials, assignments, and related links.

ADDITIONAL READINGS

Chaplin, R. "Predicting Real Estate Rents: Walking Backwards into the Future." *Journal of Property Investment & Finance* 18.3 (2000): 352–370.

Egan, D.J. and K. Nield. "Towards a Theory of Intraurban Hotel Location." *Urban Studies 37: 3* (March 2000): 611-621.

Isakson, H.R. and M.D. Ecker. "An Analysis of the Influence of Location in the Market for Undeveloped Urban Fringe Land." *Land Economics* 77:1 (February 2001): 30–41.

Lewis, P.G. "Looking Outward or Turning Inward? Motivations for Development Decisions in California Central Cities and Suburbs." *Urban Affairs Review* 36: 5 (2001): 696–720.

Mansour, A. and M.C. Christensen. "An Alternative Determinant of Warehouse Space Demand: A Case Study." *The Journal of Real Estate Research* 20: 1/2 (January-April 2001): 77-88.

McDonald, J.F. "Rent, Vacancy and Equilibrium in Real Estate Markets." *Journal of Real Estate Practice and Education 3:1 (2000) 55–69.*

McMillen, D.P. and J. Dombrow. "A Flexible Fourier Approach to Repeat Sales Price Indexes." *Real Estate Economics* 29:2 (Summer 2001): 207–255.

Phe, H.H. and P. Wakely. "Status, Quality and the Other Trade-off: Toward a New Theory of Urban Residential Location." *Urban Studies* 37:1 (January 2000): 7–35.

Sakashita, N. "An Economic Analysis of Convenience-store Location." *Urban Studies* 37:3 (March 2000): 471–479.

Thompson, B. and S. Tsolacos. "Industrial Land Values—A Guide to Future Markets? "*The Journal of Real Estate Research* 20 1/2 (January-April 2001): 55–76.

Thrall, G.I. "Data Resources Real Estate and Business Geography Analysis." *Journal of Real Estate Literature* 9:2 (2001): 173–225.

Investment Analysis

Learning Objectives

After studying this chapter, you should be able to:

- Distinguish equity from nonequity investments, and direct from indirect investments.
- Explain the advantages and disadvantages of investing in real estate.
- Describe the various risks associated with real estate investment.
- Analyze a direct investment.
- Describe the various means of indirect investment.

FROM THE WIRE

News flash—Pyramid schemes have come to the real estate market. In the early 1900s, the pyramid scheme created by George Ponzi was so effective that many now refer to the activity as a Ponzi scheme. In this type of adventure, a promoter promises investors huge returns on their investment. The problem is the underlying asset (e.g., stocks, tax stamps, unclaimed freight) does not exist, and early investors are actually paid from money obtained from newer investors.

In December 2000, a southwest Missouri evangelical minister pleaded guilty in federal court to ten felony charges and was sentenced to three years and ten months for selling phony home mortgages to 73 victims in at least six states. In addition, he was ordered to pay $2.38 million in restitution to victims in Missouri, Alabama, Georgia,

Indiana, West Virginia, and North Carolina. The minister admitted to acting as a middleman for investors and borrowers through a business called Creative Funding. Prosecutors said he promised exceedingly high rates of return to investors to finance loans for borrowers who put their property up for collateral. He usually gave investors promissory notes or deeds of trust for properties that did not exist or were owned by others.

Whether the minister still has funds available to make the court ordered payments is not clear. The good news for him is that his sentence will run concurrent with the 25 years he is already serving on some 80 related felony fraud convictions in Alabama.

Go to money.cnn.com and use "real estate" as your search term, then click on one or more of the results to learn about recent real estate investment opportunities.

INTRODUCTION

People may use their money in two ways: to purchase goods and services for current consumption, or to save and use it for future consumption. In essence, investment involves the sacrifice of current consumption in exchange for future benefits. There is an old investment adage that suggests that the best way to profit by investing money is to, "buy low and sell high." Although such advice is usually offered tongue-in-cheek, historically, real estate has been a good way for investors to accomplish such a goal. The old adage is incomplete, however, in that an investor's total return stems not only from the difference between the sale and purchase prices; it also is a function of returns generated during the investment period.

In this chapter, we describe a number of ways in which you can participate in the real estate market. You can make equity (ownership) investments, or nonequity (debt) investments. In addition, both types of investments can be accomplished either directly or indirectly. Investors make **direct investment** in real estate by purchasing real property, or by originating mortgage loans. Most individuals, however, lack the funds required to make extensive direct investments.

Indirect investment usually involves an intermediary pooling the funds of many individuals in order to invest in larger and/or more diversified investments than are possible for most individuals. Indirect equity investment occurs when an investor purchases an interest in a business organization that makes direct equity real estate investments. Indirect nonequity investment occurs when an investor purchases an interest in an organization that specializes in mortgage investment. Investors can also participate indirectly in the mortgage loan market by investing in mortgage-backed securities.

The material presented in this chapter should enable you to make more informed real estate investment decisions. Conceptually, as summarized in the following highlighted material, the chapter may be divided into two parts. In the first part, the focus is on direct equity investments. We begin by presenting the advantages and disadvantages associated with direct equity investments. As you will see, direct real estate investment offers investors several of each. As the chapter opener "From the Wire," suggests, one risk factor involved in just about any investment opportunity, including real estate, is the possibility of fraud. But, there are several other risk factors associated with real estate investments and these are explained in this chapter. Then, we demonstrate how to analyze direct equity investments. In the second part of the chapter, indirect investment vehicles are described, specifically real estate investment trusts, and mortgage-backed securities.

Real Estate Investment Opportunities

	Direct Investment	Indirect Investment
Equity Investment	1. Purchase of real property	1. Real estate investment trust
Nonequity Investment	1. Originate a mortgage loan	1. Mortgage-backed securities
		2. Real estate investment trust

ADVANTAGES OF DIRECT REAL ESTATE INVESTMENTS

There are both financial and nonfinancial advantages associated with direct equity invest-ment in real estate. "Pride of ownership" is an example of a nonfinancial advantage. Most investors do, however, have certain financial objectives when making an investment. Investors generally want the highest return available given the risk associated with an investment. Real estate investments offer the possibility of handsome returns. Data on direct equity real estate investment returns is difficult to secure because investors keep such information confidential, but compared with other investments, real estate offers signifi-cant returns. High returns may be realized because a real estate investment enjoys one, or more, of the following advantages: positive cash flow, income tax benefits, and appreciation in the value of the property. Another advantage for real estate investors is the fact that oper-ating returns can be increased by employing financial leverage (i.e., using borrowed funds). In addition, investors may value real estate investments because such investments may pro-vide opportunities for portfolio diversification. These, and other, advantages are described in the following sections.

PORTFOLIO DIVERSIFICATION

Many people prefer to hold a variety of assets in their investment portfolio because they realize that a diversified portfolio tends to reduce overall investment risk. With a well-diversified portfolio, a loss in value for one type of investment (e.g., common stocks) may be offset by gains in other types of investment (e.g., bonds or real estate). Adding any asset to a portfolio in which the asset is not already represented will provide some **diversifica-tion** benefits. But, diversification works best when the returns associated with the asset being added are not closely correlated with the returns of other assets already in the port-folio. Several studies conclude that real estate investments provide excellent diversification benefits to portfolios containing stocks and bonds.

You should be aware of one caveat regarding diversification. An investor of modest wealth may actually increase risk by including real estate in their investment portfolio. For such individuals, their home represents the largest investment they will make in their life-time. Additional real estate investment may increase risk by adding real estate to a portfo-lio already heavily weighted in this area. Some diversification benefits are possible, however, even for these individuals by investing either in other types of real estate (e.g., commercial or agricultural) and/or in geographically dispersed real estate.

CASH FLOW

Some real estate investments generate more cash than is required to cover the mortgage payment and maintain the property. When this is the case, the investment is said to have

positive cash flow. Positive cash flow is attractive to some people because it provides them with an additional source of income that they can use at their discretion.

Not all real estate investments provide positive cash flow. When the amount of cash required by the investment each month exceeds the cash that the investment generates, the investment is said to have **negative cash flow.** Certain types of real property are likely to have a negative cash flow, undeveloped land, for example. Other types of real property, such as small apartment complexes, are more likely to have a positive cash flow. Exceptions are, however, possible in both cases. Agricultural land may be profitably leased, and a variety of factors may result in negative cash flows for apartment complexes (e.g., mismanagement, increase in expenses, decrease in rents). If a property has negative cash flow it does not necessarily mean that it is a bad investment. Other factors such as the tax benefits associated with real property investments, and an increase in the value of the property, may be enough to offset the negative cash flow that occurs over the investor's holding period.

TAX BENEFITS

Investors can use the funds generated by an investment only after all obligations, including income tax, have been satisfied. Investors should, therefore, be familiar with the tax implications of each investment opportunity they contemplate. Investors in income-producing real property are entitled to several income tax benefits that were presented in Chapter 7. Recall that some expenditures may be used as deductions and that others result in tax credits. Also recall that in some cases, losses resulting from real estate investments may be used to offset other taxable income, and recognition of gains may be deferred through exchanges or installment sales. All of these tax implications may result in a greater after-tax cash flow (and after-tax return) on real estate investments compared with other types of investments.

APPRECIATION IN PROPERTY VALUE

As suggested above, increases in property value may be large enough to offset negative cash flow over an investor's holding period. To illustrate this, assume that you paid $100,000 for an investment property, and that it had annual negative cash flow of $5,000 after taxes for each of the three years that you owned it. So far, this does not appear to be a good investment. But, assume that you can sell the property for $200,000 at the end of the third year. Further, assume that you are in the 40 percent marginal income tax bracket (federal and state), and that any taxable loss resulting from the operation of the property cannot be used to offset other taxable income. The after-tax cash flows associated with the investment would be as follows:

Year	Net Cash Flow
0	−$100,000
1 and 2	−$5,000
3	$155,000*

*Item		Amount
sale price		$200,000
− purchase price	100,000	
taxable gain	100,000	
× tax rate	.4	
income tax		40,000
year 3 negative cash flow from operations		5,000
year 3 net cash flow		$155,000

Using the information from Chapter 17, your after-tax rate of return is 12.7 percent. Investors must remember, however, that the price of real property may go up or down, just like the price of other assets. In essence, when making an investment one cannot rely on price appreciation.

FINANCIAL LEVERAGE

Because real property tends to be durable, immobile, and relatively stable in value, lenders usually consider it an excellent source of loan collateral. Therefore, compared with other types of investments, lenders are willing to lend large amounts of money at relatively low interest rates and for relatively long periods of time. The willingness of lenders to lend enables investors to use financial leverage in acquiring real estate investments. Using **financial leverage** means that the investor uses some borrowed funds to make an investment. The term "leverage" is descriptive in that the use of financial leverage magnifies investment returns.

When the rate of return on an investment is greater than the interest rate on the borrowed funds, the investor is said to be positively (or favorably) levered. In essence, any earnings above that promised to the lender are retained by the borrower, not shared with the lender. To demonstrate favorable leverage, reconsider the above example, and assume that the investor borrowed $70,000 to acquire the $100,000 property. Further, assume that the loan terms call for annual payments of interest only (to simplify the example), and that the loan interest rate is 10 percent. Under these assumptions, the investor's after tax return increases from 12.7 percent to 22.8 percent; based on the following after-tax cash flows.

Year	Net Cash Flow
0	−$30,000
1 and 2	−$9,200*
3	$80,800**

*Item	Amount
negative after tax cash flow from operations	$5,000
+ interest payment	7,000
− interest tax shield (interest × tax rate)	2,800
net negative cash flow in years 1 and 2	9,200

**Item	Amount	
sale price		$200,000
− purchase price	100,000	
taxable gain	100,000	
× tax rate	.4	
income tax		40,000
year 3 negative cash flow from operations		9,200
− loan repayment		70,000
year 3 net cash flow	80,800	

It is important to realize that financial leverage will also magnify negative returns because the investor has introduced a fixed cost (the mortgage payment) which must be covered even if the investment does not provide enough cash to do so. Therefore, the use of leverage increases risk. When the return on investment is less than the interest rate on the loan, the investor is said to be negatively (or unfavorably) levered.

Decision Point

What would the after tax return on the investment in the previous example be if the investor used $80,000 in borrowed funds with a 12 percent interest-only loan?

OTHER ADVANTAGES OF REAL ESTATE AS AN INVESTMENT

Investors may value real estate for a number of other reasons. In this section, we briefly describe two possible reasons: the tangible nature of real estate, and the fact that it is non-homogeneous. All investments may be classified into one of two categories—tangible and intangible. A tangible asset is an asset that exists in a physical sense. An asset that is not physical in nature is intangible. Examples of intangible assets include a copyright, a life insurance policy, or corporate stock. While such investments may be valuable, some investors find it difficult to understand the benefits that intangible assets can provide. Such people may prefer tangible assets, like real estate, and be willing to pay a premium for them.

People may also be willing to pay a premium for real property because of its nonho-mogeneous nature. In essence, no two parcels of real estate are identical. Even tract houses, with identical improvements on the same size lots, are unique in that no two parcels have the same location. The owner of each parcel, in effect, has a monopoly on that particular location.

DISADVANTAGES OF DIRECT REAL ESTATE INVESTMENTS

There are also several disadvantages associated with real estate investment that prudent investors must consider. The disadvantages include: the need for property management, the immobility of real estate, and the large financial investment required.

NEED FOR MANAGEMENT

Most real estate investments require more management attention than many other types of investments. The amount of time required to manage real property tends to be directly related to the size of the property, but is also affected by the use to which the property is put. For example, an investor who leases farmland has very few managerial responsibilities. If, however, the land is used as a trailer court, at least some maintenance will be required. If, instead, a shopping center is built on the property, the property will require constant management attention.

Individual investors may not have the time or expertise required to properly manage a real property. Fortunately, investors need not also act as managers. Professional property management firms are available to provide required services. For large properties, fees of 2 to 3 percent of gross income are common. For smaller properties, such as an apartment building with forty units, management fees can be 6 to 7 percent of gross income. For even smaller properties, professional management may be either unavailable, or available at a prohibitive cost.

IMMOBILITY

We noted previously that the immobility of real estate adds to its value as loan collateral. Unfortunately, the immobility of real estate may also work to the disadvantage of investors. To illustrate, consider the owner of an automobile (or any other portable asset). The owner decides to sell the automobile and discovers that while the local market is poor, autos are commanding excellent prices in another part of the country. If the price differential exceeds the cost of transporting the car, the owner can profit by selling in the higher-priced market. This option is generally unavailable to real property owners. Land is completely immobile and improvements tend to be either impossible, or expensive, to move. It may also be expensive (but as the following "DOING BUSINESS" makes clear, not impossible) to modify existing improvements to meet changing demand.

LARGE DOLLAR INVESTMENT REQUIREMENT

Most direct equity investments in real estate require large dollar amounts. This fact can result in both financial and emotional barriers that restrict the value of real property. In many cases, an investor can borrow a substantial portion of the funds he or she may need to purchase a property. Still, the large amounts involved may serve as an emotional barrier that prevents some potential investors from making direct equity real estate investments.

INVESTMENT RISKS

All investment opportunities involve some degree of risk, and real estate has more risks associated with it than most other types of investment. Some people may consider these risks as additional disadvantages of real estate investments, but many experts disagree. In fact, it is the presence of risk factors that results in real estate investors requiring (and often achieving) relatively high rates of return. Rational investors will invest in more risky investments only if the returns they expect the investment to generate adequately compensate them for assuming the risk. In essence, prudent investors boost their required return as compensation for assuming increased levels of risk, and they will lower their return requirements for investments with low levels of risk. This process is sometimes referred to as the risk-return trade off.

In investment analysis, it is important to consider all risks. In the following sections, we describe the risks that investors should consider before purchasing real estate.

DOING BUSINESS

REHABILITATION

Property that once housed the operations of the Quaker Oats Company in downtown Akron, Ohio sat vacant for years after the company moved to another city. On the property were several dozen cylindrical grain silos, constructed of cement more than one foot thick, which stood in clusters nearly one hundred feet high. Next to the cement monoliths were outdated brick buildings, once used by the company as mills and office space.

A real estate developer announced plans to convert the mill buildings into a mini-mall of gift shops and restaurants, and to convert the silos into an apartment building. Many people in the area were skeptical. Conversion of the office space did, however, proceed. The developer left as much of the old structure and fixtures in place as possible, providing those who visit the thriving Quaker Square project with visual entertainment.

Converting cement grain silos into apartments, however, probably sounds unlikely to you, and, as a matter of fact, this was not done. Instead, most of the silos were demolished and the remainder converted into one of the most unique Hilton Hotels in the world (every room is round, and so are the hallways)! In essence, office space became retail space and industrial space became hotel space. Sometimes, the use to which a property may be put is limited not so much by the structure itself, as by the imagination of people.

Go to www.realestatelink.net, click "articles," then enter "rehab" as your search term and click on one or more of the titles displayed to learn more about rehabilitating residential properties.

MARKET RISK

Market risk refers to the variability in investment returns resulting from changes in general market conditions such as inflation and interest rate levels. The factors that constitute market risk are beyond the control of individual investors and are sometimes referred to as nondiversifiable risk or systematic risk. In essence, these are risks that every market participant faces, and they cannot be eliminated through diversification. Investors are generally unconcerned with market conditions that increase their return; the risk is the possibility that an investment may not perform as well as expected. In the worst case, market risk could result in the loss of the entire investment. Many people choose to put their money into defensive investments, those on which the return is little affected by economic conditions (e.g., United States Treasury Bills) because they fear losing their entire investment. For people making aggressive investments, those on which return is more sensitive to economic conditions, there is the possibility that the investment will fail to provide the anticipated income. For example, investors frequently purchase rental apartments for the current income they produce. If supply and demand conditions cause rents to be less than expected, the investors must look to appreciation of the value of the property for their return. If, however, rental demand does not increase, increases in the property value are likely to be lower than anticipated.

BUSINESS RISK

Business risk is used to describe the variability of operating returns that result from operating decisions. In general, the higher the fixed operating costs as a percentage of total operating costs, the higher the business risk. Unlike variable operating costs, fixed operating costs cannot be adjusted as revenue changes. Therefore, when fixed costs represent a large portion of total operating costs, operating returns will be lower (higher) as revenues fall (increase) compared with a similar property where a small portion of operating costs are fixed.

Real estate investors may have some control over the extent to which they incur fixed costs. For example, using short-term leases to rent equipment rather than purchasing it gives the investor periodic opportunities to adjust operating costs downward, if needed, by canceling (or electing not to renew) the lease. When equipment is purchased, (fixed) depreciation expenses will continue to be reflected on the income statement (unless the equipment is sold) despite a slow-down in the operation of the project. In many cases, however, the extent to which operating costs are employed is beyond the control of the investor. Synonyms for business risk include nonsystematic risk and diversifiable risk. As the latter term implies, such risk can be diversified by making other investments.

LIQUIDITY RISK

In investment terminology, liquidity is a relative term that refers to how rapidly an investment can be sold at a price close to its true value. **Liquidity risk** becomes particularly important if one must convert an investment to cash quickly because of some short-term need or emergency. Direct equity investments in real estate are considered to be less liquid than most other investments.

There are several possible explanations for the illiquid nature of direct equity real estate investments. In no small part, the illiquidity stems from the fact that local and national real estate markets are less developed than those for other investment vehicles. The proliferation of local multiple listing services and national real estate franchises only moderately negate the historical differences between real estate markets and security markets. It is unlikely that the real estate markets will ever become as liquid as securities markets, primarily because of the nonhomogeneous nature of real estate. When investors decide to purchase shares of IBM common stock, for example, they can rely on the fact that one share is identical to another. Therefore, investors are not required to devote resources investigating the peculiarities of the shares to be acquired. In the real estate market, however, a number of factors, including the location, income producing ability, and desirability of each parcel, are unique, and should be investigated before transactions occur.

There are several ways in which real estate investments could be made more liquid. An investor may gain increased liquidity by indirect investment (e.g., purchasing shares in a REIT, described later in the chapter). One price of the liquidity gain is the loss of control exercised by the direct investor. The liquidity of real estate could also be improved if prices were determined like securities, in essence, by auction. Real estate investors, however, have generally been unwilling to risk selling their investment too cheaply under such a system and prefer to set a price and wait for a buyer willing to meet the price.

PURCHASING POWER RISK

Purchasing power risk, also known as inflationary risk, is the risk that the dollars recovered from an investment may not buy the same number of other goods as would the dollars originally invested. All forms of investment are subject to inflationary risk. Experts suggest that this risk can best be avoided by either being in debt, or by investing in aggressive rather than defensive investments. Historically, real estate has been one of the best inflation hedges available to investors. An inflation hedge is an investment that will preserve an investor's purchasing power by increasing in value at a rate at least equal to prices in general. It is important to remember, however, that there is no guarantee that a particular investment will serve as an inflation hedge, or even increase in value.

OTHER INVESTMENT RISKS

Investors should also consider several additional risks, including legislative risk, financial risk, and interest rate risk. Legislative risk describes any variation from expected investment return resulting from changes in the tax law, zoning ordinances, rent controls, and other regulations. Changes in laws related to real estate can greatly affect the return on investment. It is, therefore, important for an investor to know (or consult with someone who does know) current laws, regulations, proposed regulatory changes, and their effect on investment decisions.

Financial risk is the risk of loss that results from the use of debt financing. This risk increases as an investor increases the amount of debt used to finance an investment. In essence, it is the risk of incurring unfavorable financial leverage discussed earlier in the chapter.

Interest rate risk refers to the fact that any change in interest rates affects either the price, or realized return, of all securities and investments that pay a fixed rate of return. Interest rate risk can be divided into two components: price risk, and reinvestment rate risk. Price risk refers to the fact that the market value of an investment will decrease if interest rates increase subsequent to acquisition of the investment. You should be able to demonstrate this risk using the concepts presented in Chapter 17. Reinvestment risk refers to the fact that investors must reinvest cash generated by the investment at a lower rate of interest than originally anticipated if interest rates drop. A decrease in interest rates may also affect real estate investments in less obvious ways. For example, when interest rates are low, investors tend to shift funds out of savings accounts and government securities into higher yielding equity investments (common stocks). This can affect the supply of mortgage money available from lending institutions.

DOING BUSINESS
AN ETHICAL ISSUE

Anyone viewing cable television in recent years is likely to have seen an infomercial that offers to teach people who attend a seminar how to get rich quick by investing in real estate. Several money-making techniques are presented in such seminars, including, but not limited to: buying foreclosure property, using discount bonds or existing mortgages to acquire property, and buying real property for no money down. In some cases, the infomercial claims that not only is a down payment unnecessary, but that the purchaser can walk away from the closing table with a check in a large amount. There are serious disadvantages associated with each of these money-making techniques. You may wish to discuss these with your fellow students and instructor.

To facilitate the discussion, consider buying real property without a down payment. For example, as we learned in Chapter 15, using a VA loan involves virtually no initial out-of-pocket cash, but such loans are only available for properties in which the borrower intends to live. Virtually any property can be acquired for no money down. All too often, however, this strategy serves to disguise the fact that the purchaser paid too much for the property.

A valid question to ask before attending a get-rich-quick by investing in real estate seminar is: "If this is such a great idea, why is the speaker giving seminars instead of doing it himself or herself?" There is a simple answer to this question. The speakers are rational economic beings, and rational economic beings act to maximize their own wealth. They realize that getting people to pay them several hundreds (or even thousands) of dollars for a seminar is a more certain way to get rich quick than the techniques they espouse. And when you perform the following Internet assignment you will see that "Get Rich Quick" seminars are not limited to this country.

Go to www.asic.gov.au, click "Visit FIDO," click Search This Site, and use "investment seminar homepage" as your search words, then click on one or more of the titles to learn about this activity in Australia.

FORMULATING A DIRECT INVESTMENT STRATEGY

To implement a successful investment plan, potential investors must consider the advantages, disadvantages, and risks enumerated above. Some people may decide that real estate does not fit into their investment objectives; others may not have the temperament to make direct equity real estate investments. Those who do must make decisions regarding: the ownership form to be employed; the specific type of investment to be made; and investment timing. The decisions made on these issues constitute the investor's investment strategy.

OWNERSHIP FORM

Title to real property can be held in several forms, including sole proprietorship, corporation, general partnership, limited partnership, limited liability entity, and trust. For a detailed discussion of ownership forms see Chapter 5. The particular ownership form an investor selects is important because it may affect several variables that include personal liability, management responsibility and control, access to external funds, income taxes, and the liquidity of the investment.

TYPE OF INVESTMENT

The specific type of property in which the investment is made may also affect investment return. For example, recall that residential income property may be depreciated faster than nonresidential property, thereby providing a greater annual tax shield. More importantly, the performance of each real property submarket (e.g., commercial, or industrial) may fluctuate independent from other submarkets. Increased demand for a particular use will tend to drive up prices within the submarket and stimulate the creation of property designed for the submarket. The most profit will go to those individuals who can predict such changes accurately.

INVESTMENT TIMING

An ongoing decision that investors face is when to make, or sell, an investment. There are two aspects of investment timing; one involves the market in general, and the other involves the individual project. Proper market timing is generally not crucial for defensive investments, but it is important for an aggressive investment like real estate. Many real estate investors have been disappointed because they either missed investment opportunities at market bottoms or missed sales opportunities at market peaks. In effect, they were disappointed that they were unable to carry the investment adage "buy low, sell high" to the extreme. Attempting to buy at the absolute market bottom and sell at the very top of market peaks is likely to be a futile effort. By following the market analysis procedures outlined in Chapter 20, however, one may greatly reduce the odds of doing the opposite.

Regardless of market conditions, investment returns are likely to be affected by the stage of a project's life cycle at the time one makes the investment. There are several stages in the life cycle of real estate projects. First, is the acquisition stage, in which the developer acquires the needed land. Next, is the construction stage, in which improvements are made to the land. This is followed by the rent-up stage, when leases are secured (although construction on large projects, such as a shopping mall, generally will not begin until one or more anchor tenants sign a lease). Finally, there is the stage in which the project is fully rented and in operation.

The risk-return tradeoff suggests that required return should be inversely related to the stage of development. In essence, highest returns should be associated with the earliest stage of development because at the acquisition stage the investor faces the greatest risk. Initially, there may be uncertainty as to whether the required land can be acquired at an acceptable price, or once acquired, that any necessary zoning changes will be granted. Meeting other regulatory requirements may also impede the project's development. Once construction begins, construction costs may be higher than anticipated, labor disputes or other legal problems may arise and delay the project. There is also uncertainty at this point regarding whether revenues from the completed project will be as high as estimated, or that expenses will be as low as estimated.

An investor considering investment in a newly completed project faces less risk because the once uncertain construction costs are known (and irrelevant to the one deciding to make an investment at this stage). Those investing at this stage should, therefore, have a lower required return. There may, however, still be uncertainty regarding revenues and expenses from the operation of the project. Existing real estate projects have even lower risk because prospective investors can check the financial performance of the property. Previous demand for the property also provides some assurance, but no guarantee, that such demand will continue in the future. As a result, required returns for existing projects can be even lower than for new projects.

At some point in the life of each real estate project, the trend toward lower risk is reversed, and investors should raise their required returns for such investments. To illustrate, consider a structurally sound warehouse that was state-of-the-art when it was built fifty years ago, but now has some functional shortcomings. Perhaps the interior support columns are too close by today's standards, or it has outdated loading docks. There is likely to be greater demand for newer warehouses and expensive renovations may have to be made, or rent concessions granted, to keep the older building rented.

ANALYSIS OF REAL ESTATE INVESTMENT OPPORTUNITIES

Assuming that the results of the market analysis (conducted according to the guidelines in Chapter 20) are acceptable, an investor may scrutinize individual projects further. To help ensure that a particular investment opportunity is feasible, an investor must gather, verify and analyze financial information about the investment. To illustrate this process, assume you are considering purchasing the Peach Blossom Apartment Building for $400,000 (appraised 90 percent improvements, 10 percent; land). You plan to put $100,000 down, and secure a thirty-year, $300,000 mortgage loan with a fixed interest rate of 10 percent.

There are several steps that you, as a prospective investor, should take. First you should secure operating and cash flow statements for the property. For existing projects, you can obtain this information from the seller. Once obtained, you should attempt to verify the accuracy of the information provided because sellers sometimes exaggerate income levels and understate expenses. You can verify rents and vacancy levels by examining copies of the existing leases. You can determine the reasonableness of rents, occupancy levels, and operating expenses by gathering data for similar properties and comparing them to the subject property. Organizations such as BOMA (Building Owners and Managers Association) International (www.boma.org) and the Institute of Real Estate Managers (www.irem.org) gather and publish operating expense data and other information that may prove useful. Operating expenses generally fall within a narrow range for similar properties located within the same geographic market. Unique features associated with a particular property may, however, justify a deviation from the norm. You can also check operating expenses by obtaining bids from professional property management and insurance companies, and by checking with utility companies and the county tax assessor's office.

For relatively small projects, like Peach Blossom, you should pay particular attention to whether the operating statements include amounts for management fees and replacement reserves. In some cases, management fees are not included because the seller managed the property. Failure to include management fees in the operating statements will result in an overstatement of the return the purchaser will realize, especially if outside management is to be employed. In examining Exhibit 21.1, you will note that an allowance is made for replacement reserves. Replacement reserves are amounts set aside for the eventual replacement of items that will wear out before the structure itself, such as draperies, refrigerators, and stoves. The reserve recognizes the fact that these items wear out over time; placing funds in a reserve helps to ensure that money will be available to keep the project functional by making the expenditures when needed. Unlike the other costs reflected in the statement, replacement reserves are not deductible for income tax purposes in the year the amount is placed in reserve. Such expenditures are deductible in the year they are actually incurred.

Once you determine that the numbers in the operating statement are accurate, you must determine whether the investment makes financial sense. It is important to consider the loan-to-value ratio, the debt coverage ratio, and the break-even occupancy ratio because lenders use these measures to evaluate loan applications. Investors may also employ several other measures to determine the feasibility of an investment. Some commonly used measures include the gross income multiplier, cash-on-cash return, and the pay back period. More sophisticated techniques, including: the internal rate of return, net present value, and the profitability index, are recommended because each considers all after-tax cash flows, and takes into account the time value of money.

LOAN-TO-VALUE RATIO

The loan-to-value ratio expresses the relationship of the mortgage loan amount to the lower of the appraised value of the property or the purchase price. Investors generally prefer higher loan-to-value ratios compared with lenders, because it enables them to increase their financial leverage. In contrast, lenders realize that the more equity a borrower has in a property the lower the probability of default. Typically, loan-to-value ratios for real estate investment loans range from 70 to 80 percent with each lender setting its own standard.

Assuming the appraised value of Peach Blossom Apartments equals or exceeds the purchase price, the loan to value ratio is 75 percent.

$$\text{Loan-to-value ratio} = \frac{\text{loan amount}}{\text{lower of appraised value or purchase price}}$$

$$.75 = \$300,000/\$400,000$$

DEBT COVERAGE RATIO

The debt coverage ratio expresses the relationship between annual net operating income and annual debt service (mortgage loan interest and principle). The purpose of this ratio

EXHIBIT	21.1	PEACH BLOSSOM APARTMENTS ANNUAL STATEMENT OF REVENUE, EXPENSES, AND CASH FLOW

Potential Gross Income	$60,000	
– Allowance for Vacancies and Bad Debts	3,000	
Effective Gross Income		$57,000
– Operating Expenses:		
–Hazard Insurance	1,400	
–Maintenance and Repairs	2,400	
– Professional Management Fees	2,400	
– Real Property Taxes	2,600	
– Utilities	2,500	
–Advertising	1,200	
– Replacement Reserves	1,200	
Net Operating Income		$43,300
Other Expenses:		
– Debt Service	31,593	
– Depreciation**	12,545	
Income Before Tax		$ (838)
– Income Tax*		812
Income After Tax		$ (1,650)
+ Depreciation	12,545	
After Tax Cash Flow		$10,895

* Calculation of Income Tax

Income Before Tax	$ (838)
Plus: replacement reserves	1,200
Plus: debt principal	1,668
Taxable income	$2,030
× Tax rate (federal and state)	.4
Income tax	$ 812

** Calculation of Depreciation

Purchase price	$400,000
× Improvements as a percentage of value	.90
Depreciable basis	$360,000

Monthly depreciation: $360,000 / 330 = $1,090.91

First year depreciation (assuming purchase made in January: $1,090.91 × 11.5 = $12,545

is to determine whether the project will generate sufficient income to meet the debt service and to provide the lender with a margin of safety. Generally, this ratio should be no lower than 1.25. In essence, net operating income must be at least 125 percent of annual mortgage principal and interest payments. Most lenders would find the debt coverage ratio of 1.37 for Peach Blossom to be acceptable.

$$\text{Debt coverage ratio} = \frac{\text{annual net income}}{\text{annual debt service}}$$

$$1.37 = \$43,300/\$31,593$$

BREAK-EVEN OCCUPANCY RATIO

The break-even occupancy ratio, sometimes called the default ratio or break-even ratio, reflects the occupancy rate at which rental income equals the combination of debt service and all required operating expenses requiring a cash outlay (i.e., depreciation allowance is not included). Basically, this ratio shows how low the occupancy rate could go before negative cash flows would occur. If a property's income goes below the break-even point, the investor must use other sources of income to pay the debt service. In large commercial projects, where it is common to acquire temporary loans to finance construction and then replace such loans with permanent financing after construction is complete, permanent lenders frequently require that a project be leased up to its break-even point before providing the permanent financing. For Peach Blossom the break-even occupancy ratio is 75.5 percent.

$$\text{Break even occupancy ratio} = \frac{\text{debt service \& cash expenses}}{\text{potential gross income}}$$

$$.755 = \$45,293/\$60,000$$

GROSS INCOME MULTIPLIER

The gross income multiplier expresses the relationship between the gross income a property generates and its purchase price. This measure provides investors with a relatively quick way to determine the reasonableness of the purchase price. First, the investor gathers information on selling price and gross income for recently sold comparable properties. Next, the investor calculates the multiplier for both the comparables and the proposed investment. Then, the investor compares the figures. If economic conditions have not changed dramatically since the comparable sales, and the gross income multiplier for the proposed investment is higher than the comparable's multiplier, this is an indication that the purchase price may be too high. The gross income multiplier for Peach Blossom is 6.7.

$$\text{Gross income multiplier} = \frac{\text{purchase price}}{\text{gross income}}$$

$$6.7 = \$400,000/\$60,000$$

CASH-ON-CASH RETURN

The cash-on-cash return shows the relationship of an investment's after tax cash flow to the initial equity investment (some investors calculate this measure on a before-tax basis). For Peach Blossom, the cash-on-cash return is approximately 10.9 percent. This figure can be compared to the cash-on-cash return for comparable properties.

$$\text{Cash-on-cash return} = \frac{\text{after tax cash flow}}{\text{equity investment}}$$

$$.10895 = \$10,895/\$100,000$$

It is best to use the gross income multiplier and the cash-on-cash return as preliminary screening devices to determine if an investment opportunity merits additional research. Note that both measures use information from only one year. The return an investor earns, however, occurs over the entire holding period. One should not base investment decisions solely on measures that require such a small amount of information.

PAY BACK PERIOD

The pay back period is a slight improvement over the two previous measures because it considers cash flows that occur beyond the first year. The pay back period represents the number of years it will take for an investor to recover the initial investment. Other things constant, investors prefer short pay back periods, reasoning that the faster a project promises to pay back the initial investment, the smaller the chances that they will lose the investment. Assuming that the figures shown in Exhibit 21.1 are applicable for each year of the investment, the pay back period for Peach Blossom is approximately nine years and two months.

$$\text{Payback period} = \frac{\text{equity investment}}{\text{annual after tax cash flow}}$$

$$9.17 = \$100,000/\$10,895$$

As a measure of investment feasibility, the pay back approach has two serious shortcomings. First, the approach ignores any cash flows beyond the pay back period. To illustrate this point, consider the following two investment opportunities.

Investment Opportunity	A	B
Equity Investment	$10,000	$10,000
Cash Inflows		
Year 1	4,000	2,000
Year 2	4,000	2,000
Year 3	4,000	2,000
Year 4	4,000	4,000
Year 5	0	12,000

Based solely on the pay back approach, one would prefer investment A because its pay back period is two-and-one-half years, compared with a four-year pay back period for investment B. The total cash flows associated with investment B are, however, clearly larger than those for investment A. The second problem with the pay back approach is that it ignores the time value of money. The following techniques are, therefore, recommended because they recognize that a dollar in your pocket today is more valuable than a dollar to be received in the future.

NET PRESENT VALUE

The **net present value** (NPV) is a single dollar value that represents the discounted value of all after tax cash flows associated with a particular investment. In effect, it tells you how many dollars (in present value terms) you expect the project to generate for each dollar invested. Therefore, to apply this technique, an investor needs two things: an estimate of the investment's after tax cash flows, and the investor's discount rate. The required cash flow estimates include both the cash flows from operation of the investment and those realized when the property is sold (the reversion value).

The NPV is used to determine whether an investment will generate enough cash flow to meet the investor's required return. If the present value of the outflows is greater than the present value of the inflows, the NPV is negative, and this suggests the investor should reject the investment opportunity. If the present value of the inflows exceeds the present value of the outflows, the NPV is positive. A positive (or zero) NPV indicates that an investment is acceptable.

To illustrate the NPV technique, we continue the Peach Blossom Apartment example. Assume you plan to hold Peach Blossom for five years. You estimate that rental income, operating expenses, and the property value will increase at a rate of six percent per year. The figures shown in Exhibit 21.2 were based on these assumptions. You also require an 18 percent

| EXHIBIT | 21.2 | PEACH BLOSSOM APARTMENTS: PROJECTED STATEMENT OF ANNUAL REVENUE, EXPENSES, AND CASH FLOW (IN THOUSANDS); PROJECTED AFTER TAX REVERSION VALUE: END OF YEAR 5; CALCULATION OF NPV |

Projected Statement of Annual Revenue, Expenses, and Cash Flow (in Thousands)

Year	1	2	3	4	5
Potential Gross Income	$60.0	$63.6	$67.4	$71.5	$75.7
– Vacancies and bad debts	3.0	3.2	3.4	3.6	3.8
Effective Gross Income	57.0	60.4	64.0	67.9	71.9
– Operating Expenses	13.7	14.5	15.4	16.3	17.3
Operating Income	43.3	45.9	48.6	51.6	54.6
– Depreciation	12.5	13.1	13.1	13.1	13.1
– Debt Service	31.6	31.6	31.6	31.6	31.6
Income Before Tax	(.8)	1.2	3.9	6.9	9.9
– Income Tax	.8	1.7	2.9	4.1	5.4
Income After Tax	(1.6)	(0.5)	1.0	2.8	4.5
+ Depreciation	12.5	13.1	13.1	13.1	13.1
After Tax Cash Flow	10.9	12.6	14.1	15.9	17.6

Projected After Tax Reversion Value: End of Year 5

Gross Selling Price ($400,000 × 1,065)			$535,290
– Selling Expenses (7%)			37,470
Net Selling Price		497,820	
Purchase Price	400,000		
– Accumulated Depreciation	64,914		
Adjusted Basis		335,086	
Taxable Gain		162,734	
× Marginal Tax Rate		.4	
– Tax on Gain			65,094
Profit on sale			432,726
– Mortgage Loan Payoff			289,723
After Tax Cash Flow From Reversion			143,003

Calculation of NPV

Year		1	2	3	4	5
Annual Net Cash Flow	(100)	10.9	12.6	14.1	15.9	160.6
× PVIF	1.000	.8475	.7182	.6086	.5159	.4371
Present Value	(100)	9.2	9.0	8.6	8.2	70.2

Therefore: NPV = $5.2 (105.2 – $100)

return for investments such as Peach Blossom Apartments. At the bottom of Exhibit 21.2, we see that the NPV for the investment is a positive $5,200. Based on the estimated cash flows, the investment is acceptable and your wealth will increase by $5,200 (in present value terms) by making the investment.

Decision Point

Using the figures from Exhibit 21.2, would the investment still be acceptable if you require a 15 percent rate of return? What if you require a 25 percent return?

INTERNAL RATE OF RETURN

The **internal rate of return** (IRR) is the interest (discount) rate that equates the present values of an investment's cash inflows and outflows. In other words, the IRR is the interest rate that results in an NPV of zero. An investment decision based on the IRR is made by comparing the investment's IRR with the investor's required return. If the IRR is less than the investor's required return, the investment should be rejected. If the IRR is greater than or equal to the investor's required return, the investment is acceptable.

The IRR for Peach Blossom Apartments is 19.47 percent (determined by calculator). This exceeds your (assumed) required return of 18 percent. Therefore, this technique suggests (as did NPV) that the investment is acceptable. In fact, the IRR, NPV and the profitability index (described in following section) will always result in the same accept/reject decision because each uses all after tax cash flows, and each considers the time value of money.

PROFITABILITY INDEX

The profitability index (PI) expresses the discounted cash inflows and outflows as a ratio, or index number. In effect, it tells you how many dollars you expect the project to generate for each dollar invested in present value terms. Therefore, a PI of less than 1.0 indicates that one should reject an investment. A PI greater than or equal to 1.0 suggests that the investment is acceptable. For Peach Blossom, the PI is 1.05.

$$\text{Profitability index} = \frac{\text{present value of cash inflows}}{\text{present value of cash outflows}}$$

$$1.05 = \$105,200/\$100,000$$

INDIRECT REAL ESTATE INVESTMENT

Relatively few individuals have the resources to invest directly either in the financing or ownership of large real estate projects such as shopping centers, hotels, or high-rise office buildings. Investment vehicles are available, however, which enable investors to finance or own such projects indirectly. Several different types of securities, backed by mortgages, offer investors a means of participating in the real estate mortgage market. These securities are discussed later in this section. Indirect equity ownership of large-scale real estate projects can be achieved by investing in real estate investment trusts.

REAL ESTATE INVESTMENT TRUSTS

A **real estate investment trust** (REIT) is a business organization that pools individual investor's money to make real estate investments. In addition to allowing investors to invest in large-scale real estate projects, REITs offer other advantages. A REIT is entitled to some of the tax advantages of a partnership while retaining many of the advantages of the corporate ownership form if (among other requirements) it invests at least 75 percent of its funds in real estate and distributes at least 90 percent of its income to its investors. In particular, the shareholders of a tax-qualified REIT, like corporate shareholders, enjoy limited legal liability; the most they can lose is what they have invested. Most REITs distribute nearly all income to shareholders as dividends that are not taxed at the REIT level. REIT shareholders, therefore, avoid the double taxation of earnings typically incurred by corporate shareholders. REIT shares are readily transferable, and small investments are possible. REIT share prices generally range from $10 to $30. Finally, although shareholders have the right to vote in company elections, they have no management responsibilities.

REIT investors may also gain diversification benefits both within the real estate market, and in a larger portfolio sense. Diversification within the real estate market is possible because some REITs diversify their portfolios; both geographically and by property type. In the larger sense, REIT returns have a low correlation with common stock and bond returns. Thus, investors holding portfolios that contain no real estate investments can lower their portfolio risk by incorporating REIT shares into their portfolios. There are some disadvantages associated with REITs. For example, losses incurred by a REIT cannot be passed through to investors and used to offset income from other sources.

REIT Classifications

REITs are commonly classified according to the type of investment in which they specialize. A mortgage REIT is defined as one that holds at least 75 percent of their invested assets in real estate mortgages. An equity REIT is one that holds at least 75 percent of their invested assets in the ownership of real estate or other equity interests. A hybrid REIT combines the two investment strategies.

At mid-year 2001, there were 189 publicly traded REITs. Examination of Exhibit 21.3 will reveal that most of them are equity REITs, and that they control the lion's share of all REIT assets. Exhibit 21.4 shows that REITs invest in a variety of property uses. As of mid-year 2001, more than 100 REITs focused their investments in industrial/office, retail, and residential properties. The shares of these REITs accounted for more than 70 percent of the market value of all REIT shares. Most REITs concentrate in a particular type of use, but 20 hold "diversified" portfolios.

OTHER REIT CLASSIFICATIONS

As the following definitions imply, REITs may be classified in a number of ways. One classification is based on whether the specific investments to be made are disclosed at the time funds are acquired from investors. Other classifications are based on either the amount of funds solicited, whether borrowed funds are to be used in property acquisitions, and according to the expected life of the trust.

EXHIBIT 21.3 ASSETS CONTROLLED BY REITS IN 2001

REIT Type	Number of	Total Assets (in thousands of $)	Percent of Total
Equity	158	$285,820,379	88.2
Hybrid	9	7,947,100	2.5
Mortgage	22	30,152,792	9.3
Total	189	323,920,271	100.0

Source: National Association of Real Estate Investment Trusts

EXHIBIT **21.4** **REITS INVESTMENTS AND EQUITY MARKET CAPITALIZATION IN 2001**

Sector	Number of REITs	Equity Market Capitalization (in millions of $)	Percent of total Capitalization
Industrial/Office	36	$ 48,262.5	31.8
Retail	46	31,506.9	20.7
Residential	25	31,393.5	20.7
Diversified	20	13,171.5	8.7
Lodging/Hotels	15	9,292.9	6.1
Self Storage	4	5,618.1	3.7
Health Care	13	6,568.7	4.3
Specialty	8	3,405.0	2.2
Mortgage	22	2,785.2	1.8
Total	189	152,004.3	100.0

Source: National Association of Real Estate Investment Trusts

- **Fully specified or purchasing trust**—The projects in which the REIT will invest are identified up front.
- **Blind pool or check trust**—The projects in which the REIT will invest are not identified up front. The managers of the blind pools must have excellent performance records to attract investment dollars because of the uncertainty associated with the investment.
- **Mixed trust**—The REIT invests some funds in specific properties and the rest on a blind pool basis.
- **Close-end**—The total number of shares that may be issued is limited because the REIT specifies the maximum amount of funds sought.
- **Open-end**—The number of shares issued may increase over time as new investments are discovered. Investors in open-end REITs should be aware that the issue of additional shares may dilute the value of existing shares.
- **Unleveraged**—Uses no borrowed funds to make property acquisitions.
- **Leveraged**—In soliciting funds, specifies that borrowed funds may be used in property acquisitions. In some cases, borrowed funds may be used to finance up to 90 percent of the value of purchased assets. Other things constant, investors should require a higher rate of return from a leveraged REIT because of the extra risk entailed in borrowing.
- **Perpetual**—Created to operate indefinitely. Traditionally, REITs were set up in this manner.
- **Finite-life or self-liquidating**—Such REITs have a specified length of existence; typically ten to twenty years.

MORTGAGE-BACKED SECURITIES

Several mortgage-backed securities are available for investors who wish to participate indirectly in the financing of real property. Included are pass-through securities, mortgage-backed bonds, mortgage pay-through bonds, and collateralized mortgage obligations (or real estate mortgage investment conduits).

MORTGAGE PASS-THROUGHS

Mortgage pass-throughs are securities that are collateralized by a pool of mortgages and issued either by the Federal National Mortgage Association (FNMA), the Federal Home Loan Mortgage Corporation (FHLMC), or by a private mortgage originator through the Government National Mortgage Association (GNMA). Prepayment risk is the risk that borrowers will pay on the underlying mortgages faster than anticipated. At the end of 1999, these securities, as a group, constituted the largest segment of the mortgage-backed security market with more than $4 trillion held by investors.

Mortgage pass-throughs were originally designed to appeal to institutional investors rather than individuals. The minimum denomination for trading any mortgage pass-throughs in the secondary market is $25,000. Most large securities firms, however, make these securities available to their customers in denominations as small as $1,000 by splitting up large blocks they have acquired. Individuals with limited means can also incorporate these securities into their investment portfolio by purchasing shares in an investment fund that specializes in these types of securities.

Mortgage Pass-Through Risks

In general, mortgage investors face two principle risks: interest rate, and prepayment. Prepayment risk is the risk that those who hold the underlying mortgages will pay them faster than anticipated. Prepayments tend to accelerate as interest rates decline and borrowers refinance existing mortgages to lock in a lower rate. In a sense, prepayment is the opposite of default. So, if default is a risk, a reasonable question is, "how can prepayment constitute a risk?" The answer is straightforward. The calculation of an investment's yield to maturity is an internal rate of return calculation (Chapter 17). Implicit in such a calculation is that all future cash flows will be invested at the internal rate of return of the investment being analyzed. So, if interest rates drop subsequent to making the investment, and prepayments occur faster than anticipated, the investor's expected yield to maturity will not be realized because the reinvestment rate assumption has been violated. To (at least partially) address the problem of prepayment risk, FHLMC issued the first collateralized mortgage obligation, (described next) in the amount of $1 billion, in 1983.

DOING BUSINESS
INFORMATION SERVICES

In March 2002, Moody's Investors Service became the first rating agency to provide ratings for real estate funds. The new system, called Moody's Real Estate Ratings, is designed for commingled open-end and closed-end funds, unit trusts, partnerships, joint ventures and similar funds that invest in real property and/or real property mortgages. The product is designed to boost transparency and to allow for increased investor confidence in the industry. The first funds rated were seven German property funds. "We are pleased to provide this new rating system to the global real estate community," said John J. Kriz, managing director of real estate finance at Moody's. "The market's excellent reception has clearly delivered the message that Moody's Real Estate Ratings will be important to fulfilling the needs of investors, consultants and investment managers for an independent, transparent and respected rating system for property funds' asset quality and management quality." When you perform the following Internet assignment you will see that another rating service also rates real estate securities.

Go to www.standardandpoors.com, click Search and use "real estate investments" as your search words, then click on one or more of the results to see real estate investments rated by Standard and Poors.

One risk that investors in pass-throughs need not be concerned about is default risk. While the default risk associated with investing in a single mortgage may be too high for most investors, there is no default risk associated with pass-throughs. Investors in pass-throughs have a pro rata, undivided ownership interest in the pool of mortgages. The common minimum size of a mortgage pool securing a pass-through is $100 million and can include more than a thousand residential mortgages. This diversification reduces greatly the risk of individual default. In addition, each agency guarantees the full and timely payment of principal and interest to investors; if the borrower fails to pay, the agency will.

Collateralized Mortgage Obligations

A **collateralized mortgage obligation** (CMO) is a multiple-class debt security backed either by mortgages, or by mortgage pass-through securities. Most CMOs are issued by FNMA and FHLMC; some are offered by private issuers (mortgage originators, security dealers, and builders). The multiple-class feature is what distinguishes CMOs from the pass-throughs described previously. In effect, a CMO issuer breaks up a pool of thirty-year mortgages into a series of securities, and predetermines a particular interest rate, cash flow schedule, and maturity for each class. Typically, a CMO has ten to twenty different classes, but some have been issued with fifty classes.

It is important to understand the difference between a CMO and a "regular" pass-through. Under a pass-through, each investor's claim is on a pro rata share of the entire mortgage pool. Therefore, all investors in a pass-through (assuming identical holding periods) earn an identical return, and each investor has an investment with the same maturity as all other investors in the security. The multiple class structure of a CMO enables investors to select a class that best meets their investment objectives. It also provides CMO investors with a measure of protection from prepayment risk. Although, if prepayment rates increase dramatically, the actual maturity of any class may be shorter than anticipated because any prepayments are passed through to the investor.

The mortgages, or pass-throughs, serving as CMO collateral are held by a trustee who is also responsible for distributing the cash flows generated by the collateral to the CMO investors in the predetermined order. Investors in the short-maturity classes receive both principal and interest on their share of the pool, as well as principal payments from other classes. Principal received from the other classes serves to liquidate the claim of the nearby class. Other CMO classes receive only interest (or nothing) until the claims of the short-maturity classes have been eliminated.

These securities have become very popular. As of September 2001, Ginnie Mae, Fannie Mae, and Freddie Mac alone had $723 billion in outstanding CMOs. Like pass-throughs, CMOs were originally designed to appeal to institutional investors, but are available from security dealers in $1,000 denominations.

Real Estate Mortgage Investment Conduit (REMIC)

The Tax Reform Act of 1986 authorized a new type of mortgage-backed security, the Real Estate Mortgage Investment Conduit (REMIC). The distinction between REMICs and CMOs is that issuers of REMICs avoid tax and other disadvantages associated with CMOs. From an investor's perspective, REMICs are indistinguishable from CMOs, and virtually all CMOs issued now are actually REMICs.

Mortgage-Backed Bonds and Mortgage Pay-Through Bonds

A mortgage-backed bond is a long-term debt instrument issued by a mortgage originator (e.g., savings and loan, or commercial bank) that is collateralized by mortgages owned by the bond issuer. These securities are very much like a mortgage bond issued by any corporation, which are usually secured by the issuer's long-term assets. Other features of mortgage-backed bonds include the following

1. Interest is paid to bondholders every six months.
2. Most carry a fixed interest rate, although variable rates or zero coupons are possible.
3. They come in denominations of $1,000 and are usually sold through securities dealers.

Investors in mortgage-backed bonds do not have to be concerned with prepayment risk because the security is a bond, not a pass-through. The default risk associated with these bonds is also low because issuers are ordinarily required to over-collateralize the issue, pledging from $125 to $240 of mortgages for every $100 of bond. In addition, issuers are usually required to pledge additional mortgages as collateral if defaults or prepayment of the underlying mortgages brings the over-collateralization ratio too low.

A mortgage pay-through bond is another long-term debt instrument secured by a pool of mortgages and issued by mortgage originators. A pay-through bond may be characterized as a hybrid security. In essence, it has some characteristics of a bond, but in other respects it resembles a pass-through security. Unlike a pass-through, the investor owns the bond itself and not an undivided interest in the underlying mortgage pool. Unlike a mortgage-backed bond, however, payments are ordinarily passed-through to the bondholder each month (although pay-throughs with quarterly or semi-annual payments are also available). Therefore, although mortgage pay-through bonds are over-collateralized, the bondholder bears some prepayment risk. Like mortgage-backed bonds, pay-through bonds may carry a fixed, variable, or zero coupon, and are normally sold through security dealers.

SUMMARY

Investors have the opportunity to make equity and nonequity investments in real estate. An individual can make both types of investment directly or indirectly, and there are disadvantages and advantages associated with each investment type. Advantages of direct equity investments include the opportunity to realize portfolio diversification, income tax benefits, positive cash flow, appreciation in the value of the property, and favorable financial leverage. The disadvantages of direct equity investment include the need for management, the illiquid nature of, and large dollar amount required to make such investments.

Indirect investment in real estate also offers several advantages and disadvantages. The degree of control indirect investors can exercise over the investment is usually quite limited; control is generally retained by the party making the direct investment. Indirect investors frequently face less risk than direct investors. For example, the default risk associated with a single mortgage loan may be high, especially compared to a security backed by hundreds of mortgages (and guaranteed by a government, or quasi-government agency). A factor several of the indirect investment vehicles have in common is the pooling of resources. Indirect investment is, therefore, more affordable, and enables more people to include real estate in their investment portfolios, compared with direct investment.

Several measures are commonly used to evaluate direct real estate investments. Some measures, like the gross income multiplier, loan to value ratio, debt coverage ratio, break-even occupancy level, and cash-on-cash return, are best used as screening devices because they fail to consider all appropriate information. Preferred measures include the net present value, internal rate of return, and profitability index, because each considers all after tax cash flows associated with an investment, and each also factors in the time value of money.

All investments are subject to a number of risks and real estate investments are subject to more risks than many other investments. When making a financial investment, risk is not necessarily a disadvantage. Prudent investors recognize risk and require higher rates of return to accept higher risk. Knowledge of the material presented in this chapter should enable you to make better-informed investment decisions.

KEY TERMS

business risk
collateralized mortgage
    obligation
direct investment
diversification
financial leverage
internal rate of return

indirect investment
interest rate risk
liquidity risk
market risk
mortgage-backed security
negative cash flow
net present value

participation certificate
pass through security
positive cash flow
purchasing power risk
real estate investment trust

REVIEW QUESTIONS

1. Distinguish a direct real estate investment from an indirect investment. What risk factors do you think are most important for direct investors, and for indirect investors?

2. Distinguish an equity real estate investment from a nonequity investment. What risk factors do you think are most important for equity investors, and for nonequity investors?

3. Define positive and negative financial leverage. How can a measure of financial leverage based on operating returns for a single year be misleading?

4. On pages 380 and 381, we demonstrated how appreciation in property value may overcome negative cash flows and result in a positive return. Specifically, it was assumed you purchased a property for $100,000 and sold it for $200,000 five years later despite the fact that it had generated nothing but negative cash flows over your holding period. Why would anyone pay you $200,000 for a property that has not generated positive cash flows in five years?

5. What are the advantages and disadvantages of real estate investment trusts as an investment vehicle?

6. Assume that you have decided to invest in a REIT. In which type of REIT would you invest? Why?

7. What does it mean if an investment opportunity has a zero net present value? Is such an investment a good investment?

8. What is the primary difference between a CMO and other mortgage-backed securities? How does this difference benefit investors?

9. What are the advantages and disadvantages of indirect investment compared with direct investment?

10. What are your answers to the questions in the two "Decision Point" sections in this chapter?

PROBLEMS

1. An investor requires a return of 11 percent. What is the payback period, net present value, internal rate of return, and profitability index for an investment with the following cash flows? Initial investment $40,000, annual after tax cash flows for each of the next ten years $6,000.

2. What are the payback period, net present value, internal rate of return, and profitability index for the investment in problem one if the investor requires a return of 9 percent? Twelve percent?

3. Using the data from Exhibit 21.1, what will happen to the breakeven occupancy ratio if rents decrease by 10 percent and operating expenses increase by 10 percent?

4. Recalculate the following measures assuming that the investor in the Peach Blossom Apartments example presented in the chapter pays the entire purchase price with his or her own funds:

    a. Break-even occupancy ratio

    b. Gross income multiplier

    c. Cash-on-cash return

    d. Payback period

    e. Net present value

    f. Internal rate of return

5. Use the following information about three comparable properties to estimate the maximum price that should be paid for the subject property if its annual gross income is estimated to be $17,500.

Property	Selling Price	Gross Monthly Income
1	$123,000	$1,025
2	$137,500	$1,273
3	$152,000	$1,600

REAL ESTATE ON THE WEB

Use your favorite search engine to:

    1. Locate currently available real estate investment opportunities in your area.

    2. Determine if there is a real estate investor's club in your area.

    3. Learn if vacancy rates vary by property type or region of the country.

    4. Find an example of an investor who successfully converted a property from one type of usage to another.

Refer to the companion Web site at www.wiley.com/college/larsen for a variety of online activities including additional chapter content, review materials, assignments, and related links.

ADDITIONAL READINGS

Boyd, J. C. and J. L. Smith. "Closely Held REIT Structures in Jeopardy." *Real Estate Finance* Journal 16 (Winter 2001) 83–86.

Duffie, D. and N. Garleanu. "Risk and Valuation of Collateralized Debt Obligations." *Financial Analysts Journal* 16 (January/February 2001) 41–59.

Eichholtz, P., K. Koedijk, and M. Schweitzer. "Global Property Investment and the Cost of International Diversification." *Journal of International Money and Finance* 20 (June, 2001) 349–366.

Lusvardi, W. C. and C. B. Warren. "Three Rules for Real Estate Valuation: Deduction, Adduction, or Reduction." *Real Estate Review* 30 (Winter 2001) 11–18.

Olsen, B.A. "German Investment in the U. S. Real Estate Market." *Real Estate Finance Journal* 16 (Winter 2001) 25–35.

Parli, R. "What's Financial Feasibility Got To Do With It?" *Appraisal Journal* 69 (October2001) 419–423.

Riggs, K. P. Jr. and R. W. Harms. "Realized vs. Required Rates of Return & What it Means to the Real Estate Industry." *Real Estate Issues* 25 (Fall 2000) 6–14.

Solomon, J. "How is the Risk of Investing in Real Estate Changing?" *Real Estate Finance* Journal 16 (Winter 2001) 6–9.

Yang, S. X. "Is Bigger Better/A Re-examination of the Scale Economies of REITs." *Journal of Real Estate Portfolio Management* 7 (January-March 2001) 67–77.

Appendix: Time Value of Money Interest Factors

Interest Rate: 6%

	Annual Compounding				Monthly Compounding				
YEARS	Future value of a dollar	Future value of annuity	Present value of a dollar	Present value of annuity	Future value of a dollar	Future value of annuity	Present value of a dollar	Present value of annuity	YEARS
1	1.060000	1.000000	0.943396	0.943396	1.061678	12.335562	0.941905	11.618932	1
2	1.123600	2.060000	0.889996	1.833393	1.127160	25.431955	0.887186	22.562866	2
3	1.191016	3.183600	0.839619	2.673012	1.196681	39.336105	0.835645	32.871016	3
4	1.262477	4.374616	0.792094	3.465106	1.270489	54.097832	0.787098	42.580318	4
5	1.338226	5.637093	0.747258	4.212364	1.348850	69.770031	0.741372	51.725561	5
6	1.418519	6.975319	0.704961	4.917324	1.432044	86.408856	0.698302	60.339514	6
7	1.503630	8.393838	0.665057	5.582381	1.520370	104.073927	0.657735	68.453042	7
8	1.593848	9.897468	0.627412	6.209794	1.614143	122.828542	0.619524	76.095218	8
9	1.689479	11.491316	0.591898	6.801692	1.713699	142.739900	0.583533	83.293424	9
10	1.790848	13.180795	0.558395	7.360087	1.819397	163.879347	0.549633	90.073453	10
11	1.898299	14.971643	0.526788	7.886875	1.931613	186.322629	0.517702	96.459599	11
12	2.012196	16.869941	0.496969	8.383844	2.050751	210.150163	0.487626	102.474743	12
13	2.132928	18.882138	0.468839	8.852683	2.177237	235.447328	0.459298	108.140440	13
14	2.260904	21.015066	0.442301	9.294984	2.311524	262.304766	0.432615	113.476990	14
15	2.396558	23.275970	0.417265	9.712249	2.454094	290.818712	0.407482	118.503515	15
16	2.540352	25.672528	0.393646	10.105895	2.605457	321.091337	0.383810	123.238025	16
17	2.692773	28.212880	0.371364	10.477260	2.766156	353.231110	0.361513	127.697486	17
18	2.854339	30.905653	0.350344	10.827603	2.936766	387.353194	0.340511	131.897876	18
19	3.025600	33.759992	0.330513	11.158116	3.117899	423.579854	0.320729	135.854246	19
20	3.207135	36.785591	0.311805	11.469921	3.310204	462.040895	0.302096	139.580772	20
21	3.399564	39.992727	0.294155	11.764077	3.514371	502.874129	0.284546	143.090806	21
22	3.603537	43.392290	0.277505	12.041582	3.731129	546.225867	0.268015	146.396927	22
23	3.819750	46.995828	0.261797	12.303379	3.961257	592.251446	0.252445	149.510979	23
24	4.048935	50.815577	0.246979	12.550358	4.205579	641.115782	0.237779	152.444121	24
25	4.291871	54.864512	0.232999	12.783356	4.464970	692.993962	0.223966	155.206864	25
26	4.549383	59.156383	0.219810	13.003166	4.740359	748.071876	0.210954	157.809106	26
27	4.822346	63.705766	0.207368	13.210534	5.032734	806.546875	0.198699	160.260172	27
28	5.111687	68.528112	0.195630	13.406164	5.343142	868.628484	0.187156	162.568844	28
29	5.418388	73.639798	0.184557	13.590721	5.672696	934.539150	0.176283	164.743394	29
30	5.743491	79.058186	0.174110	13.764831	6.022575	1004.515042	0.166042	166.791614	30
31	6.088101	84.801677	0.164255	13.929086	6.394034	1078.806895	0.156396	168.720844	31
32	6.453387	90.889778	0.154957	14.084043	6.788405	1157.680906	0.147310	170.537996	32
33	6.840590	97.343165	0.146186	14.230230	7.207098	1241.419693	0.138752	172.249581	33
34	7.251025	104.183755	0.137912	14.368141	7.651617	1330.323306	0.130691	173.861732	34
35	7.686087	111.434780	0.130105	14.498246	8.123551	1424.710299	0.123099	175.380226	35
36	8.147252	119.120867	0.122741	14.620987	8.624594	1524.918875	0.115947	176.810504	36
37	8.636087	127.268119	0.115793	14.736780	9.156540	1631.308097	0.109212	178.157690	37
38	9.154252	135.904206	0.109239	14.846019	9.721296	1744.259173	0.102867	179.426611	38
39	9.703507	145.058458	0.103056	14.949075	10.320884	1864.176824	0.096891	180.621815	39
40	10.285718	154.761966	0.097222	15.046297	10.957454	1991.490734	0.091262	181.747584	40

Interest Rate: 7%

	Annual Compounding				Monthly Compounding				
YEARS	Future value of a dollar	Future value of annuity	Present value of a dollar	Present value of annuity	Future value of a dollar	Future value of annuity	Present value of a dollar	Present value of annuity	YEARS
1	1.070000	1.000000	0.934579	0.934579	1.072290	12.392585	0.932583	11.557120	1
2	1.144900	2.070000	0.873439	1.808018	1.149806	25.681032	0.869712	22.335099	2
3	1.225043	3.214900	0.816298	2.624316	1.232926	39.930101	0.811079	32.386464	3
4	1.310796	4.439943	0.762895	3.387211	1.322054	55.209236	0.756399	41.760201	4
5	1.402552	5.750739	0.712986	4.100197	1.417625	71.592902	0.705405	50.501994	5
6	1.500730	7.153291	0.666342	4.766540	1.520106	89.160944	0.657849	58.654444	6
7	1.605781	8.654021	0.622750	5.389289	1.629994	107.998981	0.613499	66.257285	7
8	1.718186	10.259803	0.582009	5.971299	1.747826	128.198821	0.572139	73.347569	8
9	1.838459	11.977989	0.543934	6.515232	1.874177	149.858909	0.533568	79.959850	9
10	1.967151	13.816448	0.508349	7.023582	2.009661	173.084807	0.497596	86.126354	10
11	2.104852	15.783599	0.475093	7.498674	2.154940	197.989707	0.464050	91.877134	11
12	2.252192	17.888451	0.444012	7.942686	2.310721	224.694985	0.432765	97.240216	12
13	2.409845	20.140643	0.414964	8.357651	2.477763	253.330789	0.403590	102.241738	13
14	2.578534	22.550488	0.387817	8.745468	2.656881	284.036677	0.376381	106.906074	14
15	2.759032	25.129022	0.362446	9.107914	2.848947	316.962297	0.351007	111.255958	15
16	2.952164	27.888054	0.338735	9.446649	3.054897	352.268112	0.327343	115.312587	16
17	3.158815	30.840217	0.316574	9.763223	3.275736	390.126188	0.305275	119.095732	17
18	3.379932	33.999033	0.295864	10.059087	3.512539	430.721027	0.284694	122.623831	18
19	3.616528	37.378965	0.276508	10.335595	3.766461	474.250470	0.265501	125.914077	19
20	3.869684	40.995492	0.258419	10.594014	4.038739	520.926660	0.247602	128.982506	20
21	4.140562	44.865177	0.241513	10.835527	4.330700	570.977075	0.230910	131.844073	21
22	4.430402	49.005739	0.225713	11.061240	4.643766	624.645640	0.215342	134.512723	22
23	4.740530	53.436141	0.210947	11.272187	4.979464	682.193909	0.200825	137.001461	23
24	5.072367	58.176671	0.197147	11.469334	5.339430	743.902347	0.187286	139.322418	24
25	5.427433	63.249038	0.184249	11.653583	5.725418	810.071693	0.174660	141.486903	25
26	5.807353	68.676470	0.172195	11.825779	6.139309	881.024427	0.162885	143.505467	26
27	6.213868	74.483823	0.160930	11.986709	6.583120	957.106339	0.151904	145.387946	27
28	6.648838	80.697691	0.150402	12.137111	7.059015	1038.688219	0.141663	147.143515	28
29	7.114257	87.346529	0.140563	12.277674	7.569311	1126.167659	0.132112	148.780729	29
30	7.612255	94.460786	0.131367	12.409041	8.116497	1219.970996	0.123206	150.307568	30
31	8.145113	102.073041	0.122773	12.531814	8.703240	1320.555383	0.114900	151.731473	31
32	8.715271	110.218154	0.114741	12.646555	9.332398	1428.411024	0.107154	153.059383	32
33	9.325340	118.933425	0.107235	12.753790	10.007037	1544.063557	0.099930	154.297770	33
34	9.978114	128.258765	0.100219	12.854009	10.730447	1668.076622	0.093193	155.452669	34
35	10.676581	138.236878	0.093663	12.947672	11.506152	1801.054601	0.086910	156.529709	35
36	11.423942	148.913460	0.087535	13.035208	12.337932	1943.645569	0.081051	157.534139	36
37	12.223618	160.337402	0.081809	13.117017	13.229843	2096.544450	0.075587	158.470853	37
38	13.079271	172.561020	0.076457	13.193473	14.186229	2260.496403	0.070491	159.344418	38
39	13.994820	185.640292	0.071455	13.264928	15.211753	2436.300456	0.065739	160.159090	39
40	14.974458	199.635112	0.066780	13.331709	16.311411	2624.813398	0.061307	160.918839	40

Interest Rate: 8%

	Annual Compounding				Monthly Compounding				
YEARS	Future value of a dollar	Future value of annuity	Present value of a dollar	Present value of annuity	Future value of a dollar	Future value of annuity	Present value of a dollar	Present value of annuity	YEARS
1	1.080000	1.000000	0.925926	0.925926	1.083000	12.449926	0.923361	11.495782	1
2	1.166400	2.080000	0.857339	1.783265	1.172888	25.933190	0.852596	22.110544	2
3	1.259712	3.246400	0.793832	2.577097	1.270237	40.535558	0.787255	31.911806	3
4	1.360489	4.506112	0.735030	3.312127	1.375666	56.349915	0.726921	40.961913	4
5	1.469328	5.866601	0.680583	3.992710	1.489846	73.476856	0.671210	49.318433	5
6	1.586874	7.335929	0.630170	4.622880	1.613502	92.025325	0.619770	57.034522	6
7	1.713824	8.922803	0.583490	5.206370	1.747422	112.113308	0.572272	64.159261	7
8	1.850930	10.636628	0.540269	5.746639	1.892457	133.868583	0.528414	70.737970	8
9	1.999005	12.487558	0.500249	6.246888	2.049530	157.429535	0.487917	76.812497	9
10	2.158925	14.486562	0.463193	6.710081	2.219640	182.946035	0.452523	82.421481	10
11	2.331639	16.645487	0.428883	7.138964	2.403869	210.580392	0.415996	87.600600	11
12	2.518170	18.977126	0.397114	7.536078	2.603389	240.508387	0.384115	92.382800	12
13	2.719624	21.495297	0.367698	7.903776	2.819469	272.920390	0.354677	96.798498	13
14	2.937194	24.214920	0.340461	8.244237	3.053484	308.022574	0.327495	100.875784	14
15	3.172169	27.152114	0.315242	8.559479	3.306921	346.038222	0.302396	104.642592	15
16	3.425943	30.324283	0.291890	8.851369	3.581394	387.209149	0.279221	108.116871	16
17	3.700018	33.750226	0.270269	9.121638	3.878648	431.797244	0.257822	111.326733	17
18	3.996019	37.450244	0.250249	9.371887	4.200574	480.086128	0.238063	114.290596	18
19	4.315701	41.446263	0.231712	9.603599	4.549220	532.382966	0.219818	117.027313	19
20	4.660957	45.761964	0.214548	9.818147	4.926803	589.020416	0.202971	119.554292	20
21	5.033834	50.422921	0.198656	10.016803	5.335725	650.358746	0.187416	121.887606	21
22	5.436540	55.456755	0.183941	10.200744	5.778588	716.788127	0.173053	124.042099	22
23	5.871464	60.893296	0.170315	10.371059	6.258207	788.731114	0.159790	126.031475	23
24	6.341181	66.764759	0.157699	10.528758	6.777636	866.645333	0.147544	127.868388	24
25	6.848475	73.105940	0.146018	10.674776	7.340176	951.026395	0.136237	129.564523	25
26	7.396353	79.954415	0.135202	10.809978	7.949407	1042.411042	0.125796	131.130668	26
27	7.988061	87.350768	0.125187	10.935165	8.609204	1141.380571	0.116155	132.576786	27
28	8.627106	95.338830	0.115914	11.051078	9.323763	1248.564521	0.107253	133.912076	28
29	9.317275	103.965936	0.107328	11.158406	10.097631	1364.644687	0.099033	135.145031	29
30	10.062657	113.283211	0.099377	11.257783	10.935730	1490.359449	0.091443	136.283494	30
31	10.867669	123.345868	0.092016	11.349799	11.843390	1626.508474	0.084435	137.334707	31
32	11.737083	134.213537	0.085200	11.434999	12.826385	1773.957801	0.077964	138.305357	32
33	12.676050	145.950620	0.078889	11.513888	13.890969	1933.645350	0.071989	139.201617	33
34	13.690134	158.626670	0.073045	11.586934	15.043913	2106.586886	0.066472	140.029190	34
35	14.785344	172.316804	0.067635	11.654568	16.292550	2293.882485	0.061378	140.793338	35
36	15.968172	187.102148	0.062625	11.717193	17.644824	2496.723526	0.056674	141.498923	36
37	17.245626	203.070320	0.057986	11.775179	19.109335	2716.400273	0.052330	142.150433	37
38	18.625276	220.315945	0.053690	11.828869	20.695401	2954.310082	0.048320	142.752013	38
39	20.115298	238.941221	0.049713	11.878582	22.413109	3211.966288	0.044617	143.307488	39
40	21.724521	259.056519	0.046031	11.924613	24.273386	3491.007831	0.041197	143.820392	40

Interest Rate: 9%

	Annual Compounding				Monthly Compounding				
YEARS	**Future value of a dollar**	**Future value of annuity**	**Present value of a dollar**	**Present value of annuity**	**Future value of a dollar**	**Future value of annuity**	**Present value of a dollar**	**Present value of annuity**	**YEARS**
1	1.090000	1.000000	0.917431	0.917431	1.093807	12.507586	0.914238	11.434913	1
2	1.188100	2.090000	0.841680	1.759111	1.196414	26.188471	0.835831	21.889146	2
3	1.295029	3.278100	0.772183	2.531295	1.308645	41.152716	0.764149	31.446805	3
4	1.411582	4.573129	0.708425	3.239720	1.431405	57.520711	0.698614	40.184782	4
5	1.538624	5.984711	0.649931	3.889651	1.565681	75.424137	0.638700	48.173374	5
6	1.677100	7.523335	0.596267	4.485919	1.712553	95.007028	0.583924	55.476849	6
7	1.828039	9.200435	0.547034	5.032953	1.873202	116.426928	0.533845	62.153965	7
8	1.992563	11.028474	0.501866	5.534819	2.048921	139.856164	0.488062	68.258439	8
9	2.171893	13.021036	0.460428	5.995247	2.241124	165.483223	0446205	73.839382	9
10	2.367364	15.192930	0.422411	6.417658	2.451357	193.514277	0.407937	78.941693	10
11	2.580426	17.560293	0.387533	6.805191	2.681311	224.174837	0.372952	83.606420	11
12	2.812665	20.140720	0.355535	7.160725	2.932837	257.711570	0.340967	87.871092	12
13	3.065805	22.953385	0.326179	7.486904	3.207957	294.394279	0.311725	91.770018	13
14	3.341727	26.019189	0.299246	7.786150	3.508886	334.518079	0.284991	95.334564	14
15	3.642482	29.360916	0.274538	8.060688	3.838043	378.405769	0.260549	98.593409	15
16	3.970306	33.003399	0.251870	8.312558	4.198078	426.410427	0.238204	101.572769	16
17	4.327633	36.973705	0.231073	8.543631	4.591887	478.918252	0.217775	104.296613	17
18	4.717120	41.301338	0.211994	8.755625	5.022638	536.351674	0.199099	106.786856	18
19	5.141661	46.018458	0.194490	8.950115	5.493796	599.172747	0.182024	109.063531	19
20	5.604411	51.160120	0.178431	9.128546	6.009152	667.886870	0.166413	111.144954	20
21	6.108808	56.764530	0.163698	9.292244	6.572851	743.046852	0.152141	113.047870	21
22	6.658600	62.873338	0.150182	9.442425	7.189430	825.257358	0.139093	114.787589	22
23	7.257874	69.531939	0.137781	9.580207	7.863848	915.179777	0.127164	116.378106	23
24	7.911083	76.789813	0.126405	9.706612	8.601532	1013.537539	0.116258	117.832218	24
25	8.623081	84.700896	0.115968	9.822580	9.408415	1121.121937	0.106288	119.161622	25
26	9.399158	93.323977	0.106393	9.928972	10.290989	1238.798495	0.097172	120.377014	26
27	10.245082	102.723135	0.097608	10.026580	11.256354	1367.513924	0.088839	121.488172	27
28	11.167140	112.968217	0.089548	10.116128	12.312278	1508.303750	0.081220	122.504035	28
29	12.172182	124.135356	0.082155	10.198283	13.467255	1662.300631	0.074254	123.432776	29
30	13.267678	136.307539	0.075371	10.273654	14.730576	1830.743483	0.067886	124.281866	30
31	14.461770	149.575217	0.069148	10.342802	16.112406	2014.987436	0.062064	125.058136	31
32	15.763329	164.036987	0.063438	10.406240	17.623861	2216.514743	0.056741	125.767832	32
33	17.182028	179.800315	0.058200	10.464441	19.277100	2436.946701	0.051875	126.416664	33
34	18.728411	196.982344	0.053395	10.517835	21.085425	2678.056697	0.047426	127.009850	34
35	20.413968	215.710755	0.048986	10.566821	23.063384	2941.784474	0.043359	127.552164	35
36	22.251225	236.124723	0.044941	10.611763	25.226888	3230.251735	0.039640	128.047967	36
37	24.253835	258.375948	0.041231	10.652993	27.593344	3545.779215	0.036241	128.501250	37
38	26.436680	282.629783	0.037826	10.690820	30.181790	3890.905350	0.033133	128.915659	38
39	28.815982	309.066463	0.034703	10.725523	33.013050	4268.406696	0.030291	129.294526	39
40	31.409240	337.882445	0.031838	10.757360	36.109902	4681.320273	0.027693	129.640902	40

Interest Rate: 10%

	Annual Compounding				Monthly Compounding				
YEARS	Future value of a dollar	Future value of annuity	Present value of a dollar	Present value of annuity	Future value of a dollar	Future value of annuity	Present value of a dollar	Present value of annuity	YEARS
1	1.100000	1.000000	0.909091	0.909091	1.104713	12.565568	0.905212	11.374508	1
2	1.210000	2.100000	0.826446	1.735537	1.220391	26.446915	0.819410	21.670855	2
3	1.331000	3.310000	0.751315	2.486852	1.348182	41.781821	0.741740	30.991236	3
4	1.464100	4.641000	0.683013	3.169865	1.489354	58.722492	0.671432	39.428160	4
5	1.610510	6.105100	0.620921	3.790787	1.645309	77.437072	0.607789	47.065369	5
6	1.771561	7.715610	0.564474	4.355261	1.817594	98.111314	0.550178	53.978665	6
7	1.948717	9.487171	0.513158	4.868419	2.007920	120.950418	0.498028	60.236667	7
8	2.143589	11.435888	0.466507	5.334926	2.218176	146.181076	0.450821	65.901488	8
9	2.357948	13.579477	0.424098	5.759024	2.450448	174.053713	0.408089	71.029355	9
10	2.593742	15.937425	0.385543	6.144567	2.707041	204.844979	0.369407	75.671163	10
11	2.853117	18.531167	0.350494	6.495061	2.990504	238.860493	0.334392	79.872986	11
12	3.138428	21.384284	0.318631	6.813692	3.303649	276.437876	0.302696	83.676528	12
13	3.452271	24.522712	0.289664	7.103356	3.649584	317.950102	0.274004	87.119542	13
14	3.797498	27.974983	0.263331	7.366687	4.031743	363.809201	0.248032	90.236201	14
15	4.177248	31.772482	0.239392	7.606080	4.453920	414.470346	0.224521	93.057439	15
16	4.594973	35.949730	0.217629	7.823709	4.920303	470.436376	0.203240	95.611259	16
17	5.054470	40.544703	0.197845	8.021553	5.435523	532.262780	0.183975	97.923008	17
18	5.559917	45.599173	0.179859	8.201412	6.004693	600.563216	0.166536	100.015633	18
19	6.115909	51.159090	0.163508	8.364920	6.633463	676.015601	0.150751	101.909902	19
20	6.727500	57.274999	0.148644	8.513564	7.328074	759.368836	0.136462	103.624619	20
21	7.400250	64.002499	0.135131	8.648694	8.095419	851.450244	0.123527	105.176801	21
22	8.140275	71.402749	0.122846	8.771540	8.943115	953.173779	0.111818	106.581856	22
23	8.954302	79.543024	0.111678	8.883218	9.879576	1065.549097	0.101219	107.853730	23
24	9.849733	88.497327	0.101526	8.984744	10.914097	1189.691580	0.091625	109.005045	24
25	10.834706	98.347059	0.092296	9.077040	12.056945	1326.833403	0.082940	110.047230	25
26	11.918177	109.181765	0.083905	9.160945	13.319465	1478.335767	0.075078	110.990629	26
27	13.109994	121.099942	0.076278	9.237223	14.714187	1645.702407	0.067962	111.844605	27
28	14.420994	134.209936	0.069343	9.306567	16.254954	1830.594523	0.061520	112.617635	28
29	15.863093	148.630930	0.063039	9.369606	17.957060	2034.847258	0.055688	113.317392	29
30	17.449402	164.494023	0.057309	9.426914	19.837399	2260.487925	0.050410	113.950820	30
31	19.194342	181.943425	0.052099	9.479013	21.914634	2509.756117	0.045632	114.524207	31
32	21.113777	201.137767	0.047362	9.526376	24.209383	2785.125947	0.041306	115.043244	32
33	23.225154	222.251544	0.043057	9.569432	26.744422	3089.330596	0.037391	115.513083	33
34	25.547670	245.476699	0.039143	9.608575	29.544912	3425.389447	0.033847	115.938387	34
35	28.102437	271.024368	0.035584	9.644159	32.638650	3796.638052	0.030639	116.323377	35
36	30.912681	299.126805	0.032349	9.676508	36.056344	4206.761236	0.027734	116.671876	36
37	34.003949	330.039486	0.029408	9.705917	39.831914	4659.829677	0.025105	116.987340	37
38	37.404343	364.043434	0.026735	9.732651	44.002836	5160.340305	0.022726	117.272903	38
39	41.144778	401.447778	0.024304	9.756956	48.610508	5713.260935	0.020572	117.531398	39
40	45.259256	442.592556	0.022095	9.779051	53.700663	6324.079581	0.018622	117.765391	40

Interest Rate: 11%

Annual Compounding

Monthly Compounding

YEARS	Future value of a dollar	Future value of annuity	Present value of a dollar	Present value of annuity	Future value of a dollar	Future value of annuity	Present value of a dollar	Present value of annuity	YEARS
1	1.110000	1.000000	0.900901	0.900901	1.115719	12.623873	0.896283	11.314565	1
2	1.232100	2.110000	0.811622	1.712523	1.244829	26.708566	0.803323	21.455619	2
3	1.367631	3.342100	0.731191	2.443715	1.388879	42.423123	0.720005	30.544874	3
4	1.518070	4.709731	0.658731	3.102446	1.549598	59.956151	0.645329	38.691421	4
5	1.685058	6.227801	0593451	3.695897	1.728916	79.518080	0.578397	45.993034	5
6	1.870415	7.912860	0.534641	4.230538	1.928984	101.343692	0.518408	52.537346	6
7	2.076160	9.783274	0.481658	4.712196	2.152204	125.694940	0.464640	58.402903	7
8	2.304538	11.859434	0.433926	5.146123	2.401254	152.864085	0.416449	63.660103	8
9	2.558037	14.163972	0.390925	5.537048	2.679124	183.177212	0.373256	68.372043	9
10	2.839421	16.722009	0.352184	5.889232	2.989150	216.998139	0.334543	72.595275	10
11	3.151757	19.561430	0.317283	6.206515	3.335051	254.732784	0.299846	76.380487	11
12	3.498451	22.713187	0.285841	6.492356	3.720979	296.834038	0.268747	79.773109	12
13	3.883280	26.211638	0.257514	6.749870	4.151566	343.807200	0.240873	82.813859	13
14	4.310441	30.094918	0.231995	6.981865	4.631980	396.216042	0.215890	85.539231	14
15	4.784589	34.405359	0.209004	7.190870	5.167988	454.689575	0.193499	87.981937	15
16	5.310894	39.189948	0.188292	7.379162	5.766021	519.929596	0.173430	90.171293	16
17	5.895093	44.500843	0.169633	7.548794	6.433259	592.719117	0.155442	92.133576	17
18	6.543553	50.395936	0.152822	7.701617	7.177708	673.931757	0.139320	93.892337	18
19	7.263344	56.939488	0.137678	7.839294	8.008304	764.542228	0.124870	95.468685	19
20	8.062312	64.202832	0.124034	7.963328	8.935015	865.638038	0.111919	96.881539	20
21	8.949166	72.265144	0.111742	8.075070	9.968965	978.432537	0.100311	98.147856	21
22	9.933574	81.214309	0.100669	8.175739	11.122562	1104.279485	0.089907	99.282835	22
23	11.026267	91.147884	0.090693	8.266432	12.409652	1244.689295	0.080582	100.300098	23
24	12.239157	102.174151	0.081705	8.348137	13.845682	1401.347165	0.072225	101.211853	24
25	13.585464	114.413307	0.073608	8.421745	15.447889	1576.133301	0.064734	102.029044	25
26	15.079865	127.998771	0.066314	8.488058	17.235500	1771.145485	0.058020	102.761478	26
27	16.738650	143.078636	0.059742	8.547800	19.229972	1988.724252	0.052002	103.417947	27
28	18.579901	159.817286	0.053822	8.601622	21.455242	2231.480981	0.046609	104.006328	28
29	20.623691	178.397187	0.048488	8.650110	23.938018	2502.329236	0.041775	104.533685	29
30	22.892297	199.020878	0.043683	8.693793	26.708098	2804.519736	0.037442	105.006346	30
31	25.410449	221.913174	0.039354	8.733146	29.798728	3141.679369	0.033558	105.429984	31
32	28.205599	247.323624	0.035454	8.768600	33.247002	3517.854723	0.030078	105.809684	32
33	31.308214	275.529222	0.031940	8.800541	37.094306	3937.560650	0.026958	106.150002	33
34	34.752118	306.837437	0.028775	8.829316	41.386816	4405.834459	0.024162	106.455024	34
35	38.574851	341.589555	0.025924	8.855240	46.176050	4928.296368	0.021656	106.728409	35
36	42.818085	380.164406	0.023355	8.878594	51.519489	5511.216962	0.019410	106.973440	36
37	47.528074	422.982490	0.021040	8.899635	57.481264	6161.592447	0.017397	107.193057	37
38	52.756162	470.510564	0.018955	8.918590	64.132929	6887.228628	0.015593	107.389897	38
39	58.559340	523.266726	0.017077	8.935666	71.554317	7696.834582	0.013975	107.566320	39
40	65.000867	581.826066	0.015384	8.951051	79.834499	8600.127195	0.012526	107.724446	40

Interest Rate: 12%

	Annual Compounding				Monthly Compounding				
YEARS	Future value of a dollar	Future value of annuity	Present value of a dollar	Present value of annuity	Future value of a dollar	Future value of annuity	Present value of a dollar	Present value of annuity	YEARS
1	1.120000	1.000000	0.892857	0.892857	1.126825	12.682503	0.887449	11.255077	1
2	1.254400	2.120000	0.797194	1.690051	1.269735	26.973465	0.787566	21.243387	2
3	1.404928	3.374400	0.711780	2.401831	1.430769	43.076878	0.698925	30.107505	3
4	1.573519	4.779328	0.635518	3.037349	1.612226	61.222608	0.620260	37.973959	4
5	1.762342	6.325847	0.567427	3.604776	1.816697	81.669670	0.550450	44.955038	5
6	1.973823	8.115189	0.506631	4.111407	2.047099	104.709931	0.488496	51.150391	6
7	2.210681	10.089012	0.452349	4.563757	2.306723	130.672274	0.433515	56.648453	7
8	2.475963	12.299693	0.403883	4.967640	2.599273	159.927293	0.384723	61.527703	8
9	2.773079	14.775656	0.360610	5.328250	2.928926	192.892579	0.341422	65.857790	9
10	3.105845	17.548735	0.321973	5.650223	3.300387	230.038689	0.302995	69.700522	10
11	3.478550	20.654583	0.287476	5.937699	3.718959	271.895856	0.268892	73.110752	11
12	3.895976	24.133133	0.256675	6.194374	4.190616	319.061559	0.238628	76.137157	12
13	4.363493	28.029109	0.229174	6.423548	4.722091	372.209054	0.211771	78.822939	13
14	4.887112	32.392602	0.204620	6.628168	5.320970	432.096982	0.187936	81.206434	14
15	5.473566	37.279715	0.182696	6.810864	5.995802	499.580198	0.166783	83.321664	15
16	6.130394	42.753280	0.163122	6.973986	6.756220	575.621974	0.148012	85.198824	16
17	6.866041	48.883674	0.145644	7.119630	7.613078	661.307751	0.131353	86.864707	17
18	7.689966	55.149715	0.130040	7.249670	8.578606	757.860630	0.116569	88.343095	18
19	8.612762	63.439681	0.116107	7.365777	9.666588	866.658830	0.103449	89.655089	19
20	9.646293	72.052442	0.103667	7.469444	10.892554	989.255365	0.091806	90.819416	20
21	10.803848	81.698736	0.092560	7.562003	12.274002	1127.400210	0.081473	91.852698	21
22	12.100310	92.502584	0.082643	7.644646	13.830653	1283.065279	0.072303	92.769683	22
23	13.552347	104.602894	0.073788	7.718434	15.584726	1458.472574	0.064165	93.583461	23
24	15.178629	118.155241	0.065882	7.784316	17.561259	1656.125905	0.056944	94.305647	24
25	17.000064	133.333870	0.058823	7.843139	19.788466	1878.846626	0.050534	94.946551	25
26	19.040072	150.333934	0.052521	7.895660	22.298139	2129.813909	0.044847	95.515321	26
27	21.324881	169.374007	0.046894	7.942554	25.126101	2412.610125	0.039799	96.020075	27
28	23.883866	190.698887	0.041869	7.984423	28.312720	2731.271980	0.035320	96.468019	28
29	26.749930	214.582754	0.037383	8.021806	31.903481	3090.348134	0.031345	96.865546	29
30	29.959922	241.332684	0.033378	8.055184	35.949641	3494.964133	0.027817	97.218331	30
31	33.555113	271.292606	0.029802	8.084986	40.508956	3950.895567	0.024686	97.831410	31
32	37.581726	304.847719	0.026609	8.111594	45.646505	4464.650520	0.021907	97.809252	32
33	42.091533	342.429446	0.023758	8.135352	51.435625	5043.562459	0.019442	98.055822	33
34	47.142517	384.520979	0.021212	8.156564	57.958949	5695.894923	0.017254	98.274641	34
35	52.799620	431.663496	0.018940	8.175504	65.309595	6430.959471	0.015312	98.468831	35
36	59.135574	484.463116	0.016910	8.192414	73.592486	7259.248603	0.013588	98.641166	36
37	66.231843	543.598690	0.015098	8.207513	82.925855	8192.585529	0.012059	98.794103	37
38	74.179664	609.830533	0.013481	8.220993	93.442929	9244.292939	0.010702	98.929828	38
39	83.081224	684.010197	0.012036	8.233030	105.293832	10429.383172	0.009497	99.050277	39
40	93.050970	767.091420	0.010747	8.243777	118.647725	11764.772510	0.008428	99.157169	40

Interest Rate: 13%

	Annual Compounding				Monthly Compounding				
YEARS	Future value of a dollar	Future value of annuity	Present value of a dollar	Present value of annuity	Future value of a dollar	Future value of annuity	Present value of a dollar	Present value of annuity	YEARS
1	1.130000	1.000000	0.884956	0.884956	1.138032	12.741460	0.878710	11.196042	1
2	1.276900	2.130000	0.783147	1.668102	1.295118	27.241655	0.772130	21.034112	2
3	1.444897	3.406900	0.693050	2.361153	1.473886	43.743348	0.678478	29.678917	3
4	1.630474	4.849797	0.613319	2.974471	1.677330	62.522811	0.596185	37.275190	4
5	1.842435	6.480271	0.542760	3.517231	1.908857	83.894449	0.523874	43.950107	5
6	2.081952	8.322706	0.480319	3.997550	2.172341	108.216068	0.460333	49.815421	6
7	2.352605	10.404658	0.425061	4.422610	2.472194	135.894861	0.404499	54.969328	7
8	2.658444	12.757263	0.376160	4.798770	2.813437	167.394225	0.355437	59.498115	8
9	3.004042	15.415707	0.332885	5.131655	3.201783	203.241525	0.312326	63.477604	9
10	3.394567	18.419749	0.294588	5.426243	3.643733	244.036917	0.274444	66.974419	10
11	3.83S861	21.814317	0.260698	5.686941	4.146687	290.463399	0.241156	70.047103	11
12	4.334S23	25.650178	0.230706	5.917647	4.719064	343.298242	0.211906	72.747100	12
13	4.898011	29.984701	0.204165	6.121812	5.370448	403.426010	0.186204	75.119613	13
14	5.534753	34.882712	0.180677	6.302488	6.111745	471.853363	0.163619	77.204363	14
15	6.254270	40.417464	0.159891	6.462379	6.955364	549.725914	0.143774	79.036253	15
16	7.067326	46.671735	0.141496	6.603875	7.915430	638.347406	0.126336	80.645952	16
17	7.986078	53.739060	0.125218	6.729093	9.008017	739.201542	0.111012	82.060410	17
18	9.024268	61.725138	0.110812	6.839905	10.251416	853.976825	0.097548	83.303307	18
19	10.197423	70.749406	0.098064	6.937969	11.666444	984.594826	0.085716	84.395453	19
20	11.523088	80.946829	0.086782	7.024752	13.276792	1133.242353	0.075319	85.355132	20
21	13.021089	92.469917	0.076798	7.101550	15.109421	1302.408067	0.066184	86.198412	21
22	14.713831	105.491006	0.067963	7.169513	17.195012	1494.924144	0.058156	86.939409	22
23	16.626629	120.204817	0.060144	7.229658	19.568482	1714.013694	0.051103	87.590531	23
24	18.788091	136.831465	0.053225	7.282883	22.269568	1963.344717	0.044904	88.162677	24
25	21.230542	155.619556	0.047102	7.329985	25.343491	2247.091520	0.039458	88.665428	25
26	23.990513	176.850098	0.041683	7.371668	28.841716	2570.004599	0.034672	89.107200	26
27	27.109279	200.840611	0.036888	7.408556	32.822810	2937.490172	0.030467	89.495389	27
28	30.633486	227.949890	0.032644	7.441200	37.353424	3355.700690	0.026771	89.836495	28
29	34.615839	258.583376	0.028889	7.470088	42.509410	3831.637843	0.023524	90.136227	29
30	39.115898	293.199215	0.025565	7.495653	48.377089	4373.269783	0.020671	90.399605	30
31	44.200965	332.315113	0.022624	7.518277	55.054699	4989.664524	0.018164	90.631038	31
32	49.947090	376.516078	0.020021	7.538299	62.654036	5691.141761	0.015961	90.834400	32
33	56.440212	426.463168	0.017718	7.556016	71.302328	6489.445641	0.014025	91.013097	33
34	63.777439	482.903380	0.015680	7.571696	81.144365	7398.941387	0.012324	91.170119	34
35	72.068506	546.680819	0.013876	7.585572	92.344923	8431.839055	0.010829	91.308095	35
36	81.437412	618.749325	0.012279	7.597851	105.091522	9608.448184	0.009516	91.429337	36
37	92.024276	700.186738	0.010867	7.608708	119.597566	10947.467591	0.008361	91.535873	37
38	103.987432	792.211014	0.009617	7.618334	136.105914	12471.315170	0.007347	91.629487	38
39	117.505798	896.198445	0.008510	7.626844	154.892951	14205.503212	0.006456	91.711747	39
40	132.781552	1013.704243	0.007531	7.634376	176.273210	16179.065533	0.005673	91.784030	40

Interest Rate: 14%

	Annual Compounding				**Monthly Compounding**				
YEARS	**Future value of a dollar**	**Future value of annuity**	**Present value of a dollar**	**Present value of annuity**	**Future value of a dollar**	**Future value of annuity**	**Present value of a dollar**	**Present value of annuity**	**YEARS**
1	1.140000	1.000000	0.877193	0.877193	1.149342	12.800745	0.870063	11.137455	1
2	1.299600	2.140000	0.769468	1.646661	1.320987	27.513180	0.757010	20.827743	2
3	1.481544	3.439600	0.674972	2.321632	1.518266	44.422800	0.658646	29.258904	3
4	1.688960	4.921144	0.592080	2.913712	1.745007	63.857736	0.573064	36.594546	4
5	1.925415	6.610104	0.519369	3.433081	2.005610	86.195125	0.498601	42.977016	5
6	2.194973	8.535519	0.455587	3.888668	2.305132	111.868425	0.433815	48.530168	6
7	2.502269	10.730491	0.399637	4.288305	2.649385	141.375828	0.377446	53.361760	7
8	2.852586	13.232760	0.350559	4.638864	3.045049	175.289927	0.328402	57.565549	8
9	3.251949	16.085347	0.307508	4.946372	3.499803	214.268826	0.285730	61.223111	9
10	3.707221	19.337295	0.269744	5.216116	4.022471	259.068912	0.248603	64.405420	10
11	4.226232	23.044516	0.236617	5.452733	4.623195	310.559534	0.216301	67.174230	11
12	4.817905	27.270749	0.207559	5.660292	5.313632	369.739871	0.188195	69.583269	12
13	5.492411	32.088654	0.182069	5.842362	6.107180	437.758319	0.163742	71.679284	13
14	6.261349	37.581065	0.159710	6.002072	7.019239	515.934780	0.142466	73.502950	14
15	7.137938	43.842414	0.140096	6.142168	8.067507	605.786272	0.123954	75.089654	15
16	8.137249	50.980352	0.122892	6.265060	9.272324	709.056369	0.107848	76.470187	16
17	9.276464	59.117601	0.107800	6.372859	10.657072	827.749031	0.093834	77.671337	17
18	10.575169	68.394066	0.094561	6.467420	12.248621	964.167496	0.081642	78.716413	18
19	12.055693	78.969235	0.082948	6.550369	14.077855	1120.958972	0.071034	79.625696	19
20	13.743490	91.024928	0.072762	6.623131	16.180270	1301.106005	0.061804	80.416829	20
21	15.667578	104.768418	0.063826	6.686957	18.596664	1508.285522	0.053773	81.105164	21
22	17.861039	120.435996	0.055988	6.742944	21.373928	1746.336688	0.046786	81.704060	22
23	20.361585	138.297035	0.049112	6.792056	24.565954	2019.938898	0.040707	82.225136	23
24	23.212207	158.658620	0.043081	6.835137	28.234683	2334.401417	0.035417	82.678506	24
25	26.461916	181.870827	0.037790	6.872927	32.451308	2695.826407	0.030815	83.072966	25
26	30.166584	208.332743	0.033149	6.906077	37.297652	3111.227338	0.026811	83.416171	26
27	34.389906	238.499327	0.029078	6.935155	42.867759	3588.665088	0.023328	83.714781	27
28	39.204493	272.889233	0.025507	6.960662	49.269718	4137.404359	0.020296	83.974591	28
29	44.693122	312.093725	0.022375	6.983037	56.627757	4768.093467	0.017659	84.200641	29
30	50.950159	356.786847	0.019627	7.002664	65.084661	5492.970967	0.015365	84.397320	30
31	58.083181	407.737006	0.017217	7.019881	74.804537	6326.103143	0.013368	84.568442	31
32	66.214826	465.820186	0.015102	7.034983	85.975998	7283.656968	0.011631	84.717330	32
33	75.484902	532.035012	0.013248	7.048231	98.815828	8384.213825	0.010120	84.846871	33
34	86.052788	607.519914	0.011621	7.059852	113.573184	9649.130077	0.008805	84.959580	34
35	98.100178	693.572702	0.010194	7.070045	130.534434	11102.951488	0.007661	85.057645	35
36	111.834203	791.672881	0.008942	7.078987	150.028711	12773.889538	0.006665	85.142966	36
37	127.490992	903.507084	0.007844	7.086831	172.434303	14694.368868	0.005799	85.217202	37
38	145.339731	1030.998076	0.006880	7.093711	198.185992	16901.656478	0.005046	85.281792	38
39	165.687293	1176.337806	0.006035	7.099747	227.783490	19438.584899	0.004390	85.337989	39
40	188.883514	1342.025099	0.005294	7.105041	261.801139	22354.383358	0.003820	85.386883	40

Interest Rate: 15%

	Annual Compounding				**Monthly Compounding**				
YEARS	**Future value of a dollar**	**Future value of annuity**	**Present value of a dollar**	**Present value of annuity**	**Future value of a dollar**	**Future value of annuity**	**Present value of a dollar**	**Present value of annuity**	**YEARS**
1	1.150000	1.000000	0.869565	0.869565	1.160755	12.860361	0.861509	11.079312	1
2	1.322500	2.150000	0.756144	1.625709	1.347351	27.788084	0.742197	20.624235	2
3	1.520875	3.472500	0.657516	2.283225	1.563944	45.115505	0.639409	28.847267	3
4	1.749006	4.993375	0.571753	2.854978	1.815355	65.228388	0.550856	35.931481	4
5	2.011357	6.742381	0.497177	3.352155	2.107181	88.574508	0.474568	42.034592	5
6	2.313061	8.753738	0.432328	3.784483	2.445920	115.673621	0.408844	47.292474	6
7	2.660020	11.066799	0.375937	4.160420	2.839113	147.129040	0.352223	51.822185	7
8	3.059023	13.726819	0.326902	4.487322	3.295513	183.641059	0.303443	55.724570	8
9	3.517876	16.785842	0.284262	4.771584	3.825282	226.022551	0.261419	59.086509	9
10	4.045558	20.303718	0.247185	5.018769	4.440213	275.217058	0.225214	61.982847	10
11	4.652391	24.349276	0.214943	5.233712	5.153998	332.319805	0.194024	64.478068	11
12	5.350250	29.001667	0.186907	5.420619	5.982526	398.602077	0.167153	66.627722	12
13	6.152788	34.351917	0.162528	5.583147	6.944244	475.539523	0.144004	68.479668	13
14	7.075706	40.504705	0.141329	5.724476	8.060563	564.845011	0.124061	70.075134	14
15	8.137062	47.580411	0.122894	5.847370	9.356334	668.506759	0.106879	71.449643	15
16	9.357621	55.717472	0.106865	5.954235	10.860408	788.832603	0.092078	72.633794	16
17	10.761264	65.075093	0.092926	6.047161	12.606267	928.501369	0.079326	73.653950	17
18	12.375454	75.836357	0.080805	6.127966	14.632781	1090.622520	0.068340	74.532823	18
19	14.231772	88.211811	0.070265	6.198231	16.985067	1278.805378	0.058875	75.289980	19
20	16.366537	102.443583	0.061100	6.259331	19.715494	1497.239481	0.050722	75.942278	20
21	18.821518	118.810120	0.053131	6.312462	22.884848	1750.787854	0.043697	76.504237	21
22	21.644746	137.631638	0.046201	6.358663	26.563691	2045.095272	0.037645	76.988370	22
23	24.891458	159.276384	0.040174	6.398837	30.833924	2386.713938	0.032432	77.405455	23
24	28.625176	184.167841	0.034934	6.433771	35.790617	2783.249347	0.027940	77.764777	24
25	32.918953	212.793017	0.030378	6.464149	41.544120	3243.529615	0.024071	78.074336	25
26	37.856796	245.711970	0.026415	6.490564	48.222525	3777.802015	0.020737	78.341024	26
27	43.535315	283.568766	0.022970	6.513534	55.974514	4397.961118	0.017865	78.570778	27
28	50.065612	327.104080	0.019974	6.533508	64.972670	5117.813598	0.015391	78.768713	28
29	57.575454	377.169693	0.017369	6.550877	75.417320	5953.385616	0.013260	78.939236	29
30	66.211772	434.745146	0.015103	6.565980	87.540995	6923.279611	0.011423	79.086142	30
31	76.143538	500.956918	0.013133	6.579113	101.613606	8049.088447	0.009841	79.212704	31
32	87.565068	577.100456	0.011420	6.590533	117.948452	9355.876140	0.008478	79.321738	32
33	100.699829	664.665524	0.009931	6.600463	136.909198	10872.735858	0.007304	79.415671	33
34	115.804803	765.165353	0.008635	6.609099	158.917970	12633.437629	0.006293	79.496596	34
35	133.175523	881.170156	0.007509	6.616607	184.464752	14677.180163	0.005421	79.566313	35
36	153.151852	1014.345680	0.006529	6.623137	214.118294	17049.463544	0.004670	79.626375	36
37	176.124630	1167.497532	0.005678	6.628815	248.538777	19803.102194	0.004024	79.678119	37
38	202.543324	1343.622161	0.004937	6.633752	288.492509	22999.400699	0.003466	79.722696	38
39	232.924823	1546.165485	0.004293	6.638045	334.868983	26709.518627	0.002986	79.761101	39
40	267.863546	1779.090308	0.003733	6.641778	388,700685	31016.054774	0.002573	79.794186	40

Interest Rate: 16%

	Annual Compounding				**Monthly Compounding**				
YEARS	Future value of a dollar	Future value of annuity	Present value of a dollar	Present value of annuity	Future value of a dollar	Future value of annuity	Present value of a dollar	Present value of annuity	**YEARS**
1	1.160000	1.000000	0.862069	0.862069	1.172271	12.920310	0.853045	11.021609	1
2	1.345600	2.160000	0.743163	1.605232	1.374219	28.066412	0.727686	20.423539	2
3	1.560896	3.505600	0.640658	2.245890	1.610957	45.821745	0.620749	28.443811	3
4	1.810639	5.066496	0.552291	2.798181	1.888477	66.635803	0.529527	35.285465	4
5	2.100342	6.877135	0.476113	3.274294	2.213807	91.035516	0.451711	41.121706	5
6	2.436396	8.977477	0.410442	3.684736	2.595181	119.638587	0.385330	46.100283	6
7	2.826220	11.413873	0.353830	4.038565	3.042255	153.169132	0.328704	50.347235	7
8	3.278415	14.240093	0.305025	4.343591	3.566347	192.476010	0.280399	53.970077	8
9	3.802961	17.518508	0.262953	4.606544	4.180724	238.554316	0.239193	57.060524	9
10	4.411435	21.321469	0.226684	4.833227	4.900941	292.570569	0.204042	59.696816	10
11	5.117265	25.732904	0.195417	5.028644	5.745230	355.892244	0.174057	61.945692	11
12	5.936027	30.850169	0.168463	5.197107	6.734965	430.122395	0.148479	63.864085	12
13	6.885791	36.786196	0.145227	5.342334	7.895203	517.140233	0.126659	65.500561	13
14	7.987518	43.671987	0.125195	5.467529	9.255316	619.148703	0.108046	66.596549	14
15	9.265521	51.659505	0.107927	5.575456	10.849737	738.730255	0.092168	68.087390	15
16	10.748004	60.925026	0.093041	5.668497	12.718830	878.912215	0.078624	69.103231	16
17	12.467685	71.673030	0.080207	5.748704	14.909912	1043.243434	0.067069	69.969789	17
18	14.462514	84.140715	0.069144	5.817848	17.478455	1235.884123	0.057213	70.709003	18
19	16.776517	98.603230	0.059607	5.877455	20.489482	1461.711177	0.048806	71.339585	19
20	19.460759	115.379747	0.051385	5.928841	24.019222	1726.441638	0.041633	71.877501	20
21	22.574481	134.840506	0.044298	5.973139	28.157032	2036.777427	0.035515	72.336367	21
22	26.186398	157.414987	0.038188	6.011326	33.007667	2400.575011	0.030296	72.727801	22
23	30.376222	183.601385	0.032920	6.044247	38.693924	2827.044294	0.025844	73.061711	23
24	35.236417	213.977607	0.028380	6.072627	45.359757	3326.981781	0.022046	73.346552	24
25	40.874244	249.214024	0.024465	6.097092	53.173919	3913.043898	0.018806	73.589534	25
26	47.414123	290.088267	0.021091	6.118183	62.334232	4600.067404	0.016043	73.796809	26
27	55.000382	337.502390	0.018182	6.136364	73.072600	5405.444997	0.013685	73.973623	27
28	63.800444	392.502773	0.015674	6.152038	85.660875	6349.565632	0.011674	74.124454	28
29	74.008515	456.303216	0.013512	6.165550	100.417742	7456.330682	0.009958	74.253120	29
30	85.849877	530.311731	0.011648	6.177198	117.716787	8753.759030	0.008495	74.362878	30
31	99.585857	616.161608	0.010042	6.187240	137.995952	10274.696396	0.007247	74.456506	31
32	115.519594	715.747465	0.008675	6.195897	161.768625	12057.646856	0.006182	74.536375	32
33	134.002729	831.267059	0.007463	6.203359	189.636635	14147.747615	0.005273	74.604507	33
34	155.443166	965.269789	0.006433	6.209792	222.305489	16597.911700	0.004498	74.662626	34
35	180.314073	1120.712955	0.005546	6.215338	260.602233	19470.167508	0.003837	74.712205	35
36	209.164324	1301.027028	0.004781	6.220119	305.496388	22837.229116	0.003273	74.754498	36
37	242.630616	1510.191352	0.004121	6.224241	358.124495	26784.337116	0.002792	74.790576	37
38	281.451515	1752.821968	0.003553	6.227794	419.818887	31411.416562	0.002382	74.821352	38
39	326.483757	2034.273483	0.003063	6.230857	492.141422	36835.606677	0.002032	74.847605	39
40	378.721158	2360.757241	0.002640	6.233497	576.923018	43194.226353	0.001733	74.870000	40

Interest Rate: 17%

	Annual Compounding				Monthly Compounding				
YEARS	Future value of a dollar	Future value of annuity	Present value of a dollar	Present value of annuity	Future value of a dollar	Future value of annuity	Present value of a dollar	Present value of annuity	YEARS
1	1.170000	1.000000	0.854701	0.854701	1.183892	12.980593	0.844672	10.964341	1
2	1.368900	2.170000	0.730514	1.585214	1.401600	28.348209	0.713471	20.225611	2
3	1.601613	3.538900	0.624371	2.209585	1.659342	46.541802	0.602648	28.048345	3
4	1.873887	5.140513	0.533650	2.743235	1.964482	68.081048	0.509040	34.655988	4
5	2.192448	7.014400	0.456111	3.199346	2.325733	93.581182	0.429972	40.237278	5
6	2.565164	9.206848	0.389839	3.589185	2.753417	123.770579	0.363185	44.951636	6
7	3.001242	11.772012	0.333195	3.922380	3.259747	159.511558	0.306772	48.933722	7
8	3.511453	14.773255	0.284782	4.207163	3.859188	201.825006	0.259122	52.297278	8
9	4.108400	18.284708	0.243404	4.450566	4.568860	251.919548	0.218873	55.138379	9
10	4.806828	22.393108	0.208037	4.658604	5.409036	311.226062	0.184876	57.538177	10
11	5.623989	27.199937	0.177810	4.836413	6.403713	381.438553	0.156159	59.565218	11
12	6.580067	32.823926	0.151974	4.988387	7.581303	464.562540	0.131903	61.277403	12
13	7.698679	39.403993	0.129892	5.118280	8.975441	562.972341	0.111415	62.723638	13
14	9.007454	47.102672	0.111019	5.229299	10.625951	679.478890	0.094109	63.945231	14
15	10.538721	56.110126	0.094888	5.324187	12.579975	817.410030	0.079491	64.977077	15
16	12.330304	66.648848	0.081101	5.405288	14.893329	980.705566	0.067144	65.848648	16
17	14.426456	78.979152	0.069317	5.474605	17.632089	1174.029800	0.056715	66.584839	17
18	16.878953	93.405608	0.059245	5.533851	20.874484	1402.904761	0.047905	67.206679	18
19	19.748375	110.284561	0.050637	5.584488	24.713129	1673.867935	0.040464	67.731930	19
20	23.105599	130.032936	0.043280	5.627767	29.257669	1994.658995	0.034179	68.175595	20
21	27.033551	153.138535	0.036991	5.664758	34.637912	2374.440878	0.028870	68.550346	21
22	31.629255	180.172086	0.031616	5.696375	41.007538	2824.061507	0.024386	68.866887	22
23	37.006228	211.801341	0.027022	5.723397	48.548485	3356.363651	0.020598	69.134261	23
24	43.297287	248.807569	0.023096	5.746493	57.476150	3986.551756	0.017399	69.360104	24
25	50.657826	292.104856	0.019740	5.766234	68.045538	4732.626240	0.014696	69.550868	25
26	59.269656	342.762681	0.016872	5.783106	80.558550	5615.897651	0.012413	69.712000	26
27	69.345497	402.032337	0.014421	5.797526	95.372601	6661.595368	0.010485	69.848104	27
28	81.134232	471.377835	0.012325	5.809851	112.910833	7899.588246	0.008857	69.963067	28
29	94.927051	552.512066	0.010534	5.820386	133.674202	9365.237774	0.007481	70.060174	29
30	111.064650	647.439118	0.009004	5.829390	158.255782	11100.408126	0.006319	70.142196	30
31	129.945641	758.503768	0.007696	5.837085	187.357711	13154.661953	0.005337	70.211479	31
32	152.036399	888.449408	0.006577	5.843663	221.811244	15586.676066	0.004508	70.270000	32
33	177.882587	1040.485808	0.005622	5.849284	262.600497	18465.917458	0.003808	70.319431	33
34	208.122627	1218.368395	0.004805	5.854089	310.890557	21874.627526	0.003217	70.361184	34
35	243.503474	1426.491022	0.004107	5.858196	368.060758	25910.171179	0.002717	70.396451	35
36	284.899064	1669.994496	0.003510	5.861706	435.744087	30687.817929	0.002295	70.426241	36
37	333.331905	1954.893560	0.003000	5.864706	515.873821	36344.034396	0.001938	70.451403	37
38	389.998329	2288.225465	0.002564	5.867270	610.738749	43040.382285	0.001637	70.472657	38
39	456.298045	2678.223794	0.002192	5.869461	723.048553	50968.133160	0.001383	70.490609	39
40	533.868713	3134.521839	0.001873	5.871335	856.011201	60353.731845	0.001168	70.505773	40

Interest Rate: 18%

	Annual Compounding				**Monthly Compounding**				
YEARS	**Future value of a dollar**	**Future value of annuity**	**Present value of a dollar**	**Present value of annuity**	**Future value of a dollar**	**Future value of annuity**	**Present value of a dollar**	**Present value of annuity**	**YEARS**
1	1.180000	1.000000	0.847458	0.847458	1.195618	13.041211	0.836387	10.907505	1
2	1.392400	2.180000	0.718184	1.565642	1.429503	28.633521	0.699544	20.030405	2
3	1.643032	3.572400	0.608631	2.174273	1.709140	47.275969	0.585090	27.660684	3
4	1.938778	5.215432	0.515789	2.690062	2.043478	69.565219	0.489362	34.042554	4
5	2.287758	7.154210	0.437109	3.127171	2.443220	96.214652	0.409296	39.380269	5
6	2.699554	9.441968	0.370432	3.497603	2.921158	128.077197	0.342330	43.844667	6
7	3.185474	12.141522	0.313925	3.811528	3.492590	166.172636	0.286321	47.578633	7
8	3.758859	15.326996	0.266038	4.077566	4.175804	211.720235	0.239475	50.701675	8
9	4.435454	19.085855	0.225456	4.303022	4.992667	266.177771	0.200294	53.313749	9
10	5.233836	23.521309	0.191064	4.494086	5.969323	331.288191	0.167523	55.498454	10
11	6.175926	28.755144	0.161919	4.656005	7.137031	409.135393	0.140114	57.325714	11
12	7.287593	34.931070	0.137220	4.793225	8.533164	502.210922	0.117190	58.854011	12
13	8.599359	42.218663	0.116288	4.909513	10.202406	613.493716	0.098016	60.132260	13
14	10.147244	50.818022	0.098549	5.008062	12.198182	746.545446	0.081979	61.201371	14
15	11.973748	60.965266	0.083516	5.091578	14.584368	905.624513	0.068567	62.095562	15
16	14.129023	72.939014	0.070776	5.162354	17.437335	1095.822335	0.057348	62.843452	16
17	16.672247	87.068036	0.059980	5.222334	20.848395	1323.226308	0.047965	63.468978	17
18	19.673251	103.740283	0.050830	5.273164	24.926719	1595.114630	0.040118	63.992160	18
19	23.214436	123.413534	0.043077	5.316241	29.802839	1920.189249	0.033554	64.429743	19
20	27.393035	146.627970	0.036506	5.352746	35.632816	2308.854370	0.028064	64.795732	20
21	32.323781	174.021005	0.030937	5.383683	42.603242	2773.549452	0.023472	65.101841	21
22	38.142061	206.344785	0.026218	5.409901	50.937210	3329.147335	0.019632	65.357866	22
23	45.007632	244.486847	0.022218	5.432120	60.901454	3993.430261	0.016420	65.572002	23
24	53.109006	289.494479	0.018829	5.450949	72.814885	4787.658998	0.013733	65.751103	24
25	62.668627	342.603486	0.015957	5.466906	87.058800	5737.253308	0.011486	65.900901	25
26	73.948980	405.272113	0.013523	5.480429	104.089083	6872.605521	0.009607	66.026190	26
27	87.259797	479.221093	0.011460	5.491889	124.450799	8230.053258	0.008035	66.130980	27
28	102.966560	566.480890	0.009712	5.501601	148.795637	9853.042439	0.006721	66.218625	28
29	121.500541	669.447450	0.008230	5.509831	177.902767	11793.517795	0.005621	66.291930	29
30	143.370638	790.947991	0.006975	5.516806	212.703781	14113.585393	0.004701	66.353242	30
31	169.177353	934.318630	0.005911	5.522717	254.312506	16887.500372	0.003932	66.404522	31
32	199.629277	1103.495983	0.005009	5.527726	304.060653	20204.043526	0.003289	66.447412	32
33	235.562547	1303.125260	0.004245	5.531971	363.540442	24169.362788	0.002751	66.483285	33
34	277.963805	1538.687807	0.003598	5.535569	434.655558	28910.370554	0.002301	66.513289	34
35	327.997290	1816.651612	0.003049	5.538618	519.682084	34578.805589	0.001924	66.538383	35
36	387.036802	2144.648902	0.002584	5.541201	621.341343	41356.089521	0.001609	66.559372	36
37	456.703427	2531.685705	0.002190	5.543391	742.887000	49459.133344	0.001346	66.576927	37
38	538.910044	2988.389132	0.001856	5.545247	888.209197	59147.279782	0.001126	66.591609	38
39	635.913852	3527.299175	0.001573	5.546819	1061.959056	70730.603711	0.000942	66.603890	39
40	750.378345	4163.213027	0.001333	5.548152	1269.697544	84579.836287	0.000788	66.614161	40

Interest Rate: 19%

	Annual Compounding				Monthly Compounding				
YEARS	Future value of a dollar	Future value of annuity	Present value of a dollar	Present value of annuity	Future value of a dollar	Future value of annuity	Present value of a dollar	Present value of annuity	YEARS
1	1.190000	1.000000	0.840336	0.840336	1.207451	13.102168	0.828191	10.851097	1
2	1.416100	2.190000	0.706165	1.546501	1.457938	28.922394	0.685900	19.837878	2
3	1.685159	3.606100	0.593416	2.139917	1.760389	48.024542	0.568056	27.280649	3
4	2.005339	5.291259	0.498669	2.638586	2.125583	71.089450	0.470459	33.444684	4
5	2.386354	7.296598	0.419049	3.057635	2.566537	98.939196	0.389630	38.549682	5
6	2.839761	9.682952	0.352142	3.409777	3.098968	132.566399	0.322688	42.777596	6
7	3.379315	12.522713	0.295918	3.705695	3.741852	173.169599	0.267247	46.279115	7
8	4.021385	15.902028	0.248671	3.954366	4.518103	222.195973	0.221332	49.179042	8
9	4.785449	19.923413	0.208967	4.163332	5.455388	281.392918	0.183305	51.580735	9
10	5.694684	24.708862	0.175602	4.338935	6.587114	352.870328	0.151812	53.569796	10
11	6.776674	30.403546	0.147565	4.486500	7.953617	439.175798	0.125729	55.217118	11
12	8.064242	37.180220	0.124004	4.610504	9.603603	543.385424	0.104128	56.581415	12
13	9.596448	45.244461	0.104205	4.714709	11.595879	669.213441	0.086238	57.711314	13
14	11.419773	54.840909	0.087567	4.802277	14.001456	821.144606	0.071421	58.647086	14
15	13.589530	66.260682	0.073586	4.875863	16.906072	1004.594042	0.059150	59.422084	15
16	16.171540	79.850211	0.061837	4.937700	20.413254	1226.100247	0.048988	60.063930	16
17	19.244133	96.021751	0.051964	4.989664	24.648004	1493.558135	0.040571	60.595501	17
18	22.900518	115.265884	0.043667	5.033331	29.761257	1816.500430	0.033601	61.035743	18
19	27.251616	138.166402	0.036695	5.070026	35.935259	2206.437425	0.027828	61.400348	19
20	32.429423	165.418018	0.030836	5.100862	43.390065	2677.267240	0.023047	61.702310	20
21	38.591014	197.847442	0.025913	5.126775	52.391377	3245.771169	0.019087	61.952393	21
22	45.923307	236.438456	0.021775	5.148550	63.260020	3932.211806	0.015808	62.159509	22
23	54.648735	282.361762	0.018299	5.166849	76.383375	4761.055238	0.013092	62.331041	23
24	65.031994	337.010497	0.015377	5.182226	92.229182	5761.843068	0.010843	62.473102	24
25	77.388073	402.042491	0.012922	5.195148	111.362218	6970.245332	0.008980	62.590755	25
26	92.091807	479.430565	0.010859	5.206007	134.464421	8429.331851	0.007437	62.688195	26
27	109.589251	571.522372	0.009125	5.215132	162.359199	10191.107326	0.006159	62.768894	27
28	130.411208	681.111623	0.007668	5.222800	196.040777	12318.364881	0.005101	62.835728	28
29	155.189338	811.522831	0.006444	5.229243	236.709632	14886.924139	0.004225	62.891079	29
30	184.675312	966.712169	0.005415	5.234658	285.815282	17988.333579	0.003499	62.936920	30
31	219.763621	1151.387481	0.004550	5.239209	345.107947	21733.133503	0.002898	62.974886	31
32	261.518710	1371.151103	0.003824	5.243033	416.700935	26254.795909	0.002400	63.006328	32
33	311.207264	1632.669812	0.003213	5.246246	503.145960	31714.481694	0.001987	63.032369	33
34	370.336645	1943.877077	0.002700	5.248946	607.524092	38306.784745	0.001646	63.053935	34
35	440.700607	2314.213721	0.002269	5.251215	733.555571	46266.667644	0.001363	63.071796	35
36	524.433722	2754.914328	0.001907	5.253122	885.732406	55877.836195	0.001129	63.086589	36
37	624.076130	3279.348051	0.001602	5.254724	1069.478478	67482.851256	0.000935	63.098840	37
38	742.650594	3903.424180	0.001347	5.256071	1291.342851	81495.338274	0.000774	63.108986	38
39	883.754207	4646.074775	0.001132	5.257202	1559.233220	98414.729710	0.000641	63.117389	39
40	1501.667507	5529.828982	0.000951	5.258153	1882.697708	118844.065787	0.000531	63.124348	40

Interest Rate: 20%

	Annual Compounding				**Monthly Compounding**				
YEARS	**Future value of a dollar**	**Future value of annuity**	**Present value of a dollar**	**Present value of annuity**	**Future value of a dollar**	**Future value of annuity**	**Present value of a dollar**	**Present value of annuity**	**YEARS**
1	1.200000	1.000000	0.833333	0.833333	1.219391	13.163465	0.820081	10.795113	1
2	1.440000	2.200000	0.694444	1.527778	1.486915	29.214877	0.672534	19.647986	2
3	1.728000	3.640000	0.578704	2.106481	1.813130	48.787826	0.551532	26.908062	3
4	2.073600	5.368000	0.482253	2.588735	2.210915	72.654905	0.452301	32.861916	4
5	2.488320	7.441600	0.401878	2.990612	2.695970	101.758208	0.370924	37.744561	5
6	2.985984	9.929920	0.334898	3.325510	3.287442	137.246517	0.304188	41.748727	6
7	3.583181	12.915904	0.279082	3.604592	4.008677	180.520645	0.249459	45.032470	7
8	4.299817	16.499085	0.232568	3.837160	4.888145	233.288730	0.204577	47.725406	8
9	5.159780	20.798902	0.193807	4.030967	5.960561	297.633662	0.167769	49.933833	9
10	6.191736	25.958682	0.161506	4.192472	7.268255	376.095300	0.137585	51.744924	10
11	7.430084	32.150419	0.134588	4.327060	8.862845	471.770720	0.112831	53.230165	11
12	8.916100	39.580502	0.112157	4.439217	10.807275	588.436476	0.092530	54.448184	12
13	10.699321	48.496603	0.093464	4.532681	13.178294	730.697658	0.075882	55.447059	13
14	12.839185	59.195923	0.077887	4.610567	16.069495	904.169675	0.062230	56.266217	14
15	15.407022	72.035108	0.064905	4.675473	19.594998	1115.699905	0.051033	56.937994	15
16	18.488426	87.442129	0.054088	4.729561	23.893966	1373.637983	0.041852	57.488906	16
17	22.186111	105.930555	0.045073	4.774634	29.136090	1688.165376	0.034322	57.940698	17
18	26.623333	128.116666	0.037561	4.812195	35.528288	2071.697274	0.028147	58.311205	18
19	31.948000	154.740000	0.031301	4.843496	43.322878	2539.372652	0.023082	58.615050	19
20	38.337600	186.688000	0.026084	4.869580	52.827531	3109.651838	0.018930	58.864229	20
21	46.005120	225.025600	0.021737	4.891316	64.417420	3805.045193	0.015524	59.068575	21
22	55.206144	271.030719	0.018114	4.909430	78.550028	4653.001652	0.012731	59.236156	22
23	66.247373	326.236863	0.015095	4.924525	95.783203	5686.992197	0.010440	59.373585	23
24	79.496847	392.484236	0.012579	4.937104	116.797184	6947.831050	0.008562	59.486289	24
25	95.396217	471.981083	0.010483	4.947587	142.421445	8485.286707	0.007021	59.578715	25
26	114.475460	567.377300	0.008735	4.956323	173.667440	10360.046428	0.005758	59.654512	26
27	137.370552	681.852760	0.007280	4.963602	211.768529	12646.111719	0.004722	59.716672	27
28	164.844662	819.223312	0.006066	4.969668	258.228656	15433.719354	0.003873	59.767648	28
29	197.813595	984.067974	0.005055	4.974724	314.881721	18832.903252	0.003176	59.809452	29
30	237.376314	1181.881569	0.004213	4.978936	383.963963	22977.837794	0.002604	59.843735	30
31	284.851577	1419.257883	0.003511	4.982447	468.202234	28032.134021	0.002136	59.871850	31
32	341.821892	1704.109459	0.002926	4.985372	570.921630	34195.297782	0.001752	59.894907	32
33	410.186270	2045.931351	0.002438	4.987810	696.176745	41710.604726	0.001436	59.913815	33
34	492.223524	2456.117621	0.002032	4.989842	848.911717	50874.703014	0.001178	59.929321	34
35	590.668229	2948.341146	0.001693	4.991535	1035.155379	62049.322767	0.000966	59.942038	35
36	708.801875	3539.009375	0.001411	4.992946	1262.259241	75675.554472	0.000792	59.952466	36
37	850.562250	4247.811250	0.001176	4.994122	1539.187666	92291.259933	0.000650	59.961018	37
38	1020.674700	5098.373500	0.000980	4.995101	1876.871717	112552.303043	0.000533	59.968032	38
39	1224.809640	6119.048200	0.000816	4.995918	2288.640640	137258.438381	0.000437	59.973784	39
40	1469.771568	7343.857840	0.000680	4.996598	2790.747993	167384.879555	0.000358	59.978500	40

Glossary

A

absorption rate—the time that may elapse between a project's completion and its eventual sale, or lease

abstractor—an expert in title search and abstract preparation, who searches the public records for all documents that have been filed concerning a particular property and prepares a document that summarizes the results of the search

abstractor—one who searches the public records in order to prepare a title abstract

acceptance—an indication of a willingness to be bound by the terms of an offer; one of the requirements for a valid contract

accretion—the gradual increase in land area created by sedimentary deposits from a stream or river

acknowledgement—a formal declaration, before a duly authorized official (frequently a notary public), by the person who has executed an instrument that such execution was a voluntary act

active income—income derived from salaries, wages, fees for services, bonuses, and income from a trade or business in which the taxpayer materially participates

actual cash value—used in calculating insurance claims; equal to the current price of the damaged item minus accumulated depreciation

actual cash value—used in calculating insurance claims; equal to the current price of the damaged item minus accumulated depreciation

actual consideration—the actual amount paid for the property

actual notice—Knowledge that one has obtained based on what has been seen, heard, read, or observed

adjoiner—property owned by someone other than the owner of the subject parcel

adjustable rate mortgage—a mortgage in which the lender may periodically adjust the interest rate to reflect the change in the interest rate of a specified index

adjusted sales price—the gross (full) sale price, less the selling and fixing-up expenses

adverse possession—acquiring title to property by occupying land without the permission of the owner

adverse selection—a problem in the insurance industry; those most likely to suffer a loss are also the most likely to purchase a policy

adverse selection—a problem in the insurance industry; those most likely to suffer a loss are also the most likely to purchase a policy

agency—a legal relationship where one party (the agent) is employed to represent another (the principal) in business or legal affairs with third parties

agent (real estate)—a person who works under the supervision of a broker, and represents the real estate seller or buyer

air lot—air space owned by a condominium owner

amortization schedule—shows the breakdown of each loan payment into components representing interest and the amount of principal reduction

amortized loan—a mortgage loan in which payments consist of both principal and interest

amortized loan—loans with equal periodic payments with each payment including interest and partial debt reduction; an addition to land that benefits a single parcel

anchor—Gives the general location of the property in a real property description

annual percentage rate—an interest rate calculated according to procedures set by the Federal Reserve Board; designed to facilitate loan comparison

annuity due—an annuity where the periodic cash flows occur at the beginning of each time period

annuity—a series of equal cash flows paid, or received, over uniform time periods

appraiser—a person who gives a professional opinion of the value of a particular parcel of real property

appurtenance—something that has been added to a property and usually is transferred with the property when title to the property is conveyed (e.g., rights of way and other easements)

architect—a person who provides designs for individual buildings or more complex projects

articles of incorporation—a document that specifies the powers of a corporation

asset manager—the individual who responsible for enhancing the value of a managed property by establishing operating procedures that are carried out by the property manager.

assignment of lease—the transfer of the entire term of the lease by the lessee (assignor) to another party (assignee)

assignment—the transfer of one party's contractual rights and obligations to a third party (e.g., a lease)

B

back-to-back escrow—an escrow set up to facilitate the concurrent sale of one property and the purchase of another

bargain and sale deed—a deed in which the grantor asserts ownership but makes no warranties regarding the title (sometimes referred to as a deed without warranty)

base industry—a business that exports goods or services from the local area and, therefore, brings in money from outside the area

base line—in the rectangular government survey system, the primary imaginary line running east and west from which township lines are established

basis—For income tax purposes, one's net investment in property

benchmark—a permanent reference point used to facilitate surveying

bill of sale—a document used to transfer ownership of personal property

blanket mortgage—a mortgage that is secured by more than one parcel of real estate

blind ad—an advertisement that does not include the name of the brokerage firm that placed the ad

blockbusting—introducing people of another class or race into a neighborhood to play on the prejudices or fears of property owners to induce them to sell at depressed prices

boot—cash or the market value of personal property received or offered in a tax deferred exchange of real property

breach of contract—When a party fails, without legal excuse, to fulfill their contractual obligations

broker (real estate)—a person, licensed by the state, who assists others in the selling, leasing, or acquisition of real property

budget mortgage—a mortgage on which the regular payment includes amounts for the payment of property taxes and hazard insurance premiums in addition to interest and debt reduction

business risk—the variability of an investment's operating returns; affected by the proportion of total operating costs that are fixed costs.

buyer's broker—a broker hired by a buyer to act as the buyer's agent

C

call—instructions in a metes and bounds description that explain how to trace the boundary of the property

check—a quadrangle measuring twenty-four miles on each side; the largest unit of measure in the rectangular government survey system

closing costs—costs incurred in conjunction with a real estate transaction that are paid at the closing

closing—a meeting at which the buyer pays for the property, takes delivery of the deed, and all other matters pertaining to the sale are concluded; the final step in a real estate transaction

collateralized mortgage obligation—a mortgage-backed security in which the investor may select a particular maturity class

collateralized mortgage obligation—a pass through security comprised of multiple investment classes each with a predetermined interest rate and maturity

community property—property acquired by a wife and husband during their marriage, with each owning a one-half interest

competent party—a person legally qualified to enter into a contract; one of the requirements for a valid contract

compound interest—interest is earned on both the original principal and on accrued interest

concurrent ownership—ownership of a particular property by two or more parties at the same time

condominium bylaws—specify the rules and regulations for the unit owners and for the operation of the units

condominium—individual ownership of a unit of space plus an undivided ownership of common areas

consideration—something of value given or received as a part of a contractual agreement; one of the requirements for a valid contract

constructive eviction—conduct by a landlord that so disturbs the tenant's enjoyment of the leased premises that the tenant is effectively forced to vacate the property

constructive notice—Knowledge presumed of everyone, by law, resulting from the entering of documents into the public record

consumer surplus—the difference between what one must pay for an asset and the amount at which one values it

contingency—an event included in a contract, that may or may not occur, which would allow one of the parties to withdraw from the contract

contour map—a map showing the elevation of land in detail using lines which connect all points on the property having the same elevation

contract rent—the periodic rent payment specified in a lease

contract—a legally binding agreement between competent parties who, for consideration, agree to perform or not to perform certain acts

contractor—a person who contracts to supply labor and materials to construct buildings and other improvements

conventional mortgage—a mortgage that is not FHA-insured or VA-guaranteed

cooperating broker—a broker who assists the listing broker in locating a buyer; usually deemed to be a sub-agent of the listing agent

cooperative—a living arrangement in which the dwellers purchase ownership shares in a business organization that owns the building.

corporation—an association of individuals having a continuous existence

correction line—sometimes called a standard parallel, is an adjustment made every fourth township line to compensate for the curvature of the earth's surface

counter-offer—an offer (rather than an acceptance) made in response to an offer

curtesy—the right of a surviving husband to a life estate in the real property of his deceased wife

D

damages—the amount permitted by law as compensation for loss or injury caused by another

datum—any line, point, or surface from which a distance, vertical depth, or height is measured

deductible—an amount the insured is required to pay toward each insured loss

deductible—an amount the insured is required to pay toward each insured loss

deduction—an amount that can be used to reduce a taxpayer's taxable income

deed—a document by which title to real property is conveyed from one party to another

deed of trust—also called a trust deed; similar to a mortgage but with a third party trustee (with the power of sale allowing the trustee to foreclose non-judicially), who is charged with the task of ensuring that both parties to the contract perform as agreed

deed restriction—a clause in a deed that limits the nature or intensity of use of the subject real property

deed—a document used to convey ownership of real property

defeasible fee—a property interest that may be of less value to the owner than a fee simple absolute because the right to use the property is restricted

deficiency judgment—a judicial order entered against the mortgagor when the amount realized at the foreclosure sale is less than the amount due on the mortgage

demographics—statistics about the size, density and distribution of the human population

depreciable basis—the total amount that may be depreciated by a property owner over the life of the investment

depreciation allowance—the amount of depreciation that may be expensed for income tax purposes

dereliction (or reliction)—the gradual increase of land area by the permanent receding of water

derived demand—When the demand for an asset is based on the goods or services that the asset can provide; real estate is said to have a derived demand

developer—a person who builds homes or other improvements on undeveloped land

direct investment—in real estate, the purchase of real property or the origination of mortgage loans

discount rate—the interest rate applied to future amounts in order to determine their present value

diversification—Risk reduction accomplished by spreading ones investments among several different assets

dominant tenement—the parcel of real property benefited by an easement (sometimes called the dominant estate)

dower—the right of a surviving wife to a life estate in the real property of her deceased husband

dual agency—Where an agent represents two principals; illegal without
the knowledge and consent of both principals

E

earnest money—a deposit made by the purchaser at the time an offer is made as evidence of the intent to complete the transaction

easement—a nonpossessory property interest that allows a party limited use or enjoyment of property owned by another

economic rent—the rent that a real property can command in the open market

eminent domain—the power of the federal, state, and local governments to appropriate private property for public use by payment of just compensation

encroachment—the unauthorized intrusion of a building or other improvement onto the land or into the air-space of another's property, generally reducing the value of the invaded property

encumbrance—any impediment to clear title such as an easement, lease, or lien, that may diminish the value of the property, or restrict its use, but does not prevent the passing of title

endorsement—an addition to an insurance policy whereby the insurer agrees to extend coverage to losses not included in the basic policy in exchange for an additional premium

endorsement—an addition to an insurance policy whereby the insurer agrees to extend coverage to losses not included in the basic policy in exchange for an additional premium

equilibrium price—the price that occurs where the supply and demand for a good or service are equal

equitable right of redemption—the right of a borrower in default to redeem their interest in the property by paying all sums due no later than the conclusion of the foreclosure proceedings

equity build-up—occurs in one, or both, of two ways— by reducing the mortgage principal, or with increases in the value of the property

escheat—the reversion of property ownership to the state or county, as provided by state law, if the owner dies without a valid will or legal heirs

escrow agent—person engaged in the business of receiving and holding escrows for deposit or delivery

escrow agent—a person who is responsible for ensuring that all parties perform in accordance with the contract, and for processing the paperwork associated with the transaction; employed when no meeting of the parties to the transaction occurs

escrow arrangement—the deposit of money, documents, or other valuables with a neutral third party who is under instructions that the items are to be held until all conditions of a contract have been met

escrow instructions—instructions that detail the tasks to be performed by the escrow agent

estate—an interest in real property

estoppel certificate—a document signed by the borrower that attests to the loan balance as of a particular date

eviction—the legal process of removing a tenant from leased premises for some breach of the lease

excise tax—a direct tax imposed on the manufacture, sale, or consumption of a commodity

F

fast-pay mortgage—sometimes called an accelerated payment mortgage, enables the borrower to payoff the loan principal more quickly than the traditional thirty-year mortgage.

feasibilty study—the study of a proposed project to determine if it makes financial sense; an extension of a market study for a particular property

Federal Truth-in-Lending Law—law designed to enable borrowers to compare the cost of different loans by requiring lenders to make full disclosure of their lending terms to loan applicants in a uniform manner

fee simple absolute—the most complete ownership interest that can be held in real estate

fee simple determinable—created when the conveyance contains words effective to create a fee simple and a provision for automatic expiration of the estate upon the occurrence of a stated event

fee simple subject to a condition subsequent—similar to the fee simple determinable, but the holder does not automatically lose title upon the occurrence of the named event

FHA-insured mortgage—a mortgage in which the Federal Housing Administration provides the lender with insurance against loss on a loan due to default

financial leverage—sometimes called trading on equity, involves the use of borrowed funds to make an investment

first mortgage—When there is more than one mortgage or debt claim on a property, the mortgage with the first claim on the proceeds from the sale of the property acting as collateral for the loan

fixture—an item of personal property so affixed to real property that it is deemed a part of the real property

flat-fee broker—a broker who agrees to perform his or her services for a fee that is independent of the eventual selling price

forbearance—occurs when a lender elects to postpone foreclosure on a loan in default

foreclosure—a legal process to force the sale of pledged property to satisfy an unpaid debt

freehold estate—an ownership interest in real property

future interest—may give the holder the right of possession in the future

future value—the value of a sum after investing it over one or more time periods; the present value multiplied by the appropriate future value interest factor

G

general agency—an agency where the agent is given broad authority to act on behalf of the principal in a number of acts. Real property managers often serve as general agents

general market study—one conducted to determine the potential for a particular type of development without reference to a specific property

general partnership—a partnership in which all partners are personally liable for the debts of the partnership

general warranty deed—the most desirable deed type from the grantee's perspective because the grantor agrees that he will forever guarantee title to the conveyed real property

geographic information system—a computerized system in which a complete inventory of all real property within a jurisdiction is stored and can be accessed to provide detailed information about the number, size, and location of various property types

good faith estimate—a reasonable approximation made by the mortgage lender at the time of loan application concerning the costs that will be incurred by the applicant at the time of closing

government lot—in the rectangular government survey system, a section that intentionally contains less than 640 acres

graduated lease—a lease in which the rent increases by prescribed amounts over the life of the lease

graduated payment mortgage—carries a fixed interest rate, but payments start low and increase over time

grantee index—a document in the recorder's office that summarizes all real property conveyances, listed in chronological and alphabetical order of the grantee

grantee—the party receiving title to real property by deed

grantor index—a document in the recorder's office that summarizes all real property conveyances, listed in chronological and alphabetical order of the grantor

grantor—the party conveying title to real property by deed

gross lease—the tenant pays a fixed rent and the landlord pays all property expenses

ground lease—a long-term, triple-net lease of raw land upon which the lessee erects improvements

growing equity mortgage—a type of graduated payment mortgage, but unlike a GPM there is no interest deferral or negative amortization with a GEM

H

hidden defect—a title risk that cannot be discovered by an examination of the public records

holdover tenant—a lessee who stays in the leased premises after the lease has expired

holographic will—a will written by its maker entirely in the maker's handwriting

home equity loan—a form of second mortgage, frequently in the form of a line of credit, made popular by the 1986 Tax Reform Act

home inspector—a person who examines a real property and prepares a report that details its condition

home warranty policy—an insurance policy that will pay to repair or replace most appliances and major systems if they become inoperative due to normal wear and tear during the term of coverage

homeowner's policy—the most popular package insurance policy used by homeowners; perils covered include both personal liability and property losses

homeowner's policy—the most popular package insurance policy used by homeowners; perils covered include both personal liability and property losses

house poor—term used to describe those who, in acquiring their home, extended themselves financially to the point where they cannot afford to do much more than live in the home

household—a social unit comprised of those living together in the same dwelling

I

improvement in common—an addition to land that benefits more than one parcel of property—improvement to land

improvements—permanent attachments to land that are intended to enhance the value of the land

imputed rent—the rent that owners would have to pay to lease their homes if they did not own them, considered as taxable income in some countries

index lease—calls for a rental payment that fluctuates in direct proportion to some general economic indicator, such as the Consumer Price Index

indirect investment—occurs when an intermediary pools the funds of many individuals in order to invest in larger and/or more diversified investments than is possible for the individuals

inflation hedge—any investment that preserves one's purchasing power by increasing in value by at least the same rate as general price levels

inquiry notice—anyone interested in obtaining an interest in a property is responsible for making further inquiry of others who demonstrate that they may have some rights in the property

installment land contract—an arrangement for purchasing and financing property in which the seller retains title while the buyer takes possession and makes payments over time

installment sale—a sale of property that involves two or more payments over an extended period of time; for income tax purposes, tax on installment sale gains are spread over the time periods in which the payments are received

insurable interest—in real estate, when the beneficiary has a serious stake in the safety of the insured property; must exist for an insurance policy to be issued

insurable interest—in real estate, when the beneficiary has a serious stake in the safety of the insured property; must exist for an insurance policy to be issued

insurable title—a title that can be insured by a title insurance company

intangible property—property that has no material being, or no intrinsic value

interest rate cap—With an adjustable rate mortgage, the upper limit on the increase in the mortgage interest rate at each adjustment date

interest rate risk—the risk that interest rates may change after one has made an investment in a fixed-income investment

interim financing—temporary financing, usually to provide funds for construction of real estate improvements

internal rate of return—a measure of expected investment performance; the interest rate that results in a zero net present value

inverse condemnation—a legal action wherein a property owner demands that a public agency purchase his or her land because some government action has reduced its value

J

joint tenancy—undivided co-ownership of property that features the right of survivorship

joint venture—the union of two or more parties to accomplish a specific business venture

judicial foreclosure—a foreclosure proceeding overseen by a court of law

L

lease—an oral or written agreement that transfers the right of exclusive possession and use of real property from the landlord to the tenant

leasehold estate—only allows the holder to use the property for a period of time

legal or proper objective—another requirement for a valid contract; agreements to perform acts that are illegal or against public policy are not enforceable contracts

lessee—the tenant

lessor—the landlord

leverage—the use of borrowed funds to make an investment

license revocation—the permanent prohibition of the right to practice real estate brokerage

license suspension—temporary prohibition of the right to practice real estate brokerage; recovery fund is funded by fees levied on all licensees to indemnify members of the public who have suffered financial harm as a result of negligence or fraud by a licensed real estate person

license—a temporary, nonexclusive, right to do something on the property of another that is granted by the property owner

lien—a claim that one party has on the property of another as security for a debt or other obligation

life estate—an ownership interest in property that generally cannot be passed on by will

life tenant—one who has a possessory interest in a life estate

like-kind exchange—occurs when real property is traded for other real property; no income tax is due upon the exchange

limited liability company—LLC, a hybrid between a corporation and a partnership in that it combines the income/loss pass through treatment of a partnership with the limited liability of a corporation

limited partnership—a partnership with two classes of partners; general partners have personal liability for partnership debts, limited partners do not

liquidated damages—an amount, specified by contract, to be paid by one party to the other for breach of contract

liquidity risk—the possibility that an investor will be unable to quickly convert an investment into cash equal to the investment's fair market value

listing contract—an agreement between a property owner and a broker to sell or lease the owner's property

loan origination fee—an amount charged by a mortgage originator to provide the originator with a profit and to compensate the originator for expenses incurred in processing the application

loan-to-value ratio—the amount borrowed against a property divided by its purchase price or appraised value, usually expressed as a percentage

M

market risk—the variability in investment returns that result from changes in general market conditions such as inflation and interest rate levels

market study—analysis conducted to evaluate the factors external to a property that influence the property's value, utilization, ability to generate rent, and/or its sales potential. there are two types of market study: a general market study, conducted to determine the potential for a particular type of development without reference to a specific property; and a site-specific study, conducted to determine the strength of the market for a project at a particular location

marketable title—one that a court would order the buyer to accept if asked to decree specific performance of a sales contract

marketable title—title that is free from reasonable or plausible objections

master deed—Deed that describes in detail the real property involved in a condominium

master plan—a comprehensive document to guide a community's future physical growth (sometimes called a comprehensive plan)

mechanic's lien—a specific lien paced on real property when payment was not received for work performed or materials provided

metes and bounds—method of land description that specifies the shape and boundary dimensions of the tract

misrepresentation—making a false statement or concealing a material fact known to one party that is not reasonably ascertainable by the other party

modified accelerated cost recovery system (MACRS)—a depreciation system that allows a greater amount to be written off as a tax deduction during the early years of ownership than would be deductible under the straight-line method

mortgage banker—one who makes mortgage loans with the expectation of selling them to an institutional investor while retaining the servicing rights

mortgage broker—one who finds a mortgage lender for a borrower, or vice versa

mortgage covenants—clauses in a mortgage that specify the rights and responsibilities of both the lender and borrower

mortgage lender—a person or institution that lends money to individuals and businesses to finance the acquisition, or improvement of, real property

mortgage networking—the use of a computer network to inform interested parties about mortgage interest rates and loan origination charges and, in some cases, to tentatively qualify a loan applicant

mortgage pool—a group of mortgages used as collateral for a mortgage-backed security

mortgage-backed security—mortgage pass-through security issued by the Federal National Mortgage Association

mortgagee—the lender of a mortgage loan

mortgage—used to pledge the borrower's interest in the real property as security for a loan; creates a right, or security interest, in the real property for the lender

mortgagor—the borrower in a mortgage loan

multiple listing service (MLS)—an arrangement whereby member brokers agree to bring their listings to the attention of other member brokers and split the commission with the broker who locates the buyer

mutual assent—the agreement of the parties to a contract to be bound by the terms of the contract; a meeting of the minds

N

negative amortization—occurs when the loan balance increases with a payment because the payment is not large enough to cover the interest on the debt

negative cash flow—occurs when an investment generates less cash flow than is required to cover the mortgage payment and maintain the property

negative fraud—a form of misrepresentation involving the failure of a broker to mention a problem with a property to prospective purchasers

net lease—lease in which the tenant pays not only the rent but also some or all of the property taxes, insurance, and maintenance expenses (usually a commercial lease)

net listing—a listing contract in which the agent's commission equals the difference between the selling price and the reservation price specified by the principal; highly discouraged by state real estate commissions

net present value—a measure of the expected investment performance; the present value of all after tax cash flows from an investment less the cost of the investment

nominal consideration—a small amount specified in a deed to satisfy the contractual requirement, but where the amount stated is less than the actual amount paid

nominal income—income unadjusted for inflation

nonconforming use—use of an existing real property that is inconsistent with current zoning, but permitted because the use was established before the zoning ordinance was enacted

nonpossessory land interest—Entitles the holder to use, but not own, real property (e.g., easements, profits, and licenses)

O

offer—a proposal made by one party to another indicating a willingness to do or refrain from doing something on condition that the other party do or refrain from doing something

open-end mortgage—mortgage that allows for future loan amounts

opinion of title—a document in which an attorney states an opinion concerning the marketability of the seller's title

option contract—the right to purchase or lease a property at a stipulated price within a stated time

ordinary annuity—an annuity where the periodic cash flows occur at the end of each time period

ownership in severalty—ownership by a single party

P

package mortgage—mortgage used to finance the acquisition of both real property and other items such as appliances

participation certificate—mortgage pass-through security issued by the Federal Home Loan Mortgage Corporation

partition—Division of concurrently owned property into separately owned interests

partnership agreement—an oral or written agreement that specifies the duties and responsibilities of each partner

partnership—Exists when two or more parties agree to combine their time, effort, money, and property for the purpose of operating a business

pass through security—mortgage pass-through security with Government National Mortgage Association payment guarantee

passive activity loss limitation—may prevent a taxpayer from using passive losses to offset either active or portfolio income in the year the passive loss is incurred; requires that passive losses be used first to offset passive income earned during the tax year; any unused passive losses can be carried forward indefinitely

passive income—income derived from a trade or business in which the taxpayer does not materially participate

pass-through security—in mortgage finance, a security collateralized by a pool of mortgages where the payments of the underlying mortgages are passed through to the investor

payment cap—in an adjustable rate mortgage, a limit on how much the payment may be increased on each adjustment date

percentage lease—the rent is calculated as a proportion of sales or other income generated by the leased property

perils—Events that may result in a loss for the owner of an asset

perils—Events that may result in a loss for the owner of an asset

periodic tenancy—a tenancy that provides for continued automatic renewal until cancelled

personal property—all property other than real property; most personal property is movable

plat map—a map of real property that indicates its subdivision into smaller parcels

plottage—increasing the value of real property by combining two or more parcels into a single parcel

police power—the constitutional authority that state and local governments have to protect the property, health, and well being of their citizens (e.g., master planning and zoning)

portfolio income—income derived from securities such as dividends on stocks and interest on bonds

positive cash flow—occurs when an investment generates more cash flow than is required to cover the mortgage payment and maintain the property

possessory interest—current possession of property vested in the holder

potential interest in real property—interest in real property that may result in ownership (e.g., mortgage interests and liens)

power of attorney—a written instrument that authorizes one person to act as the agent for another to the extent indicated in the document

power of sale foreclosure—a foreclosure proceeding that is not overseen by a court of law

present value—the current value of an amount to be paid or received in the future; the future value multiplied by the appropriate present value interest factor

primary data—obtained directly from prospective renters or purchasers using written questionnaires, telephone, or face-to-face interviews

primary mortgage market—term used to describe the origination of mortgage loans

principal meridian—in the rectangular government survey system, the primary imaginary line running north and south from which other meridians are surveyed

principle of indemnity—Holds that an insured may not be compensated in an amount exceeding the economic loss

principle of indemnity—Holds that an insured may not be compensated in an amount exceeding the economic loss

profit—a right to remove something from the land of another

promissory note—Document by which the buyer assumes a personal obligation to repay the loan

property manager—the individual in charge of the operation of a managed property; directly responsible for maintaining or increasing its market value by developing and following an owner-approved management plan.

property—anything that is or can be owned

proprietary lease—used in cooperatives, many proprietary leases do not stipulate a specific termination date

prorated item—an expenditure or revenue associated with a property that is split between the buyer and seller

puffing—making exaggerated statements to induce a purchase

purchase contract—a written contract wherein one party agrees to sell, and another agrees to purchase, certain real estate under the terms of the contract

purchasing power risk—the possibility that the funds derived from selling an investment will not purchase as many real goods as would the dollars originally invested

Q

quiet title suit—a court action to remove title defects

quitclaim deed—a deed that contains no warranties; used to release any interest the grantor may have in the property

R

raiding—an attempt by some lenders to attract mortgage loan business away from their competitors based on information in the public record

range lines—imaginary lines that mark the eastern and western boundary of a township

real estate investment trust—a mutual fund that specializes in real property investments

real estate investment trust—a mutual fund that specializes in real estate investments

Real Estate Settlement Procedures Act (RESPA)—the federal law that regulates the activities of real estate professionals in the preparation and conduct of a closing

real income—income adjusted to account for inflation

real property—land and anything permanently attached to the land

REALTOR®—a real estate broker who belongs to the National Association of REALTORS®

reappraisal lease—a lease where the rent amount may be adjusted in the future to reflect the market value of the leased premises

recital clause—portion of a deed that contains all, or part, of the title chain to show the derivation of the grantor's title

recording acts—provide for the recording of documents by which an interest or right in real property is created, transferred, or encumbered

rectangular government survey system—developed by the federal government for the subdivision of public lands; used in 30 states to describe rural and suburban land

remainderman—one who has a future interest in a life estate

renegotiable rate mortgage—payment is based on a long-term amortization period with periodic (every three to five years) adjustments to the interest rate

rent control—state or local government regulations that restrict the amount of rent that landlords can charge

rent—periodic payment made by a tenant to the landlord for the possession and use of the leased premises

replacement cost—used in calculating insurance claims; equal to the amount a builder would charge to replace the damaged property at the time of the loss

replacement cost—used in calculating insurance claims; equal to the amount a builder would charge to replace the damaged property at the time of the loss

reservation—a clause in a deed that creates an independent right that did not exist before the conveyance

retaliatory eviction—the unlawful removal of the tenant from the leased premises by the landlord in response to some complaint made by the tenant

reverse annuity mortgage—a mortgage designed to enable homeowners to convert some of the equity in their home into cash

right of entry for condition broken—the future interest in a fee simple subject to a conditional subsequent

S

sale and leaseback—the sale of property ownership with the simultaneous renting back of the premises to the seller

satisfaction of mortgage—a document that signifies that a mortgage debt has been paid or forgiven second mortgage—mortgage that is legally subordinate to the first mortgage

secondary data—aggregated data collected and tabulated by individuals other than an analyst

secondary mortgage market—term used to describe the trading of existing mortgages

section—an area one mile square containing 640 acres

separate property—property owned by a spouse that is excluded from community property status because it was received as a gift or inheritance after marriage or was owned prior to marriage

service industry—a business that produces goods and services that are used within the market area

servicing fee—an amount charged by the party responsible for ensuring that property taxes and hazard insurance premiums are paid on a timely basis, and attending to foreclosure details

servient tenement—the parcel of real property encumbered by an easement

settlement agent—a person who is responsible for ensuring that all parties perform in accordance with the contract, and for processing the paperwork associated with the transaction; employed when a meeting of the parties to the transaction occurs

settlement statement—a recapitulation of the cash requirements for the purchase of real estate and the disposition of the proceeds

shared appreciation mortgage—lender offers a lower interest rate in exchange for a portion of any increase in property value

simple interest—interest accrues only on the original principal

site manager—individual who performs a caretaker role; overseeing the daily operation of a property and provides a critical link between tenants and the property manager.

site-specific study—used to determine the strength of the market for a project at a particular location, in most cases, the way in which the land will be used is predetermined

special agency—an agency where the agent's authority is limited to a particular task; usually a real estate broker acts as a special agent

special warranty deed—a deed in which the grantor warrants the title only against defects arising during the grantor's ownership

specific performance—a court order requiring a party to a contract to do as was promised

State Housing Finance Agencies—Government agencies that address a broad spectrum of housing needs through financing the development and preservation of affordable rental and ownership housing for lower-income citizens

state plane coordinate system—an automated system that can be used to describe real property boundaries

Statute of Frauds—state laws that require that certain agreements be in writing to be enforceable in court; almost all contracts pertaining to real estate must be written

statutory redemption—the right of a borrower in default to redeem their interest in a property after the equitable right of redemption has expired, only allowed in some states

steering—Directing prospective home purchasers to particular areas to either maintain the homogeneity of the area, or to create blockbusting opportunities

sublease—a lease given by a lessee

subsurface—the area below the surface of a property; may be sold separately from the surface rights

supersurface—the area above the surface of a property (sometimes called air space); may be sold separately from the surface rights

syndicate—a group of investors who pool their resources to make investments, not a form of ownership

T

takeout loan—permanent financing that replaces a construction loan

tangible property—property that is of material substance

tax avoidance—Reduction in one's tax liability accomplished through legal means

tax credit—a dollar-for-dollar offset against one's tax liability

tax evasion—Reduction in one's tax liability accomplished through illegal means

tax shelter—any tax advantage that allows one to reduce, postpone, or even eliminate certain taxes

tenancy at sufferance—the renter's estate when continuing in possession of the premises without the permission of the landlord after the lease has expired

tenancy at will—the renter's estate when the renter occupies property for an unspecified term with the permission of the landlord

tenancy by the entireties—concurrent ownership form that may be held by only husband and wife

tenancy for years—a lease wherein both the beginning and expiration dates of the lease term are specified

tenancy in common—concurrent ownership of real property where ownership interests need not be equal and no right of survivorship exists

tier—an east-west row of townships

title abstract—a summary of all deeds and other recorded documents pertaining to the title of a particular parcel of real property

title chain—shows the successive changes of ownership, each one "linked" to the next

title insurance—insurance against financial loss resulting from defects not listed in a title abstract or report

title insurer—an insurance company that issues policies that provide financial protection to mortgage lenders and/or real property buyers who may subsequently suffer a loss due to title defects

title report—a report made before title insurance is issued which discloses the condition of the title

title—the right to or ownership of real property

Torrens certificate—issued after certain legal requirements are met to signify that the property has been registered under the Torrens system

township lines—imaginary lines that mark the northern and southern boundary of a township

township—a six-mile square (36 square miles) containing 36 sections

tract index—Record filing system where all documents affecting each parcel of property are summarized on a single document

trade fixture—personal property affixed to leased premises by a tenant as a necessary part of the tenant's business

transactional broker—a broker that acts as a facilitator and represents neither the buyer nor the seller

trust—a legal relationship by which one party (trustee) holds property for the use and benefit of another (beneficiary) in accordance with the directions of the creator of the relationship (trustor)

V

vacancy rate—Expresses the number of empty units as a percentage of total units on the market

VA-guaranteed mortgage loan—a mortgage loan in which the Veterans Administration provides the lender with a guarantee against loss

variance—an exception to a zoning ordinance authorized by the zoning board in the event of special circumstances or unusual hardship

W

will—a document used to specify to whom a person's property is to be distributed after the property owner's death

wraparound loan—a mortgage that envelops an existing mortgage even though the wraparound loan is subordinate to the existing mortgage

Z

zoning ordinances—a set of regulations that regulate land use (e.g., type of use, building size, and setback requirements)

Index